Managing Human Resources

ARTHUR SHERMAN
PROFESSOR OF PSYCHOLOGY
CALIFORNIA STATE UNIVERSITY, SACRAMENTO

GEORGE BOHLANDER
PROFESSOR OF MANAGEMENT
ARIZONA STATE UNIVERSITY

SCOTT SNELL
ASSOCIATE PROFESSOR OF BUSINESS
PENNSYLVANIA STATE UNIVERSITY

SOUTH-WESTERN College Publishing

An International Thomson Publishing Company

Sponsoring Editor: Randy G. Haubner
Developmental Editor: Alice Denny
Production Editor: Holly Terry
Production House: Lachina Publishing Services
Cover Designer: Michael H. Stratton
Cover Illustrator: Robin Jareaux
Internal Designer: Michael H. Stratton
Marketing Manager: Stephen E. Momper

GJ83JA
Copyright © 1996
by SOUTH-WESTERN COLLEGE PUBLISHING
Cincinnati, Ohio

I(T)P
International Thomson Publishing
South-Western College Publishing is an ITP Company. The trademark
ITP is used under license.

1 2 3 4 5 KI 9 8 7 6 5
Printed in the United States of America

Library of Congress Cataloging-in-Publication Data:
Sherman, Arthur W., Jr.
    Managing human resources / Arthur W. Sherman, Jr., George W.
  Bohlander, Scott Snell.—10th ed.
        p. cm.
    Includes bibliographical references and index.
    1. Personnel management. I. Bohlander, George W. II. Snell,
  Scott III. Title.
  HF5549.C465
  658.3—dc20   95-8634
                                                      CIP

    ISBN 0-538-83925-2

To my wife, Leneve Sherman, and to our children, Judy, Beverly, and Sandy

To my wife, Ronnie Bohlander, and to our children, Ryan and Kathryn

To my wife, Marybeth Snell, and to our children, Sara, Jack, and Emily

ABOUT THE AUTHORS

Arthur W. Sherman, Jr.

Arthur W. Sherman, Jr., is Professor of Psychology, California State University, Sacramento. During most of his academic career he has taught undergraduate and graduate courses in organizational psychology, personnel psychology, human resources management, psychological testing, and professional development in psychology. Dr. Sherman has served as a personnel consultant to several organizations, including the Department of Consumer Affairs of the State of California and the Social Security Administration. He has been a participant in seminars and workshops, for twelve consecutive years as a lecturer in the management development program conducted by the CSUS School of Business Administration for the federal government. For over twenty years he had a private practice as a Licensed Psychologist specializing in career counseling.

During World War II and the Korean War, Dr. Sherman served in the U.S. Air Force as a Personnel Classification Officer, as an Aviation Psychologist, and as head of a proficiency test development unit for the Airman Career Program. Later he was active in the planning of the psychology curriculum at the U.S. Air Force Academy.

As an undergraduate, Dr. Sherman attended Oberlin College and Ohio University, receiving an A.B. in psychology from Ohio University. He received an A.M. from Indiana University and a Ph.D. in industrial and counseling psychology from the Ohio State University. His professional affiliations include the American Psychological Association, the Society for Industrial and Organizational Psychology, and the Academy of Management.

He has been an author of this book since its beginning as well as *Personnel Practices of American Companies in Europe*, published by the American Management Association.

George W. Bohlander

George W. Bohlander is Professor of Management at Arizona State University. He teaches undergraduate, graduate, and executive development programs in the field of human resources and labor relations. His areas of expertise include employment law, training and development, work teams, public policy, and labor relations. He is the recipient of five outstanding teaching awards at ASU and has received the Outstanding Undergraduate Teaching Excellence Award given by the College of Business at ASU.

Dr. Bohlander is an active researcher and author. He has published over 40 articles and monographs covering various topics in the human resources area ranging from labor–management cooperation to employee productivity. His articles appear in such academic and practitioner journals as *Labor Studies Journal, Personnel Administrator, Labor Law Journal, Journal of Collective Negotiations in the Public Sector, Public Personnel Management, National Productivity Review, Personnel,* and *Employee Relations Law Journal.*

Before beginning his teaching career, Dr. Bohlander served as Personnel Administrator for General Telephone Company of California. His duties included recruitment and selection, training and development, equal employment opportunity, and labor relations. He was very active in resolving employee grievances and in arbitration preparation. Dr. Bohlander continues to be a consultant to both public- and private-sector organizations, and he has worked with such organizations as the U.S. Postal Service, Kaiser Cement, McDonnell Douglas, Arizona Public Service, American Productivity Center, Rural Metro Corporation, and Del Webb. Dr. Bohlander is also an active labor arbitrator. He received his Ph.D. from the University of California at Los Angeles and his M.B.A. from the University of Southern California.

Scott A. Snell

Scott A. Snell is Associate Professor of Business Administration at Penn State University. During his career Dr. Snell has taught courses in human resource management, principles of management, and strategic management to undergraduates, graduates, and executives. He is actively involved in executive education and serves as Faculty Director for Penn State's Strategic Leadership Program as well as faculty leader for programs in Human Resources, Developing Managerial Effectiveness, Engineer/Scientist as Manager, and Managing the Global Enterprise. Dr. Snell also serves as Director of Research for Penn State's Institute for the Study of Organizational Effectiveness.

As an industry consultant, Professor Snell has worked with companies such as Arthur Andersen, AT&T, GE, IBM, and Shell Chemical to redesign human resource systems to cope with changes in the competitive environment. His specialization is the realignment of staffing, training, and reward systems to complement technology, quality, and other strategic initiatives. Recently, his work has centered on the development of transnational teams in global network organizations.

Dr. Snell's research has been published in the *Academy of Management Journal, Human Resource Management Review, Industrial Relations, Journal of Business Research, Journal of Management, Journal of Managerial Issues, Personnel Administrator, Strategic Management Journal*, and *Working Woman*. In addition, Dr. Snell is on the editorial boards of *Journal of Managerial Issues, Digest of Management Research*, and *Journal of Quality Management*. He is author of two books, *Management: Building Competitive Advantage*, with Thomas S. Bateman (Irwin Publishing), and *Strategic Human Resource Management* (Austin Press).

He holds a B.A. in Psychology from Miami University, as well as M.B.A. and Ph.D. degrees in Business Administration from Michigan State University. His professional associations include the Strategic Management Society, Academy of Management, and the Society for Human Resource Management.

PREFACE

In today's rapidly changing world of business, managers, supervisors, and human resource management professionals must be able to anticipate and respond to problems before they occur. Meeting challenges head-on and using human resources (HR) effectively are critical to the success of any work organization. To ensure effectiveness, HR policies and procedures must be placed into a comprehensive program that managers can follow in their day-to-day interactions with employees.

Managing Human Resources, 10th Edition, emphasizes the role managers and supervisors play in determining the success of the HR program. While the focus is on the HR role of managers, we do not exclude the impact and importance of the HR department's role—the responsibility for developing, coordinating, and enforcing policies and procedures relating to HR functions.

Our intent is to appeal to the diverse interests and career goals of your students. We recognize that the majority of students at some point in their careers will occupy a managerial position while few will become members of the HR department staff. Whether the reader becomes a manager, an HR staff member, or is employed in other areas of the organization, *Managing Human Resources* provides a functional understanding of HR programs to enable students to see how HR affects all employees, the organization, the community, and the larger society.

As we approach the close of the twentieth century, those of us who have studied work organizations are gratified to observe the increased attention and recognition given to human resources and their management. The HR manager has achieved a status equal to that of managers in charge of such major functions as marketing, production, and finance. Top management has become aware that HR managers can play a vital role in determining the success of an organization.

The role of HR managers is no longer viewed as limited to service functions such as recruiting and selecting employees. Today they assume an active role in the strategic planning and decision making at the upper echelons of their organizations. Their contributions to the achievement of organizational objectives have finally earned them the recognition they deserve. Their contributions in the past also signal even greater potential for the future.

In this edition we recognize the manager's changing role and emphasize current issues and real-world problems and the policies and practices of HRM used to meet them. As authors, we present a realistic picture of HR management as it is today and offer suggestions as to how it contributes to greater productivity and employee satisfaction.

What's New in the 10th Edition

With this edition we have gained a new author and a new emphasis on global HR issues. Scott A. Snell of The Pennsylvania State University brings a wealth of knowledge, solid research background, and practical experience, particularly in global HR issues. We are pleased to offer his expertise on the pages of this text for the benefit of students who will soon enter the workplace.

This edition also represents an extensive revision. We introduce new pedagogical features and overall text improvements that more accurately reflect

HR in today's business world and help the reader understand HR issues more effectively.

- Integrated Learning System. The text and supplements are organized around the learning objectives presented at the beginning of each chapter. Numbered icons identifying the objectives appear next to the material throughout the text and in the *Review and Applications*, *Instructor's Resource Guide*, and *Test Bank* where each objective is fulfilled. When students need further review to meet a certain objective, they can quickly identify the relevant material by simply looking for the icon. This integrated structure creates a comprehensive teaching and testing system.
- Complete update of all laws and court decisions governing HRM includes such recent developments as the 1993 Supreme Court rulings concerning harassment and the 1993 Family and Medical Leave Act.
- Greater emphasis on current issues and problems of the actual business world establishes a clear understanding of working relationships within today's organizations.
- References and examples of the policies and practices of hundreds of organizations show HR concepts in action in the business world today.
- Increased attention to the impact of internal and external environments upon HR activities shows how HR plays a key role in all business activities.
- Expanded discussions cover major current issues such as:

  Conflict resolution

  Diversity in the workplace

  Employee empowerment

  Employee rights concerning drug testing, smoking, and searches

  Employee teams

  Global perspective of HR

  HR in small businesses

  Total-quality management

  Violence in the workplace

- Many new "Highlights in HRM" boxes present the student with up-to-date real-world examples from a variety of large and small organizations.
- Greater use of charts depicting trends further clarifies these concepts for the student.
- Twelve new case studies and four new comprehensive cases reinforce critical thinking skills and problem-solving techniques.
- A glossary of all the key terms introduced in the text provides students with easy access to their definitions.
- The revised student study guide includes a greater number of review questions in addition to projects providing students with a variety of practical HR experiences.

- A completely revised test bank, almost 25 percent larger, plays a strategic role in the Integrated Learning System.
- The inclusion of 101 new color acetates and 101 new transparency masters makes teaching and preparation easier and more convenient.

Features of the Book

Designed to facilitate understanding and retention of the material presented, each chapter contains the following material:

- Learning objectives listed at the beginning of each chapter provide the basis for the Integrated Learning System. Icons for identifying the learning objectives appear throughout the text material.
- Key terms appear in boldface and are defined in margin notes next to the text discussion. The key terms are also listed at the end of the chapter and appear in the glossary at the end of the text.
- Figures. An abundance of graphic materials, flow charts, and summaries of research data provide a visual, dynamic presentation of concepts and HR activities. All figures are systematically referenced in the text discussion.
- "Highlights in HRM." This popular boxed feature provides real-world examples of how organizations perform HR functions. Highlights are introduced in the text discussion and include topics such as small businesses and international issues.
- Illustrations. Captioned, full-color photographs and carefully selected cartoons reinforce points made in the text and maintain student interest.
- Summary. A paragraph or two for each learning objective provides a brief review of the chapter.
- Discussion questions following the chapter summary offer an opportunity to focus on major points in the chapter and to stimulate critical thinking and discussion.
- A case study presents current HRM issues in a real-life setting that allows for student consideration and critical analysis.
- Notes and References. Each chapter includes references from academic and practitioner journals and books. Author notes cite some historical information as well as personal observations and experiences.

In addition to the features found in each of the twenty chapters, the text provides:

- Eleven comprehensive cases at the end of the main text that portray current issues/problems in HRM. "Managing Diversity," "Lake Superior Paper Co.: Self-Managed Teams," "Ill-Fated Love," "International Training at GE Medical Systems," and "Coping with AIDS" are just a few that enable students to put concepts into practice.
- Name, organization, and subject indexes that allow the text to become a valuable reference source.

....

Organization of the Text

Consistent with former editions, this book is organized into seven parts and twenty chapters covering the following major topics:

Part 1. Human Resources Management in Perspective
The Role of Human Resources Management, The Environment for Human Resources Management, Equal Employment Opportunity and Human Resources Management

Part 2. Meeting Human Resources Requirements
Job Requirements, Human Resources Planning and Recruitment, Selection

Part 3. Developing Effectiveness in Human Resources
Training, Career Development, Appraising and Improving Performance

Part 4. Implementing Compensation and Security
Managing Compensation, Incentive Compensation, Employee Benefits, Safety and Health

Part 5. Creating a Productive Work Environment
Motivation and Leadership, The Role of Communication in HRM, Employee Rights and Discipline

Part 6. Enhancing Employee-Management Relations
The Dynamics of Labor Relations, Collective Bargaining and Contract Administration

Part 7. International Human Resources Management and HR Audits
International Human Resources Management and Auditing the HRM Program

Supplementary Materials

All printed supplementary materials were prepared by the text authors to guarantee full integration with the text. Multimedia and additional text supplements were prepared by experts in those fields.

Review and Applications to accompany *Managing Human Resources*. Additional opportunities to apply the theories and principles presented in this textbook may be found in *Review and Applications*, 10th Edition. This study guide includes review questions that can be used to check the student's understanding of each chapter in this textbook. It also contains sixty projects designed to give students a variety of experiences similar to those they are likely to find on the job.

Instructor's Resource Guide. For each chapter in the textbook, the resource guide for the 10th Edition contains the following:

- Chapter synopsis and learning objectives.
- A very detailed lecture outline, based on the textbook chapter outline, complete with notes on the transparencies and transparency masters.

- An annotated list of audiovisual materials pertinent to the chapter's subject matter and available from various sources.
- Answers to the end-of-chapter discussion questions in the textbook.
- Analysis of the end-of-chapter case study in the textbook.
- Answers to the *Review and Applications* projects.

The resource guide also contains the solutions to the comprehensive cases in the textbook. Finally, the resource guide includes supplementary handouts that instructors can copy and distribute to students to enhance the following areas of discussion: Work Force Projections and Jobs in HRM, Developing an Action Plan for Career Development, Developing an Action Plan for Job Search, and Interpreting Test Scores.

Multicolor Transparencies and Transparency Masters. Also available with this edition is a set of 101 multicolor transparencies. Only a few of these transparencies duplicate the figures in the textbook. The set of masters includes each chapter's learning objectives, outline, and other useful information.

Test Bank and Computerized Test Bank. The test bank has been expanded to include 1,800 test questions. Each test bank chapter includes a matrix table that classifies each question according to type and learning objective. There are true/false, multiple-choice, and essay items for each chapter, arranged by learning objective. Page references from the text are included. Each objective question is coded to indicate whether it covers knowledge of key terms, understanding of concepts and principles, or application of principles.

South-Western's automated testing program, **MicroExam 4.0,** contains all the questions from the printed test bank, with a pull-down menu that allows you to edit, add, delete, or randomly mix questions for customized tests.

Human Resource Manager CD-ROM from The Institute for the Learning Sciences, Northwestern University. This new interactive multimedia CD-ROM-based simulation uses personnel information for a fictitious company to allow students to interact with managers as they make decisions just as an HR manager would on issues of productivity, morale, and profits. The program covers five years, including one year of history and four years of work time. Students advance one month at a time as they learn how to manage people throughout the employee life cycle.

Video. Part-opener videos sourced from real companies as well as professionally produced, short video segments developed from business features on CNBC, the cable business news network. The tape is accompanied by an instructor's guide, which includes descriptions of the segments and other information designed to help you integrate the videos with the text material. Use them to introduce a topic, cover lecture material, or stimulate discussion.

Applications in Human Resource Management: Cases, Exercises, and Skill Builders, 3d Edition, by Stella M. Nkomo, Myron D. Fottler, and R. Bruce McAfee. This text supplement includes seventy-five new and updated cases, experiential exercises, skill builders, and term projects. These activities will supplement many of the topics covered in *Managing Human Resources,* 10th Edition.

The Mescon Group's *Performance Through Participation*™ *(PTP) Series.* This series of flexible instructional modules allows students to learn through experiential learning projects, group projects, and coverage of practical topics that influence the workplace.

···

Acknowledgments

We were fortunate in having the expertise of a number of reviewers. Some presented suggestions for changes for this new edition and others offered insights on the manuscript itself. Our appreciation and thanks go to:

Robert Allen, California State Polytechnic University
Timothy Barnett, Louisiana Tech University
Walter Bogumil, University of Central Florida
Alan Cabelly, Portland State University
Roy Cook, Fort Lewis College
Barbara Chrispin, California State University–Dominguez Hills
Jack Dustman, Northern Arizona University
Wendy Eager, Eastern Washington University
Jan Feldhauer, Austin Community College
Mary Gowan, University of Texas at El Paso
Vicki Kaman, Colorado State University
Harriet Kandelman, Barat College
Katherine Karl, Western Michigan University
Richard Kogelman, Delta College
Corrine Livesay, Liberty University
Richard Magjuka, Indiana University
Wayne E. Nelson, Central Missouri State University
Floyd Patrick, Eastern Michigan University
Alex S. Pomnichowski, Ferris State University
Rodney Sherman, Central Missouri State University
Nestor St. Charles, Duchess Community College
Charles Toftoy, George Washington University
Robert Ulbrich, Parkland College
Sandy J. Wayne, University of Illinois
Jon Werner, University of South Carolina

In preparing the manuscript for this edition, we have drawn not only on the current literature but also on the current practices of organizations that furnished information and illustrations relating to their HR programs. We are indebted to the leaders in the field who have developed the available heritage of information and practices of HRM and who have influenced us through their writings and personal associations. We have also been aided by students in our classes, by former students, by the participants in the management development programs with whom we have been associated, by HR managers, and by our colleagues. In particular, we would like to express our appreciation to David Lepak, Mark Youndt, Chon Day, James F. White, Dennis A. Joiner, and Sharon Watkins.

We appreciate the efforts of the Marketing/Management Team at South-Western College Publishing who helped to develop and produce this text. They include Chris Sofranko, Team Director; Randy Haubner, Sponsoring Editor; Alice Denny, Developmental Editor; Holly Terry, Production Editor; Steve Momper, Marketing Manager. Others who contributed include Mike Stratton, Designer at South-Western; Alix Roughen, Photo Researcher; and at Lachina Publishing, Jeff Lachina, Project Manager.

PREFACE

· ·

Our greatest indebtedness is to our wives—Leneve Sherman, Ronnie Boh-lander, and Marybeth Snell—who have contributed in so many ways to this book over the years. They are always sources of invaluable guidance and assistance. Furthermore, by their continued enthusiasm and support, they have made the process a more pleasant and rewarding experience. We are most grateful to them for their many contributions to this publication, to our lives, and to our families.

Arthur W. Sherman, Jr.
California State University, Sacramento

George W. Bohlander
Arizona State University

Scott A. Snell
The Pennsylvania State University

BRIEF CONTENTS

CONTENTS

· ·

....

....

**PART 6 ENHANCING EMPLOYEE-
MANAGEMENT RELATIONS**

....

COMPREHENSIVE CASES

Part 1

Human Resources Management in Perspective

The three chapters in Part 1 provide an overview of the field of human resources management. Chapter 1 describes the development of HR management, including the programs and policies required for HR departments to succeed. Chapter 2 discusses both the internal and the external factors that affect the supervision of an organization's human resources. It reviews important demographic changes in the U.S. work force and discusses how organizations are evolving to meet the needs of today's employees. Chapter 3 is concerned with the many federal laws, executive orders, and court rulings that influence how managers must treat present and prospective employees. It takes a look at equal employment opportunity and affirmative action, pervasive topics that have an impact on all HR activities. When managers and supervisors understand the environment of managing employees, they are in a better position to utilize these valuable organizational resources effectively.

Chapter

The Role of Human Resources Management

After studying this chapter you should be able to

 Cite the reasons for studying human resources management (HRM).

 Describe the major forces in the development of HRM.

 List the characteristics of HRM that enable us to refer to it as a profession.

 Identify the principal elements of an HR program and their importance in managing HR.

 Describe the various responsibilities of the HR department and the nature of its relationship with other departments.

 Describe the types of changes that are forecast for HRM.

I*f an organization is to achieve its goals, it must not only have the required resources, it must also use them effectively. The resources available to a manager are human, financial, physical, and informational.[1] While human resources (HR) have always been critical to the success of any organization, they have assumed an increasingly greater importance that is being recognized inside and outside work organizations.*

Human resources departments typically include individuals with a wide variety and range of knowledge, skills, and abilities who are expected to perform job activities in a manner that contributes to the attainment of organizational goals. How effectively employees contribute to the organization depends in large part upon the quality of the HR program (including staffing, training, and compensation) as well as the ability and willingness of management—from the CEO to first-line supervisors—to create an environment that fosters the effective use of human resources.

objective

Why Study Human Resources Management (HRM)?

Anyone who embarks on a course of specialized study typically wonders about its relevance to his or her interests and goals. The answer to the question "Why study HRM?" should become apparent as we explore the importance of HRM and examine the contributions it can make to an organization.

The Importance of HRM

Personnel management
Basic functions of selection, training, compensation, etc., in the management of an organization's personnel

For many decades such responsibilities as selection, training, and compensation were considered basic functions of the area historically referred to as **personnel management.** These functions were performed without much regard for how they related to each other. From this narrow view we have seen the emergence of what is now known as human resources management. **Human resources management (HRM),** as it is currently perceived, represents the extension rather than the rejection of the traditional requirements for managing personnel effectively. An understanding of human behavior and skill in applying that understanding are still required. Also required are knowledge and understanding of the various personnel functions performed in managing human resources, as well as the ability to perform those functions in accordance with organizational objectives. An awareness of existing economic, social, and legal constraints upon the performance of these functions is also essential. Attention will be given to these constraints in the next chapter.

Human resources management (HRM)
Extension of the traditional requirements of personnel management, which recognizes the dynamic interaction of personnel functions with each other and with the strategic and planning objectives of the organization

HRM, as it is practiced today, recognizes the dynamic interaction of personnel functions with each other and with the objectives of the organization. Most important, it recognizes that HR planning must be coordinated closely with the organization's strategic and related planning functions. As a result, efforts in HRM are being directed toward providing more support for the achievement of the organization's goals, whether it be a profit, not for profit, or governmental organization.

HRM: Current Challenges

According to a survey of senior HR executives in *Personnel Journal*'s top 100 companies (based on 1992 revenues), the most challenging HR issues are health care costs, reorganizing and downsizing organizations, and mergers and acquisitions.

These issues are followed by problems in managing diverse groups of workers who have different attitudes, values, and work behaviors; managing for top-quality performance (TQM); team building; and responding to the needs of the families of employees. Other areas presenting challenges are workers' compensation, labor relations, and management development. International companies face increased global competition.[2] One may expect to see new issues and challenges emerging in the future that require appropriate action. Evolving business and economic factors forge changes in the HR field requiring that preparation for change be an ongoing process.[3]

Role of the HR Department

Top management generally recognizes the contributions that the HR program can make to the organization and thus expects HR managers to assume a broader role in the overall organizational strategy. Thus HR managers must remember the bottom line if they are to fulfill their role. In an award-winning study, Mark Huselid has demonstrated quite conclusively that investment in sophisticated HR practices contributes to greater financial performance and productivity and to reduced turnover.[4]

In the process of managing human resources, increasing attention is being given to the personal needs of the participants. Thus throughout this book we will not only emphasize the importance of the contributions that HRM makes to the organization but also give serious consideration to its effects on the individual and on society.

Increasingly, employees and the public at large are demanding that employers demonstrate greater social responsibility in managing their human resources. Complaints that some jobs are devitalizing the lives and injuring the health of employees are not uncommon. Charges of discrimination against women, minorities, the physically disabled, and the aged with respect to hiring, training, advancement, and compensation are being leveled against some employers. Issues such as comparable pay for comparable work, the rising costs of health benefits, day care for children of employees, and alternative work schedules are concerns that many employers must address.

All employers are finding that privacy and confidentiality of information about employees are serious matters and deserve the greatest protection that can be provided.

Where employees are organized into unions, employers can encounter costly collective bargaining proposals, strike threats, and charges of unfair labor practices. Court litigation, demands for corrective action by governmental agencies, sizable damage awards in response to employee lawsuits, and attempts to erode the employment-at-will doctrine valued by employers are still other hazards that contemporary employers must try to avoid. (We will discuss these issues in detail in Chapter 16.)

The HR Role of Managers and Supervisors

Students who are now preparing for careers in organizations will find that the study of HRM will provide a background of understanding that will be valuable in managerial and supervisory positions. Although HR managers have the responsibility for coordinating and enforcing policies relating to the HR functions,

PEANUTS reprinted by permission of UFS, Inc.

all managers and supervisors are responsible for performing these functions in their relations with subordinates. It is in such positions of leadership that the majority of students using this book will be employed. This book is therefore oriented to help them in managing subordinates more effectively, whether they become first-line supervisors or chief executive officers. Discussions concerning the role of the HR department can serve to provide one with a better understanding of the functions performed by this department. A familiarity with the role of the HR department should help one to cooperate more closely with the department's staff and to utilize more fully the assistance and services available from this resource.

We should recognize that the present status of HRM was achieved only after years of evolutionary development. We hope that this chapter will help readers not only to understand the forces that have contributed to this process but also to become more aware of forces acting today that will have an effect on HRM in the future.

objective

Development of Human Resources Management

HRM, at least in a primitive form, has existed since the first attempts at group effort. Certain HR functions, even though informal in nature, were performed whenever people came together for a common purpose. During the course of this century, however, the processes of managing people have become more formalized and specialized, and a growing body of knowledge has been accumulated by practitioners and scholars. An understanding of the events contributing to the growth of HRM (see Figure 1–1) can provide a perspective for contemporary policies and practices.

In the discussion that follows, major trends will be noted and some significant events described. While most of the books and articles cited in the Notes and References section (at the end of each chapter) are current, the reader should always be aware that the philosophy and practices reflected in contemporary HRM have evolved from a history encompassing several decades.

FIGURE 1-1 *Important Events in the Development of HRM*

YEAR	EVENT
1796	Earliest authenticated strike in America; Philadelphia printers seek to gain minimum weekly wage of $6.
1848	Passage of a law in Philadelphia setting a minimum wage for workers in commercial occupations.
1881	Beginning of Frederick W. Taylor's work in scientific management at the Midvale Steel Plant in Philadelphia.
1883	Establishment of the U.S. Civil Service Commission.
1886	Founding of the American Federation of Labor (AFL).
1912	Passage in Massachusetts of the first minimum wage law.
1913	Establishment of the U.S. Department of Labor.
1915	First course in personnel administration, offered at Dartmouth College.
1920	First text in personnel administration, published by Ordway Tead and Henry C. Metcalf.
1924	Point method of job evaluation developed by the National Electric Manufacturers' Association and the National Metal Trades Association.
1927	Hawthorne studies begun by Mayo, Roethlisberger, and Dickson.
1935	Establishment of the Congress of Industrial Organizations (CIO) by several unions previously affiliated with the AFL.
1939	Publication of the first edition of the *Dictionary of Occupational Titles*.
1941	Beginning of U.S. involvement in World War II, demanding the mobilization of individuals trained in personnel management and the rapid development of personnel programs in the military and in industry.
1955	Merger of the AFL and CIO.
1967	Federal Women's Program established by the U.S. Civil Service Commission to enhance the employment and advancement of women.
1975	Beginning of a professional accreditation (now certification) program by the Personnel Accreditation Institute.
1978	Passage of the Civil Service Reform Act, which established the Office of Personnel Management (OPM), the Merit Systems Protection Board (MSPB), and the Federal Labor Relations Authority (FLRA).
1982	Beginning of the erosion of the employment-at-will doctrine, with increasing attention to "just cause" terminations.
1985	Increased emphasis on employee participation in organizational decision making to improve productivity and competitive position.
1990	Heightened awareness of privacy rights of employees as employers monitor employee performance.
1991-1995	Increased emphasis on global HR practices; greater use of temporary employees; observed emphasis on sexual harassment; heightened attention to greater diversity in the workforce; increased emphasis on total quality management; and downsizing or "rightsizing" of organizations.

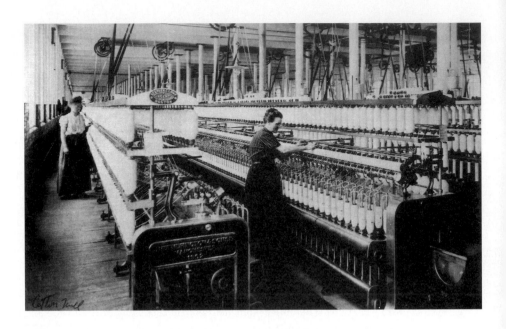

Though the work remained hard, regulations in the late 1880s improved the safety for many factory workers.

The Factory System

During the nineteenth century, the development of mechanical power made possible a factory system of production. The concentration of workers in factories served to focus public attention on their conditions of employment, which were often unhealthy and hazardous. During the late 1880s, laws were passed in some states to regulate hours of work for women and children, to establish minimum wages for male labor, and to regulate working conditions that affect employee health and safety. It was also at this time that laws were enacted to provide payments for injuries suffered in industrial accidents. Eventually, as the result of legislation and collective bargaining, employment conditions began to improve.

The Mass Production System

Mass production was made possible by the availability of standardized and interchangeable parts designed to be used in assembly-line production. With this system came improvements in production techniques and the use of labor-saving machinery and equipment. The accompanying increases in overhead costs and wage rates, however, forced companies to seek ways of using production facilities and labor more efficiently. Frederick W. Taylor's work at the Midvale Steel plant in Philadelphia stimulated the scientific management movement.

Scientific management
Substitution of exact scientific investigation and knowledge for individual judgment of either the worker or the boss

   According to Taylor, **scientific management** required accurate performance standards based on objective data gathered from time studies and other sources. These standards provided a basis for rewarding the superior workers financially and for eliminating the unproductive ones. Taylor's approach was in sharp contrast to the then-prevailing practice of attempting to gain more work from employees by threatening them with the loss of their jobs.[5]

Among Taylor's contemporaries in this movement were Frank B. Gilbreth and his wife, Lillian M. Gilbreth,[6] Henry L. Gantt, and Harrington Emerson.[7] Lillian Gilbreth was one of the first women to gain an international reputation as a management consultant. Professionally active until her death at age 94, she became the first psychologist to be honored on a U.S. postage stamp—the Great Americans series, issued in 1984.[8]

Contributions of Industrial-Organizational Psychology

By the early 1900s some of the knowledge and research from the field of psychology was beginning to be applied to the management of personnel. One of the best-known pioneers in industrial psychology was Hugo Münsterberg. His book *Psychology and Industrial Efficiency* called attention to the contributions that psychology could make in the areas of employment testing, training, and efficiency.[9]

Many psychologists whose work before World War I had been largely theoretical and experimental followed Münsterberg's lead by making practical contributions to the personnel field in business and industry. Walter Dill Scott received acclaim for his early work in the rating of sales personnel and for his classic book in personnel management, which he co-authored with Robert C. Clothier.[10]

James McKeen Cattell, another leader in the field, is noted for his activities in test development and for his leadership in establishing the Psychological Corporation, an organization that offers personnel services.[11] These services include publishing and distributing employment tests and conducting validation studies for employers; the latter activity has become a very important aspect of HRM and will be examined in detail in Chapters 3 and 6. A contemporary of Cattell, Walter Van Dyke Bingham gained prominence as an author of books on interviewing and aptitude testing that were widely used by personnel practitioners.[12]

Over the years, industrial-organizational psychology has broadened its scope and has become one of the major areas of psychology. A separate division of the American Psychological Association, the Society for Industrial and Organizational Psychology, has more than 3,500 members who are academic and professional practitioners in the field.[13]

The Hawthorne Studies

Hawthorne studies

Experiments in the 1920s to determine what effect hours of work, periods of rest, and lighting have upon worker fatigue and productivity

Begun in the 1920s, the **Hawthorne studies** were an effort to determine what effect hours of work, periods of rest, and lighting might have on worker fatigue and productivity. These experiments constituted one of the first cooperative industry-university research efforts. As the studies progressed, however, it was discovered that the social environment could have an equivalent if not greater effect on productivity than the physical environment.

Conducted by Elton Mayo, Fritz J. Roethlisberger, and W. J. Dickson at the Western Electric Company's Hawthorne Works near Chicago, Illinois, these studies were a pioneering endeavor to examine factors affecting productivity.[14] While there has been considerable controversy over interpretation of the findings, HR specialists generally agree that the Hawthorne studies played a very important role in the development of HRM.[15] The studies spurred efforts to humanize the workplace and to find more-sensitive ways to motivate workers. Out of the interviewing techniques used by the Hawthorne researchers grew the nondirective approach to counseling, which recognizes the importance of feelings—a concept that until that time was generally considered inappropriate in employment situations. It is interesting to note that what the Hawthorne studies revealed about human relations had been anticipated some years earlier by a sociologist, Mary Parker Follett. In her writings Follett continually emphasized the important role of informal groups in work situations.[16]

The Human Relations Movement

Human relations movement

Movement that focused attention on individual differences among employees and on the influence that informal groups have upon employee performance and behavior

Along with the work of Kurt Lewin at the National Training Laboratories, the Hawthorne studies helped to give rise to the **human relations movement** by providing new insights into human behavior.[17] This movement focused attention on individual differences among employees and on the influence that informal groups can have upon employee performance and behavior. It also focused attention on the necessity for managers to improve their communications and to be more sensitive to the needs and feelings of their subordinates. Furthermore, the movement emphasized the need for a more participative and employee-centered form of supervision. You will observe later that various principles and practices currently applied in employee involvement, work teams, and employee empowerment grew out of the work of researchers and practitioners of the human relations movement.

Contributions of the Behavioral Sciences

Behavioral sciences

Various disciplines of psychology, sociology, anthropology, social economics, political science, linguistics, and education

As the human relations movement evolved, it became broader in scope. The understanding of human behavior was enhanced by contributions not only from the traditional disciplines of psychology, sociology, and anthropology, but also from social economics, political science, linguistics, and education. More important, the interrelationships of these various disciplines became more widely recognized, so that they are now referred to collectively as the **behavioral sciences.**

The behavioral science approach is oriented toward economic objectives, concerned with the total climate or milieu, and consistent with the development of interpersonal competence. It stresses a humanistic approach—the use of groups and employee participation in the achievement of organizational objectives, including the management of change.[18] All of these issues of importance to managers are discussed throughout the text.

Growth of Governmental Regulations

Prior to the 1930s, employer relations with employees and with their labor organizations were subject to very few federal or state laws and regulations. However, political pressures for social reform created by the depression of the 1930s gave rise to both federal and state legislation affecting these relations. Starting with the National Labor Relations Act in 1935, federal regulations have expanded to the point where they govern the performance of virtually every HR function.

Important federal legislation, executive orders, and major court decisions affecting HRM activities will be cited throughout this book. While we must emphasize federal laws and regulations, you should be aware that HR managers and supervisors are also responsible for compliance with all state and local laws and regulations that govern work environments. These requirements are often more stringent than federal laws. Although employers are often critical of the demands these laws and regulations impose on their operations, most legislation is a response to employers' lack of social responsibility, as manifested by their poor treatment of employees in the past.

Increased Specialization of HR Functions

Initially, the management of human resources was limited largely to hiring, firing, and record keeping, functions carried out by managerial and supervisory personnel. Eventually, clerical personnel were employed to assist in keeping records relating to hours worked and to payroll.

By the 1940s the typical personnel department in a medium-sized or large firm included individuals with specific training and/or experience in carrying out various specialized functions.[19] The major functions performed in organizations today are shown in Figure 1–2, which provides an overview of the functions that will be discussed in detail in this book. (At the end of this chapter, we will outline the order in which we will study the functions.)

Increasing Emphasis on Strategic Management

We have mentioned the fact that top management expects HR managers to assume a broader role in overall organizational strategy. In the 1990s, HRM is playing a vital role in creating and sustaining the competitive advantage of an organization. In order to carry out their expanded role, many HR professionals will need to acquire competencies in related areas. These competencies are summarized below.

1. *Business capabilities*. HR professionals will need to know the business of their organization thoroughly. This requires an understanding of its economic and financial capabilities.
2. *State-of-the-art HRM practices*. HR professionals will be the organization's behavioral science experts. In areas such as staffing, development, appraisal, rewards, team building, and communication, HR professionals should develop competencies that keep them abreast of changes.
3. *Management of change process*. HR professionals will have to be able to manage change processes so that HR activities are effectively merged with the business needs of the organization.

The ability to integrate business, HRM, and management of change is essential.[20] By helping their organizations build a sustained competitive advantage and by learning to manage many activities well, HR professionals will become strategic business partners. Many of the most forward-looking CEOs are seeking top HR managers who will report directly to them and help them address key issues. Highlights in HRM 1 illustrates what Digital, a decentralized, high-technology computer company with 118,900 employees worldwide—including approximately 2,000 HR professionals—is doing to meet the challenges it faces in carrying out its global HRM functions.

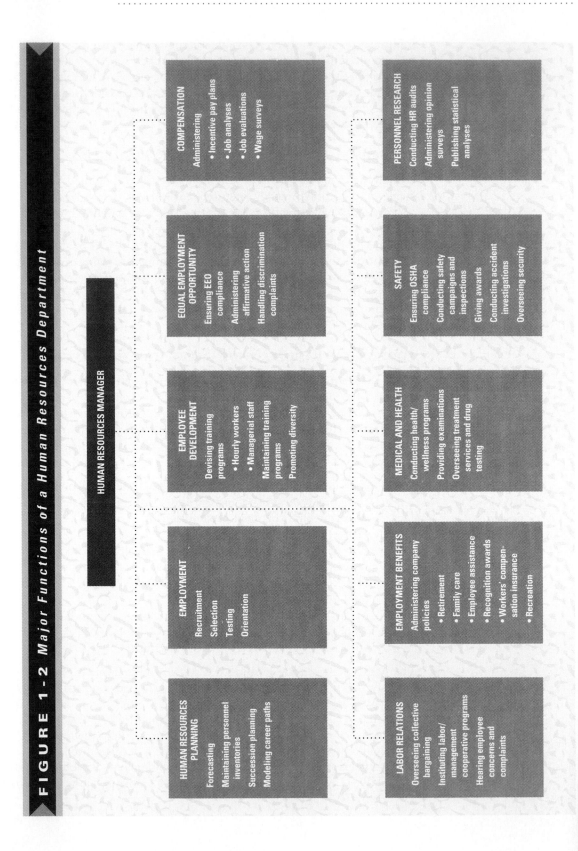

FIGURE 1-2 Major Functions of a Human Resources Department

HUMAN RESOURCES MANAGER

HUMAN RESOURCES PLANNING
Forecasting
Maintaining personnel inventories
Succession planning
Modeling career paths

EMPLOYMENT
Recruitment
Selection
Testing
Orientation

EMPLOYEE DEVELOPMENT
Devising training programs
• Hourly workers
• Managerial staff
Maintaining training programs
Promoting diversity

EQUAL EMPLOYMENT OPPORTUNITY
Ensuring EEO compliance
Administering affirmative action
Handling discrimination complaints

COMPENSATION
Administering
• Incentive pay plans
• Job analyses
• Job evaluations
• Wage surveys

LABOR RELATIONS
Overseeing collective bargaining
Instituting labor/management cooperative programs
Hearing employee concerns and complaints

EMPLOYMENT BENEFITS
Administering company policies
• Retirement
• Family care
• Employee assistance
• Recognition awards
• Workers' compensation insurance
• Recreation

MEDICAL AND HEALTH
Conducting health/wellness programs
Providing examinations
Overseeing treatment services and drug testing

SAFETY
Ensuring OSHA compliance
Conducting safety campaigns and inspections
Giving awards
Conducting accident investigations
Overseeing security

PERSONNEL RESEARCH
Conducting HR audits
Administering opinion surveys
Publishing statistical analyses

HIGHLIGHTS IN HRM

HRM
highlights

1   HRM AT DIGITAL LOOKS TO THE FUTURE

One way to conceive of the human resources professional of the future is as an architect of *organization, programs,* and *information management,* who at the same time maintains and values the earlier work functions.

As an *organizational architect* the human resources professional would:

- Address globalization of management teams and international awareness
- Adapt design for temporary project/work organization teams and drive transformation of working and management teams
- Create multiple methods to manage new work environments across all employee levels
- Develop stress management methods relating to shortened time to market and technology curves
- Invent and implement optimal communications to provide direction and manage an organizational culture that provides psychological safety in times of rapid change.

In the role of programs architect, the HR manager would:

- Create programs to address use of temporary labor
- Design cooperative training ventures with local and federal government
- Promote skill transitioning that addresses obsolescence
- Respond humanely to redeployment and change management tactics.

All of these functions involve identifying the people issues—to obtain and develop the human resources necessary to competitive business practices—at the same time addressing longer-term issues. Creative programs can prevent a reactive approach and contribute to competitive advantage. This role encourages HR professionals to be activists, to address situations before they become problems that result in productivity loss.

As information management architect, the HR professional would use current computer systems and artificial intelligence to create business models and simulations to:

- Plan and administer compensation programs
- Provide simulations of organization design options
- Track development
- Manage succession.

The information management architect must be able to assess and manipulate information necessary for management decision making, allow for on-line benefits changes, and provide more information for employee decision making. These kinds of applications could free up time from other HR professionals for consultation and employee contact.

Source: Betty Bailey, "Ask What HR Can Do for Itself," *Personnel Journal* 70, no. 7 (July, 1990): 37. Reprinted with permission of *Personnel Journal,* Costa Mesa, Calif. All rights reserved.

Professionals improve
and broaden their
expertise through
seminars.

three
objective

Professionalization of Human Resources Management

Because of the changes occurring in the workforce and its environment, HR managers can no longer function simply as technical specialists who perform the various HRM functions. Instead, they must concern themselves with the total scope of HRM and its role within the organization and in society as a whole. Therefore HR managers today should be professionals with respect to both their qualifications and their performance.

One of the characteristics of a profession is the development through research and experimentation of an organized body of knowledge. This knowledge is exchanged through conferences, seminars, and workshops sponsored by professional associations. The latest information in the field is communicated through the literature published by the professional associations, as well as by various nonprofit organizations and educational institutions. Other characteristics of a profession include the establishment of a code of ethics and of certification requirements for its members. HRM exhibits all these characteristics.

Professional Associations and Certification

Today a number of professional organizations represent general, as well as specialized, areas of HRM. The professional association with the largest membership—more than 47,000—is the Society for Human Resource Management (SHRM). Affiliated with SHRM are more than 400 local chapters in major cities throughout the United States, many of which sponsor student conferences, seminars, and workshops. The national annual meeting of the society is held in a different city each year. The society publishes *HR Magazine* (formerly *Personnel Administrator*) and *HR News* (formerly *Resource*), as well as various books and bulletins. While *HR Magazine* is available to the general public and is found in most libraries, *HR News* is generally available only by personal or organizational subscription. SHRM frequently collaborates with the Bureau of National Affairs (BNA) in conducting surveys in various areas of HRM.[21]

Other leading professional associations in the field include the International Personnel Management Association, the International Association for Personnel Women, the American Management Association (AMA), and the Conference Board (CB). AMA and CB are prominent nonprofit organizations that provide publications and educational services relating to HRM and other functional areas. Organizations that represent specialized areas of interest include the Human Resource Planning Society, the American Compensation Association, the International Foundation of Employee Benefit Plans, the American Society for Training and Development, the Association for Industrial Research, and the Society for Industrial and Organizational Psychology of the American Psychological Association. For professors in the field, there is the Personnel and Human Resources Division of the Academy of Management.[22] All of these organizations sponsor meetings and workshops that promote the professional growth of their members. They also provide opportunities for contact with other organizations, including government agencies.

Certification
Recognition of having met certain professional standards

The professionalization of a field generally leads to some form of **certification** for practitioners to enhance their status and to recognize their competency. The Human Resource Certification Institute of SHRM has developed such a program for professionals in HRM. The program offers two types of certification, each of which reflects the number of specialties and the amount of experience and/or academic training possessed by the recipient.[23]

To qualify for either certification, an applicant must provide verification of experience and pass an intensive four-hour written examination to demonstrate mastery of knowledge. The certifications, which must be renewed every three years, serve largely to indicate the qualifications of recipients and encourage others to qualify for certification. In addition to the SHRM certification for generalists in HRM, there are other certifying agencies with specific certification designations in the areas of compensation, employee benefits, and safety and health. (See Figure 1–3.) As the reputations of these programs grow and the programs become more widely recognized by top management, certification will become an important qualification for individuals seeking positions in HRM.[24]

Code of Ethics

It is typical for professional associations to develop a code of ethics that members are expected to observe. The code shown in Highlights in HRM 2 was developed for HR managers by the SHRM. Many large corporations have their own code of ethics to govern corporate relations with employees and the public at large.

Adherence to a code often creates a dilemma for professionals, including those in HRM. Referring to principles in the SHRM code, Fran A. Wallace notes, "With an observation toward profitable business, whom do HR professionals service? Who is the client—management or the individual employees? In the course of serving the employees and management and maintaining respect and regard for human values, whose needs are paramount? What happens when—as

FIGURE 1-3 *Certification Options in HR Management*

CERTIFYING AGENCY	CERTIFICATION DESIGNATION
Human Resource Certification Institute	Professional in Human Resources Senior Professional in Human Resources
American Compensation Association	Certified Compensation Professional
International Foundation of Employee Benefit Plans	Certified Employee Benefit Specialist
Board of Certified Safety Professionals	Associate Safety Professional Certified Safety Professional
American Board of Industrial Hygiene/ Board of Certified Safety Professionals	Occupational Health and Safety Technologist

Source: Carolyn Wiley, "The Certified HR Professional," *HR Magazine* 37, no. 8 (August 1992): 77-84. Reprinted with permission of *HR Magazine* (formerly *Personnel Administrator*), published by the Society for Human Resource Management, Alexandria, Va.

is frequently the case in HR work—the confidential issues of management and/or the employees are in conflict?"[25] These and similar questions are not easy to answer. However, the fact that there *is* a code in itself focuses attention on ethical values and provides a basis for HR professionals to evaluate their plans and actions.

The HR staff is, of course, concerned with monitoring ethics in its own operations. More recently, however, HR departments have been given a greater role in communicating the organization's values and standards, monitoring compliance with its code of ethics, and enforcing the standards throughout the organization. Many organizations have ethics committees and ethics ombudsmen to provide training in ethics to employees. The general objectives of ethics training are stated in Highlights in HRM 2.

The ultimate goal of ethics training is to avoid unethical behavior, adverse publicity, and potential lawsuits and to gain a strategic advantage. To achieve these objectives, two approaches are frequently used: (1) developing employee awareness of ethics in business and (2) drawing attention to potential ethical issues to which an employee may be exposed.[26]

Professional Literature

Personal development in any profession requires knowledge of the current literature in the field. A number of periodicals contain articles on general or specialized areas of interest in HRM. Some of the more important journals students and practitioners should be familiar with are shown in Figure 1–4.

HIGHLIGHTS IN HRM

highlights

2

SOCIETY FOR
HUMAN
RESOURCE
MANAGEMENT

Code of Ethics

As a member of the Society for Human Resource Management, I pledge myself to:

✻ Maintain the highest standards of professional and personal conduct.

✻ Strive for personal growth in the field of human resource management.

✻ Support the Society's goals and objectives for developing the human resource management profession.

✻ Encourage my employer to make the fair and equitable treatment of all employees a primary concern.

✻ Strive to make my employer profitable both in monetary terms and through the support and encouragement of effective employment practices.

✻ Instill in the employees and the public a sense of confidence about the conduct and intentions of my employer.

✻ Maintain loyalty to my employer and pursue its objectives in ways that are consistent with the public interest.

✻ Uphold all laws and regulations relating to my employer's activities.

✻ Refrain from using my official positions, either regular or volunteer, to secure special privilege, gain or benefit for myself.

✻ Maintain the confidentiality of privileged information.

✻ Improve public understanding of the role of human resource management

This Code of Ethics for members of the Society for Human Resource Management has been adopted to promote and maintain the highest standards of personal conduct and professional standards among its members. Adherence to this code is required for membership in the Society and serves to assure public confidence in the integrity and service of human resource management professionals.

Source: Reprinted with the permission of *HR Magazine* (formerly *Personnel Administrator*) published by the Society for Human Resource Management, Alexandria, Va.

FIGURE 1-4 *Some Important Professional Journals*

Compensation and Benefits Review

Employee Relations Law Journal

Employee Responsibility and Rights

HR Focus

HR Magazine

HR News

Human Relations

Human Resource Management

Human Resource Management Review

Human Resource Planning

Human Resources: Journal of the International
Association for Personnel Women

Industrial and Labor Relations Review

Industrial Relations

International Journal of Human Resources
Management

International Journal of Selection and
Assessment

Journal of Applied Psychology

Journal of Collective Negotiation in the Public
Sector

Journal of Labor Research

Journal of Management

Labor Law Journal

Monthly Labor Review

National Productivity Review

Personnel

Personnel Journal

Personnel Psychology

Public Personnel Management

Supervisory Management

Training and Development Journal

Other periodicals that cover the general field of business and management often contain articles pertaining to HRM. Among these are *Academy of Management Executive, Academy of Management Journal, Academy of Management Review, Business Horizons, California Management Review, Canadian Business Review, European Management Journal, Fortune, Harvard Business Review, Journal of Business Ethics, Management Review, Business Week,* and *The Wall Street Journal.*

The vast number of books and articles being published on HRM makes it virtually impossible to locate, let alone read, all of the literature in the field. Consequently, students and practitioners will find four references invaluable in locating those books and articles having information most pertinent to them. One is *Personnel Management Abstracts,* which contains abstracts from journals and books and an index of periodical literature.[27] The second is *Work Related Abstracts,* organized into broad categories with a cumulative guide to specific subjects, organizations, and individuals.[28] The third is *Human Resources Abstracts,* which provides abstracts of current literature from more than 250 sources.[29] The fourth is *Business Periodicals Index,* which provides a broader coverage of subjects and periodicals.[30] Also, the reader should not overlook various computerized compilations of periodical literature that are available in most libraries. One major source is the Dialogue Data Base System, which includes the ABI/INFORM as one of its databases. ABI/INFORM contains an index to business information and provides 150-word summaries of significant articles. Members of the SHRM can subscribe to an on-line database system that provides access to SHRM's entire library-information center.

Research Organizations

Throughout this book we will report on many of the findings of a number of different research organizations and individuals. The primary function of these organizations is to conduct research and to make their findings available to all who are interested. Many such organizations are found at universities. Probably the largest university research center in the behavioral sciences is the Institute for Social Research at the University of Michigan. Its three divisions—the Survey Research Center, the Research Center for Group Dynamics, and the Center for Political Studies—have together published over 5,000 books, articles, and reports.

A number of state universities have centers for the study of labor and industrial relations, including the Universities of California, Minnesota, Illinois, and New York. The School of Industrial and Labor Relations at Cornell University is also well known for its publications. Organizations sponsored by industry, such as the American Management Association (AMA) and the Conference Board (CB), publish research studies that benefit managers in HRM. Rand Corporation of Santa Monica, California, and the Brookings Institution of Washington, D.C., are also recognized for their contributions to this field.

The Bureau of National Affairs (BNA), Commerce Clearing House (CCH), and Prentice-Hall (PH) also conduct surveys relating to HRM policies and practices. Survey results from these organizations may be found in loose-leaf volumes that contain a wealth of information about policies and practices and the legal aspects of HRM. The student of HRM should become familiar with the various BNA, CCH, and PH publications that are updated regularly. These volumes are available in many college and university libraries, city libraries, and the libraries of the larger work organizations.

Academic Training

With so much attention focused on the behavioral sciences during the 1960s and 1970s, the subject of HRM suffered from neglect at some colleges and universities. Since then, however, equal employment opportunity, international HRM, employee rights, concern for productivity, cost of employee benefits, and other current issues have rekindled interest in HRM courses and in HRM as a major field of study.

In the past, many HR professionals entered the field with degrees in liberal arts and sciences, having perhaps taken a few business courses as electives. However, as certification requirements and other factors became essential for professional status, a bachelor's degree and even a master's degree in business have become more important.

In addition to business courses, students planning careers in HRM should take courses in such areas as personnel and organizational psychology, industrial sociology, economics, industrial engineering, and electronic data processing.

A knowledge of computer operations is essential for processing and reporting personnel data to gauge the performance of HR programs. While learning about the uses of computers, future HR professionals should become knowledgeable in research design and the use of statistics in research.

Programs for Managing Human Resources

An HR program constitutes the overall plan for managing HR and for guiding managers and supervisors in decisions relating to their subordinates. It establishes the objectives, policies, procedures, and budget pertaining to the HR functions to be performed. Although HR managers are responsible for coordinating and enforcing policies relating to HR functions, responsibility for performing these functions rests with *all* managers and supervisors within an organization.

Objectives

HR objectives
Goals to be achieved in the area of HRM

HR policies
Guides to actions required to achieve the HR objectives

HR objectives are determined by the organization's objectives as a whole. More and more, HR objectives are reflecting the increased social responsibilities of firms, which include not only traditional responsibilities to customers, employees, and shareholders but also responsibilities to the community and to the total society. Creating employment opportunities for the disadvantaged and providing a favorable work environment and greater financial security represent but a few ways in which firms can exercise greater social responsibility.

Employment opportunities for the disabled reflect socially responsible HR objectives.

Policies

Closely related to HR objectives are **HR policies** that serve to guide the actions required to achieve these objectives. Policies provide the means for carrying out the management processes and as such are an aid to decision making. Like objectives, they may be idealistic or realistic, general or specific, flexible or inflexible, qualitative or quantitative, broad or narrow in scope. However, while objectives determine what is to be done, policies explain how it is to be done.

Need for Policies

Carefully developed policies are vital to HRM because employees are sensitive to any differences, no matter how slight, in the treatment they may receive compared with others. The quickest way to impair employee efficiency and morale is for a manager to show favoritism in decisions such as those relating to vacations, schedules, raises and promotions, overtime, and disciplinary action. Decisions can be made more rap-

....

idly and more consistently if policies relating to these and other subjects have been formulated and communicated throughout the organization.

Formulation of Policies

The formulation of HR policies for approval by top management should be a co-operative endeavor among managers, supervisors, and members of the HR staff. In some cases it may be important to have employees' input. For example, BankAmerica Corporation uses suggestions from both managers and employees to formulate its policy regarding employees with life-threatening illnesses, discussed in Chapter 3.

Policy committees facilitate the pooling of experience and knowledge. Participation by operating managers is particularly important because they are often more familiar with the specific areas in which problems arise—and also because their cooperation is required for policy enforcement. On the other hand, the manager and staff of the HR department have the responsibility for exercising leadership in formulating policies that are consistent with overall organizational objectives. They also must make certain that these policies are compatible with current economic conditions; collective bargaining trends; and laws and regulations at the federal, state, and local levels.

Written Policy Statements

Organizations can make their HR policies more authoritative by putting them in writing. To strengthen their effectiveness, these statements, which may be compiled into a policy manual, should include the reasons the policy is needed. Written policy statements can serve as invaluable aids in orienting and training new personnel, administering disciplinary action, and resolving grievance issues with employees and their unions. When distributed to employees, these policy statements can provide answers to many questions that might otherwise have to be referred to supervisors. Throughout this book you will occasionally find a sample policy statement relating to the particular HR function being discussed.

In recent years, HR policy statements as well as employee handbooks have assumed the force of a legal contract between employer and employee. Just as employers refer to policy statements as a basis for their personnel actions, employees now cite organizational failure to adhere to established policies as a violation of their rights. It is therefore advisable for firms to insert a disclaimer or waiver in employee manuals to the effect that the contents of the manual do not constitute a contract. The disclaimer should be prominently placed, not buried in a footnote. Wording the manual carefully (avoiding "always" and "never," for example), using a conversational tone rather than legalistic jargon, and having an outside labor counsel check the manual can help in avoiding problems.

Procedures

HR procedures

Prescribed sequence of steps to be followed in carrying out HR policies

HR procedures serve to implement policies by prescribing the chronological sequence of steps to follow in carrying out the policies. Procedures relating to employee selection, for example, might provide that individuals first be required to complete an application form, followed by an interview with an HR office representative. Grievances, promotions, transfers, and wage adjustments likewise must be administered according to established procedure in order to avoid problems resulting from oversights. For example, as a step in the disciplinary procedure, the failure to give an employee written warning of a violation might prevent the organization from discharging the employee for a second violation.

HR procedures, like HR policies, must be treated as means to an end, not as ends in themselves. As we mentioned earlier, when organizations become more bureaucratic, complaints may be raised about excessive red tape, inflexibility, and impersonality in making HR decisions. Unfortunately, when procedures become too detailed or numerous, they can impair rather than further the interests of the organization and its employees. To avoid this hazard, procedures must be reviewed periodically and modified to meet changing conditions.

Throughout this book the discussion of policies and procedures for the various HRM functions will reflect what is typical of the large or medium-sized firm. In smaller organizations HRM is often carried out on an informal basis, and attention to policies and formal procedures may vary considerably. Since most federal laws governing work organizations apply to large firms, small organizations have greater latitude in the way they manage their employees and perform HR activities.

Human Resources Information Systems

Effective HRM requires an **HR information system (HRIS)** to provide current and accurate data for purposes of control and decision making. The system is composed of procedures, equipment, information, methods to compile and evaluate information, the people who use the information, and information management.

HR information system (HRIS)
Network of procedures, equipment, information, and personnel to provide data for purposes of control and decision making

The use of HRIS was enhanced by advancements in computer technology. According to one survey of a randomly selected group of subscribers to *Personnel Journal*, 99.8 percent of the respondents have automated one or more HR functions. Computers are not only used for storage and retrieval of information but for broader applications. These applications include production of basic reports, HR calculations, long-range forecasting and strategic planning, career and promotion planning, and evaluation of HR policies and practices—a topic discussed further in Chapter 2.

A well-designed HRIS can serve as the main management tool in the alignment of HR department goals with the goals of long-term strategic planning. As HR issues have been increasingly recognized as critical factors in strategic planning decisions, the ability of the HRIS to quantify, analyze, and model change has enhanced the status of the HRIS in many organizations. Global competition is putting increasing pressure on U.S. managers to make better and faster decisions. HR information technology can improve HRM and contribute to the competitive advantage.[31]

In addition to the major uses of computer technology, with a PC, the HR professional can take advantage of a variety of information services. An on-line service designed especially for HR departments is the Human Resource Information Network, a subsidiary of BNA. It provides up-to-the-minute information in several categories, including news, research, software, and services, covering all disciplines of HRM. As noted earlier, SHRM has an on-line database that permits users to quickly search more than 24,000 citations of books and articles.

In developing an effective HRIS, an organization must address privacy issues in advance. A data-privacy policy can make the HRIS a positive factor in employee relations rather than a mistrusted disseminator of sensitive personnel information. A comprehensive discussion of privacy issues will be presented in the next chapter.

The Budget

HR budget

Financial plan and a control for the expenditure of funds necessary to support the HR program

Statements relating to objectives, policies, and procedures or to a program as a whole can be meaningful only if they are supported financially through the budget. An **HR budget** is both a financial plan and a control for the expenditure of funds necessary to support the HR program. As such, it is one of the best indicators of management's real attitude toward the program. Thus, while a firm's selection policy may be to hire only fully qualified applicants to fill vacancies, its ability to observe this policy will depend on whether it budgets enough money to screen applicants carefully. Securing adequate funds for the HR budget further requires the HR staff to be able to convince top management that the HR program is cost-effective and is producing results.

Evaluating the Human Resources Program

Just as financial audits are conducted, audits or evaluations of the HRM program should be conducted periodically to assure that its objectives are being accomplished. Audits typically involve analyzing data relative to the program, including employee turnover, grievances, absences, accidents, and similar indicators. Special attention is usually given to assessing compliance with laws and regulations governing various specific areas such as equal employment opportunity and safety and health. A comprehensive audit, as discussed in Chapter 20, should encompass all aspects of the HR function as performed by both the HR department and the operating and line managers.

Nearly 1,000 *Fortune* 500 companies use the *Human Resource Effectiveness Report* co-sponsored by SHRM and the Saratoga Institute to measure their results against practices in other firms. In 1992 Saratoga released its first *Best Practices Report*. The report revealed that departments that had high levels of HR effectiveness cultivated communication, interdependence, strategy and planning, commitment, customer focus, continued improvement, risk taking, and culture consciousness and relationships.[32]

The Human Resources Department

five
objective

We observed earlier that the HR manager is assuming a greater role in top-management planning and decision making. This trend reflects a growing awareness of the contributions that HRM can make to the success of the firm.

Although managerial personnel at all levels are engaged in HRM activities, the top manager of the HR department has the primary responsibility for developing a program that will help the organization to meet its HRM objectives.

Responsibilities of the Human Resources Manager

Since the early 1960s, federal and state legislation and court decisions have had a major influence on HR policies and practices. More recently, concern for productivity improvement, employee desires for balancing family and job demands, and desire of workers for more equitable treatment have added to the responsibilities of the HR manager. These influences have thus required HR managers not only to be more knowledgeable about many issues but also to be more versatile in handling several activities. The major activities for which an HR manager is typically responsible are as follows:

1. *Policy initiation and formulation.* The HR manager generally proposes and drafts new policies or policy revisions to cover recurring problems or prevent anticipated problems. Ordinarily, these are proposed to the senior executives of the organization, who actually issue the policy.
2. *Advice.* The HR manager generally counsels and advises line managers. The HR staff is expected to be fully familiar with HR policy, labor agreements, past practices, and the needs and welfare of both the organization and the employees in order to develop sound solutions to problems.
3. *Service.* The HR manager generally engages in activities such as recruiting, selection, testing, planning of training programs, and hearing employee concerns and complaints.
4. *Control.* The HR manager generally monitors performance of line departments and other staff departments to ensure conformity with established HR policy, procedures, and practice.

The HR manager's authority in carrying out these activities is restricted to staff authority (policy initiation and formulation and advice giving) and functional authority (service and control). Within the scope of functional authority, the HR manager generally has the right and is expected to issue policies and procedures for HR functions—i.e., selection, training, performance evaluation, and so on—throughout an organization. The only line authority the HR manager has is over subordinates in his or her department.

In-House Consultants

A major contribution that the HR department staff can make to the organization is to serve as in-house consultants to the managers and supervisors of other departments. Alerting top management to contemporary issues and changes within society that affect the organization is also an important responsibility. Closely related is the responsibility of monitoring new developments taking place in the HR field and, when feasible, getting top management to adopt them.

Any consultation provided by the HR staff must be based on managerial and technical expertise. Furthermore, the staff should be concerned with the operating goals of the managers and supervisors who are their consulting clients and should help them to make sound decisions. These managers and supervisors must be convinced that the HR staff is there to assist them in increasing their productivity rather than to impose obstacles to their goals. This requires not only the ability to consider problems from the viewpoint of the line managers and supervisors, but also skill in communicating with the managers and supervisors.[33] Highlights in HRM 3 provides the reader with a better understanding of the variety of activities in the day of a generalist HR manager.

Outside Consultants and Outsourcing

HR managers often go outside the organization for professional assistance from qualified consultants. These consultants are hired to solve a variety of HR problems. In the past most consulting firms specialized in one or two areas of expertise, though many have now broadened their backgrounds in order to meet the expanding needs of their clients more effectively. The areas for which consultants are used most frequently are pension plans, executive recruitment, health and welfare plans, psychological assessment, wage and salary administration, job evaluation, and executive compensation. When using the services of a consultant, it is important to select an experienced, reputable individual, to educate him or her about the corporate environment, and to have a clear and mutual understanding of what the consultant is to do.[34]

Outsourcing

Practice of contracting with outside vendors to handle specified HR functions

In recent years, **outsourcing**—the practice of contracting with outside firms to handle some HR functions previously performed in-house—has become a trend at companies of all sizes. A recent survey of 927 firms by the Wyatt Company shows that 32 percent of employers already outsource some or all of the administration of the HR and benefit programs.

Unlike one-time vendor contracts, outsourcing contracts require months of study and negotiation to make certain that all the major and minor issues have been carefully examined and resolved. When outsourcing is used, the vendors are actually integrated into the firm. In a comprehensive article, Brenda Sunoo and Jennifer Laabs provide detailed instructions on how to proceed in making outsourcing arrangements.[35]

Department Organization

In a small firm the HR department may consist only of a manager and a few assistants. In a larger firm many additional staff members may be required. Increased size eventually leads to the establishment of departmental units.

The relative pressures of each HR function will help determine the need for specialization. For example, changes in the legal environment have forced many firms to establish a unit to oversee and coordinate equal employment opportunity and affirmative action (EEO/AA) efforts. The passage of the Employee Retirement Income Security Act (ERISA), together with employee pressure for expanded benefits, similarly has led firms to establish units to supervise these functions. Safety units have been formed to ensure compliance with the Occupational Safety and Health Act (OSHA). When a firm becomes unionized, a separate unit is likely to be established to oversee the labor relations function.

HIGHLIGHTS IN HRM

highlights

3   A DAY IN THE LIFE OF A GENERALIST HR MANAGER

Mike Rogers leans back in his chair, cradling the phone to his ear, scrawling notes to himself on squares of paper. The telephone is his tool, his lifeline to his constituency. He's not an elected official, although legislative issues rank high on his agenda. He's not an educator, although he believes improving education is vital to the nation's future. He's not a recruiter, trainer, or benefits specialist either, although he's conversant in all those areas. He's an HR generalist, beginning what he would call a typical day.

Rogers is vice president of human resources for BancFirst in Oklahoma City. The bank has about 600 employees in approximately thirty locations, primarily in the eastern part of the state. There are no human resource representatives in the branches.

"There's no personnel department—I'm it," says Rogers, who sees himself as the internal consultant to his BancFirst customers. Like any HR generalist, he must be able to move from one item on the agenda to the next—affirmative action, vacation policy, the United Way campaign, performance evaluations, employee assistance programs—dispatching each with aplomb. Or as Rogers puts it, "I'm like a bumblebee; I try to meet with each branch manager once a month to put out fires and teach the managers to teach others. Their job is to train. We fought the urge to create a bureaucracy. We've all become trainers—training is a big deal."

On the job, Rogers pretty much follows a daily ritual. After an early breakfast meeting, he's in the office by 8:30, going through a folder of papers with HR assistant Tina Strunk. The papers include a memo on new vacation policy, another on plans for a loan officer training class. This "to do" folder is his way of staying on track, of making sure that nothing falls through the cracks.

His next task of the morning is a reference check on a potential employee, followed by a phone call to discuss a meeting with another job applicant. "We're going through the budgeting process," he tells the applicant. "We will have some slots open and we've got to fill up our pipeline with just the right kind of people."

On a day-to-day basis, Rogers estimates he spends much of his time on laws and regulations. "You've got to spend a lot of your time staying current," he says. Legislative affairs is a subject dear to Rogers' heart. He is a member of the SHRM's Legislative Affairs Committee and is known to hand out silver dollars to people who can name their elected state officials. During the legislative session he canvasses the capitol—twisting arms, as he puts it, to win support for HR issues. Rogers has a creed: "Legislative affairs needs to be a competency just like my other responsibilities. It's like knowing the right questions to ask when you hire and fire; you need to have competency."

Another part of Rogers' day, today and almost every day lately, is taken up by the new health care proposal. "It's a project and I'm a project guy," he says. "The other things are ongoing." BancFirst is considering (and will later accept) a self-insured health care plan. Today Rogers is working on a presentation to explain why the change should be made and how the company can go about it.

As part of the health care puzzle, Rogers is asking himself the generalist's basic question—what to handle himself and what to turn over to outside experts. "The key, if you're a generalist, is to develop the trait of being able to evaluate outside people," he observes. "Generalists also have to be able to ne-gotiate with consultants or it can be like a runaway taxicab meter."

Rogers next meets with CEO David Rainbold to go over an upcoming all-day planning meeting, the bank's Presidents' Day, where the health care proposal will be presented. The annual budget is due the same day. "This is what happens to generalists," Rogers jokes. "At least the Sooners are playing an away game this weekend so I can concentrate on my work at home."

A few minutes later, Rogers is back on the phone again, this time bargaining over the cost of an HR information service.

At lunch, he proudly takes a visitor on a short tour of downtown Oklahoma City, showing off the skyline of the state capital from the top floor of one of the city's tallest buildings.

Right after lunch, Rogers takes time to look over the wording of BankFirst's employee handbook, which he says has long been a work-in-progress. "I want you to know this policy forward and back-ward," he now tells assistant Tina Strunk.

At 2 p.m., a simple ceremony takes place in Rogers' office. The vice president of human resources presents a BancFirst pin to new employee Valerie Pautsch, a loan administration specialist. The ceremony itself is brief, but Rogers takes time to answer Pautsch's questions about the details of BancFirst's 401(k) plan.

Controller Randy Foraker stops by Rogers' open door, and they confer on a range of tax and bene-fits issues, including the proposed health care policy. "We've got to try to anticipate every attack and be prepared to respond to it," Rogers tells the controller. CEO Rainbold stops by and joins in the discussion.

In late afternoon Rogers drives across town to meet with Mike Seney, director of the manufactur-ers' department of the Oklahoma State Chamber of Commerce and Industry. They discuss plans for a pro-gram on alternative dispute resolution. The two work easily together, a relationship based on long experience in fighting legislative battles together, furthering mutual interests. Rogers sees much advan-tage to working with the chamber. "They have something we don't; they walk the halls of the state capi-tol. (Seney) knows our issues and we're his resource." Seney is equally supportive of the collaborative process. "It doesn't do them any good to wail about a law after it passes," he says.

The Chamber of Commerce visit may be the last *official* stop of the day, but it's not the end of Rogers' day by any means. Rogers, who preaches the importance of education, makes it a point to prac-tice what he preaches. This evening he stops by Oklahoma City's Alternative Middle School to attend an Open House where he hopes to meet with the student he is mentoring. The student doesn't show up— "Sometimes it's hard to tell if I'm doing any good," Rogers observes—but he sticks with it, talking with teachers, urging them to encourage the boy's talent for art.

Later, looking back over the events of the day, Rogers seems pleased. "We're moving things along," he says. "At least there weren't any crises today." Yesterday, there was a meeting to define skill-based pay. Tomorrow there'll be an employee meeting in Hugo, Oklahoma. Next week there's the Presi-dents' Day meeting. "The key to being a generalist is the ability to juggle," Rogers says, "to do multiple things at once. You need to be disciplined enough to be competent, not just muddle through."

At the end of a long day, what does a garden-variety generalist ask himself? For Mike Rogers the question is simple: "Was what I did today good for the company and good for the employee?"

Source: Adapted from Stephenie Overman, "A Day in the Life of an HR Generalist," *HR Magazine* 38, no. 3 (March 1993): 78–83. Reprinted with the permission of *HR Magazine* (formerly *Personnel Administrator*), published by the Society for Human Resource Management, Alexandria, Va.

objective

HRM in the Future

During the 1990s HRM has been in the throes of a radical transformation. According to a study by IBM and the consulting firm of Towers Perrin and another by the SHRM Foundation—as well as many articles by respected scholars—the HR function is being transformed into a significant management function. Where HR departments fail to recognize their responsibilities to become vital members of the management team, line managers are reaching out to take control and ownership of the various HR functions.[36]

The IBM–Towers Perrin study (1992) conducted in twelve countries with 2,961 individuals—line executives, HR executives, faculty, and consultants—provides valuable information on the new and potentially stronger role of HRM in work organizations. Looking to the year 2000, both line and HR executives agree that a proactive and strategically oriented HR function will be critical. Almost all respondents see the need for dramatic changes from centralized and functionally organized HR units to more flexible and decentralized units. This will necessitate more supervisory involvement in HR activities.

In the IBM–Towers Perrin study the respondents were asked about various attributes of the HR role through a series of six paired alternative choices (shown in Figure 1–5). The response clearly shows that the current HR roles are not what they should be in the year 2000. Figure 1–6 shows how much the existing roles differ from those described for 2000. What it ultimately shows is a new

FIGURE 1-5 *Alternative Attributes of the HR Role*

Concentrate on operational matters	Participate in strategic planning matters
Respond to management's view of needed changes	Proactively create and manage change
Assume full responsibility for the management of all human resources	Advise and counsel line management, who takes responsibility for HR
Focus on individual employees	Focus on teams and groups of employees
Focus on internal business needs	Actively address societal issues
Represent the views and concerns of employees	Represent the views and concerns of management

Source: Towers Perrin, *Priorities for a Competitive Advantage, an IBM–Towers Perrin Study* (New York: Towers Perrin, 1992), 20. Reproduced with permission.

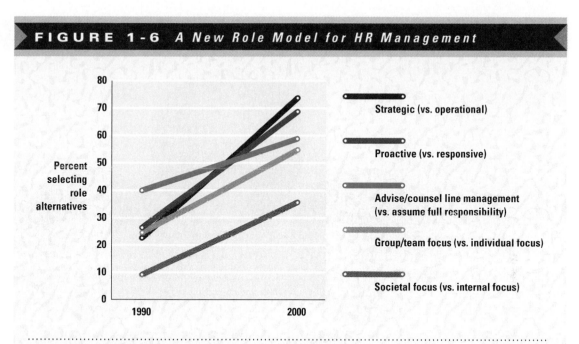

> **FIGURE 1-6** *A New Role Model for HR Management*

Percent selecting role alternatives

- Strategic (vs. operational)
- Proactive (vs. responsive)
- Advise/counsel line management (vs. assume full responsibility)
- Group/team focus (vs. individual focus)
- Societal focus (vs. internal focus)

1990   2000

Source: Towers Perrin, *Priorities for a Competitive Advantage, an IBM–Towers Perrin Study* (New York: Towers Perrin, 1992), 21. Reproduced with permission.

role model for the HR department and its functions. The study itself shows that both line and HR executives support the concept of shared responsibilities between line managers and HR managers and that the single greatest attribute of the HR staff will be the ability to educate and influence line managers on HR issues.[37]

An earlier study prepared for the Society for Human Resource Management was conducted to determine what pressures organizations face today, what they must do to remain competitive, what the role of HR is in providing a competitive advantage, and how this role is changing. A leading question in the survey was "What distinguishes superior HR performance from average performance?" The study found a clear link between an organization's level of success and the effectiveness of its HR leadership.

During the course of the study more than twenty CEOs and more than fifty practitioners participated in determining the role they expect HR to play in meeting competitive and organizational challenges. This information was obtained to create the Senior-Level HR Competency Model shown in Figure 1–7. The purpose of this model is to define and describe the competencies required of superior HR leaders from the perspective of both CEOs and HR practitioners.[38] Study the individual competencies within each of the five clusters: goal and action management, functional and organizational leadership, influence management, business knowledge, and HR technical proficiency.

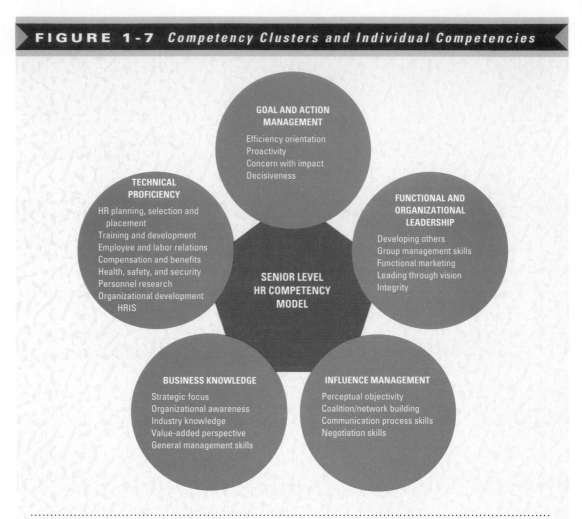

FIGURE 1-7 *Competency Clusters and Individual Competencies*

GOAL AND ACTION MANAGEMENT

Efficiency orientation
Proactivity
Concern with impact
Decisiveness

TECHNICAL PROFICIENCY

HR planning, selection and
    placement
Training and development
Employee and labor relations
Compensation and benefits
Health, safety, and security
Personnel research
Organizational development
    HRIS

FUNCTIONAL AND ORGANIZATIONAL LEADERSHIP

Developing others
Group management skills
Functional marketing
Leading through vision
Integrity

SENIOR LEVEL HR COMPETENCY MODEL

BUSINESS KNOWLEDGE

Strategic focus
Organizational awareness
Industry knowledge
Value-added perspective
General management skills

INFLUENCE MANAGEMENT

Perceptual objectivity
Coalition/network building
Communication process skills
Negotiation skills

Source: Tom E. Lawson, *The Competency Initiative Standards of Excellence for Human Resource Executives* (Alexandria, Va., SHRM Foundation, 1990), 25. Used with permission from the Society for Human Resource Management, Alexandria, Va. Copyright, 1989.

While the HR competency model was prepared as guidance for HR leaders and those who aspire to such positions, the knowledge and skills within the individual clusters can be used as a guide by anyone who wishes to succeed in a work organization or as an entrepreneur.

Organization of the Text

This book is divided into seven parts. In Part 1 we show why and how the various HRM functions have evolved and examine the different environments that must be considered. Because of their importance in performing all of the HRM functions, equal employment opportunity and affirmative action are introduced early in the book, in Chapter 3.

The chapters in Part 2 focus on the way that the HR requirements are met through analyzing job requirements, planning, recruiting personnel, and selecting those individuals who are most likely to be successful.

Once individuals are hired, it is necessary to provide training, to assist in their career development, and to appraise their performance on the job. These topics are discussed in Part 3.

In Part 4 we study the importance of implementing compensation and providing economic, physical, and emotional security for employees. The creation of a productive work environment is of fundamental concern to all managers. It is a topic that is emphasized in Part 5 and throughout this text.

In Part 5 we also focus on the motivation and leadership of employees, on the role of communication in HRM, and on employee rights and discipline.

Part 6, Enhancing Employee-Management Relations, discusses the dynamics of labor relations, collective bargaining, and contract administration. While these activities are typically handled by specialists in labor relations, all managers must be alert to the constraints of employee-management agreements.

In the last part of the book—Part 7—there is a chapter on international HRM. The rapid growth of global enterprises in recent years demands that managers have an understanding of the types of differences that one encounters in operations outside one's homeland.

The topic of the final chapter is the auditing of the HRM program. As with other organizational programs, there should be formal procedures for determining the extent to which HR objectives are being met.

Following Part 7 there is a major section containing eleven extended cases portraying current issues and problems in HRM. "Ill-Fated Love," "Toxic Substances at Lukens Chemical Industries," and "Managing Diversity" are a few of them.

The section of comprehensive cases is followed by:

- A glossary
- A name index
- An organization index
- A subject index

SUMMARY

objective

HRM represents a new concept of and approach to performing personnel functions. It still requires the performance of those personnel functions that have evolved over the years in response to emerging needs. However, instead of treating these functions as separate and distinct, HRM considers them interrelated parts of a management system that must be integrated closely with strategic organizational planning. Accordingly, HR managers are becoming more involved in the decision making of top management in a wide variety of issues and problems. Knowledge of HRM is important for individuals who will occupy managerial and supervisory roles, since they will also perform HR functions.

The present status of HRM was achieved only after years of evolutionary development. During the nineteenth century the factory system enabled products to be manufactured more cheaply than before. The concentration of workers in factories in turn focused public attention on the need for better working conditions and greater consideration for employee health and safety. During this period an objective and systematic approach to improving worker efficiency known as scientific management emerged. By the early 1900s some of the knowledge and research from the field of psychology was beginning to be applied to the management of personnel.

Since the late 1920s several forces have contributed significantly to the HRM movement. The Hawthorne studies were influential in humanizing the workplace, and the human relations movement focused attention on individual differences and informal groups. As the human relations movement evolved, it became broader in scope and included the various behavioral sciences, focusing on the achievement of organizational objectives. During this period political pressures gave rise to federal and state legislation affecting HRM. Now there is increasing specialization of HR functions and an emphasis on strategic management.

HRM may be referred to as a profession because it has the following characteristics: (1) It is based upon an organized body of knowledge developed through research and experimentation, (2) the knowledge is disseminated through publications and professional meetings, (3) professional associations promote the professional growth of their members, (4) various types of certification allow practitioners to increase their competency, and (5) the various HRM professional associations have developed codes of ethics that their members are expected to observe.

A code of ethics focuses attention on ethical values and provides a basis for HR professionals to evaluate their plans and their actions. HR departments have been given a greater role in communicating the organization's values and standards and in monitoring compliance with its code of ethics.

The principal elements of an HR program are objectives, policies, and procedures. HR objectives are determined by the organization's objectives as a whole. Policies serve to guide the actions required to achieve these objectives. HR policies must be compatible with current economic conditions, collective bargaining trends, and laws and regulations at all levels. HR procedures implement policies by prescribing the steps to follow in carrying out the policies. Statements relating to objectives, policies, and procedures can be meaningful only if they are supported financially by the budget. It is important that the HRM program be audited periodically to assure that its objectives are being accomplished.

The HR department is responsible for initiating and formulating policy; counseling and advising line managers; providing services such as recruiting, selection, and planning of training programs; and monitoring the performance of line and staff departments to ensure conformity with established HR policy and procedures. The HR manager's authority in carrying out these activities is restricted to staff authority and functional authority. HR managers often use the

objective

services of outside consultants, and more recently, they have outsourced some of the HR functions to vendors on a long-term basis.

HRM is in the midst of a radical transformation. Line managers are reaching out to take control over the HR functions where HR departments fail to recognize their responsibilities. Comprehensive research studies have shown that a proactive, strategically oriented perspective is critical. Both line and HR executives support the concept of shared responsibility between line and HR managers. An HR competency model emphasizes goal and action management, functional and organizational leadership, influence management, business knowledge, and HR technical proficiency.

KEY TERMS

behavioral sciences

certification

Hawthorne studies

HR budget

HR information system (HRIS)

HR objectives

HR policies

HR procedures

human relations movement

human resources management (HRM)

outsourcing

scientific management

DISCUSSION QUESTIONS

1. In what respects does HRM differ from the traditional approach of personnel management?
2. Why is HRM playing an increasingly important role in organizations?
3. What specific HRM responsibilities do line managers and supervisors have?
4. HRM is referred to as a profession. On what basis can this statement be made?
5. Cite the reasons why policy statements are needed and describe the manner in which they should be disseminated.
6. What contributions has the Society for Human Resource Management made to HRM?
7. What should be the role of the HR staff in its relations with personnel outside the HR department?
8. Of those functions performed in HRM, which do you consider to be most important? State your reasons.

CASE STUDY: The Business of HR at IBM

HR departments are typically viewed by management personnel as cost centers rather than as profit-generating centers. Until a major restructuring of International Business Machines (IBM) in 1992, its HR department was no exception to this rule. At that time IBM was divided into thirteen separate divisions, each with increased autonomy. While not one of the thirteen new divisions, HR was restructured into a more autonomous organization and a separate company known as Workforce Solutions (WFS) was formed. In the process, hundreds of IBM HR professionals joined WFS—all with impressive academic credentials and training, in-depth HR experience, industry association involvement, and dedication to quality and customer satisfaction.

With the formation of WFS, HR personnel were retained in the major divisions of IBM to provide advice and counsel and to report to line management, as they always had. HR strategy, responsibility, and decision making remains in the major divisions. WFS is designed to deliver quality programs and services that *support* the HR strategies, plans, and functions of the major divisions. Every division still has an HR department, but now it serves only the advise and counsel function. At IBM there are about 500 HR professionals and about 1,300 staff members at WFS.

WFS is headquartered in Westchester County, New York; operating nationwide, it provides, for a charge, the following programs and services to IBM companies:

- Human resource research and consulting services
- Leadership development programs
- Workforce diversity programs
- Equal opportunity programs and compliance monitoring
- Resources planning services
- Compensation and benefits programs
- Recruiting and employment services
- Occupational health services
- Relocation programs
- International assignment services
- Employee involvement and suggestion programs
- Testing and assessment services

The results have been excellent: HR services delivered at a lower cost, enhancement of the commitment to HR, flexibility and responsiveness to customer needs, streamlining of HR processes, and innovative HR programs for the workplace. WFS innovations include introduction of a world-class employee suggestion program, design of cost-saving medical plan changes, establishment of centralized employee-benefits support using state-of-the-art technology, and increased employee involvement in the organization through incentive pay programs.

While WFS was primarily designed to provide quality, cost-effective service to the IBM community of businesses, its services are now available to outside organizations.

Source: IBM brochure, "Workforce Solutions," and Jennifer J. Laabs, "HR Becomes a Separate Business at IBM," *Personnel Journal* 72, no. 4 (April 1993): 25–29.

....

Questions

1. How can the WFS concept make an HR program more cost-effective?

2. What effect is the availability of a WFS type of organization likely to have on HR personnel in their advising and counseling roles?

3. Do you foresee other corporations developing similar structures? Why or why not?

NOTES AND REFERENCES

1. Andrew J. DuBrin and R. Duane Ireland, *Management & Organization,* 2d ed. (Cincinnati: South-Western, 1993); 6–8. See also Lee Dyer, ed., *Human Resource Management—Evoking Roles and Responsibilities* (Washington, D.C.: Bureau of National Affairs, 1988).

2. For discussions of these issues, see Robert J. Nobile, "Can There Be Too Much Diversity?" *Personnel* 68, no. 9 (August 1991): 11; Lawrence M. Baytos, "Launching Successful Diversity Initiatives," *HR Magazine* 37, no. 3 (March 1992): 91–97; Jim Spoor, "HRIS Can Make Downsizing Strategic and Fair," *Personnel* 68, no. 8 (August 1991): 87; "The Right Family Values in the Workplace," *Business Week* (June 28 1993): 134; "Work and the Family," *Business Week* (June 28, 1993): 80–84; Charlene Marmer Solomon, "Managing Today's Immigrants," *Personnel Journal* 72, no. 2 (February 1993): 56–65; Cresencio Torres and Mary Bruxelles, "Capitalizing on Global Diversity," *HR Magazine* 37, no. 12 (December 1992): 30–33.

3. Charlene Marmer Solomon, "Managing the HR Career in the '90s," *Personnel Journal* 73, no. 6 (June 1994): 62–76; see also Shannon Peters Talbott, "How HR Keeps Current in Century-Old Companies," *Personnel Journal* 37, no. 10 (October 1994): 86–94.

4. Mark A. Huselid, "Documenting the HR's Effect on Company Performance," *HR Magazine* 39, no. 1 (January 1994): 79–85. See also George C. Tokesky and Joanne F. Kornides, "Strategic HR Management Is Vital," *Personnel Journal* 73, no. 12 (December 1994): 115–17.

5. Frederick W. Taylor, "What Is Scientific Management?" in *Classics in Management,* ed. Harwood F. Merrill (New York: American Management Association, 1960), 80. See also Edwin A. Locke, "The Ideas of Frederick W. Taylor: An Evaluation," *Academy of Management Review* 7, no. 1 (January 1982): 14–24. See also Hindy Lauer Schacter, "Frederick Winslow Taylor and the Idea of Worker Participation: A Brief against Easy Administrative Dichotomies," *Administration and*

Society 21, no. 1 (May 1989): 20–30; Charles D. Wrege and Ronald G. Greenwood, *Frederick W. Taylor, Father of Scientific Managment: Myth and Reality* (Homewood, Ill.: Business One Irwin, 1991).

6. For the collected works of the Gilbreths, see William R. Spriegel and Clark E. Myers, eds., *The Writings of the Gilbreths* (Homewood, Ill.: Richard D. Irwin, 1953). For many years Dr. Lillian Gilbreth combined a career as a management consultant with that of a homemaker and mother of twelve children, who, her husband alleged, were "cheaper by the dozen." For an entertaining account of the lives of Lillian and Frank Gilbreth as parents, see Frank B. Gilbreth, Jr., and Ernestine Gilbreth Carey, *Cheaper by the Dozen* (New York: Grosset & Dunlap, 1948).

7. Harrington Emerson, *The Twelve Principles of Efficiency* (New York: The Engineering Magazine Co., 1913). See also Alex W. Rathe, ed., *Gantt on Management* (New York: American Management Association, 1961).

8. John Bales, "Lillian Gilbreth Honored on U.S. Postage Stamp," *APA Monitor* (February 1984): 2. Dr. Gilbreth's portrait appears on a 40-cent stamp.

9. Hugo Münsterberg, *Psychology and Industrial Efficiency* (Boston: Houghton Mifflin, 1913).

10. Walter Dill Scott and Robert C. Clothier, *Personnel Management: Practices and Point of View* (New York: A. W. Shaw, 1923). See also Edmund C. Lynch, *Walter Dill Scott, Pioneer in Personnel Management* (Austin: Bureau of Business Research, University of Texas, 1968), 2223.

11. For extensive references to Cattell, see Ernest R. Hilgard, ed., *American Psychology in Historical Perspective* (Washington, D.C.: American Psychological Association, 1978). The address of the Psychological Corporation is 555 Academic Court, San Antonio, Texas 78204-0952.

12. Walter Van Dyke Bingham and Bruce Victor Moore, *How to Interview* (New York: Harper & Brothers, 1931). See also Bingham, *Aptitudes and Aptitude Testing* (New York: Harper & Brothers, 1937).

13. For a comprehensive view of the many aspects of organizational psychology, see a special issue of the

American Psychologist 45, no. 2 (February 1990), edited by Lynn R. Offermann and Marilyn K. Gowing.

14. F.J. Roethlisberger and W.J. Dickson, *Management and the Worker* (Cambridge, Mass.: Harvard University Press, 1939).

15. John G. Adair, "The Hawthorne Effect: A Reconsideration of the Methodological Artifact," *Journal of Applied Psychology* 69, no. 2 (May 1984): 334–45. This article includes a comprehensive bibliography of articles that contain critiques and reinterpretations of the Hawthorne experiments. See also Berkeley Rice, "The Hawthorne Defect: Persistence of a Flawed Theory," *Psychology Today* 16, no. 2 (February 1982): 70–74.

16. For an appreciation of Mary Parker Follett's contributions, see Elliot M. Fox, "Mary Parker Follett: The Enduring Contribution," *Public Administration Review* 28, no. 6 (November– December 1968): 520–29.

17. Kurt Lewin, *The Research Center for Group Dynamics* (New York: Beacon House, 1947). See also Alfred J. Marrow, *The Practical Theorist: The Life and Work of Kurt Lewin* (New York: Basic Books, 1969).

18. Harold M. F. Rush, *Behavioral Science: Concepts and Management Application*, Personnel Policy Study No. 216 (New York: National Industrial Conference Board, 1969), 2.

19. Harold E. Burtt, *Principles of Employment Psychology*, rev. ed. (New York: Harper & Brothers, 1942), 62–66. One of Burtt's former doctoral students, Frank Stanton, president emeritus of CBS, and Ruth Stanton honored Burtt on his 100th birthday on April 26, 1990, by donating $1.25 million to Ohio State University to establish the Harold E. Burtt Chair in Industrial Psychology. As an author of ten books and a university professor for over forty years, Dr. Burtt (1890–1991) had widespread influence in the area of personnel and industrial psychology.

20. David Ulrich, Wayne Brockbank, and Arthur Yeung, "HR Competencies in the 1990s," *Personnel Administrator* 34, no. 11 (November 1989): 91–93.

21. Membership Department, Society for Human Resource Management.

22. Addresses of these associations may be found in the latest edition of the *Encyclopedia of Associations* (Detroit, Mich.: Gale Research), available in most libraries.

23. The certifications and requirements for achieving them are
    - Professional in Human Resources (PHR)—Four years of professional HRM experience, or two years of HRM experience and a related bachelor's degree, or one year's HRM experience and a related graduate degree.
    - Senior Professional in Human Resources (SPHR)—Eight years of professional HRM experience, or six years of professional HRM experience and a related bachelor's degree, or five years of professional HRM experience and a related graduate degree. The most recent three years' experience must include policy-developing responsibility.

24. Carolyn Wiley, "The Certified HR Professional," *HR Magazine* 37, no. 8 (August 1992): 77–84.

25. Fran A. Wallace, "Walking a Tightrope: Ethical Issues Facing HR Professionals," *Personnel* 62, no. 6 (June 1985): 32–36.

26. Susan J. Harrington, "What Corporate America Is Teaching about Ethics," *The Executive* V, no. 1 (February 1991): 21–30. See also Alan Weis, "Seven Reasons to Examine Workplace Ethics," *HR Magazine* 36, no. 3 (March 1991): 69–74: Paul G. Kaponya, "March to a Different Drummer," *HR Magazine* 37, no. 4 (April 1992): 66–68; Bernard J. Reilly," *Business Horizons* 33, no. 6 (November– December 1990): 23–27; Michael R. Hyman, Robert Skipper, and Richard Tansey, "Ethical Codes Are Not Enough," *Business Horizons* 33, no. 2 (March–April 1990): 15–22.

27. Issued quarterly, *Personnel Management Abstracts* includes abstracts of articles and recent books, a subject and author index of articles, and a list of journals abstracted with addresses of publishers.

28. Issued monthly, *Work Related Abstracts* extracts significant information from over 250 management, labor, government, professional, and university publications.

29. *Human Resources Abstracts* is published quarterly in March, June, September, and December by Sage Periodicals Press.

30. *Business Periodicals Index* is published monthly (except August) by the H.W. Wilson Company.

31. Scott A. Snell, Patricia Pedigo, and George M. Krawiec, "Managing the Impact of Information Technology on Human Resources Management," Chapter 9 in Geral R. Ferris, Sherman D. Rosen, and Darold T. Barnum, eds., *Handbook of Human Resources Management* (Oxford, U.K.: Blackwell Publishers, 1994). See also Samuel Greengard, "How Technology Is Advancing HR," *Personnel Journal* 72, no. 9 (September 1993): 80–90; Renae Broderick and John W. Boudreau, "Human Resource Management, Information Technology, and the Competitive Edge," *Academy of Management Executive* 6, no. 2 (May 1992): 7–17.

32. Linda Thornburg, "The White Knight of HR Effectiveness," *HR Magazine* 37, no. 11 (November 1992): 67–78.

33. "Building a Customer-Oriented HR Department," *HR Magazine* 36, no. 10 (October 1991): 64–66.

34. Robert S. Seeley, "HR Redesigns to Optimize Effectiveness," *HR Magazine* 37, no. 11 (November 1992): 44–46; Peter Rosik, "Four Ways

to Profit from Consultants," *HR Magazine* 37, no. 11 (November 1992): 77–85.

35. Brenda Paik Sunoo and Jennifer J. Laabs, "Winning Strategies for Outsourcing Contracts," *Personnel Journal* 73, no. 3 (March 1994): 69–78.

36. Randall S. Schuler, "Repositioning the Human Resource Function," *Academy of Management Executive* 4, no. 3 (August 1990): 49–60.

37. Towers Perrin, *Priorities for a Competitive Advantage, an IBM–Towers Perrin Study* (New York: Towers Perrin, 1992).

38. Tom E. Lawson, *The Competency Initiative Standards of Excellence for Human Resource Executives* (Alexandria, Va.: SHRM Foundation, 1990).

Chapter

The Environment for Human
Resources Management

After studying this chapter you should be able to

After studying this chapter you should be able to

Explain why managers should be concerned with the external and internal environments of their organizations.

Explain how technological changes affect employee jobs and HRM.

Describe the federal regulatory system as it pertains to HRM.

Identify the major demographic trends that influence HRM.

Explain how an organization's concern about quality is reflected in its approach to HRM.

Identify the elements of a strong organizational culture.

An HRM *program functions in a complex environment comprising several elements both inside and outside the firm. In order to have an effective HR program, HR managers must give careful attention to all aspects of the* **environment.** *Rapid changes are occurring within society and therefore in the environment within which organizations operate. These changes present challenges that require early solutions if an HR program is to be successful and make its full contribution to the organization and to all its members. One specific example well known to most of us is the declining number of middle-manager jobs, coupled with a growing number of baby boomers competing for those positions. Other issues such as unemployment, the influx of immigrants, the education and skills gap, the adoption of advanced technology, lifestyle adjustments for dual-career couples, and the like all have significant implications for HRM.*

From the broadest perspective, HRM balances the needs of the organization with the realities of the internal and external environments. In this chapter we will consider the kinds of changes that are anticipated and their effects on HRM. How to improve an organization's internal environment is one of the major challenges confronting employers today, so we will give special emphasis to ways the internal environment can be changed to improve the quality of work life.

one
objective

Environment
The conditions, circumstances, and influences that affect the organization's ability to achieve its objectives

External environment
The environment that exists outside an organization

Environmental scanning
Analyzing the environment and the changes occurring within it

Issues management
Process by which managers keep abreast of current issues and bring organizational policies in line with prevailing public opinion

Elements of an Organization's Environment

The **environment** of an organization consists of the conditions, circumstances, and influences that affect the firm's ability to achieve its objectives. Figure 2–1 shows that every organization exists in an environment that has both external and internal components. It also illustrates that both the external and the internal environment are composed of five elements: physical, technological, social, political, and economic. As shown by the arrows, the five elements of the external environment influence how HR functions will be performed. The internal environment influences both HR policies and procedures and the individuals who make up the workforce of the organization. One could further argue that performance of the HR functions also has some influence on the external environment. In fact, more than a decade ago, the president of the Conference Board of Canada observed: "For an increasing number of HR executives, their role goes beyond the sensing and interpreting of the impact of the environment on the firm. For them it is equally important to participate in and influence the environment."[1]

The External Environment

The environment that exists outside the firm, the **external environment,** has a significant impact on HRM policies and practices. It helps to determine the values, attitudes, and behavior that employees bring to their jobs. This is why many organizations engage in **environmental scanning,** which involves analyzing the environment and changes occurring within it. The purpose here is to determine the environment's possible impact on organizational policies and practices. Another closely related practice is **issues management,** by which managers attempt to keep abreast of current issues. This may include bringing the organization's policies in line with prevailing public opinion.

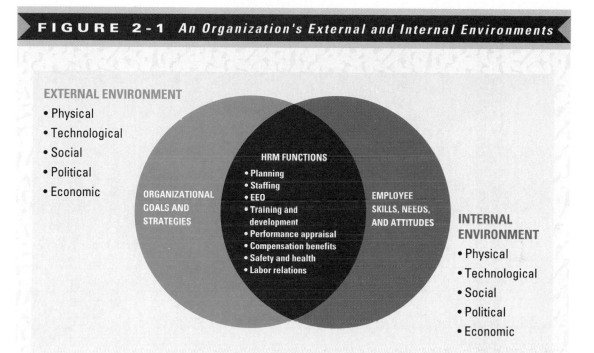

FIGURE 2-1 *An Organization's External and Internal Environments*

EXTERNAL ENVIRONMENT
• Physical
• Technological
• Social
• Political
• Economic

ORGANIZATIONAL GOALS AND STRATEGIES

HRM FUNCTIONS
• Planning
• Staffing
• EEO
• Training and development
• Performance appraisal
• Compensation benefits
• Safety and health
• Labor relations

EMPLOYEE SKILLS, NEEDS, AND ATTITUDES

INTERNAL ENVIRONMENT
• Physical
• Technological
• Social
• Political
• Economic

Physical Element

The physical element of the external environment includes the geography, climate, and other physical characteristics of the area in which the organization is located. Physical surroundings can help or hinder a firm's ability to attract and retain employees. Housing, commuting, and living costs can vary from one location to another and can have a significant impact on the compensation employees will expect. Recent population shifts to the Sun Belt and to small towns and rural areas can be attributed, at least in part, to the desire of the migrants to work and live in what they perceive to be a more desirable physical environment. For example, the Bureau of the Census projects that the population in the West will increase about 19 percent between 1990 and 2005. In the South, the population is expected to increase about 15 percent. The number of people in the Northeast is projected to increase slightly, by about 4 percent, while in the Midwest the population is expected to remain about the same. Ironically, this movement has created, and will continue to create, congestion, pollution, and other problems of growth in the areas to which people are moving.

Geographic shifts in the population alter the demand for and the supply of workers in local job markets. Organizations that depend on scientists and engineers, for example, pay particular attention to geographic regions where they can recruit "knowledge workers." Figure 2–2 shows *Fortune*'s list of the top ten U.S. metropolitan areas for business in 1993. These cities are among the best for

FIGURE 2-2 Top 10 U.S. Metropolitan Areas for Business (1993)

	1 RALEIGH/DURHAM	2 NEW YORK	3 BOSTON	4 SEATTLE	5 AUSTIN
Population 1993	925,448	17,033,162	5,033,657	2,171,534	918,123
Research centers	248	788	650	153	174
Education of people age 25+					
BA or higher	31.7%	25.4%	28.8%	29.5%	30.7%
Graduate degree	11.6%	10.5%	11.2%	8.8%	10.3%
Patents issued 1988-92	1,745	7,482	9,013	3,424	2,121
Presence of innovative firms (rank)	7	16	3	2	4
Pro-business attitude (rank)	16	46	55	30	28

	6 CHICAGO	7 HOUSTON	8 SAN JOSE	9 PHILADELPHIA	10 MINNEAPOLIS
Population 1993	7,612,116	3,536,757	1,524,168	4,981,082	2,660,189
Research centers	516	199	91	469	235
Education of people age 25+					
BA or higher	24.5%	25.0%	32.6%	22.6%	26.9%
Graduate degree	8.7%	7.9%	12.0%	8.3%	7.7%
Patents issued 1988-92	11,793	5,765	10,138	8,565	7,513
Presence of innovative firms (rank)	20	30	6	23	18
Pro-business attitude (rank)	27	11	48	32	56

Source: *Fortune.* Copyright 1993, Time Inc. All rights reserved.

finding high-tech talent, and many companies are moving their operations to those particular locations. For example, Data General, DuPont, Sumitomo, Ciba-Geigy, BASF, CompuChem, the U.S. Environmental Protection Agency, and the National Institutes of Health all have facilities located in Raleigh-Durham's 7,000-acre Research Triangle Park. More than 34,000 scientists and researchers and over fifty corporate, academic, and government tenants occupy this area at the center of three universities: University of North Carolina, Duke, and North Carolina State. Austin, Texas, has also become a hub for emerging high-tech companies. Dell Computer is located there, and Apple Computer recently relocated its payroll facilities, employee travel services, and customer service telephone lines to Austin. Further, a dozen technology-oriented companies, including Hewlett-Packard, Digital Equipment, NCR, and Rockwell have formed a semiconductor research consortium in Austin.[2]

objective

Technological Element

We live in an extremely competitive age. Only through technological innovation can firms develop new products and services and improve existing ones in order to stay competitive. Technology also provides a basis for an organization to attain the productivity and quality it needs to gain a competitive advantage.

Advancements in computer technology have enabled firms to take advantage of the information explosion. With computers, unlimited amounts of data can be stored, retrieved, and used in a wide variety of ways, from simple record keeping to controlling complex equipment. In our everyday living we see bank tellers, airline reservation clerks, and supermarket cashiers using computers to perform their jobs. At the bank's automated teller machine and at the library's computerized card catalog we become computer operators ourselves.

Less visible are the systems that monitor employees' speed, efficiency, and accuracy. Companies such as AT&T, United Airlines, Equitable Life Insurance, and American Express use sophisticated devices to measure employee work output.[3] But while large businesses and computer firms tout computerized monitoring as an effective means of improving productivity, the computerized control systems used for this purpose have been linked to increased stress, loss of job privacy rights, health risks, and job dissatisfaction among employees. Supporters argue that such systems improve the consistency, clarity, and objectivity of performance measurement and so are an improvement over stressful, subjective evaluations by human supervisors.

The introduction of advanced technology affects the number of employees as well as the skills they need on the job. In particular, technological advancements have tended to reduce the number of jobs that require little skill and to increase the number of jobs that require considerable skill. In general, this transformation is referred to as a shift from "touch labor," where employee responsibilities are limited to only physical execution of work, to **"knowledge workers,"** where their responsibilities expand to include a richer array of activities such as planning, decision making, and problem solving.[4] In many cases, current employees can be retrained to assume new roles and responsibilities. However, those employees who are displaced also require retraining. We thus experience the paradox of having pages and pages of newspaper advertisements for applicants

Knowledge workers
Employees whose responsibilities include a rich array of activities such as planning, decision making, and problem solving

"OPEN THE DOOR, CLAYTON— YOU KNEW IT WAS INEVITABLE..."

Reprinted with permission of Dave Carpenter

with technical or scientific training while several million job seekers without such training register for work with employment agencies.

Because of the implications of advanced technology for HRM, the HR manager should play a major role in planning for its implementation. In the new era, employees are increasingly viewed as assets to be fully utilized, rather than costs to be minimized. Communication with employees clearly plays a crucial role, as management must demonstrate a real commitment to supporting change through staffing, training, job redesign, and reward systems.[5]

HR can play an important role in helping line managers cope with the organizational changes caused by new technology. HR can, for example, identify methods for introducing new technology that minimizes disruption and disarms the threat perceived by employees. In addition, HR can provide guidance to line managers in ensuring that the right technological skills are identified and sought in new employees, as well as in developing technology-literacy training programs. HR can also identify and evaluate the changes in organizational relationships brought about by new technology. Finally, HR should work with line managers to develop new structures that use technology to improve service, increase productivity, and reduce costs.[6]

Information technology has, of course, changed the face of HR in organizations around the world. In the United Kingdom alone several companies have made significant changes in their HR systems. Smith Kline Beecham, for example, has developed a news service based on voice-mail technology that is available to all its employees. The London Underground has developed a computer-based training program to help staff with evacuation procedures in the event of fire. The Miller Group, the largest privately owned construction company in Britain, has automated its process for determining profit-based bonuses. British Gas has computerized their employee suggestion system to automatically log suggestions, check for duplicates, statistically analyze the database, produce letters, and manage other aspects of reporting. Finally, Britain's North West Regional Health Authority has developed an information system that receives data from each health authority's personnel databases and presents aggregated information for senior line managers. Each of these examples shows that technology is changing the face of HRM: altering the methods of collecting employment information, speeding up the processing of that data, and improving the process of internal and external communication.[7]

In the United States, the impact of advanced technology is no less significant. For example, the U.S. Army's Career and Alumni Program (ACAP) uses information technology to integrate all available federal and local transition activities for army alumni. Their computerized database matches the skills of army veterans with the needs of private industry.[8] Other organizations such as AT&T and IBM have also begun to use relational databases to match up jobs and job seekers.

Social Element

Increasingly, employers are expected to demonstrate a greater sense of responsibility toward employees and toward society as a whole. Employees, furthermore,

Organizational changes place new demands on families by changing the roles of parents.

are expecting the same freedoms, rights, and benefits on the job that they enjoy as members of society. Health care, retirement, and safety issues, for example, represent just a few of the important areas where organizations must balance economic and social concerns. Employers who fail to accept this fact are encountering difficulties with their employees. In addition, employers are being constrained by legislation and court decisions that support their employees' rights in the workplace.

Many employees today are less obsessed with the acquisition of wealth and now view life satisfaction as more likely to result from balancing the challenges and rewards of work with those in their personal lives. Though most people still enjoy work, and want to excel at it, they also appear to be seeking ways of living that are less complicated but more meaningful. These new lifestyles cannot help but have an impact on the way employees must be motivated and managed. Consequently, HRM has become more complex than it was when employees were concerned primarily with economic survival.[9]

objective

Political Element

Governments have a significant impact on HRM. Each of the functions per-formed in the management of human resources—from employee recruitment to termination—is in some way affected by laws and regulations established at the state and federal levels.

As mentioned earlier, managers must follow all laws and government regula-tions—federal, state, and local—relating to HRM. In this book we will empha-size federal laws and regulations, however, because they apply to all organizations within the United States, except those specifically exempted from their provi-sions. Occasionally, state laws will be mentioned to illustrate differences among the states and to emphasize that managers must abide by state as well as federal laws and regulations in performing their various HRM functions.

While federal legislation and the agencies to enforce it have existed for many decades—e.g., the Interstate Commerce Commission (1887) and the Fed-eral Communications Commission (1934)—those agencies regulating the activi-ties relating to HRM are relatively new. Unlike agencies overseeing particular industries, the newer agencies regulate a specific management function across several industries, such as equal employment opportunity, labor relations, and worker safety and health.

Today's manager must understand the federal regulatory system in order to function effectively in the face of what has been described as a "seemingly inco-herent body of agency directives, inspections, reviews, regulations, and determi-nations."[10] Figure 2–3 shows that regulation begins with social and political problems that prompt lawmakers to pass laws empowering agencies to take regu-latory actions that in turn trigger management responses. Finally, the courts oversee the process by settling disputes between the litigating parties. Careful study of Figure 2–3 will give you a better understanding of how acts of Congress (laws) and presidential executive orders influence the activities of managers.

Federal regulations in particular are made more complex by the different in-terpretations placed upon them. The federal agency charged with administering a certain law typically develops guidelines for its interpretation, which are pub-lished in the *Federal Register*.[11] This interpretation may differ from what Congress intended in passing the law. Furthermore, subsequent court decisions may pro-vide still a different interpretation. To keep abreast of the latest interpretations, most managers find it advisable to use one of the principal labor information ser-vices listed at the end of this chapter.[12] We will refer in this book to federal laws and court decisions that are currently viewed as having a major influence on HRM. Be aware, however, that each week brings news of pending legislation and court decisions that may change the course of HRM policies and practices.

Economic Element

The economic environment has a profound influence on business in general and on the management of human resources in particular. Economic conditions often dictate whether a firm will need to hire or lay off employees. They also affect an employer's ability to increase employees' pay and/or benefits. While economic recessions can force the curtailment of operations in the private sector, they may

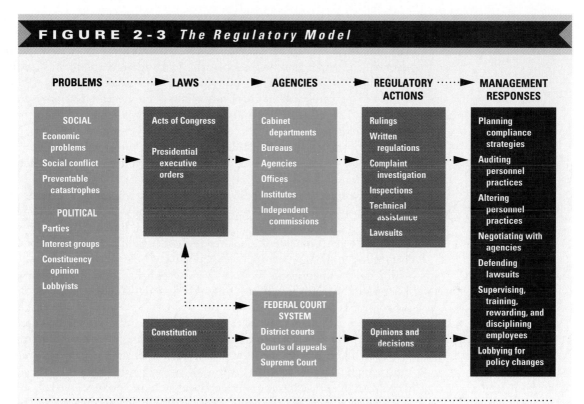

FIGURE 2-3 *The Regulatory Model*

PROBLEMS	LAWS	AGENCIES	REGULATORY ACTIONS	MANAGEMENT RESPONSES
SOCIAL Economic problems Social conflict Preventable catastrophes **POLITICAL** Parties Interest groups Constituency opinion Lobbyists	Acts of Congress Presidential executive orders	Cabinet departments Bureaus Agencies Offices Institutes Independent commissions	Rulings Written regulations Complaint investigation Inspections Technical assistance Lawsuits	Planning compliance strategies Auditing personnel practices Altering personnel practices Negotiating with agencies Defending lawsuits Supervising, training, rewarding, and disciplining employees Lobbying for policy changes
	Constitution	**FEDERAL COURT SYSTEM** District courts Courts of appeals Supreme Court	Opinions and decisions	

Source: James Ledvinka and Vida Scarpello, *Federal Regulation of Personnel and Human Resource Management,* 2d ed. (Boston: PWS-Kent Publishing, 1990), 18. Reproduced with permission.

have the opposite effect in the public sector. Unemployment generated by a recession usually necessitates the expansion of agencies that provide welfare and other social services. Expanding federal programs to combat a recession may mean that these agencies need more employees to supervise the programs.

Economists have long argued that a critical determinant of economic growth is the quality and quantity of inputs such as labor, private- and public-sector capital, and knowledge. U.S. productivity growth has dropped from its 3.3 percent annual level in the 1960s and 1970s to its current annual level of about 2.5 percent. Put in perspective, this drop-off is significant: Had our growth rate been as high from 1970 to 1990 as it was from 1900 to 1970, we would currently have a standard of living at least 25 percent higher than it is today. A large part of the drop in productivity growth is the result of technological change that has not yet paid off. As Robert Solow, Nobel Prize winner for economics, noted, "[W]e see the computer age everywhere but in the productivity statistics."[13]

But for all the concern about growth, it is important to keep in mind that the United States still remains the most productive country in the world. Contrary to some suspicions, Japan's productivity rate is less than 70 percent of that of the United States, and productivity in Germany is only about 80 percent of that of the United States.[14] These comparisons are important, as we now live in a global economy. Competition and cooperation with foreign companies has become an increasingly important focal point for business since the early 1980s. Indeed, nearly 17 percent of U.S. corporate assets are overseas. Nations such as Japan, Germany, France, Taiwan, Brazil, and South Korea represent both formidable rivals and important partners in our transformation to a global economy. In every country of the world, political leaders are under pressure to provide jobs for their unemployed—not just jobs, but "decent" jobs that will provide the standard of living to which their citizens aspire. These jobs can be created only if employers are able to compete successfully in the domestic and foreign markets. The North American Free Trade Agreement (NAFTA), for example, was created to establish a free-trade zone between Mexico, Canada, and the United States. (Plans are underway to include Argentina and other South American countries by the beginning of the next century.) Proponents of NAFTA argue that the agreement will remove impediments to trade and investment, thereby creating jobs. But opponents of NAFTA fear that jobs will be lost to Canada and particularly Mexico where wages are lower.[15]

Figure 2–4 shows fluctuations in the U.S. civilian unemployment rates from 1980 to 1994. When our economy is healthy, companies hire more workers to fill demand, and unemployment rates fall. But the economic picture is neither simple nor completely predictable. Perennially successful corporations, such as Sears, IBM, and General Motors are undergoing profound change, restructuring to compete better in a global economy. Particularly in the manufacturing sector, where capacity utilization rates are only about 80 percent, job growth is projected to move slowly, around 1.5 percent, over the next few years, though government spending may stimulate this growth rate somewhat.[16]

The Internal Environment

Internal environment (organizational climate)
The environment that exists within an organization

The environment that exists within an organization is known as the **internal environment,** or **organizational climate.** Like the external environment, the internal environment consists of physical, technological, social, political, and economic elements. These elements affect and are affected by the policies, procedures, and employment conditions that managers oversee. Therefore the program developed for managing human resources must take into account the internal as well as the external environment.

Physical Element

The physical element of the internal environment includes such factors as air quality, temperature, noise, dust, radiation, and other conditions affecting employee health and safety. One study of government employees revealed a high percentage of dissatisfaction with aspects of the physical environment of the workplace. Seventy-one percent of employees were dissatisfied with air quality and temperature; 54 percent with elevator operation; 46 percent with workplace appearance; 46 percent with maintenance and repairs; and 28 percent with

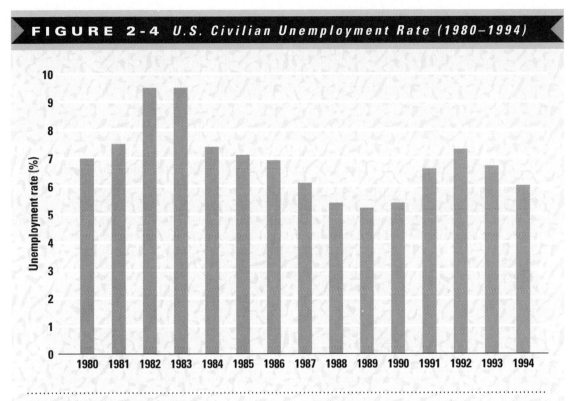

FIGURE 2-4 *U.S. Civilian Unemployment Rate (1980–1994)*

Source: U.S. Bureau of Labor Statistics

washroom cleanliness.[17] These responses would seem to indicate that there is much room for improvement in such areas, and organizations would be well advised to be attentive to these aspects of the internal environment.

Technological Element

The technological element of the internal environment relates closely to the physical element. It consists of the layout of the workplace; the process by which the work is performed; and the tools, equipment, and machinery used to perform the work. These factors in turn determine both the way work is processed and the requirements of the jobs performed.

The way in which work is organized affects interpersonal relations and interaction among employees within a work area. It influences the formation of informal work groups and the degree of cooperation or conflict among employees. More and more, technological systems are being integrated with the social systems of an organization, creating what is referred to as a **sociotechnical system.** Under this system, which is discussed more fully in Chapter 4, job design is based on human as well as technological considerations.[18]

Sociotechnical system

Environment in which the technical and social systems are integrated so that job design is based on human as well as technological considerations

Social Element

The social element reflects the attitudes and behaviors of managers and employees, individually and in groups. Because of their influential place in the organizational hierarchy, top managers play an extremely important role in determining the quality of the social element. The rules and regulations they devise, the concern they have for employees, the rewards and support they provide, and the tolerance they have for varying opinions are major factors in determining the organizational climate. In recent years there has been considerable interest in "the corporate culture." We will examine later in this chapter how the culture influences the type of climate as well as the course that HRM will take.

Political Element

Politics is an important social process found in all organizations. Organizational politics, of course, has the potential for being helpful or harmful to organizations and individuals. There are several tactics used in organizational politics. These include attacking or blaming others, using (or withholding or distorting) information, building images, building support for ideas, praising others, creating power coalitions, associating with the influential, and performing services or favors to create obligations. Which of these tactics an individual will use depends on that individual's nature or disposition and on the particular situation confronting him or her.

Power is the capacity to influence the behavior of others. The degree of power that managers possess is determined in part by where they fit into the formal organization structure, the number of subordinates they supervise, and the authority delegated to them. Power may also be derived from personal expertise and from informal leadership skills.

Power is an important aid in HRM. It can provide a means of gaining the type of performance and behavior desired of employees. As noted in Chapter 1, two recent studies, one by the Society for Human Resource Management (SHRM) and the other by IBM–Towers Perrin, suggest that HR departments must play a more active role in influencing change in their firms. This means having both the political power and leadership capabilities to overcome resistance to change.[19] Companies such as AT&T, Exxon, and Pepsico have designed programs to ensure that HR executives develop these types of competencies. The more power HR managers have in their organizations, the more successful they will be in getting other managers to carry out their own HR responsibilities and to comply with established policies and procedures.

In order to build a broad base of influence, HR managers should learn to adopt the perspective and language of business and focus on the bottom line. Too often HR managers view themselves as performing strictly a service function. Once HR managers establish themselves as business partners, they become more involved in strategic matters shaping the business.[20]

Economic Element

The economic element of a firm's internal environment reflects the organization's financial condition. The more favorable this condition, the more financial resources the organization will have to support its human resources, including employee compensation and benefits. Furthermore, when the financial health of a firm is strong, there is a tendency to expand HRM activities such as training and development, employee assistance programs, and recreational activities. If the organization is growing, there is the possibility of expansion leading to employee recruitment, selection, and orientation. Conversely, when financial resources are low, an organization tends to reduce its HR budget and to cut back the HR services it offers to its employees.

Changes That Challenge Managers of Human Resources

objective

In the preceding section we briefly mentioned some of the environmental changes that may precipitate changes in an HR program. Increasingly, HR managers are involved in issues management directed toward early identification of trends that may require adjustments in HR policies and procedures. Beginning in the fall of 1986, SHRM began an organizational effort known as the Issues Management Program. After reviewing the trends and patterns of development of more than 200 specific issues, SHRM identified five basic areas where change is occurring. These five areas are shown in Highlights in HRM 1. The goals of the departments of SHRM are now directly related to these areas so that the Society can provide the services most relevant to the needs of its members.

In our discussion of changes that challenge managers we will incorporate key issues from the SHRM Issues Management Program under the following categories: demographic changes, job trends, cultural changes, and total-quality management.

Demographic Changes

Among the most significant challenges to managers are the demographic changes occurring in the United States. Because they affect the workforce of an employer, these changes—in population growth, in age and gender distribution of the population, and in education trends—are important topics for discussion. According to Frank Doyle, General Electric's vice president for external and industrial relations, demographic changes "will turn the professional human resources world on its ear." Jean Fraser, vice president of employee relations at American Express, echoes these views but adds, "We're not just sitting around and waiting for demographic changes to take place. To us, the year 2000 is already here."[21]

Population Growth and Ethnic Background

Population growth is the single most important factor governing the size and composition of the labor force. The U.S. civilian labor force totaled about 125 million in 1990 and is expected to reach approximately 151 million in the year 2005. Though this projected increase of 20 percent for the fifteen-year period sounds quite high, it is substantially lower than the 33 percent increase for the period 1975–1990.[22] This difference represents a slowing in both the number of people joining the labor force and the rate of labor-force growth, which is now projected at 1.3 percent per year.

HIGHLIGHTS IN HRM

highlights

1   CURRENT ISSUES IN HUMAN RESOURCES MANAGEMENT

Employer/Employee Rights

This is clearly an important and growing area of debate and concern. To some degree, it reflects the shift in employer/employee negotiations from the bargaining table to the courtroom, as organizations and individuals attempt to define rights, obligations, and responsibilities. Among the many specific issues covered in this broad area are

- Job as an entitlement
- Employment at will
- Privacy (testing)
- Whistle-blowing
- Mandated benefits
- Smoking

- Plant closing notification
- Right to know
- Comparable worth
- Right to manage
- AIDS

Work and Family Relationships

There is a new and important perception that the individual at work is not "detached" from family concerns and responsibilities. Due, in part, to the rapid increase of women in the workplace, as well as a growing interest in and concern with the family, there is increasing demand for recognition and support of family-related employee concerns. Among the issues in this area are

- Day care
- Child care leave
- Alternative work plans
- Elder care

- Parental leave
- Cafeteria plans
- Mandated benefits

Education/Training/Retraining

As organizations trim personnel and gear up for the tough competition within the global economy, the skills and competence of the available pool of employees are becoming a pivotal issue. This issue spans the range of skill development from the earliest stages of the education experience to the challenges of retraining an aging workforce. If "human resources are our most important asset," it is here that the investments must be made if that asset is to be productive. Among the key issues in this area are

- Literacy
- Employee education/training
- Management development
- Plant closings

- Dropout prevention
- Retraining
- Industry obsolescence

Changing Demographics

The next 20 years will bring a constant aging of the workforce. This has major implications for all aspects of human resource management as it alters traditional experience and expectations regarding the labor pool. Among the issues in this area are

- Shrinking pool of entry-level workers
- Retirement health benefits funding

- Social Security
- "Plateauing" and motivation

- Increasing number of "nonpermanent/ contract" employees
- Elder care
- Pension fund liabilities

Productivity/Competitiveness

The calls for increased productivity, quality, and competitiveness will only grow in intensity over the coming years. A persistent trade deficit and continued successes in the global market of our international competitors will serve to intensify the quest for a more productive workforce. Among the issues in this area are

- Productivity improvement
- Worker participation
- Foreign competition
- Mergers
- Quality programs and measurement
- Incentive/performance pay
- Globalization
- Downsizing

Source: Catherine Downes Bower and Jeffrey J. Hallett, "Issues Management at ASPA," *Personnel Administrator* 34, no. 1 (January 1989): 40–43. Reprinted with the permission of *HR Magazine* (formerly *Personnel Administrator*), published by the Society for Human Resource Management, Alexandria, Va.

Of course, American workers will continue to be a diverse group. In the year 2005 minorities will make up an even larger share of the U.S. labor force than they did in 1986. Although white males will still constitute approximately 38 percent of the labor force, blacks will increase their share from 10 to 13 percent, Hispanics from 7 to 16 percent, and Asians and others from 3 to nearly 6 percent. These nonwhite groups are expected to account for about 65 percent of the labor-force growth between 1986 and 2005. In cities such as New York, Houston, Chicago, Los Angeles, Atlanta, and Detroit, minorities currently represent more than half the population.[23]

The arrival of immigrants also has significant implications for the labor force. Figure 2–5 shows that between 1980 and 1990, immigrants accounted for 39 percent of total population growth in the United States. Too often these individuals are of working age but have different educational and occupational backgrounds from those of the U.S. population as a whole.[24]

To accommodate the shift in demographics, many organizations have increased their efforts to recruit and train a more diverse workforce.[25] Kathleen Alexander, vice president of personnel services at Marriott Corporation, argues, "Companies have a great need to include all the talented people they can find. So we want to use personnel policies not to discriminate but to attract and retain."[26] In this regard, a group of 600 firms such as Chevron, AT&T, and Monsanto, has developed an organization called Inroads, which for the past twenty years has identified promising minority students during their senior year in high school and offered them summer internships. Chevron alone has tripled its spending on minority recruitment since 1989.

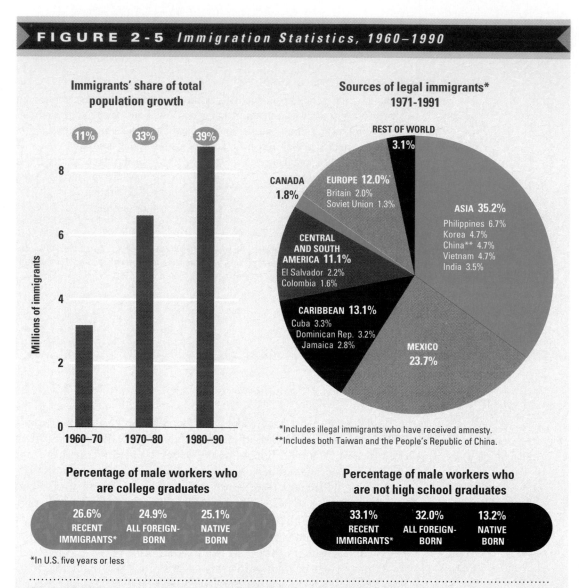

FIGURE 2-5 *Immigration Statistics, 1960–1990*

Immigrants' share of total population growth

11% 33% 39%

Millions of immigrants

8

6

4

2

0

1960–70 1970–80 1980–90

Sources of legal immigrants*
1971-1991

REST OF WORLD 3.1%

CANADA 1.8%

EUROPE 12.0%
Britain 2.0%
Soviet Union 1.3%

ASIA 35.2%
Philippines 6.7%
Korea 4.7%
China** 4.7%
Vietnam 4.7%
India 3.5%

CENTRAL AND SOUTH AMERICA 11.1%
El Salvador 2.2%
Colombia 1.6%

CARIBBEAN 13.1%
Cuba 3.3%
Dominican Rep. 3.2%
Jamaica 2.8%

MEXICO 23.7%

*Includes illegal immigrants who have received amnesty.
**Includes both Taiwan and the People's Republic of China.

Percentage of male workers who are college graduates

| 26.6% RECENT IMMIGRANTS* | 24.9% ALL FOREIGN-BORN | 25.1% NATIVE BORN |

*In U.S. five years or less

Percentage of male workers who are not high school graduates

| 33.1% RECENT IMMIGRANTS* | 32.0% ALL FOREIGN-BORN | 13.2% NATIVE BORN |

Sources: The Urban Institute; Census Bureau; Immigration and Naturalization Service

Age Distribution of the Population

Past fluctuations in the birthrate are producing abrupt changes in the makeup of major U.S. labor-force groups. The number of younger workers (16 to 24 years of age) will decline until the mid-1990s, then turn upward as the children of the "baby boom" generation enter the workforce. From 1990 to 2005, this sector of the labor force is expected to grow at 13.2 percent, and concerns about the lack of entry-level workers should ease somewhat.[27]

Older workers find greater job satisfaction as they acquire new skills.

The number of older workers (55 and above) will decline through the mid-1990s, then start to rise sharply as the baby boomers themselves approach retirement age. By 2005, older employees will constitute about 15 percent of the labor force, approximately the same proportion they did in 1970. Declining labor-force participation of older persons will largely offset the increase in the number of persons in this population group. The youth share of the labor force is projected to drop to only 16 percent by 2005, down from 24 percent in 1975. Many firms with a primary interest in this younger age group—such as fast-food restaurants and other retail establishments—can expect to see the population from which they draw part-time workers, as well as customers, shrink throughout most of the 1986–2000 period.[28]

Despite the fact that the pool of younger workers is shrinking and labor shortages loom ahead, public policy can discourage the employment of older workers beyond traditional retirement age, regardless of substantial evidence of the value of their training and experience. Some employers, however, are making positive efforts to attract more older workers, especially those who have taken early retirement, by expanding the number of part-time hours available and offering sabbaticals and job sharing. McDonald's, for example, places a great deal more emphasis on hiring retirees and other older workers as an alternative for dealing with the coming youth shortage.[29] John Snodgrass, president of the Days Inn hotel chain, argues that "Corporate America is walking past an unbelievable resource of talent—reliable, trained, educated." Companies such as Corning Glass, Grumman, Varian Associates, and Wells Fargo Bank are also providing retraining programs for older employees.[30]

But there are a number of barriers to overcome before firms can succeed in making continued employment attractive to older workers. The economic disincentives of the Social Security tax for wage earners between ages 65 and 70 need to be reduced, and discriminatory pension arrangements must be eliminated.

Also, many employers fall victim to the myth that older people don't want to work or are incapable of it. There is a continuing need to counteract this and other inaccurate perceptions of the older worker.[31]

Older workers, for example, have significantly lower accident rates and absenteeism than younger workers. Further, they tend to report higher job satisfaction scores. And while some motor skills and cognitive abilities may start to decline (starting around age 25), most individuals find ways to compensate for this fact so that there is no discernible impact on their performance.

There is an old cliche that "You can't teach an old dog new tricks." Probably we should revise this to say, "You can't teach an old dog the same way you teach a puppy." To address the fact that seniors learn in different ways, McDonald's, a heavy recruiter of older workers, has developed its McMasters program in which newly hired seniors work alongside experienced employees so that in a matter of four weeks, they can be turned loose to work on their own. The training program is designed to help seniors "unlearn" old behaviors while acquiring new skills.

Imbalance in the age distribution of our labor force has significant implications for employers. At Bethlehem Steel, for example, the average age of employees is almost 46 years, with an average service record of 22 years. Before the year 2000, close to 50 percent of Bethlehem's current workforce is likely to retire.[32] On the other hand, those who constitute the population bulge are experiencing greater competition for advancement from others of approximately the same age. This situation challenges the ingenuity of managers to develop career patterns for members of this group and to motivate their performance. In addition, providing pension and social security benefits for this group when they reach retirement age early in the next century will present a very serious problem for employers and society. Because of the drop in the birthrate following the baby boom, the labor force available to support the retirees will be smaller. The solutions to this and other problems created by the imbalance in the age distribution of our labor force will require long-range planning on the part of both organization and government leaders.

Gender Distribution of the Workforce

According to projections by the Bureau of Labor Statistics, women will continue to join the U.S. labor force, but at a slower rate than between 1975 and 1990. Women made up only about one-third of the labor force in 1970; by 2005 they are expected to account for over 47 percent.[33] The increase of women in the labor force is a trend that organizations continue to recognize. Employers are under constant pressure to ensure equality for women with respect to employment, advancement opportunities, and compensation. They also need to accommodate working mothers and fathers through parental leaves, part-time employment, flexible work schedules, job sharing, telecommuting, and child care assistance. More and more, benefit programs are being designed to meet the needs of the two-wage-earner family.

Because more women are working, employers are more sensitive to the growing need for policies and procedures to eliminate sexual harassment in the workplace. Some organizations have special orientation programs to acquaint all personnel with the problem and to warn potential offenders of the consequences. Many employers are demanding that managers and supervisors enforce their sexual harassment policy vigorously. (The basic components of such policies will be presented in Chapter 3.)

Typically, sexual harassment involves one individual taking advantage of another. However, instead of a single individual being charged with harassment, there are an increasing number of cases in which the whole environment is seen as the source of sexual harassment. Characteristic of the "whole environment" syndrome are risque jokes, pornographic magazines, slides in video presentations, and pinup posters. While some employers argue that it isn't always easy to define what constitutes an environment of sexual harassment, a spokesman for DuPont says that, to be safe, "We tell people: It's harassment when something starts bothering somebody."[34]

Rising Levels of Education

In recent years the educational attainment of the U.S. labor force has risen dramatically. Between 1972 and 1990 the proportion of the labor force age 18 to 64 with at least one year of college increased from 28 to 47 percent, while the proportion with four years of college or more increased from 14 to 26 percent. The emphasis on education is expected to continue; Figure 2–6 shows the average payoff in monthly earnings from education.

For the past few decades, the most secure and fastest-growing sectors of employment have been in those areas requiring higher levels of education. For example, three of the four fastest-growing occupational groups are (1) executive,

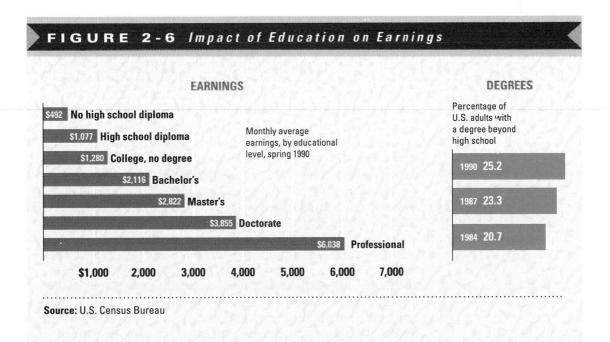

FIGURE 2-6 *Impact of Education on Earnings*

EARNINGS

$492	**No high school diploma**
$1,077	**High school diploma**
$1,280	**College, no degree**
$2,116	**Bachelor's**
$2,822	**Master's**
$3,855	**Doctorate**
$6,038	**Professional**

Monthly average earnings, by educational level, spring 1990

$1,000 2,000 3,000 4,000 5,000 6,000 7,000

DEGREES

Percentage of U.S. adults with a degree beyond high school

1990	25.2
1987	23.3
1984	20.7

Source: U.S. Census Bureau

administrative, and managerial occupations; (2) professional specialty occupations; and (3) technicians and related support occupations—occupations that generally require the highest levels of education and skill.[35]

On the other hand, opportunities for high school dropouts will be increasingly limited. In 1990, for example, the unemployment rate for dropouts was more than twice that of individuals with a high school education.[36] At the same time, college graduates may find that to be employed will require taking a job that does not fully utilize the knowledge and skills they acquired in college. To compensate their employees for this lack of parity, employers must try harder to improve the quality of work life. We will discuss some suggested improvements later in the chapter.

It is important to observe that while the educational level of the workforce has continued to rise over the past several decades, the United States still grants the smallest proportion of science and engineering degrees of all industrialized nations in the world—and could face a deficit of 700,000 scientists and engineers by the year 2010. Although women now make up nearly half of the labor force, less than 30 percent of them are engineers and scientists. Even further, while minorities are expected to make up approximately one-third of the labor force by the turn of the century, they account for less than 2 percent of the doctoral degrees awarded in science and engineering.[37]

There is a widening gap between the educated and noneducated. At the lower end of the educational spectrum, many employers are having to cope with individuals who are functionally illiterate—i.e., unable to read, write, calculate, or solve problems at a level that enables them to perform even the simplest technical tasks. Here are some frightening statistics: A recent study by the U.S. Department of Education suggests that less than half of all high school seniors are able to handle mathematics problems involving fractions, decimals, percents, elementary geometry, and simple algebra. Estimates vary, but experts believe that anywhere from 20 million to 80 million American adults are functionally illiterate. Further, a joint study by the Society for Human Resource Management and the Commerce Clearing House suggests that nearly 64 percent of organizations surveyed either knowingly or unknowingly hire workers lacking basic skills. The U.S. Department of Education estimates that the functionally illiterate now account for 30 percent of unskilled, 29 percent of semiskilled, and 11 percent of all managerial, professional, and technical employees.[38] In a speech to the Commonwealth Club of California, David Kearns, chairman and CEO of Xerox Corporation, said, "The American work force is in grave jeopardy. We are running out of qualified people. If current demographic and economic trends continue, American business will have to hire a million new workers a year who can't read, write, or count."[39]

Clearly, there is much work to be done. Modernization makes basic skill deficiencies that much more noticeable, and many believe that without immediate action, we are running down a path toward a national crisis. To rectify the situation, both private- and public-sector organizations are working together. General Motors, for example, spent nearly $2 billion from 1984 to 1990 on education and training, making it the largest privately funded educational institution in the United States.[40] Many other organizations and educational institutions are establishing much-needed partnerships to ensure that future employees have the skills they need for work. Sears and IBM, for example, have begun developing apprenticeship-type programs that combine academic and vocational instruction with on-the-job training. (See Chapter 7 for a discussion of apprenticeship programs.) In Portland, Oregon, alone, more than 90 percent of the students who have participated in such programs have gone on to college, work, or the military. Another popular effort is referred to as "tech prep." This type of program is an alternative to college preparation; in tech prep high school students prepare for two years of community college. In North Carolina's Richmond County, enrollment in tech prep has reached 30 percent, roughly equal to the enrollment in college prep.[41]

Another, related problem is technological illiteracy. In Ottawa, Ontario, a coalition of high-technology businesses and educators launched the Partners Summer Institute for high school teachers as part of a larger program that is encouraging students to pursue technologically oriented careers. IBM alone has spent more than $60 million since 1982 working with Canadian educational institutions to help bolster technological skills. In the United States, nearly forty states now have some kind of technology education program. In New York State, for example, all junior high school students are required to take a one-year introductory technology course. The program stresses hands-on laboratory work, problem-solving activities, and a curriculum that treats technology as a set of systems.[42] Similarly, Focus: Hope is a Detroit-based nonprofit organization dedicated to building the technological skills of inner-city youths.

While estimates vary, U.S. organizations spend over $50 billion a year on employee education. Highlights in HRM 2 shows a list of some of the organizations most dedicated to education and training and indicates the percent of payroll they spend on training as well as the number of hours per employee spent per year on training.[43] Unfortunately, only about 12 percent of the workforce receives any formal on-the-job training. Many of the larger employers have instituted programs in basic skills. Ford Motor Company offers reading courses at twenty-five plants. AT&T spends $6 million a year on remedial courses for employees. Aetna Life and Casualty spent $750,000 to teach 500 employees basic reading, writing, and math skills. Domino's Pizza Distribution Corporation developed a videodisc program designed to improve employees' reading and math skills while also teaching them how to make pizza dough.[44] Siemens Stromberg-Carlson recently launched an Americanized version of its technical apprenticeship with local community colleges and high schools in Florida. After students complete the 2-1/2 year program, they will be certified as Siemens electronics technicians and will be awarded an associate's degree in telecommunications engineering technology. Siemens Stromberg-Carlson then considers them for hire or works to place them in another U.S. Siemens operation.[45]

Job and Occupational Trends

Government studies show that as incomes and living standards have risen, the desire for services has grown more rapidly than the desire for goods. As a result, employment in service-producing industries has increased faster than employment in goods-producing industries. Furthermore, imports of foreign-made goods have been limiting the growth of goods-producing industries in the United States.

HIGHLIGHTS IN HRM

highlights

2   GO TO THE HEAD OF THE CLASS

COMPANY Employees worldwide	TRAINING		COMMENTS
	Percent of payroll spent in 1992	Avg. hours per employee per year	
Motorola 107,000	3.6	36	The gold standard of corporate training. The company says every $1 spent on education returns $30 in productivity gains.
Target 100,000	N.A.	N.A.	Rapidly expanding retail chain has used Disney-type training to empower front-line employees and improve customer service.
Federal Express 93,000	4.5	27	Workers take computer-based job competency tests every six to twelve months. Low scores lead to remedial action.
General Electric Aircraft Engines 33,000	N.A.	N.A.	Training budget has shrunk, but new focus on teamwork has helped the division boost productivity in a slumping industry.
Andersen Consulting 26,700	6.8	109	Replaced forty-hour Business Practices class with interactive video, saving $4 million per year, mostly on travel and lodging.
Corning 14,000 (domestic)	3.0	92	Ordinary employees, not professional educators, do most training. Pay of factory workers rises as they learn new skills.
Solectron 3,500	3.0	95	Training helped this fast-growing Silicon Valley company win a Baldrige in 1991.
Dudek Manufacturing 3,500	5.0	25	Had to teach basic literacy and math before introducing quality management. Hefty investment has paid off in profits.

Source: *FORTUNE*, copyright 1993, Time Inc. All rights reserved.

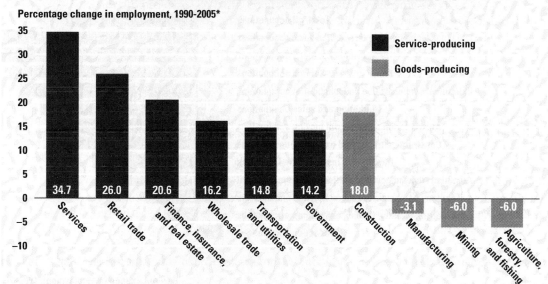

FIGURE 2-7 *Growth of Service- and Goods-Producing Firms*

SOME INDUSTRIES WILL GROW MORE RAPIDLY THAN OTHERS

Percentage change in employment, 1990-2005*

■ Service-producing
▬ Goods-producing

Services 34.7
Retail trade 26.0
Finance, insurance, and real estate 20.6
Wholesale trade 16.2
Transportation and utilities 14.8
Government 14.2
Construction 18.0
Manufacturing -3.1
Mining -6.0
Agriculture, forestry, and fishing -6.0

*Wage and salary employment, except for agriculture, forestry, and fishing, which includes self-employed and unpaid family workers.

Source: U.S. Bureau of Labor Statistics

Increase in Service Jobs

Employment is expected to continue to increase much faster in service-producing industries than in goods-producing industries, as shown in Figure 2–7. By 2005, the largest projected change in employment is in services (34 percent); retail and wholesale trade (16.2 percent); and finance, insurance, and real estate (20.6 percent). In addition, the growth rate of government employment is expected to rise as state and local governments respond to issues such as education and road repair and other elements of the nation's infrastructure.[46]

Employment in the goods-producing industries peaked in the late 1970s and has not recovered from the recessionary period of the early 1980s. Construction is the only goods-producing area expected to show an increase in employment between 1986 and 2005 in response to projected economic conditions and demographic trends. Nevertheless, this growth rate is less than one-half that of the previous fifteen years. Employment in manufacturing is expected to continue its decline. Employment in this sector reached its peak at 21 million in 1979 and is projected to drop to 18.5 million by 2005. Most of the jobs that will disappear

. . . .

Telecommuting

Telecommuting
Use of microcomputers, networks, and other communications technology such as fax machines to do work in the home that is traditionally done in the workplace

One of the more recent changes and potentially the most far-reaching is telecommuting. **Telecommuting** is the use of microcomputers, networks, and other communications technology such as facsimile (fax) machines to do work in the home that is traditionally done in the workplace. As technology becomes both more sophisticated and user-friendly, employees can hook up with their offices and perform their tasks while still remaining miles away. The number of telecommuters and corporate homeworkers increased from 14 million in 1990 to 16 million in 1991. Projections are that by 2000, approximately 25 percent of the workforce will be telecommuting either full-time or part-time.[52] Since, according to the Bureau of Labor Statistics, about 75 percent of new jobs are in the suburbs, but 57 percent of blacks and Hispanics live in the city, telecommuting holds promise of closing the rather serious geographic gap between jobs and the people who can fill them.[53]

Not all jobs lend themselves to at-home work, but many do: travel agent, architect, writer, salesperson, data entry clerk, insurance agent, real estate agent, bookkeeper, accountant, computer programmer, word-processing secretary, engineer, and others. Numerous organizations have developed some sort of telecommuting policy. Among them are Bell Atlantic, Control Data, J. C. Penney, American Express, International Banking Corporation, Blue Cross/Blue Shield of South Carolina, Chevron Chemical Company, Pacific Bell, and Travelers Insurance.

What potential benefits do HR managers see in telecommuting? The most common responses of over 100 HR managers surveyed in the Raleigh-Durham, North Carolina, area were decreased production costs, increased employee satisfaction, and increased productivity.[54] Yet despite the increasing use and value of telecommuting, managers may not feel comfortable supervising a telcommuting employee. Managers of telecommuters must be innovative thinkers and risk takers. According to Jack Nilles, who coined the term "telecommuter," "The major obstacle to telecommuting in the last 15 years has been conservative management with industrial revolution mind-sets."[55] Many employers have been reluctant to consider telecommuting because they fear they will lose control if employees are not physically present. When Continental Corporation rolled out a series of programs including telecommuting and job sharing, many were skeptical. However, within fifteen months of initiating the program, the company found that productivity jumped 15 percent and that the voluntary employee turnover rate had been cut to less than 5 percent, better than a 50 percent improvement.[56]

Ironically, many employers now report that there is a tendency for telecommuters to become workaholics. In choosing telecommuters, organizations should try to fill the positions with people whose jobs have not required interaction with others, who have been with the organization for some time, who have the appropriate psychological characteristics to work at home, and who above all are self-starters. Preparing managers to supervise employees who are not physically present is a special requirement for success. Managers have to work harder at planning and communicating with their telecommuting subordinates, and they have to be clearer about their objectives. Ultimately, the key to putting together a successful telecommuting program is to have quality HR leadership guiding and managing the process.

Cultural Changes

The attitudes, beliefs, values, and customs of people in a society are an integral part of their culture. Naturally, their culture affects their behavior on the job and the environment within the organization, influencing their reactions to work assignments, leadership styles, and reward systems. Like the external and internal environments of which it is a part, culture is undergoing continual change. HR policies and procedures therefore must be adjusted to cope with this change.

Employee Rights

Over the past few decades, federal legislation has radically changed the rules for management of employees by granting them many specific rights. Among these are laws granting the right to equal employment opportunity (Chapter 3), union representation if desired (Chapters 17 and 18), a safe and healthful work environment (Chapter 13), a pension plan that is fiscally sound (Chapter 12), equal pay for men and women performing essentially the same job (Chapter 10), and privacy in the workplace. An expanded discussion of the specific areas in which rights and responsibilities are of concern to employers and employees, including the often-cited employment-at-will doctrine, will be presented in Chapter 16.

Concern for Privacy

HR managers and their staffs, as well as line managers in positions of responsibility, generally recognize the importance of discretion in handling all types of information about employees. Since the passage of the federal Privacy Act of 1974, increased attention to privacy has been evident. While the act applies almost exclusively to records maintained by federal government agencies, it has drawn attention to the importance of privacy and has led to the passage of privacy legislation in several states.

Employer responses to the issue of information privacy vary widely. IBM was one of the first companies to show concern for how personal information about employees was handled. It began restricting the release of information as early as 1965 and in 1971 developed a comprehensive privacy policy. Cummins Engine Company, Dow Corning Corporation, Avid, and Corning Glass Works are among other employers that have developed privacy programs.[57] We will discuss the content of such programs and present some recommended privacy guidelines in Chapter 16.

Changing Attitudes Toward Work

Changing attitudes toward authority have become prevalent in today's labor force. Employees increasingly expect to exercise certain freedom from management control without jeopardizing their job security or chances for advancement. They are more demanding, more questioning, and less willing to accept the "I'm the boss" approach.

Another well-established trend is for employees to define success in terms of personal self-expression and fulfillment of potential on the job, while still receiving adequate compensation for their efforts. A greater proportion of the workforce now strives for challenging jobs. More people are also seeking rewarding careers and multiple careers rather than being satisfied with just having a job.

Workers also seem to value free time more than they did in earlier decades. Many polls report that Americans feel they have less free time than they once did. Contrary to their reported feelings, however, a use-of-time project at the Survey Research Center at the University of Maryland found that Americans today actually have more free time than ever before. Men have forty hours of free time a week and women have thirty-nine hours. ("Free time" is defined as what is left over after subtracting the time people spend working and commuting to work, taking care of their families, doing housework, shopping, sleeping, eating, and engaging in other personal activities.) According to the report, free time has increased because women are doing much less housework than they did several decades ago and because the number of actual work hours that workers record in their daily diaries—not the number of "official" hours of work—has fallen significantly for both men and women. The findings, however, do hide much individual variation. Working parents, especially, are under severe time pressures. On balance, though, more people are gaining free time than are losing it.[58]

Personal and Family Life Orientation

We noted earlier that HRM has become more complex than it was when employees were concerned primarily with economic survival. Today's employees have greater expectations from society and from their employment. In many cases, having time to develop a satisfying personal life and pursue cultural and other nonwork-related interests is valued by workers today as much as having a full-time job.[59] Employers are thus being forced to recognize the fact that as individuals strive for a greater balance in their lives, organizations will have to alter their attitudes and their HRM policies to satisfy employee desires.

Many companies encourage employees to volunteer their time and experience at schools.

Work and the family are connected in many subtle and not-so-subtle social, economic, and psychological ways. Because of the new forms that the family has taken—e.g., the two-wage-earner and the single-parent family—work organizations find it necessary to provide employees with more flexibility and options. "Flexibility" is a broad term and may include unconventional hours, day care, part-time work, job sharing, pregnancy leave, parental leave, executive transfers, spousal involvement in career planning, assistance with family problems, and telecommuting. These issues have become important considerations for all managers. Some of the most progressive companies, such as American Express, Levi Strauss, NationsBank, PepsiCo, and Schering-Plough promote flexibility throughout their organizations.[60] In general, these companies calculate that accommodating individual needs and circumstances is a powerful way to attract and retain top-caliber people. Aetna Life and Casualty, for example, has cut turnover by 50 percent since it began to offer six-month parental leaves, coupled with an option for part-time work when employees return to the job. Nations-Bank provides up to six weeks of paid leave for fathers. Further, NationsBank encourages all its employees to spend two hours each week visiting their children's schools or volunteering at any school—on company time. Hugh McColl, the company's chairman, sees it this way: "It may seem inconsistent that we're asking employees to work harder now, but the need to pinch pennies and reduce head count plays to the short term, while flexibility is important to our long-term health."[61]

Arthur Andersen has developed a flexible work program that allows new parents to lighten their workloads for up to three years. There are acknowledged costs, however. In professional firms, such as accounting and law, career paths and promotion sequences are programmed in a lockstep manner. Time away from work can slow down—and in some cases derail—an individual's career advancement.

Human Resources and Total-Quality Management

As noted early, in absolute terms, the United States remains the world's most productive nation. However, of major concern to most Americans is the fact that the United States now ranks twelfth among the top thirteen industrialized nations in "growth in output per worker." U.S. annual growth in output per worker averaged 1 percent for the period 1981–1985. In recent years productivity in basic manufacturing operations has improved slightly. Following a cycle of downsizing, the forging of new union agreements, and the closing or modernization of obsolete plants, the U.S. manufacturing sector recovered from the 1970s slowdown and was back on a 3 percent growth track in the late 1980s.[62] More recently there have been periods of decline, but prospects for the future are encouraging.

Intense international competition has forced U.S. organizations to enhance quality, as well as productivity, to regain their competitive edge.[63] **Total-quality management (TQM)** is a set of principles and practices whose core ideas include doing things right the first time, striving for continuous improvement, and understanding customer needs. Through TQM initiatives, companies such as Motorola, Xerox, Ford, Corning, General Electric, 3M, Hewlett-Packard, Boeing, A. O. Smith, Cummins Engine, Maytag, and Allied-Signal have substantially improved productivity and bolstered their competitive advantage. However, quality programs are certainly no panacea. Unfortunately, too many organizations view quality as a quick fix. As a consequence, 75 percent of all quality programs begun in 1982 had been discontinued by 1986.[64] Further, the number of applications for the Malcolm Baldrige National Quality Award peaked in 1991 and has fallen sharply ever since. If quality initiatives are to work, an organization must make major changes in its philosophy, its operating mechanisms, and its HR programs.

A survey asked 307 executives from *Fortune* 1000 companies and 308 executives from smaller firms (twenty-plus employees) to rate the importance of eight quality-improvement techniques. Those techniques that stressed human factors—employee motivation, change in corporate culture, and employee education—received higher ratings than those emphasizing processes or equipment. Organizations known for product and service quality strongly believe that

Total-quality management (TQM)

A set of principles and practices whose core ideas include doing things right the first time, striving for continuous improvement, and understanding customer needs

> **FIGURE 2-9** *The Evolution of a Total-Quality HR Paradigm*

HUMAN RESOURCE CHARACTERISTICS	TRADITIONAL PARADIGM	TOTAL-QUALITY PARADIGM
Corporate culture	Individualism Differentiation Autocratic leadership Profits Productivity	Collective efforts Cross-functional work Coaching/enabling Customer satisfaction Quality
Communications	Top-down	Top-down Horizontal, lateral; Multidirectional
Voice and involvement	Employment-at-will Suggestion systems	Due process Quality circles Attitude surveys
Job design	Efficiency Productivity Standard procedures Narrow span of control Specific job descriptions	Quality Customization Innovation Wide span of control Autonomous work teams Empowerment
Training	Job-related skills Functional, technical Productivity	Broad range of skills Cross-functional Diagnostic, problem-solving Productivity and quality
Performance measurement and evaluation	Individual goals Supervisory review Emphasize financial performance	Team goals Customer, peer, and supervisory review Emphasize quality and service
Rewards	Competition for individual merit increases and benefits	Team/group-based awards Financial rewards, financial and nonfinancial recognition
Health and safety	Treat problems	Prevent problems Safety and wellness programs Employee assistance
Selection/promotion Career development	Selected by manager Narrow job skills Promotion based on individual accomplishment Linear career path	Selected by peers Problem-solving skills Promotion based on group facilitation Horizontal career path

Source: Richard Blackburn and Benson Rosen, "Total Quality and Human Resources Management: Lessons Learned from Baldrige Award-Winning Companies," *Academy of Management Executive* 7, no. 3 (1993); 51. Reproduced with permission.

employees are the key to that quality. They believe that proper attention to employees will naturally improve quality and productivity.[65] In other words, they believe that HRM is the most promising strategy for reversing the productivity slide. Figure 2–9 shows how organizations tend to change their HR practices to support quality initiatives.[66]

To test the validity of this belief that HRM is instrumental for improving quality and productivity, two researchers designed an empirical study. The study was conducted at two autonomous divisions of a large service-recreation corporation, each with a separate profit center. Using a list of activities the company believed to be important and a set of critical employee attitude statements, an employee opinion survey was developed and administered. The results showed that when a firm is committed to good HR department programs and activities, employees will see this commitment in a positive manner, and attitudes will be affected, thus contributing to organizational effectiveness in many ways. These findings add empirical support to the literature and other reported HR surveys.[67]

The fact that many organizations in the United States have found it difficult to compete successfully with those in Japan has stimulated interest in uncovering differences between the two countries. Cultural and sociological differences between Japanese and American workers may explain to some extent why workers in Japan are credited with being more productive and more dedicated to their work. For example, the Japanese tradition in the larger companies of providing lifetime employment and avoiding layoffs, even at a financial sacrifice, has generated a sense of loyalty and commitment to employers among Japanese workers. In addition, evidence suggests that Japanese workers tend to identify more than American workers with their employers and their employers' goals. However, they tend to be very similar to American workers with respect to their dedication to the work ethic or to doing a decent job.[68]

One of the keys to the increased productivity of Japanese workers lies in the coordinated efforts of individuals—through interdependence, collaboration, and teamwork. Teamwork has also become one of the mainstays of work organization in the United States, both in manufacturing and service firms.[69] Levi Strauss, for example, has converted its entire Roswell, New Mexico, facility from assembly lines to modular manufacturing teams. Sewing machine operators, rather than acting as "living extensions of their machines," now work as a self-managed team to coordinate scheduling, maintenance, and trouble shooting. As a result, Levi Strauss has reduced the time it takes to get out a sixty-pair bundle of jeans from six days to one. Equally important is the concern for quality, and here Levi has lowered its defect rate from 3.9 to 1.9 percent.[70] (Work teams are discussed in Chapter 14.)

Another philosophy borrowed from the Japanese is employee management, which rests on respect for the worker's intelligence and need for self-esteem. Some Japanese subsidiaries, such as Nissan in Smyrna, Tennessee, and GM-Toyota in Fremont, California, have been able to apply this philosophy to the management of their American employees. These companies have translated the philosophy into action by encouraging their American workers to participate in decision making and to identify with company goals.

Many American organizations have adopted certain aspects of Japanese management practices to their advantage. It should be observed, however, that the Japanese business and management system is undergoing significant changes.

Lifetime employment, seniority-based promotion systems, and company-wide unions—all characteristic of Japanese-style management—have recently been called into serious question.

Quality of Work Life

Quality of work life (QWL)
The extent to which work is rewarding and free of anxieties and stresses

Improving a firm's external environment is, to a large extent, beyond an employer's control. However, improving the organization's internal environment is definitely within the realm of an employer's influence. A major challenge confronting employers today is that of improving the **quality of work life (QWL).** This challenge stems not only from the need to meet foreign competition but also from the demographic and cultural changes that have just been discussed.

Many of our largest private and public organizations are making changes to try to improve the QWL of their employees. These efforts consist of looking for ways to make work more rewarding and reduce anxieties and stresses in the work environment. Several different approaches are being used, including restructuring work organization and job design, increasing employee involvement in shaping the organization and its functions, and developing an organizational culture that will encourage members to behave in ways that will maximize productivity, strengthen human relationships, meet employee expectations, and sustain desired attitudes and beliefs.[71]

Work Organization and Job Design

If quality is to be improved, there is no better place to start than with the way work is organized and the way jobs are designed. Since each industry and its jobs present special problems to be solved, it is only possible to present some general prescriptions. Jacquie Mansell and Tom Rankin of the Ontario (Canada) Quality of Working Life Centre have developed criteria for designing organizational structures and processes, including jobs, for high QWL. These criteria are presented in Highlights in HRM 3. We will discuss specific ways of making jobs more meaningful and more satisfying in Chapter 4. Other aspects of job design and such work arrangements as job rotation, flexible working hours, and job sharing that contribute to QWL will also be discussed in that chapter.

Empowerment and Participative Management

Participative management
A system of management that enables employees to participate in decisions relating to their work and employment conditions, thereby creating a psychological partnership between management and employees

Essential to TQM is employee empowerment and the development of **participative management.** By involving employees in decisions relating to their work and employment conditions, firms can create a solid psychological partnership with employees. Unfortunately, at times efforts to provide a more participative environment are resisted by managers and viewed with suspicion by employees. Nevertheless, empowerment and participation are realities of today's business environment.

Enlightened organizational leaders recognize that basic changes in relations between employers and employees are essential.[72] Many are also convinced that bringing workers into the decision-making process offers the best opportunity to improve quality and productivity. If only for reasons of survival, both sides must recognize that they have a mutual interest in working together to reduce costs and avoid becoming victims of foreign and domestic competition. Thus there is a

HIGHLIGHTS IN HRM

highlights

3   CRITERIA FOR ORGANIZATIONAL STRUCTURES AND PROCESSES

1. Decisions are made at the *lowest* level possible. *Self-regulation* for individuals and groups is a primary goal.
2. Individuals or integrated groups of workers are responsible for a *whole job*. People do not work on fragmented, meaningless tasks.
3. The *potential* (technical and social) of individuals, of groups, and of the overall organization is developed to the fullest.
4. Hierarchies are minimized and *artificial barriers do not exist* between people or between functions.
5. *Quality and quality control* are built directly into the primary production system.
6. *Safety and health* are built directly into the total system.
7. Support systems and structures promote and support *self-regulation, integration, and flexibility.* For example, information systems provide immediate feedback directly to those who need the information in order to perform their job; information is not used to retain power or to police others.
8. *Problems are resolved on the basis of joint control and shared responsibility* between all groups. Structures and processes for the sharing of decision-making powers are guaranteed at all levels in the organization.

Source: Jacquie Mansell and Tom Rankin, *Changing Organizations: The Quality of Working Life Process* (Toronto, Ontario, Canada: Ontario Quality of Working Life Centre, September 1983), 10–11. Reproduced with permission of the authors.

strong incentive to work jointly to reduce costs and improve quality. Caterpillar, Champion International, and General Motors, through their QWL programs, are making substantial progress in providing avenues for employee input. Other firms with employee participation programs will be examined in detail in Chapters 14 and 15.

objective

Supportive Organizational Culture

Over the years much has been written about firms such as 3M, Procter & Gamble, and Hewlett-Packard that are noted for the quality of their products and services and their relationships with people both outside and inside the organization.

Organizational culture

The shared philosophies, values, assumptions, beliefs, expectations, attitudes, and norms that knit an organization together

These companies are well known for the attention they give to HR and the work environments they have created and nurtured. The credo of Johnson & Johnson, reproduced in Highlights in HRM 4, conveys the attitudes characteristic of these companies.

In the past decade, **organizational culture** has been viewed as an intangible but real and important factor in determining the organizational climate. The conventional wisdom about culture is that it is "the glue that holds the organization together." Organizational culture is defined as the shared philosophies, values, assumptions, beliefs, expectations, attitudes, and norms that knit an organization together. It may also be defined as "the way things are done around here."[73] For example, everyone at Hewlett-Packard knows that employees are expected to be innovative. Everyone at Mary Kay Cosmetics knows the philosophy of the chair emeritus of the board, Mary Kay Ash:

> People come first at Mary Kay Cosmetics—our beauty consultants, sales directors and employees, our customers, and our suppliers. We pride ourselves as a "company known for the people it keeps." Our belief in caring for people, however, does not conflict with our need as a corporation to generate a profit. Yes, we keep our eye on the bottom line, but it's not an overriding obsession. To me, P and L doesn't only mean profit and loss— it also means people and love.[74]

In her book *Mary Kay on People Management*, Ash describes how managers can develop an organizational culture and provide leadership that is based on the golden rule. Unlike most management books, which are written by and for men, her book is written for women and men who aspire to be effective managers.[75]

We do find an increasing number of larger American firms receiving widespread acclaim for their supportive cultures, including Wal-Mart, Herman Miller, and others that have been recognized in a series of *Fortune* articles. While each of these companies has its own unique culture, team spirit is a characteristic they all share. In addition to what observers have noted about these and other companies, the findings from two research studies of employees show a positive correlation between employees' perception of being valued and cared about by the firm and (1) conscientiousness in carrying out conventional job responsibilities, (2) expressed emotional involvement in the organization, and (3) innovative work for the organization, even in the absence of anticipated reward or personal recognition.[76]

Elements of culture. Terrence Deal and Allan Kennedy made an exhaustive study of the organizational literature from the 1950s to the early 1980s to understand better the elements that make up a strong culture. They found five elements, which they describe as follows:

1. *Business environment.* Each organization carries on certain kinds of activities—e.g., selling, inventing, conducting research. Its business environment is the single greatest influence in shaping its culture.

HIGHLIGHTS IN HRM

highlights

4   SOCIAL OBJECTIVES OF JOHNSON & JOHNSON

Our Credo

We believe our first responsibility is to the doctors, nurses and patients,
to mothers and fathers and all others who use our products and services.
In meeting their needs everything we do must be of high quality.
We must constantly strive to reduce our costs
in order to maintain reasonable prices.
Customers' orders must be serviced promptly and accurately.
Our suppliers and distributors must have an opportunity
to make a fair profit.

We are responsible to our employees,
the men and women who work with us throughout the world.
Everyone must be considered as an individual.
We must respect their dignity and recognize their merit.
They must have a sense of security in their jobs.
Compensation must be fair and adequate,
and working conditions clean, orderly and safe.
We must be mindful of ways to help our employees fulfill
their family responsibilities.
Employees must feel free to make suggestions and complaints.
There must be equal opportunity for employment, development
and advancement for those qualified.
We must provide competent management,
and their actions must be just and ethical.

We are responsible to the communities in which we live and work
and to the world community as well.
We must be good citizens — support good works and charities
and bear our fair share of taxes.
We must encourage civic improvements and better health and education.
We must maintain in good order
the property we are privileged to use,
protecting the environment and natural resources.

Our final responsibility is to our stockholders.
Business must make a sound profit.
We must experiment with new ideas.
Research must be carried on, innovative programs developed
and mistakes paid for.
New equipment must be purchased, new facilities provided
and new products launched.
Reserves must be created to provide for adverse times.
When we operate according to these principles,
the stockholders should realize a fair return.

Johnson & Johnson

Source: Johnson & Johnson. Reproduced by permission.

2. *Values.* These are basic concepts and beliefs that define "success" in concrete terms for employees—e.g., "If you do this, you too will be a success."
3. *Heroes.* People who personify the culture's values provide tangible role models for employees to follow. Organizations with strong cultures have many heroes.
4. *Rites and rituals.* The systematic and programmed routines (rituals) of day-to-day life in the organization show employees the kind of behavior that is expected of them and what the organization stands for.
5. *Cultural network.* Through informal communication the corporate values are spread throughout the firm.[77]

A strong culture not only spells out how people are to behave, it also enables people to feel better about what they do, causing them to work harder.

Keeping culture contemporary. We observed earlier in this chapter that there are many changes taking place in our society that affect HRM. Organizations with strong cultures must be able to adapt to these changes and at the same time retain their basic philosophy. And organizations must find ways to keep their cultures current—that is, support efforts to adapt to changes in the competitive environment. IBM, for example, is making feverish attempts to reinvent itself to be more flexible and responsive to compete with foreign and domestic competition. When Louis Gerstner was brought in as the company's new CEO, he noted that fixing a "broken culture" is the most crucial—and difficult—part of a corporate transformation. To revamp the culture, Gerstner is working to encourage cooperation among divisions, as well as to foster trust and teamwork. Left unchecked, managers and employees over time may become risk-averse and turf-conscious. To stay on top, Gerstner argues that he must eliminate unnecessary bureaucracy and infuse the firm with "china breakers," employees with innovative ideas who challenge the status quo.[78]

Along these lines, other organizations have also pushed hard to encourage employees to become entrepreneurs, or innovators on the job. Since they remain in the employ of the firm but are given freedom to create new products, services, and production methods, these innovative workers are referred to as **intrapreneurs**. G. Pinchot defines this people-based approach to innovative management as allowing "entrepreneurs...freedom and incentive to do their best in small groups within large corporations."[79] Often the results of such activities lead to the organization of a new division or subsidiary. Among the better-known divisions or subsidiaries devoted to intrapreneurship are the Colgate Venture Company, General Foods' Culinova Unit, and Scott Paper's Do-It-Yourself Group.[80]

Employers are beginning to recognize that if the spirit of intrapreneurism is to exist beyond the life span of a fad, it must be nurtured. Not only should intrapreneurs be given special recognition, but incentives and rewards should be

Intrapreneurs
Employees who remain in the organization but are given freedom to create new products, services, and/or production methods

customized on an individual basis. To quote one writer, "A major roadblock to the nurturing of intrapreneurs is often the compensation manager whose traditional interests are control and consistency."[81]

The challenge for management in the coming decades will be to maintain a balance between the fact of rapid change and the need for stability. Since the focus of managers is on human performance and everything that affects it, they should not lose sight of their responsibility to keep the culture open and flexible.

SUMMARY

one objective

The internal and external environments of an organization can have a significant impact on the productivity of its human resources and on their management. For this reason managers must be aware of the impact these environments—and the changes occurring within them—may have on their programs. The failure of management in many organizations to anticipate and cope effectively with these changes is one of the principal causes for the declining rate of productivity growth in the United States.

two objective

Technology influences both the number of employees needed as well as the skills they require. This has the effect of reducing the number of jobs for "touch labor" and increasing the number of jobs for "knowledge workers." HR must take a leadership role in helping managers cope with technological change, identifying the skills needed of employees, training new employees, and retraining current employees. Technology has also changed HRM by altering the methods of collecting employment information, speeding data-processing efforts, and improving the process of internal and external communication.

three objective

The regulatory system begins with social and political problems that prompt lawmakers to pass laws. These laws then empower agencies such as the EEOC, OSHA, and NLRB to ensure compliance. These agencies make certain that management has initiated actions that bring their practices under compliance with the law. In those cases where compliance is not met, courts oversee the process of settling disputes between the parties involved.

four objective

While changes are taking place in many areas that affect HRM, those related to demographics include the rising number of minorities and immigrants, the aging workforce and decreasing number of 16- to 24-year-olds, the influx of women in the workforce, and the education and skills gap.

five objective

To improve quality and increase productivity, many organizations have begun to rethink their approaches to human resource management. These efforts include an emphasis on teamwork, job design, empowerment and participative management, and the building of a supportive organizational culture. All of these efforts reflect the increasing responsiveness of employers to the changes that affect the management of their human resources.

objective

The elements of organizational culture include the business environment, values and beliefs that define success, heroes and role models, rites and rituals that show employees the kind of behavior expected, and an informal communications network through which organizational values are spread throughout the firm.

KEY TERMS

environment

environmental scanning

external environment

internal environment (organizational climate)

intrapreneurs

issues management

knowledge workers

organizational culture

participative management

quality of work life (QWL)

sociotechnical system

telecommuting

total-quality management

DISCUSSION QUESTIONS

1. What impact will the growing proportion of women and the rising level of education in the workforce have on HRM?
2. What are some of the problems employers may encounter with respect to the federal regulation of HRM?
3. What are some of the jobs that can be performed by telecommuting? How is telecommuting likely to affect superior-subordinate relationships?
4. How do employee demands for more rights affect HRM?
5. It is generally recognized that today's employees are seeking a more balanced lifestyle. What effect does this have on HR policies and procedures?
6. Describe the culture of an organization with which you have been associated. What are its values, who are its heroes, and what rites and rituals does it use to reinforce the culture?
7. What can the management of an organization do to encourage intrapreneuring? Can you name some of the outstanding intrapreneurs in American industry?
8. What is your opinion concerning the governmental regulation of HRM? Do you consider the amount of regulation to be excessive? Insufficient? About right? What would your viewpoint be if you were an employer? A union leader?

CASE STUDY: Quality and Human Resources at AT&T Universal Card Services

AT&T Universal Card Services (UCS) is committed to continuous improvement in quality and customer satisfaction. Because of this commitment, UCS won the Malcolm Baldrige National Quality Award, one component of which focuses on human resources management. AT&T launched UCS in 1990, and shortly thereafter the firm's leaders established what they called the "seven values" to guide their business: continuous improvement, customer delight, teamwork, commitment, trust and integrity, mutual respect, and sense of urgency. These seven values are the foundation for UCS's human resource strategy—and the keys to their winning the Baldrige award.

When the business was just beginning, UCS conducted its first self-assessment, using Baldrige quality criteria. Each time they conduct another assessment, managers learn more about their business, their customers, and their associates—and then leverage this learning to improve quality. UCS pursues quality through a four-step human resource plan:

Step 1.   Employee involvement: UCS strives for continuous improvement by involving each employee in its award-winning suggestion program, "Your Ideas—Your Universe." Employee suggestions total nearly 10,000 annually (three times greater than U.S. industry standards). In addition, UCS empowers employees to work in self-directed teams. These teams have responsibility for reporting their own daily quality measurements, thereby assuming responsibility for their goals rather than requiring an external audit.

Step 2.   Education and training: To provide a comprehensive platform for education and training, UCS has created "Universal Card University." UCS addresses any competency gaps by providing basic job skills training, career-based skills development, quality training, and personal development. To ensure transfer of training to the job, UCS conducts a thirty-day follow-up evaluation. After that time, trainers are responsible for their students' results.

Step 3.   Performance recognition: Appraisal and rewards play a big role in UCS's HR quality plan. Managers and employees set mutually agreeable objectives and performance standards annually (to align individual, departmental, and corporate goals). Bonuses are then based on the number of days UCS achieves these quality standards. In addition, both teams and individuals are eligible for a variety of other awards such as the President's Circle Award and the Power of One Award, which is given spontaneously for exceptional accomplishments.

Step 4.   Wellness and morale: The final step in UCS's HR quality plan focuses on creating a well-rounded team of individuals. Their proactive and preventive approach to wellness includes professionally staffed fitness centers, smoke-free workstations, and medical services teams. All of these factors are incorporated into a ongoing survey in which employees give feedback as to how they think the system can be improved.

According to Pamela Vosmik, vice president of human resources, the HR quality plan creates a win-win situation: "Both customers and employees benefit as they work together to meet strategic goals in an arena that involves, empowers, and values everyone."

Source: Pamela Vosmik, "In Pursuit of Quality Human Resources at AT&T Universal Card Services," *Employment Relations Today* (Spring 1993): 29–35.

Questions
1. What other ways could UCS push to improve quality through HR practices?
2. Do you see any potential problems with the system?
3. How closely does the HR quality plan at UCS correspond to our discussion of a supportive culture in Chapter 2?

NOTES AND REFERENCES

1. James R. Nininger, "Human Resource Priorities in the 1980s," *Canadian Business Review* 7, no. 4 (Winter 1980): 11.
2. Kenneth Labich, "The Best Cities for Knowledge Workers," *Fortune* (November 15, 1993): 50–56. See also Patricia Sellers, "The Best Cities for Business," *Fortune* (October 22, 1990): 48–51.
3. Gary T. Marx and Sanford Sherizen, "Corporations That Spy on Their Employees," *Business and Society Review* 60 (Winter 1987): 32–37; Rebecca Grant and Christopher Higgins, "Monitoring Service Workers via Computer: The Effect on Employees, Productivity, and Service," *National Productivity Review* 8, no. 2 (Spring 1989): 101–112; Marco A. Monsalve and Arlene Triplett, "Maximizing New Technology," *HR Magazine* (March 1990): 85–87.
4. James W. Dean, Jr., and Scott A. Snell, "Integrated Manufacturing and Job Design: Moderating Effects of Organizational Inertia," *Academy of Management Journal* 34, no. 4 (1991): 776–804. See also Walter Kiechel, III, "How We Will Work in the Year 2000," *Fortune* (May 17, 1993): 38–52.
5. Scott A. Snell and James W. Dean, Jr., "Integrated Manufacturing and Human Resource Management: A Human Capital Perspective," *Academy of Management Journal* 35, no. 3 (1992): 467–504.
6. Monsalve and Triplett, "Maximizing New Technology."
7. Colin Richards-Carpenter, "Bright Ideas from Systems Users," *Personnel Management* (February 1992): 19–20.
8. Scott A. Snell, Patricia Pedigo, and George M. Krawiec, "Managing the Impact of Information Technology on Human Resource Management," in Gerald R. Ferris, Sherman D. Rosen, and Darold T. Barnum (eds.) *Handbook of Human Resources Management* (Oxford, U.K.: Blackwell Publishers), in press; Easy Klein, "Heroes for Hire," *D&B Reports* (January/February 1993): 26–27. See also Laura M. Herren, "The Right Technology for the 1990s," *Personnel Administrator* 34, no. 4 (April 1989): 48–52.
9. Brian Dumaine, "Why Do We Work?" *Fortune* (December 26, 1994): 196–204; Myron Magnet, "You Don't Have to Be a Workaholic," *Fortune* (August 9, 1993): 64. See also Marlys Harris, "What's Wrong with This Picture?" *Working Woman* (December 1990): 72–76; Charlene Marmer Solomon, "Managing the Baby Busters," *Personnel Journal* (March 1992): 52–59.
10. James Ledvinka and Vida Scarpello, *Federal Regulation of Personnel and Human Resource Management*, 2d ed. (Boston: PWS-Kent Publishing, 1990), 18.
11. The *Federal Register* provides a uniform system for making available to the public those regulations and legal notices issued by federal agencies. These include presidential proclamations and executive orders; federal agency documents having general applicability and legal effect; documents required to be published by act of Congress; and other federal agency documents of public interest. It is published daily, Monday through Friday, except holidays.
12. Prentice-Hall, Commerce Clearing House, and the Bureau of National Affairs are the leading publishers of such services.

13. John W. Mayo, "The U.S. Economic Outlook: A Turn for the Better?" *Survey of Business* (Winter 1993): 16–20. See also Evangelos O. Simos and John E. Triantis, eds., "International Economic Outlook," *Journal of Business Forecasting* (Spring 1993): 30–37.

14. Mayo, "U.S. Economic Outlook," 16–20; Simos and Triantis, "International Economic Outlook," 30–37.

15. "North American Free Trade Agreement," *HR Magazine* (December 1991): 85–86. See also "The Mexican Worker," *Business Week* (April 19, 1993): 84–92.

16. Mayo, "U.S. Economic Outlook," 16–20; see also "Men Working Less: Which Groups Are Affected?" *The New York Times* (December 1, 1994): D15; Gener Koretz, "Where Has All the Labor Gone?" *Business Week* (December 12, 1994): 30.

17. *Government Executive,* October 1989, as cited in *USA Today* (January 25, 1990): 1A.

18. Alistair Mant, "Putting Humanity Back into Human Resources," *Personnel Management* (January 1992): 24–27.

19. "The Competency Initiative: Standards of Excellence for Human Resource Executives," Society for Human Resource Management Foundation (1990). See also "Priorities for Competitive Advantage" in *A 21st Century Vision: A Worldwide Human Resource Study,* an IBM study conducted by Towers Perrin (1992); Stephenie Overman, "Reaching for the 21st Century," *HR Magazine* (April 1992): 61–63.

20. Donna Brown, "HR Is the Key to Survival in the '90s," *HR Magazine* (March 1991): 5–6.

21. William H. Miller, "A New Perspective for Tomorrow's Workforce," *Industry Week* (May 6, 1991): 7–8.

22. "Tomorrow's Jobs," *Occupational Outlook Handbook,* 1992–1993 edition (Washington, D.C.: Bureau of Labor Statistics, bulletin no. 2400, May 1992): 8–14. See also Ronald E. Kutscher, "Outlook 1990–2005: Major Trends and Issues," *Occupational Outlook Quarterly* (Spring 1992): 2–5.

23. Margaret L. Usdansky, "Minority Majorities in One in Six Cities," *USA Today* (June 9, 1993): 10A.

24. "The Immigrants," *Business Week* (July 13, 1992): 114–22. See also Jaclyn Fierman, "Is Immigration Hurting the U.S.? *Fortune* (August 9, 1993): 76–79, "The Price of Open Arms," *Business Week* (June 21, 1993): 32–35.

25. Anthony Redwood, "Human Resources in the 1990s," *Business Horizons* (January/February 1990): 6–12.

26. Nancy J. Perry, "Workers of the Future," *Fortune* (Spring/Summer 1991): 68–72.

27. Perry, "Workers of the Future."

28. "Tomorrow's Jobs."

29. Redwood, "Human Resources in the 1990's."

30. Walter Kiechel III, "How to Manage Older Workers," *Fortune* (November 5, 1990): 183–86. See also Anthony Ramirez, "Making Better Use of Older Workers," *Fortune* (January 30, 1989): 179–87.

31. Perry, "Workers of the Future."

32. Miller, "New Perspective."

33. Walecia Konrad, "Welcome to the Woman-Friendly Company Where Talent Is Valued and Rewarded," *Business Week* (August 6, 1990): 48–55.

34. Joseph Pereira, "Women Allege Sexist Atmosphere in Offices Constitutes Harassment," *The Wall Street Journal* (February 10, 1988): 23; Louise F. Fitzgerald, "Sexual Harassment: Violence against Women in the Workplace," *American Psychologist* (October 1993): 1070–76; Ronni Sandroff, "Sexual Harassment: The Inside Story," *Working Woman* (June 1992): 47–78.

35. Kutscher, "Outlook 1990–2005."

36. Donald J. Ford, "Toward a More Literate Workforce," *Training and Development* (November 1992): 52–55. See also "Workplace Literacy Problems," *Supervision* (January 1991): 24–25; "Why Ellis Can Read—At Last," *Business Week* (May 24, 1993): 26.

37. Alfred S. Warren, "Creating a Competitive Workforce," *Economic Development Review* (Winter 1990): 10–12.

38. Kutscher, "Outlook 1990–2005"; Ford, "Toward a More Literate Workforce"; "Workplace Literacy Problems"; "Why Ellis Can Read—At Last."

39. Ron Zemke, "Workplace Illiteracy—Shall We Overcome?" *Training* 26, no. 6 (June 1989): 33–39. See also William H. Wagel, "On the Horizon: HR in the 1990s," *Personnel* (January 1990): 11–16.

40. Warren, "Creating a Competitive Workforce."

41. Perry, "Workers of the Future."

42. John Eberlee, "Schools, Businesses Partner to Encourage High-Tech Careers," *Computing Canada* 16, no. 18 (1990): 13; Mimi Bluestone and Douglas A. Harbrecht, "Reading, 'Riting, 'Rithmetic—and Now Tech Ed," *Business Week* (October 19, 1987): 114–16.

43. Ronald Henkoff, "Companies That Train Best," *Fortune* (March 22, 1993): 62–75. Anita K. Ross, "IBM Canada's Involvement in Education," *Canadian Business Review* 17, no. 3 (Autumn 1990): 21–23. See also Perry, "Workers of the Future."

44. Zemke, "Workplace Illiteracy," 33–39.

45. Dianne Hammer, "U.S. Takes a Lesson from German Education System," *Telephone Engineer and Management* 97, no. 12 (June 15, 1993): 8. See also "From High Schools to High Skills," *Business Week* (April 26, 1993): 110–12.

46. Kutscher, "Outlook 1990–2005."

47. Kutscher, "Outlook 1990–2005"; see also "Tomorrow's Jobs."

48. "Tomorrow's Jobs."

49. "Tomorrow's Jobs."

50. Jaclyn Fierman, "The Contingency Workforce," *Fortune* (January 1994): 30–36. See also Michael R. Losey, "Temps: They're Not Just for Typing

Anymore," *Modern Office Technology* (August 1991): 58–59; Louis S. Richman, "CEOs to Workers: Help Not Wanted," *Fortune* (July 12, 1993): 42–43; Linda Dickens, "Part-Time Employees: Workers Whose Time Has Come?" *Employee Relations* 14, no. 2 (1992): 3–12.

51. "The Truth about Temping," *U.S. News and World Report* (November 1993): 95; Valerie A. Personick, "A Second Look at Industry Output and Employment Trends through 1995," *Monthly Labor Review* 108, no. 11 (November 1985): 37.

52. Barbara J. Farrah and Cheryl D. Dagen, "Telecommuting Policies That Work," *HR Magazine* (July 1993): 64–71. See also "Lone Eagles: The Ultimate Commuters," *American Demographics* (August 1993): 10–14.

53. Easy Klein, "Tomorrow's Workforce," *D&B Reports* (January/February 1990): 33–35.

54. Barbara J. Risman, and Donald Tomaskovic-Devey, "The Social Construction of Technology: Microcomputers and the Organization of Work," *Business Horizons* 32, no. 3 (May-June 1989): 71–75.

55. Lynne F. McGee, "Setting Up Work at Home," *Personnel Administrator* 33, no. 12 (December 1988): 58–62.

56. John Mascotte, "Business Is Still Structured like Fourth Grade," *Business Week* (June 28, 1993): 86; Farrah and Dagen, "Telecommuting Policies That Work." See also "Vanishing Offices," *The Wall Street Journal* (June 4, 1993): A1.

57. For practical recommendations on how to avoid lawsuits over invasion of privacy, see John Corbett O'Meara, "The Emerging Law of Employees' Right to Privacy," *Personnel Administrator* 30, no. 6 (June 1985): 159–65. See also Lee Smith, "What the Boss Knows about You," *Fortune* (August 9, 1993): 88–93; "Privacy Issues in the Workplace," *HR Magazine* (August 1992): 93–94; "Claims Gone Wrong," *HR Magazine* (January 1990): 60–62; "Debate Is Brewing over Employees' Right to Privacy," *HR Focus* (February 1993): 1–4; Michael R. Losey, "Workplace Privacy: What You Do Know May Hurt You," *Modern Office Technology* (May 1993): 56–58.

58. John P. Robinson, "Time's Up," *American Demographics* 11, no. 7 (July 1989): 33–35; see also Dumaine, "Why Do We Work?"

59. Harris, "What's Wrong with This Picture?" See also Patricia Sellers, "Don't Call Me a Slacker," *Fortune* (December 12, 1994): 180–96.

60. Alan Deutschman, "Pioneers of the New Balance," *Fortune* (May 20, 1991): 60–68; Miller, "New Perspective for Tomorrow's Workforce."

61. Deutschman, "Pioneers"; Miller, "New Perspective."

62. Thomas Rollins and Jerrold R. Bratkovich, "Productivity's People Factor," *Personnel Administrator* 33, no. 2 (February 1988): 50–57.

63. R. Krishnan, A. B. Rami Shani, R. M. Grant, and R. Baer, "In Search of Quality Improvement: Problems of Design and Implementation," *Academy of Management Executive* (November 1993): 7–20.

64. Thomas A. Stewart, "Allied-Signal's Turnaround Blitz," *Fortune* (November 30, 1992): 72–76.

65. Y. K. Shetty, "The Human Side of Product Quality," *National Productivity Review* 8, no. 2 (Spring 1989): 175–82. See also Rosabeth Moss Kanter, Barry A. Stein, and Todd Jick, *The Challenge of Organizational Change—How People Experience It and Manage It* (New York: Free Press, 1991).

66. Richard Blackburn and Benson Rosen, "Total Quality and Human Resources Management: Lessons Learned from Baldrige Award–Winning Companies," *Academy of Management Executive* 7, no. 3 (1993): 49–66.

67. George W. Bohlander and Angelo J. Kinicki, "Where Personnel and Productivity Meet," *Personnel Administrator* 33, no. 9 (September 1988): 122–130.

68. Richard G. Linowes, "The Japanese Manager's Traumatic Entry into the United States: Understanding the American-Japanese Cultural Divide," *Academy of Management Executive* (November 1993): 21–40.

69. Jon R. Katzenbach and Douglas K. Smith, *The Wisdom of Teams: Creating the High Performance Organization* (Cambridge, Mass.: Harvard Business School, 1993), See also Perry, "Workers of the Future." For a discussion of instances when teams are illegal forms of company unions, see "Making Teamwork Work—And Appeasing Uncle Sam," *Business Week* (January 25, 1993): 101.

70. Perry, "Workers of the Future."

71. Robert T. Golembiewski and Ben-chu Sun, "QWL Improves Worksite Quality: Success Rates in a Large Pool of Studies," *Human Resource Development Quarterly* 1, no. 1 (Spring 1990): 35–43. See also "Evolution of the Workplace: Reich Presses Worker Involvement," *USA Today* (July 28, 1993): 4B.

72. Brian O'Reilly, "The New Deal: What Companies and Employees Owe One Another," *Fortune* (June 13, 1994): 44–52.

73. An interesting technique for studying an organization's culture is outlined in W. Jack Duncan, "Organizational Culture: 'Getting a Fix' on an Elusive Concept," *Academy of Management Executive* 3, no. 3 (August 1989): 229–36.

74. Mary Kay Ash, *Mary Kay on People Management* (New York: Warner Books, 1984), xix. See also Mary Kay Ash, *Mary Kay* (New York: Harper & Row, 1981); Richard E. Hattwick, "Mary Kay Ash," *The Journal of Behavioral Economics* 16 (Winter 1987): 61–69; Alan Farnham, "Mary Kay's Lessons in Leadership," *Fortune* (September 20, 1993): 68–77.

75. Ash, *Mary Kay on People Management*, xviii–xix.

76. Kenneth Labich, "Hot Company, Warm Culture," *Fortune* (February 27, 1989): 74–78; John Huey,

"Wal-Mart—Will It Take Over the World?" *Fortune* (January 30, 1989): 52–61. See also Robert Eisenberger, Peter Fasolo, and Valerie Davis-LaMastro, "Perceived Organizational Support and Employee Diligence, Commitment, and Innovation," *Journal of Applied Psychology* 75, no. 1 (1990): 51–59.

77. Terrence E. Deal and Allan A. Kennedy, *Corporate Cultures: The Rites and Rituals of Corporate Life* (Reading, Mass.: Addison-Wesley, 1982), 7. See also Benjamin Schneider, ed., *Organizational Climate and Culture* (San Francisco: Jossey-Bass, 1990).

78. Patricia Sellers and David Kirkpatrick, "Can This Man Save IBM?" *Fortune* (April 19, 1993): 63–67.

79. G. Pinchot, "Intrapreneurialism for Corporations," *The Futurist* (February 1984): 82–83. See also Peter F. Drucker, *Innovation and Entrepreneurship—Practice and Principles* (New York: Harper & Row, 1985); and Philip R. Harris, *Management in Transition* (San Francisco: Jossey-Bass, 1985), Chapter 3. For an interesting biography of probably America's greatest intrapreneur, see Stuart W. Leslie, *Boss Kettering—Wizard of General Motors* (New York: Columbia University Press, 1983).

80. Ronald Alsop, "Consumer-Product Grants Relying on 'Intrapreneurs' in New Ventures," *The Wall Street Journal* (April 22, 1988): A25.

81. Kirkland Ropp, "Bringing Up Baby: Nurturing Intrapreneurs," *Personnel Administrator* 32, no. 6 (June 1987): 92–96. See also W. Jack Duncan, Peter M. Guites, Andrew C. Ruchs, and T. Douglas Jacobs, "Intrapreneurship and the Reinvention of the Corporation," *Business Horizons* 31, no. 3 (May-June 1988): 16–21.

Chapter

Equal Employment Opportunity
and Human Resources Management

3

After studying this chapter you should be able to

one
objective

Explain the reasons behind passage of EEO legislation.

two
objective

Identify and describe the major laws affecting equal employment opportunity.

three
objective

Explain the use of the Uniform Guidelines on Employee Selection Procedures.

four
objective

Explain the concept of adverse impact and apply the four-fifths rule.

five
objective

Discuss significant court cases impacting equal employment opportunity.

six
objective

Describe sexual harassment, bona fide occupational qualification, and religious preference as equal employment opportunity issues.

seven
objective

Explain various enforcement procedures affecting equal employment opportunity.

eight
objective

Describe affirmative action and the basic steps in developing an affirmative action program.

Equal employment opportunity

The treatment of individuals in all aspects of employment—hiring, promotion, training, etc.—in a fair and nonbiased manner

Within the field of HRM perhaps no topics have received more attention during the past thirty years than equal employment opportunity (EEO) and affirmative action (AA). **Equal employment opportunity,** *or the employment of individuals in a fair and nonbiased manner, has consumed the attention of the media, the courts, practitioners, and legislators. Not surprisingly, along with this attention have come a myriad of legal requirements affecting all aspects of the employment relationship. These mandates create legal responsibilities for an organization and each of its managers to comply with various laws and administrative guidelines. All functions of HRM should be carried out according to these legal standards.*

When managers ignore the legal aspects of HRM, they risk incurring costly and time-consuming litigation, negative public attitudes, and damage to organizational morale. In one highly publicized case, State Farm Insurance Company was sued by a group of women claiming sex-bias employment discrimination. The court award of $157 million to 800 women is the largest sex-based court settlement in U.S. history. Experts agree that this court case with its record award is a dramatic example of what women can accomplish in undoing corporate discrimination.[1]

Equal employment opportunity is not only a legal topic, it is also an emotional issue. It concerns all individuals regardless of their sex, race, religion, age, national origin, color, or position in an organization. Supervisors should be aware of their personal biases and how these attitudes can influence their dealings with subordinates. It should be emphasized that covert, as well as blatantly intentional, discrimination in employment is illegal.

In recent decades, employers have been compelled to develop employment policies that incorporate different laws, executive orders (EOs), administrative regulations, and court decisions (case law) designed to end job discrimination. The role of these legal requirements in shaping employment policies will be emphasized in this chapter. We will also discuss the process of affirmative action, which attempts to correct past practices of discrimination by actively recruiting minority group members.

objective

Historical Perspective of EEO Legislation

Equal employment opportunity as a national priority has emerged slowly in the United States. Not until the mid-1950s and early 1960s did nondiscriminatory employment become a strong social concern. Three factors seem to have influenced the growth of EEO legislation: (1) changing attitudes toward employment discrimination; (2) published reports highlighting the economic problems of women, minorities, and older workers; and (3) a growing body of disparate laws and government regulations covering discrimination.

Changing National Values

The United States was founded on the principles of individual merit, hard work, and equality. The Constitution grants to all citizens the right to life, liberty, and the pursuit of happiness. The Fifth, Thirteenth, and Fourteenth Amendments expanded these guarantees by providing for due process of law (Fifth Amendment), outlawing slavery (Thirteenth Amendment), and guaranteeing equal protection under the law (Fourteenth Amendment). A central aim of political action has been to establish justice for all people of the nation.

In spite of these constitutional guarantees, employment discrimination has a long history in the United States. Organizations that claim to offer fair treat-

A group of black students was refused service at an F. W. Woolworth lunch counter in 1960.

ment to employees have openly or covertly engaged in discriminatory practices. Well-known entities such as American Telephone and Telegraph, New York City, Shoney's Restaurants, and Rockwell International have violated equal employment laws.[2] While in theory the American dream of economic prosperity has existed for all citizens, in reality many have believed that women and minorities should be excluded from equal consideration.

Public attitudes changed dramatically with the beginning of the civil rights movement. During the late 1950s and early 1960s, minorities—especially blacks—publicized their low economic and occupational position through marches, sit-ins, rallies, and clashes with public authorities. The low employment status of women also gained recognition during this period. Supported by concerned individuals and church and civic leaders, the civil rights movement and the women's movement received wide attention through television and print media. These movements had a pronounced influence on changing the attitudes of society at large, of the business community, of civic leaders, and of government officials, resulting in improvements in the civil rights of all individuals. No longer was blatant discrimination to be accepted.

Economic Disparity

The change in government and societal attitudes toward discrimination was further prompted by increasing public awareness of the economic imbalance between nonwhites and whites. Even today, civil rights activists cite government statistics to emphasize this disparity. For example, the July 1994 unemployment rate for black males over 20 years old was 10.5 percent, compared with 4.9 percent for white males the same age. When employed, nonwhites tend to hold unskilled or semiskilled jobs characterized by unstable employment, low status, and low pay. In the third quarter of 1994, the median weekly earnings of white males were $534; of black males, $388; and of Hispanic males, $342.[3] The

Equal Pay Act of 1963

The Equal Pay Act outlaws discrimination in pay, employee benefits, and pensions based on the worker's gender. Employers are prohibited from paying employees of one gender at a rate lower than that paid to members of the other gender for doing equal work.[5] Jobs are considered "equal" when they require substantially the same skill, effort, and responsibility under similar working conditions and in the same establishment. For example, male and female flight attendants working for Delta Airlines must not be paid differently because of their gender. However, other airlines may pay their flight attendants wage rates that differ from those at Delta, based on different job content or economic conditions.

Employers do not violate the Equal Pay Act when differences in wages paid to men and women for equal work are based on seniority systems, merit considerations, or incentive pay plans. However, these exceptions must not be based on the employee's gender or serve to discriminate against one particular gender. Employers may not lower the wages of one gender to comply with the law; rather, they must raise the wages of the gender being underpaid.

The Equal Pay Act was passed as an amendment to the Fair Labor Standards Act (FLSA) and is administered by the Equal Employment Opportunity Commission (EEOC). It covers employers engaged in interstate commerce and most government employees.

Civil Rights Act of 1964

Title VII of the Civil Rights Act of 1964 is the broadest and most significant of the antidiscrimination statutes. The act bars discrimination in all HR activities, including hiring, training, promotion, pay, employee benefits, and other conditions of employment. Discrimination is prohibited on the basis of race, color, religion, sex (also referred to as gender), or national origin. Also prohibited is discrimination based on pregnancy.[6] The law protects hourly employees, supervisors, professional employees, managers, and executives from discriminatory practices. Section 703(a) of Title VII of the Civil Rights Act specifically provides that

> It shall be unlawful employment practice for an employer:
> 1. To fail or refuse to hire or to discharge any individual, or otherwise to discriminate against any individual with respect to his [or her] compensation, terms, conditions, or privileges of employment because of such individual's race, color, religion, sex, or national origin; or
> 2. To limit, segregate, or classify his [or her] employees or applicants for employment in any way which would deprive or tend to deprive any individual of employment opportunities or otherwise adversely affect his [or her] status as an employee because of such individual's race, color, religion, sex, or national origin.

While the purpose and the coverage of Title VII are extensive, the law does permit various exemptions. For example, as with the Equal Pay Act, managers are permitted to apply employment conditions differently if those differences are based on such objective factors as merit, seniority, or incentive payments. Nowhere does the law require employers to hire, promote, or retain workers who are not qualified to perform their job duties. And managers may still reward employees differently, provided these differences are not predicated on the employees' race, color, sex, religion, or national origin.

The Civil Rights Act of 1964, as amended by the Equal Employment Opportunity Act of 1972 and the Civil Rights Act of 1991, covers a broad range of organizations. The law includes under its jurisdiction the following:

1. All private employers in interstate commerce who employ fifteen or more employees for twenty or more weeks per year
2. State and local governments
3. Private and public employment agencies, including the U.S. Employment Service
4. Joint labor-management committees that govern apprenticeship or training programs
5. Labor unions having fifteen or more members or employees
6. Public and private educational institutions
7. Foreign subsidiaries of U.S. organizations employing U.S. citizens

Certain employers are excluded from coverage of the Civil Rights Act. Broadly defined, these are (1) U.S. government-owned corporations, (2) bona fide, tax-exempt private clubs, (3) religious organizations employing persons of a specific religion, and (4) organizations hiring Native Americans on or near a reservation.

The Civil Rights Act of 1964 established the Equal Employment Opportunity Commission to administer the law and promote equal employment opportunity. The commission's structure and operations will be reviewed later in this chapter.

Age Discrimination in Employment Act of 1967

A special study by the U.S. Department of Labor notes that by the year 2000, the average age of the workforce will be 39 years.[7] Since older workers are less likely to agree to relocate or adapt to new job demands, they are prone to employer discrimination. To make employment decisions based on age illegal, the Age Discrimination in Employment Act (ADEA), as amended, was passed in 1967. The act prohibits specific employers from discriminating against persons 40 years of age or older in any area of employment, including selection, because of age. Employers affected are those with twenty or more employees; unions with twenty-five or more members; employment agencies; and federal, state, and local governments.

Exceptions to the law are permitted where age is a bona fide occupational qualification (BFOQ).[8] (BFOQs are discussed more fully later in the chapter.) A BFOQ may exist where an employer can show that advanced age may affect public safety or organizational efficiency. For example, such conditions might exist for bus or truck drivers or for locomotive engineers. The greater the safety factor, measured by the likelihood of harm through accidents, the more stringent may be the job qualification designed to ensure safety. A BFOQ does not exist where an employer argues that younger employees foster a youthful or more energetic organizational image. Employers must also be careful to avoid making offhanded remarks (e.g., "the old man") or expressing negative opinions (e.g., "People over 50 years old have more accidents") about older individuals. These remarks and attitudes can be used as proof of discrimination in age-bias suits.

Equal Employment Opportunity Act of 1972

In 1972 the Civil Rights Act of 1964 was amended by the Equal Employment Opportunity Act. Two important changes were made. First, the coverage of the act was broadened to include state and local governments and public and private educational institutions. Second, the law strengthened the enforcement powers of the EEOC by allowing the agency itself to sue employers in court to enforce the provisions of the act. Regional litigation centers were established to provide faster and more effective court action.

Pregnancy Discrimination Act of 1978

Prior to the passage of the Pregnancy Discrimination Act, pregnant women could be forced to resign or take a leave of absence because of their condition. In addition, employers did not have to provide disability or medical coverage for pregnancy. The Pregnancy Discrimination Act amended the Civil Rights Act of 1964 by stating that pregnancy is a disability and that pregnant employees in covered organizations must be treated on an equal basis with employees having other medical conditions. Under the law, it is illegal for employers to deny sick leave for morning sickness or related pregnancy illness if sick leave is permitted for other medical conditions such as flu or surgical operations.

Furthermore, the law prohibits discrimination in the hiring, promotion, or termination of women because of pregnancy. Women must be evaluated on their ability to perform the job, and employers may not set arbitrary dates for mandatory pregnancy leaves. Leave dates are to be based on the individual pregnant employee's ability to work.

Americans with Disabilities Act of 1990

Discrimination against the disabled was first prohibited in federally funded activities by the Vocational Rehabilitation Act of 1973 (to be discussed below). However, the disabled were not among the protected classes covered by the Civil Rights Act of 1964. To remedy this shortcoming, Congress in 1990 passed the Americans with Disabilities Act, prohibiting employers from discriminating against individuals with physical and mental handicaps and the chronically ill. The law defines a disability as "(a) a physical or mental impairment that substantially limits one or more of the major life activities; (b) a record of such impairment; or (c) being regarded as having such an impairment." Note that the law also protects persons "regarded" as having a disability—for example, individuals with disfiguring burns. The act does not cover

1. Homosexuality or bisexuality
2. Gender-identity disorders not resulting from physical impairment or other sexual-behavior disorders

3. Compulsive gambling, kleptomania, or pyromania
4. Psychoactive substance-use disorders resulting from current illegal use of drugs
5. Current illegal use of drugs
6. Infectious or communicable diseases of public health significance (applied to food-handling jobs only and excluding AIDS)

The act requires employers to make a reasonable accommodation for disabled persons who are otherwise qualified to work, unless doing so would cause undue hardship to the employer. "Undue hardship" refers to unusual work modifications or excessive expenses that might be incurred by an employer in providing an accommodation.[9] **Reasonable accommodation** "includes making facilities accessible and usable to disabled persons, restructuring jobs, permitting part-time or modified work schedules, reassigning to a vacant position, changing equipment, and/or expense." "Reasonable" is to be determined according to (1) the nature and cost of the accommodation and (2) the financial resources, size, and profitability of the facility and parent organization. Furthermore, employers cannot use selection procedures that screen out or tend to screen out disabled persons, unless the selection procedure "is shown to be job-related for the position in question and is consistent with business necessity" and acceptable job performance cannot be achieved through reasonable accommodation. ("Essential functions," a pivotal issue for ensuring reasonable accommodation, will be discussed in Chapter 4.)

The act prohibits covered employers from discriminating against a qualified individual regarding application for employment, hiring, advancement, discharge, compensation, training, or other employment conditions.[10] The law incorporates the procedures and remedies found in Title VII of the Civil Rights Act, allowing job applicants or employees initial employment, reinstatement, back pay, and other injunctive relief against employers who violate the statute.[11] The act covers employers with fifteen or more employees. The EEOC enforces the law in the same manner that Title VII of the Civil Rights Act is enforced.

Reasonable accommodation
Attempt by employers to adjust, without undue hardship, the working conditions or schedules of employees with disabilities or religious preferences

Civil Rights Act of 1991

After extensive U.S. House and Senate debate, the Civil Rights Act of 1991 was signed into law. The act amends Title VII of the Civil Rights Act of 1964. One of the major elements of the law is the awarding of damages in cases of intentional discrimination or unlawful harassment. For the first time under federal law, damages are provided to victims of intentional discrimination or unlawful harassment on the basis of sex, religion, national origin, and disability. An employee who claims intentional discrimination can seek compensatory or punitive damages. Compensatory damages include payment for future money losses, emotional pain, suffering, mental anguish, and other nonmonetary losses. Punitive damages are awarded if it can be shown that the employer engaged in discrimination with malice or reckless indifference to the law. Most significantly, the act allows juries rather than federal judges to decide discrimination claims. Compensatory or punitive damages cannot be awarded in cases where an employment practice not intended to be discriminatory is shown to have an unlawful adverse impact on persons of a protected class. The total damages any one person can receive cannot be more than

$ 50,000 for employers having between 15 and 100 employees
$100,000 for employers having between 101 and 200 employees
$200,000 for employers having between 201 and 500 employees
$300,000 for employers having over 500 employees

In each case the aggrieved individual must have been employed with the organization for twenty or more calendar weeks.

The act requires that employers defending against a charge of discrimination demonstrate that employment practices are *job-related* and consistent with *business necessity*.[12] Additionally, the act provides that an employer may not avoid liability in mixed-motive discrimination cases by proving it would have taken the same action without the discriminatory motive.

Under its other provisions, the law

- Extends coverage of Title VII and Americans with Disabilities Act to U.S. citizens employed abroad by American firms
- Prohibits employers from adjusting employment test scores or using different cutoff test scores on the basis of race, color, religion, sex, or national origin
- Prohibits litigation involving charges of reverse discrimination where employers are under a consent order (court order) to implement an affirmative action program

The act mandates the Equal Employment Opportunity Commission to establish a Technical Assistance Training Institute (TATI). The institute is to provide technical assistance and training regarding government regulations enforced by the commission. The commission must also provide educational and outreach activities to persons who have historically faced job discrimination.

Uniformed Services Employment and Reemployment Rights Act of 1994

Under this act, individuals who enter the military for a short period of service can return to their private-sector jobs without risk of loss of seniority or benefits. The act protects against discrimination on the basis of military obligation in the areas of hiring, job retention, and advancement. Other provisions under the act require employers to make reasonable efforts to retrain or upgrade skills to qualify employees for reemployment, expand health care and employee pension plan coverage, and extend the length of time an individual may be absent for military duty from four to five years. For their part, service members must provide their employers advance notice of their military obligations in order to be protected by the reemployment rights statute. The Labor Department's Veterans Employment and Training Service is responsible for enforcing the law.

Other Federal Laws and Executive Orders

Because the major laws affecting equal employment opportunity do not cover agencies of the federal government and because state laws do not apply to federal employees, it has at times been necessary for the president to issue executive orders to protect federal employees. Executive orders are also used to provide equal employment opportunity to individuals employed by government contractors. Since many large employers—like General Dynamics, AT&T, Allied-Signal, and Motorola—and numerous small companies have contracts with the federal government, managers are expected to know and comply with the provisions of executive orders and other laws. The federal laws and executive orders that apply to government agencies and government contractors are summarized in Figure 3–2.

Vocational Rehabilitation Act of 1973

Disabled individual
Any person who (1) has a physical or mental impairment that substantially limits one or more of such person's major life activities, (2) has a record of such impairment, or (3) is regarded as having such an impairment

Often considered a forgotten group, people with disabilities experience discrimination both because of negative attitudes regarding their ability to perform work and because of physical barriers imposed by organizational facilities.[13] The Vocational Rehabilitation Act was passed in 1973 to correct these problems by requiring private employers with federal contracts over $2,500 to take affirmative action to hire disabled individuals with a mental or physical disability. Recipients of federal financial assistance, such as public and private colleges and universities, are also covered. Employers must make a reasonable accommodation to hire disabled individuals but are not required to employ unqualified persons. In applying the safeguards of this law, the term **disabled individual** means "any person who (1) has a physical or mental impairment which substantially limits one or more of such person's major life activities, (2) has a record of such an impairment, or (3) is regarded as having such an impairment." This definition closely parallels the definition of disabled individual provided in the Americans with Disabilities Act just discussed.

FIGURE 3-2 *EEO Rules Applicable to Federal Contractors, Agencies*

LAW	PROVISIONS
Vocational Rehabilitation Act of 1973 (amended in 1974)	Prohibits federal contractors from discriminating against disabled individuals in any program or activity receiving federal financial assistance; requires federal contractors to develop affirmative action plans to hire and promote disabled persons.
Executive Order 11246 (1965), as amended by Order 11375 (1966)	Prohibits employment discrimination based on race, color, religion, sex, or national origin by government contractors with contracts exceeding $10,000; requires contractors employing fifty or more workers to develop affirmative action plans when government contracts exceed $50,000 a year.
Executive Order 11478 (1969)	Obligates the federal government to ensure that all personnel actions affecting applicants for employment be free from discrimination based on race, color, religion, sex, or national origin.

Individuals may be regarded as "substantially limited" when they experience difficulty in securing, retaining, or advancing in employment because of their disability. Since the act was passed, a growing number of mental and physical impairments have been classified as disabilities within the meaning of the law. For example, disabilities such as blindness and paralysis are clearly covered. But other, less obvious impairments such as diabetes, high blood pressure, and heart disease also fall within the definition of disability established under the act.

In 1987, the Supreme Court ruled in *Nassau County, Florida v Arline* that employees afflicted with contagious diseases, such as tuberculosis, are disabled individuals and subject to the act's coverage.[14] In cases where persons with contagious diseases are "otherwise qualified" to do their jobs, the law requires employers to make a reasonable accommodation to allow the disabled to perform their jobs.[15] Individuals with AIDS are also disabled within the meaning of the Rehabilitation Act. Therefore, discrimination on the basis of AIDS violates the law, and employers must accommodate the employment needs of AIDS victims.[16] Public interest in AIDS has presented management with a challenge to address work-related concerns about AIDS. Many organizations, including BankAmerica Corporation, have developed specific policies to deal with the issue of AIDS in the workplace. (See Highlights in HRM 1.)

The Rehabilitation Act does not require employers to hire or retain a disabled person if he or she has a contagious disease that poses a direct threat to the health or safety of others and the individual cannot be accommodated. Also, employment is not required when some aspect of the employee's disability prevents that person from carrying out essential parts of the job; nor is it required if the disabled person is not otherwise qualified.

Nevertheless, because of the success experienced in the employment of disabled persons, the slogan "Hire the disabled—it's good business" has become standard policy for many organizations. This slogan does not suggest that disabled persons can be placed in any job without careful consideration being given to their disabilities, but rather that it is good business to hire qualified disabled persons who can work safely and productively. Members of the HR staff should be trained to assess individual types and degrees of limitations and should be aware of how these restrictions relate to different jobs in the organization. In many cases the restructuring of jobs or the use of special equipment permits disabled persons to qualify for employment.

Executive Order 11246

Federal agencies and government contractors with contracts of $10,000 or more must comply with the antidiscrimination provisions of Executive Order 11246. The order prohibits discrimination based on race, color, religion, sex, or national origin in all employment activities. Furthermore, it requires that government contractors or subcontractors having fifty or more employees with contracts in excess of $50,000 develop affirmative action plans; such plans will be discussed later in the chapter.

Executive Order 11246 created the Office of Federal Contract Compliance Programs (OFCCP) to ensure equal employment opportunity in the federal procurement area. The agency issues nondiscriminatory guidelines and regulations similar to those issued by the EEOC. Noncompliance with OFCCP policies can

HIGHLIGHTS IN HRM

highlights

1   BANK OF AMERICA NT & SA CORPORATION'S POLICY ON ASSISTING EMPLOYEES WITH LIFE-THREATENING ILLNESSES

The company recognizes that employees with life-threatening illnesses—including but not limited to cancer, heart disease, and HIV disease—may wish to continue to engage in as many of their normal pursuits as their condition allows, including work. As long as these employees are able to meet acceptable performance standards, and medical evidence indicates that their conditions are not a threat to themselves or others, managers should be sensitive to their conditions and ensure that they are treated consistently with other employees. At the same time, the company seeks to provide a safe work environment for all employees and customers. Therefore, precautions should be taken to ensure that an employee's condition does not present a health and/or safety threat to other employees or customers.

Consistent with this concern for employees with life-threatening illnesses, the company offers the following range of resources available through your Human Resources representative:

- Management and employee education and information on terminal illness and specific life-threatening illnesses.
- Referral to agencies and organizations that offer supportive services to employees and dependents directly or indirectly affected by life-threatening illnesses.
- Benefits consultation to assist employees in effectively managing health, leave, and other benefits.

Guidelines to help you deal with a situation

When dealing with situations involving employees with life-threatening illnesses, managers should:

- Remember that an employee's health condition is personal, should be treated as confidential, and reasonable precautions should be taken to protect information regarding an employee's health condition.
- Contact your Human Resources representative if you believe that you or other employees need information about terminal illness, or a specific life-threatening illness, or if you need further guidance in managing a situation that involves an employee with a life-threatening illness.
- Contact your Human Resources representative if you have any concern about the possible contagious nature of an employee's illness.
- Contact your Human Resources representative to determine if a statement should be obtained from the employee's attending physician that continued presence at work will pose no threat to the employee, co-workers, or customers. The company reserves the right to require an examination by a medical doctor appointed by the company.
- If warranted, make reasonable accommodation, consistent with the business needs of the unit, for employees with life-threatening illnesses.
- Make a reasonable attempt upon request to transfer employees who have life-threatening illnesses and are experiencing undue emotional stress.

(*continued*)

result in the cancellation or suspension of contracts. The OFCCP is further charged with requiring that contractors provide job opportunities to the disabled, disabled veterans, and veterans of the Vietnam war.

Fair Employment Practice Laws

Federal laws and executive orders provide the major regulations governing equal employment opportunity. But, in addition, almost all states and many local governments have passed laws barring employment discrimination. Referred to as **fair employment practices (FEPs),** these statutes are often more comprehensive than the federal laws. While state and local laws are too numerous to review here, managers should be aware of them and how they affect HRM in their organizations.

Fair employment practices (FEPs)

State and local laws governing equal employment opportunity that are often more comprehensive than federal laws

State and local FEPs also promote the employment of individuals in a fair and unbiased way. They are patterned after federal legislation, although they frequently extend jurisdiction to employers exempt from federal coverage and therefore pertain mainly to smaller employers. While Title VII of the Civil Rights Act exempts employers with fewer than fifteen employees, many states extend antidiscrimination laws to employers with one or more workers. Thus managers and entrepreneurs operating a small business must pay close attention to these laws. Local or state legislation may bar discrimination based on physical appearance, marital status, sexual orientation, arrest records, color blindness, or political affiliation.

States with FEPs establish independent agencies to administer and enforce the statutes. The Ohio Civil Rights Commission, Massachusetts Commission against Discrimination, Colorado Civil Rights Division, and Pittsburgh Commission on Human Relations are examples. State agencies play an important role in the investigation and resolution of employment discrimination charges. FEP agencies and the Equal Employment Opportunity Commission often work together to resolve discrimination complaints.

Uniform Guidelines on Employee Selection Procedures

objective

In the past, employers have been uncertain about the appropriateness of specific selection procedures, especially those related to testing. To remedy this concern, in 1978 the Equal Employment Opportunity Commission, along with three other government agencies, adopted the current **Uniform Guidelines on Employee Selection Procedures.**[17] Since it was first published in 1970, the *Uniform Guidelines* has become a very important procedural document for managers because it applies to employee selection procedures in the areas of hiring, retention, promotion, transfer, demotion, dismissal, and referral. It is designed to assist employers, labor organizations, employment agencies, and licensing and certification boards in complying with the requirements of federal laws prohibiting discrimination in employment.

Essentially the *Uniform Guidelines* recommends that an employer be able to demonstrate that selection procedures are valid in predicting or measuring performance in a particular job. It defines "discrimination" as follows:

> The use of any selection procedure which has an adverse impact on the hiring, promotion, or other employment or membership opportunities of members of any race, sex, or ethnic group will be considered to be discriminatory and inconsistent with these guidelines, unless the procedure has been validated in accordance with these guidelines (or, certain other provisions are satisfied).[18]

Validity

When using a test or other selection instrument to choose individuals for employment, employers must be able to prove that the selection instrument bears a direct relationship to job success. This proof is established through validation studies that show the job relatedness or lack thereof for the selection instrument under study.[19] The *Uniform Guidelines*, along with several of the court cases we discuss later, provides strict standards for employers to follow as they validate selection procedures. The different methods of testing validity are reviewed in detail in Chapter 6.

Adverse Impact

objective

For an applicant or employee to pursue a discrimination case successfully, the individual must establish that the employer's selection procedures resulted in an adverse impact on a protected class. **Adverse impact** refers to the rejection for employment, placement, or promotion of a significantly higher percentage of a protected class when compared with a nonprotected class.[20] There are three basic ways to show that adverse impact exists:

Adverse rejection rate, or four-fifths rule. According to the *Uniform Guidelines*, a selection program has an adverse impact when the selection rate for any racial, ethnic, or sex class is less than four-fifths (or 80 percent) of the rate of the class with the highest selection rate. The Equal Employment Opportunity

Commission has adopted the **four-fifths rule** as a rule of thumb to determine adverse impact in enforcement proceedings. The four-fifths rule is not a legal definition of discrimination; rather, it is a method by which the EEOC or any other enforcement agency monitors serious discrepancies in hiring, promotion, or other employment decisions. Highlights in HRM 2 explains how adverse impact is determined and gives a realistic example of how the four-fifths rule is computed.

An alternative to the four-fifths rule is to apply standard deviation analysis to the observed applicant flow data. This statistical procedure determines whether the difference between the expected selection rates for protected groups and the actual selection rates could be attributed to chance. If chance is eliminated for the lower selection rates of the protected class, it is assumed that the employer's selection technique has an adverse impact on the employment opportunities of that group.

Statistical evidence.   Employees may use statistical evidence to show underrepresentation of women and minorities in job discrimination claims. In *Watson v Fort Worth Bank and Trust* (1988), the Supreme Court ruled that Clara Watson, a black bank teller seeking promotion to supervisor, could use, as proof of job discrimination, statistical evidence showing that white supervisors hired only 3.5 percent of black applicants but 14.8 percent of white applicants.[21] This ruling expands antidiscrimination laws, making it easier for women and minority workers to prove adverse impact discrimination in hirings and promotions.

Restricted policy.   Any evidence that an employer has a selection procedure that excludes members of a protected class, whether intentional or not, constitutes adverse impact.

While the *Uniform Guidelines* does not require an employer to conduct validity studies of selection procedures where no adverse impact exists, it does encourage employers to use selection procedures that are valid. Organizations that validate their selection procedures on a regular basis and use interviews, tests, and other procedures in such a manner as to avoid adverse impact will generally be in compliance with the principles of equal employment legislation. Affirmative action programs also reflect employer intent. The motivation for using valid selection procedures, however, should be the desire to achieve effective management of human resources rather than the fear of legal pressure.

Bottom-Line Concept

The 1978 revision of the *Uniform Guidelines* introduced the **bottom-line concept,** which specifies that an employer is not required to evaluate individually each component of the selection process unless there is adverse impact. However, the end result of the selection process must be predictive of future job performance if adverse impact is present. The *Uniform Guidelines* also requires that if adverse impact is present, employers consider alternative selection devices and maintain detailed records from which adverse impact can be detected.

Significant Court Cases

The *Uniform Guidelines* has been given added importance through three leading Supreme Court cases. Each case is noteworthy because it elaborates on the con-

objective

HIGHLIGHTS IN HRM

highlights

2 DETERMINING ADVERSE IMPACT: THE FOUR-FIFTHS RULE

Employers can determine adverse impact by using the method outlined in the interpretive manual on the *Uniform Guidelines on Employee Selection Procedures.*

A. Calculate the rate of selection for each group (divide the number of persons selected from a group by the number of total applicants from that group).

B. Observe which group has the highest selection.

C. Calculate the impact ratios by comparing the selection rate for each group with that of the highest group (divide the selection rate for a group by the selection rate for the highest group).

D. Observe whether the selection rate for any group is substantially less (i.e., usually less than four-fifths, or 80 percent) than the selection rate for the highest group. If it is, adverse impact is indicated in most circumstances.

Example

	JOB APPLICANTS	NUMBER HIRED	SELECTION RATE PERCENT HIRED
Step A	Whites 100	52	52/100 = 52%
	Blacks 50	14	14/50 = 28%

Step B The group with the highest selection rate is whites, 52 percent.

Step C Divide the black selection rate (28 percent) by the white selection rate (52 percent). The black rate is 53.8 percent of the white rate.

Step D Since 53.8 percent is less than four-fifths, or 80 percent, adverse impact is indicated.

Source: Adoption of Questions and Answers to Clarify and Provide a Common Interpretation of the *Uniform Guidelines on Employee Selection Procedures, Federal Register* 44, no. 43 (2 March 1979): 11998.

cepts of adverse impact, validity testing, and job relatedness. Managers of both large and small organizations must constantly be alert to new court decisions and be prepared to implement those rulings. The Bureau of National Affairs, Commerce Clearing House, and Prentice-Hall provide legal information on a subscription basis to interested managers.

The benchmark case in employment selection procedures is *Griggs v Duke Power Company* (1971). Willie Griggs had applied for the position of coal handler with the Duke Power Company. His request for the position was denied because he was not a high school graduate, a requirement for the position. Griggs claimed the job standard was discriminatory because it did not relate to job success and because the standard had an adverse impact on a protected class.

In the *Griggs* decision, the Supreme Court established two important principles affecting equal employment opportunity.[22] First, the Court ruled that employer discrimination need not be overt or intentional to be present. Rather, employment practices can be illegal even when applied equally to all employees. For example, under this ruling, cities requiring all firefighters to be six feet tall would impose an adverse impact on Asians and women, limiting their employment opportunities.

In EEO cases it is important to distinguish between adverse impact and disparate treatment discrimination. Adverse impact cases such as *Griggs* deal with unintentional discrimination; disparate treatment cases involve instances of purposeful discrimination. For example, disparate treatment would arise where an employer hires men, but no women, with school-age children. Allowing men to apply for craft jobs, such as carpentry or electrical work, but denying this opportunity to women would also show disparate treatment. To win a disparate treatment case, the plaintiff must prove that the employer's actions intended to discriminate, a situation often difficult to substantiate.

Second, under *Griggs*, employment practices must be job-related. When discrimination charges arise, employers have the burden of proving that employment requirements are job-related or constitute a business necessity. Where employers use education, physical, or intelligence standards as a basis for hiring or promotion, these requirements must be absolutely necessary for job success. Under Title VII, good intent, or absence of intent to discriminate, is not a sufficient defense.

In 1975 the Supreme Court decided *Albemarle Paper Company v Moody*.[23] The Albemarle Paper Company required job applicants to pass a variety of employment tests, some of which were believed to be poor predictors of job success. The *Albemarle* case is important because in it the Supreme Court strengthened the principles established in *Griggs*. Specifically, more-stringent requirements were placed on employers to demonstrate the job relatedness of tests. Where tests are used for hiring or promotion decisions (tests are defined to include performance appraisals), they must be valid predictors of job success. To ensure the validity of selection, the Court defined the proper method for employers to use when validating selection tools. The Supreme Court's ruling in *Albemarle* placed great importance on the EEOC *Uniform Guidelines* for employee selection procedures. Today HR managers follow these procedures to ensure the legality of their HRM practices.

In *Wards Cove Packing Co. v Antonio*, decided in 1989, the Supreme Court handed down a major decision involving the burden of proof in a discrimination charge.[24] The Court ruled that in an adverse impact case, the burden of proving a charge of discrimination fell on the charging party. This decision made it more difficult for individuals to substantiate discrimination claims. The *Wards Cove* case, in effect, reversed the *Griggs* decision, which required employers to justify their employment practices. Additionally, the Court held that a statistical disparity among protected members of a workforce does not, in itself, show proof of discrimination. Rather, the relevant statistical comparison is to *qualified applicants* in the employer's relevant labor market.

Disparate treatment
Situation in which protected-class members receive unequal treatment or are evaluated by different standards

The Civil Rights Act of 1991 overturned important parts of *Wards Cove.* The act once again places the burden of persuasion back upon the employer. If a discrimination case is made by showing a statistical disparity, the employer must again prove that the employment practice bears a relationship to the requirements of the job—a business necessity defense. Thus the Civil Rights Act of 1991 supports the *Griggs* decision.

Workforce Utilization Analysis

While employers must be aware of the impact of their selection procedures on protected-class members, they must also be concerned with the composition of their internal workforce when compared with their external labor market. The EEOC refers to this comparison as "workforce utilization analysis." This concept simply compares an employer's workforce by race and sex for specific job categories against the surrounding labor market. The employer's relevant labor market is that area from which employees are drawn who have the skills needed to successfully perform the job. For example, if an employer is hiring computer technicians from a labor market composed of 10 percent black workers, 8 percent Hispanic workers, and 2 percent Native American workers, all of whom possess the qualifications for the job, the employer's internal workforce should reflect this racial composition. When this occurs, the employer's workforce is said to be *at parity* with the relevant labor market. If the employer's racial workforce composition is below external figures, then the protected class is said to be *underutilized* and the employer should take affirmative steps to correct the imbalance.[25]

six
objective

Other Equal Employment Opportunity Issues

Federal laws, executive orders, court cases, and state and local statutes provide the broad legal framework for equal employment opportunity. Within these major laws, specific issues are of particular interest to supervisors and HR managers. The situations discussed here occur in the day-to-day supervision of employees.

Sexual Harassment

Sexual situations in the work environment are not new to organizational life. Sexual feelings are a part of group dynamics, and people who work together may come to develop these kinds of feelings for one another. Unfortunately, however, often these encounters are unpleasant and unwelcome, as witnessed by the many reported instances of sexual harassment. In one study, 90 percent of *Fortune* 500 companies had received complaints regarding sexual harassment. More than a third of the companies surveyed had been sued. In addition to legal expenses, the survey estimated sexual harassment complaints cost a typical *FORTUNE* 500 company $6.7 million per year in employee absenteeism, turnover, and loss of productivity.[26] Nationwide, 11,908 sexual harassment complaints were filed with the EEOC in 1993 by employees of both small and large organizations.[27] Figure 3–3 illustrates various types of sexual harassment and their percentages as reported in a recent study.

The EEOC guidelines on sexual harassment are specific, stating that "unwelcome advances, requests for sexual favors, and other verbal or physical

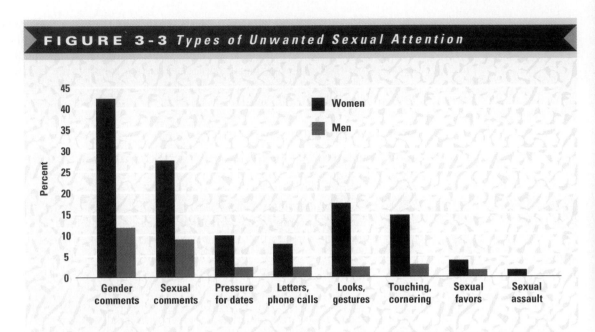

FIGURE 3-3 *Types of Unwanted Sexual Attention*

Source: Stephen H. Crow and Clifford M. Koen, "Sexual Harassment: New Challenges for Labor Arbitrators?" *Arbitration Journal*, 47, no. 2 (June 1992), p. 9. Used with permission.

Sexual harassment

Unwelcome advances, requests for sexual favors, and other verbal or physical conduct of a sexual nature in the working environment

conduct of a sexual nature" constitute **sexual harassment** when submission to the conduct is tied to continuing employment or advancement. The conduct is also illegal when it interferes with an employee's work performance or creates an "intimidating, hostile, or offensive working environment." If a supervisor promotes a female employee only after she agrees to an after-work date, the conduct is clearly illegal. Also, dirty jokes, vulgar slang, swearing, and personal ridicule and insult constitute sexual harassment when an employee finds them offensive.

For example, the Paradise Valley Unified School District of Phoenix, Arizona, defines sexual harassment as including, but not limited to, suggestive or obscene letters, notes, or invitations; derogatory comments, slurs, jokes, and epithets; assault; blocking movements; leering gestures; and displays of sexually suggestive objects, pictures, or cartoons where such conduct may create a hostile environment for the employee.[28]

In 1986 the Supreme Court issued its first sexual harassment decision, in *Meritor Savings Bank v Vinson*.[29] This ruling provided employers with the Court's interpretation of how sexual harassment is viewed under the EEOC guidelines. It is noteworthy that both the Supreme Court and the EEOC hold employers strictly accountable to prevent the sexual harassment of both female and male employees. The EEOC considers an employer guilty of sexual harassment when the employer knew, or should have known, about the unlawful conduct and failed to remedy it or take corrective action. Employers are also guilty of sexual harassment when they allow nonemployees (customers or salespersons) to sexu-

. . . .

ally harass employees. Where charges of sexual harassment have been proved, the EEOC has imposed remedies including back pay; reinstatement; and payment of lost benefits, interest charges, and attorney's fees. Sexual harassment involving physical conduct can invite criminal charges, and damages may be assessed against both the employer and the individual offender.[30]

In 1993 the Supreme Court held in *Harris v Forklift Systems Inc.* that an individual alleging hostile work environment harassment need not show that the defendant's conduct caused psychological injury. As long as a reasonable person would perceive the conduct to be hostile or abusive, and the individual perceives the conduct as such, there is no need for the conduct to cause psychological injury as well. To determine whether the misconduct is hostile or abusive, courts must look at all the circumstances surrounding the charge of harassment. Important factors include the frequency of the misconduct; the severity of the misconduct; whether it is physically threatening or humiliating, as opposed to merely offensive; and whether it unreasonably interferes with the employee's work performance.

Despite legislation against it, however, sexual harassment is still common in the workplace. Managers and supervisors must take special precautions to try to prevent it. Highlights in HRM 3 presents the Court's suggestions and the EEOC guidelines for an effective policy to minimize sexual harassment in the work environment.[31]

Bona Fide Occupational Qualification

Bona fide occupational qualification (BFOQ)
Suitable defense against a discrimination charge only where age, religion, sex, or national origin is an actual qualification for performing the job

Under Title VII of the Civil Rights Act of 1964, employers are permitted limited exemptions from antidiscrimination regulations if employment preferences are based on a bona fide occupational qualification. A **bona fide occupational qualification (BFOQ)** permits discrimination where employer hiring preferences are a reasonable necessity for the normal operation of the business. However, a BFOQ is a suitable defense against a discrimination charge only where age, religion, sex, or national origin is an actual qualification for performing the job.[32] For example, an older person could legitimately be excluded from consideration for employment as a model for teenage designer jeans. It is reasonable to expect the San Francisco 49ers of the National Football League to hire male locker-room attendants or for Macy's department store to employ females as models for women's fashions. Likewise, religion is a BFOQ in organizations that require employees to share a particular religious doctrine.

Business necessity
Work-related practice that is necessary to the safe and efficient operation of an organization

The EEOC does not favor BFOQs, and both the EEOC and the courts have construed the concept narrowly. The exception does not apply to discrimination based on race or color. Where an organization claims a BFOQ, it must be able to prove that hiring on the basis of sex, religion, age, or national origin is a business necessity. **Business necessity** has been interpreted by the courts as a practice that is necessary to the safe and efficient operation of the organization.

Religious Preference

Freedom to exercise religious choice is guaranteed under the U.S. Constitution. Title VII of the Civil Rights Act also prohibits discrimination based on religion

HIGHLIGHTS IN HRM

highlights

3   BASIC COMPONENTS OF AN EFFECTIVE SEXUAL HARASSMENT POLICY

1. Develop a comprehensive organization-wide policy on sexual harassment and present it to all current and new employees. Stress that sexual harassment will not be tolerated under any circumstances. Emphasis is best achieved when the policy is publicized and supported by top management.
2. Hold training sessions with supervisors to explain Title VII requirements, their role in providing an environment free of sexual harassment, and proper investigative procedures when charges occur.
3. Establish a formal complaint procedure in which employees can discuss problems without fear of retaliation. The complaint procedure should spell out how charges will be investigated and resolved.
4. Act immediately when employees complain of sexual harassment. Communicate widely that investigations will be conducted objectively and with appreciation for the sensitivity of the issue.
5. When an investigation supports employee charges, discipline the offender at once. For extremely serious offenses, discipline should include penalties up to and including discharge. Discipline should be applied consistently across similar cases and among managers and hourly employees alike.
6. Follow up on all cases to ensure a satisfactory resolution of the problem.

in employment decisions, though it permits employer exemptions. The act defines religion to "include all aspects of religious observance and practice, as well as belief."

Title VII does not require employers to grant complete religious freedom in employment situations. Employers need only make a reasonable accommodation for a current employee's or job applicant's religious observance or practice without incurring undue hardship in the conduct of the business. What constitutes "reasonable accommodation" has been difficult to define. In 1977, in the leading case of *TWA v Hardison,* the Supreme Court attempted to settle this dispute by ruling that employers had only to bear a minimum cost to show accommodation.[33] The Court said that to require otherwise would be discrimination against other employees for whom the expense of permitting time off for religious observance was not incurred. The *Hardison* case is important because it supported union management seniority systems where the employer had made a reasonable attempt to adjust employee work schedules without undue hardship. While *Hardison* permits reasonable accommodation and undue hardship as a defense against religious discrimination charges, the EEOC will investigate complaints on a case-by-case basis; and employers are still responsible for supporting their decisions to deny an employee's religious requests.[34]

Immigration Reform and Control

Good employment is the magnet that attracts many people to the United States. Unfortunately, illegal immigration has adversely affected welfare services and educational and Social Security benefits. To preserve our tradition of legal immigration while closing the door to illegal entry, in 1986 Congress passed the Immigration Reform and Control Act. The act was passed to control unauthorized immigration by making it unlawful for a person or organization to hire, recruit, or refer for a fee persons not legally eligible for employment in the United States.

Employers must comply with the law by verifying and maintaining records on the legal rights of applicants to work in the United States. The *Handbook for Employers*, published by the U.S. Department of Justice, lists five actions that employers must take to comply with the law:

1. Have employees fill out their part of Form I-9
2. Check documents establishing an employee's identity and eligibility to work
3. Complete the employer's section of Form I-9
4. Retain Form I-9 for at least three years
5. Present Form I-9 for inspection to an Immigration and Naturalization Service officer or to a Department of Labor officer upon request[35]

Section 102 of the law also prohibits discrimination. Employers with four or more employees may not discriminate against any individual (other than an unauthorized alien) in hiring, discharge, recruiting, or referring for a fee because of that individual's national origin, or in the case of a citizen or intending citizen, because of citizenship status. Employers found to have violated the act will be ordered to cease the discriminatory practice. They may also be directed to hire, with or without back pay, individuals harmed by the discrimination and pay a fine of up to $1,000 for each person discriminated against. Charges of discrimination based on national origin or citizenship are filed with the Office of Special Counsel in the Department of Justice.

In 1990 Congress passed the Immigration Act, which enables a more diverse group of skilled immigrants to enter the United States. It is hoped that the act will accomplish its objectives by increasing the number of foreign nationals who can be admitted to the United States because they possess needed employment abilities and skills. Additionally, the 1990 law amends various employer sanctions and antidiscrimination provisions of the Immigration Reform and Control Act. Employers who "overdocument" prospective employees may face civil fines, and employers are subject to unfair immigration-related charges if they retaliate against grieving individuals.[36]

seven
objective

Enforcing Equal Employment Opportunity Legislation

The law requires EEOC posters to be prominently displayed.

Along with prohibiting employment discrimination, Title VII of the Civil Rights Act created the Equal Employment Opportunity Commission. As the federal government's leading civil rights agency, the EEOC is responsible for ensuring that covered employers comply with the intent of this act. The commission accomplishes this goal primarily by (1) issuing various employment guidelines and monitoring the employment practices of organizations and (2) protecting employee rights through the investigation and prosecution of discrimination charges.

It is important to remember that the EEOC's guidelines are not federal law but administrative rules and regulations published in the *Federal Register*. However, the different guidelines have been given weight by the courts as they interpret the law and therefore should not be taken lightly. In addition to enforcing Title VII, the EEOC has the authority to enforce the Age Discrimination in Employment Act and the Equal Pay Act. Executive Order 12067, which requires the coordination of all federal equal employment opportunity regulations, practices, and policies, is also administered by the EEOC.

The Equal Employment Opportunity Commission

The EEOC consists of five commissioners and a general counsel, all appointed by the president of the United States and confirmed by the Senate. The president appoints commissioners for staggered five-year terms, and no more than three members of the commission can be of the same political party. One commissioner is appointed to be the EEOC chairperson, who is responsible for the overall administration of the agency. The commission's work consists of formulating EEO policy and approving all litigation involved in maintaining equal employment opportunity.

Appointed for a four-year term, the general counsel is responsible for investigating discrimination charges, conducting agency litigation, and providing legal opinions, in addition to reviewing EEOC regulations, guidelines, and contracts.

The day-to-day operation of the commission is performed through administrative headquarters, districts, and area offices. *District offices* handle discrimination charges and all compliance and litigation enforcement functions. *Area offices* are less than full-service organizations and generally serve as charge-processing and initial investigation units. Much of the EEOC's work is delegated to the district offices and other designated representatives. District directors have authority to receive or consent to the withdrawal of Title VII charges, issue subpoenas, send notices of the filing of charges, dismiss charges, enter into and sign conciliation agreements (voluntary employer settlements), and send out notices of the employee's right to sue. Employees who wish to file discrimination charges and employers responding to complaints work with district or area office personnel.

Record-Keeping and Posting Requirements

Organizations subject to Title VII are required by law to maintain specific employment records and reports. In addition, employers are required to post selected equal employment opportunity notices and to summarize the composition of their workforce in order to determine the distribution of protected individuals. These records are for establishing minority-group statistical reports. Equal employment opportunity legislation covering federal contractors and subcontractors has special reporting requirements for these employers. Those failing to comply with record-keeping and posting requirements or willfully falsifying records can incur penalties, including fines and imprisonment.

It is important to note that record-keeping requirements are both detailed and comprehensive. For example, managers must generate and retain for specific time periods different employment data under each of the following laws: Title VII, the Age Discrimination in Employment Act, and the Equal Pay Act. Where federal contractors are required to have written affirmative action programs, these must be retained along with supporting documents (e.g., names of job applicants, rejection ratios, and seniority lists).

EEO-1 report

An employer information report that must be filed annually by employers of 100 or more employees (except state and local government employers) and government contractors and subcontractors to determine an employer's workforce composition

Employers of 100 or more employees (except state and local government employers) and government contractors and subcontractors subject to Executive Order 11286 must file annually an **EEO-1 report** (Employer Information Report). Figure 3–4 shows Section D of the EEO-1 report, which requires the reporting of minority employees. This comprehensive report is the EEOC's basic document for determining an employer's workforce composition. In preparing the EEO-1 report, the organization may collect records concerning racial or ethnic identity either by visual survey or through postemployment questionnaires, if not prohibited by state fair employment practice law.

To show evidence of its equal employment opportunity and affirmative action efforts, an organization should retain copies of recruitment letters sent to minority agencies, announcements of job openings, and other significant information concerning employee recruitment. Other employment records to keep include data on promotions, demotions, transfers, layoffs or terminations, rates of pay or other terms of compensation, and selections for training or apprenticeship programs. Title VII requires retention of all personnel or employment records, including application forms, for at least six months or until resolution of any HR action, whichever occurs later.

During the employment process, employers are permitted to collect racial data on job applicants for compiling statistical reports; however, these data must be collected on a separate information sheet, not on the formal job application form. Where a charge of discrimination has been filed, the respondent organization must retain all HR records relevant to the case until final disposition of the charge.

Posters explaining to individuals what their employment rights are and how to file complaints of discrimination have been developed by the EEOC and other

FIGURE 3-4 *Section D, EEO-1 Report*

Section D—EMPLOYMENT DATA

Employment at this establishment—Report all permanent full-time and part-time employees including apprentices and on-the-job trainees unless specifically excluded as set forth in the instructions. Enter the appropriate figures on all lines and in all columns. Blank spaces will be considered as zeros.

JOB CATEGORIES		OVERALL TOTALS (SUM OF COL. B THRU K)	MALE					FEMALE				
			WHITE (NOT OF HISPANIC ORIGIN)	BLACK (NOT OF HISPANIC ORIGIN)	HISPANIC	ASIAN OR PACIFIC ISLANDER	AMERICAN INDIAN OR ALASKAN NATIVE	WHITE (NOT OF HISPANIC ORIGIN)	BLACK (NOT OF HISPANIC ORIGIN)	HISPANIC	ASIAN OR PACIFIC ISLANDER	AMERICAN INDIAN OR ALASKAN NATIVE
		A	B	C	D	E	F	G	H	I	J	K
Officials and Managers	1											
Professionals	2											
Technicians	3											
Sales Workers	4											
Office and Clerical	5											
Craft Workers (Skilled)	6											
Operatives (Semi-Skilled)	7											
Laborers (Unskilled)	8											
Service Workers	9											
TOTAL	10											
Total employment reported in previous EEO-1 report	11											

NOTE: Omit questions 1 and 2 on the Consolidated Report.

1. Date(s) of payroll period used: _____
2. Does this establishment employ apprentices?
   1 ☐ Yes   2 ☐ No

administrative agencies. (See Highlights in HRM 4.) The law requires that employers display these posters and other federally required posters related to HRM in prominent places easily accessible to employees. HR employment offices, cafeterias, centrally located bulletin boards, and time clocks are popular locations. Posting requirements should not be taken lightly. For example, EEO posters show the time limits for filing a charge of discrimination. Failure to post these notices may be used as a basis for excusing the late filing of a discrimination charge.

Processing Discrimination Charges

Charge form

Discrimination complaint filed with the EEOC by employees or job applicants

Employees or job applicants who believe they have been discriminated against may file a discrimination complaint, or **charge form,** with the EEOC. Filing a charge form initiates an administrative procedure that can be lengthy, time-consuming, and costly for the employer. Both parties, the plaintiff (employee) and the defendant (organization), must be prepared to support their beliefs or actions. If litigation follows, employers will normally take an aggressive approach to defend their position.[37]

Figure 3–5 summarizes the process of filing a discrimination charge with the EEOC. Under the law, charges must be filed within 180 days of the alleged

HIGHLIGHTS IN HRM

highlights

4   EEOC POSTER

Equal Employment Opportunity is
THE LAW

Employers Holding Federal Contracts or Subcontracts

Applicants to and employees of companies with a Federal government contract or subcontract are protected under the following Federal authorities:

RACE, COLOR, RELIGION, SEX, NATIONAL ORIGIN

Executive Order 11246, as amended, prohibits job discrimination on the basis of race, color, religion, sex or national origin, and requires affirmative action to ensure equality of opportunity in all aspects of employment.

INDIVIDUALS WITH HANDICAPS

Section 503 of the Rehabilitation Act of 1973, as amended, prohibits job discrimination because of handicap and requires affirmative action to employ and advance in employment qualified individuals with handicaps who, with reasonable accommodation, can perform the essential functions of a job.

VIETNAM ERA AND SPECIAL DISABLED VETERANS

38 U.S.C. 4212 of the Vietnam Era Veterans Readjustment Assistance Act of 1974 prohibits job discrimination and requires affirmative action to employ and advance in employment qualified Vietnam era veterans and qualified special disabled veterans.

Any person who believes a contractor has violated its nondiscrimination or affirmative action obligations under the authorities above should contact immediately:

The Office of Federal Contract Compliance Programs (OFCCP), Employment Standards Administration, U.S. Department of Labor, 200 Constitution Avenue, N.W., Washington, D.C. 20210 or call (202) 523-9368, or an OFCCP regional or district office, listed in most telephone directories under U.S. Government, Department of Labor.

Private Employment, State and Local Governments, Educational Institutions

Applicants to and employees of most private employers, state and local governments, educational institutions, employment agencies and labor organizations are protected under the following Federal laws:

RACE, COLOR, RELIGION, SEX, NATIONAL ORIGIN

Title VII of the Civil Rights Act of 1964, as amended, prohibits discrimination in hiring, promotion, discharge, pay, fringe benefits, job training, classification, referral, and other aspects of employment, on the basis of race, color, religion, sex or national origin.

DISABILITY

The Americans with Disabilities Act of 1990, as amended, protects qualified applicants and employees with disabilities from discrimination in hiring, promotion, discharge, pay, job training, fringe benefits, classification, referral, and other aspects of employment on the basis of disability. The law also requires that covered entities provide qualified applicants and employees with disabilities with reasonable accommodations that do not impose undue hardship.

AGE

The Age Discrimination in Employment Act of 1967, as amended, protects applicants and employees 40 years of age or older from discrimination on the basis of age in hiring, promotion, discharge, compensation, terms, conditions or privileges of employment.

SEX (WAGES)

In addition to sex discrimination prohibited by Title VII of the Civil Rights Act (see above), the Equal Pay Act of 1963, as amended, prohibits sex discrimination in payment of wages to women and men performing substantially equal work in the same establishment.

Retaliation against a person who files a charge of discrimination, participates in an investigation, or opposes an unlawful employment practice is prohibited by all of these Federal laws.

If you believe that you have been discriminated against under any of the above laws, you immediately should contact:

The U.S. Equal Employment Opportunity Commission (EEOC), 1801 L Street, N.W., Washington, D.C. 20507 or an EEOC field office by calling toll free (800) 669-4000. For individuals with hearing impairments, EEOC's toll free TDD number is (800) 800-3302.

Programs or Activities Receiving Federal Financial Assistance

RACE, COLOR, NATIONAL ORIGIN, SEX

In addition to the protection of Title VII of the Civil Rights Act of 1964, Title VI of the Civil Rights Act prohibits discrimination on the basis of race, color or national origin in programs or activities receiving Federal financial assistance. Employment discrimination is covered by Title VI if the primary objective of the financial assistance is provision of employment, or where employment discrimination causes or may cause discrimination in providing services under such programs. Title IX of the Education Amendments of 1972 prohibits employment discrimination on the basis of sex in educational programs or activities which receive Federal assistance.

INDIVIDUALS WITH HANDICAPS

Section 504 of the Rehabilitation Act of 1973, as amended, prohibits employment discrimination on the basis of handicap in any program or activity which receives Federal financial assistance. Discrimination is prohibited in all aspects of employment against handicapped persons who, with reasonable accommodation, can perform the essential functions of a job.

If you believe you have been discriminated against in a program of any institution which receives Federal assistance, you should contact immediately the Federal agency providing such assistance.

EEOC-P/E-1

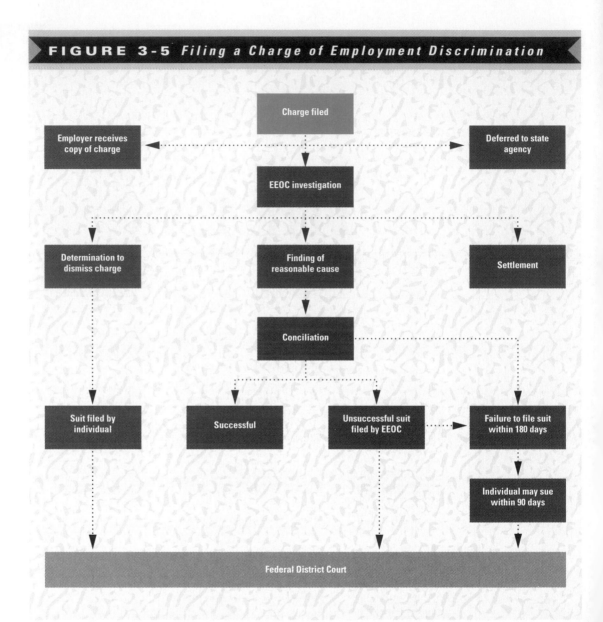

FIGURE 3-5 *Filing a Charge of Employment Discrimination*

unlawful practice. The processing of a charge includes notifying the employer that a charge of employment discrimination has been filed. Employers will receive a copy of the charge within ten days of filing. Organizations may not retaliate against individuals for their legal right to file charges or to support other employees during EEOC proceedings. The commission has the power to prosecute employers in court if retaliation takes place.

In states that have FEP laws with appropriate enforcement machinery, the discrimination charge is deferred to the state agency for resolution before action is taken by the EEOC. The EEOC will accept the recommendation of the state agency because deferral states must comply with federal standards. If the state agency fails to resolve the complaint or if the sixty-day deferral period lapses, the case is given back to the EEOC for final investigation.

EEOC investigations are conducted by fully trained equal opportunity specialists (EOSs) who have extensive experience in investigative procedures, theories of discrimination, and relief and remedy techniques. The EOS will gather facts from both sides through telephone calls, letters and questionnaires, field visits, or jointly arranged meetings. While it is generally advisable for them to cooperate in EEOC investigations, employers may legally resist the commission's efforts by refusing to submit documents or give relevant testimony. However, the EEOC may obtain this information through a court subpoena. Employers who then refuse to supply the information will face contempt-of-court charges.

Once the investigation is under way or completed, several decision points occur. First, the employer may offer a settlement to resolve the case without further investigation. If the offer is accepted, the case is closed. Second, the EEOC may find no violation of law and dismiss the charge. In this case, the charging party is sent a *right-to-sue* notice, which permits the individual to start private litigation, if he or she so desires, in federal court within ninety days. Third, if the EEOC finds "reasonable cause" of discrimination, the commission will attempt to conciliate (settle) the matter between the charging party and the employer. The conciliation process is a voluntary procedure and will not always lead to a settlement.

Employers should keep in mind that when the EEOC negotiates a settlement, it will attempt to obtain full remedial, corrective, and preventive relief. Back pay, reinstatement, transfers, promotions, seniority rights, bonuses, and other "make whole" perquisites of employment are considered to be appropriate remedies. These settlements can frequently be costly.

If the employer and the EEOC cannot reach a negotiated settlement, the commission has the power to prosecute the organization in court. However, this decision is made on a case-by-case basis and may depend on the importance of the issue. Failure of the EEOC to take court action or to resolve the charge in 180 days from filing permits employees to pursue litigation within 90 days after receiving a right-to-sue letter issued by the commission.

Using Testers to Uncover Discrimination

In a study of job applicants conducted by the Urban Institute, it was found that black job applicants, as compared with white applicants, experienced entrenched and widespread discrimination during employment processing. In response to findings such as this, the EEOC has issued its "Policy Guidance on the Use of Testers in the Employment Selection Process."[38] The EEOC defines testers as "individuals who apply for employment which they do not intend to accept, for the sole purpose of uncovering unlawful discriminatory hiring practices." Testers are individuals of all races, sexes, ages, nationalities, and disabilities. As job applicants, testers are difficult to identify from regular job seekers. As noted by one employment expert, "Testers will be well prepared for the hiring process, well qualified for the jobs they apply for, and otherwise entirely suitable applicants."[39] Testers are employed and trained by civil rights organizations or government

SUMMARY

objective

Employment discrimination against blacks, Hispanics, women, and other groups has long been practiced by U.S. employers. Prejudice against minority groups is a major cause in their lack of employment gains. Government reports show that the wages and job opportunities of minorities typically lag behind those for whites.

objective

Effective management requires knowing the legal aspects of the employment relationship. Pertinent legislation includes the Equal Pay Act, Title VII of the Civil Rights Act of 1964, Age Discrimination in Employment Act, Equal Employment Opportunity Act of 1972, Pregnancy Discrimination Act, Americans with Disabilities Act, Civil Rights Act of 1991, and various executive orders.

objective

The *Uniform Guidelines on Employee Selection Procedures* are guidelines designed to assist employers in complying with federal prohibitions against employment practices that discriminate on the basis of race, color, religion, gender, or national origin. The *Uniform Guidelines* provide employers a framework for making legally enforceable employment decisions. Employers must be able to show that selection procedures are valid in predicting job performance.

objective

Adverse impact plays an important role in proving employment discrimination. Adverse impact means that an employer's employment practices result in the rejection of a significantly higher percentage of members of minority and other protected groups for some employment activity. The four-fifths rule is a guideline to determine whether employment discrimination might exist. Highlights in HRM 2 demonstrates calculation of the four-fifths rule.

objective

The United States court system continually interprets employment law, and managers must formulate organizational policy in response to court decisions. Violations of the law will invite discrimination charges from protected groups or self-initiated investigation from government agencies. *Griggs v Duke Power, Albemarle Paper Company v Moody,* and *Wards Cove Packing Co. v Antonio* provided added importance to the *Uniform Guidelines. Meritor Savings Bank v Vinson, Harris v Forklift Systems Inc.,* and *TWA v Hardison* are instructive in the areas of sexual harassment and religious preference. Important cases in affirmative action include *University of California v Bakke, United Steelworkers of America v Weber, Firefighters Local 93 v City of Cleveland,* and *City of Richmond v Croson.*

objective

Sexual harassment and religious preference are two areas of particular importance to managers. Extensive efforts should be made to ensure that employees are free from all forms of sexually harassing conduct and that their religious preferences are accommodated as required by law. Employers are permitted to discriminate against selected protected classes where hiring preferences are a reasonable necessity, constituting a bona fide occupational qualification for the normal operation of the business.

objective

To ensure that organizations comply with antidiscrimination legislation, the EEOC was established to monitor employers' actions. Employers subject to federal laws must maintain required records and report requested employment statistics where mandated. The EEOC maintains a complaint procedure for individuals who believe they have been discriminated against. Figure 3–5 illustrates the steps in filing a charge of employment discrimination.

Affirmative action goes beyond providing equal employment opportunity to employees. Affirmative action requires employers to become proactive and correct areas of past discrimination. This is accomplished by employing protected classes for jobs where they are underrepresented. The employer's goal is to have a balanced internal workforce representative of the employer's relevant labor market.

KEY TERMS

adverse impact

affirmative action

bona fide occupational qualification (BFOQ)

bottom-line concept

business necessity

charge form

disabled individual

disparate treatment

EEO 1 report

equal employment opportunity

fair employment practices (FEPs)

four-fifths rule

protected classes

reasonable accommodation

reverse discrimination

sexual harassment

Uniform Guidelines on Employee Selection Procedures

DISCUSSION QUESTIONS

1. EEO legislation was prompted by significant social events. List those events and describe how they influenced the passage of various EEO laws.
2. Cite and describe the major federal laws and court decisions that affect the employment process of both large and small organizations.
3. What is the *Uniform Guidelines on Employee Selection Procedures*? To whom do the guidelines apply? What do they cover?
4. What is meant by adverse impact? How is it determined? Give an example in calculating the four-fifths rule.
5. After receiving several complaints of sexual harassment, the HR department of a city library decided to establish a sexual harassment policy. What should be included in the policy? How should it be implemented?
6. Describe the structure of the EEOC.
   a. What purpose does the EEOC serve?
   b. What are some of its reporting and posting requirements?

....

7. Explain how affirmative action differs from equal employment opportunity.
8. What are the arguments for and against affirmative action programs? If you were asked to implement such a program, what steps would you follow?

CASE STUDY: Misplaced Affections: Discharge for Sexual Harassment*

Peter Lewiston was terminated on July 15, 1994, by the governing board of the Pine Circle Unified School district (PCUSD) for violation of the district's sexual harassment policy. Prior to Lewiston's termination he was a senior maintenance employee with an above-average work record who had worked for the PCUSD for eleven years. He had been a widower since 1989 and was described by his co-workers as a friendly, outgoing, but lonely individual. Beverly Gilbury was a fifth-grade teacher working in the district's Advanced Learning Program. She was 28 years old, married, and had worked for PCUSD for six years. At the time of the incidents, Lewiston and Gilbury both worked at the Simpson Elementary School where their relationship was described as "cooperative." The following sequence of events was reported separately by Lewiston and Gilbury during the district's investigation of this sexual harassment case.

Gilbury reported that her relationship with Lewiston began to change during the last month of the 1993–1994 school year. She believed that Lewiston was paying her more attention and that his behavior was "out of the ordinary" and "sometimes weird." He began spending more time in her classroom talking with the children and with her. At the time she didn't say anything to Lewiston because "I didn't want to hurt his feelings since he is a nice, lonely, older man." However, on May 25, when Lewiston told Gilbury that he was "very fond" of her and that she had "very beautiful eyes," she replied, "Remember, Peter, we're just friends." For the remainder of the school year there was little contact between them; however, when they did see each other, Lewiston seemed "overly friendly" to her.

June 7, 1994. On the first day of summer school, Gilbury returned to school to find a dozen roses and a card from Lewiston. The card read, "Please forgive me for thinking you could like me. I played the big fool. Yours always, P.S." Later in the day Lewiston asked Gilbury to lunch. She replied, "It's been a long time since anyone sent me roses, but I can't go to lunch. We need to remain just friends." Gilbury told another teacher that she was uncomfortable about receiving the roses and card and that Lewiston wouldn't leave her alone. She expressed concern that Lewiston might get "more romantic" with her.

June 8, 1994. Gilbury arrived at school to find another card from Lewiston. Inside was a handwritten note that read, "I hope you can someday return my affections for you. I need you so much." Later in the day Lewiston again asked her to lunch and she declined saying, "I'm a happily married woman." At the close of the school day, when Gilbury went to her car, Lewiston suddenly appeared. He asked to explain himself but Gilbury became agitated and shouted, "I

*This case is adapted from an actual experience. The background information is factual. All names are fictitious.

have to leave right now." Lewiston reached inside the car, supposedly to pat her shoulder, but touched her head instead. She believed he meant to stroke her hair. He stated that he was only trying to calm her down. She drove away, very upset.

June 9, 1994. Gilbury received another card and a lengthy letter from Lewiston, stating that he was wrong in trying to develop a relationship with her and he hoped they could still remain friends. He wished her all happiness with her family and job.

June 11, 1994. Gilbury obtained from the Western Justice Court an injunction prohibiting sexual harassment by Lewiston. Shortly thereafter Lewiston appealed the injunction. A notice was mailed to Gilbury giving the dates of the appeal hearing. The notice stated in part, "If you fail to appear, the injunction may be vacated and the petition dismissed." Gilbury failed to appear at the hearing and the injunction was set aside. Additionally, on June 11 she had filed with the District's EEOC officer a sexual harassment complaint against Lewiston. After the investigation the district concluded that Lewiston's actions created an intimidating, hostile, and offensive employment environment for Gilbury. The investigative report recommended dismissal based upon the grievous conduct of Lewiston and the initial injunction granted by the Justice Court.

Questions

1. Evaluate the conduct of Peter Lewiston against the EEOC's definition of sexual harassment.
2. Should the intent or motive behind Lewiston's conduct be considered when deciding sexual harassment activities? Explain.
3. If you were the district's EEOC officer, what would you conclude? What disciplinary action, if any, would you take?

NOTES AND REFERENCES

1. "Sex-bias Settlement: $157 Million," *The Arizona Republic* (December 12, 1992): A-1.
2. For recent stories regarding employment discrimination see "Denny's: The Stain That Isn't Coming Out," *Business Week* (June 28, 1993): 98–99; "The Angry Voices at Kidder," *Business Week* (February 1, 1993): 60–63; and "Record Race Discrimination Settlement: Shoney's to Pay $132 Million," *The Arizona Labor Letter* 1, no. 1 (January 1993): 1.
3. "Current Labor Statistics—Table 6," *Monthly Labor Review* 117, no. 9 (September 1994): 70; U.S. Department of Labor, Bureau of Labor Statistics, *Employment and Earnings* 41, no. 10 (October 1994): 73. See also Barry T. Hirsch and Edward J. Schumacher, "Labor Earnings, Discrimination, and the Racial Composition of Jobs," *The Journal of Human Resources* 27, no. 4 (Fall 1992): 602–27.
4. "Getting Serious about Sexual Harassment," *Business Week* (November 9, 1992): 78–82.
5. Sue Ann Unger, "Should Men Benefit from Same Presumption of Unlawful Sex Discrimination That Helps Women Claimants under the Equal Pay Act?" *Labor Law Journal* 44, no. 3 (March 1993): 186–91.
6. For an overview of EEO law, see Nancy J. Sedmak and Michael D. Levin-Epstein, *Primer on Equal Employment Opportunity* (Washington, D.C.: Bureau of National Affairs, 1991); James H. Coil, *The New Supervisor's EEO Handbook* (New York: Executive Enterprises Publications Company, 1992).
7. *Workforce 2000: Work and Workers for the 21st Century,* Executive Summary (Washington, D.C.: U.S. Department of Labor, n.d.): 19.
8. Joseph M. Pellicciotti, "Exemptions and Employer Defenses under the ADEA," *Public Personnel Management* 20, no. 2 (Summer 1991): 233–51.
9. Paul S. Greenlaw and John P. Kohl, "The ADA: Public Personnel Management, Reasonable

their managers, or from other individuals who are familiar with or perform the same job. It is common practice to have the descriptions for each job reviewed by the jobholders and their managers. The job description summaries contained in the *Dictionary of Occupational Titles* can also serve as a basis for the job analyst's review.

Finally, the traditional approach to job analysis assumes a static job environment. However, as jobs change, job analysis data become inaccurate. Outdated job analysis information can hinder an organization's ability to adapt to change. Downsizing, computerization, the demands of small organizations, or the need to respond to global changes can alter the nature of jobs and the characteristics of individuals needed to successfully perform them. Therefore a future-oriented approach to job analysis is recommended when organizations anticipate rapid change.[8]

The *DOT* and Job Analysis

Commonly referred to as the *DOT*, the *Dictionary of Occupational Titles* is compiled by the U.S. Department of Labor. It contains standardized and comprehensive descriptions of about 20,000 jobs. The purpose of the *DOT* is to "group occupations into a systematic occupational classification structure based on interrelationships of job tasks and requirements." This grouping of occupational classifications is done under a coding system.[9]

The *DOT* has helped to bring about a greater degree of uniformity in the job titles and descriptions used by employers in different sections of the country. This uniformity has facilitated the movement of workers from sections of the country that may be experiencing widespread unemployment to areas where employment opportunities are greater. The *DOT* code numbers also facilitate the exchange of statistical information about jobs. In addition, these code numbers are useful in reporting research in the HR area, in vocational counseling, and in charting career paths through job transfers and/or advancements.

Approaches to Job Analysis

The systematic and quantitative definition of job content that job analysis provides is the foundation of many HRM practices. Specifically, it serves to justify job descriptions and other HRM selection procedures. It should be emphasized that a major goal of modern job analysis is to help the organization establish the *job relatedness* of its selection requirements. Therefore these procedures help both large and small employers to meet their legal duty under EEO law. Section 14.C.2 of the *Uniform Guidelines* states: "There shall be a job analysis which includes an analysis of the important work behaviors required for successful performance.... Any job analysis should focus on work behavior(s) and the tasks associated with them." Several different job analysis approaches are used, each with specific advantages and disadvantages. Three of the more popular methods are functional job analysis, the position analysis questionnaire system, and the critical incident method.

Functional Job Analysis

Developed by the U.S. Training and Employment Service, the **functional job analysis (FJA)** approach utilizes an inventory of the various types of functions

Functional job analysis (FJA)

Quantitative approach to job analysis that utilizes a compiled inventory of the various functions or work activities that can make up any job and that assumes that each job involves three broad worker functions: (1) data, (2) people, and (3) things

FIGURE 4-3 *Difficulty Levels of Worker Functions*

DATA (4TH DIGIT)	PEOPLE (5TH DIGIT)	THINGS (6TH DIGIT)
0 Synthesizing	0 Mentoring	0 Setting-up
1 Coordinating	1 Negotiating	1 Precision working
2 Analyzing	2 Instructing	2 Operating-controlling
3 Compiling	3 Supervising	3 Driving-operating
4 Computing	4 Diverting	4 Manipulating
5 Copying	5 Persuading	5 Tending
6 Comparing	6 Speaking-signaling*	6 Feeding-offbearing
	7 Serving	7 Handling
	8 Taking instructions—helping	

* Hyphenated factors are single factors.

Source: U.S. Department of Labor, Employment and Training Administration, *Revised Handbook for Analyzing Jobs* (Washington, D.C.: U.S. Government Printing Office, 1991), 5.

or work activities that can constitute any job. FJA thus assumes that each job involves performing certain functions. Specifically, there are three broad worker functions that form the bases of this system: (1) data, (2) people, and (3) things. These three categories are subdivided to form a hierarchy of worker-function scales, as shown in Figure 4–3. The job analyst, when studying the job under review, will indicate the functional level for each of the three categories (for example, "copying" under "DATA") and then reflect the relative involvement of the worker in the function by assigning a percentage figure to each function (i.e., 50 percent to "copying"). This is done for each of the three areas, and the three functional levels must equal 100 percent. The end result is a quantitatively evaluated job. FJA can easily be used to describe the content of jobs and to assist in writing job descriptions and specifications; it is used as a basis for the *DOT* code.

The Position Analysis Questionnaire System

Position analysis questionnaire (PAQ)
Questionnaire covering 194 different tasks which, by means of a five-point scale, seeks to determine the degree to which different tasks are involved in performing a particular job

The **position analysis questionnaire (PAQ)** is a quantifiable data collection method covering 194 different worker-oriented tasks. Using a five-point scale, the PAQ seeks to determine the degree, if any, to which the different tasks, or job elements, are involved in performing a particular job. The 194 different elements are grouped into the six divisions shown in Figure 4–4.[10]

A sample page from the PAQ covering eleven elements of the Information Input Division is shown in Figure 4–5. The person conducting an analysis with this questionnaire would rate each of the elements using the five-point scale shown in the upper right-hand corner of the sample page. The results obtained

FIGURE 4-4 Divisions and Number of Job Elements in the PAQ

DIVISION	NUMBER OF JOB ELEMENTS
Information input (where and how does the worker get the information used in the job)	35
Mental processes (what reasoning, decision making, planning, etc., are involved in the job)	14
Work output (what physical activities do the workers perform, and what tools or devices do they use)	49
Relationships with other persons (what relationships with other people are required in the job)	36
Job context (in what physical and social contexts is the work performed)	19
Other job characteristics	41

with the PAQ are quantitative and can be subjected to statistical analysis. The PAQ also permits dimensions of behavior to be compared across a number of jobs and permits jobs to be grouped on the basis of common characteristics.

The Critical Incident Method

Critical incident method

Job analysis method by which important job tasks are identified for job success

The objective of the **critical incident method** is to identify critical job tasks. Critical job tasks are those important duties and job responsibilities performed by the jobholder that lead to job success. Information about critical job tasks can be collected through interviews with employees or managers or through self-report statements written by employees.

Suppose, for example, that the job analyst is studying the job of reference librarian. The interviewer will ask the employee to describe the job on the basis of what is done, how the job is performed, and what tools and equipment are used. The reference librarian may describe the job as follows:

> I assist patrons by answering their questions related to finding books, periodicals, or other library materials. I also give them directions to help them find materials within the building. To perform my job I may have to look up materials myself or refer patrons to someone who can directly assist them. Some individuals may need training in how to use reference materials or special library facilities. I also give library tours to new patrons. I use computers and a variety of reference books to carry out my job.

After the job data are collected, the analyst will then write separate task statements that represent important job activities. For the reference librarian one task statement might be "Listens to patrons and answers their questions related to locating library materials." Typically the job analyst will write five to ten important task statements for each job under study. The final product will be written task statements that are clear, complete, and easily understood by those

FIGURE 4-5 *A Sample Page from the PAQ*

INFORMATION INPUT

		Extent of Use (U)
	NA	Does not apply
1	INFORMATION INPUT	1	Nominal/very infrequent
1.1	Sources of Job Information	2	Occasional

1   INFORMATION INPUT

1.1   Sources of Job Information

Rate each of the following items in terms of the extent to which it is used by the worker as a source of information in performing his job.

	Extent of Use (U)
NA	Does not apply
1	Nominal/very infrequent
2	Occasional
3	Moderate
4	Considerable
5	Very substantial

1.1.1   Visual Sources of Job Information

1 U   Written materials (books, reports, office notes, articles, job instructions, signs, etc.)

2 U   Quantitative materials (materials which deal with quantities or amounts, such as graphs, accounts, specifications, tables of numbers, etc.)

3 U   Pictorial materials (pictures or picturelike materials used as *sources* of information, for example, drawings, blueprints, diagrams, maps, tracings, photographic films, x-ray films, TV pictures, etc.)

4 U   Patterns/related devices (templates, stencils, patterns, etc., used as *sources* of information when *observed* during use; do *not* include here materials described in item 3 above)

5 U   Visual displays (dials, gauges, signal lights, radarscopes, speedometers, clocks, etc.)

6 U   Measuring devices (rulers, calipers, tire pressure gauges, scales, thickness gauges, pipettes, thermometers, protractors, etc., used to obtain visual information about physical measurements; do *not* include here devices described in item 5 above)

7 U   Mechanical devices (tools, equipment, machinery, and other mechanical devices which are *sources* of information when *observed* during use or operation)

8 U   Materials in process (parts, materials, objects, etc., which are *sources* of information when being modified, worked on, or otherwise processed, such as bread dough being mixed, workpiece being turned in a lathe, fabric being cut, shoe being resoled, etc.)

9 U   Materials *not* in process (parts, materials, objects, etc., not in the process of being changed or modified, which are *sources* of information when being inspected, handled, packaged, distributed, or selected, etc., such as items or materials in inventory, storage, or distribution channels, items being inspected, etc.)

10 U   Features of nature (landscapes, fields, geological samples, vegetation, cloud formations, and other features of nature which are observed or inspected to provide information)

11 U   Man-made features of environment (structures, buildings, dams, highways, bridges, docks, railroads, and other "man-made" or altered aspects of the indoor or outdoor environment which are *observed or inspected* to provide job information; do not consider equipment, machines, etc., that an individual uses in his work, as covered by item 7)

Source: *Position Analysis Questionnaire,* copyright 1969, 1989 by Purdue Research Foundation, West Lafayette, Indiana 47907. Reprinted with permission.

unfamiliar with the job. The critical incident method is an important job analysis method since it teaches the analyst to focus on employee behaviors critical to job success.

three
objective

Job Descriptions

As previously noted, a job description is a written description of a job and the types of duties it includes. Since there is no standard format for job descriptions, they tend to vary in appearance and content from one organization to another. However, most job descriptions will contain at least three parts: the job title, a job identification section, and a job duties section. If the job specifications are not prepared as a separate document, they are usually stated in the concluding section of the job description. Highlights in HRM 1 shows a job description for an HR employment assistant. This sample job description includes both job duties and job specifications and should satisfy most of the job information needs of managers who must recruit, interview, and orient a new employee.

Job Title

Selection of a job title is important for several reasons. First, the job title is of psychological importance, providing status to the employee. For instance, "sanitation engineer" is a more appealing title than "garbage collector." Second, if possible, the title should provide some indication of what the duties of the job entail. Titles like "meat inspector," "electronics assembler," "salesperson," and "engineer" obviously hint at the nature of the duties of these jobs. The job title also should indicate the relative level occupied by its holder in the organizational hierarchy. For example, the title "junior engineer" implies that this job occupies a lower level than that of "senior engineer." Other titles that indicate the relative level in the organizational hierarchy are "welder's helper" and "laboratory assistant."

Certain kinds of job titles should be avoided altogether. For example, a series of identical titles with qualifiers, such as "inventory clerk I" and "inventory clerk II," makes it difficult to distinguish one job from another.[11] Job titles quali-

" 'Overqualified'? You don't mean you *believe* all that stuff!"

From *The Wall Street Journal*—Permission, Cartoon Features Syndicate

....

HIGHLIGHTS IN HRM

highlights

1   JOB DESCRIPTION FOR AN EMPLOYMENT ASSISTANT

Job Identification

JOB TITLE: Employment Assistant

Division:	Southern Area
Department:	Human Resources Management
Job Analyst:	Virginia Sasaki
Date Analyzed:	12/3/94
Wage Category:	Exempt
Report to:	HR Manager
Job Code:	11–17
Date Verified:	12/17/94

Brief Listing of Major Job Duties

JOB STATEMENT

Performs professional human resources work in the areas of employee *recruitment* and *selection, testing, orientation, transfers,* and maintenance of employee human resources files. May handle special assignments and projects in *EEO/Affirmative Action, employee grievances, training,* or *classification and compensation.* Works under general supervision. Incumbent exercises initiative and independent judgment in the performance of assigned tasks.

Essential Functions and Responsibilities

ESSENTIAL FUNCTIONS

1. Prepares recruitment literature and job advertisements for applicant placement.
2. Schedules and conducts personal interviews to determine applicant suitability for employment. Includes reviewing mailed applications and resumes for qualified personnel.
3. Supervises administration of testing program. Responsible for developing or improving testing instruments and procedures.
4. Presents orientation program to all new employees. Reviews and develops all materials and procedures for orientation program.
5. Coordinates division job posting and transfer program. Establishes job posting procedures. Responsible for reviewing transfer applications, arranging transfer interviews, and determining effective transfer dates.
6. Maintains a daily working relationship with division managers on human resource matters, including recruitment concerns, retention or release of probationary employees, and discipline or discharge of permanent employees.
7. Distributes new or revised human resources policies and procedures to all employees and managers through bulletins, meetings, memorandums, and/or personal contact.
8. Performs related duties as assigned by the human resource manager.

(continued)

HIGHLIGHTS IN HRM *(continued)*

JOB SPECIFICATION

Job Specifications and Requirements

1. Four-year college or university degree with major course work in human resources management, business administration, or industrial psychology; OR a combination of experience, education, and training equivalent to a four-year college degree in human resources management.
2. Considerable knowledge of principles of employee selection and assignment of personnel.
3. Ability to express ideas clearly in both written and oral communications.
4. Ability to independently plan and organize one's own activities.
5. Knowledge of human resource computer applications desirable.

fied by the terms "man" or "woman" are also being discarded to avoid the implication that the jobs can be performed only by members of one gender. Thus, a repairman is now a "repairer"; and a steward or stewardess, a "flight attendant."

Job Identification Section

The job identification section of a job description usually follows the job title. It includes such items as the departmental location of the job, the person to whom the jobholder reports, and the date the job description was last revised. Sometimes it also contains a payroll or code number, the number of employees performing the job, the number of employees in the department where the job is located, and the *DOT* code number. "Statement of the Job" usually appears at the bottom of this section and serves to distinguish the job from other jobs—something the job title may fail to do.

Essential Functions Section

Statements covering job duties are typically arranged in order of importance. These statements should indicate the weight, or value, of each duty. Usually, but not always, the weight of a duty can be gauged by the percentage of time devoted to it. The statements should stress the responsibilities all the duties entail and the results they are to accomplish. It is also general practice to indicate the tools and equipment used by the employee in performing the job.

Job Specifications Section

As stated earlier, the personal qualifications an individual must possess in order to perform the duties and responsibilities contained in a job description are compiled in the job specification. Typically the job specification covers two areas: (1) the skill required to perform the job and (2) the physical demands the job places upon the employee performing it.

Skills relevant to a job include education or experience, specialized training, personal traits or abilities, and manual dexterities. The physical demands of a job refer to how much walking, standing, reaching, lifting, or talking must be done on the job. The condition of the physical work environment and the hazards employees may encounter are also among the physical demands of a job.

Problems with Job Descriptions

Managers consider job descriptions a valuable tool for performing HRM functions. Nevertheless, several problems are frequently associated with these documents, including the following:

1. If they are poorly written, using vague rather than specific terms, they provide little guidance to the jobholder.
2. They are sometimes not updated as job duties or specifications change.
3. They may violate the law by containing specifications not related to job success.
4. They can limit the scope of activities of the jobholder.

Writing Clear and Specific Job Descriptions

When writing a job description, it is essential to use statements that are terse, direct, and simply worded. Unnecessary words or phrases should be eliminated. Typically, the sentences that describe job duties begin with a present-tense verb, with the implied subject of the sentence being the employee performing the job. The term "occasionally" is used to describe those duties that are performed once in a while. The term "may" is used in connection with those duties performed only by some workers on the job.

Even when set forth in writing, job descriptions and specifications can still be vague. To the consternation of many employers, however, today's legal environment has created what might be called an "age of specifics." Federal guidelines and court decisions now require that the specific performance requirements of a job be based on *valid* job-related criteria.[12] Personnel decisions that involve either job applicants or employees and are based on criteria that are vague or not job-related are increasingly successfully challenged. Managers of small businesses, where employees may perform many different job tasks, must be particularly concerned about writing specific job descriptions.

When preparing job descriptions, managers also must adhere to the legal mandates of the Americans with Disabilities Act. (See Chapter 3.) The act requires that job duties and responsibilities be *essential functions* for job success. The purpose of essential functions is to help match and accommodate human capabilities to job requirements.[13] For example, if the job requires the jobholder to read extremely fine print, to climb ladders, or to memorize stock codes, these physical and mental requirements should be stated within the job description. Section 1630.2(n) of the act gives three guidelines for rendering a job function essential. These include (1) the reason the position exists is to perform the function, (2) a limited number of employees are available among whom the performance of the function may be distributed, and (3) the function may be highly specialized, requiring needed expertise or abilities to complete the job.[14] Managers who write job descriptions in terms of essential functions reduce the risk of discriminating on the basis of a disability.

The Value of Written Job Requirements

Spelling out job requirements in job descriptions and job specifications is essential in order for members of the HR staff to perform their duties. Job descriptions, in particular, are of value to both the employees and the employer. From the employees' standpoint, job descriptions can be used to help them learn their job duties and to remind them of the results they are expected to achieve. From the employer's standpoint, written job descriptions can serve as a basis for minimizing the misunderstandings that occur between managers and their subordinates concerning job requirements. They also establish management's right to take corrective action when the duties covered by the job description are not performed as required.

Job design

Outgrowth of job analysis that improves jobs through technological and human considerations in order to enhance organization efficiency and employee job satisfaction

Industrial engineering

A field of study concerned with analyzing work methods and establishing time standards

Job Design

An outgrowth of job analysis, **job design** is concerned with structuring jobs in order to improve organization efficiency and employee job satisfaction. The design of a job should reflect both technological and human considerations. It should facilitate the achievement of organizational objectives and the performance of the work the job was established to accomplish. At the same time, the design should recognize the capacities and needs of those who are to perform it.

As Figure 4–6 illustrates, job design is a combination of four basic considerations: (1) the organizational objectives the job was created to fulfill; (2) industrial engineering considerations, including ways to make the job technologically efficient; (3) human engineering concerns, including workers' physical and mental capabilities; and (4) quality-of-work-life changes. Quality-of-work-life considerations in job design or redesign are reflected in contemporary programs. Three of the more popular programs are job enrichment, job enlargement, and employee teams, all of which are discussed later in the chapter.

Industrial Engineering Considerations

The study of work is an important contribution of the scientific management movement. **Industrial engineering,** which evolved with this movement, is concerned with analyzing work methods and establishing time standards. Specifically, it involves both analyzing the elements of the work cycle that compose a particular job activity and determining the time required to complete each element. For example, the Methods Improvement Group of First Interstate Bank employs the principles of industrial engineering to improve the work flow of its tellers. This may include eliminating any seemingly duplicate processes in the work cycle, or it may involve combining the tasks of two employees.

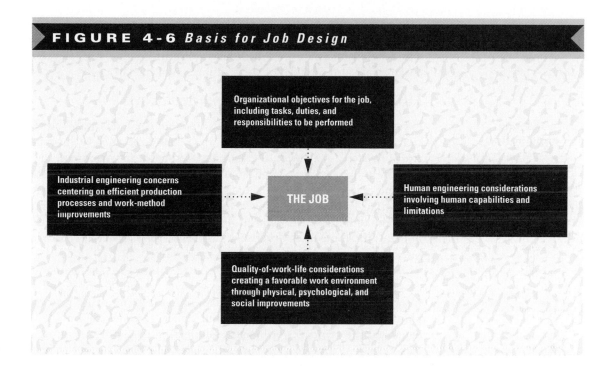

FIGURE 4-6 *Basis for Job Design*

Development of Time Standards

Identifying and timing the elements in a work cycle are generally the responsibilities of the industrial engineering staff. They study the work cycle to determine which, if any, of its elements can be modified, combined, rearranged, or eliminated to reduce the time needed to complete the cycle.

To establish time standards, the industrial engineering staff measures and records the time required to complete each element in the work cycle, using a stopwatch or work-sampling techniques. By combining the times for each element, they determine the total time required. This time is subsequently adjusted to allow for the skill and effort demonstrated by the observed worker and for interruptions that may occur in performing the work. The adjusted time becomes the time standard for that particular work cycle. This standard then provides an objective basis for evaluating and improving employee performance and for determining incentive pay.

Benefits and Limitations of Industrial Engineering

Since jobs are created primarily to enable an organization to achieve its objectives, the efficiency goals of industrial engineering cannot be ignored. Industrial engineering does constitute a disciplined and objective approach to job design. Unfortunately, the concern of industrial engineering for improving efficiency and simplifying work methods may cause the human considerations in job design to be neglected. What may be improvements in job design and efficiency from an engineering standpoint can sometimes prove to be psychologically unsound. For example, the assembly line with its simplified and repetitive tasks embodies sound principles of industrial engineering, but these tasks are often not psychologically rewarding for those who must perform them. Thus, to be effective, job design must also provide for the satisfaction of human needs.

Human Engineering Considerations

Human engineering attempts to accommodate the human capabilities and deficiencies of those who are to perform a job. It is concerned with adapting the entire job system—the work, the work environment, the machines, the equipment, and the processes—to match human characteristics. In short, *it seeks to fit the machine to the person rather than the person to the machine*. Also referred to as *human factors engineering, ergonomics*, and *engineering psychology*, human engineering attempts to minimize the harmful effects of carelessness, negligence, and other human fallibilities that otherwise may cause product defects, damage to equipment, or even the injury or death of employees.

Machine design must take into consideration the physical ability of operators to use the machines and to react through vision, hearing, and touch to the information that the machines convey. Building on earlier research with airplanes, the National Aeronautics and Space Administration (NASA) widely employed the principles of human engineering to improve the visual and auditory display of information through dials, instruments, and indicators on the space shuttle *Discovery*. Designing equipment controls to be compatible with both the physical characteristics and reaction capabilities of the people who must operate them and the environment in which they work is increasingly important in the design of work systems. At Chrysler's Jefferson North assembly facility, the plant uses ergonomically designed equipment to accommodate an experienced workforce whose average age is 51 years. Instead of dangling auto chassis from overhead assembly lines, which would require workers to crane upward, auto

Human engineering

An interdisciplinary approach to designing machines and systems that can be easily and efficiently used by human beings.

The complex array of instruments aboard the space shuttle *Discovery*.

chassis are tilted at an angle for ease of access.[15] While human engineering ordinarily focuses on what is the best arrangement for a large percentage of workers, it can also aid in the design of jobs for specific groups, such as the disabled or the elderly.[16]

Job Design and the Problem of Overspecialization

Organizations typically combine similar duties and tasks into one job in order to facilitate the selection, training, and supervision of personnel who are to perform it. In doing so, organizations may unintentionally create jobs that are monotonous to perform. The employees performing such jobs face a problem referred to as "overspecialization."

Recognizing the problems created by overspecialization, some employers have initiated programs to consolidate the duties of several jobs under a single title. For example, the jobs of typist, receptionist, and file clerk might be consolidated under the single title of "administrative assistant." This process is essentially one of enlarging the job duties of employees to relieve the boredom and feeling of low achievement that overspecialization creates.

objective

Behavioral Considerations

Management thought pertaining to job design has evolved from preoccupation with work simplification, standardization, and division of labor to concerns with human needs in job performance. This change has been caused in part by the limitations of overspecialization and industrial engineering noted earlier. Another major challenge confronting employers today is that of improving the quality of work life (QWL). In large and small organizations, efforts are under way to use job design to improve the well-being of employees while also improving organizational productivity. These efforts consist of making work more satisfying and reducing anxieties and stresses of the work environment. They include job enrichment programs, changes in job characteristics, creation of employee participation teams, and adjustments in traditional work schedules.

Job Enlargement

Job enlargement

An increase in the number and variety of tasks in a job in order to offer additional variety to the jobholder

Job enlargement, sometimes referred to as the *horizontal loading* of jobs, consists of increasing the number and variety of tasks a job includes. The tasks that are added are similar to current job duties; however, the new duties relieve boredom by offering additional variety to the jobholder. For example, a salesclerk's job may be enlarged by having that individual perform inventory control, merchandise returns, or shipping and receiving duties.

Job Rotation

Employees participate in job rotation when they do entirely different jobs on a rotating schedule. For example, employees working for an airline could be trained in reservations-sales, in-flight services (flight attendant), and ramp service work. Organizations may allow employees to rotate between jobs on a daily, weekly, or monthly basis, depending on organizational needs or the seniority of the employee.

Job Enrichment

Any effort that makes work more rewarding or satisfying by adding more meaningful tasks to an employee's job is called **job enrichment.** Originally popularized by Frederick Herzberg, job enrichment is touted as fulfilling the high motivational needs of employees, such as self-fulfillment and self-esteem, while achieving long-term job satisfaction and performance goals.[17] Job enrichment, or the *vertical expansion* of jobs, may be accomplished by increasing the autonomy and responsibility of employees.[18] Herzberg discusses five factors for enriching jobs and thereby motivating employees: achievement, recognition, growth, responsibility, and performance of the whole job versus only parts of the job. For example, managers can use these five factors to enrich the jobs of employees by

- Increasing the level of difficulty and responsibility of the job
- Allowing employees to retain more authority and control over work outcomes
- Providing unit or individual job performance reports directly to employees
- Adding new tasks to the job that require training and growth
- Assigning individuals specific tasks, thus enabling them to become experts

These factors allow employees to assume a greater role in the decision-making process and become more involved in planning, organizing, directing, and controlling their own work. Vertical job enrichment can also be accomplished by organizing workers into teams and giving these teams greater authority for self-management.

In spite of the benefits to be achieved through job enrichment, it must not be considered a panacea for overcoming production problems and employee discontent. Job enrichment programs are more likely to succeed in some jobs and work situations than in others. They are *not* the solution to such problems as dissatisfaction with pay, with employee benefits, or with employment insecurity. Moreover, not all employees object to the mechanical pacing of an assembly line, nor do all employees seek additional responsibility or challenge. Some prefer routine jobs because they can let their minds wander while performing their work.

Furthermore, managerial attitudes can be a factor that limits the success of a job enrichment program.[19] Granting employees more job responsibility and allowing them to make job decisions once made by supervisors can be demotivating and unsettling to managers. First-level managers who feel threatened with the possible loss of their jobs can be formidable sources of resistance to change. This point is well illustrated by a statement, made to one of the authors of this text at the completion of a job enrichment program: "Now that you've enriched the jobs of my employees, what's left for me to do?" Moreover, where managers hold low beliefs about participative decision making, this may discourage employees from participating in the redesign of work.

Job Characteristics

objective

Job design studies explored a new field when behavioral scientists focused on identifying various job dimensions that would improve simultaneously the effi-

Job enrichment
Enhancing a job by adding more meaningful tasks and duties to make the work more rewarding or satisfying

Job characteristics model

Job design that purports that three psychological states (experiencing meaningfulness of the work performed, responsibility for work outcomes, and knowledge of the results of the work performed) of a jobholder result in improved work performance, internal motivation, and lower absenteeism and turnover

ciency of organizations and the job satisfaction of employees. Perhaps the theory that best exemplifies this research is the one advanced by Richard Hackman and Greg Oldham.[20] Their **job characteristics model** proposes that three psychological states of a jobholder result in improved work performance, internal motivation, and lower absenteeism and turnover. The motivated, satisfied, and productive employee is one who (1) experiences *meaningfulness* of the work performed, (2) experiences *responsibility* for work outcomes, and (3) has *knowledge of the results* of the work performed. Achieving these three psychological states serves as reinforcement to the employee and as a source of internal motivation to continue doing the job well. As Hackman and Oldham state, "The net result is a self-perpetuating cycle of positive work motivation powered by self-generated rewards, that is predicted to continue until one or more of the three psychological states is no longer present, or until the individual no longer values the internal rewards that derive from good performance."[21]

Hackman and Oldham believe that five core job dimensions produce the three psychological states. As Figure 4–7 illustrates, three of these job characteristics foster meaningful work, while one contributes to responsibility and one to knowledge of results. The five job characteristics are as follows:

1. *Skill variety.* The degree to which a job entails a variety of different activities, which demand the use of a number of different skills and talents by the jobholder

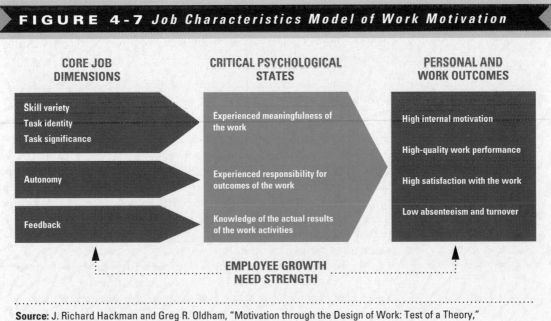

FIGURE 4-7 *Job Characteristics Model of Work Motivation*

CORE JOB DIMENSIONS

Skill variety
Task identity
Task significance

Autonomy

Feedback

CRITICAL PSYCHOLOGICAL STATES

Experienced meaningfulness of the work

Experienced responsibility for outcomes of the work

Knowledge of the actual results of the work activities

PERSONAL AND WORK OUTCOMES

High internal motivation

High-quality work performance

High satisfaction with the work

Low absenteeism and turnover

EMPLOYEE GROWTH NEED STRENGTH

Source: J. Richard Hackman and Greg R. Oldham, "Motivation through the Design of Work: Test of a Theory," *Organizational Behavior and Human Performance,* copyright August 1976. Reprinted with permission.

2. *Task identity.* The degree to which the job requires completion of a whole and identifiable piece of work, that is, doing a job from beginning to end with a visible outcome

3. *Task significance.* The degree to which the job has a substantial impact on the lives or work of other people, whether in the immediate organization or in the external environment

4. *Autonomy.* The degree to which the job provides substantial freedom, independence, and discretion to the individual in scheduling the work and in determining the procedures to be used in carrying it out

5. *Feedback.* The degree to which carrying out the work activities required by the job results in the individual being given direct and clear information about the effectiveness of his or her performance[22]

It is important to realize that each of the five job characteristics affects employee performance differently. Therefore employees will experience the greatest motivation when all five characteristics are present, since the job characteristics combine to produce the three psychological states. Since the works of Hackman and Oldham and Herzberg are similar, suggestions for redesigning jobs through job enrichment also apply to the job characteristics model.

The job characteristics model appears to work best when certain conditions are met. One of these conditions is that employees must have the psychological desire for the autonomy, variety, responsibility, and challenge of enriched jobs. When this personal characteristic is absent, employees may resist the job redesign effort. In addition, job redesign efforts almost always fail when employees lack the physical or mental skills, abilities, or education needed to perform the job. Forcing enriched jobs on individuals lacking these traits can result in frustrated employees.

Employee Teams

Employee teams

Teams of employees offering production or service suggestions to improve organizational performance

A logical outgrowth of job enrichment and the job characteristics model has been the growth of **employee teams.** Teams are groups of employees who assume a greater role in the production or service process.[23] Teams provide a forum through which employees can express their beliefs about daily operations or identify and solve organizational problems. Involvement can include joint decision making in which employees are encouraged to share their knowledge to resolve operations concerns. Inherent in the concept of employee involvement is that employees, not managers, are in the best position to contribute to workplace improvements.

Team members often acquire multiple skills, enabling them to perform a variety of job tasks. Lechmere Inc., a retail chain having twenty-seven stores, believes that the multiple skills of team members enhance employee performance and interpersonal relationships. Utilizing the multiple skills of its employees, Lechmere has created a more stable workforce by scheduling employees when and where needed.[24]

Employee teams incorporate the motivational factors of job enrichment and the core job dimensions from the job characteristics model to produce a work environment that is intrinsically fulfilling to employees. One key ingredient of teams is their ability to foster among all team members a sense of ownership, involvement, and responsibility for completing the assigned tasks. Additionally, teams can foster feelings of employee empowerment, an important component of total-quality management.[25] Because of the growing attention being paid to work teams, they will receive an extended treatment in Chapter 14.

Adjustments in Work Schedules

seven
objective

Another form of job design is to alter the normal workweek of five eight-hour days in which all employees begin and end their workday at the same preset time. Employers may depart from the traditional workday or workweek in their attempt to improve organizational productivity and morale by giving employees increased control over the hours they work. The more common alternative work schedules include the four-day workweek, flextime, and job sharing.

The Four-Day Workweek

Under the four-day workweek (or compressed workweek), the number of days in the workweek is shortened by lengthening the number of hours worked per day. This schedule is best illustrated by the four-day, forty-hour week, generally referred to as 4/10 or 4/40. Employees working a four-day workweek might work ten hours a day, Monday through Thursday. Although the 4/10 schedule is probably the best known, other compressed arrangements include reducing weekly hours to thirty-eight or thirty-six hours or scheduling eighty hours over nine days (9/80), taking one day off every other week.[26]

Organizations that operate batch-processing systems (e.g., oil companies like Exxon or Shell Oil) use shorter workweeks to coordinate work schedules with production schedules. Compressed workweeks may assist with scheduling arrangements by improving plant and equipment utilization. The keying of work schedules to processing time for a specific operation rather than to a standard workweek reduces startup and closedown time and often results in higher weekly output.

Two of the strongest advantages for the compressed work schedule are that it accommodates the leisure-time activities of employees and facilitates the employee's scheduling of medical, dental, and other types of personal appointments. Other advantages include the improvement of employee job satisfaction and morale, reduced absenteeism, and the facilitation of recruitment.

The major disadvantage of the compressed workweek involves federal laws regarding overtime. The Fair Labor Standards Act has stringent rules requiring the payment of overtime to nonsupervisory employees who work more than forty hours a week. (See Chapter 10.) Another disadvantage of the compressed workweek is that it increases the amount of stress on managers. There is no apparent problem of employee fatigue from working ten-hour days nor is there a loss of coordination of work activities between departments.

. . . .

Flextime

Flexible working hours
that permit employees
the option of choosing
daily starting and
quitting times, provided
that they work a set
number of hours per
day or week

Flextime

Data from the Current Population Survey of the U.S. Census Bureau shows that in May 1991, 12.1 million, or 15.1 percent, of the country's full-time wage and salary workers were allowed to use flextime.[27] **Flextime**, or flexible working hours, permits employees the option of choosing daily starting and quitting times, provided that they work a certain number of hours per day or week. With flextime, employees are given considerable latitude in scheduling their work. However, there is a "core period" during the morning and afternoon when *all* employees are required to be on the job.

Some variations of flextime allow employees to work as many or as few hours per day as they desire, so long as the total hours worked per week meet the minimum specified by management, usually forty hours. Flexible working hours are most common in service-type organizations—financial institutions, government agencies, or other organizations with large clerical operations. The regional office of Sentry Insurance Company in Scottsdale, Arizona, has found that flextime provides many advantages for employees working in claims, underwriting, and HR areas. Highlights in HRM 2 illustrates the flextime schedule used by Sentry Insurance.

Flextime provides both employees and employers with several advantages. By allowing employees greater flexibility in work scheduling, employers can reduce some of the traditional causes of tardiness and absenteeism. Employees can adjust their work to accommodate their particular lifestyles and, in doing so, gain greater job satisfaction.[28] Employees can also schedule their working hours for the time of day when they are most productive. In addition, variations in arrival and departure times can help reduce traffic congestion at the peak com-

Flextime alleviates the
burden of rush hour
traffic on many
employees.

**2   SENTRY INSURANCE COMPANY'S
     FLEXTIME SCHEDULE**

Flextime (arrival)			Core Time (everyone present)			Lunch	Core Time (everyone present)			Flextime (departure)		
6	7	8	9	10	11	12 12:30	1:30	2:30	3:30	4:30	5:30

HOURS

- Employees arriving at 6:00 a.m. would leave at 2:30 p.m.
- Employees arriving at 9:00 a.m. would leave at 5:30 p.m.

muting hours. In some cases, employees require less time to commute, and the pressures of meeting a rigid schedule are reduced.

From the employer's standpoint, flextime can be most helpful in recruiting and retaining personnel. It has proved invaluable to organizations wishing to improve service to customers or clients by extending operating hours. US West, a telecommunications company, uses flextime to keep its business offices open for customers who cannot get there during the day. Research demonstrates that flextime can have a positive impact on the performance measures of reliability, quality, and quantity of employee work.[29]

There are, of course, several disadvantages to flextime. First, it is not suited to some jobs. It is not feasible, for example, where specific workstations must be staffed at all times. Second, it can create problems for managers in communicating with and instructing employees. Flextime schedules may also force these managers to extend their workweek if they are to exercise control over their subordinates. Finally, keeping premises open for a longer period will increase energy consumption, resulting in higher costs for the employer.

Job Sharing

The arrangement whereby two part-time employees perform a job that otherwise would be held by one full-time employee is called "job sharing." Job sharers usually work three days a week, "creating an overlap day for extended face-to-face conferencing."[30] Their pay is three-fifths of a regular salary; however, job sharers usually take on additional responsibilities beyond what the original job would require. Companies that use job sharing are primarily in the legal, advertising, and financial-services businesses. Among more notable national programs, US Sprint began an extensive jobsharing program for its attorneys, and Kaiser Permanente, one of the nation's largest health maintenance organizations, developed a job sharing program for physicians in its Northern California region. American Express, Lotus Development Company, and Carter Hawley Hale Stores also use job sharing extensively. Employers note that without job sharing two good employees might otherwise be lost.

Job sharing is suited to the needs of families where one or both spouses desire to work only part-time. It is suited also to the needs of older workers who want to phase into retirement by shortening their workweek. For the employer, the work of part-time employees can be scheduled to conform to peaks in the daily workload. Job sharing can also limit layoffs in hard economic times. A final benefit is that employees engaged in job sharing have time off during the week to accommodate personal needs, so they are less likely to be absent.

Job sharing does have several problems, however. Employers may not want to employ two people to do the work of one because the time required to orient and train a second employee constitutes an added burden. They may also want to avoid prorating the employee benefits between two part-time employees. This problem may be reduced, however, by permitting the employees to contribute the difference between the health insurance (or life insurance) premiums for a full-time employee and the pro rata amount the employer would otherwise contribute for a part-time employee. The key to making job sharing work is good communications between partners who use a number of ways to stay in contact—phone calls, written updates, electronic mail, and voice mail.

A variation of job sharing is work sharing. A work-sharing program permits all employees in the organization to shorten their workweeks (usually to under thirty-two hours) while continuing to receive normal employee benefits. Work sharing is used almost exclusively to reduce the harmful effects of extensive layoffs due to poor economic conditions.

Shift Work

In order to meet various service requirements, some industries, such as transportation, communications, and health care, must provide continuous operations. For economic reasons, some businesses—for example, refinery operations—must maintain twenty-four-hour production schedules. Employees working in these organizations are subject to round-the-clock work schedules, or shift work. The most common shift schedules are days (7 a.m. to 3 p.m.), evenings (3 p.m. to 11 p.m.), and nights (11 p.m. to 7 a.m.). Employees doing shift work may have their shifts rotated on a daily, weekly, or monthly basis. Rotating employees through the different shifts permits everyone to share in the favored daytime hours. Employees can be assigned to shifts by management; in unionized organizations, the seniority rights of employees will dictate their ability to choose their work hours.[31]

SUMMARY

Job requirements reflect the different duties, tasks, and responsibilities contained in jobs. Job requirements, in turn, influence the HR function performed by managers, including recruitment, selection, training and development, performance appraisal, compensation, and various labor relations activities.

Job analysis data may be gathered using one of several collection methods—interviews, questionnaires, observations, or diaries. Other more quantitative approaches include use of the functional job analysis, the position analysis questionnaire system, and the critical incident method. It is the prevailing opinion of the courts that HRM decisions on employment, performance appraisal, and promotions must be based on specific criteria that are job-related. These criteria can be determined objectively only by analyzing the requirements of each job.

The format of job descriptions varies widely, often reflecting the needs of the organization and the expertise of the writer. As a minimum, job descriptions should contain a job title, a job identification section, and an essential functions section. A job specification section also may be included. Job descriptions should be written in clear and specific terms with consideration given to their legal implications.

Job design is a combination of four basic considerations: industrial engineering concerns of analyzing work methods and establishing time standards; human engineering considerations, which accommodate human capabilities and limitations to job tasks; behavioral considerations, which make jobs more psychologically rewarding; and quality-of-life concerns, which foster a favorable work environment through physical, psychological, and social job improvements.

To improve the internal environment of organizations and thereby increase American productivity, greater efforts are being made by many organizations to enhance the quality of work life. These efforts include the establishment of job enrichment programs offering opportunities for employees to experience achievement, responsibility, growth, and recognition in performing their jobs, thus giving them greater job satisfaction. Job enlargement programs reduce boredom by introducing variety into the job. This is accomplished by giving the jobholder additional and different tasks to perform. Job rotation programs allow employees to perform entirely different jobs on a selected schedule. Employee involvement teams allow employees to make suggestions to improve operations and services, thereby giving them a greater commitment to the organization.

In the job characteristics model, five job factors contribute to increased job performance and satisfaction—skill variety, task identity, task significance, autonomy, and feedback. All factors should be built into jobs since each factor influences different employee psychological states. When jobs are enriched through the job characteristics model, then employees experience more meaningfulness in their jobs, they acquire more job responsibility, and they receive direct feedback from the tasks they perform.

Changes in work schedules—which include the four-day workweek, flex-time, and job sharing—permit employees to adjust their work periods to accommodate their particular lifestyles. Employees can select from among these HR techniques to accommodate diverse employee needs while fostering organizational effectiveness.

KEY TERMS

critical incident method	job description
employee teams	job design
flextime	job enlargement
functional job analysis (FJA)	job enrichment
human engineering	job requirements
industrial engineering	job specification
job	position
job analysis	position analysis questionnaire (PAQ)
job characteristics model	

DISCUSSION QUESTIONS

1. What does job analysis entail? Who within an organization participates in the job analysis process?
2. Clearly differentiate between job analysis, job descriptions, and job specifications.
3. The courts have been fairly consistent in ruling that selection, performance appraisal, and similar decisions must be based on job-related criteria. What are the implications of these rulings for job analysis?
4. To what extent, if any, can the absence of formal job descriptions contribute to employee dissatisfaction?
5. As a project, prepare a description of a job at which you are currently working or have worked. Develop specifications listing the minimum qualifications required for the job. How do the qualifications required for the job compare with your own qualifications? Are/were you underemployed or overemployed?
6. Considering your present job, or a recent job, how would you incorporate into the position the five job characteristics that motivate employees? Could all five characteristics be included?

7. As a small business employer, explain how nontraditional work schedules might make it easier for you to recruit employees.
8. Assume the role of a manager. What are the advantages and disadvantages you see with flextime?

CASE STUDY: Job Design, Saturn Style

Industry experts agree that Saturn Corporation, a General Motors subsidiary, has made a remarkable impact on the automobile market. Consider these facts. In 1991 Saturn sold more cars per dealer than any other manufacturer, including Honda, the leader for the previous two years. It was the first time in fifteen years that a U.S. car maker claimed the number 1 spot. Furthermore, 70 percent of Saturn buyers would have bought a non-GM car as their second choice. For 1991 Saturn placed sixth among all makes in the degree of satisfaction buyers had with the sales and delivery experience. Only luxury models like Lexus, Cadillac, and Mercedes-Benz outpaced Saturn.

Saturn did not achieve these results by resorting to traditional production methods. Rather, it uses state-of-the-art manufacturing and job design techniques, including industrial engineering, ergonomics, and behavioral considerations. For example, workers stand on soft birch-wood floors instead of hard concrete. Cars pass through the assembly line on hydraulic lifts called "skillets," which allow employees to raise or lower the cars to the employee's height. Employees are allowed to ride the platform and take up to six minutes to correctly finish tasks. On traditional assembly lines, employees are given less than one minute to complete their individual duties. Industrial engineers videotape employees in action, looking for wasted motion. In one instance, employees were saved one-third of the steps walking to and from cars, thereby conserving employee energy.

Saturn managers agree, however, that the introduction of employee involvement teams is the key feature of the company's success. Teams are the basic organizational building block at Saturn. On the production floor, employees are formed into teams of five to fifteen people who manage themselves. Each team elects a leader called a "work-team counselor." Teams make decisions regarding scheduling, hiring, budgeting, and various production and quality concerns. Decisions are made by consensus, which requires a 70 percent "agreement rate" and a 100 percent "support rate" once a decision is reached.

Teams monitor themselves to ensure maximum efficiency. For example, one team member may check scrap and receive weekly reports on employee waste. Team members know the cost of parts and can calculate the added expense of wasted materials. Interestingly, each team forecasts yearly the amount of resources it plans to use in the coming year. Teams receive monthly breakdowns on budgeted items, even including telephone bills.

Above shop-floor teams are groups of employees called "work-unit module advisors." Advisors serve as troubleshooters and coordinators for all work teams within each of three business units—powertrain, body system, and vehicle systems. The entire Saturn complex is overseen by the manufacturing advisory committee composed of union and management representatives from each of the business units. At the pinnacle is the Strategic Action Committee (SAC), which is responsible for long-range planning and policy making for the company.

Questions

1. What arguments could be advanced both for and against the use of employee involvement teams?
2. At Saturn, since team members are responsible for hiring decisions, what job specifications would be important for the hiring of employees?

NOTES AND REFERENCES

1. *Workplace 2000: Work and Workers for the 21st Century, Executive Summary* (Washington, D.C.: U.S. Department of Labor, m.d.): 1; see also "The New World of Work," *Business Week* (October 17, 1994): 76–87.
2. For a good review of workforce trends, see "Tomorrow's Jobs," *Occupational Outlook Handbook,* 1994–1995 ed. (Washington, D.C.: Bureau of Labor Statistics, Bulletin No. 2450, May 1994): 8.
3. Adapted from job description, *Senior Personnel Analyst,* City of Mesa, Arizona. Provided by John Smoyer, personnel director, City of Mesa.
4. George T. Milkovich and Jerry M. Newman, *Compensation,* 4th rev. ed. (Homewood, Ill.: Irwin, 1993): 61; see also Ronald A. Ash, "Job Analysis in the World of Work," in *The Job Analysis Handbook for Business, Industry, and Government,* ed. Sidney Gall (New York: John Wiley and Sons, 1988): 3.
5. Richard Henderson, *Compensation Management,* 6th ed. (Englewood Cliffs, N.J.: Prentice-Hall, 1993).
6. John G. Veres, Samuel B. Green, and Wiley R. Boyles, "Racial Differences on Job Analysis Questionnaires: An Empirical Study," *Public Personnel Management* 20, no. 2 (Summer 1991): 135–44.
7. Frank J. Landy and Joseph Vasey, "Job Analysis: The Composition of SME Samples," *Personnel Psychology* 44, no. 1 (Spring 1991): 27–50.
8. Bob Cardy and Greg Dobbins, "Job Analysis in a Dynamic Environment," *News* (Academy of Management, Human Resources Division) 16, no. 1 (Fall 1992): 4; see also Benjamin Schneider and Andrea Marcus Konz, "Strategic Job Analysis," *Human Resource Management* 28, no. 1 (Spring 1989): 51–63.
9. U.S. Department of Labor, *Dictionary of Occupational Titles,* 4th ed. (Washington, D.C.: U.S. Government Printing Office, 1991): xiv.
10. Milkovich and Newman, *Compensation,* 68.
11. Jai V. Ghorpade, *Job Analysis: A Handbook for the Human Resource Director* (Englewood Cliffs, N.J.: Prentice-Hall, 1988): 97–98.
12. Chapter 3 discussed the *Uniform Guidelines on Employee Selection Procedures* and the necessity for performance standards to be based on valid job-related criteria.
13. Matt Chalker, "Tooling Up for ADA," *HR Magazine* 36, no. 12 (December 1991): 61–64.
14. Elliot H. Shaller and Dean A. Rosen, "A Guide to the EEOC's Final Regulations on the Americans with Disabilities Act," *Employee Relations Law Journal* 17, no. 3 (Winter 1991–1992): 413.
15. "Evolved Assembly," *Business Week* (April 2, 1993): 46.
16. Bob Filipczak, "Adaptive Technology for the Disabled," *Training* 30, no. 3 (March 1993): 23–29.
17. For Herzberg's important article on job enrichment, see Frederick Herzberg, "One More Time: How Do You Motivate Employees?" *Harvard Business Review* 46, no. 2 (January-February 1968): 53–62.
18. Ebrahim A. Maidani, "Comparative Study of Herzberg's Two-Factor Theory of Job Satisfaction among Public and Private Sectors," *Public Personnel Management* 20, no. 4 (Winter 1991): 441–48.
19. Dean B. McFarlin, Paul D. Sweeney, and John L. Cotton, "Attitudes toward Employee Participation in Decision-Making: A Comparison of European and American Managers in a United States Multinational Company," *Human Resource Management* 31, no. 4 (Winter 1992): 363–83.
20. For the original article on the job characteristics model, see J. Richard Hackman and Greg R. Oldham, "Motivation through the Design of Work: Test of a Theory," *Organizational Behavior and Human Performance* 16, no. 2 (August 1976): 250–79.
21. Ibid., 256.
22. Ibid., 257–58.
23. Richard J. Magjuka, "The 10 Dimensions of Employee Involvement," *Training and Development Journal* 47, no. 4 (April 1993): 61–67.

24. D. Keith Denton, "Multi-Skilled Teams Replace Old Work Systems," *HR Magazine* 37, no. 9 (September 1992): 48.

25. John H. Dobbs, "The Empowerment Environment," *Training and Development Journal* 47, no. 2 (February 1993): 55–57.

26. Jon L. Pierce and Randall B. Dunham, "The 12-Hour Work Day: A 48-Hour, Eight-Day Week," *Academy of Management Journal* 35, no. 5 (December 1992): 1086–98.

27. The Current Population Survey (CPS), or household survey, is conducted each month by the U.S. Census Bureau for the Bureau of Labor Statistics. The CPS collects a variety of information on the household population, most notably unemployment and employment data. In addition, every few years, supplementary questions are asked, such as questions on flexible work schedules.

28. Charles S. Rogers, "The Flexible Workplace: What Have We Learned?" *Human Resource Management* 31, no. 3 (Fall 1992): 183–99; see also David A. Ralston, "How Flextime Eases Work/Family Tensions," *Personnel* 67, no. 8 (August 1990): 45–48; Sue Shellenbarger, "Employees Take Pains to Make Flextime Work," *The Wall Street Journal* (August 18, 1992): B1.

29. Sue Shellenbarger, "More Companies Experiment with Workers Schedules," *Wall Street Journal* (January 13, 1994): B1, see also *1987 American Society for Personnel Administration and Commerce Clearing House Survey* (June 26, 1987): 4.

30. Sue Shellenbarger, "Two People, One Job: It Really Can Work," *The Wall Street Journal* (December 7, 1994): B1; see also Alan Deutschman, "Pioneers of the New Balance," *Fortune* (May 20, 1991): 61, 64, 68.

31. Charlene Marmer Solomon, "HR is Solving Shift-Work Problems," *Personnel Journal* 72, no. 8 (August 1993): 36–48.

Chapter

Human Resources
Planning and Recruitment

5

After studying this chapter you should be able to

Identify the advantages of integrating human resources planning and strategic planning.

Describe the basic approaches to human resources planning.

Explain the advantages and disadvantages of recruiting from within the organization.

Explain the advantages and disadvantages of external recruitment.

Describe how recruitment activities are integrated with affirmative action and equal employment initiatives.

4. Social concerns, including child care and educational priorities
5. Demographic trends, including age, composition, and literacy of the workforce

The labor-force trends listed earlier, for example, illustrate the importance of monitoring demographic changes in the population as a part of HRP. Such changes can affect the composition and performance of an organization's workforce. These changes are important because EEO/AA plans must take into account the demographic composition of the population in the area where the organization is located. Furthermore, with a "maturing" American workforce, HRP must consider the many implications of this demographic fact on recruitment and replacement policies. McDonald's and other fast-food chains, for example, have made a stronger effort in recent years to hire older workers.

objective

Elements of Effective HRP

Managers follow a systematic process, or model, when undertaking HRP, as shown in Figure 5–1. The three key elements of the process are forecasting the demand for labor, performing a supply analysis, and balancing supply and demand considerations. Careful attention to each factor will help top managers and supervisors to meet their staffing requirements.

FIGURE 5-1 *Human Resources Planning Model*

EMPLOYMENT FORECASTING	Leads to →	SUPPLY ANALYSIS	Resulting in →	BALANCING SUPPLY AND DEMAND CONSIDERATIONS
CONSIDERATIONS		**INTERNAL**		**RECRUITMENT (SHORTAGE)**
• Product/service demand		• Staffing tables		• Full-time
• Economics		• Markov analysis		• Part-time
• Technology		• Skills inventories		• Recalls
• Financial resources		• Management inventories		
• Absenteeism/turnover		• Replacement charts		**REDUCTIONS (SURPLUS)**
• Organizational growth		• Succession planning		• Terminations
• Management philosophy				• Layoffs
TECHNIQUES		**EXTERNAL**		• Demotions
• Trend analysis		• Demographic changes		• Retirement
• Managerial estimate		• Education of workforce		
• Delphi technique		• Labor mobility		
		• Governmental policies		
		• Unemployment rate		

Forecasting Demand for Employees

A key component of HRP is forecasting the *number* and *type* of people needed to meet organizational objectives. A variety of organizational factors, including competitive strategy, technology, structure, and productivity, can influence the demand for labor. For example, as noted in Chapter 2, utilization of advanced technology is generally accompanied by less demand for low-skilled workers and more demand for knowledge workers. External factors such as business cycles—economic and seasonal trends—can also play a role. The Internal Revenue Service, for example, relies heavily on temporary employees between January and April when tax returns are received for processing. For other organizations, the drivers of labor demand may not be quite so predictable.

Forecasting is frequently more an art than a science, providing inexact approximations rather than absolute results. The ever-changing environment in which an organization operates contributes to this problem. For example, estimating changes in product or service demand is a basic forecasting concern, as is anticipating changes in national or regional economics. A hospital anticipating internal changes in technology, organization, or administration must consider these environmental factors in its forecasts of staffing needs. Also, the forecasted staffing needs must be in line with the organization's financial resources.

There are two approaches to HR forecasting: quantitative and qualitative. When concentrating on human resources needs, forecasting is primarily quantitative in nature, and in large organizations is accomplished by highly trained specialists. Quantitative approaches to forecasting can employ sophisticated analytical models, although forecasting may be as informal as having one person who knows the organization anticipate future HR requirements. Organizational demands will ultimately determine which technique to use. Regardless of the method, however, forecasting should not be neglected, even in relatively small organizations.

Quantitative Approaches

Trend analysis
A quantitative approach to forecasting labor demand based on an organizational index such as sales

Quantitative approaches to forecasting involve the use of statistical or mathematical techniques; they are the approaches used by theoreticians and professional planners. One example is **trend analysis,** which forecasts employment requirements based on some organizational index and is one of the most commonly used approaches for projecting HR demand.[12] Trend analysis is typically done by following several steps:

First, select an appropriate *business factor*. This should be the best available predictor of human resources needs. Frequently, sales or value added (selling price minus costs of materials and supplies) are used as predictors in trend analysis. Second, plot an historical trend of the business factor in relation to number of employees. The ratio of employees to the business factor will provide a *labor productivity ratio* (for example, sales per employee). Third, compute the productivity ratio for at least the past five years. Fourth, calculate human resources demand by dividing the business factor by the productivity ratio. Finally, project human resources demand out to the target year. This procedure is summarized in Figure 5–2 for a housing contractor.

FIGURE 5-2 *Example of Trend Analysis of HR Demand*

YEAR	BUSINESS FACTOR (Sales in thousands)	LABOR PRODUCTIVITY (Sales/employee)	HUMAN RESOURCES DEMAND (Number of employees)
1989	$2,351	14.33	164
1990	$2,613	11.12	235
1991	$2,935	8.34	352
1992	$3,306	10.02	330
1993	$3,613	11.12	325
1994	$3,748	11.12	337
1995	$3,880	12.52	310
1996*	$4,095	12.52	327
1997*	$4,283	12.52	342
1998*	$4,446	12.52	355

*Projected figures

Other, more sophisticated statistical-planning methods include modeling or multiple-predictive techniques. Whereas trend analysis relies on a single factor (e.g., sales) to predict employment needs, the more advanced methods combine several factors, such as interest rates, gross national product, disposable income, and sales, to predict employment levels. Because of the high costs of developing these forecasting methods, they are used only by large organizations in relatively stable industries such as transportation, communications, and utilities.

Qualitative Approaches

In contrast to quantitative approaches, qualitative approaches to forecasting are less statistical, attempting to reconcile the interests, abilities, and aspirations of individual employees with the current and future staffing needs of an organization. In both large and small organizations, HR planners may rely on experts who assist in preparing forecasts to anticipate staffing requirements. **Management forecasts** are the opinions (judgments) of supervisors, department managers, experts, or others knowledgeable about the organization's future employment needs.

Another forecasting method, the *Delphi technique,* attempts to decrease the subjectivity of forecasts by soliciting and summarizing the judgments of a preselected group of individuals. The final forecast thus represents a composite group judgment. The Delphi technique requires a great deal of coordination and cooperation in order to ensure satisfactory forecasts. This method works best in organizations where dynamic technological changes affect staffing levels.

Ideally, HRP should include the use of both quantitative and qualitative approaches. In combination, the two approaches serve to complement each other,

Management forecasts

The opinions (judgments) of supervisors, department managers, or others knowledgeable about the organization's future employment needs

providing a more complete forecast by bringing together the contributions of both theoreticians and practitioners.

Supply Analysis

Once an organization has forecast its future requirements for employees, it must then determine if there are sufficient numbers and types of employees available to staff anticipated openings. Supply analysis will encompass two sources—internal and external.

Internal Labor Supply

An internal supply analysis may begin with the preparation of staffing tables. **Staffing tables** are a pictorial representation of all organizational jobs, along with the numbers of employees currently occupying those jobs and future employment requirements. Another technique, called **Markov analysis,** shows the percentage (and actual number) of employees who remain in each job from one year to the next, as well as the proportions of those who are promoted, demoted, transferred, or exit the organization. As shown in Figure 5–3, Markov analysis can be used to track the pattern of employee movements through various jobs and develop a transition matrix for forecasting labor supply.

In conjunction with quantitative techniques that forecast the number of employees, **skill inventories** can also be prepared that list each employee's education, past work experience, vocational interests, specific abilities and skills, compensation history, and job tenure. Of course, confidentiality is a vital concern in setting up any such inventory. Nevertheless, well-prepared and up-to-date skill inventories allow an organization to quickly match forthcoming job openings with employee backgrounds. Organizations like Zenith Data Systems, Westinghouse, and the State of Illinois use computers and special programs to perform

Staffing tables

Pictorial representations of all organizational jobs, along with the numbers of employees currently occupying those jobs and future (monthly or yearly) employment requirements

Markov analysis

Method for tracking the pattern of employee movements through various jobs

Skill inventories

Files of education, experience, interests, skills, etc., that allow managers to quickly match job openings with employee backgrounds

FIGURE 5-3 Hypothetical Markov Analysis for a Retail Company

1994 \ 1995	STORE MANAGERS	ASST. STORE MANAGERS	SECTION MANAGERS	DEPT. MANAGERS	SALES ASSOCIATES	EXIT
STORE MANAGERS (n=12)	90% / 11					10% / 1
ASSISTANT STORE MANAGERS (n=36)	11% / 4	83% / 30				6% / 2
SECTION MANAGERS (n=96)		11% / 11	66% / 63	8% / 8		15% / 14
DEPARTMENT MANAGERS (n=288)			10% / 29	72% / 207	2% / 6	16% / 46
SALES ASSOCIATES (n=1440)				6% / 86	74% / 1066	20% / 288
FORECASTED SUPPLY	15	38	92	300	1072	351

☐ Transition percentage   ☐ Actual number of employees

**Replacement
charts**

Listings of current
jobholders and persons
who are potential
replacements if an
opening occurs

**Succession
planning**

The process of
identifying, developing,
and tracking key
individuals for executive
positions

this task. When data are gathered on managers, these inventories are called *management inventories*.

Both skill and management inventories can be used to develop employee **replacement charts,** which list current jobholders and identify possible replacements should openings occur. Figure 5–4 shows an example of how an organization might develop a replacement chart for the managers in one of its divisions. Note that this chart provides information on the current job performance and promotability of possible replacements. As such, it can be used side by side with other pieces of information for **succession planning**—the process of identifying, developing, and tracking key individuals so that they may eventually assume top-level positions.

External Labor Supply

When an organization lacks an internal supply of employees for promotions, or when it is staffing entry-level positions, managers must consider the external

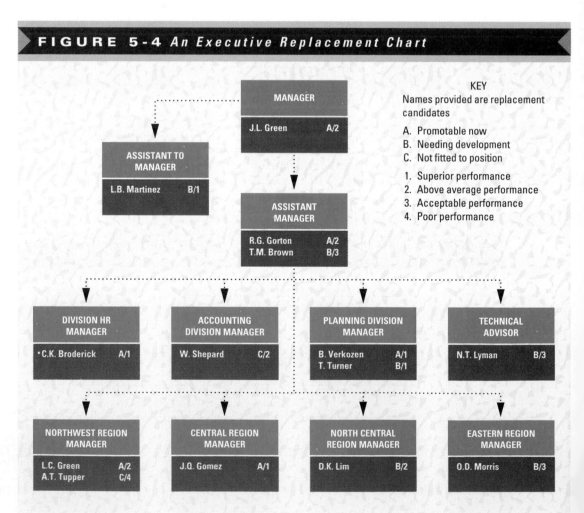

FIGURE 5-4 *An Executive Replacement Chart*

supply of labor. As noted in Chapter 2, many factors influence labor supply, including demographic changes in the population, national and regional economics, education level of the workforce, demand for specific employee skills, population mobility, and governmental policies. National and regional unemployment rates are often considered a general barometer of labor supply.

Fortunately, labor market analysis is aided by various published documents. Unemployment rates, labor-force projection figures, and population characteristics are reported by the U.S. Department of Labor.[13] Chambers of commerce and individual state development and planning agencies also may assist with labor market analysis.[14] The *Monthly Labor Review,* published by the Bureau of Labor Statistics of the U.S. Department of Labor, frequently contains articles on jobholder characteristics and predicted changes in the workforce.[15]

Balancing Supply and Demand Considerations

HRP should strive for a proper balance not only between forecasting techniques and their application, but also between the emphasis placed on *demand considerations* and that placed on *supply considerations.* Demand considerations are based on forecasted trends in business activity. Supply considerations involve the determination of where and how candidates with the required qualifications are to be found to fill vacancies. Because of the difficulty in locating applicants for the increasing number of jobs that require advanced training, this aspect of planning is receiving more attention. Greater planning effort is also needed in recruiting members of protected classes for managerial jobs and technical jobs that require advanced levels of education.

In an effort to meet the demand for labor, organizations have several staffing possibilities, including hiring full-time employees, having employees work overtime, recalling those laid off, and using temporary employees. However, when HRP shows a surplus of jobholders, organizations may use terminations, work sharing, layoffs, or demotions or rely on attrition (a gradual reduction of employees through resignations, retirements, or deaths) to achieve workforce balance. Over the past decade, early retirements have become a more and more common means for organizations to reduce excess labor supply. Organizations as diverse as state colleges, health care facilities, and travel companies encourage employees to accept early retirement by offering "sweetened" retirement benefits. The various types of benefits are discussed in Chapter 12.

Organizational Downsizing

In recent years a host of organizations have undertaken the extremely painful task of downsizing and restructuring. Because of either economic or competitive pressures, organizations have found themselves with too many employees or with employees that have the wrong kinds of skills. In an effort to reconcile supply and demand considerations, companies such as Sara Lee, Digital, and America West Airlines have eliminated literally thousands of jobs. In fact, since 1979, *Fortune* 500 companies have cut nearly 5 million jobs—more than one out of four they once provided. These cuts are not simply restricted to hourly workers. Technical, professional, and managerial positions are being eliminated at an unprecedented rate.[16] Furthermore, the layoffs are not simply a result of a stagnant economy. In many cases, downsizing is part of a longer-term process of restructuring to take advantage of new technology, corporate partnerships, and cost minimization.

Layoff Decisions

Decisions about employee layoffs are usually based on seniority and/or performance. In some organizations, especially those with labor agreements, seniority may be the primary consideration. In other organizations, such factors as ability and fitness may take precedence over seniority in determining layoffs.

In the case of unionized organizations, the criteria for determining an employee's eligibility for layoff are typically set forth in the union agreement. As a rule, seniority on the job receives significant weight in determining which employees are laid off first. Similar provisions in the union agreement provide for the right of employees to be recalled for jobs they are still qualified to perform. Organizational policy, as well as provisions in the labor agreement, should therefore establish and define clearly the employment rights of each individual and the basis upon which layoff selections will be made and reemployment effected. The rights of employees during layoffs, the conditions concerning their eligibility for recall, and their obligations in accepting recall should also be clarified. It is common for labor agreements to preserve the reemployment rights of employees laid off for periods of up to two years, providing that they do not refuse to return to work if recalled sooner.

It has become customary, however, for employers to give some degree of recognition to seniority even among employees who are not unionized. Unions generally advocate recognition of seniority because they feel that their members should be entitled to certain rights proportionate to the years they have invested in their jobs. Nevertheless, whenever seniority provides a basis for determining or even influencing HR decisions, the discretion of management is reduced accordingly. One of the major disadvantages of overemphasizing seniority is that the less competent employees receive the same rewards and security as the more competent ones. Also, the practice of using seniority as the basis for deciding which workers to lay off may well have a disparate impact on women and minority workers, who often have less seniority than other groups.

In cases where economic conditions have brought about layoffs, employees who were let go while in good standing may be recalled to their jobs when the economic outlook brightens and job openings occur. However, in many cases these new job openings require a different set of skills than the ones they replaced. Identifying individuals for these jobs can be accomplished by searching among previous employees or among current employees who can be transferred; but frequently it requires searching externally in the broader labor market.

Recruiting within the Organization

Recruitment is the process of locating and encouraging potential applicants to apply for existing or anticipated job openings. During this process, efforts are made to inform the applicants fully about the qualifications required to perform the job and the career opportunities the organization can offer them. Whether or not a particular job vacancy will be filled by someone from within the organization or from outside will, of course, depend upon the availability of personnel, the organization's HR policies, and the requirements of the job to be staffed.

Advantages of Recruiting from Within

Most organizations try to follow a policy of filling job vacancies above the entry-level position through promotions and transfers. By filling vacancies in this way, an organization can capitalize on the investment it has made in recruiting, selecting, training, and developing its current employees.

Promotion-from-within policies at Canondale Corporation, maker of racing and mountain bikes, as well as Stew Leonard's, the world's largest dairy store, have contributed to the companies' overall growth and success.[17] Promotion serves to reward employees for past performance and is intended to encourage them to continue their efforts. It also gives other employees reason to anticipate that similar efforts by them will lead to promotion, thus improving morale within the organization. This is particularly true for members of protected classes who have encountered difficulties in finding employment and have often faced even greater difficulty in advancing within an organization. Most organizations have integrated promotion policies as an essential part of their EEO/AA programs.

If an organization's promotion policy is to have maximum motivational value, employees must be made aware of that policy. The following is an example of a policy statement that an organization might prepare:

> "Promotion from within" is generally recognized as a foundation of good employment practice, and it is the policy of our museum to promote from within whenever possible when filling a vacancy. The job vacancy will be posted for five calendar days to give all qualified full- and part-time personnel an equal opportunity to apply.

While a transfer lacks the motivational value of a promotion, it sometimes can serve to protect employees from layoff or to broaden their job experiences. Furthermore, the transferred employee's familiarity with the organization and its operations can eliminate the orientation and training costs that recruitment from the outside would entail. Most importantly, the transferee's performance record is likely to be a more accurate predictor of the candidate's success than the data gained about outside applicants.

Methods of Locating Qualified Job Candidates

The effective use of internal sources requires a system for locating qualified job candidates and for enabling those who consider themselves qualified to apply for the opening. Qualified job candidates within the organization can be located by computerized record systems, by job posting and bidding, and by recalling those who have been laid off.

Computerized Record Systems

Computers have made possible the creation of data banks that contain the complete records and qualifications of each employee within an organization.

Westinghouse Electric, for example, has developed a computer program named HuRBIE (Human Resource Basic Information Environment) that allows managers to access information from the Personnel Records Information Systems Management (PRISM) database. Similarly, Employment Solutions, a subsidiary of IBM, has developed a resume-tracking system that allows managers to query an on-line database of resumes. Similar to the skills inventories mentioned earlier, these information systems allow an organization to screen its entire workforce in a matter of minutes to locate suitable candidates to fill an internal opening.[18] These data can also be used to predict the career paths of employees and to anticipate when and where promotion opportunities may arise. Since the value of the data depends on how current the data are, the record system must include provisions for recording changes in employee qualifications and job placements as they occur.

Job Posting and Bidding

Job posting and bidding

Posting vacancy notices and maintaining lists of employees looking for upgraded positions

Organizations may communicate information about job openings through a process referred to as **job posting and bidding.** This process consists largely of posting vacancy notices on bulletin boards, but may also include use of designated posting centers, employee publications, special "announcement handouts," direct mail, and public-address messages. Intel Corporation has computerized its job posting and bidding program by maintaining voluntary lists of employees looking for upgraded positions. As a position becomes available, the list of employees seeking that position is retrieved from the computer and their records are reviewed to select the best-qualified candidate.

The system of job posting and bidding can provide many benefits to an organization. However, these benefits may not be realized unless employees believe the system is being administered fairly. Therefore, to reap the full advantages of job posting, organizations should follow the administrative guidelines for job posting and bidding programs presented in Highlights in HRM 2.

Furthermore, job bidding is more effective when it is part of a career development program in which employees are made aware of opportunities available to them within the organization. For example, HR departments may provide new employees with literature on job progression that describes the lines of job advancement, training requirements for each job, and skills and abilities needed as they move up the job-progression ladder.

Limitations of Recruiting from Within

Sometimes certain jobs at the middle and upper levels that require specialized training and experience cannot be filled from within the organization and must be filled from the outside. This is especially common in small organizations. Also, for certain openings it may be necessary to hire individuals from the outside who have gained from another employer the knowledge and expertise required for these jobs.

Even though HR policy encourages job openings to be filled from within the organization, potential candidates from the outside should be considered in order to prevent the inbreeding of ideas and attitudes. Applicants hired from the outside, particularly for certain technical and managerial positions, can be a source

of new ideas and may bring with them the latest knowledge acquired from their previous employers. Indeed, excessive reliance upon internal sources can create the risk of "employee cloning." Furthermore, it is not uncommon for firms in competitive fields such as high technology to attempt to gain secrets from competitors by hiring away their employees.

objective

Recruiting Outside the Organization

Unless there is to be a reduction in the workforce, a replacement from outside must eventually be found to fill a job left vacant when a jobholder moves to a new slot in the organization. Thus, when the president or CEO of the organization retires, a chain reaction of promotions may subsequently occur. This creates other managerial openings throughout the organization. The question to be resolved therefore is not whether to bring people into the organization, but rather at which level they are to be brought in.

In the past few years, organizations such as Eastman Kodak, Westinghouse, and Goodyear have brought in outsiders to be their new CEOs. In fact, an astounding 31 percent of *Fortune* 500 companies who replaced their CEOs in 1993, did so by hiring executives from outside their companies. In many of these cases, hiring someone from the outside was seen as essential for revitalizing the organizations.[19]

The Labor Market

The **labor market,** or the area from which applicants are to be recruited, will vary with the type of job to be filled and the amount of compensation to be paid for the job. Recruitment for executive and technical jobs requiring a high degree of knowledge and skill may be national or even international in scope. Most colleges and universities, for example, conduct national employment searches to fill top administrative positions. Recruitment for jobs that require relatively little skill, however, may encompass only a small geographic area. The reluctance of people to relocate may cause them to turn down offers of employment, thereby eliminating them from employment consideration beyond the local labor market. However, by offering an attractive level of compensation and by helping to defray moving costs, employers may induce some applicants to move.

The ease with which employees can commute to work will also influence the boundaries of the labor market. Insufficient public transportation or extreme traffic congestion on the streets and freeways can limit the distance employees are willing to travel to work, particularly to jobs of low pay. Also, population migration from the cities to the suburbs has had its effect on labor markets. If suitable employment can be obtained near where they live or if they can work at home (see Chapter 2), many suburbanites are less likely to accept or remain in jobs in the central city.

One organization, Kentucky Fried Chicken (KFC), has adopted several nontraditional recruiting strategies to attract needed managerial and hourly employees. Faced with high turnover and labor shortages in the central Florida labor market, KFC recruited from outside established geographical boundaries. Areas with high unemployment were chosen as recruitment locations and jobs were offered in other areas. KFC also recruited from inner-city areas for hourly positions in its suburban stores. Anticipating the potential transportation problems of inner-city employees, it established a van service and provided public-transportation coupons to recruits.[20]

Outside Sources of Recruitment

The outside sources from which employers recruit will vary with the type of job to be filled. A computer programmer, for example, is not likely to be recruited from the same source as a machine operator. Trade schools can provide applicants for entry-level positions, though these recruitment sources are not as useful when highly skilled employees are needed.[21]

The condition of the labor market may also help to determine which recruiting sources an organization will use. During periods of high unemployment, organizations may be able to maintain an adequate supply of qualified applicants from unsolicited resumes alone. A tight labor market, one with low unemployment, may force the employer to advertise heavily and/or seek assistance from local employment agencies. How successful an organization has been in reaching its affirmative action goals may be still another factor in determining the sources from which to recruit. Typically, an employer at any given time will find it necessary to utilize several recruitment sources.

Several studies have suggested that an employee's recruitment source can affect that employee's subsequent tenure and job performance with an organization.[22] In general, applicants who find employment as "walk-ins" or through referral by a current employee tend to remain with the organization longer and give higher-quality performance than those employees recruited through the formal recruitment sources of advertisements and employment agencies. Informal recruiting sources may also yield higher selection rates than formal sources. In one study, an examination of recruitment sources showed that women and African Americans use formal recruiting sources more frequently than men, nonminorities, and Hispanics.[23] Employers are cautioned, however, that relying on only one or two recruitment sources to secure job applicants could have an adverse effect on protected classes.

Advertisements

One of the most common methods of attracting applicants is through advertisements. While newspapers and trade journals are the media used most often, radio, television, billboards, posters, and electronic mail are also utilized. Advertising has the advantage of reaching a large audience of possible applicants. Some degree of selectivity can be achieved by using newspapers and journals directed toward a particular group of readers. Professional journals, trade journals, and publications of unions and various fraternal or nonprofit organizations fall into this category.

As Highlights in HRM 3 illustrates, the preparation of recruiting advertisements is not only time-consuming, it also requires creativity in developing design and message content. Well-written advertisements highlight the major assets of the position while showing the responsiveness of the organization to the job and career needs of the applicants. Also, there appears to be a correlation between the accuracy and completeness of information provided in advertisements and the recruitment success of the organization. Among the information typically included in advertisements is that the recruiting organization is an *equal opportunity employer*.

Advertising can sometimes place a severe burden on an organization's employment office. Even though the specifications for the openings are described thoroughly in the advertisement, many applicants who know they do not meet the job requirements may still be attracted. They may apply with the hope that the employer will not be able to find applicants who do meet the specifications.

Public Employment Agencies

Each of the fifty states maintains an employment agency that is responsible for administering its unemployment insurance program. Many of the state agencies bear such titles as Department of Employment or Department of Human Resources. They are subject to certain regulations and controls administered by the U.S. Employment Services (USES).

State agencies maintain local public employment offices in most communities of any size. Individuals who become unemployed must register at one of these offices and be available for "suitable employment" in order to receive their weekly unemployment checks. Consequently, public employment agencies are able to refer to employers with job openings those applicants with the required skills who are available for employment.

HIGHLIGHTS IN HRM

highlights

**3 EIGHT POINTS FOR DEVELOPING
EFFECTIVE NEWSPAPER ADVERTISEMENTS**

1. Determine the readership and geographic area served by the newspaper. Consider placing ads in sections of the paper such as the sports, entertainment, or television section to reach people who are currently employed and who may not be reading the classified section.
2. Use small community newspapers or weekly classified publications that reach only a specific market segment or geographical area.
3. Develop ads that are creative and distinctive. Employ eye-catching images and borders. Use language that is clear and creates interest in the position.
4. Consult your organization's marketing or advertising department for suggestions for copy and graphics that will attract readers' attention.
5. Use different copy formats to reach different types of applicants.
6. To reach impulse applicants, consider using weekend telephone numbers to attract applicants currently employed or those without prepared resumes.
7. Attach "clip-out" coupons to the ad that applicants can send in to the organization to obtain additional information about the advertised position. The convenience of this feature might attract potential applicants who have given only slight consideration to a job change.
8. Make sure that job specifications clearly define applicant skill, ability, and educational requirements.

Source: Adapted from Catherine D. Fyock, "New Ways to Say 'Help Wanted,'" *Personnel Administrator* 33, no. 9 (September 1988): 100.

USES has developed a nationwide computerized job bank that lists job openings, and state employment offices are connected to this job bank. The computerized job bank helps facilitate the movement of job applicants to different geographic areas. Most of these offices now have a local job bank book that is published as a daily computer printout. Employer openings are listed along with other pertinent information, such as number of openings, pay rates, and job specifications. The local job bank makes it possible for employment interviewers in an agency to have a list of all job openings in the geographic area for which applicants assigned to them might qualify. Furthermore, applicants looking for a specific job can review the computer printout and apply directly to the organization having the opening.

In addition to matching unemployed applicants with job openings, public employment agencies may assist employers with employment testing, job analysis, evaluation programs, and community wage surveys.

Private Employment Agencies

Charging a fee enables private employment agencies to tailor their services to the specific needs of their clients. It is common for agencies to specialize in serving a specific occupational area or professional field. For example, Remedy Perm Personnel Services places clerical, data-processing, and accounting personnel with requesting organizations. Depending upon who is receiving the most service, the fee may be paid by either the employer or the jobseeker or both. It is not uncommon for private employment agencies to charge an employer a 25 to 30 percent fee, based on the position's annual salary, if they hire an applicant found by the agency.

Private employment agencies differ in the services they offer, their professionalism, and the caliber of their counselors. If counselors are paid on a commission basis, their desire to do a professional job may be offset by their desire to earn a commission. Thus they may encourage jobseekers to accept jobs for which they are not suited. As one management consultant has noted, "Take the time to find a recruiter who is knowledgeable, experienced, and professional. Discuss openly your philosophies and practices with regard to recruiting strategies, including advertising, in-house recruiting, screening procedures, and costs for these efforts. Find a recruiter who is flexible and who will consider your needs and wants."[24]

Executive Search Firms

In contrast to public and private employment agencies, which help jobseekers find the right job, executive search firms (often called "headhunters") help employers find the right person for a job. They seek out candidates with qualifications that match the requirements of the positions their client firm is seeking to fill. Executive search firms do not advertise in the media for job candidates, nor do they accept a fee from the individual being placed.

The fees charged by search firms may range from 30 to 40 percent of the annual salary for the position to be filled. For the recruitment of senior executives, this fee is paid by the client firm whether or not the recruiting effort results in a hire. It is for this practice that search firms receive the greatest criticism.

Nevertheless, as noted earlier, it is an increasingly common occurrence that new chief executive officers (CEOs) are brought in from outside the organization. A large number of these new CEOs are placed in those positions through the services of an executive search firm. Since high-caliber executives are in short supply, a significant number of the nation's largest corporations, including Texaco, Pillsbury, MONY Financial Services, as well as the Rockefeller Foundation, use search firms to fill their top positions. Recently, when BMW opened its new plant in the United States, it used an executive search firm to lure two senior executives away from Honda USA. The tactic was designed to help BMW duplicate Honda's success in the U.S. market.[25]

Educational Institutions

Educational institutions typically are a source of young applicants with formal training but with relatively little full-time work experience. High schools are usually a source of employees for clerical and blue-collar jobs. Community colleges, with their various types of specialized training, can provide candidates for technical jobs. These institutions can also be a source of applicants for a variety of white-collar jobs, including those in the sales and retail fields. Some management-trainee jobs are also staffed from this source.

For technical and managerial positions, colleges and universities are generally the primary source. However, the suitability of college graduates for open positions often depends on their major field of study. Organizations seeking applicants in the technical and professional areas, for example, are currently faced with a shortage of qualified candidates. To attract graduates in areas of low supply, managers are employing innovative recruitment techniques such as work-study programs, internships, low-interest loans, and scholarships. Writing on the subject of educational assistance programs, one professional journal noted that "the object is to ensure the company meets its personnel needs by targeting potential employees at a younger age, and nurturing their educational—and professional—development through college and even high school."[26]

Some employers fail to take full advantage of college and university resources because of a poor recruitment program. Consequently, their recruitment efforts fail to attract many potentially good applicants. Another common weakness is the failure to maintain a planned and continuing effort on a long-term basis. Furthermore, some recruiters sent to college campuses are not sufficiently trained or prepared to talk to interested candidates about career opportunities or the requirements of specific openings. Attempts to visit too many campuses instead of concentrating on selected institutions and the inability to use the campus placement office effectively are other recruiting weaknesses. Mismanagement of applicant visits to the organization's headquarters and the failure to follow up on individual prospects or to obtain hiring commitments from higher management are among other mistakes that have caused employers to lose well-qualified prospects.

Employee Referrals

The recruitment efforts of an organization can be aided by employee referrals, or recommendations made by current employees. Managers have found that the quality of employee-referred applicants is normally quite high, since employees are generally hesitant to recommend individuals who might not perform well. The effectiveness of this recruitment effort can be increased by paying commissions to employees when they make a successful "recruitment sale." Other recruitment incentives used by organizations include complimentary dinners, discounts on merchandise, all-expense-paid trips, and free insurance.[27]

Negative factors associated with employee referrals include the possibility of inbreeding and the violation of EEO regulations. Since employees and their referrals tend to have similar backgrounds, employers who rely heavily on employee referrals to fill job openings may intentionally or unintentionally screen out, and

Recruitment efforts
take many forms.

thereby discriminate against, protected classes. Furthermore, organizations may choose not to employ relatives of current employees. The practice of hiring relatives, referred to as **nepotism**, can invite charges of favoritism, especially in appointments to desirable positions.

Nepotism
A preference for hiring
relatives of current
employees

Unsolicited Applications and Resumes

Many employers receive unsolicited applications and resumes from individuals who may or may not be good prospects for employment.[28] Even though the percentage of acceptable applicants from this source may not be high, it is a source that cannot be ignored. In fact, it is often believed that individuals who on their own initiative contact the employer will be better employees than those recruited through college placement services or newspaper advertisements.

　　Good public relations dictates that any person contacting an organization for a job be treated with courtesy and respect. If there is no possibility of employment in the organization at present or in the future, the applicant should be tactfully and frankly informed of this fact. Telling applicants, "Fill out an application, and we will keep it on file," when there is no hope for their employment is not fair to the applicant.

Professional Organizations

Many professional organizations and societies offer a placement service to members as one of their benefits. Listings of members seeking employment may be advertised in their journals or publicized at their national meetings. A placement center is usually established at national meetings for the mutual benefit of employers and jobseekers.

Labor Unions

Labor unions can be a principal source of applicants for blue-collar and some professional jobs. Some unions, such as those in the maritime, printing, and construction industries, maintain hiring halls that can provide a supply of applicants, particularly for short-term needs. Employers wishing to use this recruitment source should contact the local union under consideration for employer eligibility requirements and applicant availability.

Temporary Help Agencies

The temporary services industry is one of the fastest-growing recruitment sources. An estimated nine out of ten U.S. companies use temporary employees, and the U.S. Department of Commerce predicts that of all American industries, temporary services will be one of the strongest employers through the 1990s.[29] Organizations such as Citibank, General Mills, and Avis use "temps" for occasional short-term assignments. Small business managers use temporary help when they cannot justify hiring a full-time employee, such as for vacation fill-ins, during peak work periods, and as a replacement during an employee's pregnancy leave or sick leave.

Temporary employees, however, are being used more and more to fill positions once staffed by permanent employees. This practice is growing because temporaries can be laid off quickly, and with less cost, when work lessens. Some companies use a *just-in-time staffing* approach where a core staff of employees is augmented by a trained and highly skilled supplementary workforce.[30] The use of temporaries thus becomes a viable way to maintain proper staffing levels. Also, the employment costs of temporaries are often lower than those of permanent employees because temps are not provided with benefits and can be dismissed without the need to file unemployment insurance claims. Used predominantly in office clerical positions, temporaries are becoming more and more common in legal work, engineering, computer programming, and other jobs requiring advanced professional training.[31]

Employee Leasing

National Staff Network, Staff Services, Inc., and Action Staffing are three of a growing number of employee-leasing firms. Employee leasing, also called "contract staffing" or "staff leasing," became popular after 1982 with passage of the Tax Equity and Fiscal Responsibility Act. Unlike temporary help agencies, which supply workers only for limited periods, employee-leasing companies place their employees with subscribers on a permanent basis. Already there is a leased workforce of more than 50,000 employees in Texas alone.[32]

In its most common form, **employee leasing** is a process whereby an employer terminates a number of employees who are then hired by a third party—the employee-leasing company—which then leases the employees back to the original organization. However, leasing companies also hire workers on a continual basis and then lease them to requesting organizations. The leasing company performs all the HR duties of an employer—hiring, payroll, performance appraisal,

Employee leasing
Process of dismissing employees who are then hired by a leasing company (that handles all HR-related activities) and then contracting with that company to lease back the employees

benefits administration, and other day-to-day HR activities—and in return is paid a placement fee of normally 5 to 10 percent of payroll cost.[33] Some leasing companies charge payroll cost plus a fixed fee per employee that might be $5 to $25 per week.[34]

Improving the Effectiveness of External Recruitment

With all of the uncertainties inherent in external recruiting, it is sometimes difficult to determine whether or not an organization's efforts to locate promising talent are effective and/or cost-efficient. However, there are several things the HR department can do to maximize the probability of success. These include calculating yield ratios on recruiting sources, training organizational recruiters, and conducting realistic job previews.

Yield Ratios

Yield ratio

The percentage of applicants from a recruitment source that made it to the next phase of the selection process

Yield ratios help indicate which recruitment sources are most effective at producing qualified job candidates. Quite simply, a **yield ratio** is the percentage of applicants from a particular source that make it to the next stage in the selection process. For example, if 100 resumes were obtained from an employment agency, and 17 of these applicants were invited for an on-site interview, the yield ratio for that agency would be 17 percent (17/100). This yield ratio could then be recalculated for each subsequent stage in the selection process (e.g., after the interview and again after the final offer), which would result in a cumulative yield ratio. By calculating and comparing yield ratios for each recruitment source, it is possible not only to find out which sources produce qualified applicants, but which sources are the most cost-effective.

Organizational Recruiters

Who performs the recruitment function depends mainly on the size of the organization. For large employers, professional HR recruiters are hired and trained to find new employees. In smaller organizations, recruitment may be done by an HR generalist; or if the organization has no HR position, recruitment may be carried out by managers and/or supervisors. At companies like Macy's, members of work teams take part in the selection of new team members.

Regardless of who does the recruiting, it is imperative that these individuals have a good understanding of the knowledge, skills, abilities, experiences, and other characteristics required for the job. All too often, a new person in the HR department or a line manager may be given a recruitment assignment, even before they have been given interview training, before they fully understand the job, or before they fully comprehend the values and goals of the organization.

It is important to remember that recruiters have an influence on applicants' job decisions. Recruiters are often a main reason why applicants select one organization over another. One study showed that recruiters may have significant impacts on perceived job attractiveness, regard for job and company, and intention to accept a job.[35] Therefore choosing personable, enthusiastic, competent recruiters would seemingly have an impact on the success of an organization's recruitment program.

Realistic Job Previews

Realistic job preview (RJP)

Informing applicants about all aspects of the job, including both its desirable and undesirable facets

Another way organizations may be able to increase the effectiveness of their recruitment efforts is to provide job applicants with a **realistic job preview (RJP).** An RJP informs applicants about all aspects of the job, including both its desirable and undesirable facets. In contrast, a typical job preview only presents the job in positive terms. The RJP may also include a tour of the working area, combined with a discussion of any negative health or safety considerations. Proponents of the RJP believe that applicants who are given realistic information regarding a position are more likely to remain on the job and be successful, because there will be fewer unpleasant surprises. In fact, since 1980 a number of research studies on RJP report these positive results:

- Improved employee job satisfaction
- Reduced voluntary turnover
- Enhanced communication through honesty and openness
- Realistic job expectations[36]

Like other HR techniques, however, RJPs must be tailored to the needs of the organization and should include a balanced presentation of positive and negative job information.[37] (RJPs are discussed further in Chapter 15.)

objective

Recruitment of Protected Classes

In meeting their legal obligation to provide equal employment opportunity, employers often develop a formal EEO/AA program. An essential part of any EEO/AA policy must be an affirmative effort to recruit members of protected classes. The steps the EEOC recommends for organizations to follow in developing such a program were discussed in Chapter 3.

Recruitment of Women

Women constitute the largest numbers among the protected classes. In 1993, they accounted for 45 percent of all workers and 60 percent of the total labor-force growth.[38] Women will be the major source of new entrants into the U.S. labor force over the next thirteen years. They will make up 62 percent of the net labor-force growth, or 15 million workers, by the year 2005.[39] Within this group, women of Hispanic and Asian origin will increase their labor-force participation by 80 percent between 1990 and 2005.[40] However, even with the large numbers of women in the labor force, employers today often have difficulty in recruiting women for clerical, secretarial, and other jobs in which they have traditionally been employed. Furthermore, women still encounter barriers to landing the better-paying jobs that have been traditionally performed by men, particularly in rising to positions of top managerial responsibility.

Contrary to a once-common belief, most women do not go to work merely to "get out of the house" or to fulfill psychological needs. It is essential for employers to recognize that a majority of women, like men, work because of economic necessity. In recent years, over 60 percent of all women in the work-

An increasing number of women enter the labor force in managerial positions.

force have been responsible for supporting themselves, and three out of five of them are heads of households. These women have the employment disadvantage of having completed, on average, fewer years of school than married women not in the workforce, and they are concentrated in lower-skilled, lower-paying jobs.[41]

A major employment obstacle for women is the stereotyped thinking that persists within our society. For example, a recent study comparing male and female personality types concluded that females are still viewed as possessing fewer characteristics of the "ideal" manager profile.[42] Still another barrier has been that women in the past were not as likely as men to have professional training and preparation for entrance or advancement into management positions. This situation is changing, however, with a significant increase in the enrollment of women in programs leading to degrees in management. In addition, more women are enrolling in management seminars and certification programs that will further prepare them for higher managerial positions.

Entrance of Men into Traditional Jobs for Women

EEO/AA requirements have also led to the recruitment of men for jobs traditionally held by women. More and more men are working as secretaries, phone operators, flight attendants, and nurses. While the entrance of males into jobs once exclusively held by women will deprive women of employment opportunities, in the long run both groups will benefit. The willingness of men and women to assert themselves in jobs traditionally held by one sex will help make employment conditions better and more equal for both sexes. Higher wages, better working conditions, and greater job status for both men and women could be the result.

Recruitment of Minorities

Since the passage of the Civil Rights Act of 1964, many members of minority groups have been able to realize a substantial improvement in their social and economic well-being. Increasing numbers of African Americans and Hispanics are now in the upper income-tax brackets by virtue of their entrance into professional, engineering, and managerial positions. However, the proportion of minorities in these areas is still substantially below their proportions in the total population. Unemployment among minorities, particularly the youth, continues to be at a critically high level. Undoubtedly, these rates are considerably higher during periods of economic downturn when employment opportunities become harder to find.

For many minorities who live predominantly in the inner cities, employment opportunities still remain exceedingly limited because of educational and

CASE STUDY: British Airways

British Airways (BA) has the largest centralized commercial recruitment operation in the United Kingdom, recruiting nearly 5,000 people each year. A team of only ninety people, supported by a mainframe computer system, has the rather arduous task of handling 72,000 applications, 13,000 job applicants, and 169,000 unsolicited inquiries—all for a workforce of 50,000 employees.

At the beginning of the 1990s, senior human resources executives at BA took significant steps to deal with changes they had observed in the labor market. For some time it had been increasingly difficult to find skilled recruits in areas such as information technology, finance, and engineering. In addition, there had been a clear downturn in the supply of skilled young people. All of these trends were occurring side-by-side with an increase, driven by business growth, in demand for skilled labor.

The widening gap between supply and demand led to the creation of a recruitment marketing team within BA. The primary purpose of the team was to ensure consistency in the promotion of BA as a first-choice employer and to extend the company's customer-focused approach to the recruitment field.

The team's first priority was to apply some basic customer service principles to the recruitment operation as a whole. Having identified that there were, in fact, two customers for recruitment—external applicants and line managers—the team drew up basic guidelines and targets for measuring the quantity, quality, timing, and cost of services provided to each. Within career services, measures were developed to ensure excellent response to telephone inquiries (e.g., answer all calls within twenty seconds) and graduate recruitment (e.g., acknowledge receipt of a candidate's application within three days).

In addition to establishing quality standards, BA also developed four different training programs for line managers to help increase their understanding of the recruitment marketplace, emphasize the importance of equal opportunity in recruitment, and improve their basic skills in assessment and selection. This training was a crucial element of BA's strategy of meeting the needs of the airline while simultaneously reducing the head count in the recruitment department itself. As a consequence of the reorganization and training, many of the traditional HR functions were handed over to line managers themselves.

In order to promote BA as a first-choice employer, the company worked with Barkers Advertising to develop a recruitment advertising style that was consistent with the company's £40 million advertising budget. The philosophy was to convey a consistent corporate message while targeting different niches, especially for positions that were difficult to fill.

In their efforts to promote BA as first choice among employers, the recruitment department made special efforts to maintain a delicate balance between projecting the genuine opportunities of working for a company of the size and diversity of British Airways and the tendency to paint too rosy a picture of the realities of life within a large corporation. This was seen as especially important since retaining talented employees in a diminishing labor market was perhaps more important than attracting them in the first place.

These efforts at BA are indicative of the company's overall effort to build a more flexible and capable workforce. Flexibility and capability are two vital ingredients in the company's strategy to become a world-class carrier in the airline industry.

Source: This case is a summary of an article written by Chris Wyche, "British Airways Flies the Marketing Flag," *Personnel Management* (October 1990): 125–27.

Questions
1. What is the relationship between strategy, human resource planning, and recruitment at British Airways?
2. Do you agree with BA's decision to shift responsibility for recruitment and selection over to line managers? Explain.
3. What else could British Airways do to attract qualified candidates?

NOTES AND REFERENCES

1. Martha I. Finney, "The ASPA Labor Shortage Survey," *Personnel Administrator* 34, no. 2 (February 1989): 35–42. See also William B. Johnson, "The Coming Labor Shortage," *Journal of Labor Research* (Winter 1992): 5–10. For a broader treatment of these issues see Louis S. Richman, "The Coming World Labor Shortage," *Fortune* (April 9, 1990): 70–77; Dave Jensen, "What's All This about a Labor Shortage?" *Management Review* (June 1991): 42–44.
2. Ronald E. Kutscher, "Outlook 1990–2005: Major Trends and Issues," *Occupational Outlook Quarterly* (Spring 1992): 2–5. See also Martha I. Finney, "Planning Today for the Future's Changing Shape," *Personnel Administrator* 34, no. 1 (January 1989): 44–45; Gilbert Fuchsberg, "Many Businesses Responding Too Slowly to Rapid Work Force Shifts, Study Says," *The Wall Street Journal* (July 19, 1990): B1; Kenneth A. Kovach and John A. Pearce, "HR Strategic Mandates for the 1990s," *Personnel* 67, no. 4 (April 1990): 50–55.
3. James W. Walker and Gregory Moorhead, "CEOs: What They Want from HRM," *Personnel Administrator* 32, no. 12 (December 1987): 51.
4. James W. Walker, "Human Resource Planning, 1990s Style," *Human Resource Planning* 13, no. 4 (1990): 229–40. See also Patrick Wright and G. McMahan, "Theoretical Perspectives for Strategic Human Resource Management," *Journal of Management* 18 (1992): 295–320.
5. A. D. Chandler, Jr., *Strategy and Structure: Chapters in the History of American Industrial Enterprise*

(Cambridge, Mass.: MIT Press, 1962). See also R. E. Miles and C. C. Snow, *Organization Strategy, Structure, and Process* (New York: McGraw-Hill, 1978).
6. Dave Ulrich, "Strategic and Human Resource Planning: Linking Customers and Employees," *Human Resource Planning* 15, no. 2 (1992): 47–62. See also William E. Fulmer, "Human Resource Management: The Right Hand of Strategy Implementation," *Human Resource Planning* 12, no. 1 (1990): 1–11.
7. Charles C. Snow and Scott A. Snell, "Staffing as Strategy," in N. Schmitt, W. C. Borman, and Associates, eds., *Personnel Selection in Organizations* (San Francisco: Jossey-Bass, 1993): 448–80.
8. Walker, "Human Resource Planning, 1990s Style."
9. "Human Resources Managers Aren't Corporate Nobodies Anymore," *Business Week* (December 2, 1985): 59.
10. Brian J. Smith, John W. Boroski, and George E. Davis, "Human Resource Planning," *Human Resource Management* (Spring/Summer 1992): 81–93. For other examples of how strategic planning and HRP are combined, see D. F. Beatty and F. M. K. Tampoe, "Human Resource Planning for ICL," *Long Range Planning* 23, no. 1 (1990): 17–28; Paul Michael Swiercz and Barbara A. Spencer, "HRM and Sustainable Competitive Advantage: Lessons from Delta Airlines," *Human Resource Planning* 15, no. 2 (1992): 35–46; Alan F. White, "Organizational Transformation at BP: An Interview with Chairman

and CEO Robert Horton," *Human Resource Planning* 15, no. 1 (1992): 3–14.

11. R. S. Schuler, "Scanning the Environment: Planning for Human Resource Management and Organizational Change," *Human Resource Planning* 12, no. 4 (1989).

12. W. F. Cascio, *Applied Psychology in Personnel Management*, 4th ed. (Englewood Cliffs, N.J.: Prentice-Hall, 1991).

13. For example, see U.S. Department of Labor, Bureau of Labor Statistics, *Geographic Profiles of Employment and Unemployment, 1992*, Bulletin 2428 (July 1993).

14. For example, each month the Arizona Department of Economic Security publishes the *Arizona Labor Market Information Newsletter*, providing information on labor market conditions in Arizona.

15. The *Monthly Labor Review* is published each month by the U.S. Department of Labor, Bureau of Labor Statistics.

16. Jaclyn Fierman, "The Contingency Workforce," *Fortune* (January 24, 1994): 30–36; Ronald Henkoff, "Getting beyond Downsizing," *Fortune* (January 10, 1994): 58–64; Susan Caminiti, "What Happens to Laid-Off Managers?" *Fortune* (June 13, 1994): 68–78; Del Jones, "Kodak to Eliminate 10,000 Jobs by '96," *USA Today* (August 19, 1993): B1; Tim Jones, "Retooling Unleashes Huge Wave of Layoffs," *Chicago Tribune* (June 22, 1994).

17. Barbara Carlson, "A Freewheeler on Firm Ground," *New England Business* (March 1989): 34–39. "Interview with Les Slater," *Review of Business* (Summer/Fall 1991): 10–12. See also Von Johnston and Herff Moore, "Ride Drives Wal-Mart to Service Excellence," *HR Magazine* (October 1991): 79–82; Gerald R. Ferris, Ronald M. Buckley, and Gillian M. Allen, "Promotion Systems in Organizations," *Human Resource Planning* 15, no. 3 (1992): 47–68.

18. B. G. Clayton, "A Helping Hand Named HuRBIE," *Human Resource Planning* 13, no. 3 (1990): 179–87. See also Nicholas Kandel, Jean-Pierre Remy, Christian Stein, and Thomas Durand, "Who's Who in Technology: Identifying Technological Competence within the Firm," *R&D Management* (July 1991): 215–28; Renae Broderick and John Boudreau, "Human Resource Management, Information Technology and the Competitive Edge," *The Executive* (May 1992): 7–17; Pai-Cheng Chu, "Developing Expert Systems for Human Resource Planning and Management," *Human Resource Planning* 13, no. 3 (1990): 159–78.

19. Brian Dumaine, "What's So Hot about Outsiders?" *Fortune* (November 29, 1993): 63–67.

20. "Innovative Recruiting Practices at Kentucky Fried Chicken Attract Middle Managers and Reduce Turnover," paper presented at the annual meeting of the American Society for Personnel Administration, Kansas City, 1987.

21. L. Amante, "Help Wanted: Creative Recruitment Tactics," *Personnel* 66, no. 10 (1989): 32–36. See also R. Wayne Mondy, Robert M. Noe, and Robert E. Edwards, "Successful Recruitment: Matching Sources and Methods," *Personnel* 64, no. 9 (September 1987): 42–46.

22. Jean Powell Kirnan, John A. Farley, and Kurt F. Geisinger, "The Relationship between Recruiting Source, Applicant Quality, and Hire Performance: An Analysis by Sex, Ethnicity, and Age," *Personnel Psychology* 42, no. 2 (Summer 1989): 293–308. See also David F. Caldwell and A. Austin Spivey, "The Relationship between Recruiting Source and Employee Success: An Analysis by Race," *Personnel Psychology* 36, no. 1 (Spring 1983): 67–72.

23. Kirnan, Farley, and Geisinger, "Relationship between Recruiting Source, Applicant Quality, and Hire Performance," 293–308.

24. Donald A. Levenson, "Needed: Revamped Recruiting Services," *Personnel* 65, no. 7 (July 1988): 52. See also J. A. Breaugh, *Recruitment: Science and Practice* (Boston: PWS-Kent, 1992).

25. J. Mitchell, "BMW Names Two Honda Executives to Oversee New U.S. Assembly Plant," *The Wall Street Journal* (November 29, 1992): B4. See also Julie Amparano Lopez, "Headhunting On-Line: Job Seekers Firms Link Up in Cyberspace," *Arizona Republic* (November 7, 1994): E1.

26. Holly Rawlinson, "Scholarships Recruit Future Employees Now," *Recruitment*, a supplement of *Personnel Journal* (August 1988): 14.

27. Allan Halcrow, "Employees Are Your Best Recruiters," *Personnel Journal* 67, no. 11 (November 1988): 42–49.

28. For an excellent article on the contents of job resumes, see William H. Holly, Jr., Early Higgins, and Sally Speights, "Résumés and Cover Letters," *Personnel* 65, no. 12 (December 1988): 49–51.

29. Michael R. Losey, "Temps: They're Not Just for Typing Anymore," *Modern Office Technology* (August 1991): 58–59. See also Louis S. Richman, "CEOs to Workers: Help Not Wanted," *Fortune* (July 12, 1993): 42–43; "The Temporary Services: A Lasting Impact on the Economy," *Personnel Administrator* 33, no. 1 (January 1988): 60–62.

30. Frank N. Liguori, "Get Ready for Just-In-Time Staffing," *Chief Executive* (April 1993): 30–32; see also William E. Gruer and Herff L. Moore, "Staffing a Company with the Just-In-Time Employee," *Industrial Management* (January/February 1992): 31–32.

31. Linda Dickens, "Part-Time Employees: Workers Whose Time Has Come?" *Employee Relations* 14, no. 2 (1992): 3–12; see also Jack L. Simonetti, Nick

Nykodym, and Louella M. Sell, "Temporary Employees," *Personnel* 65, no. 8 (August 1988): 52.

32. Gruer and Moore, "Staffing a Company," 31–32. See also "Rightsizing the Human Resources Department," *Institutional Investor* (July 1993): 48; George Munchus III, "Employee Leasing: Benefits and Threats," *Personnel* 65, no. 7 (July 1988): 59–61.

33. Virginia Gibson, "Staffing Alternatives for Today's Business Needs," *HR Focus* (March 1992): 11; see also Howard E. Potter, "Getting a New Lease on Employees," *Management Review* 78, no. 4 (April 1989): 28–31.

34. Paul N. Keaton and Janine Anderson, "Leasing Offers Benefits to Both Sides," *HR Magazine* (July 1990): 53–58; see also "Give Your Employees a Break—by Leasing Them," *Business Week* (August 14, 1989): 135.

35. Michael M. Harris and Laurence S. Fink, "A Field Study of Applicant Reactions to Employment Opportunities: Does the Recruiter Make a Difference?" *Personnel Psychology* 40, no. 1 (Winter 1987): 781. See also G. N. Powell, "Applicant Reactions to the Initial Employment Interview: Exploring Theoretical and Methodological Issues," *Personnel Psychology* 44 (1991): 67–83.

36. Breaugh, *Recruitment*. See also Patricia Buhler, "Managing in the 90s: Hiring the Right Person for the Job," *Supervision* (July 1992): 21–23.

37. John P. Wanous, "Installing a Realistic Job Preview: Ten Tough Choices," *Personnel Psychology* 42, no. 1 (Spring 1989): 117–33.

38. U.S. Department of Labor, Women's Bureau, *Facts on Working Women*, No. 93-2 (June 1993).

39. U.S. Department of Labor, Women's Bureau, *Facts on Working Women*, No. 93-1 (January 1992).

40. Ibid.

41. Ibid.

42. Kenneth P. Carson, "Effects of Applicant Gender and Trait Characteristics on Selection Decision Behavior and Outcome," unpublished manuscript (September 1989): 1–14. See also Madeline E. Heilman, Caryn J. Block, Richard F. Martell, and

Michael C. Simon, "Has Anything Changed? Current Characterizations of Men, Women, and Managers," *Journal of Applied Psychology* 74, no. 6 (December 1989): 935–42.

43. Jennifer J. Laabs, "Affirmative Outreach," *Personnel Journal* (May 1991): 86–93. See also Wendy Hickey, "Balancing Act: Coordinated Strategy, Commitment Critical to Wooing Minority Staffers," *Advertising Age* (July 29, 1991): 13.

44. Barbara Ettorre, "Operation Enterprise: Training Tomorrow's Workers," *Management Review* (September 1993): 45–49; L. Winter, "Employers Go to School on Minority Recruiting," *The Wall Street Journal* (December 15, 1992): B1. See also Stu Borman, "College Science Studies: Women, Minority Recruitment Lags," *Chemical and Engineering News* (November 4, 1991): 6–7.

45. Sharon Nelton, "Winning with Diversity," *Nation's Business* (September 1992): 18–22. See also *Out of the Job Market: A National Crisis*, President's Committee on Employment of the Handicapped (n.d.), 13.

46. "320-Pound Woman Wins $100,000 Legal Appeal Over Lost Job," *Arizona Republic* (November 24, 1993): A3.

47. Donald J. Ford, "Toward a More Literate Workforce," *Training and Development* (November 1992): 52–55. See also "Functional Illiteracy: It's Your Problem, Too," *Supervisory Management* 34, no. 6 (June 1989): 22.

48. Donald J. Ford, "The Magnavox Experience," *Training and Development* (November 1992): 55–56. See also "Managing Now for the 1990s," *Fortune* (September 26, 1988): 46.

49. Benson Rosen and Thomas H. Jerdee, "Investing in the Older Worker," *Personnel Administrator* 34, no. 4 (April 1989): 70–74. See also David V. Lewis, "Make Way for the Older Worker," *HR Magazine* 36, no. 5 (May 1990): 75–77; Walter Kiechel III, "How to Manage Older Workers," *Fortune* (November 5, 1990): 183–86; "The Rising Tide of Older Workers," *Nation's Business* (September 1992): 22–23.

Chapter

Selection

6

After studying this chapter you should be able to

one
objective

Explain the objectives of the personnel selection process.

two
objective

Identify the various sources of information used for personnel selection.

three
objective

Explain the value of different types of employment tests.

four
objective

Discuss the different approaches to conducting a selection interview.

five
objective

Describe the various decision strategies for selection.

Obtaining Reliable and Valid Information

The degree to which interviews, tests, and other selection procedures yield comparable data over a period of time is known as **reliability.** For example, unless interviewers judge the capabilities of a group of applicants to be the same today as they did yesterday, their judgments are unreliable (i.e., unstable). Likewise, a test that gives widely different scores when it is administered to the same individual a few days apart is unreliable.

Reliability also refers to the extent to which two or more methods (interviews and tests, for example) yield similar results or are *consistent*. Interrater reliability—agreement between two or more raters—is one measure of a method's consistency. Unless the data upon which selection decisions are based are reliable, in terms of both stability and consistency, they cannot be used as predictors.

In addition to having reliable information pertaining to a person's suitability for a job, the information must be as valid as possible. **Validity** refers to *what* a test or other selection procedure measures and *how well* it measures it. In the context of personnel selection, validity is essentially an indicator of the extent to which data from a procedure (interview or test, for example) are related to or predictive of job performance or some other relevant criterion. Like a new medicine, a selection procedure must be validated before it is used. There are two reasons for validating a procedure. First, validity is directly related to increases in employee productivity, as we will demonstrate later. Second, EEO regulations emphasize the importance of validity in selection procedures.[2] Although we commonly refer to "validating" a test or interview procedure, validity in the technical sense refers to the inferences made from the use of a procedure, not to the procedure itself.

The *Uniform Guidelines* (see Chapter 3) recognizes and accepts different approaches to validation. These are criterion-related validity, content validity, and construct validity.

Criterion-related Validity

The extent to which a selection tool predicts or significantly correlates with important elements of work behavior is known as **criterion-related validity.** Performance on a test, for example, is compared with actual production records, supervisory ratings, training outcomes, and other measures of success that are appropriate to each type of job. In a sales job, for example, it is common to use sales figures as a basis for comparison. In production jobs, quantity and quality of output may provide the best criteria of job success.

There are two types of criterion-related validity, concurrent and predictive. **Concurrent validity** involves obtaining criterion data at about the same time that test scores (or other predictor information) are obtained from *current employees*. For example, a supervisor is asked to rate a group of clerical employees on the quantity and quality of their performance. These employees are then given a clerical aptitude test, and the test scores are compared with the supervisory ratings to determine the degree of relationship between them. **Predictive validity,** on the other hand, involves testing *applicants* and obtaining criterion data *after* they have been on the job for some indefinite period. For example, applicants are

Cross-validation

Verifying the results
obtained from a
validation study by
administering a test or
test battery to a
different sample (drawn
from the same
population)

given a clerical aptitude test, which is then filed away for later study. After the individuals have been on the job for several months, supervisors, who should not know the employees' test scores, are asked to rate them on the quality and quantity of their performance. Test scores are then compared with the supervisors' ratings.

Regardless of the method used, cross-validation is essential. **Cross-validation** is a process in which a test or test battery is administered to a different sample (drawn from the same population) for the purpose of verifying the results obtained from the original validation study.

Correlational methods are generally used to determine the relationship between predictor information such as test scores and criterion data. The correlation scatterplots in Figure 6–2 illustrate the difference between a selection test of zero validity (A) and one of high validity (B). Each dot represents a person. Note that in scatterplot A there is no relationship between test scores and success on the job; in other words, the validity is zero. In scatterplot B, those who score low on the test tend to have low success on the job, whereas those who score high on the test tend to have high success on the job, indicating high validity. In actual practice we would apply a statistical formula to the data to obtain a coefficient of correlation referred to as a validity coefficient. Correlation coefficients range from 0.00, denoting a complete absence of relationship, to +1.00 and to −1.00, indicating a perfect positive and perfect negative relationship, respectively.

A thorough survey of the literature shows that the averages of the maximum validity coefficients are 0.45 where tests are validated against *training* criteria

FIGURE 6-2 *Correlation Scatterplots*

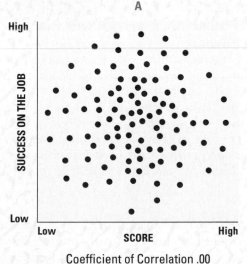

A

Coefficient of Correlation .00

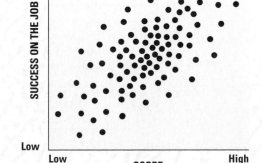

B

Coefficient of Correlation .75

and 0.35 where tests are validated against job *proficiency* criteria. These figures represent the predictive power of single tests.[3] A higher validity may be obtained by combining two or more tests or other predictors (interview or biographical data, for instance), using the appropriate statistical formulas. The higher the overall validity, the greater the chances of hiring individuals who will be the better performers. The criterion-related method is generally preferred to other validation approaches because it is based on empirical data.

For several decades, personnel psychologists believed that validity coefficients had meaning only for the specific situation (job and organization). More recently, as a result of several research studies—many involving clerical jobs—it appears that validity coefficients can often be generalized across situations, hence the term **validity generalization.** Where there are adequate data to support the existence of validity generalization, the development of selection procedures can become less costly and time-consuming. The process involves analyzing jobs and situations and, on the basis of these analyses, consulting tables of generalized validities from previous studies using various predictors in similar circumstances. It is advisable for organizations to employ the services of an industrial-organizational psychologist experienced in test validation to develop the selection procedures.[4]

Validity generalization
The extent to which validity coefficients can be generalized across situations

Content Validity

Where it is not feasible to use the criterion-related approach, often because of limited samples of individuals, the content method is used. **Content validity** is assumed to exist when a selection instrument, such as a test, adequately samples the knowledge and skills needed to perform a particular job.

Content validity
The extent to which a selection instrument, such as a test, adequately samples the knowledge and skills needed to perform a particular job

The closer the content of the selection instrument is to actual work samples or behaviors, the greater its content validity. For example, a civil service examination for accountants has high content validity when it requires the solution of accounting problems representative of those found on the job. Asking an accountant to lift a sixty-pound box, however, is a selection procedure that has content validity only if the job description indicates that accountants must be able to meet this requirement.

Content validity is the most direct and least complicated type of validity to assess. It is generally used to evaluate job knowledge and skill tests, to be described later. Unlike the criterion-related method, content validity is not expressed in correlational terms. Instead, an index that indicates the relationship between the content of the test items and performance on the job is computed from evaluations of a panel of experts.[5] While content validity does have its limitations, it has made a positive contribution to job analysis procedures and to the role of expert judgment in sampling and scoring procedures.

Construct Validity

The extent to which a selection tool measures a theoretical construct, or trait, is known as **construct validity.** Typical constructs are intelligence, mechanical comprehension, and anxiety. They are in effect broad, general categories of human functions that are based on the measurement of many discrete behaviors.

Construct validity
The extent to which a selection tool measures a theoretical construct or trait

The strength of these two workers was tested before they were hired.

For example, the *Bennett Mechanical Comprehension Test* consists of a wide variety of tasks that measure the construct of mechanical comprehension.

Measuring construct validity requires showing that the psychological trait is related to satisfactory job performance and that the test accurately measures the psychological trait. There is a lack of literature covering this concept as it relates to employment practices, probably because it is difficult and expensive to validate a construct and to show how it is job-related.[6]

objective

Sources of Information about Job Candidates

Many sources of information are used to provide as reliable and valid a picture as possible of an applicant's potential for success on the job. In this section, we will study the potential contributions of application forms, biographical information blanks, background investigations, lie detector tests, honesty tests, and medical examinations. Because interviewing plays such a major role in selection and because testing presents unique challenges, there will be expanded discussions of these sources of information later in the chapter. Assessment centers, which are often used in managerial selection, will be discussed in Chapter 8.

Application Forms

Most organizations require application forms to be completed because they provide a fairly quick and systematic means of obtaining a variety of information about the applicant. As with interviews, the EEOC and the courts have found that many questions asked on application forms disproportionately discriminate against females and minorities and often are not job-related. Application forms should therefore be developed with great care and revised as often as necessary. Because of differences in state laws on fair employment practices (FEPs) (see Chapter 3), organizations operating in more than one state will find it difficult to develop one form that can be used nationally.

Application forms serve several purposes. They provide information for deciding whether an applicant meets the minimum requirements for experience, education, etc. They provide a basis for questions the interviewer will ask about the applicant's background. They also offer sources for reference checks. For certain jobs, a short application form is appropriate. For example, McDonald's uses a form that is quite brief, but asks for information that is highly relevant to job performance. It also provides information regarding the employer's conformity with various laws and regulations. For scientific, professional, and managerial jobs, a more extended form is likely to be used.

Even when applicants come armed with elaborate resumes, it is important that they complete an application form early in the process. Individuals frequently exaggerate or overstate their qualifications on a resume. One technique for anticipating problems of misrepresentation is to ask applicants to transcribe specific resume material onto a standardized application form. The applicant is then asked to sign a statement that the information contained on the form is true and that he or she accepts the employer's right to terminate the candidate's employment if any of the information is subsequently found to be false.[7]

Biographical Information Blanks

One of the oldest methods for predicting job success uses biographical information about job applicants. As early as 1917, the Life Insurance Agency Management Association constructed and validated a biographical information blank (BIB) for life insurance salespersons. It covers such items as hobbies, club memberships, sales experience, and investments. Certain responses to these items were found to be predictive of success on the job.

Like application blanks, BIBs reveal information about a person's history that may have shaped their behavior. Sample questions from a BIB might include:

- At what age did you leave home?
- How large was the town/city in which you lived as a child?
- Did you ever build a model airplane that flew?
- Were sports a big part of your childhood?
- Do you play any musical instruments?

Both the BIB and the application form can be scored like tests. And because biographical questions rarely have obviously right or wrong answers, BIBs are difficult to fake. The development of a scoring system requires that the items that are valid predictors of job success be identified and that weights be established for different responses to these items. By totaling the scores for each item, it is possible to obtain a composite score on the blank as a whole for each applicant. Studies have shown that an objective scoring of BIB and application forms is one of the most potentially valid methods that can be used to predict job success. This method has been useful in predicting all types of behavior, including employee theft.[8]

Background Investigations

When the interviewer is satisfied that the applicant is potentially qualified, information about previous employment as well as other information provided by the applicant is investigated. Former employers, school and college officials, credit bureaus, and individuals named as references may be contacted for verification of pertinent information such as length of time on the job, type of job, performance evaluation, highest wages, academic degrees earned, possible criminal record, and credit rating. Most of this information is now readily available on existing computer databases. An Employment Management Association survey found that 93 percent of companies participating in the survey investigate information supplied by job applicants.[9] The most common ruse, according to employers, is to exaggerate one's college background.

Checking References

Organizations ranging from Canon to the Boston Philharmonic use both the mail and the telephone to check references. But while references are commonly used to screen and select employees, they have not proved successful for predicting employee performance. Written letters of reference are notoriously inflated, and this limits their validity. Generally, telephone checks are preferable because they save time and provide for greater candor. The most reliable information usually comes from supervisors, who are in the best position to report on an applicant's work habits and performance. It is often advisable, however, to obtain written verification of information relating to job titles, duties, and pay levels from the former employer's HR office.[10]

Since enactment of the Family Educational Rights Privacy Act of 1974 (FERPA), which gave students and their parents the right to inspect student personnel files, university administrators and faculty have been reluctant to provide anything other than general and often meaningless positive statements about student performance. The principles involved in FERPA came to apply to employees and their personnel records as well. As a result, most employers prefer using the telephone to check references.

Inadequate reference checking can contribute to high turnover, employee theft, and white-collar crime. By using sources in addition to former employers, organizations can obtain valuable information about an applicant's character and habits. For example, it is legal to use court records, litigation, bankruptcy, and workers' compensation records of applicants as long as the prospective employer is consistent in the use of information from these records.

In recent years there have been a growing number of cases in which organizations have been charged with "negligently" hiring or retaining employees who later commit crimes. Typically, the suits charge that the organization has failed to adequately check references, criminal records, or general background that would have shown the employee's likelihood for aberrant behavior. Rulings in the cases, which range from theft to homicide, are making employers even more aware of the importance of checking applicant references. The recent kidnapping of Sidney Reso, Exxon's head of International Operations, may become a classic case of what can happen when a company fails to adequately investigate the background of a prospective employee.[11]

Requiring Signed Requests for References

As a legal protection for all concerned, it is important to ask the applicant to fill out forms permitting information to be solicited from former employers and other reference sources. Even with these safeguards, many organizations are reluctant to put into writing an evaluation of a former employee. One reason is that several firms have been sued by former employees who discovered that they had been given poor recommendations. As a result of such experiences, some employers even hesitate to answer questions and/or verify information about former employees over the phone.

Individuals have a legal right to examine letters of reference about them (unless they waive the right to do so) where protected by the Privacy Act of 1974 or state laws. While the Privacy Act applies only to the records maintained by federal government agencies, it has influenced many employers to "clean up" personnel files and open them up to review and challenge by the employees concerned. Furthermore, over half of the states have privacy legislation.[12]

Using Credit Reports

The use of consumer credit reports by employers as a basis for establishing an applicant's eligibility for employment has become more restricted. Under the federal Fair Credit Reporting Act, an employer must advise applicants if such reports will be requested. If the applicant is rejected on the basis of the report, the applicant must be advised of this fact and be provided with the name and address of the reporting agency.

If an employer plans to use a more comprehensive type of consumer report, such as an investigative consumer report, the applicant must be advised in writing. An investigative consumer report includes information based upon personal interviews with the applicant's friends, neighbors, and associates. The applicant must be told that, upon written request, additional disclosure concerning the complete nature and scope of the investigation will be provided.[13]

The Polygraph

The polygraph, or lie detector, is a device that measures the changes in breathing, blood pressure, and pulse of a person who is being questioned. It consists of a rubber tube around the chest, a cuff around the arm, and sensors attached to the fingers that record the physiological changes in the examinee as the examiner asks questions that call for an answer of yes or no. Questions typically cover such items as whether a person uses drugs, has stolen from an employer, or has committed a serious undetected crime.

The growing swell of objections to the use of polygraphs in employment situations culminated in the passage of the federal Employee Polygraph Protection Act of 1988. The act prohibits the use of a lie detector for prehire screening and random testing and applies to all private employers except pharmaceutical companies and companies that supply security guards for health and safety operations.[14] It defines the term "lie detector" to include the polygraph, deceptograph, voice stress analyzer, psychological stress evaluator, and any similar mechanical or electrical device used to render a diagnostic opinion about the honesty or dishonesty of an individual. There are some exemptions, as stated in the poster reproduced in Highlights in HRM 1.

Other provisions of the act set qualification standards for polygraph examiners, conditions for examinations, and disclosure of information where the use of the polygraph is authorized. Because of the law, employers have had to resort to such alternatives as written tests of honesty and background checks of applicants. Among the organizations most affected are Wall Street firms, banks, and retail companies, which used to rely heavily on polygraphs.[15]

Honesty and Integrity Testing

In response to the Employee Polygraph Protection Act, many employers have dramatically increased their use of pencil-and-paper honesty and integrity tests. These tests have commonly been used in settings such as retail stores where employees have access to cash or merchandise. Common areas of inquiry include beliefs about frequency and extent of theft in our society, punishment for theft, and perceived ease of theft.[16]

A comprehensive analysis of honesty tests reveals that they are valid for predicting job performance as well as a wide range of disruptive behaviors such as theft, disciplinary problems, and absenteeism.[17] Nevertheless, HRM specialists should use the results from such tests very cautiously and most certainly in conjunction with other sources of information.

Graphology

Graphology, a term that refers to a variety of systems of handwriting analysis, is being used by a some employers to make employment decisions. Graphologists obtain a sample of handwriting and then examine such characteristics as the size and slant of letters, amount of pressure applied, and placement of the writing on the page. From their observations they draw inferences about the writer's personality traits, temperament, cognitive abilities, and social traits. Graphology is used extensively in France, Germany, Switzerland, Israel, and the United Kingdom in making employment decisions.[18] Now handwriting analysis is quietly spreading through corporate America. Companies such as Ford and General Electric have used it for selection, as has the U.S. Central Intelligence Agency (CIA). In fact, CIA agents operating in the former Soviet Union were encouraged to send any New Year's cards they received to the United States so that graphologists could check whether their acquaintances were suspicious.[19]

Organizations using handwriting analysis say they prefer it to typical personality tests because it only requires job candidates to take a few minutes to jot down a short essay. By contrast, a battery of personality tests and interviews with psychologists can take several hours and can cost thousands of dollars. In addition, the available evidence shows graphology to be a reliable predictor of personality when compared with other psychological tests. However, its predictive validity for job performance and occupational success remains questionable. In the academic community, where formal and rigorous validity studies are customary, use of graphology for employment decisions has been viewed with considerable skepticism.

HIGHLIGHTS IN HRM

1   EMPLOYEE POLYGRAPH PROTECTION ACT

U.S. DEPARTMENT OF LABOR

EMPLOYMENT STANDARDS ADMINISTRATION

Wage and Hour Division
Washington, D.C. 20210

NOTICE

EMPLOYEE POLYGRAPH PROTECTION ACT

The Employee Polygraph Protection Act prohibits most private employers from using lie detector tests either for pre-employment screening or during the course of employment.

PROHIBITIONS

Employers are generally prohibited from requiring or requesting any employee or job applicant to take a lie detector test, and from discharging, disciplining, or discriminating against an employee or prospective employee for refusing to take a test or for exercising other rights under the Act.

EXEMPTIONS*

Federal, State and local governments are not affected by the law. Also, the law does not apply to tests given by the Federal Government to certain private individuals engaged in national security-related activities.

The Act permits *polygraph* (a kind of lie detector) tests to be administered in the private sector, subject to restrictions, to certain prospective employees of security service firms (armored car, alarm, and guard), and of pharmaceutical manufacturers, distributors and dispensers.

The Act also permits polygraph testing, subject to restrictions, of certain employees of private firms who are reasonably suspected of involvement in a workplace incident (theft, embezzlement, etc.) that resulted in economic loss to the employer.

EXAMINEE RIGHTS

Where polygraph tests are permitted, they are subject to numerous strict standards concerning the conduct and length of the test. Examinees have a number of specific rights, including the right to a written notice before testing, the right to refuse or discontinue a test, and the right not to have test results disclosed to unauthorized persons.

ENFORCEMENT

The Secretary of Labor may bring court actions to restrain violations and assess civil penalties up to $10,000 against violators. Employees or job applicants may also bring their own court actions.

ADDITIONAL INFORMATION

Additional information may be obtained, and complaints of violations may be filed, at local offices of the Wage and Hour Division, which are listed in the telephone directory under U.S. Government, Department of Labor, Employment Standards Administration.

THE LAW REQUIRES EMPLOYERS TO DISPLAY THIS POSTER WHERE EMPLOYEES AND JOB APPLICANTS CAN READILY SEE IT.

*The law does not preempt any provision of any State or local law or any collective bargaining agreement which is more restrictive with respect to lie detector tests.

U.S. DEPARTMENT OF LABOR
EMPLOYMENT STANDARDS ADMINISTRATION
Wage and Hour Division
Washington, D.C. 20210

WH Publication 1462
September 1988

Medical Examination

The medical examination is one of the later steps in the selection process because it can be costly. The use of the preemployment medical examination varies according to industry, but about one-half of the companies surveyed by the Bureau of National Affairs give preemployment examinations to prospective employees.[20]

The results of this employee's medical exam will be compared against his preemployment baseline exam.

A medical examination is generally given to ensure that the health of applicants is adequate to meet the job requirements. It also provides a baseline against which subsequent medical examinations can be compared and interpreted. The latter objective is particularly important in determinations of work-caused disabilities under workers' compensation law.

In the past, requirements for such physical characteristics as strength, agility, height, and weight were often determined by an employer's unvalidated notion of what should be required. Many such requirements that tend to discriminate against women have been questioned and modified so as to represent typical job demands.

While there is much publicity about acquired immune deficiency syndrome (AIDS), corporate testing for the presence of the HIV virus is conducted in only 6 percent of the companies surveyed by the American Management Association. Nearly two-thirds of those firms reporting that they were conducting HIV tests were health care providers; an additional 14 percent were government and military units.[21]

In some cases, medical testing can be considered an invasion of privacy and may be in violation of the law. For example, the Americans with Disabilities Act severely limits the types of medical inquiries and examinations that employers may use. The ADA prohibits companies from screening out a prospective employee because he or she has an elevated risk of on-the-job injury or a medical condition that could be aggravated because of job demands. However, the ADA does not prevent testing of applicants or employees for illegal drug use, a topic discussed below.[22]

Drug Testing

A growing number of employers use drug tests to screen applicants and current employees for drug use. Urine sampling is the preferred form of drug testing; it is used by 96 percent of AMA-surveyed employers who do drug testing. More sophisticated tests are used to validate positive findings. Some of the sharpest criticism of drug testing attacks the technology and standards by which tests are conducted—a topic we will discuss in detail in Chapter 16, in the context of employee rights.

The wide range of firms that report using drug tests includes Federal Express, General Electric, Georgia Power, Westinghouse, Southern Pacific Railroad, and the New York Times Company. With most employers, applicants who test positive have virtually no chance of being hired. However, employees who test positive are typically referred for treatment or counseling or receive some sort of disciplinary action.[23]

Since passage of the Drug-Free Workplace Act of 1988, applicants and employees of federal contractors, Department of Defense contractors, and those under Department of Transportation regulations are subject to testing for illegal drug use. (See Chapter 13 for an extended discussion of this topic, including a sample policy statement for a drug-free workplace.)

three

objective

Employment Tests

Since the development of the Army Alpha Test of mental ability during World War I, tests have played an important part in the HR programs of both public and private organizations. Before the passage of the Civil Rights Act of 1964, over 90 percent of companies surveyed by the Bureau of National Affairs reported using tests. By 1976, however, only 42 percent were using tests. In the past decade, there has been a dramatic resurgence of employment testing.[24] In part, this indicates both that employers today are less fearful of lawsuits challenging the soundness of their tests and that there is a return to a focus on individual competence. Objective standards are coming back in both education and employment. Concurrently, methodological changes have made it easier to demonstrate test validity.[25] Too often employers have relied exclusively on the interview to measure or predict skills and abilities that can be measured or predicted more accurately by tests.

Tests have played a more important part in government HR programs where hiring on the basis of merit is required by law. Government agencies experienced the same types of problems with their testing programs as did organizations in the private sector. However, their staffs were forced to improve their testing programs rather than to abandon them.

Many organizations utilize professional test consultants to improve their testing programs and to meet EEO requirements. While it is often advisable to use consultants, especially if an organization is considering the use of personality tests, managers should have a basic understanding of the technical aspects of testing and the contributions that tests can make to the HR program.

The Nature of Employment Tests

An employment test is an objective and standardized measure of a sample of behavior that is used to gauge a person's knowledge, skills, abilities, and other characteristics (KSAOs) in relation to other individuals.[26] The proper sampling of behavior—whether verbal, manipulative, or some other type—is the responsibility of the test author. It is also the responsibility of the test author to develop tests that meet accepted standards of reliability.[27] Data concerning reliability are ordinarily presented in the manual for the test. While high reliability is essential, it offers no assurance that the test provides the basis for making valid judgments. It is the responsibility of the HR staff to conduct validation studies before a test is adopted for regular use. Other considerations are cost, time, ease of administration and scoring, and the apparent relevance of the test to the individuals being tested—commonly referred to as "face validity." While face validity is desirable, it is no substitute for technical validity, described earlier in this chapter. Adopting a test just because it appears relevant is bad practice; many a "good-looking" test has poor validity.

Classification of Employment Tests

Employment tests may be classified in different ways. Generally, they are viewed as measuring either aptitude or achievement. **Aptitude tests** refer to measures of a person's capacity to learn or acquire skills. **Achievement tests** refer to measures of what a person knows or can do right now.

Aptitude tests
Measures of a person's capacity to learn or acquire skills

Achievement tests
Measures of what a person knows or can do right now

Cognitive Ability Tests

Cognitive ability tests measure mental capabilities such as general intelligence, verbal fluency, numerical ability, and reasoning ability. There are a host of paper-and-pencil tests that measure cognitive abilities, including the *General Aptitude Test Battery* (GATB), the *Scholastic Aptitude Test* (SAT), the *Graduate Management Aptitude Test* (GMAT), and the *Bennett Mechanical Comprehension Test.* Figure 6–3 shows some items that could be used to measure different cognitive abilities.

Although cognitive ability tests can be developed to measure very specialized areas such as reading comprehension and spatial relations, many experts believe that the validity of cognitive ability tests simply reflects their connection to general intelligence. Measures of general intelligence (e.g., IQ) have been shown to be good predictors of performance across a wide variety of jobs.[28]

Personality and Interest Inventories

Whereas cognitive ability tests measure a person's mental capacity, personality tests measure dispositional characteristics such as extroversion, inquisitiveness, and dependability. Interest tests, such as the *Kuder Inventory*, measure an applicant's preferences for certain activities over others (such as sailing versus poker). The predictive validity of personality and interest inventories historically has been quite low.[29] However, since 1944 Sears has successfully employed an "executive battery" composed of several attitudinal and interest tests to predict managerial success.[30] Beyond the initial hiring decision, personality and interest inventories may be most useful for helping with occupational selection and career planning.

Physical Ability Tests

In addition to learning about a job candidate's mental capabilities, employers frequently need to assess a person's physical abilities as well. Particularly for demanding and potentially dangerous jobs like those held by firefighters and police officers, physical abilities such as strength and endurance tend to be not only good predictors of performance, but of accidents and injuries.[31]

Despite their potential value, physical ability tests tend to work to the disadvantage of women and disabled job applicants, a tendency that has led to several recent lawsuits. As with other methods for screening potential employees, the

FIGURE 6-3 *Sample Measures of Cognitive Ability*

Verbal

1. What is the meaning of the word "surreptitious"?

   a. covert   c. lively
   b. winding   d. sweet

2. How is the noun clause used in the following sentence? "I hope that I can learn this game."

   a. subject   c. direct object
   b. predicate nominative   d. object of the preposition

Quantitative

3. Divide 50 by 0.5 and add 5. What is the result?

   a. 25   c. 95
   b. 30   d. 105

4. What is the value of 144^2?

   a. 12   c. 288
   b. 72   d. 20736

Reasoning

5. _____ is to *boat* as *snow* is to _____ .

   a. Sail, ski   c. Water, ski
   b. Water, winter   d. Engine, water

6. Two women played 5 games of chess. Each woman won the same number of games, yet there were no ties. How can this be?

   a. There was a forfeit.   c. They played different people.
   b. One player cheated.   d. One game is still in progress.

Mechanical

7. If gear A and gear C are both turning counterclockwise, what is happening to gear B?

   a. It is turning counterclockwise.   c. It remains stationary.
   b. It is turning clockwise.   b. The whole system will jam.

A   B   C

Answers: 1. a, 2. c, 3. d, 4. d, 5. c, 6. c, 7. b

use of physical ability tests should be carefully validated on the basis of the essential functions of the job.[32]

Job Knowledge Tests

Government agencies and licensing boards usually develop job knowledge tests, a type of achievement test designed to measure a person's level of understanding about a particular job. Most civil service examinations, for example, are used to determine whether an applicant possesses the information and understanding that will permit placement on the job without further training.[33] Job knowledge tests also have had a major role in the enlisted personnel programs of the U.S. Army, Navy, Air Force, and Marines. They should be considered as useful tools for private and public organizations.

Job Sample Tests

Job sample tests, or work sample tests, require the applicant to perform tasks that are actually a part of the work required on the job. Like job knowledge tests, job sample tests are constructed from a carefully developed outline that experts agree includes the major job functions; the tests are thus considered content-valid. They are often used to measure skills for office and clerical jobs. Job sample tests have also been devised for many diverse jobs: a map-reading test for traffic control officers, a lathe test for machine operators, a complex coordination test for pilots, an in-basket test for managers, a group discussion test for supervisors, a judgment and decision-making test for administrators, to name a few. The City of Miami Beach has used job sample tests for jobs as diverse as plumber, planner, and assistant chief accountant. The U.S. Air Force has also used job samples for enlisted personnel in eight different specialty areas. In an increasing number of cases, job sample tests are aided by computer simulations, particularly when testing a candidate might prove to be dangerous. The reports are that this type of test is cost-effective, reliable, valid, fair, and acceptable to applicants.[34]

The Employment Interview

Traditionally, the employment interview has had a very important role in the selection process — so much so that it is rare to find an instance where an employee is hired without some sort of interview. Depending upon the type of job, applicants may be interviewed by one person, by members of a work team, or other individuals in the organization. While researchers have raised some doubts about its validity, the interview remains a mainstay of selection because (1) it is especially practical when there are only a small number of applicants; (2) it serves other purposes, such as public relations; and (3) interviewers maintain great faith and confidence in their judgments. Nevertheless, the interview can be plagued by problems of subjectivity and personal bias. In such cases, some interviewers' judgments are more valid than those of others in the evaluation of applicants.[35]

Interviewing Methods

Employment or selection interviews differ according to the methods used to obtain information and to find out an applicant's attitudes and feelings. The most significant difference lies in the amount of structure, or control, that is exercised by the interviewer. In the highly structured interview, the interviewer determines the course that the interview will follow as each question is asked. In the less-structured interview, the applicant plays a larger role in determining the course the discussion will take. An examination of the different types of interviews from the least structured to the most structured will reveal the differences.

The Nondirective Interview

Nondirective interview

An interview in which the applicant is allowed the maximum amount of freedom in determining the course of the discussion, while the interviewer carefully refrains from influencing the applicant's remarks

In the **nondirective interview,** the interviewer carefully refrains from influencing the applicant's remarks. The applicant is allowed the maximum amount of freedom in determining the course of the discussion. The interviewer asks broad, open-ended questions—such as "Tell me more about your experiences on your last job"— and permits the applicant to talk freely with a minimum of interruption. Generally, the nondirective interviewer listens carefully and does not argue, interrupt, or change the subject abruptly. The interviewer also uses follow-up questions to allow the applicant to elaborate, makes only brief responses, and allows pauses in the conversation; the pausing technique is the most difficult for the beginning interviewer to master.

The greater freedom afforded to the applicant in the nondirective interview is particularly valuable in bringing to the interviewer's attention any information, attitudes, or feelings that may often be concealed by more-structured questioning. However, because the applicant determines the course of the interview and no set procedure is followed, little information that comes from these interviews enables interviewers to cross-check agreement with other interviewers. Thus the reliability and validity of the nondirective interview may be expected to be minimal. This method is most likely to be used in interviewing candidates for high-level positions and in counseling, which we will discuss in Chapter 15.

The Structured Interview

Structured interview

An interview in which a set of standardized questions having an established set of answers is used

More attention is being given to the **structured interview** as a result of EEO requirements and a concern for maximizing validity of selection decisions.[36] Because a structured interview has a set of standardized questions (based on job analysis)

The interview plays a crucial role in the selection process.

and an established set of answers against which applicant responses can be rated, it provides a more consistent basis for evaluating job candidates. For example, staff members of Weyerhauser Company's HR department have developed a structured interviewing process with the following characteristics. The program:

1. Is based exclusively on job duties and requirements critical to job performance
2. Uses four types of questions: situational questions, job knowledge questions, job sample/simulation questions, and worker requirements questions
3. Has sample answers, determined in advance, to each question and interviewee responses are rated on a five-point scale explicitly defined in advance
4. Uses an interview committee so that interviewee responses are evaluated by several raters
5. Consistently follows the same procedures in all instances to ensure that each applicant has exactly the same chance as every other applicant
6. Is documented for future reference and in case of legal challenge[37]

A structured interview is more likely to provide the type of information needed for making sound decisions. It also helps to reduce the possibility of legal charges of unfair discrimination. Employers must be aware that the interview is highly vulnerable to legal attack and that more litigation in this area can be expected in the future.

Most employment interviewers will tend toward either a nondirected or a structured format. However, there are other methods that are utilized for special purposes.

The Situational Interview

Situational interview

An interview in which an applicant is given a hypothetical incident and asked how he or she would respond to it

One variation of the structured interview is called the **situational interview.**[38] With this approach, an applicant is given a hypothetical incident and asked how he or she would respond to it. The applicant's response is then evaluated relative to preestablished benchmark standards. Interestingly, many organizations are using the situational interview to select new college graduates. Highlights in HRM 2 shows a sample question from a situational interview used to select analyzer technicians at a chemical plant.

The Behavioral Description Interview

Behavioral description interview (BDI)

An interview in which an applicant is asked questions about what he or she actually did in a given situation

Similar to a situational interview, a **behavioral description interview (BDI)** focuses on real work incidents. However, while a situational interview addresses hypothetical situations, the BDI format asks the job applicant what he or she *actually did* in a given situation. For example, to assess a potential manager's ability to handle a problem employee, an interviewer might ask, "Tell me about the last time you disciplined an employee." Such an approach to interviewing, based on a critical incidents job analysis, assumes that past performance is the best predictor of future performance.

2 SAMPLE SITUATIONAL INTERVIEW QUESTION

QUESTION:

It is the night before your scheduled vacation. You are all packed and ready to go. Just before you get into bed, you receive a phone call from the plant. A problem has arisen that only you can handle. You are asked to come in to take care of things. What would you do in this situation?

RECORD ANSWER:

_____

_____

_____

SCORING GUIDE:

Good: "I would go in to work and make certain that everything is O.K. Then I would go on vacation."
Good: "There are no problems that *only I* can handle. I would make certain that someone qualified was there to handle things."
Fair: "I would try to find someone else to deal with the problem."
Poor: "I would go on vacation."

The Panel Interview

Panel interview
An interview in which a board of interviewers questions and observes a single candidate

Another type of interview involves a panel of interviewers who question and observe a single candidate. In a typical **panel interview** the candidate meets with three to five interviewers who take turns asking questions. After the interview they pool their observations to reach a consensus about the suitability of the candidate. HRM specialists using this method at Philip Morris USA and Virginia Power report that panel interviews provide several significant advantages over traditional one-to-one interviews, including higher validity because of multiple inputs, greater acceptance of the decision, and faster decision time.[39]

The Computer Interview

Recently, a growing number of organizations have begun using computers to help with the interviewing process. Cigna Insurance and Pinkerton Security and Investigation Services, for example, have developed expert systems to gather preliminary information as well as compare candidates.[40] Typically, the system asks candidates 75 to 125 multiple-choice questions tailored to the job and then compares the applicant's responses with either an ideal profile or with profiles developed on the basis of other candidates' responses. The computer can generate a printed report that contains the applicant's response summary, an itemized list of contradictory responses, a latency response report (time delays for each answer), a summary of potentially problematic responses, and a list of structured interview questions for the job interviewer to ask.[41] In addition to the benefits of objectivity, some research evidence suggests that applicants may be less likely to engage in "impression management" in computerized interviews than in face-to-face interviews.[42] So far, organizations have used the computer mainly as a complement to, rather than as a replacement for, conventional interviews.

Guidelines for Employment Interviewers

Organizations should exercise considerable caution in the selection of employment interviewers. Qualities that are desirable include humility; the ability to think objectively; freedom from overtalkativeness, extreme opinions, and biases; maturity; and poise. Given the importance of diversity in the workforce, experience in associating with people from a variety of backgrounds is also desirable.

A training program should be provided on a continuing basis for employment interviewers and at least periodically for managers and supervisors in other departments. Many books on employment interviewing are available as guides. For the individual who desires to explore the topic in depth, a wealth of information is available in books and journals.[43]

There have been several reviews of research studies on the employment interview.[44] Each of these reviews discusses and evaluates numerous studies concerned with such questions as "What traits can be assessed in the interview?" and "How do interviewers reach their decisions?" Highlights in HRM 3 presents some of the major findings of these studies. It shows that information is available that can be used to increase the validity of interviews.

Figure 6–4 summarizes the variables and processes involved in the employment interview. The figure shows that a number of applicant characteristics may influence the perception of the interviewer and thus the hiring decision. In addition, many interviewer and situational factors may also influence the perceptual and judgmental processes. For example, knowing the race and sex of an applicant may shape the expectations, biases, and behaviors of an interviewer, which in turn may affect the interview outcome. Even a limited understanding of the variables shown in Figure 6–4 can help increase the interviewing effectiveness of managers and supervisors.

Interviewer training programs should include practice interviews conducted under guidance. Practice interviews may be recorded on videotape and evaluated later in a group training session. Some variation in technique is only natural. However, the following list presents ten ground rules for employment interviews that are commonly accepted and supported by research findings. Their apparent simplicity should not lead one to underestimate their importance.

1. *Establish an interview plan.* Examine the purposes of the interview and determine the areas and specific questions to be covered. Review job requirements, application-form data, test scores, and other available information *before* seeing the applicant.

HIGHLIGHTS IN HRM

3 SOME MAJOR FINDINGS FROM RESEARCH STUDIES ON THE INTERVIEW

1. Structured interviews are more reliable than unstructured interviews.
2. Interviewers are influenced more by unfavorable than by favorable information.
3. Interrater reliability is increased when there is a greater amount of information about the job to be filled.
4. A bias is established early in the interview, and this tends to be followed by either a favorable or an unfavorable decision.
5. Intelligence is the trait most validly estimated by an interview, but the interview information adds nothing to test data.
6. Interviewers can explain why they feel an applicant is likely to be an unsatisfactory employee but not why the applicant may be satisfactory.
7. Factual written data seem to be more important than physical appearance in determining judgments. This increases with interviewing experience.
8. An interviewee is given a more extreme evaluation (positive/negative) when preceded by an interviewee of opposing value (positive/negative).
9. Interpersonal skills and motivation are probably best evaluated by the interview.
10. Allowing the applicant time to talk makes rapid first impressions less likely and provides a larger behavior sample.
11. Nonverbal as well as verbal interactions influence decisions.
12. Experienced interviewers rank applicants in the same order, although they differ in the proportion that they will accept. There is a tendency for experienced interviewers to be more selective than less experienced ones.

2. *Establish and maintain rapport.* This is accomplished by greeting the applicant pleasantly, by explaining the purpose of the interview, by displaying sincere interest in the applicant, and by listening carefully.
3. *Be an active listener.* Strive to understand, comprehend, and gain insight into what is only suggested or implied. A good listener's mind is alert, and face and posture usually reflect this fact.
4. *Pay attention to nonverbal cues.* An applicant's facial expressions, gestures, body position, and movements often provide clues to that person's attitudes and feelings. Interviewers should be aware of what they themselves are communicating nonverbally.

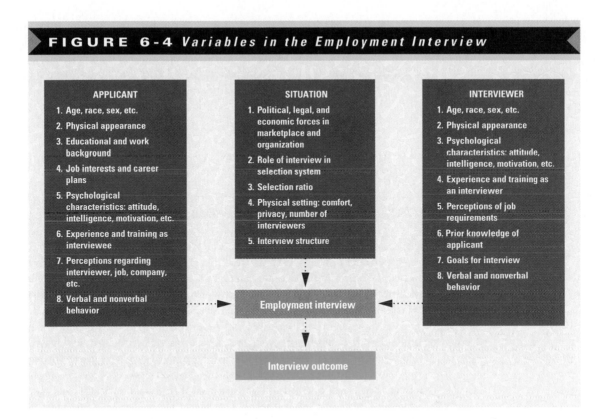

FIGURE 6-4 *Variables in the Employment Interview*

APPLICANT

1. Age, race, sex, etc.
2. Physical appearance
3. Educational and work background
4. Job interests and career plans
5. Psychological characteristics: attitude, intelligence, motivation, etc.
6. Experience and training as interviewee
7. Perceptions regarding interviewer, job, company, etc.
8. Verbal and nonverbal behavior

SITUATION

1. Political, legal, and economic forces in marketplace and organization
2. Role of interview in selection system
3. Selection ratio
4. Physical setting: comfort, privacy, number of interviewers
5. Interview structure

INTERVIEWER

1. Age, race, sex, etc.
2. Physical appearance
3. Psychological characteristics: attitude, intelligence, motivation, etc.
4. Experience and training as an interviewer
5. Perceptions of job requirements
6. Prior knowledge of applicant
7. Goals for interview
8. Verbal and nonverbal behavior

Employment interview

Interview outcome

5. *Provide information as freely and honestly as possible.* Answer fully and frankly the applicant's questions. Present a realistic picture of the job.

6. *Use questions effectively.* To elicit a truthful answer, questions should be phrased as objectively as possible, giving no indication of what response is desired.

7. *Separate facts from inferences.* During the interview, record factual information. Later, record your inferences or interpretations of the facts. Compare your inferences with those of other interviewers.

8. *Recognize biases and stereotypes.* One typical bias is for interviewers to consider strangers who have interests, experiences, and backgrounds similar to their own to be more acceptable. *Stereotyping* involves forming generalized opinions of how people of a given gender, race, or ethnic background appear, think, feel, and act. The influence of sex-role stereotyping is central to sex discrimination in employment. Avoid the influence of "beautyism." Discrimination against unattractive persons is a persistent and pervasive form of employment discrimination. Also avoid "halo error," or judging an individual favorably or unfavorably overall on the basis of only one strong point (or weak point) on which you place high value.

9. *Control the course of the interview.* Establish an interview plan and stick to it. Provide the applicant with ample opportunity to talk, but maintain control of the situation in order to reach the interview objectives.

10. *Standardize the questions asked.* To increase reliability and avoid discrimination, ask the same questions of all applicants for a particular job. Keep careful notes; record facts, impressions, and any relevant information, including what was told to the applicant.

Types of Preemployment Questions to Ask

The entire subject of preemployment questioning is complex. There are differing and sometimes contradictory interpretations by the courts, the EEOC, and the OFCCP about what is lawful and unlawful. Under federal laws there are no questions that are expressly prohibited. However, the EEOC looks with disfavor on direct or indirect questions related to race, color, age, religion, sex, or national origin. Some of the questions that interviewers once felt free to ask are now potentially hazardous. Federal courts have severely limited the area of questioning. An interviewer, for example, can ask about physical disabilities if the job involves manual labor, but not otherwise. Several states have fair employment practice laws that are more restrictive than federal legislation. In general, if a question is job-related, is asked of everyone, and does not discriminate against a certain class of applicants, it is likely to be acceptable to government authorities.

Particular care has to be given to questions asked of female applicants about their family responsibilities. It is inappropriate, for example, to ask, "Who will take care of your children while you are at work?" or "Do you plan to have children?" or "What is your husband's occupation?" or "Are you engaged?" It is, in fact, inappropriate to ask applicants of either gender questions about matters that have no relevance to job performance.

Employers have found it advisable to provide interviewers with instructions on how to avoid potentially discriminatory questions in their interviews. The examples of appropriate and inappropriate questions shown in Highlights in HRM 4 may serve as guidelines for application forms as well as preemployment interviews. Complete guidelines may be developed from current information available from district and regional EEOC offices and from state FEP offices. Once the individual is hired, the information needed but not asked in the interview may be obtained if there is a valid need for it and if it does not lead to discrimination.

Reaching a Selection Decision

objective five

While all of the steps in the selection process are important, the most critical step is the decision to accept or reject applicants. Because of the cost of placing new employees on the payroll, the short probationary period in many organizations, and EEO/AA considerations, the final decision must be as sound as possible. Thus it requires systematic consideration of all the relevant information about applicants. It is common to use summary forms and checklists to ensure that all of the pertinent information has been included in the evaluation of applicants.

HIGHLIGHTS IN HRM

highlights

4   APPROPRIATE AND INAPPROPRIATE INTERVIEW QUESTIONS

	APPROPRIATE QUESTIONS	INAPPROPRIATE QUESTIONS
National origin	What is your name? Have you ever worked under a different name? Do you speak any foreign languages that may be pertinent to this job?	What's the origin of your name? What is your ancestry?
Age	Are you over 18? If hired, can you prove your age?	How old are you? What is your date of birth?
Gender	(Say nothing unless it involves a bona fide occupational qualification)	Are you a man or a woman?
Race	(Say nothing)	What is your race?
Disabilities	Do you have any disabilities that may inhibit your job performance? Are you willing to take a physical exam if the job requires it?	Do you have any physical defects? When was your last physical? What color are your eyes, hair, etc.?
Height and weight	(Not appropriate unless it is a bona fide occupational qualification)	How tall are you? How much do you weigh?
Residence	What is your address? How long have you lived there?	What are the names/relationships of those with whom you live?
Religion	(You may inform a person of the required work schedule.)	Do you have any religious affiliation?
Military record	Did you have any military education/ experience pertinent to this job?	What type of discharge did you receive?
Education and experience	Where did you go to school? Did you finish school? What is your prior work experience? Why did you leave? What is your salary history?	Is that a church-affiliated school? When did you graduate? What are your hobbies?
Criminal record	Have you ever been convicted of a crime?	Have you ever been arrested?
Citizenship	Do you have a legal right to work in the United States?	Are you a U.S. citizen?
Marital/family status	What is the name, address, and telephone number of a person we may contact in case of an emergency?	Are you married, divorced, single? Do you prefer Miss, Mrs., or Ms.? Do you have any children? How old are they?

Summary of Information about Applicants

Fundamentally, an employer is interested in what an applicant *can do* and *will do*. An evaluation of candidates on the basis of assembled information should focus on these two factors, as shown in Figure 6–5.[45] The "can-do" factors include knowledge and skills, as well as the aptitude (the potential) for acquiring new knowledge and skills. The "will-do" factors include motivation, interests, and other personality characteristics. Both factors are essential to successful performance on the job. The employee who has the ability *(can do)* but is not motivated to use it *(will not do)* is little better than the employee who lacks the necessary ability.

It is much easier to measure what individuals can do than what they will do. The "can-do" factors are readily evident from test scores and verified information. What the individual will do can only be inferred. Responses to interview and application-form questions may be used as a basis for obtaining information for making inferences about what an individual will do.

Decision Strategy

The strategy used for making personnel decisions for one category of jobs may differ from that used for another category. The strategy for selecting managerial and executive personnel, to be discussed in Chapter 8, will differ from that used in selecting clerical and technical personnel. While many factors are to be considered in hiring decisions, the following are some of the questions that managers must consider:

1. Should the individuals be hired according to their highest potential or according to the needs of the organization?
2. At what grade or wage level should the individual be started?
3. Should initial selection be concerned primarily with an ideal match of the employee to the job, or should potential for advancement in the organization be considered?
4. To what extent should those who are not qualified but are qualifiable be considered?
5. Should overqualified individuals be considered?
6. What effect will a decision have on meeting affirmative action goals and diversity considerations?

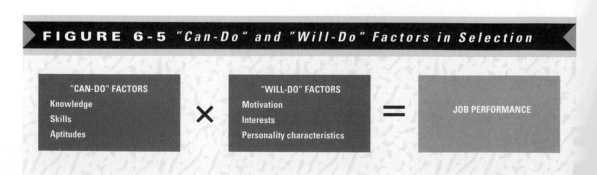

FIGURE 6-5 *"Can-Do" and "Will-Do" Factors in Selection*

"CAN-DO" FACTORS
Knowledge
Skills
Aptitudes

×

"WILL-DO" FACTORS
Motivation
Interests
Personality characteristics

=

JOB PERFORMANCE

"What I lack in skills, I make up for with intangible shmoozing abilities."

From *The Wall Street Journal*—Permission, Cartoon Features Syndicate

In addition to these types of factors, managers must also consider which approach they will use in making hiring decisions. There are two basic approaches to selection: clinical and statistical.

Clinical Approach

In the clinical approach to decision making, those making the selection decision review all the data on applicants. Then, based on their understanding of the job and the individuals who have been successful in that job, they make a decision. Different individuals often arrive at different decisions about an applicant when they use this approach because each evaluator assigns different weights to the applicant's strengths and weaknesses. Furthermore, personal biases and stereotypes are frequently covered up by what appear to be rational bases for acceptance or rejection.

Statistical Approach

Compensatory model

Selection decision model in which a high score in one area can make up for a low score in another area

Multiple cutoff model

Selection decision model that requires an applicant to achieve some minimum level of proficiency on all selection dimensions

In contrast to the clinical approach, the statistical approach to decision making is more objective. It involves identifying the most valid predictors and weighting them through statistical methods such as multiple regression.[46] Quantified data such as scores or ratings from interviews, tests, and other procedures are then combined according to their weighted value. Individuals with the highest combined scores are selected. A comparison of the clinical approach with the statistical approach in a wide variety of situations has shown that the statistical approach is superior.[47] Although this superiority has been recognized for many decades, the clinical approach continues to be the one most commonly used.

With a strictly statistical approach, a candidate's high score on one predictor (e.g., cognitive ability test) will make up for a low score on another predictor (e.g., the interview). For this reason, this model is a **compensatory model.** However, it is frequently important that applicants achieve some minimum level of proficiency on all selection dimensions. When this is the case, a **multiple cutoff** model can be used in which only those candidates who score above the cutoff on all dimensions are considered. The selection decision is made from that subset of candidates.

Multiple hurdle model

A sequential strategy in which only the applicants with the highest scores at an initial test stage go on to subsequent stages

A variation of the multiple cutoff is referred to as the **multiple hurdle** model. This decision strategy is sequential in that after candidates go through an initial evaluation stage, the ones who score well are provisionally accepted and are assessed further at each successive stage. The process may continue through several stages (hurdles) before a final decision is made regarding the candidates. This approach is especially useful when either the testing or training procedures are lengthy and expensive.[48]

Each of the statistical approaches requires that a decision be made about where the cutoff lies—that point in the distribution of scores above which a person should be considered and below which the person should be rejected. The score that the applicant must achieve is the cutoff score. Depending upon the labor supply, it may be necessary to lower or raise the cutoff score.

The effects of raising and lowering the cutoff score are illustrated in Figure 6–6. Each dot in the center of the figure represents the relationship between the test score (or a weighted combination of test scores) and the criterion of success for one individual. In this instance, the test has a fairly high validity, as represented by the elliptical pattern of dots. Note that the high-scoring individuals are concentrated in the satisfactory category on job success, whereas the low-scoring individuals are concentrated in the unsatisfactory category.

If the cutoff score is set at A, only the individuals represented by areas 1 and 2 will be accepted. Nearly all of them will be successful. If more employees are needed (i.e., there is an increase in the selection ratio), the cutoff score may be lowered to point B. In this case, a larger number of potential failures will be accepted, as shown in quadrants 2 and 4. Even if the cutoff is lowered to C, the total number of satisfactory individuals selected (represented by the dots in areas 1, 3, and 5) exceeds the total number selected who are unsatisfactory (areas 2, 4, and 6). Thus the test serves to maximize the selection of probable successes and to minimize the selection of probable failures. This is all we can hope for in predicting job success: the probability of selecting a greater proportion of individuals who will be successful rather than unsuccessful.

Selection ratio

The number of applicants compared with the number of persons hired

While the most valid predictors should be used with any selection strategy, there is a related factor that contributes to selecting the best-qualified persons. It is selectivity, or having an adequate number of applicants or candidates from which to make a selection. Selectivity is typically expressed in terms of a **selection ratio,** which is the ratio of the number of applicants to be selected to the total number of applicants. A ratio of 0.10, for example, means that 10 percent of the applicants will be selected. A ratio of 0.90 means that 90 percent will be selected. If the selection ratio is low, only the most promising applicants will normally be hired. When the ratio is high, very little selectivity will be possible, since even applicants having mediocre ability will have to be hired if the vacancies are to be filled.

It should be noted that how much of a contribution any predictor will make to the improvement of a given selection process is a function not only of the validity of the predictor and the selection ratio, but also of the proportion of persons who are judged successful using current selection procedures.[49]

> **FIGURE 6-6** *Test Score Scatterplot with Hypothetical Cutoffs*

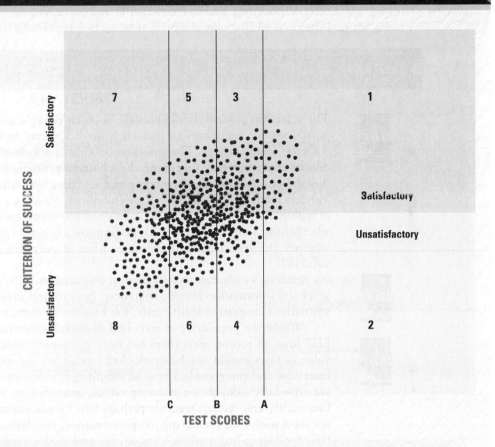

The Final Decision

After a preliminary selection has been made in the employment department, those applicants who appear to be most promising are then referred to departments having vacancies. There they are interviewed by the managers or supervisors, who usually make the final decision and communicate it to the employment department. Because of the weight that is usually given to their choices, managers and supervisors should be trained so that their role in the selection process does not negate the more scientific efforts of personnel in the HR department.

In large organizations, notifying applicants of the decision and making job offers is often the responsibility of the HR department. This department should confirm the details of the job, working arrangements, wages, etc., and specify a deadline by which the applicant must reach a decision. If, at this point, findings from the medical examination are not yet available, an offer is often made contingent upon the applicant's passing the examination.

In government agencies, the selection of individuals to fill vacancies is made from lists or registers of eligible candidates. Ordinarily, three or more names of

7. The Supreme Court has consistently interpreted Title VII of the Civil Rights Act of 1964 as prohibiting not only intentional discrimination but also neutral practices that have a discriminatory effect. Thus practices that are discriminatory in intent *and* effect are prohibited by Title VII. What are some employment practices that are discriminatory in effect, even if not in intent? What should be done with respect to these practices?

CASE STUDY: # Pinkerton Selects Security Personnel for the Emmy Awards

With a "galaxy of stars" attending the Annual Primetime Emmy Awards in August 1992, Pinkerton Security and Investigation Services brought out all of its high-tech selection tools to ensure that it hired the most-qualified security officers. Pinkerton has provided security for the Emmys since 1977 and staffs the event with approximately 250 officers. However, each year the company screens more than 1 million job applicants, both for its own operations as well as for other clients.

The selection process developed by Pinkerton is a five-step multiple hurdle approach that includes: (1) a job application and initial interview, (2) an honesty test, (3) a computerized structured interview, (4) a face-to-face interview, and (5) a background check.

Pinkerton uses the job application as a starting point to learn more about each candidate's education, work history, and ability to meet minimum qualifications of the job. To assess the person's integrity, Pinkerton has developed the *STANTON* survey. This thirty-minute paper-and-pencil survey measures an applicant's attitude toward honesty and his or her propensity to follow company rules. If the applicant does not meet the company's high standards for integrity—and in the past more than 40 percent of all applicants have not—Pinkerton wastes no further time, money, or effort in the selection process.

The third step in the selection process is a computerized, structured interview session referred to as *IntelliView*. Using the keypad of a touch-tone telephone, an applicant answers 100 yes/no questions regarding job stability, policy compliance, career ambition, productivity and enthusiasm, work ethic, performance initiative, and competency skills. The ten-minute computer interview allows Pinkerton to handle a greater number of applicants, with a more objective method of collecting information about each applicant. The expert system, which is linked back to Pinkerton's information services office in Charlotte, North Carolina, does not actually score the applicants answers but simply provides information about key areas that should be addressed during the face-to-face interview. *IntelliView* even provides specific follow-up questions for the interviewer.

The fourth step in the selection process is a traditional interview. Since each applicant has been prequalified, the interviewer can develop a one-on-one relationship and focus on a key set of issues for each candidate. In the final stage of selection, Pinkerton undertakes a background check that may include a Social Security trace, a report from the department of motor vehicles, reference checks with previous employers, and an investigation into potential criminal records.

In the case of the Emmy Awards, if an applicant passed each of Pinkerton's five hurdles, he or she was selected to become one of the officers who would be in charge of the event's highly sensitive security requirements.

Source: This case is adapted from Peter C. Sawyers, "Structured Interviewing: Your Key to the Best Hires," *Personnel Journal,* Special Supplement (December 1992); and Bob Smith, "Pinkerton Keeps Its Eye on Recruitment," *HR Focus* (September 1993): 1, 8.

Questions

1.   Do you think the selection system used by Pinkerton is valid? Discuss.
2.   Are there any possible problems of discrimination with this selection system? Discuss.

NOTES AND REFERENCES

1.   Frank J. Landy and Laura J. Shankster, "Personnel Selection and Placement," in *Annual Review of Psychology* 45 (Palo Alto, Calif.: Annual Reviews 1994), 261–96. See also Neal Schmitt and Ivan Robertson, "Personnel Selection," in *Annual Review of Psychology* (Palo Alto, Calif.: Annual Reviews, 1990). See also Charlene Marmer Solomon, "Testing Is Not at Odds with Diversity Efforts," *Personnel Journal* (March 1993): 100–104.

2.   Scott E. Maxwell and Richard D. Arvey, "The Search for Predictors with High Validity and Low Adverse Impact: Compatible or Incompatible Goals?" *Journal of Applied Psychology* 78, no. 3 (June 1993): 433–37. See also James H. Coil III and Charles M. Rice, "Managing Work-Force Diversity in the Nineties: The Impact of the Civil Rights Act of 1991," *Employee Relations Law Journal* 18, no. 4 (Spring 1993): 547–65.

3.   Frank J. Landy, "Test Validity Yearbook," *Journal of Business Psychology* 7, no. 2 (1992): 111–257. See also Edwin E. Ghiselli, "The Validity of Aptitude Tests in Personnel Selection," *Personnel Psychology* 26, no. 4 (Winter 1973): 461–77. See also J. E. Hunter and R. H. Hunter, "Validity and Utility of Alternative Predictors of Job Performance," *Psychological Bulletin* 96 (1984): 72–98; N. Schmitt, R. Z. Gooding, R. A. Noe, and M. Kirsch, "Meta-Analysis of Validity Studies Published between 1964 and 1982 and the Investigation of Study Characteristics," *Personnel Psychology* 37 (1984): 407–22.

4.   Society for Industrial and Organizational Psychology, *Principles for the Validation and Use of Personnel Selection Procedures* (College Park, Md.: University of Maryland Press, 1987). See also R. L. Schmidt and J. E. Hunter, "The Future of

Criterion-Related Validity," *Personnel Psychology* 33 (1980): 41–60.

5.   Richard S. Barrett, "Content Validation Form," *Public Personnel Management* 21 (Spring 1992): 41–52. See also C. H. Lawshe, "A Quantitative Approach to Content Validity," *Personnel Psychology* 28 (1975): 563–75; M. L. Tenopyr, "Content-Construct Confusion," *Personnel Psychology* 30 (1977): 47–54.

6.   R. D. Arvey, S. M. Nutting, and T. E. Landon, "Validation Strategies for Physical Ability Testing in Police and Fire Settings," *Public Personnel Management* 21 (1992): 301–12.

7.   Marlene Brown, "Checking the Facts on a Resume," *Personnel Journal* 72 (January 1993): SS6–SS7. See also T. Lammers, "How to Read between the Lines: Tactics for Evaluating a Resume," *Inc.* (March 1993): 105–7; Robert P. Vecchio, "The Problem of Phony Resumes: How to Spot a Ringer among the Applicants," *Personnel* 61, no. 2 (March–April 1984): 22–27.

8.   A. N. Kluger, R. R. Reilly, and C. J. Russell, "Faking Biodata Tests: Are Option-Keyed Instruments More Resistant?" *Journal of Applied Psychology* 76 (December 1991): 889–96. See also T. E. Becker and A. L. Colquitt, "Potential Versus Actual Faking of a Biodata Form: An Analysis along Several Dimensions of Item Type," *Personnel Psychology* 45 (Summer 1992): 389–406; F. A. Mael, "A Conceptual Rationale for the Domain and Attributes of Biodata Items," *Personnel Psychology* 44 (Winter 1991): 763–92.

9.   BNA *Policy and Practice Series—Personnel Management,* 1989 (Washington, D.C.: Bureau of National Affairs), 201:283. See also L. Barani,

"Background Investigations: How HR Stays on the Cutting Edge," *HR Focus* 70 (June 1993): 12.

10. P. Falcone, "Reference Checking: Revitalize a Critical Selection Tool," *HR Focus* 69 (December 1992): 19. See also M.G. Aamodt, D.A. Bryan, and A.J. Whitcomb, "Predicting Performance with Letters of Recommendation," *Public Personnel Management* 22 (Spring 1993): 81–90.

11. W.M. Carley and A. Sullivan, "Reso Kidnapping Offers Security Lesson," *Wall Street Journal* (June 25, 1992): B1. See also "Firms Face Lawsuits for Hiring People Who Then Commit Crimes," *The Wall Street Journal* (April 30, 1987): 29.

12. For a continuously updated listing of employment policy changes, see *Fair Employment Practices Bulletin* (Washington, D.C.: Bureau of National Affairs). See also Suzanne Cook, "Privacy Rights: Whose Life Is It Anyway?" *Personnel Administrator* 67, no. 9 (April 1987): 58–69.

13. *BNA Policy and Practice Series—Personnel Management,* 1988, 201:279. See also Gilbert Fuchsberg, "More Employers Check Credit Histories of Job Seekers to Judge Their Character," *The Wall Street Journal* (May 30, 1990): B1.

14. With some exceptions for jobs in law enforcement, government agencies, and drug-dispensing firms, the following states have banned compulsory or involuntary polygraphing in employment situations: Alaska, California, Connecticut, Delaware, Georgia, Hawaii, Idaho, Iowa, Kansas, Maine, Maryland, Massachusetts, Michigan, Minnesota, Montana, Nebraska, Nevada, New Jersey, New York, Oregon, Pennsylvania, Rhode Island, Tennessee, Texas, Utah, Vermont, Virginia, Washington, West Virginia, and Wisconsin. The District of Columbia also prohibits such testing. Several states have some restrictions. See *BNA Policy and Practice Series—Personnel Management,* 1988, 201:251.

15. Albert R. Karr, "Law Limiting Use of Lie Detectors Is Seen Having Widespread Effect," *The Wall Street Journal* (July 1, 1988): 13.

16. P.R. Sackett, L.R. Burris, and C. Callahan, "Integrity Testing for Personnel Selection: An Update," *Personnel Psychology* 42 (Autumn 1989): 491–529. See also C. Gorman, "Honestly, Can We Trust You?" *Time* (January 23, 1989): 44.

17. D.S. Ones, C. Viswesvaran, and F.L. Schmidt, "Comprehensive Meta-analysis of Integrity Test Validities: Findings and Implications for Personnel Selection and Theories of Job Performance," *Journal of Applied Psychology* 78 (August 1993): 679–703. See also Gilbert Fuchsberg, "Attorney General in New York Urges Integrity Test Ban," *The Wall Street Journal* (March 6, 1991).

18. A. Fowler, "An Even-Handed Approach to Graphology," *Personnel Management* 23 (March 1991): 40–43. See also J. Gooding, "By Hand, By Jove," *Across the Board* 28 (December 1991): 43–47; M.A. Hopper and K.S. Stanford, "A Script for Screening," *Security Management* 36 (May 1992): 72–81.

19. "Graphology: The Power of the Written Word," *The Economist* 315 (June 16, 1990): 97–98. See also G. Ben-Shakar, M. Bar-Hillel, Y. Bilu, E. Ben-Abba, and A. Flug, "Can Graphology Predict Occupational Success? Two Empirical Studies and Some Methodological Ruminations," *Journal of Applied Psychology* 71 (1986): 645–53.

20. *BNA Policy and Practice Series—Personnel Management,* 1988, 201:254. See also Craig Zwerling and James Ryan, "Preemployment Drug Screening," *Journal of Occupational Medicine* 34, no. 6 (June 1992): 595.

21. Stephen J. Vodanovich and Milano Reyna, "Alternatives to Workplace Testing," *Personnel Administrator* 33, no. 5 (May 1988): 78–84; Judy D. Olian, "AIDS Testing for Employment Purposes? Facts and Controversies," *Journal of Business and Psychology* 3, no. 2 (Winter 1988): 135–53; Eric Rolfe Greenberg, "Workplace Testing: Who's Testing Whom?" *Personnel* 66, no. 5 (May 1989): 39–45.

22. David Warner, "Rules on Medical Tests for New Hires," *Nation's Business* 79 (August 1991): 29–31. See also Jonathan A. Segal, "Pre-employment Physicals under the ADA," *HR Magazine* 37 (October 1992): 103–7.

23. Zwerling and Ryan, "Preemployment Drug Screening," 595; Greenberg, "Workplace Testing," 39–45.

24. Eric Rolfe Greenberg, "Workplace Testing: The 1990 AMA Survey, Part 1," *Personnel* (June 1990): 43–51. See also *Resource* (Alexandria, VA: American Society for Personnel Administration, June 1988), 2.

25. Todd J. Maurer and Ralph A. Alexander, "Methods of Improving Employment Test Critical Scores Derived by Judging Test Content: A Review and Critique," *Personnel Psychology* 45 (Winter 1992): 727–62.

26. For books with comprehensive coverage of testing, including employment testing, see Anne Anastasi, *Psychological Testing,* 5th ed. (New York: Macmillan, 1982); Lee J. Cronbach, *Essentials of Psychological Testing,* 4th ed. (New York: Harper & Row, 1984).

27. Standards that testing programs should meet are described in *Standards for Educational and Psychological Tests* (Washington, D.C.: American Psychological Association, 1985). HR managers who want to examine paper-and-pencil tests can obtain specimen sets that include a test manual, a copy of the test, an answer sheet, and a scoring key. The test manual provides the essential information about the construction of the test; its recommended use; and instructions for administering, scoring, and interpreting the test. Test users should not rely

entirely on the material furnished by the test author and publisher. Since 1934 a major source of consumer information about commercially available tests—the *Mental Measurements Yearbook* (MMY)—has been available in most libraries. Published periodically, the MMY contains descriptive information plus critical reviews by experts in the various types of tests. The reviews are useful in evaluating a particular test for tryout in employment situations. Other sources of information about tests include *Test Critiques,* a set of volumes containing professional reviews of tests, and *Tests: A Comprehensive Reference for Assessments in Psychology, Education, and Business.* The latter describes more than 3,100 tests published in the English language. Another source, *Principles for the Validation and Use of Personnel Selection Procedures,* published by the Society for Industrial and Organizational Psychology, is a valuable guide for employers who use tests. Other publications are available that present detailed information on how to avoid discrimination and achieve fairness in testing.

28. F. L. Schmidt and J. E. Hunter, "Tacit Knowledge, Practical Intelligence, General *Mental Ability,* and *Job Knowledge," Current Directions in Psychological Science* 2, no. 1 (1993): 3–13. See also Bruce J. Avolio and David A. Waldman, "An Examination of Age and Cognitive Test Performance across Job Complexity and Occupational Types," *Journal of Applied Psychology* 75 (February 1990): 43–50. See also Linda S. Gottredson, ed., "The g Factor in Employment," *Journal of Vocational Behavior* 29 (1986): 293–450; Hunter and Hunter, "Validity and Utility," 72–98.

29. Schmitt, Gooding, Noe, and Kirsch, "Meta-Analysis of Validity Studies," 407–22. See also M. R. Barrick and M. K. Mount, "The Big Five Personality Dimensions and Job Performance: A Meta-Analysis," *Personnel Psychology* 44 (1991): 1–26.

30. V. J. Bentz, "The Sears Experience in the Investigation, Description, and Prediction of Executive Behavior," in J. A. Myers, Jr., ed., *Predicting Managerial Success* (Ann Arbor, Mich.: Foundation for Research on Human Behavior, 1968). See also V. J. Bentz, "Executive Selection at Sears: An Update," paper presented at the Fourth Annual Conference of Frontiers of Industrial Psychology, Virginia Polytechnic Institute, Blacksburg, Va: (August 1983).

31. J. Hogan, "The Structure of Physical Performance," *Journal of Applied Psychology* 76 (1991): 495–507. See also Richard D. Arvey, Timothy E. Landon, and Steven M. Nutting, "Development of Physical Ability Tests for Police Officers: A Construct Validation Approach," *Journal of Applied Psychology* 77 (December 1992): 996–1009; J. Hogan, "Physical

Abilities," in M. D. Dunnette and L. M. Hough, eds., *Handbook of Industrial and Organizational Psychology* (Palo Alto, Calif.: Consulting Psychologists Press, 1991).

32. Arvey, Nutting, and Landon, "Validation Strategies," 301–12.

33. It is interesting to note that the origins of the civil service system go back to 2200 B.C., when the Chinese emperor examined officials every three years to determine their fitness for continuing in office. In 1115 B.C. candidates for government posts were examined for their proficiency in music, archery, horsemanship, writing, arithmetic, and the rites and ceremonies of public and private life. See Philip H. DuBois, *A History of Psychological Testing* (Boston: Allyn & Bacon, 1970), Chapter 1.

34. Jerry W. Hedge and Mark S. Teachout, "An Interview Approach to Work Sample Criterion Measurement," *Journal of Applied Psychology* 44 (August 1992): 453–61. See also Wayne F. Cascio and Niel F. Phillips, "Performance Testing: A Rose among Thorns?" *Personnel Psychology* 32, no. 4 (Winter 1979): 751–66.

35. Robert L. Dipboye, *Selection Interviews: Process Perspectives* (Cincinnati: South-Western Publishing, 1992).

36. Michael M. Harris, "Reconsidering the Employment Interview: A Review of Recent Literature and Suggestions for Future Research," *Personnel Psychology* 42 (Winter 1989): 691–726. See also Willi H. Wiesner and Steven F. Cronshaw, "A Meta-Analytic Investigation of the Impact of Interview Format and Degree of Structure on the Validity of the Employment Interview," *Journal of Occupational Psychology* 61 (December 1988): 275–90; Robert W. Eder and Gerald R. Ferris, eds., *The Employment Interview—Theory, Research, and Practice* (Newbury Park, Calif.: Sage Publications, 1989).

37. A. I. Huffert and D. J. Woehr, "A Conceptual Analysis of Interview Structure and the Effects of Structure on the Interview Process," paper presented at the annual meeting of the Society for Industrial and Organizational Psychology (Montreal, 1992). See also Patrick M. Wright, Philip A. Lichtenfels, and Elliot D. Pursell, "The Structured Interview: Additional Studies and a Meta-Analysis," *Journal of Occupational Psychology* 62 (September 1989): 191–99; Elliott D. Pursell, Michael A. Campion, and Sarah R. Gaylord, "Structured Interviewing: Avoiding Selection Problems," *Personnel Journal* 59, no. 11 (November 1980): 907–12.

38. T. R. Lin, G. H. Dobbins, and J. L. Fahr, "A Field Study of Race and Age Similarity Effects on Interview Ratings in Conventional and Situational Interviews," *Journal of Applied Psychology* 77, no. 3 (1992): 367–71; see also Ivan T. Robertson, Lynda

Gratton, and Usharani Rout, "The Validity of Situational Interviews for Administrative Jobs," *Journal of Organizational Behavior* 11 (January 1990): 69–76. See also Gerald T. Gabris and Steven M. Rock, "Situational Interviews and Job Performance: The Results in One Public Agency," *Public Personnel Management* 20 (Winter 1991): 469–83; Thung-Rung Lin, G. H. Dobbins, and Jiing-Lih Farh, "A Field Study of Race and Age Similarity Effects on Interview Ratings in Conventional and Situational Interviews," *Journal of Applied Psychology* 77 (June 1992): 363–71.

39. Philip L. Roth and James E. Campion, "An Analysis of the Predictive Power of the Panel Interview and Pre-Employment Tests," *Journal of Occupational and Organizational Psychology* 65 (March 1992): 51–60. See also David J. Weston and Dennis L. Warmke, "Dispelling the Myths about Panel Interviews," *Personnel Administrator* 33, no. 5 (May 1988): 109–11.

40. Peter C. Sawyers, "Structured Interviewing: Your Key to the Best Hires," *Personnel Journal,* Special Supplement (December 1992). See also Bob Smith, "Pinkerton Keeps Its Eye on Recruitment," *HR Focus* (September 1993): 1, 8; Elizabeth Daniele, "PC-Based Screening Passes the Test at Cigna," *Insurance & Technology* 17 (January 1992): 15, 18; Mitchell Brooks and Pat Engler-Parish, "The Computer—A Valuable Addition to the Recruiting Process," *Insurance Sales* 133 (May 1990): 28–29.

41. Brooks Mitchell, "Interviewing Face-to-Interface," *Personnel* (January 1990): 23–25.

42. C. L. Martin and D.H. Nagao, "Some Effects of Computerized Interviewing on Job Applicant Responses," *Journal of Applied Psychology* 74 (1989): 72–80.

43. The student who desires to study a comprehensive evaluation of research as it relates to the employment interview may wish to consult Eder and Ferris, *The Employment Interview.* A book designed for executives that contains many helpful suggestions is Auren Uris, 88 *Mistakes Interviewers Make and How to Avoid Them* (New York: AMACOM, 1988).

44. E. C. Mayfield, "The Selection Interview—A Reevaluation of Published Research," *Personnel Psychology* 17, no. 3 (Autumn 1964): 239–60; Lynn Ulrich and Don Trumbo, "The Selection Interview since 1949," *Psychological Bulletin* 63, no. 2 (February 1965): 100–16; Orman R. Wright, Jr., "Summary of Research on the Selection Interview since 1964," *Personnel Psychology* 22, no. 4 (Winter 1969): 391–414; Neal Schmitt, "Social and Situational Determinants of Interview Decisions: Implication for the Employment Interview," *Personnel Psychology* 29, no. 1 (Spring 1976): 79–101; Richard D. Arvey and James E. Campion, "The Employment Interview: A Summary and Review of Recent Literature," *Personnel Psychology* 35, no. 2 (Summer 1982): 281–322; Michael M. Harris, "Reconsidering the Employment Interview: A Review of Recent Literature and Suggestions for Future Research," 691–726.

45. These two factors are emphasized in a system developed by Robert N. McMurry, *Tested Techniques of Personnel Selection,* rev. ed. (Chicago: Dartnell, n.d.). The system includes a summary sheet for rating the applicant on "can-do" and "will-do" factors and for summarizing the ratings.

46. Multiple regression is a statistical method for evaluating the magnitude of effects of more than one independent variable (e.g., selection predictors) on a dependent variable (e.g., job performance) using principles of correlation and regression. See W. P. Vogt, *Dictionary of Statistics and Methodology* (Newbury Park, Calif.: Sage Publications, 1993): 146; F. N. Kerlinger, *Foundations of Behavioral Research,* 3d ed. (Fort Worth, Tex.: Holt, Rinehart and Winston, 1986): 527.

47. P. E. Meehl, *Clinical v. Statistical Prediction* (Minneapolis: University of Minnesota Press, 1954); J. Sawyer, "Measurement and Prediction, Clinical and Statistical," *Psychological Bulletin* 66, no. 3 (September 1966): 178–200.

48. R. R. Reilly and W. R. Manese, "The Validation of a Minicourse for Telephone Company Switching Technicians," *Journal of Applied Psychology* 32 (1979): 83–90.

49. Wayne F. Cascio, *Applied Psychology in Personnel Management,* 4th ed. (Englewood Cliffs, N.J.: Prentice-Hall, 1991). In addition to Cascio's book, the statistically oriented reader may wish to consult George F. Dreher and Paul R. Sackett, *Perspectives on Employee Staffing and Selection* (Homewood, Ill.: Richard D. Irwin, 1983).

Part 3

Developing Effectiveness in Human Resources

Part 3 contains three chapters that deal with the training and development of employees. Chapter 7 discusses the process by which an organization plans for its training activities, and it describes the many available nonmanagerial and managerial training programs to improve employees' skills and abilities. Chapter 8 looks at career development and explains how individuals can implement their own career development program. Chapter 9 provides a comprehensive review of the employee performance appraisal process, offering several suggestions for carrying out a successful employee appraisal interview. Employees perform more effectively when they receive the proper training for their jobs and their work performance is evaluated in an objective and honest manner.

Chapter

Training

After studying this chapter you should be able to

List some of the characteristics of an effective orientation program.

Describe the scope of organizational training programs.

Identify and describe the four phases of the systems approach to training.

Identify the types of training methods used primarily with nonmanagerial personnel.

List the different types of training methods for developing managers and supervisors.

Describe the special training programs that are currently popular.

Identify the preconditions for and the basic principles of learning.

Human resources training has become increasingly vital to the success of modern organizations. Rapidly changing technology requires that employees possess the knowledge, skills, and abilities (KSAs) needed to cope with new processes and production techniques. The growth of organizations into large, complex operations whose structures are continually changing makes it necessary for managers, as well as employees, to develop the KSAs that will enable them to handle new and more demanding assignments.

There are many forces that determine the types of training required in an organization. Automation and computerization will continue to have a major impact. Economic, social, and political forces likewise have implications for training programs.

Based on data from a survey of 17,150 organizations with at least 100 employees conducted by Lakewood Research for Training magazine, the total dollars budgeted for formal training in 1994 was $50.6 billion. Over 47 million individuals received some formal training from their employers in that year, totaling 1.4 billion hours. In addition to formal training there is a vast amount of informal training that goes on every day in organizations everywhere. Training experts estimate that approximately $180 billion a year is spent on informal instruction. Training and development dollars are invested in a variety of programs, ranging from new employee orientation to executive development.[1]

There has been a definite trend for organizations to create career development programs. We will give special attention to these programs in the next chapter. In this chapter the emphasis will be on the orientation of employees, the scope of training programs, a systems approach to training, training methods, new programs, and the application of learning theory.

Orientation

Orientation

Formal process of familiarizing new employees with the organization, their job, and their work unit

The first step in the training process is to get new employees off to a good start. This is generally accomplished through a formal orientation program. **Orientation** is the *formal* process of familiarizing new employees with the organization, their job, and their work unit. Its purpose is to enable new employees to get "in sync" so that they quickly become productive members of the organization.

objective

Benefits of Orientation

In some organizations a formal new-hire orientation program is almost nonexistent or, when it does exist, it is performed in a casual manner. This is unfortunate, since there are a number of very practical and cost-effective benefits from conducting a well-run program. Some of the benefits frequently reported by employers include the following:

1. Lower turnover
2. Increased productivity
3. Improved employee morale
4. Lower recruiting and training costs
5. Facilitation of learning
6. Reduction of the new employee's anxiety

The more time and effort spent in helping new employees feel welcome, the more likely they are to identify with the organization and become valuable members of it. Unlike training, which emphasizes the *what* and *how*, orientation stresses the *why*. It is designed to develop in employees a particular attitude about the work they will be doing and their role in the organization. It defines the philosophy behind the organization's rules and provides a framework for job-related tasks.

A Continuous Process

Since an organization is faced with ever-changing conditions, its plans, policies, and procedures must change with these conditions. Unless current employees are kept up to date with these changes, they may find themselves embarrassingly unaware of activities with which new employees are being oriented. While the discussion that follows focuses primarily on the needs of new employees, it is important that *all* employees be continually reoriented to changing conditions.

A Cooperative Endeavor

For a well-integrated orientation program, cooperation between line and staff is essential. The HR department ordinarily is responsible for coordinating orientation activities and for providing new employees with information about conditions of employment, pay, benefits, and other areas not directly under a supervisor's direction. However, the supervisor has the most important role in the orientation program. New employees are interested primarily in what the supervisor says and does and what their new co-workers are like. Before the arrival of a new employee, the supervisor should inform the work group that a new worker is joining the unit. It is also common practice for supervisors or other managerial personnel to recruit co-workers to serve as volunteer "sponsors" for incoming employees. In addition to providing practical help to newcomers, this approach conveys an emphasis on teamwork.

Careful Planning

An orientation program can make an immediate and lasting impression on an employee that can mean the difference between the employee's success and failure on the job. Thus careful planning—with emphasis on program goals, topics to be covered, and methods of organizing and presenting them—is essential. Successful programs emphasize the individual's needs for information, understanding, and a feeling of belonging.

To avoid overlooking items that are important to employees, many organizations devise checklists for use by those responsible for conducting the orientation. Highlights in HRM 1 suggests items to include in a supervisor's orientation checklist. Orientation should focus on matters of immediate concern such as important aspects of the job and organizational behavior rules—for example, attendance and safety.

In orientation sessions new employees are often given a packet of materials to read at their leisure. Some of the materials such a packet might include are listed in Highlights in HRM 2. Because statements regarding such matters as tenure, basis for dismissal, and benefits may be viewed by employees and the courts as legally binding on the employer, it is advisable to have the legal department review the packet and write disclaimers to the effect that the materials do not constitute an employment contract. (See Chapter 16.)

HIGHLIGHTS IN HRM

1   A MANAGER'S ORIENTATION CHECKLIST

1. A formal greeting, including introduction to fellow employees
2. Explanation of job procedures, duties, and responsibilities
3. Training to be received
4. Manager and organization expectations regarding attendance, personal conduct, and appearance
5. Job standards and production/service levels
6. Performance appraisal criteria
7. Conditions of employment, including hours of work, pay periods, and overtime requirements
8. Organization and work unit rules, regulations, and policies
9. Safety regulations
10. Those to notify or turn to if problems or questions arise
11. Chain of command for reporting purposes
12. An overall explanation of the organization's operation and purpose
13. Offers of help and encouragement

Those planning an orientation program should take into account the anxiety employees feel during their first few days on the job. It is natural to experience some anxiety, but if employees are too anxious, training costs, turnover, absenteeism, and even production costs may increase. Early in the orientation program steps should be taken to reduce the anxiety level of new employees.

Some employers think it does no harm to allow new employees to be oriented by their peers. One danger of failing to ensure that new workers are oriented by their supervisors and not their peers is that unsafe work practices and unacceptable behaviors that conflict with the organization's policies can be perpetuated. The behaviors these employees develop can undermine the organization's policies and procedures.[2]

Follow-up and Evaluation

Supervisors should always consult with their new employees after the first day and frequently throughout the first week on the job. When all of the items on the orientation checklist for the employee have been addressed, both the supervisor and the employee should sign it, and the record should then be placed in the employee's personnel file to document what has been covered. After the employee has been on the job for a month, and again after a year, management

2   ITEMS FOR AN ORIENTATION PACKET

1. Copy of specific job goals and descriptions
2. Copies of performance appraisal forms, dates of appraisals, and appraisal procedures
3. List of on-the-job training opportunities
4. Detailed outline of emergency and accident-prevention procedures
5. Copy of policy handbook
6. Telephone numbers and locations of key personnel and operations
7. Current organization chart
8. Map of the facility
9. List of key terms unique to the industry, company, and/or job
10. Copy of union contract
11. List of holidays
12. List of employee benefits
13. Copies of other required forms (e.g., supply requisition and expense reimbursement)
14. Sources of information
15. Copy of each important organization publication
16. Copies of insurance plans

Source: Adapted from Walter D. St. John, "The Complete Employee Orientation Program," *Personnel Journal* (May 1990). Reprinted with permission

should follow up to determine how effective the orientation has been. Evaluations can then be conducted through in-depth interviews, questionnaires and surveys, and discussion groups.

objective

The Scope of Training

Many new employees come equipped with most of the KSAs needed to start work. Others may require extensive training before they are ready to make much of a contribution to the organization. A majority, however, will require some type of training at one time or another to maintain an effective level of job performance.

Training can be defined as any procedure initiated by an organization to foster learning among its members. The primary purpose of a training program is to help the organization achieve its overall objectives. At the same time, an effective training program should help trainees to satisfy their own personal goals.

The primary reason that organizations train new employees is to bring their KSAs up to the level required for satisfactory performance. As they continue on the job, additional training provides opportunities for them to acquire new knowledge and skills. As a result of the training, employees may be even more effective on the job and may qualify for jobs at a higher level.

A survey of a large number of organizations reveals that the content of training programs varies widely. Figure 7–1 illustrates the diversity of subjects covered, the percentage of organizations providing different types of training, and the place where that training occurs.

FIGURE 7-1 General Types of Training

TYPES OF TRAINING	% PROVIDING[1]	IN-HOUSE ONLY (%)[2]	OUTSIDE ONLY (%)[3]	BOTH (%)[4]
Management skills/development	91	12	18	61
Basic computer skills	90	21	14	55
Communication skills	87	21	12	53
Supervisory skills	86	18	12	56
Technical skills/knowledge	82	22	6	54
New methods/procedures	80	38	5	37
Executive development	77	8	26	44
Customer relations/services	76	25	9	41
Personal growth	73	14	15	45
Clerical/secretarial skills	73	23	18	32
Employee/labor relations	67	23	12	31
Customer education	65	28	5	31
Wellness	63	21	15	28
Sales skills	56	15	11	30
Remedial/basic education	48	11	21	15

Of all organizations with 100 or more employees . . .
[1]Percent that provide each type of training
[2]Percent that say all training of this type is designed and delivered by in-house staff
[3]Percent that say all training of this type is designed and delivered by outside consultants or suppliers
[4]Percent that say training of this type is designed and delivered by a combination of in-house staff and outside suppliers

Source: Reprinted with permission from the October 1993 issue of *Training*. Copyright 1993. Lakewood Publications, Minneapolis, Minn. All rights reserved. Not for resale.

As noted earlier, there are many forces that determine the types of training required in an organization. A Work in America Institute study identifies these forces as follows:

1. Increased global and domestic competition is leading to a greater need for competitive strategies, which often include training as an essential element.
2. Rapid advances in technology have created an acute need for people with specialized technical skills.
3. Widespread mergers, acquisitions, and divestitures, which realign corporate structures but do not necessarily give people the ability to carry out their new responsibilities, require long-term training plans.
4. A better-educated workforce, which values self-development and personal growth, has brought an enormous desire for learning plus a growing need for new forms of participation at work.
5. The obsolescence of some occupations and the emergence of new occupations resulting from the changing nature of the economy; the shift from manufacturing to service industries; and the impact of research, development, and technology require flexible training policies to prevent increased turnover and lower productivity.[3]

In order to have personnel who have the KSAs required for effective organizational performance, training programs are typically organized for two major groups: nonmanagerial personnel and managerial and supervisory personnel. Training for these two major groups and special types of training programs will be discussed after we study the systems approach to training.

objective

A System Approach to Training

Since the primary goal of training is to contribute to the organization's overall goals, training programs should be developed with an eye to organizational strategy. Part of the organization's strategy must include recognition of the growing pressure from government and society to attend to the needs of workers who have been displaced by structural shifts in the economy, geographical relocation of jobs, international competition, technological changes, and industry deregulation. Ford Motor Company and General Motors even train their displaced workers who must seek jobs at other organizations.

The problem with some training programs is that one method or gimmick can sometimes become the main focus of the program. The objectives may be hazy, or evaluation may be inadequate. Too frequently the popularity of a program as indicated by the satisfaction of the participants has been used as the sole basis for judging the program's value in meeting the organizational objectives. A recommended solution to these programs is the use of a systems approach to training that involves a four-step sequence: (1) formulate instructional objectives, (2) develop learning experiences to achieve these objectives, (3) establish performance criteria, and (4) gather information to use in evaluating training programs. A model that is useful to designers of training programs is presented in Figure 7–2. Note that the model consists of four phases: needs assessment, training and development, evaluation, and training goals.

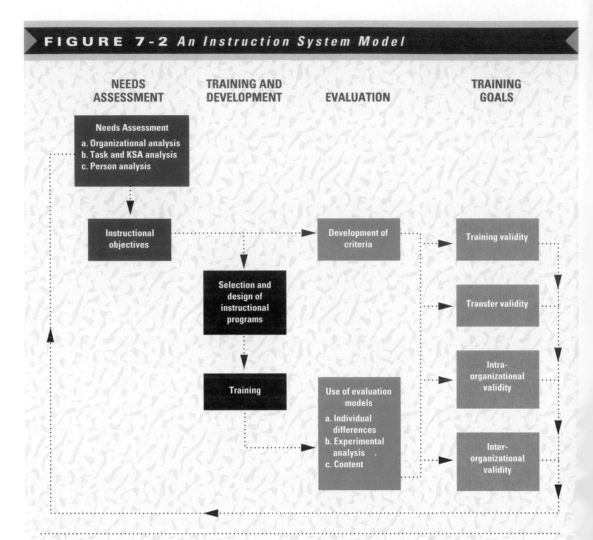

FIGURE 7-2 *An Instruction System Model*

Source: From I. L. Goldstein, *Training in Organizations: Needs Assessment, Development, and Evaluation,* 3d ed. (Pacific Grove, Calif.: Brooks/Cole Publishing, 1986), 21. Copyright 1993 by Wadsworth, Inc. Reprinted by permission of Brooks/Cole Publishing Company.

Needs Assessment Phase

Managers and HR staffs should be alert to indications of what kind of training is needed and where it is needed. The failure of workers to meet production quotas, for example, might signal a need for training. Likewise, an excessive number of rejects or a waste of material might suggest inadequate training. Managers should be careful to approach training needs systematically, however. Three different analyses are recommended for use in the needs assessment phase: organizational analysis, task analysis, and person analysis.

Organizational analysis

Examination of the goals, resources, and environment of the organization to determine where training emphasis should be placed

Organizational analysis is an examination of the goals, resources, and environment of the organization to determine where training emphasis should be placed. The resources—technological, financial, and human—that are available to meet objectives also must be considered.

HR policies and organizational climate have an impact on the goals of the training program. Similarly, external factors, such as public policy as reflected in laws, regulations, and court decisions, also influence where the training emphasis will be placed. Training programs in handling sexual harassment recently adopted by such organizations as Zenith, Smith and Barney, and the City of Minneapolis illustrate this point.

Organizations typically collect data to use in the analysis, such as information on direct and indirect labor costs, quality of goods or services, absenteeism, turnover, and number of accidents. The availability of potential replacements and the time required to train them are other important factors in organizational analysis. In recent years organizational analysis has given attention to those factors that determine whether a training program takes place in an environment that allows for behavior change back on the job.[4]

Task analysis

Process of determining what the content of a training program should be on the basis of a study of the tasks or duties involved in the job

Designing a specific training program requires an organization to review the job description that indicates the activities performed in a particular job and the conditions under which they are performed. This review is followed by a **task analysis,** which involves determining what the content of the training program should be, on the basis of a study of the tasks or duties involved in the job. Task analysis appears to be shifting from an emphasis on what is currently required to what will be required in the future for an employee to be effective in a particular job.

The first step in task analysis is to list all the tasks or duties included in the job. The second step is to list the steps performed by the employee to complete each task. Once the job is understood thoroughly, the type of performance required (e.g., speech, recall, discrimination, manipulation), along with the skills and knowledge necessary for job performance, can be defined. For example, in the task of taking a chest X-ray, a radiologist correctly positions the patient

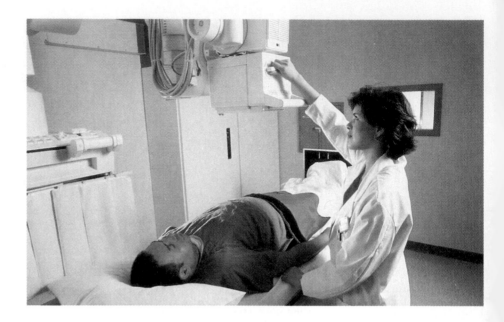

Correctly positioning the X-ray machine above a patient shows just one aspect to a radiologist's job description.

(manipulation), gives special instructions (speech), and checks the proper distance of the X-ray tube from the patient (discrimination).

The types of performance skills and knowledge that trainees need can be determined by observing and questioning skilled jobholders and/or by reviewing job descriptions. This information helps trainers to select program content and choose the most effective training method.

Once the organizational and task analyses have been made, it is necessary to perform a person analysis. **Person analysis** involves determining whether task performance by individual employees is acceptable and studying the characteristics of individuals and groups who will be placed in the training environment. It is important to determine what prospective trainees can and cannot do so that the training program can be designed to emphasize the areas in which they are deficient.

Person analysis
Determination of the specific skills, knowledge, and attitudes required of people on the job

After all the analyses have been made, a picture of the training needs emerges. The desired outcomes of training programs should then be stated formally in instructional objectives. Generally, **instructional objectives** involve the acquisition of skills or knowledge or the changing of attitudes. Robert Mager, an internationally known training expert, emphasizes the importance of instructional objectives by noting that "before you prepare for instruction, before you select instructional procedures or subject matter or material, it is important to be able to state clearly just what you intend the results of that instruction to be. A clear statement of instructional objectives will provide a sound basis for choosing methods and materials and for selecting the means for assessing whether the instruction will be successful."[5]

Instructional objectives
Desired outcomes of a training program

One type of instructional objective, the performance-centered objective, is widely used because it lends itself to an unbiased evaluation of results. For example, the stated objective for one training program might be that "Employee trained in team methods will be able to perform these different jobs within six months." Performance-centered objectives typically include precise terms, such as "to calculate," "to repair," "to adjust," "to construct," "to assemble," and "to classify."

Training and Development Phase

Once the training needs have been determined and the instructional objectives specified, the next step is to develop the type of environment necessary to achieve these objectives. This includes formulating a specific training strategy and preparing instructional plans. A major consideration in creating a training environment is choosing a method that will enable the trainee to learn most effectively. The methods commonly used in training personnel at all levels—managerial, supervisory, and nonmanagerial—will be discussed later in the chapter.

Evaluation Phase

Training, like any other HRM function, should be evaluated to determine its effectiveness. Unfortunately, however, few organizations have adequate systems to evaluate the effectiveness of their training programs.

While evaluation methods are improving, too many conclusions about training effectiveness are still based on the subjective reactions of trainers and trainees. It is easy to collect glowing comments from trainees, but this information, however gratifying to management, may not be very useful to the organization. Training is not provided for its entertainment value. The real issue is whether the training effort will translate to improved behavior and job performance.

Not only should trainees be tested before and after training, but the same evaluations should also be made of individuals in a control group. The control group contains employees who have not received the training but who match the trainees in such areas as experience, past training, and job level. Some of the criteria used in evaluating the effectiveness of training are increased productivity, fewer employee complaints, decreased costs and waste, and similar evidence of improved performance.

An evaluation should be undertaken to provide data for a specific decision, such as whether or not to adopt or continue a training course or how to improve the course. This latter question was addressed by a large midwestern police force as it evaluated a training program for police officer recruits. The objectives of this evaluation were (1) to determine the extent to which the training content was job-related and (2) to identify what changes in training content were needed to improve job relatedness.[6] Planning the evaluation around specific objectives increases the likelihood that findings will produce meaningful changes. Training directors often limit themselves by not being able to prove their effectiveness objectively in terms of the specific benefits of training to the organization and the costs of obtaining those benefits.

According to an American Society of Training and Development (ASTD) study, approximately two-thirds of training managers surveyed reported that they were coming under additional pressure to show that their programs produce "bottom-line" results.[7]

Meeting Training Goals

To help determine the effectiveness of training, the evaluation phase must address the worth of the training program. As the last column of Figure 7–2 shows, a number of goals are possible. The choice of which goal to pursue depends on the information one seeks and the constraints under which one operates. Irwin Goldstein describes the four choices as follows:

1. *Training validity:* whether the trainees learn during training
2. *Transfer validity:* whether what has been learned in training translates to enhanced performance in the organization
3. *Intraorganizational validity:* whether the performance of a new group of trainees in the organization that developed the training program is consistent with the performance of the original training group in the same organization
4. *Interorganizational validity:* whether a training program found effective in one organization can be used successfully in another organization[8]

Benchmarking

In recent years there has been an increased interest in benchmarking human resources developmental activities. **Benchmarking** is the continuous process of comparing one's own services and practices against those recognized leaders in a particular area such as HR development. While there are shortcomings in the benchmarking process, experts in this area are attempting to work out ways of measuring what training departments do. Three broad areas that most HR training and developmental practitioners consider essential are:

1. Measures of training activity (How much training is occurring?)
2. Measures of training results (How well do training and development achieve their goals?)
3. Measures of training efficiency (To what extent are resources utilized in the pursuit of this mission?)

Several companies have come together under the auspices of the ASTD and its Institute for Workplace Learning. The project provides a way for the companies to measure and benchmark against each other their practices in the area of training and development. This consortium plans to publish averaged data periodically in the journal *Training and Development*.[9]

Benchmarking
Process of measuring one's own services and practices against the recognized leaders in order to identify areas for improvement

Training Nonmanagerial Employees

four objective

A wide variety of methods is available for training personnel at all levels. Some of the methods have a long history of usage. Newer methods have emerged over the years out of a greater understanding of human behavior, particularly in the areas of learning, motivation, and interpersonal relationships. More recently technological advances, especially in electronics, have resulted in training devices that in many instances are more effective and economical than traditional training methods.

On-the-Job Training

On-the-job training (OJT) is one of the most common methods of training non-managerial employees. OJT has the advantage of providing hands-on experience under normal working conditions and an opportunity for the trainer—a manager or senior employee—to build good relationships with new employees.

Although it is used by all types of organizations, OJT is often one of the most poorly implemented training methods. Three common drawbacks include (1) the lack of a well-structured training environment, (2) poor training skills of managers, and (3) the absence of well-defined job performance criteria. To overcome these problems, training experts suggest the following:

1. Develop realistic goals and/or measures for each OJT area.
2. Plan a specific training schedule for each trainee, including set periods for evaluation and feedback.
3. Help managers to establish a nonthreatening atmosphere that is conducive to learning.
4. Conduct periodic evaluations, after training is completed, to prevent regression.[10]

Many successful trainers use a system known as Job Instruction Training (JIT) to acquaint managers with techniques in instructing their employees. (See Highlights in HRM 3.) While the principles of JIT were developed during World War II, the recommended training tips are clearly appropriate for today's organizations. The JIT card, or an adaptation of it, is used by many small business managers for instructing a new person on the job or a present worker on a new job.[11]

Off-the-Job Training

In addition to on-the-job training, it is usually necessary to provide employees with training in settings away from their ordinary workplace. Some methods involve training employees away from their usual locations but still within the organization's facilities. Other methods involve training employees in locations outside the organization.

Conference or Discussion

A method of individualized instruction frequently used where the training involves primarily the communication of ideas, procedures, and standards is the conference or discussion method. This method allows for considerable flexibility in the amount of employee participation.

Classroom Training

Classroom training enables the maximum number of trainees to be handled by the minimum number of instructors. This method lends itself particularly to training in areas where information and instructions can be presented in lectures, demonstrations, films, and videotapes, and through computer instruction. Where it is not possible to obtain videotapes, audiotapes can be very valuable. For example, to instruct flight-crew trainees, airlines might play a cockpit tape taken from a doomed aircraft. After listening to the tape, the trainees could discuss the behavior of the crew during the crisis. By listening to the recorded statements of others and observing their failure to operate as a team, pilot

HIGHLIGHTS IN HRM

3   THE JIT CARD

Practical methods to guide you in instructing a new employee on a job, or a present employee on a new job or a new skill

FIRST, here's what *you must* do to *get ready* to teach a job:

1. Decide what the employee must be taught in order to do the job efficiently, safely, economically and intelligently.
2. Have the right tools, equipment, supplies and material ready.
3. Have the work place properly arranged, just as the employee will be expected to keep it.

THEN, you should *instruct* the employee according to the following *four basic steps:*

STEP 1—PREPARATION (of the employee)

1. Put the employee at *ease.*
2. Find out what the employee already knows about the job.
3. Get the employee interested and desirous of learning the job.

STEP II—PRESENTATION (of the operations and knowledge)

1. *Tell, show, illustrate,* and *question* in order to put over the new knowledge and operations.
2. Instruct slowly, clearly, completely and patiently, one point at a time.
3. Check, question, and repeat.
4. Make sure the employee really knows.

STEP III—PERFORMANCE TRY-OUT

1. Test the employee by having him or her perform the job.
2. Ask questions beginning with *why, how, when* or *where.*
3. Observe performance, correct errors, and repeat instructions if necessary.
4. Continue until you *know the employee knows.*

STEP IV—FOLLOW-UP

1. Put the employee "on his or her own."
2. Check frequently to be sure the employee follows instructions.
3. Taper off extra supervision and close follow-up until the employee is qualified to work with normal supervision.

REMEMBER—If the employee hasn't learned, the manager hasn't taught.

Source: *The Training within Industry Report* (Washington, D.C.: Bureau of Training, Training within Industry Service, War Manpower Commission.

trainees will develop an understanding of the need for balancing their sense of self-reliance with an ability to listen to subordinates.[12]

A special type of classroom facility is used in *vestibule training*. Trainees are given instruction in the operation of equipment like that found in operating departments. The emphasis is on instruction rather than production.

Programmed Instruction

One method of instruction uses a book, manual, or computer to present programmed subject matter. Programmed instruction breaks down subject matter content into highly organized, logical sequences that demand continuous responses on the part of the trainee. After being presented with a small segment of information, the trainee is required to answer a question, either by writing it in a response frame or by pushing a button. If the response is correct, the trainee is told so and is presented with the next step (frame) in the material. If the response is incorrect, further explanatory information is given and the trainee is told to try again.

A major advantage of programmed instruction is that it incorporates a number of established learning principles, which we discuss later in the chapter. With programmed instruction, training is individualized, trainees are actively involved in the instructional process, and feedback and reinforcement are immediate.

Computer-based Training

As development of technology proceeds at a rapid pace and the cost of computers continues to decline, high-technology training methods are finding increasing use in industry, academia, and the military.[13]

Computer-based training (CBT) encompasses two distinct techniques: computer-assisted instruction and computer-managed instruction. A **computer-assisted instruction (CAI) system** delivers training material directly through a computer terminal in an interactive format. Computers make it possible to provide drill and practice, problem solving, simulation, gaming forms of instruction, and certain very sophisticated forms of individualized tutorial instruction.

A **computer-managed instruction (CMI) system** is normally used in conjunction with CAI, thereby providing an efficient means of managing the training function. CMI uses a computer to generate and score tests and to determine the level of trainee proficiency. CMI systems can also track the performance of trainees and direct them to appropriate study material to meet their specific needs. With CMI, the computer takes on some of the routine aspects of training, freeing the instructor to spend time on course development or individualized instruction.

CBT is being used more and more to train users of human resources information systems (HRIS),

Computer-assisted instruction (CAI)
System that delivers instructional material directly through a computer terminal in an interactive format

Computer-managed instruction (CMI)
System normally employed in conjunction with CAI that uses a computer to generate and score tests and to determine the level of training proficiency

This group of training instructors learns the procedures of an interactive tutorial.

HIGHLIGHTS IN HRM

highlights

4 ADVANTAGES OF COMPUTER-BASED TRAINING

1. Learning is self-paced.
2. Training comes to the employee.
3. All trainees get exactly the same training.
4. New employees do not have to wait for a scheduled training session.
5. Training can focus on specific needs as revealed by built-in tests.
6. Trainees can be referred to on-line help or written material.
7. It is easier to revise a computer program than to change classroom training materials.
8. Record keeping is facilitated.
9. The computer program can be linked to video presentations.

Source: Adapted from Ralph E. Ganger, "Computer-Based Training Improves Job Performance," *Personnel Journal* 68, no. 6 (June 1989): 116–23. Reproduced with permission.

Trainees begin with relatively simple tasks, such as entering a new employee's records in the personnel file, then proceed to more complex procedures as they master each task. The training data are often simulated, but the procedures are real. Some of the advantages of CBT are listed in Highlights in HRM 4.[14]

Simulation Method

Sometimes it is either impractical or unwise to train employees on the actual equipment that is used on the job. An obvious example is the training of personnel to operate aircraft, spacecraft, and other highly technical and expensive equipment. The simulation method emphasizes realism in equipment and its operation at minimum cost and maximum safety. For example, locomotive engineers can receive rigorous training through the use of a locomotive simulator. Employing advanced computer technology, the simulator can realistically depict train-track dynamics, provide taped train sounds and visuals, and duplicate a variety of operations.[15]

Use of Other Training Devices

To teach skills and procedures for many production jobs, certain training devices may be used. For example, devices that look like a portable TV use slides or videotape to illustrate the steps in the manufacture and assembly of electronic

Closed-circuit teletraining sessions save this staff the expense of travel.

and other components. Closed-circuit television and video recording equipment (such as camcorders) are also standard training devices. Closed-circuit television allows an instructional program to be transmitted to many locations simultaneously. The use of camcorders permits on-the-spot recording and immediate feedback to the trainees.

Two newer training techniques, the *videodisc* and *training by telephone* (or *teletraining*), incorporate positive learning principles while providing flexibility to organizational trainers. Interactive videodiscs, an extension of CBT, have an advantage over other programmed learning techniques in that they allow immediate access to any segment of the instructional program. This is especially useful for individualized instruction of employees with different levels of knowledge and ability. Videodiscs are currently used to teach doctors to diagnose illness, to help dairy farmers to increase productivity, and to teach CPR trainees in firefighting and other emergency services jobs to revive victims of heart attacks. More-recent applications tackle the difficult managerial skills of leadership, supervision, and interpersonal relations.

Teletraining is used by the Iowa Department of Social Services to provide orientation to new employees. The United Bank of Colorado presents monthly sales market training by telephone to thirty banks throughout the state. What are the benefits of teletraining? They include scheduling flexibility, reduced time and expense of staff travel, increased access to experts, and the ability to reach dispersed groups of trainees in remote locations.

Apprenticeship Training

Apprenticeship training
System of training in which a worker entering the skill trades is given thorough instruction and experience, both on and off the job, in the practical and theoretical aspects of the work

A system of training in which the employee entering industry is given thorough instruction and experience, both on and off the job, in the practical and theoretical aspects of the work in a skilled trade is known as **apprenticeship training.**

Apprenticeship programs are based on voluntary cooperation between management and labor, between industry and government, and between the organization and the school system. Although apprenticeship wages are less than those of fully qualified workers, this method does provide training with pay for individuals interested in qualifying for jobs such as machinist, laboratory technician, and electrician. U.S. Department of Labor regulations require apprenticeship-program operators to take affirmative action in recruiting and hiring women and to establish goals and timetables for doing so.

Cooperative Training, Internships, and Governmental Training

Cooperative training programs combine practical on-the-job experience with formal classes. The term "cooperative training" is also used in connection with high school and college programs that incorporate part- or full-time experiences. In recent years there has been an increased effort to expand opportunities that combine on-the-job skill training with regular classroom training so that students can pursue either technical work or a college degree program. Many organizations, including Fannie Mae, Burger King, Champion International, Pacific Telesis Foundation, Cray Research, and UNOM Life Insurance, have strong ties to public schools and invest millions of dollars in educational programs.[16] With the federal government playing a more active role in the development of a national apprenticeship program, individuals who are not planning to attend college will be able to receive training and certification in an occupation.[17]

Internship programs, jointly sponsored by colleges, universities, and a variety of organizations, offer students the chance to get real-world experience while finding out how they will perform in work organizations. Organizations benefit by getting student-employees with new ideas, energy, and eagerness to accomplish their assignments. Arizona State University and other universities allow students to earn college credits on the basis of successful job performance and fulfillment of established program requirements.

The federal government and various state governments sponsor a multitude of training programs for new and current employees. Frequently, these training efforts are aimed at the development of basic job skills for individuals lacking marketable skills.

The federal government's largest job-skills program is carried out under the provisions of the Job Training Partnership Act (JTPA). It operates on an annual budget of $4 billion and has aided thousands of employers such as Ross (Dress for Less) and the Marriott Corporation in funding local disadvantaged and disabled individuals who need job training assistance and who are likely to be qualified for jobs once they are trained. Its primary goal is to move the jobless into permanent, sustaining employment. Employers who are interested in participating in the JTPA program are advised to contact the local Private Industry Council (PIC). There are more than 600 PICs in the country that are responsible for administering the program. PICs are staffed by appointees of local elected officials and are the legal arms of the U.S. Department of Labor. Employers sign a contract with the PIC that stipulates how long the training will last, what the training consists of, and how much the company will receive in reimbursement. Ross

Cooperative training

Training program that combines practical on-the-job experience with formal educational classes

Internship programs

Programs jointly sponsored by colleges, universities, and other organizations that offer students the opportunity to gain real-life experience while allowing them to find out how they will perform in work organizations

reports that people recruited through PIC stay with the company about 50 percent longer than individuals recruited from the general market.[18]

five
objective

Training Managers and Supervisors

Training and development of managers is a multibillion-dollar business. In a survey of a representative sample of 611 companies, the percentage of companies that reported using this type of training was 93 percent for on-the-job training, 90 percent for external short courses, 80 percent for special projects or task forces, 57 percent for mentoring, 40 percent for job rotation, 31 percent for university residential programs, and 25 percent for executive MBA programs. Significant differences in training practices were found among various industries and between large and small companies.[19] Some of the training methods used for nonmanagerial personnel may also be used to train managers and supervisors.

On-the-Job Experiences

Management skills and abilities cannot be acquired just by listening and observing or by reading about them. They must be acquired through actual practice and experience in which there are opportunities to perform under pressure and to learn from mistakes. On-the-job experiences are used most commonly by organizations to develop executives. Such experiences should be well planned and supervised and should be meaningful and challenging to the participant. Methods of providing on-the-job experiences include the following:

1. *Coaching* involves a continuing flow of instructions, comments, and suggestions from the manager to the subordinate.
2. *Understudy assignment* grooms an individual to take over the manager's job by gaining experience in handling important functions of the job.
3. *Job rotation* provides, through a variety of work experiences, the broadened knowledge and understanding required to manage more effectively.
4. *Lateral transfer* involves horizontal movement through different departments along with upward movement in the organization.
5. *Project and committee assignments* provide an opportunity for the individual to become involved in the study of current organizational problems and in planning and decision-making activities.
6. *Staff meetings* enable participants to become more familiar with problems and events occurring outside their immediate area by exposing them to the ideas and thinking of other managers.
7. *Planned career progressions* (discussed in Chapter 8) utilize all these different methods to provide employees with the training and development necessary to progress through a series of jobs requiring higher and higher levels of knowledge and/or skills.
8. *Interactions with a mentor,* also discussed in Chapter 8, add a personal touch to an informal training process.

Although these methods are used most often to train managers for higher-level positions, they also provide valuable experiences for those who are being groomed for other types of positions in the organization.

Off-the-Job Experiences

While on-the-job experiences constitute the core of management training, certain methods of development away from the job can be used to supplement these experiences. Off-the-job experiences may be provided on either an individual or a group basis and may be taught by means of special programs or seminars. They may include time management, assertiveness training, strategic planning, employee appraisal, creative thinking, stress management, interpersonal skills, listening skills, and management of change.

Case Study

Particularly useful in classroom learning situations are case studies. These documented examples, which may have been developed from actual experiences within their organizations, can help managers to learn how to gather and interpret facts, to become conscious of the many variables on which a management decision may be based, and, in general, to improve their decision-making skills.

In-basket Training

In-basket technique

Training method in which trainees are given several documents, each describing some problem or situation the solution of which requires an immediate decision

A method used to simulate a problem situation is the **in-basket technique.** With this technique the participants are given several documents, each describing some problem or situation requiring an immediate response. They are thus forced to make decisions under the pressure of time and also to determine what priority to give each problem. In-basket exercises are a common instructional technique used in assessment centers, which are discussed in Chapter 8.

Leaderless Group Discussions

Leaderless group discussions

Assessment-center activities in which trainees are gathered in a conference setting to discuss an assigned topic, either with or without designated group roles

A popular assessment-center activity is **leaderless group discussions.** With this technique, trainees are gathered in a conference setting to discuss an assigned topic, either with or without designated group roles. The participants are given little or no instruction in how to approach the topic, nor are they told what decision to reach. Leaderless group trainees are evaluated on their initiative, leadership skills, and ability to work effectively in a group setting.

Management Games

Training experiences have been brought to life and made more interesting through the development of management games. Players are faced with the task of making a series of decisions affecting a hypothetical organization. The effects that every decision has on each area within the organization can be simulated with a computer that has been programmed for the game. A major advantage of this technique is the high degree of participation it requires.

Games are now widely used as a training method. Many of them have been designed for general use, and more recently the development of industry-specific games has increased, with the result that there are now simulations for a wide variety of industries.[20] More and more organizations are using simulations of organization dynamics as tools for change. General Electric, for example, uses a three-day simulation to wrap up its management development program. It is a customized computerized simulation that teaches managers to balance such variables as profit, cost, turnover, product schedules, and personnel changes.[21] Practitioners in the area of management training have come to realize that extensive preparation, planning, and debriefing are needed to realize the potential benefits of this method.

The game method does not always require a computer, however. Motorola has developed a game called "EEO: It's Your Job" to teach the basic principles of equal employment opportunity. Originally devised to fill Motorola's own affirmative action needs, it is now commercially available for use in training programs.[22] A game kit accommodates up to twenty-four players, divided into teams of four, at a single session. The players get caught up in the competitive spirit of a game and at the same time absorb and remember government regulations. They also become aware of how their own daily decisions affect their employer's compliance with these regulations. The game is reinforced with a slide presentation.

Role Playing

Role playing consists of assuming the attitudes and behavior—that is, playing the role—of others, often a supervisor and a subordinate who are involved in a personnel problem. Role playing can help participants improve their ability to understand and cope with the issues of those they deal with in their daily work. It should also help them to learn how to counsel others by helping them see situations from a different point of view. Role playing is used widely in training health care personnel to be sensitive to the concerns of patients. It is also used widely in training managers to handle employee issues relating to absenteeism, performance appraisal, and conflict situations.

Laboratory Training

Laboratory training, which typically involves interpersonal interactions in a group setting, has as its primary goal the development of greater sensitivity on the part of its participants, including self-insight and an awareness of group processes. It also provides the opportunity to improve human relations skills by helping managers and supervisors to better understand themselves and others. This is achieved by encouraging trainees to share their experiences, feelings, emotions, and perceptions with other trainees or fellow employees. The ability to participate constructively in team activities is another benefit of this technique.

One variant of laboratory training is *sensitivity training*. As the term would indicate, this training increases a person's awareness of his or her own behavior as it is seen by other training participants. Highly popular in the 1970s, sensitivity training came to be viewed as a form of brainwashing because of its often unwarranted intrusion into employees' personal lives. As the popularity of sensitivity training declined, a wide variety of "New Age" seminars and self-improvement courses emerged. However, a problem with these programs is that some individuals find that the content of the programs conflicts with their own personal moral, ethical, and religious beliefs. As a result, they resent being forced by their employer to participate. In February 1988 the EEOC issued a policy statement that referred specifically to such cases. The EEOC intends to treat religious objections to New Age programs according to the traditional guidelines of Title VII of the Civil Rights Act of 1964. In considering whether to offer such a program, an employer should examine the ethical and legal ramifications of the program.[23]

Behavior Modeling

Training programs designed simply to change managers' attitudes are no longer as useful as they might have been in the past. Managers now must be shown how to put their attitudes to work. One such approach is **behavior modeling,** or **interaction management,** which emphasizes the need to involve managerial trainees in handling real-life employee problems and to provide immediate feedback on their own performance. The main purpose of behavior modeling is to achieve behavioral change. There are four basic steps in behavior modeling:

1. Managerial trainees view films or videotapes in which a model manager is portrayed dealing with an employee in an effort to improve or maintain the employee's performance. The example shows specifically how to deal with the situation.
2. Trainees participate in extensive practice and rehearsal of the behaviors demonstrated by the models. The greatest percentage of training time is spent in these skill-practice sessions.
3. As the trainee's behavior increasingly resembles that of the model, the trainer and other trainees provide social reinforcers such as praise, approval, encouragement, and attention. Videotaping behavior rehearsals provides feedback and reinforcement.
4. Emphasis throughout the training period is placed on transferring the training to the job.[24]

Does behavior modeling work? Several controlled studies have demonstrated success in changing the behavior of managers as well as in increasing worker productivity. One study provided objective evidence that behavior modeling of marketing representatives actually resulted in increased sales.[25]

Behavior modeling (interaction management)
Approach that emphasizes the involvement of the supervisory trainees in handling real-life employee problems and receiving immediate feedback on their performance

objective

Special Training Programs

Within any large organization there are likely to be hundreds of jobs, each of which involves a variety of knowledge and skills. Thus training programs will encompass a wide range of content reflecting the particular demands of the jobs. In addition to providing training for specific jobs, many employers develop special training programs to meet special needs. Some of the areas that have been the subject of special training programs are basic education, team training, training for diversity, global training, and crisis prevention training.

Basic Education

We noted in Chapter 2 that it is estimated that from 20 million to 80 million American adults are functionally illiterate. Experts define an illiterate individual as one having a sixth-grade education or less. The U.S. Department of Education reports that illiteracy will grow in the workforce because each year 1 million teenagers leave school without elementary skills and another 1.3 million non-English-speaking persons arrive in the United States.[26] These figures have important implications for society at large and for organizations that must assimilate these individuals into the workforce.

More than half of the *Fortune* 500 companies report that they conduct remedial employee training at costs upward of $300 million each year. In a workplace increasingly dominated by technology, these basic skills have become essential occupational qualifications that have profound implications for product quality, customer service, internal efficiency, and workplace and environmental safety. While there are different possible approaches to the problem, the establishment of in-house basic skills programs has come increasingly into favor.[27]

To combat the problem of illiteracy, Polaroid and United Technologies Corporation have developed remedial training programs in math, English, and spelling. Standard Oil of Indiana hired a schoolteacher to give classes in grammar and spelling to newly hired secretaries, while RJR Nabisco offers employees at its Planters Peanuts factory in Suffolk, Virginia, four hours a week of elementary school courses on company time. A further development is that community colleges have been actively working with industry to develop cooperative programs to fight illiteracy. All of these efforts are attempts by organizations to reduce losses in productivity resulting from the poor performance of illiterate employees—losses that in the United States alone annually run into the hundreds of millions of dollars.[28]

Team Training

As organizations rely more on the use of teams to attain organizational goals the need to enhance team effectiveness has increased. Whether it be an aircrew, a research team, or a manufacturing or service unit, the contributions of the individual members of the team are not only a function of the KSAs of each individual but the interaction of the team members. Teamwork behaviors that differentiate effective teams include effective communication, coordination, mutual performance monitoring, exchange of feedback, and adaptation to varying situational demands. The fact that these behaviors are observable and measurable provides a basis for training team members to function more effectively in the pursuit of their goals.[29]

In the last few years specialists in the development of training materials have devised simulation exercises to generate enthusiasm and enhance team participation. Pfeiffer and Company, for example, published a series of exercises by Daniel Tagliere with descriptive titles like "Hurricane Disaster," "Trapped Underground," "Lost at Sea," "Wilderness Survival," and "Hostage Rescue."[30] In "Hostage Rescue," participants play the part of a security task force assigned to help gain the release of the hostages. In order to arrive at the correct responses in this "life and death" scenario, participants must sharpen their decision-making skills and work together as an effective team. The role of teams will be discussed more fully in Chapter 14.

Training for Diversity

There has been a remarkable increase in diversity training programs in a wide range of organizations in the past few years. Diversity training is based upon an awareness of the changing demographics of the national workforce, the challenges of affirmative action, the dynamics of stereotyping, and workers' changing values. Diversity training is aimed at teaching such skills as conducting performance appraisals with people from different cultures and teaching male supervisors how to coach female employees toward better career opportunities. For any proposed program, a thorough needs analysis is the first step. All of the diverse dimensions—race, gender, age, and so on—should be considered in the design of such a program.[31]

The diversity development director for Monsanto Chemicals, Thomas W. Cummins, states that their program was designed to raise the awareness of white males. "I know how white males behave and how they communicate. I'm part of the reality that needs changing," he admits. "Our mission is to have a great place to work as a means of achieving our business objectives," says Cummins. "Improving work relations by removing barriers is now seen as strategic to that mission."[32]

Diversity training is especially important for police departments. The Sacramento, California, Police Department has staff members who familiarize officers with the cultures of California's 125 ethnic groups—and with the basics of cross-cultural communication.[33]

Organizations that have been successful with diversity training realize that it is a long-term process that requires the highest level of skill. Ineffective training in this area can be very damaging and create more problems than it solves. Unfortunately, many consulting firms have added diversity training to their list of programs without adequate personnel to handle the assignment. Rita Craig of Florida Power and Light warns, "The number of brochures I get from so-called experts in the diversity training field is frightening. This is a sensitive topic and a new field."[34]

Global Training

The global business environment demands employees who can work effectively across national and cultural boundaries. The extent to which organizations have gone international will determine the emphasis given to special training. United Airlines, for example, went from a domestic airline that offered just a few flights across the Pacific to a full-fledged airline serving approximately 200,000 people a day in eighteen countries.

United started a training program in July 1991 in the customer service division, which includes public-contact employees. Half of the training time is devoted to giving employees an overview of cultural differences as they relate to customer service. Before the training sessions, the scheduled participants complete a 200-page workbook that includes exercises on such topics as technical processing, geography, cargo, and cultural diversity.[35]

Another important aspect of global training is the training of executives. The major international corporations have special programs for the U.S. personnel who are assigned to overseas operations. These individuals, who are referred to as "expatriates," require training in several areas in order to perform their assignments successfully. The training program for the expatriates will be discussed in detail in Chapter 19.

Crisis Prevention Training

One has only to turn to the daily newspaper to find accounts of individuals being physically assaulted at work. For every assault there are many instances of potential violence that require appropriate intervention before the situation becomes worse. While it is essential that certain types of organizations provide training in crisis intervention (e.g., counseling centers and hospitals), an increasing number of employers have found it necessary to provide training in managing disruptive and assaultive behavior. Learning how to recognize warning signs and how to use verbal and nonverbal techniques to avoid a violent confrontation are important aspects of such training. The National Crisis Prevention Institute is one organization providing crisis prevention training as well as instructional materials that employers can use for in-house training. Among the employers providing training to designated employees are General Motors Regional Security, Holyoke Public Schools, General Mills, Gary Job Corps Center, Massachusetts Department of Youth Services, and Metro Toronto Libraries.[36]

Psychological Principles of Learning

The success of a training program depends on more than the organization's ability to identify training needs and the care with which it prepares the program. If the trainees do not learn what they are supposed to learn, the training has not been successful. However, training experts believe that if trainees do not learn, it is probably only because some important learning principle has been overlooked. Because the success or failure of a training program is frequently related to this simple fact, those who develop instructional programs should recognize that they need to attend to the basic psychological principles of learning. Managers as well should understand that the different methods or techniques used in training personnel vary in the extent to which they utilize these principles.

objective

Preconditions for Learning

Two preconditions for learning will affect the success of those who are to receive training: *readiness* and *motivation*. Trainee readiness refers to both maturity and experience factors in the trainee's background. Prospective trainees should be screened to determine that they have the background knowledge and the skills necessary to absorb what will be presented to them. Recognizing individual differences in readiness is as important in organizational training as it is in any other teaching situation. It is often desirable to group individuals according to their capacity to learn, as determined by test scores, and to provide an alternative type of instruction for those who need it.

The receptiveness and readiness of participants in workshops and similar training programs can be increased by having them complete questionnaires about why they are attending the workshop and what they want to accomplish.

5 TRAINING AND DEVELOPMENT PREPROGRAM WORKSHEET

_____   _____
              Program Title   Program Date

Instructions: Please review and complete the questions below with your supervisor, referencing the program objectives in the Training & Development Guide.

1. The following are work situations in which I want to improve my skills.

2. As a result of this program, I want to achieve the following:

3. Any other related information:

_____   _____   _____
   Signature of Participant   Signature of Supervisor   Date

Requirements for Program Attendance. To help ensure your learning and use of new skills:

BRING one copy of this form to the program.
GIVE one copy to your supervisor.
SEND one copy to Training & Development, *at least five days before the program.*

Source: Reprinted with permission of Analog Devices, Norwood, Mass.

Participants may also be asked to give copies of their completed questionnaires to their managers. Highlights in HRM 5 offers an example of a preprogram worksheet used by Analog Devices.

The other precondition for learning is that trainees be properly motivated. That is, for optimum learning trainees must recognize the need for acquiring new information or for having new skills, and they must maintain a desire to learn as training progresses. As one management consultant advises, "It's not enough just to 'tell.' You also have to 'sell' trainees on the material they are supposed to learn if training is to succeed."[37]

It is also important to create a training environment that is conducive to learning. A motivating environment can be created by focusing on the trainees rather than on the trainer or training topic. Six strategies can be essential:

1. Use positive reinforcement.
2. Eliminate threats and punishment.
3. Be flexible.
4. Have participants set personal goals.
5. Design interesting instruction.
6. Break down physical and psychological obstacles to learning.[38]

While most workers are motivated by certain common needs, they differ from one another in the relative importance of these needs at any given time. For example, new college graduates often have a high desire for advancement, and they have established specific goals for career progression. Training objectives that are clearly related to trainees' individual needs will increase the motivation of employees to succeed in training programs.

Basic Principles of Learning for Managers

After trainees are placed in the learning situation, their readiness and motivation should be assessed further. In addition, managers should understand the following basic principles of learning.

Meaningfulness of Presentation

One principle of learning is that the material to be learned should be presented in as meaningful a manner as possible. The material should be arranged so that each experience builds upon preceding ones and so that the trainee is able to integrate the experiences into a usable pattern of knowledge and skills.

Reinforcement

Reinforcement
Anything that strengthens the trainee's response

Behavior modification
Technique that operates on the principle that behavior that is rewarded, or positively reinforced, will be exhibited more frequently in the future, whereas behavior that is penalized, or unrewarded, will decrease in frequency

Anything that strengthens the trainee's response is called **reinforcement.** It may be in the form of approval from the manager or the feeling of accomplishment that follows the performance; or it may simply be confirmation in programmed instruction that the trainee's response was correct. Reinforcement is generally most effective when it occurs immediately after a task has been performed.

In recent years some work organizations have used **behavior modification,** a technique that operates on the principle that behavior that is rewarded—positively reinforced—will be exhibited more frequently in the future, whereas behavior that is penalized or unrewarded will decrease in frequency. Behavior modification will be discussed more thoroughly in Chapter 14.

Transfer of Training

Unless what is learned in the training situation is applicable to what is required on the job, the training will be of little value. The ultimate effectiveness of

DISCUSSION QUESTIONS

1. Why is employee orientation an important process? What are some benefits of a properly conducted orientation program?
2. A new employee is likely to be anxious the first few days on the job.
   a. What are some possible causes of this anxiety?
   b. How may the anxiety be reduced?
3. What economic, social, and political forces have made employee training even more important than in the past?
4. What analyses should be made to determine the training needs of an organization? After the needs are determined, what is the next step?
5. Indicate what training methods you would use for each of the following jobs. Give reasons for your choices.
   a. File clerk
   b. Computer operator
   c. Automobile service station attendant
   d. Pizza maker
   e. Nurse's aide
6. Compare computer-assisted instruction with the lecture method in regard to the way they involve the different psychological principles of learning.
7. Suppose that you are the manager of an accounts receivable unit in a large company. You are switching to a new system of billing and record keeping and need to train your three supervisors and twenty-eight employees in the new procedures. What training method(s) would you use? Why?
8. Participants in a training course are often asked to evaluate the course by means of a questionnaire. What are the pros and cons of this approach? Are there better ways of evaluating a course?

CASE STUDY: Orientation of New Employees at Visitech

Visitech opened its first optical store in Dallas in October 1983. At the forefront of the revolution in the eyeware industry, Visitech has an on-site computerized and automated optical laboratory at each store that fabricates prescription glasses upon request. Customers can select their frames and watch as their lenses are being made in the laboratory. Each Visitech store employs about twenty employees who perform a variety of jobs.

Because of the company's rapid growth, Ronnie Gorton was recently promoted to store manager of a new facility to be opened in New Mexico. Like all new Visitech store managers, Gorton will receive a week of managerial training in Dallas. This training stresses human relations skills and customer service. One training session in particular discusses the importance of first impressions and how initial employee beliefs and experiences influence their job behavior. The training instructor emphasizes the importance of establishing a strong employee-supervisor relationship through a well-managed orientation program. The positive work attitudes that Visitech's employee relations program promotes are especially important in light of the optical industry's growing emphasis on service.

Visitech has a formal employee orientation program. The HR department is responsible for introducing new employees to the company and its benefits, but store managers are required to orient all new employees to store operations and their individual jobs. Supervisors are granted considerable freedom to perform this task.

The New Mexico store is scheduled to open in two weeks. As a new store manager, Gorton is concerned about meeting new employees and getting them started on the right foot.

Questions

1. Is Gorton's concern with the orientation program a legitimate one?
2. What should be covered during the orientation? How should the orientation be designed?
3. What principles of learning should be applied to the orientation process?

NOTES AND REFERENCES

1. "1994 Industry Report," *Training* 30, no. 10 (October 1994): 30. See also A. P. Carnevale, L. J. Gainer, and J. Villet, *Training in America: The Organization and Strategic Role of Training* (San Francisco: Jossey-Bass, 1990). For an interesting discussion of the HR development field, see "The HRD Hall of Fame," *Training* 30, no. 2 (February 1993): 43–45.

2. For an interesting discussion of the importance of orientation for younger employees, see James W. Sheehy, "New Work Ethic Is Frightening," *Personnel Journal* 69, no. 6 (June 1990): 51–55.

3. Jill Cassner-Lotto and Associates, *Successful Training Strategies* (San Francisco: Jossey-Bass, 1988), 28–36. See also William Wiggenhorn, "Motorola U: When Training Becomes an Education," *Harvard Business Review* 68, no. 4 (July-August 1990): 71–83, a comprehensive discussion of how Motorola's program widened from emphasis on specific techniques to graduate work in computer-integrated manufacturing. For an account of how four successful companies handle training in today's fast-paced environment, see Linda Thornburg, "Training in a Changing World," *HR Magazine* 37, no. 8 (August 1992): 44–47; see also Fred R. Bleakley, "Training Women for Tough Guys' Jobs," *The Wall Street Journal* (December 28, 1994): B1.

4. Scott A. Tannenbaum and Gary Yukl, "Training and Development in Work Organizations," in Mark R. Rosenzweig and Lyman W. Porter, eds., *Annual Review of Psychology* (Palo Alto, Calif.: Annual Review, Inc., 1992): 401. See also Craig Eric Schneier, Craig J. Russell, Richard W. Beatty, and Lloyd S. Baird, *Training and Development Sourcebook*, 2d ed. (Amherst, Mass.: Human Resource Development Press, 1993). This is a training classic containing more than fifty articles written by leading professionals in the field.

5. Robert F. Mager, *Preparing Instructional Objectives* (Belmont, Calif.: David S. Lake, 1984): vi. See also Robert F. Mager, *Making Instruction Work or Skillbloomers*, rev. 2d ed., (Belmont, Calif.: David S. Lake, 1988) and his *What Every Manager Should Know about Training* (Belmont, Calif.: Lake Publishing, 1992). **Author note:** Dr. Mager is a member of the HRD Hall of Fame (see reference 1).

6. J. Kevin Ford and Steven P. Wroten, "Introducing New Methods for Conducting Training Evaluation and for Linking Training Evaluation to Program Redesign," *Personnel Psychology* 37, no. 4 (Winter, 1984): 651–65. Also see Paul R. Erickson, "Evaluating Training Results," *Training and Development Journal* 44, no. 1 (January 1990): 57–59.

7. A. P. Carnevale and E. R. Schulz, "Evaluation Practices," *Training and Development* 44 (1990): S23–S29. See also Anthony R. Montebello and Maureen Haga, "To Justify Training, Test, Test

Again," *Personnel Journal* 73, no. 1 (January 1994): 83–87; Jack E. Smith and Sharon Merchant, "Using Competency Exams for Evaluating Training," *Training and Development Journal* 44, no. 8 (August 1990): 65 ff.

8. Irwin L. Goldstein, *Training in Organizations: Needs Assessment, Development, and Evaluation*, 3d ed. (Monterey, Calif.: Brooks/Cole, 1993), 23.

9. Donald J. Ford and Catherine Fisk, "Benchmarking HRD," *Training and Development* 47, no. 6 (June 1993): 37–41.

10. Robert F. Sullivan and Donald C. Miklas, "On-the-Job Training That Works," *Training and Development Journal* 39, no. 5 (May 1985): 118–21. See also Marcia Ann Pulich, "The Basics of On-the-Job Training and Development," *Supervisory Management* 29, no. 2 (January 1984): 7–11; William J. Rothwell and H. C. Kazanas, "Planned OJT Is Production OJT," *Training and Development Journal* 44, no. 10 (October 1990): 53–56.

11. For a comprehensive discussion of training in small businesses, see Sarah Vickerstaff, "The Training Needs of Small Firms," *Human Resource Management Journal* 2, no. 3 (Spring 1992): 1–15.

12. Judith Valente and Bridget O'Brian, "Airline Cockpits Are No Place to Solo," *The Wall Street Journal* (August 2, 1989): B1.

13. Tannenbaum and Yukl, "Training and Development," 408.

14. Ralph E. Ganger, "Computer-Based Training Improves Job Performance, *Personnel Journal* 68, no. 6 (June 1989): 116–23. See also Carolyn Spitz, "Multimedia Training at Hewlett-Packard," *Training and Development* 46, no. 6 (June 1992): 39–41; Ralph Ganger, "Computer-Based Training Works," *Personnel Journal* 69, no. 9 (September 1990): 85–91.

15. Walter W. Wager, Stuart Polkinghorne, and Roger Powley, "Simulation: Selection and Development," *Performance Improvement Quarterly* 5, no. 2 (1992): 47–64.

16. Charlene Marmer Solomon, "Partners in Business," *Personnel Journal* 70, no. 3 (April 1991): 57–67. See also Ralph T. King, Jr., "Job Retraining Linked Closely to Employers Works in Cincinnati," *The Wall Street Journal* (March 19, 1993): A-1.

17. Christina DelValle, "From High Schools to High Skills," *Business Week* (April 26, 1993): 110–12. See also Aaron Bernstein, "How Much Good Will Training Do?" *Business Week* (February 22, 1993): 76–77.

18. Jennifer J. Laabs, "How Federally Funded Training Helps Business," *Personnel Journal* 71, no. 3 (March 1992): 35–39.

19. Tannenbaum and Yukl, "Training and Development," 427.

20. Tannenbaum and Yukl, "Training and Development," 407–8. For information on some of the available games, see George C. Thornton III and Jeannette N. Cleveland, "Developing Managerial Talent through Simulation," *American Psychologist* 45, no. 2 (February 1990): 190–99.

21. Kim Slack, "Training for the Real Thing," *Training and Development* 47, no. 5 (May 1993): 79–89.

22. For more information, contact Corporate Affirmative Action and Compliance Department, Motorola, Inc., 1303 East Algonquin Road, Schaumburg, Ill. 60196.

23. Jack Gordon, "Where's the Line between Training and Intrusion?" *Training* 26, no. 3 (March 1989): 27–39.

24. Phillip J. Decker, "The Effects of Rehearsal Group Size and Video Feedback in Behavior Modeling Training," *Personnel Psychology* 36, no. 4 (Winter 1983): 763–73. While four basic steps in behavior modeling are normally discussed, some authors note a fifth step—the use of retention aids. See also William M. Fox, "Getting the Most from Behavior Modeling," *National Productivity Review* 7 (Summer 1988): 238–45.

25. Stephen Wehrenberg and Robert Kuhnle, "How Training through Behavior Modeling Works," *Personnel Journal* 59, no. 7 (July 1980): 576–80; Herbert H. Meyer and Michael S. Raich, "An Objective Evaluation of a Behavior Modeling Training Program," *Personnel Psychology* 36, no. 4 (Winter 1983): 755–61.

26. Richard D. Zalman, "The Basics of In-house Skills Training," *HR Magazine* 34, no. 2 (February 1990): 74–78. See also "Functional Illiteracy: It's Your Problem Too," *Supervisory Management* 34, no. 6 (June 1989): 22.

27. Richard G. Zalman, "The Basics of In-House Skill Training," *HR Magazine* 36, no. 2 (February 1991): 74–78. For a detailed account of the programs of two companies, see Patricia L. May, Sinclair E. Hugh, and Edward A. Quesada, "Back to Basics," *Personnel Journal* 69, no. 10 (October 1990): 62–71. See also Patrick J. O'Connor, "Getting Down to Basics," *Training and Development* 47, no. 7 (July 1993): 62–64; Edward E. Gordon, Judith A. Ponticell, and Ronald R. Morgan, *Closing the Literacy Gap in American Business: A Guide for Trainers and Human Resource Specialists* (New York: Quorom Books, 1991).

28. Zalman, "The Basics."

29. Tannenbaum and Yukl, "Training and Development," 430–32. See also D. Keith Denton, "Multiskilled Teams Replace Old Systems," *HR Magazine* 37, no. 9 (September 1992): 48–50; R. Glenn Ray, Jeff Hines, and Dave Wilcox, "Training Internal Facilitators," *Training and Development* 48, no. 11 (November 1994): 45–48; Paul Froiland, "Who's Getting Trained?" *Training* 30, no. 10 (October 1993): 53–60. A special section in this article is devoted to "The teaming of America."

30. Pfeiffer and Company's address is 2780 Circleport Drive, Erlanger, Ky. 41018.

31. Ann Perkins Delatte and Larry Baytos, "Guidelines for Successful Diversity Training," *Training* 30, no. 1 (January 1993): 55–60. See also Joyce E. Santora, "Kinney Shoe Steps into Diversity," *Personnel Journal* 70, no. 9 (September 1991): 72 ff.

32. Patricia A. Galagan, "Trading Places at Monsanto," *Training and Development* 47, no. 4 (April 1993): 45–49.

33. *The Sacramento Bee* (February 15, 1993): B-1.

34. Shari Caudron, "Training Can Damage Diversity Efforts," *Personnel Journal* 72, no. 4 (April 1993): 51–62.

35. Shari Caudron, "Training Helps United Go Global," *Personnel Journal* 71, no. 2 (February 1992): 103–5. See also "Trainers Network on the Net," *Training and Development* 48, no. 8 (August 1994): 35–37.

36. Information obtained from the National Crisis Prevention Institute, Inc., 3315-K North 124th Street, Brookfield, Wisc. 53005.

37. Philip C. Grant, "Employee Motivation: The Key to Training," *Supervisory Management* 34, no. 6 (June 1989): 16–21. See also Debra J. Cohen, "What Motivates Trainees," *Training and Development Journal* 44, no. 1 (November 1990): 91–93.

38. David R. Torrence, "Motivating Trainees to Learn," *Training and Development* 47, no. 3 (March 1993): 55–58.

39. *The Journal of Applied Psychology* is an excellent source of research studies of this type. Its articles are indexed in *Psychological Abstracts*.

40. Les Donaldson and Edward E. Scannell, *Human Resource Development: The New Trainers Guide* (Reading, Mass.: Addison-Wesley, 1983): 142–51.

41. For other suggestions on successful training, see Carol Haig, "A Line Manager's Guide to Training," *Personnel Journal* 63, no. 10 (October 1984): 42–45; Leslie A. Bryan, "Making the Manager a Better Trainer," *Supervisory Management* 29, no. 4 (April 1984): 28.

Chapter

Career Development

After studying this chapter you should be able to

Explain how a career development program integrates individual and organizational needs.

objective

Describe the conditions that help to make a career development program successful.

objective

Discuss how job opportunities may be inventoried and employee potential may be assessed.

objective

Describe the methods used for identifying and developing managerial talent.

objective

Cite the ways in which employers can facilitate the career development of women.

objective

Cite the ways for developing a diverse workforce.

objective

Describe the various aspects of personal career development that one should consider.

objective

The functions of human resources management that we have discussed so far have a fairly long history. In the 1970s more and more employers recognized the need employees have for satisfying careers, and they tended to establish programs that enabled employees to attain their personal goals within the organization. By the 1980s the emphasis had changed: Organizational career development was seen as a tool for addressing business needs in a vastly changed corporate environment. In the 1990s the focus is on a balance between the two. Organizational career development is now viewed as a strategic process in which maximizing an individual's career potential is a way of enhancing the success of the organization as a whole.[1]

Increased competition for promotion, constant innovation in technology, pressures for equal employment opportunities, corporate rightsizing and restructuring, globalization of our economy, and employees' desire to get the most out of their careers are all major forces pushing organizations to offer career development programs. The desire of employers to make better use of their employees' knowledge and skills and to retain those who are valuable to the organization are also important considerations. In this chapter we will not only acquaint the reader with career development as an HRM function but will provide some suggestions that may be considered in one's own career development.

Phases of a Career Development Program

Organizations have traditionally engaged in human resources planning and development. As we noted in Chapter 5, this activity involves charting the moves of large numbers of employees through various positions in an organization and identifying future staffing needs. Career development programs, with their greater emphasis on the individual, introduce a personalized aspect to the process.

A common approach to establishing a career development program is to integrate it with the existing HR functions and structures in the organization. Integrating career development with the HR program reinforces both programs. Figure 8–1 illustrates how HR structures relate to some of the essential aspects of the career development process. For example, in planning careers, employees need organizational information—information that strategic planning, forecasting, succession planning, and skills inventories can provide. Similarly, as they obtain information about themselves and use it in career planning, employees need to know how management views their performance and the career paths within the organization.[2]

objective

Determining Individual and Organizational Needs

A career development program should be viewed as a dynamic process that attempts to meet the needs of managers, their employees, and the organization. Individual employees are responsible for initiating their own career planning. It is up to them to identify their knowledge, skills, abilities, interests, and values and seek out information about career options so that they can set goals and develop career plans. Managers should encourage employees to take responsibility for their own careers, offering continuing assistance in the form of feedback on individual performance, information about the organization, job information, and information about career opportunities that might be of interest. The organization is responsible for supplying information about its mission, policies, and plans

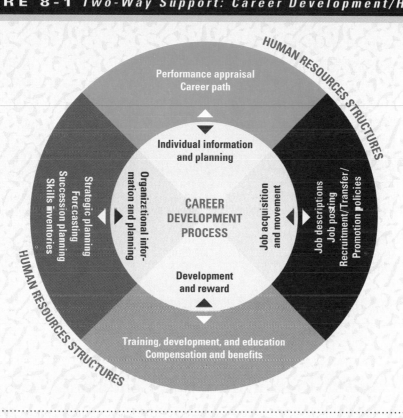

FIGURE 8-1 *Two-Way Support: Career Development/HR*

HUMAN RESOURCES STRUCTURES

Performance appraisal
Career path

Individual information
and planning

Organizational infor-
mation and planning

CAREER
DEVELOPMENT
PROCESS

Job acquisition
and movement

Strategic planning
Forecasting
Succession planning
Skills inventories

Job descriptions
Job posting
Recruitment/Transfer/
Promotion policies

Development
and reward

HUMAN RESOURCES STRUCTURES

Training, development, and education
Compensation and benefits

Source: Zandy B. Leibowitz, Caela Farren, and Beverly L. Kaye, *Designing Career Development Systems* (San Francisco: Jossey-Bass, 1986), 41. Reproduced with permission.

and for providing support for employee self-assessment, training, and development. Significant career growth can occur when individual initiative combines with organizational opportunity. Career development programs benefit managers by giving them increased skill in managing their own careers, greater retention of valued employees, increased understanding of the organization, and enhanced reputations as people-developers. As with other HR programs, the inauguration of a career development program should be based on the organization's needs as well.

Assessment of needs should take a variety of approaches (surveys, informal group discussions, interviews, etc.) and should involve personnel from different groups, such as new employees, managers, plateaued employees, minorities, and technical and professional employees. Identifying the needs and problems of these groups provides the starting point for the organization's career development efforts. As shown in Figure 8–2, organizational needs should be linked with individual career needs in a way that joins personal effectiveness and satisfaction of employees with the achievement of the organization's strategic objectives.

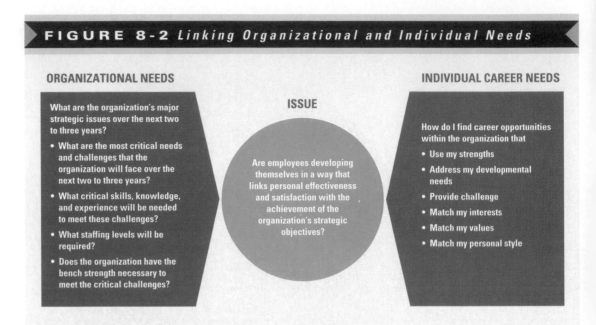

FIGURE 8-2 *Linking Organizational and Individual Needs*

ORGANIZATIONAL NEEDS

What are the organization's major strategic issues over the next two to three years?

- What are the most critical needs and challenges that the organization will face over the next two to three years?
- What critical skills, knowledge, and experience will be needed to meet these challenges?
- What staffing levels will be required?
- Does the organization have the bench strength necessary to meet the critical challenges?

ISSUE

Are employees developing themselves in a way that links personal effectiveness and satisfaction with the achievement of the organization's strategic objectives?

INDIVIDUAL CAREER NEEDS

How do I find career opportunities within the organization that

- Use my strengths
- Address my developmental needs
- Provide challenge
- Match my interests
- Match my values
- Match my personal style

Source: Forrer and Leibowitz, Conceptual Systems, Inc., copyright 1992.

Creating Favorable Conditions

objective

While a career development program requires many special processes and techniques, which we will describe later, some basic conditions must be present if it is to be successful. These conditions create a favorable climate for the program.

Management Support

If career development is to succeed, it must receive the complete support of top management. Ideally, senior line managers and HR department managers should work together to design and implement a career development system. The system should reflect the goals and culture of the organization, and the HR philosophy should be woven throughout. An HR philosophy can provide employees with a clear set of expectations and directions for their own career development. For a program to be effective, managerial personnel at all levels must be trained in the fundamentals of job design, performance appraisal, career planning, and counseling.

Goal Setting

Before individuals can engage in meaningful career planning, they must not only have an awareness of the organization's philosophy, but they must also have a clear understanding of the organization's more immediate goals. Otherwise, they may plan for personal change and growth without knowing if or how their own goals match those of the organization. For example, if the technology of a business is changing and new skills are needed, will the organization retrain to meet this need or hire new talent? Is there growth, stability, or decline in the number of employees needed? How will turnover affect this need? Clearly, an organizational plan that answers these kinds of questions is essential to support individual career planning.

Changes in HRM Policies

To ensure that its career development program will be effective, an organization may need to alter its current HRM policies. For example, a policy of lifelong job rotation can counteract obsolescence and maintain employee flexibility. Another policy that can aid development involves job transfers and promotions.

A **transfer** is the placement of an employee in another job for which the duties, responsibilities, status, and remuneration are approximately equal to those of the previous job. A transfer may require the employee to change work group, workplace, work shift, or organizational unit; it may even necessitate moving to another geographic area. Transfers make it possible for an organization to place its employees in jobs where there is a greater need for their services and where they can acquire new knowledge and skills. A downward transfer, or demotion, moves an individual into a lower-level job that can provide developmental opportunities; but such a move is ordinarily considered unfavorable, especially by the individual who is demoted.

A *promotion* is a change of assignment to a job at a higher level in the organization. The new job normally provides an increase in pay and status and demands more skill or carries more responsibility. Promotions enable an organization to utilize the skills and abilities of its personnel more effectively, and the opportunity to gain a promotion serves as an incentive for good performance. The two principal criteria for determining promotions are *merit* and *seniority*. Often the problem is to determine how much consideration to give to each factor.

Transfers and promotions require the individual to adjust to new job demands and usually to a different work environment. A transfer that involves moving to a new location within the United States or abroad places greater demands on an employee, because it requires that employee to adapt not only to a new work environment but also to new living conditions. The employee with a family has the added responsibility of helping family members adjust to the new living arrangements. Even though some employers provide all types of **relocation services**—including covering moving expenses, helping to sell a home, providing cultural orientation, and language training—there is always some loss of productive time. Pretransfer training, whether related to job skills or to lifestyle, has been suggested as one of the most effective ways to reduce lost productivity.

Many organizations now provide **outplacement services** to help terminated employees find a job somewhere else. These services can be used to enhance a productive employee's career, as well as to terminate an employee who is unproductive. If an organization cannot meet its career development responsibilities to its productive workers, HR policy should provide for assistance to be given them in finding more suitable career opportunities elsewhere.

Transfer
Placement of an individual in another b for which the duties, esponsibilities, status, nd remuneration are pproximately equal to ose of the previous job

Relocation services
ervices provided to an employee who is transferred to a new ocation, which might clude help in moving, in selling a home, in orienting to a new lture, or in learning a new language

Outplacement services
Services provided by organizations to help erminated employees get a new job

Publicizing the Program

The career development program should be announced widely throughout the organization. The objectives and opportunities can be communicated in several ways, including the following:

1. Publication in newsletters
2. Inclusion in employee manuals
3. Publication in a special career guide or as part of career planning workshops
4. Inclusion in videotaped or live presentations
5. Inclusion in computer-accessed programs

At the very least, a manual that spells out the basic job families, career progression possibilities, and related requirements should be given to each manager and made available to every employee.

objective

Inventorying Job Opportunities

While career development usually involves many different types of training experiences (as discussed in the preceding chapter), the most important of these experiences occur on the job. It is here that the individual is exposed to a wide variety of situations, and it is here that contributions are made to the organization.

Job Competencies

It is important for an organization to study its jobs carefully in order to identify and assign weights to the knowledge and skills that each one requires. This can be achieved with job analysis and evaluation systems such as those used in compensation programs. The system used at Sears measures three basic competencies for each job: *know-how, problem solving,* and *accountability.* Know-how is broken down into three types of job knowledge: technical, managerial, and human relations. Problem solving and accountability also have several dimensions. Scores for each of these three major competencies are assigned to each job, and a total value is computed for each job. For any planned job transfer, the amount of increase (or decrease) the next job represents in each of the skill areas, as well as in the total point values, can be computed. This information is then used to make certain that a transfer to a different job is a move that requires growth on the part of the employee.

Sears designs career development paths to provide the following experiences: (1) an increase in at least one skill area on each new assignment, (2) an increase of at least 10 percent in total points on each new assignment, and (3) assignments in several different functional areas.[3]

Job Progressions

Once the skill demands of jobs are identified and weighted according to their importance, it is then possible to plan **job progressions.** A new employee with no experience is typically assigned to a "starting job." After a period of time in that

Job progressions
Hierarchy of jobs a new employee might experience, ranging from a starting job to successive jobs that require more knowledge and/or skill

job, the employee can be promoted to one that requires more knowledge and/ or skill. While most organizations concentrate on developing job progressions for managerial, professional, and technical jobs, progressions can be developed for all categories of jobs. These job progressions then can serve as a basis for developing **career paths**—the lines of advancement within an organization—for individuals.

Figure 8–3 illustrates a typical line of advancement in the human resources area of a large multinational corporation. It is apparent that one must be prepared to move geographically in order to advance very far in HRM with this firm. This would also be true of other career fields within the organization.

Many organizations prepare interesting and attractive brochures to describe the career paths that are available to employees. General Motors has prepared a *Career Development Guide* that groups jobs by fields of work such as engineering, manufacturing, communications, data processing, financial, HR, and scientific. These categories give employees an understanding of the career possibilities in the various fields.

Dual Career Paths

Not too long ago moving upwards in an organization meant that an employee would eventually become a manager and perform those functions that are typical

Career paths
Lines of advancement within an organization in an occupational field

FIGURE 8-3 *Typical Line of Advancement in HR Management*

				Vice president, HR		
			Corporate HR director			
		Corporate HR manager	Division HR director			
		Asst. division HR director				
	Regional HR manager	Plant HR manager				
	Asst. plant HR manager					
Regional HR associate	HR supervisor					
HR associate						

of a managerial position. This was the only way to recognize the worth of an individual to the organization and to compensate the outstanding scientist, technical specialist, or professional person. It became apparent that there must be another way to compensate such individuals without elevating them to a management position. The solution was to develop dual career paths or tracks that provide for progression in special areas such as finance, marketing, and engineering with compensation that is comparable to that received by managers at different levels.[4] Many organizations have found that this is the solution to keeping employees with valuable knowledge and skills performing tasks that are as important to the organization as those performed by managers. Figure 8–4 shows the dual career path available to information system specialists after attaining a level 3 position.

Training Needs

There are likely to be points in one's career path where training beyond that received on the job is essential. Such points should be identified and appropriate training made available to prevent progress from being impaired by a lack of knowledge or skills. Because the training needs of individual employees differ, these needs must be monitored closely.

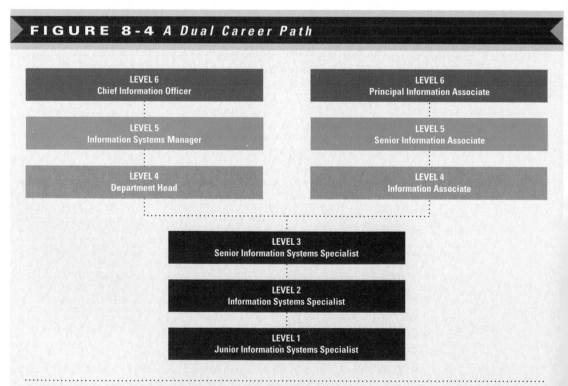

FIGURE 8-4 *A Dual Career Path*

LEVEL 6 Chief Information Officer	LEVEL 6 Principal Information Associate
LEVEL 5 Information Systems Manager	LEVEL 5 Senior Information Associate
LEVEL 4 Department Head	LEVEL 4 Information Associate

LEVEL 3
Senior Information Systems Specialist

LEVEL 2
Information Systems Specialist

LEVEL 1
Junior Information Systems Specialist

Source: Andrew J. DuBrin and R. Duane Ireland, *Management & Organization,* 2d ed. (Cincinnati, Ohio: South-Western Publishing, 1993): 555. Reprinted with permission.

Gauging Employee Potential

Probably the most important objective of any career development program is to provide the tools and techniques that will enable employees to gauge their potential for success in a career path. This objective may be achieved in various ways, all of which naturally involve the active participation of the employees themselves. Informal counseling by HR staff and supervisors is used widely. Many organizations give their employees information on educational assistance, EEO/AA programs and policies, salary administration, and job requirements. Career planning workbooks and workshops are also popular means of helping employees identify their potential and the strength of their interests.

Career Planning Workbooks

Several organizations have prepared workbooks to guide their employees individually through systematic self-assessment of values, interests, abilities, goals, and personal development plans. General Motors' *Career Development Guide* contains a section called "What Do You Want Your Future to Be?" in which the employee makes a personal evaluation. General Electric has developed an extensive set of manuals for its career development program, including two workbooks to help employees explore life issues that affect career decisions. Syntex's workbook, *How to Work for a Living and Like It*, may be used by individuals on their own or in a group workshop.

Some organizations prefer to use workbooks written for the general public. Popular ones include *Where Do I Go from Here with My Life?* by John Crystal and Richard N. Bolles—a workbook follow-up to Bolles's *What Color Is Your Parachute?* Andrew H. Souerwine's *Career Strategies: Planning for Personal Growth* and John Holland's *Self-Directed Search* are also used frequently.[5] These same books are recommended to students for help in planning their careers.

Career Planning Workshops

Workshops offer experiences similar to those provided by workbooks. However, they have the advantage of providing a chance to compare and discuss attitudes, concerns, and plans with others in similar situations. Some workshops focus on current job performance and development plans. Others deal with broader life and career plans and values.

As mentioned earlier, employees should be encouraged to assume responsibility for their own careers. A career workshop can help them do that. It can also help them learn how to make career decisions, set career goals, create career options, seek career planning information, and at the same time build confidence and self-esteem.[6]

Career Counseling

Career counseling
Process of discussing with employees their current job activities and performance, their personal job and career goals, their personal skills, and suitable career development objectives

Career counseling involves talking with employees about their current job activities and performance, personal and career interests and goals, personal skills, and suitable career development objectives. While some organizations make counseling a part of the annual performance appraisal, career counseling is usually voluntary.

Many organizations have designated career counselors who are available on a full-time basis to employees. A leader in career development as recognized by an award from the American Society for Training and Development is the Internal Revenue Service. It has twenty-seven formal counseling offices across the United States. Each office has a career counseling program. Counselors help employees on a one-to-one basis where possible and conduct organizational development and team-building sessions for employees and their managers. They also design customized workshops for different IRS divisions.[7]

As employees approach retirement, they may be encouraged to participate in preretirement programs, which often include counseling along with other helping activities. Career counseling may be provided by the HR staff, superiors, specialized staff counselors, or outside professionals. Chapter 15 includes an expanded discussion of the types of skills required for career counseling. Preretirement programs will be discussed in Chapter 12.

Career Development Programs for a Diverse Workforce

Organizations differ widely in the types of career development programs they offer. Some organizations have formal programs for all levels of employees that cover a broad array of topics. Others have offerings limited to career counseling incorporated into annual performance reviews. The more extensive career development programs also frequently include programs geared to special groups, such as management development programs or programs for women, minorities, or dual-career couples. Let's examine some of these special programs more closely.

objective

Management Development Programs

Contemporary organizations must have competent managers who can cope with the growing complexity of the problems affecting their operations. A formal management development program helps to ensure that developmental experiences both on and off the job are coordinated and in line with the individual's and the organization's needs.

Inventorying Management Requirements and Talent

An important part of a management development program is an inventory of managerial positions. The inventory directs attention to the developmental needs of employees, both in their present jobs and in managerial jobs to which they may be promoted. An equally important part of the program is identifying employees who may be groomed as replacements for managers who are reassigned, retire, or otherwise vacate a position. Replacement charts, discussed in Chapter 5, provide the information needed to fill vacancies in key positions.

Role of Managers

Identifying and developing talent in individuals is a role that all managers should take seriously. As they conduct formal appraisals, they should be concerned with their subordinates' potential for managerial or advanced technical jobs and encourage their growth in that direction. In addition to immediate managers, there should be others in the organization who have the power to evaluate, nominate, and sponsor employees with promise. Organizations that emphasize developing human assets as well as turning a profit typically have the talent they need and some to spare. Some companies—Citicorp, Xerox, Millers Outpost, and Wal–Mart, to name a few—have become "academy" companies that unintentionally provide a source of talented managers to organizations that lack good management development programs of their own.

Use of Assessment Centers

Assessment center

Process by which individuals are evaluated as they participate in a series of situations that resemble what they might be called upon to handle on the job

Pioneered in the mid-1950s by Dr. Douglas Bray and his associates at AT&T, assessment centers are considered one of the most valuable methods for evaluating personnel. An **assessment center** is a process (*not a place*) in which individuals are evaluated as they participate in a series of situations that resemble what they might be called upon to handle on the job. The popularity of the assessment center can be attributed to its capacity for increasing an organization's ability to select employees who will perform successfully in management positions or to assist and promote the development of skills for their current position. These centers may use in-basket exercises, role playing, and other approaches to employee development that we discussed in Chapter 7.

The schedule of the various activities at the California Highway Patrol Academy assessment center is shown in Highlights in HRM 1. Participation in these activities provides samples of behavior that are representative of what is required for advancement. At the end of the assessment-center period, the assessors' observations are combined and integrated to develop an overall picture of the strengths and needs of the participants. A report is normally submitted to senior management, and feedback is given to the participants.

Increasing attention is being given to the validity of assessment-center procedures. As with employment tests, the assessments provided must be valid. Before the assessment center is run, the characteristics or dimensions to be studied should be determined through job analyses. The exercises used in the center should reflect the job for which the person is being evaluated; i.e., the exercises should have content validity. While the assessment-center methodology lends itself readily to content validation, predictive validity has also been observed in many instances. A strong positive relationship is found between assessments and future performance on the job.[8]

Telephone interviews with nine organizational psychologists who have had extensive experiences with assessment centers reveal the following trends: An increasing interest in assessment centers, with a dramatic shift from sales to development; an increase in the use of computers to present stimuli and to record performance; growth in the assessment of nonmanagerial personnel; a more detailed focus on behavioral descriptions rather than on traits of successful performers; and an increasing use of assessment centers in the public sector. One respondent reported that "In the public sector there is a great temptation to call something an assessment center in order to bring an aura of validity, reliability, fairness, and job relatedness."[9]

While assessment centers have proved quite valuable in identifying managerial talent and in helping with the development of individuals, it should be noted

HRM
highlights

HIGHLIGHTS IN HRM

1 ASSESSMENT-CENTER PROGRAM OF THE CALIFORNIA HIGHWAY PATROL

One week prior to conduct of the centers	Five-day training for all assessors*
Monday—A.M.	Assessors review exercises.
	Participants go through orientation.
Monday—P.M.	Leaderless group discussion: Participants divided into two groups of six each, observed by three assessors; each assessor observes two participants.
	Assessors prepare final report on this exercise.
	In-basket exercise: Each participant works individually for three hours on a 31-item in-basket.
	Assessors review and score in-basket and prepare for in-basket interview the following day.
Tuesday—P.M.	Participants take a forty-minute reading test (*Davis Reading Test*).
	Assessors review in-basket observations with participants and prepare final report on this exercise.
Wednesday—A.M.	Participants complete an individual analysis exercise and prepare a seven-minute presentation to the panel of assessors on solution to the problem.
	Participants begin presentations to panel of assessors.
Wednesday—P.M.	Presentations continue through afternoon.
	Participants are released to return to work site.
	Assessors prepare final reports on this exercise.
	Administrator prepares for discussion of each candidate the following day.
Thursday—All day	Assessors meet in teams of three to integrate observations of each participant's overall exercises, to reach a consensual rating on each skill evaluated, and to make specific developmental recommendations.
Within 45 days	Assessors meet with participants and their supervisors at the participant's work site to discuss observations of assessor panel.
Within 60 days	Participants and supervisors develop a career plan to assist participant in skill development.

Source: California Highway Patrol Academy. Reproduced with permission.

---

*All exercises and training take place on-site at the CHP Academy.

that the method tends to favor those who are strong in interpersonal skills and have the ability to influence others. Some individuals find it difficult to perform at their best in a situation that for them is as threatening as taking a test. The manner in which assessment-center personnel conduct the exercises and provide feedback to the participants will play a major role in determining how individuals react to the experience.

Management positions are the usual targets of assessment centers. However, adaptations of the assessment-center method can be used for nonmanagerial positions, such as those in sales. One adaptation involves playing videotaped scenarios for applicants, then using a multiple-choice test to find out how they would respond to the situations depicted.

Determining Individual Development Needs

Because the requirements of each management position and the qualifications of the person performing it are different, no two managers will have identical developmental needs. For one individual, self-development may consist of developing the ability to write reports, give talks, or lead conferences. For another, it may require developing interpersonal skills in order to communicate and relate more effectively with a diverse workforce. Periodic performance appraisals can provide a basis for determining each manager's progress. Conferences in which these appraisals are discussed are an essential part of self-improvement efforts.

In helping individuals plan their careers, it is important for organizations to recognize that younger managers today seek meaningful training assignments that are interesting and involve challenge, responsibility, and a sense of empowerment. They also have a greater concern for the contribution that their work in the organization will make to society. Unfortunately, they are frequently given responsibilities they view as rudimentary, boring, and composed of too many "make-work" activities. Some organizations are attempting to retain young managers with high potential by offering a **fast-track program** that enables them to advance more rapidly than those with less potential. A fast-track program may provide for a relatively rapid progression—lateral transfers or promotions—through a number of managerial positions requiring exposure to different organizational functions, as well as providing opportunities to make meaningful decisions.

Fast-track program
Program that encourages young managers with high potential to remain with an organization by enabling them to advance more rapidly than those with less potential

Mentoring

When one talks with men and women about their employment experiences, it is common to hear them mention individuals at work who influenced them. They frequently refer to immediate managers who were especially helpful as career developers. But they also mention others at higher levels in the organization who provided guidance and support to them in the development of their careers. These executives and managers who coach, advise, and encourage employees of lesser rank are called **mentors**.

Informal mentoring goes on daily within every type of organization. Generally, the mentor initiates the relationship, but sometimes an employee will approach a potential mentor for advice. Most mentoring relationships develop over

Mentors
Executives who coach, advise, and encourage individuals of lesser rank

time on an informal basis. However, in proactive organizations there is an emphasis on formal mentoring plans that call for the assignment of a mentor to those employees considered for upward movement in the organization. Under a good mentor, learning focuses on goals, opportunities, expectations, standards, and assistance in fulfilling one's potential.[10]

**Mentoring
functions**

Functions concerned
with the career
advancement and
psychological aspects of
the person being
mentored

Analysis of a large number of research studies revealed that the **mentoring functions** can be divided into two broad categories: *career functions* and *psychosocial functions*. These functions are listed in Figure 8–5. Career functions are those aspects of the relationship that enhance career advancement; psychosocial functions are those aspects that enhance the protégé's sense of competence, identity, and effectiveness in a professional role. Both kinds of functions are viewed as critical to management development.[11]

Organizations with formal mentoring programs include The Jewel Companies, NCR, Johnson & Johnson, the Government Accounting Office, and Merrill Lynch. While NCR nurtures mentoring relationships, its mentoring programs are loosely administered among its 53,000 employees, and the company does no matching of protégés with mentors. NCR uses mentoring as an early identification program for high-potential employees who are selected by their mentors. Mentoring is viewed as an educational tool to train and track "green" talent.[12]

An alternative form of mentoring is the "mentoring circles" organized by the Association of Management Women (AMW), an in-house association of the 84,000-employee telephone giant NYNEX Corporation. The NYNEX circles' primary focus is to help AMW members attain greater leadership roles.[13]

Another new form of mentoring, sponsored by the MS Foundation for Women, provides an opportunity for girls 9 to 15 years to spend a day with mothers or friends on the job. The program is designed to give young women more attention and to provide them with career role models. Many of the larger organizations, including Nike, DuPont, Ford, and Valvoline, have participated in this program. Other groups, like the Girl Scouts in the Washington, D.C., area, have longer-term mentoring plans where young women ages 12 to 18 spend up to

---

FIGURE 8-5 *Mentoring Functions*

CAREER FUNCTIONS	PSYCHOSOCIAL FUNCTIONS
Sponsorship	Role modeling
Exposure and visibility	Acceptance and confirmation
Coaching	Counseling
Protection	Friendship
Challenging assignments	

Source: Kathy E. Kram, *Mentoring at Work,* University Press of America, Lanham, Md., 1988. Reprinted with permission.

a month a year in the offices of women scientists, accountants, and other professionals. It is hoped that through such programs young women will think more broadly in their career planning.[14]

Problems associated with mergers and the emergence of the cross-cultural organization could be ameliorated by the use of assigned mentors to improve communication and ensure the continuity of the organizational culture. Not only have formal mentoring programs been valuable for management development, but more organizations are turning to them to help a diverse workforce move more quickly throughout the organization.

objective

Career Development for Women

In Chapter 5 we discussed some of the current trends in the employment of women in jobs that until recently were held predominantly by men. Included among these jobs are management-level positions. Organizations are continually concerned, as a result of EEO/AA requirements and because of the need for strong leadership, to increase the proportion of women they employ as managers.

Eliminating Barriers to Advancement

Women in management have been at a disadvantage by not being part of the so-called *good old boys' network*, an informal network of interpersonal relationships that has traditionally provided a means for senior (male) members of the organization to pass along news of advancement opportunities and other career tips to junior (male) members. Women have typically been outside the network, lacking role models to serve as mentors.

To combat their difficulty in advancing to management positions, women in several organizations have developed their own *women's networks*. At Ralston Purina in St. Louis, a women's network that any female employee may join serves as a system for encouraging and fostering women's career development and for

Professional women today assume higher-level positions in many organizations.

sharing information, experiences, and insights. Corporate officers are invited to regularly scheduled network meetings to discuss such matters as planning, development, and company performance. Network members view these sessions as an opportunity to let corporate officers know of women who are interested in and capable of furthering their careers. Other corporations where women's networks have been established include Hoffman-LaRoche, Metropolitan Life Insurance, Atlantic Richfield, Scholastic Magazines, and CBS.[15]

An organization that is devoted to helping employers break down barriers to upward mobility for women is Catalyst, a New York City–based not-for-profit organization. Catalyst not only courts corporate officers but also offers career advice, job placement, continuing education, and related professional development for women of all ages. At its New York headquarters, Catalyst houses an extensive library and audiovisual center that is regarded as the country's leading resource for information on women and work.[16]

The advancement of women in management has been hindered by a series of sex-role stereotypes that have shaped the destiny of women, and working women in particular. Some of the more prominent myths were discussed in Chapter 5. Fortunately, there is substantial evidence that stereotyped attitudes toward women are changing. As women pursue career goals assertively and attitudes continue to change, the climate for women in management will be even more favorable. Research has shown that newer male managers tend to be more receptive to the advancement of women managers. Also, the U.S. Supreme Court ruling in *Price Waterhouse v Hopkins* (1989), which states unequivocally that sex stereotyping is discriminatory, has helped to push organizations in a progressive direction.

According to data cited in an article by Dan Dalton and Idelene Kesner, there have been some improvements in opportunities for women. From 1981 to 1991 the percentage of women managers in the workplace increased from 27 to 41 percent, the percentage of women in senior executive positions increased from 1 to 3 percent, and in senior management placements from 5.5 to 16 percent. While these data suggest there that has been some progress, there is much left to do to break the glass ceiling, that invisible barrier of attitudes, prejudices, and "old boy" networks that blocks the progress of women who seek important positions in an organization.[17]

Preparing Women for Management

As noted above, opportunities for women to move into management positions are definitely improving. In addition to breaking down the barriers to advancement, the development of women managers demands a better understanding of women's needs and the requirements of the management world.

According to Rose Mary Wentling, business today needs all the leadership, talent, quality, competence, productivity, innovation, and creativity possible, as U.S. firms face more-effective worldwide competition. Companies committed to equal opportunities for women and men will undoubtedly keep the best talent available. Wentling has devised a list of actions organizations can take to maximize the human resource represented by women. These actions are presented in Highlights in HRM 2.[18]

> ## HIGHLIGHTS IN HRM

2   MAXIMIZING THE HUMAN RESOURCES OF FEMALE MANAGERS

highlights

1. Ensure that women receive frequent and specific feedback on their job performance. Women need and want candid reviews of their work. Clearly articulated suggestions for improvement, standards for work performance, and plans for career advancement will make women feel more involved in their jobs and help make them better employees.

2. Accept women as valued members of the management team. Include them in every kind of communication. Listen to their needs and concerns, and encourage their contributions.

3. Give talented women the same opportunities given to talented men to grow, develop, and contribute to company profitability. Give them the responsibility to direct major projects and to plan and implement systems and programs. Expect them to travel and relocate and to make the same commitment to the company as men aspiring to leadership positions.

4. Give women the same level of counseling on professional career advancement opportunities as that given to men.

5. Identify women as potential managers early in their employment and facilitate their advancement through training and other developmental activities.

6. Assist women in strengthening their assertion skills. Reinforce strategic career planning to encourage women's commitment to their careers and long-term career plans.

7. Accelerate the development of qualified women through fast-track programs. Either formally or informally, this method will provide women with the exposure, knowledge, and positioning for career advancement.

8. Provide opportunities for women to develop mentoring or sponsoring relationships with employees. Women do not often have equal or easy access (compared with their male colleagues) to senior employees. The overall goal should be to provide advice, counsel, and support to promising female employees by knowledgeable, senior-level men and women.

9. Encourage company co-ed management support systems and networks. Sharing experiences and information with other men and women who are managers provides invaluable support to peers. These activities provide the opportunity for women to meet and learn from men and women in more advanced stages of their careers—a helpful way of identifying potential mentors or role models.

10. Examine the feasibility of increasing participation of women in company-sponsored planning retreats, use of company facilities, social functions, and so forth. With notable exceptions, men are still generally more comfortable with other men, and as a result, women miss many of the career and business opportunities that arise during social functions. In addition, women may not have access to information about the company's informal political and social systems. Encourage male managers to include women when socializing with other business associates.

Source: R. M. Wentling, "Women in Middle Management: Their Career Development and Aspirations." Reprinted from *Business Horizons,* January/February 1992, copyright 1992 by the Foundation for the School of Business at Indiana University. Used with permission.

Many employers now offer special training to women who are on a management career path. They may use their own staff or outside firms to conduct this training. Opportunities are also available for women to participate in seminars and workshops that provide instruction and experiences in a wide variety of management topics.

In the past several years, the number of women enrolled in college and university degree programs in management has increased significantly. At the same time, more women trained in management have joined management department faculties at business schools, thus creating an environment that fosters the mentoring and development of women as professionals capable of assuming higher-level positions in work organizations.

In addition to formal training opportunities, women today are provided with a wealth of information and guidance in books and magazines. Business sections in bookstores are stocked with numerous books written especially for women who want a better idea of the career opportunities available to them. Many books are devoted to the pursuit of careers in specific fields.[19]

Popular magazines that contain many articles about women and jobs include *Working Woman, New Woman, Savvy, The Executive Female,* and *Enterprising Women.* These magazines are also recommended reading for men who want a better understanding of the problems that women face in the world of work.

Accommodating Families

One of the major problems women have faced is that of having both a managerial career and a family. Women managers whose children are at an age requiring close parental attention often experience conflict between their responsibility to the children and their duty to the employer. If the conflict becomes too painful, they may decide to forgo their careers, at least temporarily, and leave their jobs.

In recent years many employers—including DuPont, Digital Equipment Corporation, Quaker Oats Company, Corning Glass Works, and Pacific Telesis—have inaugurated programs that are mutually advantageous to the career-oriented woman and the employer. These programs, which include alternative career paths, extended leave, flextime, job sharing, and telecommuting, provide new ways to balance career and family. The number of employers moving to protect their investment in top-flight women is still small, but more of them are defining a separate track for women managers.[20]

In a provocative article in the *Harvard Business Review,* Felice Schwartz, founder and president of Catalyst, offers justification for two separate groups, "career-primary" women and "career and family" women. She advises helping women in the latter group to be productive but not necessarily upwardly mobile.[21] Many women, as well as men, criticize Schwartz's approach as perpetuating the inequities of a double standard and as pitting women against women—those with children against those without. On the other hand, there are those who believe that this approach at least gives women choices.

Career Development for Minorities

objective

Many organizations have specific career planning programs for minority employees. These programs are intended to equip employees with career planning skills and development opportunities that will help them compete effectively for advancement.

We observed in Chapter 5 that many employers make a special effort to recruit minorities. Once individuals from minority groups are on the job, it is important for employers to provide opportunities for them to move ahead in the organization as they improve their job skills and abilities.

Advancement of Minorities to Management Positions

The area of employment that has been the slowest to respond to affirmative action appeals is the advancement of minorities to middle- and top-management positions. For example, while blacks constituted almost 10 percent of the employed U.S. civilian population in 1993, they held only 6.6 percent of executive, administrative, and managerial positions. With 7.8 percent of the employed civilian population, Hispanics held 4.0 percent of executive, administrative, and managerial positions.[22]

The male black or Hispanic manager who aspires to higher levels in an organization is likely to find that his career will start off like a rocket but that as he reaches the middle ranks a barrier makes it very difficult to move to the top. Support groups like the Black Professionals Organization at United Airlines alert management to the concerns of black employees.

In recent years black women have been rising more rapidly than black men in corporate America. Between 1982 and 1992 this group grew 125 percent. The reasons black women are overtaking black men are many and complex. However, in spite of their progress, both black women and black men need continued support in their development and advancement.[23]

While minority managers do play a part in creating a better climate for groups that are discriminated against in advancement opportunities, top management and the HR department have the primary responsibility to create conditions in the organization that are favorable for recognizing and rewarding performance on the basis of objective, nondiscriminatory criteria.

Providing Internships

One approach to helping minority students prepare for management careers is to give them employment experiences while they are still in college. An *internship program* offers students an opportunity to learn on the job and gain hands-on experience. One organization, Inroads, Inc., offers qualified minority college students a package of tutoring, counseling, and summer internships with large corporations. It has about 800 corporate sponsors that pay an annual fee for each intern they sponsor. Among the sponsors are Pitney-Bowes, Kaiser Permanente, Arthur Andersen & Company, TRW, Macys California, and Shell Oil Company. The program considers only students who graduate in the top 10 percent of their high school class. In college, the students must maintain a 2.7 grade-point average out of a possible 4.0. Participants report that Inroads has raised their aspirations and has taught them how to adjust to the corporate world. Benefits for the corporation include early access to talented minorities, opportunities to hire college graduates who understand the company's business and its culture, and a greater number of minorities pursuing careers in the traditionally underrepresented fields of engineering and business.[24]

Organizing Training Courses

Training opportunities for minority managers are offered by such organizations as the American Management Association. Specifically addressing the advancement difficulties of blacks, it conducts a course titled "Self-Development Strategies for Black Managers" in several cities throughout the country. Major topics include the realities of corporate life, race-related stresses, effective interpersonal relationships, situational leadership, handling of racial discrimination, and personal self-assessment.

Dual-Career Couples

As discussed in Chapter 2, the employment of both members of a couple has become a way of life in North America. Economic necessity and social forces have encouraged this trend to the point that the U.S. Department of Labor notes that in 1995 81 percent of all marriages will be **dual-career partnerships** in which both members follow their own careers and actively support each other's career development.[25]

As with most lifestyles, the dual-career arrangement has its positive and negative sides. A significant number of organizations are concerned with the problems facing dual-career couples and offer assistance to them. Flexible working schedules are the most frequent organizational accommodation to these couples. Other arrangements include leave policies where either parent may stay home with a newborn, policies that allow work to be performed at home, day care on organization premises, and job sharing.

The difficulties that dual-career couples face include the need for child care, the time demands, and emotional stress. However, the main problem these couples face is the threat of relocation. Many large organizations now offer some kind of job-finding assistance for spouses of employees who are relocated, including payment of fees charged by employment agencies, job counseling firms, and executive search firms. Organizations are also developing networking relationships with other employers to find jobs for the spouses of their relocating employees. These networks can provide a way to "share the wealth and talent" in a community while simultaneously assisting in the recruitment efforts of the participating organizations.

The relocating of dual-career couples to foreign facilities is a major issue that international employers face. Fewer employees are willing to relocate without assistance for their spouses. Many employers have developed effective approaches for integrating the various allowances typically paid for overseas assignments when husband and wife work for the same employer. Far more complex are the problems that arise when couples work for two different employers.[26] These problems associated with overseas assignments of dual-career couples will be examined in greater detail in Chapter 19.

Dual-career partnerships

Marriages in which both members follow their own careers and actively support each other's career development

A flexible working schedule allows this half of a dual-career couple to work at home.

objective

Personal Career Development

We have observed that there are numerous ways for an employer to contribute to an individual employee's career development and at the same time meet the organization's HR needs. The organization can certainly be a positive force in the development process, but the primary responsibility for personal career growth still rests with the individual. One's career may begin before and often continue after a period of employment with an organization. To help employees achieve their career objectives, managers and HRM professionals should have an understanding of the stages one goes through in developing a career and the actions one should take to be successful.

Stages of Career Development

Knowledge, skills, abilities, and attitudes as well as career aspirations change as one matures. While the work that individuals in different occupations perform can vary significantly, the challenges and frustrations that they face at the same stage in their careers are remarkably similar. A model describing these stages is shown in Figure 8–6. The stages are (1) preparation for work, (2) organizational entry, (3) early career, (4) midcareer, and (5) late career. The typical age range and the major tasks of each stage are also presented in the figure.

The first stage—preparation for work—encompasses the period prior to entering an organization, often extending until age 25. It is a period in which individuals must acquire the knowledge, abilities, and skills they will need to compete in the marketplace. It is a time when careful planning, based on sound information, should be the focus. The second stage, typically from ages 18 to 25, is devoted to soliciting job offers and selecting an appropriate job. During this

---

FIGURE 8-6 *Stages of Career Development*

STAGE 1: PREPARATION FOR WORK

Typical age range: 0–25

Major tasks: Develop occupational self-image, assess alternative occupations, develop initial occupational choice, pursue necessary education.

STAGE 2: ORGANIZATIONAL ENTRY

Typical age range: 18–25

Major tasks: Obtain job offer(s) from desired organization(s), select appropriate job based on accurate information.

STAGE 3: EARLY CAREER

Typical age range: 25–40

Major tasks: Learn job, learn organizational rules and norms, fit into chosen occupation and organization, increase competence, pursue goals.

STAGE 4: MIDCAREER

Typical age range: 40–55

Major tasks: Reappraise early career and early adulthood, reaffirm or modify goals, make choices appropriate to middle adult years, remain productive in work.

STAGE 5: LATE CAREER

Typical age range: 55–retirement

Major tasks: Remain productive in work, maintain self-esteem, prepare for effective retirement.

Source: From *Career Management* by Jeffrey H. Greenhaus, copyright 1987 by The Dryden Press, reproduced by permission of the publisher.

---

period one may also be involved in preparing for work. The next three stages entail fitting into a chosen occupation and organization, modifying goals, making choices, remaining productive, and finally, preparing for retirement. In the remainder of the chapter we will examine some of the activities of primary concern to the student, who is likely to be in the early stages. Retirement planning will be discussed in Chapter 12.

Developing Personal Skills

In planning a career, one should not attend only to acquiring specific job knowledge and skills. Job know-how is clearly essential, but there are other skills one must develop to be successful as an employee. To succeed as a manager, one must achieve a still higher level of proficiency in such major areas as communication, time management, self motivation, interpersonal relationships, and the broad area of leadership.

"You have to admit it's not a run of the mill resume."

From *The Wall Street Journal*—Permission, Cartoon Features Syndicate

Hundreds of self-help books have been written on these topics, and a myriad of opportunities to participate in workshops are available, often under the sponsorship of one's employer.[27] One should not overlook sources of valuable information such as articles in general-interest magazines and professional journals. For example, the pointers on the basic skills of successful career management listed in Highlights in HRM 3 are taken from a *Personnel Journal* article in which the eight skills are discussed.

Choosing a Career

When asked about career choice, Peter Drucker said, "The probability that the first job choice you make is the right one for you is roughly one in a million. If you decide your first choice is the right one, chances are that you are just plain lazy."[28] The implications of this statement are that one must often do a lot of searching and changing to find a career path that is psychologically and financially satisfying.

Use of Available Resources

A variety of resources is available to aid in the process of choosing a satisfying career. Counselors at colleges and universities, as well as those in private practice, are equipped to assist individuals in evaluating their aptitudes, abilities, interests, and values as they relate to career selection. There is broad interest

HIGHLIGHTS IN HRM

3   BASIC SKILLS OF SUCCESSFUL CAREER MANAGEMENT

1. Develop a positive attitude.
2. Take responsibility for your own career.
3. Establish goals.
4. Be aware of success factors.
5. Present yourself in a positive manner.
6. Be in the right place at the right time.
7. Establish a relationship with a mentor or guide.
8. Adopt the mindset of your superiors.

Source: Excerpted from Lewis Newman, "Career Management: Start with Goals," *Personnel Journal* 68, no. 4 (April 1989): 91–92. Reprinted with permission of *Personnel Journal*. All rights reserved.

among business schools in a formal instructional program in career planning and development, and other units in the institutions, such as placement offices and continuing education centers, offer some type of career planning assistance.

Accuracy of Self-evaluation

Successful career development depends in part on an individual's ability to conduct an accurate self-evaluation. In making a self-evaluation, one needs to consider those factors that are personally significant. The most important internal factors are one's academic aptitude and achievement, occupational aptitudes and skills, social skills, communication skills, leadership abilities, interests, and values. The latter should include consideration of salary level, status, opportunities for advancement, and growth on the job. External factors that should be assessed include family values and expectations, economic conditions, employment trends, job market information, and perceived effect of physical or psychological disabilities on success.[29]

Significance of Interest Inventories

Psychologists who specialize in career counseling typically administer a battery of tests such as those mentioned in Chapter 6. The Strong Vocational Interest

Blank (SVIB), developed by E. K. Strong, Jr., was among the first of the interest tests.[30] Somewhat later, G. Frederic Kuder developed inventories to measure degree of interest in mechanical, clerical, scientific, and persuasive activities, among others. Both the Strong and the Kuder interest inventories have been used widely in vocational counseling.

Strong found that there are substantial differences in interests that vary from occupation to occupation and that a person's interest pattern, especially after age 21, tends to become quite stable. By taking his test, now known as the *Strong Interest Inventory*, one can learn the degree to which his or her interests correspond with those of successful people in a wide range of occupations. Personality type can also be obtained by using a special scoring key on an individual's *Strong Interest Inventory* answer sheet. This key, developed by John Holland, provides scores on six personality types:

1. Realistic
2. Investigative
3. Artistic
4. Social
5. Enterprising
6. Conventional

These categories characterize not only a type of personality, but also the type of working environment that a person would find most satisfying. In the actual application of Holland's theory, combinations of the six types are examined. For example, a person may be classified as realistic-investigative-enterprising (RIE). Jobs in the RIE category include mechanical engineer, lineperson, and air-traffic controller.[31] To facilitate searching for occupations that match one's category, such as RIE, Holland has devised a series of tables that correlate the Holland categories with jobs in the *Dictionary of Occupational Titles* (DOT), described in Chapter 4.

Another inventory that measures *both* interests and skills is the *Campbell Interest and Skill Survey* (CISS).[32] The CISS can be used not only to assist employees in exploring career paths and options but to help organizations develop their employees or to reassign them because of major organizational changes. In completing the inventory, individuals report their levels of interest and skill using a six-point response scale on 200 interest items and 120 skill items. CISS item responses are translated into seven orientations—*influencing, organizing, helping, creating, analyzing, producing, and adventuring*—and further categorized into twenty-nine basic scales such as leadership and supervision, to identify occupations that reflect today's workplace.

Highlights in HRM 4 shows a sample profile for one individual. Note that at the top of the profile the range of scores is from 30 to 70, with 50 in the mid-range. Corresponding verbal descriptions of scores range from very low to very high. Also note that on the profile two types of scores are profiled: *interest* (a solid diamond ◆) and *skill* (an open diamond ◇). The interest score ◆ shows how much the individual likes the specified activities; the skill score ◇ shows how confident the individual feels about performing these activities.

HIGHLIGHTS IN HRM

4 CAMPBELL INTEREST AND SKILL SURVEY: INDIVIDUAL PROFILE

highlights

SAMPLE   **ORIENTATIONS AND BASIC SCALES**   DATE SCORED 10/20/92

Orientations and Basic Scales	Interest ◆	Skill ◇	Interest/ Skill Pattern
Influencing	**61**	**60**	Pursue
Leadership	65	64	Pursue
Law/Politics	48	57	Explore
Public Speaking	63	59	Pursue
Sales	46	58	Explore
Advertising/Marketing	47	42	
Organizing	**46**	**37**	
Supervision	68	58	Pursue
Financial Services	35	31	Avoid
Office Practices	44	42	Avoid
Helping	**60**	**68**	Pursue
Adult Development	62	58	Pursue
Counseling	58	68	Pursue
Child Development	56	43	Develop
Religious Activities	70	60	Pursue
Medical Practice	52	56	Explore
Creating	**23**	**37**	Avoid
Art/Design	19	32	Avoid
Performing Arts	41	39	Avoid
Writing	32	36	Avoid
International Activities	50	64	Explore
Fashion	35	48	
Culinary Arts	48	43	
Analyzing	**33**	**33**	Avoid
Mathematics	34	33	Avoid
Science	31	36	Avoid
Producing	**37**	**46**	
Mechanical Crafts	33	35	Avoid
Woodworking	32	39	Avoid
Farming/Forestry	46	44	
Plants/Gardens	51	51	
Animal Care	50	49	

Scale markers: Very Low 30, 35 — Low 40, 45 — Mid-Range 50, 55 — High 60 — Very High 65, 70

Adventuring	59	54		Develop
Athletics/Physical Fitness	58	47		Develop
Military/Law Enforcement	63	66		Pursue
Risks/Adventure	46	52		

There are four noteworthy patterns of combinations of the interest and skill scores:

Pursue	Interests high, skills high
Develop	Interests high, skills lower
Explore	Interests lower, skills high
Avoid	Interests low, skills low

For the individual whose scores are profiled in Highlights in HRM 4, one would interpret the scores on the seven orientation scales (as shown in the right-hand column of the profile) as follows:

Influencing	Pursue
Organizing	Indeterminate
Helping	Pursue
Creating	Avoid
Analyzing	Avoid
Producing	Indeterminate
Adventuring	Develop

On the basis of such profiles, individuals can see how their interests and skills compare with those of a sample of people happily employed in a wide range of occupations. Completed answer sheets can be mailed to a scoring center, or software is available and may be obtained for in-house scoring.

Evaluation of Long-term Employment Opportunities

In making a career choice, one should attempt to determine the probable long-term opportunities in the occupational fields one is considering. While even the experts can err in their predictions, one should give at least some attention to the opinions that are available. A source of information that has proved valuable over the years is the *Occupational Outlook Handbook*, published by the U.S. Department of Labor and available at most libraries. Many libraries also have publications that provide details about jobs and career fields. In recent years, a considerable amount of computer software has been developed to facilitate access to information about career fields and to enable individuals to match their abilities, aptitudes, interests, and experiences with the requirements of occupational areas.

Choosing an Employer

Once an individual has made a career choice, even if only tentatively, the next major step is deciding where to work. The choice of employer may be based primarily on location, immediate availability of a position, starting salary, and other basic considerations. However, the college graduate who has prepared for a professional or managerial career is likely to have more sophisticated concerns. Douglas Hall proposes that people frequently choose an organization on the basis of its climate and how it appears to fit their needs. According to Hall,

> People with high needs for achievement may choose aggressive, achievement-oriented organizations. Power-oriented people may choose influential, prestigious, power-oriented organizations. Affiliative people may choose warm, friendly, supportive organizations. We know that people whose needs fit with the climate of an organization are rewarded more and are more satisfied than those who fit in less well, so it is natural to reason that fit would also be a factor in one's choice of an organization.

Hall suggests further that because the relevant theory and measurement technology are available, the prediction of organizational choice is a promising area for researchers.[33]

The "Plateauing Trap"

Career plateau

Situation in which for either organizational or personal reasons the probability of moving up the career ladder is low

Judith Bardwick was the first to label the plateauing phenomenon.[34] A **career plateau** is a situation in which for either organizational or personal reasons the probability of moving up the career ladder is low. According to Bardwick, only 1 percent of the labor force will *not* plateau in their working lives. There are three types of plateaus: structural, content, and life. A *structural plateau* marks the end of promotions; one will now have to leave the organization to find new opportunities and challenges. A *content plateau* occurs when a person has learned a job too well and is bored with day-to-day activities. According to Susan Brooks, a *life plateau* is more profound and may feel like a midlife crisis.[35] People who experience life plateaus often have allowed work or some other major factor to become the most significant aspect of their lives, and they experience a loss of identity and self-esteem when there is no longer success in that area.

Organizations can help individuals cope with plateaus by providing opportunities for lateral growth where opportunities for advancement do not exist. Brooks makes reference to Beverly Kaye, a partner in Career Systems, Inc., and Jane Michel, training services consultant at Chevron, who work with Chevron employees in a career enrichment program. According to Michel, "It is a process for helping people learn more about what gives them satisfaction within the company, as well as what kinds of opportunities will make them happiest if they go elsewhere."[36] Other employers using an approach that encourages career self-

. . . .

management include John Hancock, Apple Computer, the Los Angeles Times, Mirror Company, and Marriott International.[37]

While employers are recognizing the importance of helping employees with their plateauing experiences, each employee must assume responsibility for his or her professional self-development and make constructive use of time and opportunities. Gone are the days when one can expect continuing employment with any employer.[38]

Becoming an Entrepreneur

Entrepreneur
One who starts, organizes, manages, and assumes responsibility for a business or other enterprise

In the decade of the 1990s no discussion of careers would be complete if entrepreneuring opportunities were not mentioned. Being an **entrepreneur**—one who starts, organizes, manages, and assumes responsibility for a business or other enterprise—offers a personal challenge that many individuals prefer over being an employee. Small businesses are typically run by entrepreneurs who accept the personal financial risks that go with owning a business but who also benefit directly from the success of the business.[39]

Small businesses are actually big employers. Over 87 percent of all businesses employ fewer than twenty people. But in total those small firms employ 27 percent of the U.S. workforce. Businesses with ninety-nine or fewer employees account for 56 percent of the workforce.[40] Hence small business is the source of nearly half of wage and salary jobs in this country.

The individual who considers starting a small business can obtain assistance from the Small Business Administration (SBA), which advises and assists the millions of small businesses in the United States. It is essential for one considering a small business to obtain as much information as possible from the SBA, from libraries, and from organizations and individuals who are knowledgeable about the type of business one is considering. For instance, valuable assistance may be obtained from members of the Service Corps of Retired Executives (SCORE), who offer advisory services under the auspices of the SBA.

Since the details of organizing a business are beyond the scope of this book, Figure 8–7 is presented to provide an overview of the basic steps in starting a new business.[41] *Nation's Business*, published monthly by the U.S. Chamber of Commerce, has a column entitled "Entrepreneur's Notebook" in each issue.

Keeping a Career in Perspective

For most people, work is a primary factor in the overall quality of their lives. It provides a setting for satisfying practically the whole range of human needs and is thus of considerable value to the individual. Nevertheless, it is advisable to keep one's career in perspective so that other important areas of life are not neglected.

Off-the-Job Interests

Satisfaction with one's life is a product of many forces. Some of the more important ingredients are physical health, emotional well-being, financial security, harmonious interpersonal relationships, freedom from too much stress, and achievement of one's goals. While a career can provide some of the satisfaction

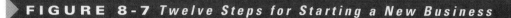

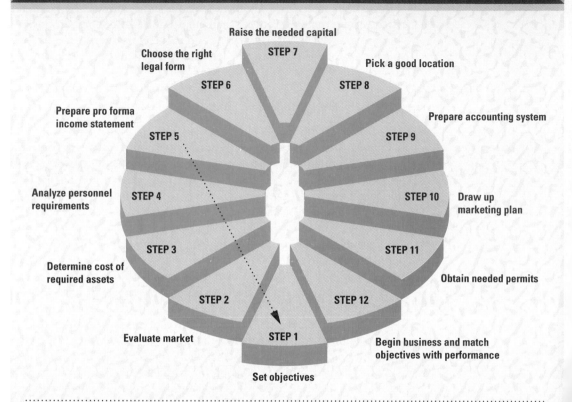

FIGURE 8-7 *Twelve Steps for Starting a New Business*

Raise the needed capital — STEP 7
Choose the right legal form — STEP 6
Pick a good location — STEP 8
Prepare pro forma income statement — STEP 5
Prepare accounting system — STEP 9
Analyze personnel requirements — STEP 4
Draw up marketing plan — STEP 10
Determine cost of required assets — STEP 3
Obtain needed permits — STEP 11
Evaluate market — STEP 2
Begin business and match objectives with performance — STEP 12
Set objectives — STEP 1

Source: William H. Cunningham, Ramon J. Aldag, and Stanley B. Block, *Business in a Changing World,* 3d ed. (Cincinnati, Ohio: South-Western Publishing, 1993), 139. Reprinted with permission.

that one needs, most people find it necessary to turn to interests and activities outside their career. Off-the-job activities not only provide a respite from daily work responsibilities but also offer satisfaction in areas unrelated to work.

Marital and/or Family Life

The career development plans of an individual as well as an organization must take into account the needs of spouses and children. As we have said, the one event that often poses the greatest threat to family needs is relocation. Conflict between a desire to advance in one's career and a strong desire to stay in one place and put down family roots often borders on the disastrous. Many employers now provide complete assistance in this area, including relocation counseling, in an effort to reduce the severity of the pain that can accompany relocations.

While relocation may be the most serious threat to employees with families, there are also other sources of conflict between career and family. Some of th

Aerobic exercise
provides an
invigorating lift from
one's daily work
responsibilities.

work-related sources of conflict are numbers of hours worked per week, frequency of overtime, and the presence and irregularity of shift work. In addition, ambiguity and/or conflict within the employee's work role, low level of leader support, and disappointments due to unfulfilled expectations affect one's life away from the job. Some of the family-related sources of conflict include having to spend an unusually large amount of time with the family and its concerns, spouse employment patterns, and dissimilarity in a couple's career orientations. Jeffrey Greenhaus and Nicholas Beutell, who have examined research studies that identify the sources of work conflict, point out the need for refined measuring devices for use in studying work-family interface more accurately. They emphasize that public policy decisions should rest on a solid foundation of accumulated knowledge.[42]

Planning for Retirement

While retirement appears to be a long way off for the individual who is still in the early stages of a career, it is never too early to make plans for it. In order to enjoy retirement one should prepare for it by giving careful attention to health, finances, family, and interpersonal relationships throughout one's adult life. While most of the larger organizations have preretirement programs, most of the participants in those programs are unfortunately already too close to actual retirement. Thus it is each individual's responsibility to plan early in order to have time to set the stage for a healthy and satisfying retirement as free as possible from worries—especially those that could have been avoided or minimized earlier in life. While employer-sponsored preretirement programs are usually considered very helpful by the participants, as we will see in Chapter 12, they are not a substitute for continual personal concern for oneself.

Maintaining a Balance

Those who are "married" to their jobs to the extent that they fail to provide the attention and caring essential to marriage and family relationships can be said to lack an appreciation for the balance needed for a satisfying life. One should always be aware that "to be a success in the business world takes hard work, long hours, persistent effort, and constant attention. To be a success in marriage takes hard work, long hours, persistent effort, and constant attention.... The problem is giving each its due and not shortchanging the other."[43]

SUMMARY

A career development program is a dynamic process that should integrate individual employee needs with those of the organization. It is the responsibility of the employee to identify his or her own KSAs as well as interests and values and to seek out information about career options. The organization should provide information about its mission, policies, and plans and what it will provide in the way of training and development for the employee.

In order to be successful, a career development program must receive the support of top management. The program should reflect the goals and the culture of the organization, and managerial personnel at all levels must be trained in the fundamentals of job design, performance appraisal, career planning, and counseling. Employees should have an awareness of the organization's philosophy and its goals, otherwise they will not know how their goals match those of the organization. HRM policies, especially those concerning rotation, transfers, and promotions, should be consistent with the goals. The objectives and opportunities of the career development program should be announced widely throughout the organization.

Job opportunities may be identified by studying jobs and determining the knowledge and skills each one requires. Once that is accomplished, it is possible to plan job progressions. These progressions can then serve as a basis for developing career paths. Once career paths are developed and employees are identified on the career ladders, it is possible to inventory the jobs and determine where individuals with the required skills and knowledge are needed or will be needed.

Identifying and developing managerial talent is a responsibility of all managers. In addition to immediate superiors, there should be others in the organization who can nominate and sponsor employees with promise. Many organizations use assessment centers to identify managerial talent and recommend developmental experiences in order that each individual may reach her or his full potential. Mentoring has been found to be valuable for providing guidance and support to potential managers.

The first step in facilitating the career development of women is to eliminate barriers to advancement. The formation of women's networks, the providing of special training for women, the acceptance of women as valued members of the organization, the providing of mentors of women, and accommodating families have been found to be effective ways to facilitate a woman's career development.

objective

While a diversified workforce is composed of many different groups, an important segment is minority groups. In addition to creating conditions that are favorable for recognizing and rewarding performance, many organizations have special programs such as internships that provide hands-on experience as well as special training opportunities. Another group that requires the attention of management is composed of dual-career couples who often need to have flexible working schedules.

objective

In choosing a career, one should use all available resources. Consideration should be given to internal factors such as academic aptitude and achievement, occupational aptitudes and skills, communication skills, leadership abilities, and interests and values. External factors such as economic conditions, employment trends, and job market information must also be considered. In choosing a career one should make use of interest and skill inventories. Long-term employment opportunities in an occupational field should be assessed by utilizing various publications, including those published by the government. Keeping a career in perspective so as to have a balanced life is desirable. While work is usually a primary factor in overall quality of life, one should give proper attention to physical health, harmonious family and interpersonal relationships, and interests and activities outside of one's career.

KEY TERMS

assessment center	job progressions
career counseling	mentoring functions
career paths	mentors
career plateau	outplacement services
dual-career partnerships	relocation services
entrepreneur	transfer
fast-track program	

DISCUSSION QUESTIONS

1. Give some reasons for the trend toward increased emphasis on career development programs.

2. Bank of America maintains a special suite of offices at its world headquarters in San Francisco for its retired executives. Two of the bank's former chief executives use their offices regularly.
    a. Of what value is this arrangement to the corporation? To the individuals?
    b. How might retired executives in any organization assist in the career development of current employees?
3. What contributions can a career development program make to an organization that is forced to downsize its operations?
4. One recruiter has said, "Next to talent, the second most important factor in career success is taking the time and effort to develop visibility." What are some ways of developing visibility?
5. Over 50 percent of all MBAs leave their first employer within five years. While the change may mean career growth for the individuals, it represents a loss to the employers. What are some of the probable reasons an MBA would leave his or her first employer?
6. What are some of the barriers that have limited advancement opportunities for women in many organizations?
7. List the advantages and disadvantages of being an entrepreneur.
8. In your opinion, what personal characteristics are employers looking for in individuals whom they are considering for long-term employment and probable advancement in the organization? To what extent can one develop these characteristics?

CASE STUDY: Preparing a Career Development Plan

Sue Ann Scott was a receptionist at the headquarters of a large corporation. A high school graduate, she had no particular skills other than an ability to organize her job duties and a pleasant personality. Nevertheless, Scott wanted very much to improve her economic position. Recognizing her educational limitations, she began taking accounting courses on a random basis in an evening adult education program. Unfortunately, she did not have any particular plan for career development.

   Scott also took advantage of the corporation's job bidding system by applying for openings that were posted, even though in many instances she did not meet the specifications listed for them. After being rejected several times, she became discouraged. Her depressed spirits were observed by Elizabeth Burroughs, one of the department managers in the corporation. Burroughs invited Scott to come to her office for a talk about the problems she was having. Scott took full advantage of this opportunity to express her frustrations and disappointments. As she unburdened herself, it became apparent both to her and to Burroughs that during interviews she invariably apologized for having "only a high school education." This made it difficult for the interviewers to select her over other candidates who were more positive about their backgrounds and skills. Burroughs suggested that perhaps Scott might try taking an equally positive approach during her interviews. For example, she could stress her self-improvement efforts at night school and the fact that she was a dependable and cooperative person who was willing to work hard to succeed in the job for which she was applying.

Following Burroughs' advice, Scott applied for a position as invoice clerk, a job for which she felt she was qualified. She made a very forceful and positive presentation during her interview, stressing the favorable qualities that she possessed. As a result of this approach, she got the job. While the pay for an invoice clerk was not much more than that for a receptionist, the position did offer an avenue for possible advancement into the accounting field, where the accounting courses she was taking would be of value.

Questions

1. What are some of the possible reasons Scott did not seek or receive advice from her immediate supervisor?

2. After reviewing the chapter, suggest all possible ways that Scott can prepare herself for career advancement.

NOTES AND REFERENCES

1. Thomas G. Gutteridge, Zandy B. Leibowitz, and Jane E. Shore, *Organizational Career Development* (San Francisco: Jossey-Bass, 1993): xvii–xix, 1–3. See also Beverly Kaye and Zandy Leibowitz, "Career Development—Don't Let It Fizzle," *HR Magazine* 39, no. 9 (September 1994): 78–83.

2. Zandy B. Leibowitz, Caela Farren, and Beverly L. Kaye, *Designing Career Development Systems* (San Francisco: Jossey-Bass, 1986): 40–42. See also Paul Herriot, *The Career Management Challenge—Balancing Individual and Organizational Needs* (Thousand Oaks, Calif.: Sage Publications, 1992).

3. K. J. Nilan, S. Walls, S. L. Davis, and M. E. Lund, "Creating Hierarchical Career Progression," *Personnel Administrator* 32, no. 6 (June 1987): 168–83; R. J. Sahl, "Succession Planning: A Blueprint for Your Company's Future," *Personnel Administrator* 32, no. 9 (September 1987): 101–8.

4. Milan Moravec, and Beverly McKee, "Designing Dual Career Paths and Compensation," *Personnel* 67, no. 8 (August 1990): 5. See also Robert Tucker, Milan Moravec, and Ken Ideus, "Designing a Dual-Track Career System," *Training and Development* 46, no. 6 (June 1992): 55–58.

5. For other sources of career information and advice on how to select a professional career counselor, see Berkeley Rice, "Why Am I in This Job?" *Psychology Today* 19, no. 1 (January 1985): 54–59. For books that provide guidance as well as an opportunity for

self-analysis, see James D. Porterfield, *Business Career Planning Guide* (Cincinnati, Ohio: South-Western Publishing, 1993); and Julie Griffin Levitt, *Your Career—How to Make It Happen*, 2d ed. (Cincinnati, Ohio: South-Western Publishing, 1990).

6. Jean R. Haskell, "Getting Employees to Take Charge of Their Careers," *Training and Development* 47, no. 2 (February 1993): 51–54. See also Harry Levinson, *Career Mastery* (San Francisco: Barrett-Koehler Publishers, 1992).

7. Deena Harkins, Zandy Leibowitz, and Stephen E. Forrer, "How the IRS Finds and Keeps Good Employees," *Training and Development* 47, no. 4 (April 1993): 76–78.

8. Dennis A. Joiner, "Exploring the Accuracy and Value of Self-Assessments," *Training and Development Journal* 43, no. 5 (1989): 88. See also Dennis A. Joiner, "Demystifying Assessment Center Exercises," *Fire Chief* (September 1990): 51–53. A classic book on assessment centers is G. C. Thornton III and W. C. Byham, *Assessment Centers and Managerial Performance* (New York: Academic Press, 1982).

9. George P. Hollenbeck, "The Past, Present, and Future of Assessment Centers," *The Industrial-Organizational Psychologist* 28, no. 2 (October 1990): 13–17.

10. George S. Odiorne, "Mentoring: An American Management Innovation," *Personnel Administrator* 30, no. 5 (May 1985): 63–70.

11. Kathy E. Kram, *Mentoring at Work* (Lanham, Md.: University Press of America, 1988), 22–24. See also Belle Rose Ragins and Terri A. Scandura, "Gender Differences in Expected Outcomes of Mentoring Relationships," *Academy of Management Journal* 37, no. 4 (August 1994): 957–71; James A. Wilson and Nancy S. Elman, "Organization Benefits of Mentoring," *The Executive* IV, no. 4 (November 1990): 88–94.

12. Beth Rogers, "Mentoring Takes a New Twist," *HR Magazine* 37, no. 8 (August 1992): 48–51.

13. Rogers, "Mentoring Takes a New Twist."

14. Lori Bongiorno, "Big Ideas for Little Girls," *Business Week* (May 3, 1993): 38–39; Sue Shellenbarger, "Women Mentors Hope to Make Lasting Impact," *The Wall Street Journal* (April 28, 1993): B1. See also Stephenie Overman, "Business Gives Students a Hand," *HR Magazine* 38, no. 4 (April 1993): 46–50.

15. Victoria A. Parker and Kathy E. Kram, "Women Mentoring Women: Creating Conditions for Connection," *Business Horizons* 36, no. 2 (March-April 1993): 42–51. See also Leslie Smith, "Rounding Out Your Network," *Executive Female* 17, no. 6 (November/December 1994): 60, 67; Carol Wolfe Konek and Sally L. Kitch, eds., *Women and Careers—Issues, Pressures, and Challenges* (Thousand Oaks, Calif.: Sage Publications, 1993).

16. Headquarters for Catalyst is at 250 Park Avenue South, 5th Floor, New York, N.Y. 10003-8900.

17. Dan R. Dalton and Idelene F. Kesner, "Cracks in the Glass: The Silent Competence of Women," *Business Horizons* 36, no. 2 (March-April 1993): 6–11. See also Peggy Stuart, "What Does the Glass Ceiling Cost You?" *Personnel Journal* 71, no. 11 (November 1992): 70–80; Charlene Marmer Solomon, "Careers under Glass," *Personnel Journal* 69, no. 4 (April 1990): 96–105; Rochelle Sharpe, "The Waiting Game: Women Make Strides but Men Stay Firmly in Top Company Jobs," *The Wall Street Journal* (March 29, 1994): A-1.

18. Rose Mary Wentling, "Women in Middle Management: Their Career Development and Aspirations," *Business Horizons* 35, no. 1 (January-February 1992): 47–54. See also Michelle Neely Martinez, "The High Potential Woman," *HR Magazine* 36, no. 6 (June 1991): 46–51.

19. The interested reader should find the following books very informative: Johanna Hunsaker and Phillip Hunsaker, *Strategies and Skills for Managerial Women* (Cincinnati, Ohio: South-Western Publishing, 1991); and Helen Gurley Brown, *Having It All* (New York: Simon and Schuster, 1982).

20. Elizabeth Ehrlich, "The Mommy Track," *Business Week* (March 20, 1989): 126–34; Elizabeth Ehrlich, "Is the Mommy Track a Blessing or Betrayal?" *Business Week* (May 15, 1989): 98–99.

21. Felice Schwartz, "Management Women and the New Facts of Life," *Harvard Business Review* 89, no. 1 (January-February 1989): 65–82. See also Hal Lancaster, "A Big Six Firm Decides Detours Won't Derail a Career," *The Wall Street Journal* (December 20, 1994): B1.

22. U.S. Department of Commerce, Bureau of the Census, *Statistical Abstract of the United States* (Washington, D.C.: U.S. Government Printing Office, 1994): 407.

23. Herminia Ibarra, "Personal Networks of Women and Minorities in Management: A Conceptual Framework," *The Academy of Management Review* 18, no. 1 (January 1993): 56–87. See also Dorothy J. Gaiter, "Black Women's Gains in Corporate America Outstrip Black Men's," *The Wall Street Journal* (March 8, 1994): A-1. For an interesting book written especially for black managers, see Floyd Dickens, Jr., and Jacqueline B. Dickens, *The Black Manager—Making It in the Corporate World*, 2d ed. (New York: AMACOM, 1991).

24. *Inroads 1993 Annual Report* and Inroads brochure, *Partnership for a Diverse Workforce*. The national headquarters of Inroads, Inc., is located at Suite 800, 1221 Locust, St. Louis, Mo. 63103.

25. Calvin Reynolds and Rita Bennett, "The Career Couple Challenge," *Personnel Journal* 70, no. 3 (March 1991): 46–49.

26. Reynolds and Bennett, "The Career Couple Challenge."

27. A selection of self-help publications on a variety of topics may be found in any bookstore. College and university bookstores typically have a very wide selection in their trade or general books department. A recent popular book that presents a principle-centered approach to time management is Stephen R. Corey, A. Roger Merrill, and Rebecca R. Merrill, *First Things First* (New York: Simon & Schuster, 1994).

28. Mary Harrington Hall, "A Conversation With Peter Drucker," *Psychology Today* 1, no. 10 (March 1968): 22.

29. Lila B. Stair, *Careers in Business: Selecting and Planning Your Career Path* (Homewood, Ill.: Richard D. Irwin, 1980): 8. See also Walter Kiechel III, "A Manager's Career in the New Economy," *Fortune* (April 4, 1994): 68–72; Sander I. Marcus and Jotham G. Friedland, "14 Steps on a New Career Path," *HR Magazine* 38, no. 3 (March 1993): 55–56; Stephenie Overman, "Weighing Career Anchors," *HR Magazine* 38, no. 3 (March 1993): 56–58.

30. E. K. Strong, Jr., of Stanford University, was active in the measurement of interests from the early 1920s to the time of his death in 1963. Since then his work has been carried on by the staff of the Measurement Research Center, University of Minnesota. *The Strong Interest Inventory* is distribute

by Consulting Psychologists Press, Inc., P.O. Box 60070, Palo Alto, Calif. 94306, to qualified persons under an exclusive license from the publisher, Stanford University Press.

31. John I. Holland, *Making Vocational Choices: A Theory of Careers,* 2d ed. (Englewood Cliffs, N.J.: Prentice-Hall, 1984).

32. The *Campbell Interest and Skill Survey* (copyright 1992) is published and distributed by NCS Assessments, P. O. Box 1416, Minneapolis, Minn. 55440.

33. Douglas T. Hall, *Careers in Organizations* (Santa Monica, Calif.: Goodyear Publishing, 1976), 36. See also Douglas T. Hall and Associates, *Career Development in Organizations* (San Francisco: Jossey-Bass, 1986).

34. Judith Bardwick, *The Plateauing Trap* (New York: AMACOM, 1986).

35. Susan Sonnsesyn Brooks, "Moving Up Is Not the Only Option," *HR Magazine* 39, no. 3 (March 1994): 79–82.

36. Brooks, "Moving Up."

37. Shari Caudron, "HR Revamps Career Itineraries," *Personnel Journal* 73, no. 4 (April 1994): 64B–64J.

38. William Bridges, *Job Shift* (Reading, Mass.: Addison-Wesley, 1994).

39. William H. Cunningham, Ramon J. Aldag, and Stanley B. Block, *Business in a Changing World,* 3rd ed. (Cincinnati, Ohio: South-Western Publishing, 1993): 130–31. See also Bruce Nussbaum, Alice Cuneo, Barbara Carlson, and Gary McWilliams, "Corporate Refugees," *Business Week* (April 12, 1993): 58–65; Ronald Henkoff, "Winning the New Career Game," *Fortune* (July 12, 1993): 46–49; John Naisbitt and Patricia Aburdene, *Megatrends 2000* (New York: William Morrow, 1990): 300–2, 311–13.

40. U.S. Department of Commerce, Bureau of the Census, *County Business Patterns,* 1992 (Washington, D.C.: U.S. Government Printing Office, 1994): IX.

41. Cunningham, Aldag, and Block, *Business in a Changing World,* Chapter 6. See also Gary Brenner, Joel Ewan, and Henry Custer, *The Complete Handbook for the Entrepreneur* (Englewood Cliffs, N.J.: Prentice-Hall, 1990). This book was written by an attorney, a bank officer, and a CPA.

42. Jeffrey H. Greenhaus and Nicholas J. Beutell, "Sources of Conflict Between Work and Family Roles," *Academy of Management Review* 10, no. 1 (January 1985): 76–88. See also Sue Shellenbarger, "How Some Companies Help Their Employees Get a Life," *The Wall Street Journal* (November 16, 1994): B1.

43. Richard W. Ogden, *How to Succeed in Business and Marriage* (New York: AMACOM, 1978): 2.

Chapter

Appraising and Improving Performance

9

one
objective

Explain the purposes of performance appraisals and the reasons they fail.

two
objective

Identify the characteristics of an effective appraisal program.

three
objective

Describe the different sources of appraisal information.

four
objective

Explain the various methods used for performance evaluation.

five
objective

Outline the characteristics of an effective performance appraisal interview.

....

In the preceding chapters, we discussed the programs that an organization uses to procure and develop a productive workforce. In this chapter we turn to performance appraisal programs, which are among the most helpful tools an organization can use to maintain and enhance its productivity. Of course, performance appraisals take place in every organization whether there is a formal program or not. Managers are constantly observing the way their employees carry out their assignments and thereby forming impressions about the relative worth of these employees to the organization. Most organizations, however, do seem to use a formal program. In a study of 324 organizations, 94 percent reported having such a program—a clear indication that performance appraisal is a potentially valuable activity.[1]

The success or failure of a performance appraisal program depends on the philosophy underlying it and the attitudes and skills of those responsible for its administration. Many different methods can be used to gather information about employee performance. However, gathering information is only the first step in the appraisal process. The information must then be evaluated in the context of organizational needs and communicated to employees so that it will result in high levels of performance.

objective

Performance Appraisal Programs

Formal programs for performance appraisal and merit ratings are by no means new to organizations. The federal government began evaluating employees in 1842, when Congress passed a law mandating yearly performance reviews for department clerks. From this early beginning, performance appraisal programs have spread to large and small organizations in both the public and private sectors. Advocates see these HR programs as among the most logical means to appraise, develop, and thus effectively utilize the knowledge and abilities of employees. However, a growing number of observers point out that performance appraisals frequently fall short of their potential.[2]

Recent interest in total-quality management (TQM), for example, has caused numerous organizations to rethink their approach to performance appraisal. The late W. Edward Deming, a pioneer in TQM, identified performance appraisal as one of seven deadly diseases of U.S. management. While most managers still recognize the benefits of performance appraisal, TQM challenges some long-standing assumptions about how it should be conducted. Motorola, General Motors, and Digital, for example, have modified their appraisal systems to better acknowledge *quality of performance* (in addition to quantity), *teamwork* (in addition to individual accomplishments), and *process improvements* (in addition to performance outcomes).[3] Each of these issues is discussed at greater length throughout the chapter.

Purposes of Performance Appraisal

A performance appraisal program can serve many purposes that benefit both the organization and the employee whose performance is being appraised. The Travelers Insurance Company has the following objectives for its performance appraisal program. They are similar to the objectives of other organizations.

1. To give employees the opportunity to discuss performance and performance standards regularly with their supervisor
2. To provide the supervisor with a means of identifying the strengths and weaknesses of an employee's performance
3. To provide a format enabling the supervisor to recommend a specific program designed to help an employee improve performance
4. To provide a basis for salary recommendations[4]

Figure 9–1 shows the most common uses of performance appraisals. In general, these can be classified as either *administrative* or *developmental*.

FIGURE 9-1 *Uses of Performance Appraisal*

RANKING	RATING*
1. Salary administration	5.85
2. Performance feedback	5.67
3. Identification of individual strengths and weaknesses	5.41
4. Documentation of personnel decisions	5.15
5. Recognition of individual performance	5.02
6. Determination of promotion	4.80
7. Identification of poor performance	4.96
8. Assistance in goal identification	4.90
9. Decision in retention or termination	4.75
10. Evaluation of goal achievement	4.72
11. Meeting legal requirements	4.58
12. Determination of transfers and assignments	3.66
13. Decision on layoffs	3.51
14. Identification of individual training needs	3.42
15. Determination of organizational training needs	2.74
16. Personnel planning	2.72
17. Reinforcement of authority structure	2.65
18. Identification of organizational development needs	2.63
19. Establishment of criteria for validation research	2.30
20. Evaluation of personnel systems	2.04

*Ratings are on a seven-point scale.

Source: Adapted from Jeanette N. Cleveland, Kevin R. Murphy, and Richard E. Williams, "Multiple Uses of Performance Appraisal: Prevalence and Correlates," *Journal of Applied Psychology* 74 (1989): 130–135. Copyright 1989 by the American Psychological Association. Adapted by permission.

Administrative Purposes

From the standpoint of administration, appraisal programs provide input that can be used for the entire range of HRM activities. For example, research has shown that performance appraisals are used most widely as a basis for compensation decisions.[5] The practice of "pay-for-performance" is found in all types of organizations. Performance appraisal is also directly related to a number of other major HR functions, such as promotion, transfer, and layoff decisions. Performance appraisal data may also be used in HR planning, in determining the relative worth of jobs under a job evaluation program, and as criteria for validating selection tests. Performance appraisals also provide a "paper trail" for documenting HRM actions that may result in legal action. Because of government EEO/AA directives, employers must maintain accurate, objective records of employee performance in order to defend themselves against possible charges of discrimination in connection with such HRM actions as promotion, salary determination, and termination. Finally, it is important to recognize that the success of the entire HR program depends on knowing how the performance of employees compares with the goals established for them. This knowledge is best derived from a carefully planned and administered HR appraisal program. Appraisal systems have the capability to influence employee behavior, thereby leading directly to improved organizational performance.

Developmental Purposes

From the standpoint of individual development, appraisal provides the feedback essential for discussing strengths and weaknesses as well as improving performance. Regardless of the employee's level of performance, the appraisal process provides an opportunity to identify issues for discussion, eliminate any potential problems, and set new goals for achieving high performance. Newer approaches to performance appraisal emphasize training as well as development and growth plans for employees. A developmental approach to appraisal recognizes that the purpose of a manager is to improve job behavior, not simply to evaluate past performance. Having a sound basis for improving performance is one of the major benefits of an appraisal program.

Reasons Appraisal Programs Sometimes Fail

In actual practice, and for a number of reasons, formal performance appraisal programs sometimes yield disappointing results. Figure 9–2 shows that the primary culprits include lack of top-management information and support, unclear performance standards, rater bias, too many forms to complete, and use of the program for conflicting purposes. For example, if an appraisal program is used to provide a written appraisal for salary action and at the same time to motivate employees to improve their work, the administrative and developmental purposes may be in conflict. As a result, the appraisal interview may become a discussion about salary in which the manager seeks to justify the action taken. In such cases, the discussion might have little influence on the employee's future job performance.

FIGURE 9-2 *Top 10 Reasons Performance Appraisals Can Fail*

1. Manager lacks information concerning an employee's actual performance.
2. Standards by which to evaluate an employee's performance are unclear.
3. Manager does not take the appraisal seriously.
4. Manager is not prepared for the appraisal review with the employee.
5. Manager is not honest/sincere during the evaluation.
6. Manager lacks appraisal skills.
7. Employee does not receive ongoing performance feedback.
8. Insufficient resources are provided to reward performance.
9. There is ineffective discussion of employee development.
10. Manager uses unclear/ambiguous language in the evaluation process.

Source: Adapted with permission from Clinton O. Longnecker and Denise R. McGinnis, "Appraising Technical People: Pitfalls and Solutions," *Journal of Systems Management* (December 1992): 12-16; and Clinton O. Longnecker and Stephen J. Goff, "Why Performance Appraisals Still Fail," *Journal of Compensation and Benefits* 6, no. 3 (November/December 1990): 36-41. Copyright 1992 and 1990 by Warren, Gorham & Lamont, Park Square Building, 31 St. James Avenue, Boston, MA 02116-4112. 1-800-950-1216. All rights reserved.

As with all HR functions, if the support of top management is lacking, the appraisal program will not be successful. Even the best-conceived program will not work in an environment where appraisers are not encouraged by their superiors to take the program seriously. To underscore the importance of this responsibility, top management should announce that effectiveness in appraising subordinates is a standard by which the appraisers themselves will be evaluated.

Other reasons why performance appraisal programs can fail to yield the desired results include the following:

1. Managers feel that little or no benefit will be derived from the time and energy spent in the process.
2. Managers dislike the face-to-face confrontation of appraisal interviews.
3. Managers are not sufficiently adept in providing appraisal feedback.
4. The judgmental role of appraisal conflicts with the helping role of developing employees.

Performance appraisal at many organizations is a once-a-year activity in which the appraisal interview becomes a source of friction for both managers and employees. An important principle of performance appraisal is that continual feedback and employee coaching must be a positive daily activity.[6] The annual

The appraisal process should take place in an environment where both parties feel free to talk.

or semiannual performance review should simply be a logical extension of the day-to-day supervision process.

One of the main concerns of employees is the fairness of the performance appraisal system, since the process is central to so many HRM decisions. Employees who believe the system is unfair may consider the appraisal interview a waste of time and leave the interview with feelings of anxiety or frustration. Also, they may view compliance with the appraisal system as perfunctory and thus play only a passive role during the interview process. By addressing these employee concerns during the planning stage of the appraisal process, the organization will help the appraisal program to succeed in reaching its goals.

Finally, organizational politics can introduce a bias even in fairly administered employee appraisals.[7] For example, managers may inflate evaluations because they desire higher salaries for their employees or because higher subordinate ratings make them look good as managers. Alternatively, managers may want to get rid of troublesome employees, passing them off to another department by inflating their ratings.

objective

Developing an Effective Appraisal Program

The HR department ordinarily has the primary responsibility for overseeing and coordinating the appraisal program. Managers from the operating departments must also be actively involved, particularly in helping to establish the objectives for the program. Furthermore, employees are more likely to accept and be satisfied with the performance appraisal program when they have the chance to participate in its development. Their concerns about fairness and accuracy in determining raises, promotions, and the like tend to be alleviated somewhat when they have been involved at the planning stage and have helped develop the performance standards themselves.

Establishing Performance Standards

Before any appraisal is conducted, the standards by which performance is to be evaluated should be clearly defined and communicated to the employee. As discussed in Chapter 4, these standards should be based on job-related requirements derived from job analysis and reflected in the job descriptions and job specifications. When performance standards are properly established, they help translate organizational goals and objectives into job requirements that convey acceptable and unacceptable levels of performance to employees.[8]

In establishing performance standards, there are four basic considerations: strategic relevance, criterion deficiency, criterion contamination, and reliability.

Strategic Relevance

This refers to the extent to which standards relate to the strategic objectives of the organization. For example, if a TQM program has established a standard that "95 percent of all customer complaints are to be resolved in one day," then it is relevant for the customer service representatives to use such a standard for their evaluations. Companies such as 3M and Rubbermaid have strategic objectives that 25 to 30 percent of their sales are to be generated from products developed within the past five years. These objectives are translated into performance standards for their employees.[9]

Criterion Deficiency

A second consideration in establishing performance standards is the extent to which the standards capture the entire range of an employee's responsibilities. When performance standards focus on a single criterion (e.g., sales revenues) to the exclusion of other important but less quantifiable performance dimensions (e.g., customer service), then the appraisal system is said to suffer from criterion deficiency.

Criterion Contamination

Just as performance criteria can be deficient, they can also be contaminated. There are factors outside an employee's control that can influence his or her performance. A comparison of performance of production workers, for example, should not be contaminated by the fact that some have newer machines than others. A comparison of the performance of traveling salespersons should not be contaminated by the fact that territories differ in sales potential.

Reliability

As discussed in Chapter 6, reliability refers to the stability or consistency of a standard, or the extent to which individuals tend to maintain a certain level of performance over time. In ratings, reliability may be measured by correlating two sets of ratings made by a single rater or by two different raters.[10] For example, two managers may rate the same individual and estimate his or her suitability for a promotion. Their ratings could be compared to determine interrater reliability.

Performance standards will permit managers to specify and communicate precise information to employees regarding quality and quantity of output. Therefore, when performance standards are written, they should be defined in quantifiable and measurable terms. For example, "ability and willingness to handle customer orders" is not as good a performance standard as "all customer orders will be filled in 4 hours with a 98 percent accuracy rate." When standards are expressed in specific, measurable terms, comparing the employee's performance against the standard results in a more justifiable appraisal.

Complying with the Law

Since performance appraisals are used as one basis for HRM actions, they must meet certain legal requirements. In *Brito v Zia*, for example, the Supreme Court ruled that performance appraisals were subject to the same validity criteria as selection procedures.[11] As the courts have made clear, a central issue is to have carefully defined and measurable performance standards. In one landmark case involving test validation, *Albemarle Paper Company v Moody* (discussed in Chapter 3), the U.S. Supreme Court found that employees had been ranked against a vague standard, open to each supervisor's own interpretation. The court stated that "there is no way of knowing precisely what criteria of job performance the supervisors were considering, whether each supervisor was considering the same criteria, or whether indeed, any of the supervisors actually applied a focused and stable body of criteria of any kind."[12] This decision has prompted organizations to try to eliminate vagueness in descriptions of traits such as attitude, cooperation, dependability, initiative, and leadership. For example, the trait "dependability" can be made much less vague if it is spelled out in terms of employee tardiness and/or unexcused absences. In general, reducing room for subjective judgments will improve the entire appraisal process.

Furthermore, other court decisions show that employers might face legal challenges to their appraisal systems when appraisals indicate acceptable or above-average performance but employees are later passed over for promotion, disciplined for poor performance, discharged, or laid off from the organization. In these cases the performance appraisals can undermine the legitimacy of the subsequent personnel decision. Therefore, in light of recent court rulings, performance appraisals should meet the following legal guidelines:

- Performance ratings must be job-related, with performance standards developed through job analysis.
- Employees must be given a written copy of their job standards in advance of appraisals.
- Managers who conduct the appraisal must be able to observe the behavior they are rating. This implies having a measurable standard with which to compare employee behavior.

- Supervisors should be trained to use the appraisal form correctly. They should be instructed in how to apply appraisal standards when making judgments.
- Appraisals should be discussed openly with employees and counseling or corrective guidance offered to help poor performers improve their performance.
- An appeals procedure should be established to enable employees to express disagreement with the appraisal.[13]

To comply with the legal requirements of performance appraisals, employers must ensure that managers and supervisors document appraisals and reasons for subsequent HRM actions. (See Chapter 16 on documentation.) This information may prove decisive should an employee take legal action. An employer's credibility is strengthened when it can support performance appraisal ratings by documenting instances of poor performance.[14]

objective

Deciding Who Should Appraise Performance

Just as there are multiple standards by which to evaluate performance, there are also multiple candidates for appraising performance. Given the complexity of today's jobs, it is often unrealistic to presume that one person can fully observe and evaluate an employee's performance. Companies such as US West, Westinghouse, and The Walt Disney Company have begun to use multiple-rater approaches to performance evaluation.[15] As shown in Figure 9–3, these raters may include supervisors, peers, team members, self, subordinates, and customers. And each may be more or less useful for the administrative and developmental purposes we discussed earlier.

Manager/Supervisor Appraisal

Manager and/or supervisor appraisal

Performance appraisal done by an employee's manager and often reviewed by a manager one level higher

Manager and/or supervisor appraisal has traditionally been the method of evaluating a subordinate's performance. In most instances they are in the best position to perform this function, although it may not always be possible for them to do so. Managers often complain that they do not have the time to fully observe the performance of employees. The result is a less-than-objective appraisal. These managers must then rely on performance records or on the observations of others to complete the appraisal. For example, American Express uses individuals as telephone monitors to gauge the quality of conversation between a service-center representative or credit analyst and a customer. This information is then given to the supervisor for use in completing the employee's performance appraisal.

Where a supervisor appraises employees independently, provision is often made for a review of the appraisals by the supervisor's superior. Having appraisals reviewed by a supervisor's superior reduces the chance of superficial or biased evaluations. Reviews by superiors generally are more objective and provide a broader perspective of employee performance than do appraisals by immediate supervisors.

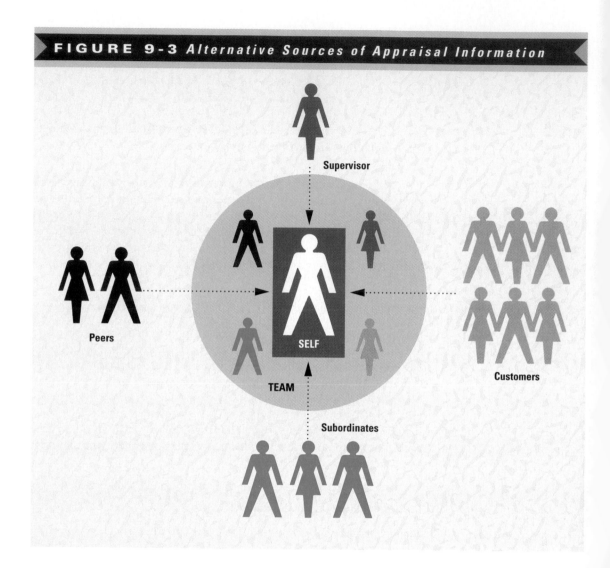

FIGURE 9-3 *Alternative Sources of Appraisal Information*

Supervisor

Peers

SELF

TEAM

Customers

Subordinates

Self-Appraisal

Sometimes employees are asked to evaluate themselves on a self-appraisal form.[16] Self-appraisals are beneficial when managers seek to increase employees' involvement in the review process. A **self-appraisal** system requires an employee to complete the appraisal form prior to the performance interview. At a minimum, this gets the employee thinking about his or her strengths and weaknesses and may lead to discussions about barriers to effective performance. During the performance interview, the manager and the employee discuss job performance and agree on a final appraisal. This approach also works well when the manager and the employee jointly establish future performance goals or employee development plans. Critics of self-appraisal argue that self-raters are more lenient than managers in their assessments and tend to present themselves in a highly favorable light.[17] For this reason, self-appraisals may be best for developmental purposes rather than for administrative decisions. Used in conjunction with other methods, self-appraisals can be a valuable source of appraisal information.

Subordinate Appraisal

Subordinate appraisal
Performance appraisal of a superior by an employee, which is more appropriate for developmental than for administrative purposes

Subordinate appraisal has been used in companies such as Xerox and IBM to give managers feedback on how their subordinates view them.[18] Subordinates are in a good position to evaluate their managers since they are in frequent contact with their superiors and occupy a unique position from which to observe many performance-related behaviors. Those performance dimensions judged most appropriate for subordinate appraisals include leadership, oral communication, delegation of authority, coordination of team efforts, and interest in subordinates. However, dimensions related to managers' specific job tasks, such as planning and organizing, budgeting, creativity, and analytical ability, are not usually seen as appropriate for subordinate appraisal.

Since subordinate appraisals give employees power over their bosses, the managers themselves may be hesitant to endorse such a system, particularly when it might be used as a basis for compensation decisions. However, when the information is used for developmental purposes, managers tend to be more open to the idea.[19] Nevertheless, to avoid potential problems, subordinate appraisals should be submitted anonymously and combined across several individual raters.

Peer Appraisal

Peer appraisal
Performance appraisal done by one's fellow employees, generally on forms that are compiled into a single profile for use in the performance interview conducted by the employee's manager

Individuals of equal rank who work together are increasingly asked to evaluate each other. A **peer appraisal** provides information that differs to some degree from ratings by a superior, since peers often see different dimensions of performance. Peers can readily identify leadership and interpersonal skills along with other strengths and weaknesses of their co-workers. A superior asked to rate a patrol officer on a dimension such as "dealing with the public" may not have had much opportunity to observe it. Fellow officers, on the other hand, have the opportunity to observe this behavior regularly.

One advantage of peer appraisals is the belief that they furnish more accurate and valid information than appraisals by superiors. The supervisor often sees employees putting their best foot forward, while those who work with their fellow employees on a regular basis may see a more realistic picture. With peer appraisals, co-workers complete an evaluation on the employee. The forms are then usually compiled into a single profile, which is given to the supervisor for use in the final appraisal.[20]

Despite the evidence that peer appraisals are possibly the most accurate method of judging employee behavior, there are reasons why they have not been used more frequently.[21] The reasons commonly cited include the following:

1. Peer ratings are simply a popularity contest.
2. Managers are reluctant to give up control over the appraisal process.
3. Those receiving low ratings might retaliate against their peers.
4. Peers rely on stereotypes in ratings.

When peers are in competition with one another, such as with sales associates, peer appraisals may not be advisable for administrative decisions such as salary or bonuses. Employers using peer appraisals must also be sure to safeguard confidentiality in handling the review forms. Any breach of confidentiality can create interpersonal rivalries or hurt feelings and bring about hostility among fellow employees.

Team Appraisal

Team appraisal
Performance appraisal, based on TQM concepts, that recognizes team accomplishment rather than individual performance

An extension of the peer appraisal is the **team appraisal.** While peers are on equal standing with one another, they may not work closely together. In a team setting, it may be nearly impossible to separate out an individual's contribution. Advocates of team appraisal argue that, in such cases, individual appraisal can be dysfunctional since it detracts from the critical issues of the team. To address this issue, organizations such as General Foods, General Motor's Cadillac division, and Digital have begun developing team appraisals to evaluate the performance of the team as a whole.[22]

A company's interest in team appraisals is frequently driven by its commitment to TQM principles and practices. At its root, TQM is a control system that involves setting standards (based on customer requirements), measuring performance against those standards, and identifying opportunities for continuous improvement. In this regard TQM and performance appraisal are perfectly complementary. However, a basic tenet of TQM is that performance is best understood at the level of the system as a whole, whereas performance appraisal traditionally has focused on individual performance. Team appraisals represent one way to break down barriers between individuals and encourage their collective effort.[23] Frequently, the system is complemented by use of team incentives or group variable pay. (See Chapter 11.)

Customer Appraisal

Customer appraisal
Performance appraisal, which, like team appraisal, is based on TQM concepts and seeks evaluation from both external and internal customers

Also driven by TQM concerns, an increasing number of organizations use internal and external **customer appraisal** as a source of performance appraisal information. External customers' evaluations, of course, have been used for some time to appraise restaurant personnel. However, companies like Ford and Honda have begun utilizing external customers as well. Within Honda's Acura division, a system has been developed that combines customer appraisals and team appraisal. Its Precision Team Program asks customers to rate a dealership on its overall service. This evaluation incorporates salespeople, customer service, and the parts department. Dealerships that score well in all three departments receive both group and individual rewards.[24]

In contrast to external customers, internal customers include anyone inside the organization who depends upon an employee's work output. For example

These customers are being asked to evaluate the overall service of the car dealership.

managers who rely on the HR department for selection and training services would be candidates for conducting internal customer evaluations. For both developmental and administrative reasons, internal customers can provide extremely useful feedback about the value added by an employee or team of employees.[25] The $3 billion Taurus/Sable program at Ford Motor represents a classic example of how internal customers were used to reengineer manufacturing processes to improve performance.[26]

Training Appraisers

A weakness of many performance appraisal programs is that managers and supervisors are not adequately trained for the appraisal task and provide little meaningful feedback to subordinates. Because they lack precise standards for appraising subordinates' performance and have not developed the necessary observational and feedback skills, their appraisals often become nondirective and meaningless. Therefore, training appraisers can vastly improve the performance appraisal process.

Establishing an Appraisal Plan

Training programs are most effective when they follow a systematic process that begins with an explanation of the objectives of the performance appraisal system.[27] It is important for the rater to know the purpose for which the appraisal is to be used. For example, using the appraisal for compensation decisions rather than development purposes may affect how the rater evaluates the employee, and it may change the rater's opinion of how the appraisal form should be completed. The mechanics of the rating system should also be explained, including how frequently the appraisals are to be conducted, who will conduct them, and what the standards of performance are. In addition, appraisal training should alert raters to the weaknesses and problems of appraisal systems so they can be avoided.

Eliminating Rater Error

Appraisal training should focus on eliminating the subjective errors made by managers in the rating process. Gary Latham and Kenneth Wexley stress the importance of performance appraisal training by noting that:

> Observer bias in performance appraisals can be largely attributed to well-known rating errors...that occur in a systematic manner when an individual observes and evaluates another. In order to minimize the occurrence of rating error and costly litigation battles, organizations, regardless of the appraisal instrument they use, are well advised to expose people who evaluate employees to a training program to minimize rating errors.[28]

With any rating method, certain types of errors can arise that should be considered. The "halo error" discussed in Chapter 6 is also common with respect to rating scales, especially those that do not include carefully developed descriptions of the employee behaviors being rated.[29] Provision for comments on the rating form tends to reduce halo error.

Some types of rating errors are *distributional* errors in that they involve a group of ratings given across various employees. For example, raters who are reluctant to assign either extremely high or extremely low ratings commit the **error of central tendency.** In this case, all employees are rated about average. To

Error of central tendency
Performance-rating error in which all employees are rated about average

such raters it is a good idea to explain that, among large numbers of employees, one should expect to find significant differences in behavior, productivity, and other characteristics.

In contrast to central tendency errors, it is also common for some raters to give unusually high or low ratings. For example, a manager may erroneously assert, "All my employees are excellent" or "None of my people are good enough." These beliefs give rise to what is called **leniency or strictness error.** One way to reduce this error is to clearly define the characteristics or dimensions of performance, and to provide meaningful descriptions of behavior, known as *anchors,* on the scale. Another approach is to require ratings to conform to a *forced distribution.* Managers appraising employees under a forced-distribution system would be required to place a certain percentage of employees into various performance categories. For example, it may be required that 10 percent of ratings be poor (or excellent). This is similar to the requirement in some schools that instructors grade on a curve. However, while a forced distribution may solve leniency and strictness error, it may create other errors in the accuracy of ratings—particularly if most employees are performing above standard. In addition, since employees are usually compared only in terms of overall suitability, this method may result in a legal challenge. (See *Albemarle Paper Company v Moody*.) Companies such as Xerox and Cadillac have recently abandoned their forced-distribution systems completely, but a modified version is still being used at Merck for determining merit pay.[30]

Some rating errors are *temporal* in that the performance review is biased either favorably or unfavorably, depending on the way performance information is selected, evaluated, and organized by the rater over time.[31] For example, when the appraisal is based largely on the employee's recent behavior, good or bad, the rater has committed the **recency error.** Managers who give higher ratings because they believe an employee is "showing improvement" may unwittingly be committing recency error. Without work-record documentation for the entire appraisal period, the rater is forced to recall recent employee behavior to establish the rating. The recency error can be minimized by having the rater routinely document employee accomplishments and failures throughout the whole appraisal period. Rater training also will help reduce this error.

Contrast error occurs when an employee's evaluation is biased either upward or downward because of another employee's performance who was just evaluated previously. For example, an average employee may appear especially productive when compared with a poor performer. However, that same employee may appear unproductive when compared with a star performer. Contrast errors are most likely when raters are required to rank employees in order from the best to the poorest. Employees are evaluated against one another, usually on the basis of some organizational standard or guideline. For example, they may be compared on the basis of their ability to meet production standards or their "overall" ability to perform their job. As with other types of rating error, contrast error can be reduced through training that focuses on using objective standards and behavioral anchors to appraise performance.

Similar-to-me error occurs when appraisers inflate the evaluations of people with whom they have something in common. For example, if both the manager and the employee are from small towns, the manager may unwittingly

---

Leniency or strictness error
Performance-rating error in which the appraiser tends to give employees either unusually high or unusually low ratings

Recency error
Performance-rating error in which the appraisal is based largely on the employee's most recent behavior rather than on behavior throughout the appraisal period

Contrast error
Performance-rating error in which an employee's evaluation is biased either upward or downward because of comparison with another employee just previously evaluated

Similar-to-me error
Performance-rating error in which an appraiser inflates the evaluation of an employee because of a mutual personal connection

have a more favorable impression of the employee. The effects of a similar-to-me error can be powerful, and when the similarity is based on race, religion, gender, or some other protected category, it may result in discrimination.

Furthermore, raters should be aware of any stereotypes they may hold toward particular groups—e.g., male/female, Caucasian/African American—because the observation and interpretation of performance can be clouded by these stereotypes. Results from a study examining how individual differences in stereotypes of women affect performance ratings suggested that women evaluated by raters who have traditional stereotypes of women will be at a disadvantage in obtaining merit pay increases and promotions.[32] This problem will be aggravated when employees are appraised on the basis of poorly defined performance standards and subjective performance traits.

A host of organizations such as Sears, Weyerhauser, and Allied Chemical have developed formal training programs to reduce the subjective errors commonly made during the rating process. This training can pay off, particularly when participants have the opportunity to (1) observe other managers making errors, (2) actively participate in discovering their own errors, and (3) practice job-related tasks to reduce the errors they tend to make.[33]

Providing Feedback

Finally, a training program for raters should provide some general points to consider for planning and conducting the feedback interview. The interview not only provides employees with knowledge of results of their evaluation, but it allows the manager and employee to discuss current problems and set future goals. Training in specific skills should cover at least three basic areas: (1) communicating effectively, (2) diagnosing the root causes of performance problems, and (3) setting goals and objectives.[34] A checklist can be used to assist supervisors in preparing for the appraisal interview. A checklist suggested by AT&T is shown in Highlights in HRM 1. The AT&T checklist reflects the growing tendency of organizations to have employees assess their own performance prior to the appraisal interview. The performance appraisal interview will be discussed in detail later in the chapter.

objective

Performance Appraisal Methods

Since the early years of their use by the federal government, methods of evaluating personnel have evolved considerably. Old systems have been replaced by new methods that represent technical improvements and legal requirements and are more consistent with the purposes of appraisal. In the discussion that follows, we will examine in some detail those methods that have found widespread use, and we will briefly touch on other methods that are used less frequently. Performance appraisal methods can be broadly classified as measuring traits, behaviors, or results. Trait approaches continue to be the more popular systems despite their inherent subjectivity. Behavioral approaches provide more action-oriented information to employees and therefore may be best for development. The results-oriented approach is gaining popularity because it focuses on the measurable contributions that employees make to the organization.

HIGHLIGHTS IN HRM

HRM highlights

5 SAMPLE ITEMS FROM BEHAVIOR OBSERVATION SCALES

INSTRUCTIONS: Please consider the Sales Representative's behavior on the job in the past rating period. Read each statement carefully, then circle the number that indicates the extent to which the employee has demonstrated this *effective* or *ineffective* behavior.

For each behavior observed, use the following scale:

5 represents *almost always*   95–100% of the time
4 represents *frequently*   85–94% of the time
3 represents *sometimes*   75–84% of the time
2 represents *seldom*   65–74% of the time
1 represents *almost never*   0–64% of the time

SALES PRODUCTIVITY	ALMOST NEVER				ALMOST ALWAYS
1. Reviews individual productivity results with manager	1	2	3	4	5
2. Suggests to peers ways of building sales	1	2	3	4	5
3. Formulates specific objectives for each contact	1	2	3	4	5
4. Focuses on product rather than customer problem	1	2	3	4	5
5. Keeps account plans updated	1	2	3	4	5
6. Keeps customer waiting for service	1	2	3	4	5
7. Anticipates and prepares for customer concerns	1	2	3	4	5
8. Follows up on customer leads	1	2	3	4	5

Requirements for a Successful MBO Program

If they are to succeed, MBO programs should meet several requirements. First objectives set at each level of the organization should be quantifiable and measurable for both the long and short term. Second, the expected results must be under the employee's control, and goals (e.g., profit, cost of product made, sales per product, quality control) must be consistent for each level (top executive, manager, and employee). Third, managers and employees must establish specific times when goals are to be reviewed and evaluated. Finally, each employee goal statement must be accompanied by a description of how that goal will be accomplished. Highlights in HRM 6 on page 326 presents the goal-setting worksheet

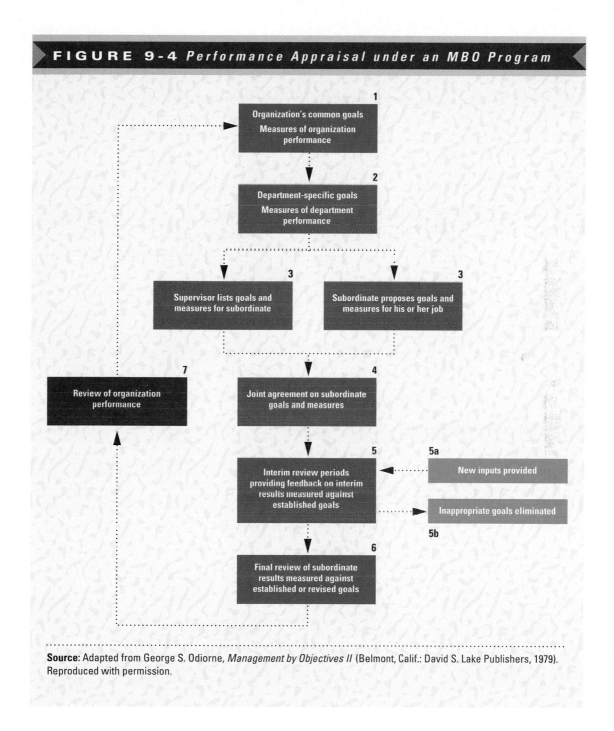

FIGURE 9-4 *Performance Appraisal under an MBO Program*

Source: Adapted from George S. Odiorne, *Management by Objectives II* (Belmont, Calif.: David S. Lake Publishers, 1979). Reproduced with permission.

used by Universal Service Corporation. Note that this worksheet contains sections for the setting of goals and the evaluation of goal achievement.

George Odiorne states that the success of an MBO program depends heavily on a behavioral change by both the supervisor and the subordinate.[42] Both individuals must be willing to *mutually* establish goals and measurable standards

HIGHLIGHTS IN HRM

**HRM
highlights**

6 EXAMPLE OF A GOAL-SETTING WORKSHEET

UNIVERSAL SERVICE CORPORATION

Employee's Rating Record

Name _____ Date _____

Job Title _____ Department _____

Appraised by _____ Date Started _____

_____

Summary of Appraisal

Development Needs

Major Responsibilities and Period Goals	Evaluation of Attainment of Goals
Responsibility	
Goal	
Responsibility	
Goal	
Responsibility	
Goal	

for employee performance. Furthermore, MBO must be viewed as part of a system of managing, not as merely an addition to the manager's job. Managers who adopt MBO as a system of managing must be willing to delegate responsibility for reaching goals to their subordinates.

A major advantage of MBO is that it requires the setting of employee-established goals. Goal setting has been shown to improve employee performance, thereby leading to increased productivity.[43] Measurable increases in job performance typically range from 10 to 25 percent, and in some cases they have been even higher.[44] Goal setting works because it allows employees to focus their efforts on important job tasks and makes them accountable for completing these tasks. Furthermore, goal setting establishes an automatic feedback system, since employees can regularly evaluate their performance against their goals. Goal setting has been of benefit to groups as diverse as clerical personnel, scientists, maintenance employees, computer analysts, and engineers.

Criticisms of MBO

The MBO system is not without its critics. One researcher contends that MBO is a lengthy and costly appraisal system that has only a moderate impact on organizational success.[45] Another criticism of MBO is that since performance data are designed to measure results, they may be affected by factors out of an individual's control. Recall that this raises the issue of *criterion contamination* discussed earlier.

MBO systems may inadvertently encourage employees to "look good" on a short-term basis, while ignoring the long-term ramifications. Line supervisors, for example, may let their equipment suffer to reduce maintenance costs. If the MBO program focuses on a narrow set of results criteria to the exclusion of other important process issues, the system may suffer from *criterion deficiency* and may unintentionally foster the attitude that "what gets measured gets done." In fact, in any job involving interaction with others, it is not enough to meet certain production or sales objectives. Factors such as cooperation, adaptability, initiative, and concern for human relations may be important to job success. If these factors are important job standards, they should be added to the appraisal review. Thus, to be realistic, both the results *and* the method used to achieve them should be considered.

Westinghouse, for example, recently modified the MBO system used in its Commercial Nuclear Fuel Division to address process issues related to TQM. As a Malcolm Baldrige National Quality Award–winning company, Westinghouse took special care to make certain that quality improvement was one of the major objectives against which employees are evaluated.[46] In addition, companies such as Roberts Express have integrated their MBO systems with measures of customer satisfaction, providing yet another means by which to merge TQM initiatives with MBO.[47]

Which Performance Appraisal Method to Use?

The choice of method should be based largely on the purpose of the appraisal. Figure 9–5 lists some of the strengths and weaknesses of trait, behavior, and results approaches to appraisal. Note that the simplest and least expensive

FIGURE 9-5 *Summary of Various Appraisal Methods*

	ADVANTAGES	DISADVANTAGES
Trait Methods	1. Are inexpensive to develop 2. Use meaningful dimensions 3. Are easy to use	1. Have high potential for rating errors 2. Are not useful for employee counseling 3. Are not useful for allocating rewards 4. Are not useful for promotion decisions
Behavioral Methods	1. Use specific performance dimensions 2. Are acceptable to employees and superiors 3. Are useful for providing feedback 4. Are fair for reward and promotion decisions	1. Can be time-consuming to develop/use 2. Can be costly to develop 3. Have some potential for rating error
Results Method	1. Has less subjectivity bias 2. Is acceptable to employees and superiors 3. Links individual performance to organizational performance 4. Encourages mutual goal setting 5. Is good for reward and promotion decisions	1. Is time-consuming to develop/use 2. May encourage short-term perspective 3. May use contaminated criteria 4. May use deficient criteria

techniques often yield the least-accurate information. However, research has not always supported a clear choice among appraisal methods. For example, results from a study comparing the relative advantages of BARS versus an overall rating scale in terms of dispersion, test/retest reliability, halo effect, and criterion-related validity showed that the BARS was not superior to the overall rating scale in the properties examined.[48] In addition, another recent study showed that an MBO-based system was no better than a graphic rating system for motivating performance.[49] However, evidence suggests that a BOS system may lead to higher satisfaction than a system based on graphic ratings.[50] While researchers and HR managers generally believe that the more sophisticated and more time consuming methods offer more useful information, this may not always be the case. Managers must make cost-benefit decisions about which methods to use.

Appraisal Interviews

The appraisal interview is perhaps the most important part of the entire performance appraisal process. The appraisal interview gives a manager the opportunity to discuss a subordinate's performance record and to explore areas of possible improvement and growth. It also provides an opportunity to identify the subordinate's attitudes and feelings more thoroughly and thus to improve communication.

Unfortunately, the interviewer can become overburdened by attempting to discuss too much, such as the employee's past performance and future development goals. Dividing the appraisal interview into two sessions, one for the performance review and the other for the employee's growth plans, can alleviate time pressures. Moreover, by separating the interview into two sessions, the interviewer can give each session the proper attention it deserves. It can be difficult for a supervisor to perform the role of both evaluator and counselor in the same review period. Dividing the sessions may also improve communication between the parties, thereby reducing stress and defensiveness.

The format for the appraisal interview will be determined in large part by the purpose of the interview, the type of appraisal system used, and the organization of the interview form. Most appraisal interviews attempt to give feedback to employees on how well they are performing their jobs and on planning for their future development. Interviews should be scheduled far enough in advance to allow the interviewee, as well as the interviewer, to prepare for the discussion. Usually ten days to two weeks is a sufficient amount of lead time.

Three Types of Appraisal Interviews

The individual who has probably studied different approaches to performance appraisal interviews most thoroughly is Norman R. F. Maier. In his classic book *The Appraisal Interview,* he analyzes the cause-and-effect relationships in three types of appraisal interviews: tell-and-sell, tell-and-listen, and problem solving.[51]

- *Tell-and-sell interview.* The skills required in the tell-and-sell interview include the ability to persuade an employee to change in a prescribed manner. This may require the development of new behaviors on the part of the employee and skillful use of motivational incentives on the part of the appraiser/supervisor.
- *Tell-and-listen interview.* In the tell-and-listen interview the skills required include the ability to communicate the strong and weak points of an employee's job performance during the first part of the interview. During the second part of the interview, the employee's feelings about the appraisal are thoroughly explored. The supervisor is still in the role of appraiser, but the method requires listening to disagreement and coping with defensive behavior without attempting to refute any statements. The tell-and-listen method assumes that the opportunity to release frustrated feelings will help to reduce or remove those feelings.
- *Problem-solving interview.* The skills associated with the problem-solving interview are consistent with the nondirective procedures of the tell-and-listen method in that listening, accepting, and responding to feelings are essential. However, the problem-solving method goes beyond an interest in the employee's feelings. It seeks to stimulate growth and development in the employee by discussing the problems, needs, innovations, satisfactions, and dissatisfactions the employee has encountered on the job since the last appraisal interview. Maier

recommends this method, since the objective of appraisal is normally to stimulate growth and development in the employee.

Managers should not assume that only one type of appraisal interview is appropriate for every review session. Rather, they should be able to use one or more of the interview types, depending on the topic being discussed or on the behavior of the employee being appraised. The interview should be seen as requiring a flexible approach.[52]

Conducting the Appraisal Interview

While there are probably no hard-and-fast rules for how to conduct an appraisal interview, there are some guidelines that may increase the employee's acceptance of the feedback, satisfaction with the interview, and intention to improve in the future. Many of the principles of effective interviewing discussed in Chapter 6 apply to performance appraisal interviews as well. Here are some other guidelines that should also be considered.

- *Ask for a self assessment.* As noted earlier in the chapter, it is useful to have employees evaluate their own performance prior to the appraisal interview. Even if this information is not used formally, the self-appraisal starts the employee thinking about his or her accomplishments. Self-appraisal also ensures that the employee knows against what criteria he or she is being evaluated, thus eliminating any potential surprises. When the employee has evaluated his or her own performance, the interview can be used to discuss those areas where the manager and the employee have reached different conclusions.

- *Invite participation.* The core purpose of a performance appraisal interview is to initiate a dialogue that will help an employee improve her or his performance. To the extent that an employee is an active participant in that discussion, the more likely it is that the root causes and obstacles to performance will be uncovered, and the more likely it is that constructive ideas for improvement will be raised. In addition, research evidence suggests that participation is strongly related to an employee's satisfaction with the appraisal feedback as well as her or his intention to improve performance.[53] As a rule of thumb, supervisors should spend only about 30 to 35 percent of the time talking during the interview. The rest of the time they should be listening to employees respond to questions.

- *Express appreciation.* Praise is a powerful motivator, and in an appraisal interview, particularly, employees are seeking out positive feedback. It is frequently beneficial to start the appraisal interview by expressing appreciation for what the employee has done well. In this way, he or she may be less defensive and more likely to talk about aspects of the job that are not going so well. However, try to avoid obvious use of the "sandwich technique," in which positive statements are followed by negative ones, which are then followed by positive statements. This approach may not work for several reasons. Praise often alerts the employee that criticism will be coming. Positive comments following

This small group discusses ways to best solve a performance problem as a team.

the criticism then suggest to the employee that no more negative comments will come for a while. If managers follow an appraisal form, the problem of the sandwich technique will oftentimes be avoided. Furthermore, if employees are kept informed of their behavior on a regular basis, there will be no need for this appraisal technique to be used.

- *Minimize criticism.* Employees who have a good relationship with their managers may be able to handle criticism better than those who do not. However, even the most stoic employees can absorb only so much criticism before they start to get defensive. If an employee has many areas in need of improvement, managers should focus on those few objective issues that are most problematic or most important to the job.[54]

- *Change the behavior, not the person.* Managers frequently try to play psychologist, to "figure out" why an employee has acted a certain way. However, when dealing with a problem area, in particular, remember that it is not the person who is bad, but the actions they have exhibited on the job. Avoid suggestions about personal traits to change; instead suggest more acceptable ways of performing. For example, instead of focusing on a person's "unreliability," a manager might focus on the fact that the employee "has been late to work seven times this month." It is difficult for employees to change who they are; it is usually much easier for them to change how they act.

- *Focus on solving problems.* In addressing performance issues, it is frequently tempting to get into the "blame game" in which both manager and employee enter into a potentially endless discussion of why a situation has arisen. Frequently, solving problems requires an analysis of the causes, but ultimately the appraisal interview should be directed at devising a solution to the problem.

- *Be supportive.* One of the better techniques for engaging an employee in the problem-solving process is for the manager to ask, "What can I do to help?" Employees frequently attribute performance problems to either real or perceived obstacles (such as bureaucratic procedures or inadequate resources). By being open and supportive, the manager conveys to the employee that he or she will try to eliminate external roadblocks and work with the employee to achieve higher standards.

- *Establish goals.* Since a major purpose of the appraisal interview is to make plans for improvement, it is important to focus the interviewee's attention on the future rather than the past. In setting goals with an employee, the manager should observe the following points:

  1. Emphasize strengths on which the employee can build rather than weaknesses to overcome.
  2. Concentrate on opportunities for growth that exist within the framework of the employee's present position.
  3. Limit plans for growth to a few important items that can be accomplished within a reasonable period of time.
  4. Establish specific action plans that spell out *how* each goal will be achieved. These action plans may also include a list of contacts, resources, and timetables for follow-up.

- *Follow up day to day.* Ideally, performance feedback should be an ongoing part of a manager's job.[55] Feedback is most useful when it is immediate and specific to a particular situation. Unfortunately, both managers and employees are frequently happy to finish the interview and file away the appraisal form. A better approach is to have informal talks periodically to follow up on the issues raised in the appraisal interview. This practice may also help the manager adopt more of a coaching role and less a judging role.

Improving Performance

In many instances the appraisal interview will provide the basis for noting deficiencies in employee performance and for making plans for improvement. Unless these deficiencies are brought to the employee's attention, they are likely to continue until they become quite serious. Sometimes underperformers may not understand exactly what is expected of them. However, once their responsibilities are clarified, they are in a position to take the corrective action needed to improve their performance.

Identifying Sources of Ineffective Performance

There are many reasons why an employee's performance might not meet the standards. First, each individual has a unique pattern of strengths and weaknesses that play a part. In addition, other factors—such as the work environment, the external environment, including home and community, and personal problems—have an impact on job performance. To provide a better understanding of possible sources of ineffective performance related to these environments, we have devised the comprehensive list shown in Figure 9–6.

> **FIGURE 9-6** *Sources of Ineffective Performance*

ORGANIZATION POLICIES AND PRACTICES

- Ineffective job placement
- Insufficient job training
- Ineffectual employment practices
- Permissiveness with enforcing policies or job standards
- Heavy-handed management
- Lack of attention to employee needs or concerns
- Inadequate communication within organization
- Unclear reporting relationships

PERSONAL PROBLEMS

- Marital problems
- Financial worries
- Emotional disorders (including depression, guilt, anxiety, fear)
- Conflict between work demands and family demands
- Physical limitations, including disabilities
- Low work ethic
- Other family problems
- Lack of effort
- Immaturity

JOB CONCERNS

- Unclear or constantly changing work requirements
- Boredom with job
- Lack of job growth or advancement opportunities
- Management-employee conflict
- Problems with fellow employees
- Unsafe working conditions
- Unavailable or inadequate equipment or materials
- Inability to perform the job
- Excessive workload
- Lack of job skills

EXTERNAL FACTORS

- Industry decline or extreme competition
- Legal constraints
- Conflict between ethical standards and job demands
- Union-management conflict

It is recommended that a diagnosis of poor employee performance focus on three interactive elements: skill, effort, and external conditions. For example, if an employee's performance is not up to standards, the cause could be a skill problem (knowledge, abilities, technical competencies), an effort problem (motivation to get the job done), and/or some problem in the external conditions of work (poor economic conditions, supply shortages, difficult sales territories).[56] Any one of these problem areas could cause performance to suffer.

Managing Ineffective Performance

Once the sources of performance problems are known, a course of action can be planned. This action may lie in providing training in areas that would increase the knowledge and/or skills needed for effective performance. A transfer to another job or department might give an employee a chance to become a more effective member of the organization. In other instances, greater attention may have to be focused on ways to motivate the individual.[57]

If ineffective performance persists, it may be necessary to transfer the employee, take disciplinary action, or discharge the person from the organization. Whatever action is taken to cope with ineffective performance, it should be done with objectivity, fairness, and a recognition of the feelings of the individual involved.

SUMMARY

objective

Performance appraisal programs serve many purposes, but in general those purposes can be clustered into two categories: administrative and developmental. The administrative purposes include decisions about who will be promoted, transferred, or laid off. They can also include compensation decisions and the like. Developmental decisions include those related to improving and enhancing an individual's capabilities. These include identifying a person's strengths and weaknesses, eliminating external performance obstacles, establishing training needs, and so on. The combination of administrative and developmental purposes of performance appraisal reflect, in a specific way, human resources management's larger role of integrating the individual with the organization. In many organizations, performance appraisals are seen as a necessary evil. Managers frequently avoid conducting appraisals because managers dislike playing the role of judge. Further, if managers are not adequately trained, subjectivity and organizational politics can distort the reviews. This situation tends to be self-defeating in that such managers frequently do not develop good feedback skills and are often not prepared to conduct an appraisal. As a consequence, the appraisal is done begrudgingly once a year and then forgotten about.

objective

The success of an organization depends largely on the performance of its human resources. To determine the contributions of each individual, it is necessary to have a formal appraisal program with clearly stated objectives. Carefully defined performance standards that are reliable, strategically relevant, and free from either criterion deficiency or contamination are essential foundations for evaluation. Appraisal systems must also comply with the law. Appraisals should be treated with the same concerns for validity as are selection tests. For example, ratings must be job-related, employees must understand their performance standards in advance, appraisers must be able to observe job performance, appraisers must be trained, feedback must be given, and an appeals procedure must be established.

objective

Using multiple raters is frequently a good idea because different individuals see different facets of an employee's performance. The supervisor, for example, has legitimate authority over an employee and is in a good position to discern whether he or she is contributing to the goals of the organization. Peers and team members, on the other hand, often have an unfiltered view of an employee's work activity, particularly related to issues such as cooperation and dependability. Subordinates often provide good information about whether an employee facilitating their work, and customers (both internal and external) can convey the extent to which an employee adds value and meets their requirements. Self-appraisal is useful, if for no other reason than it encourages employees to think about their strengths, weaknesses, and future goals. Regardless of the source of appraisal information, appraisers should be thoroughly trained in the particular methods they will use in evaluating their subordinates. Participation in developing rating scales, such as a BARS, automatically provides such training.

There are several methods that can be used for performance appraisal. These include trait approaches (such as graphic rating scales, mixed standard scales, forced-choice forms, and essays), behavioral methods (such as critical incidents ratings, checklists, BARS, and BOS), and results method (MBO). The choice of method depends on the purpose of the appraisal. Trait appraisals are simple to develop and complete, but they have problems of subjectivity and are not useful for feedback. Behavioral methods provide more-specific information for giving feedback but can be time-consuming and costly to develop. Results appraisals are more objective and can link individual performance to the organization as a whole, but they may encourage a short-term perspective (e.g., annual goals) and may not include subtle yet important aspects of performance.

The degree to which the performance appraisal program benefits the organization and its members is directly related to the quality of the appraisal interviews that are conducted. Interviewing skills are best developed through instruction and supervised practice. Although there are various approaches to the interview, research suggests that employee participation and goal setting lead to higher satisfaction and improved performance. Discussing problems, showing support, minimizing criticism, and rewarding effective performance are also beneficial practices. In the interview, deficiencies in employee performance can be discussed and plans for improvement can be made.

KEY TERMS

behaviorally anchored rating scale (BARS)

behavior observation scale (BOS)

contrast error

critical incident

customer appraisal

error of central tendency

essay method

forced-choice method

graphic rating scale method

leniency or strictness error

management by objectives (MBO)

manager/supervisor appraisal

mixed standard scale method

peer appraisals

recency error

self-appraisal

similar-to-me error

subordinate appraisal

team appraisal

DISCUSSION QUESTIONS

1. What are the major purposes of performance appraisal? In what ways might these purposes be contradictory?
2. Describe the relationships among performance appraisal and selection, compensation management, and training and development.
3. How can performance appraisals be adjusted to include the principles underlying total-quality management (TQM)?
4. Describe the characteristics of the ideal appraisal system.
5. What performance standards could be used to evaluate the performance of people working in the following jobs?
   a. Sales representative
   b. TV repairer
   c. Director of nursing in a hospital
   d. HR manager
   e. Air-traffic controller
6. Discuss the guidelines that performance appraisals should meet in order to be legally defensible.
7. What are the pros and cons of trait, behavior, and results appraisals?
8. In many organizations, evaluators submit ratings to their immediate superiors for review before discussing them with the individual employees they have rated. What advantages are there to this procedure?
9. Three types of appraisal interviews are described in this chapter.
   a. What different skills are required for each type of appraisal interview? What reactions can one expect from using these different skills?
   b. How can one develop the skills needed for the problem-solving type of interview?
   c. Which method do you feel is the *least* desirable? Why?
10. Discuss how you would diagnose poor performance. List several factors to consider.

CASE STUDY: Setting Performance Standards at General Telephone Company of California

Raymond Sanchez, a new college graduate with a degree in human resources, was recently hired by General Telephone Company of California. His job assignment was as college recruiter, with the responsibility to fill entry-level supervisory positions and staff assignments in accounting, finance, data processing, and marketing. He was in charge of a recruiting schedule that included twelve colleges and universities. Six of the schools were located in California, three in Arizona, two in Oregon, and one in Nevada.

Over the past two years, the company had made a concerted effort to develop a comprehensive and effective college recruiting program. It was decided that part of this effort should be devoted to creating a positive and continuing relationship with the college placement offices, as well as with certain professors who would be in a position to refer students for job openings. Establishing this relationship with the schools, which was viewed as critical for identifying and selecting high-potential employees, was Sanchez's responsibility, as important as filling the positions for General Telephone.

Daniel Turner, manager of the company's HR department, established yearly performance standards for each of his subordinates. Company guidelines indicated that, where possible, observable and measurable performance standards should be set. When Sanchez completed his first three months with GT&E, he and Turner agreed to set his performance standards for the upcoming recruitment period, although both acknowledged that setting measurable standards might be somewhat difficult because of the subjective nature of college recruiting. The job description stated only that the person who held the position should develop and maintain rapport with the colleges and universities, that openings should be filled in a timely manner, and that college graduates selected for company interviews should be of high quality. (GT&E's annual HR planning schedule, listing the types and numbers of college graduates needed by each department and operating area, was completed by December of each year, and managers requesting new graduates also stated on the employment requisition form the date by which the positions were to be filled.)

Now Turner asked Sanchez to come up with four to six observable and measurable performance standards that would capture the duties and responsibilities of the college recruiter's job.

Source: Based on an actual case known to the authors; employee names are fictitious.

Questions

1. Develop four to six observable and measurable performance standards suitable to Sanchez's position as college recruiter.
2. Discuss any obstacles that might make this task difficult.

NOTES AND REFERENCES

1. Alan H. Locher and Kenneth S. Teel, "Appraisal Trends," *Personnel Journal* 67, no. 9 (September 1988): 139.
2. Michael A. Verespej, "Performance Reviews Get Mixed Reviews," *Industry Week* (August 20, 1990): 49–54.
3. Richard Blackburn and Benson Rosen, "Total Quality and Human Resources Management: Lessons Learned from Baldrige Award-Winning Companies," *Academy of Management Executive* 7, no. 3 (1993): 49–66; Jeannie Coyle, "Aligning Human Resources Processes with Total Quality," *Employment Relations Today* (Autumn 1991): 273–78. See also Carol A. Norman and Robert A. Zawacki, "Team Appraisals—Team Approach," *Personnel Journal* (September 1991): 101–04.

4. *Your Guide to Performance Appraisal*, The Travelers, rev. September 1978, 2.
5. Jeanette N. Cleveland, Kevin R. Murphy, and Richard E. Williams, "Multiple Uses of Performance Appraisal: Prevalence and Correlates," *Journal of Applied Psychology* 74 (1989): 130–35. See also David A. Waldman and Ron S. Kent, "Improve Performance by Appraisal," *HR Magazine* 35, no. 7 (July 1990): 66–69.
6. Dave Day, "Performance Management Year-Round," *Personnel* 66, no. 8 (August 1989): 43–45.
7. Gerald R. Ferris and Thomas R. King, "Politics in Human Resources Decisions: A Walk on the Dark Side," *Organizational Dynamics* 20 (Autumn 1991): 59–71.

8. Stephenie Overman, "Best Appraisals Measure Goals, Not Traits," *Resource* 8, no. 2 (February 1989): 16.

9. Ashok K. Gupta and Arvind Singhal, "Managing Human Resources for Innovation and Creativity," *Research Technology Management* (May-June 1993): 41–48.

10. S. W. J. Kozlowski and K. Hattrup, "A Disagreement about Within-Group Agreement: Disentangling Issues of Consistency versus Consensus," *Journal of Applied Psychology* 77 (1992): 161–67.

11. *Brito v Zia Company* 478 F.2d 1200 (10th. Cir. 1973). See also Edmund J. Metz, "Designing Legally Defensible Performance Appraisal Systems," *Training and Development Journal* 42, no. 7 (July 1988): 47.

12. *Albemarle Paper Company v Moody,* 422 U.S. 405 (1975).

13. For a review of performance appraisal court cases, see David C. Martin and Kathryn M. Bartol, "The Legal Ramifications of Performance Appraisal: An Update," *Employee Relations* 17 (Autumn 1991): 257–86. See also Robert W. Goddard, "Is Your Appraisal System Headed for Court?" *Personnel Journal* 68, no. 1 (January 1989): 114–18.

14. David I. Rosen, "Appraisals Can Make—Or Break—Your Court Case," *Personnel Journal* (November 1992): 113–18.

15. Mark R. Edwards, "Assessment: A Joint Effort Leads to Accurate Appraisals," *Personnel Journal* (June 1990): 122–28.

16. Loriann Roberson, Steven Torkel, Audrey Korsgaard, Doug Klein, et al., "Self-Appraisal and Perceptions of the Appraisal Discussion: A Field Experiment," *Journal of Organizational Behavior* 14 (March 1993): 129–42. See also John W. Lawrie, "Your Performance: Appraise It Yourself," *Personnel* 66, no. 1 (January 1989): 21–23; Len Sandler, "Two-Sided Performance Reviews," *Personnel Journal* 69, no. 1 (January 1990): 75–78.

17. Paul E. Levy, "Self-Appraisal and Attributions: A Test of a Model," *Journal of Management* 19 (Spring 1993): 51–62. See also Shaul Fox and Yossi Dinur, "Validity of Self-Assessment: A Field Evaluation," *Personnel Psychology* 41, no. 3 (Autumn 1988): 582.

18. Edwards, "Assessment"; Robert McGarvey and Scott Smith, "When Workers Rate the Boss," *Training* 30 (March 1993): 31–34; Tom Redman and Ed Snape, "Upward and Onward: Can Staff Appraise Their Managers?" *Personnel Review* 21 (1992): 32–46.

19. Glenn M. McEvoy, "Evaluating the Boss," *Personnel Administrator* 33, no. 9 (September 1988): 115–20. See also Paul Nevels, "Why Employees Are Being Asked to Rate Their Supervisors," *Supervisory Management* 34, no. 12 (December 1989): 5–11.

20. Edwards, "Assessment." See also Mark R. Edwards, "An Alternative to Traditional Appraisal Systems," *Supervisory Management* 35 (June 1990): 3; Mark R. Edwards, "Joint-Appraisal Efforts," *Personnel Journal* 69, no. 6 (June 1990): 122–28.

21. Glenn M. McEvoy and Paul F. Buller, "User Acceptance of Peer Appraisals in an Industrial Setting," *Personnel Psychology* 40, no. 4 (Winter 1987): 785–97.

22. Kenneth P. Carson, Robert L. Cardy, and Gregory H. Dobbins, "Upgrade the Employee Evaluation Process," *HR Magazine* (November 1992): 88–92; Blackburn and Rosen, "Total Quality and Human Resources Management"; Norman and Zawacki, "Team Appraisals"; Marilyn Moats Kennedy, "Where Teams Drop the Ball," *Across the Board* (September 1993): 9–10; Joshua Hyatt, "Surviving on Chaos," *Inc.* (May 1990): 60–71.

23. David E. Bowen and E. E. Lawler III, "Total Quality-Oriented Human Resource Management," *Organizational Dynamics* 21 (1992): 29–41. Also see Nancy K. Austin, "Updating the Performance Review," *Working Woman* 17, no. 11 (November 1992): 32–35.

24. Margaret Kaeter, "Driving toward Sales and Satisfaction," *Training* (August 1990): 19–22.

25. J. M. Juran, *Juran on Quality by Design* (New York: The Free Press, 1992).

26. For a more complete description of the Taurus program, see James Brian Quinn, "Ford: Team Taurus," in Henry Mintzberg and James Brian Quinn, eds., *The Strategy Process, Concepts, Context, Cases* (Englewood Cliffs, N.J.: Prentice-Hall, 1991): 481–504.

27. Robert H. Buckham, "Appraisal Training: Not Just for Managers," *Training and Development Journal* 44, no. 6 (June 1990): 18, 21. See also Stephen B. Wehrenberg, "Train Supervisors to Measure and Evaluate Performance," *Training* 67, no. 2 (February 1988): 77–79.

28. Gary P. Latham and Kenneth N. Wexley, *Increasing Productivity through Performance Appraisal* (Reading, Mass.: Addison-Wesley, 1981), 116.

29. William K. Balzer and Lorne M. Sulsky, "Halo and Performance Appraisal: A Critical Examination," *Journal of Applied Psychology* 77, no. 6 (December 1992): 975–85; Keven Murphy, Robert A. Jako, and Rebecca L. Anhalt, "Nature and Consequences of Halo Error: A Critical Analysis," *Journal of Applied Psychology* 78, no. 2 (April 1993): 218–25; Kevin R. Murphy and William K. Balzer, "Rater Errors and Rating Accuracy," *Journal of Applied Psychology* 74, no. 4 (August 1989): 619–24.

30. Coyle, "Aligning Human Resources Processes"; Kevin J. Murphy, "Performance Measurement and Appraisal: Merck Tries to Motivate Managers to Do It Right," *Employment Relations Today* 20, no. 1 (Spring 1993): 47–62; Commerce Clearing House, "Merck's New Performance Appraisal/Merit Pay

System Is Based on Bell-Shaped Distribution," *Ideas and Trends* (May 17, 1989): 88–90.

31. Robert A. Gacalone, "Image Control: The Strategies of Impression Management," *Personnel* 66, no. 5 (May 1989): 52–55.

32. Gregory H. Dobbins, Robert L. Cardy, and Donald M. Truxillo, "The Effects of Purpose of Appraisal and Individual Differences in Stereotypes of Women on Sex Differences in Performance Ratings: A Laboratory and Field Study," *Journal of Applied Psychology* 73, no. 3 (August 1988): 551–58.

33. Kenneth N. Wexley and Gary P. Latham, *Developing and Training Human Resources in Organizations* (Glenview, Ill.: Scott, Foresman, 1981).

34. Buckham, "Appraisal Training," 18, 21.

35. Philip G. Benson, M. Ronald Buckley, and Sid Hall, "The Impact of Rating Scale Format on Rater Accuracy: An Evaluation of the Mixed Standard Scale," *Journal of Management* 14, no. 3 (September 1988): 415–23.

36. Margaret E. Griffin, "Personnel Research in Testing, Selection, and Performance Appraisal," *Public Personnel Management* 18, no. 2 (Summer 1989): 130.

37. Brendan D. Bannister, Angelo J. Kinicki, Angelo S. Dinisi, and Peter Hom, "A New Method for the Statistical Control of Rating Error in Performance Ratings," *Educational and Psychological Measurement* 47, no. 3 (Autumn 1987): 583–96.

38. For a comprehensive review of the research on BARS, see Chapter 6 in H. John Bernardin and Richard W. Beatty, *Performance Appraisal: Assessing Human Behavior at Work* (Boston: Kent, 1984). Also see Kevin R. Murphy and Jeanette N. Cleveland, *Performance Appraisal* (Boston: Allyn and Bacon, 1991).

39. Latham and Wexley, *Increasing Productivity*," 55–64.

40. U. Wiersma and G. Latham, "The Practicality of Behavioral Observation Scales, Behavioral Expectation Scales, and Trait Scales," *Personnel Psychology* 39 (1986): 619–28.

41. Peter F. Drucker, *The Practice of Management* (New York: Harper & Brothers, 1954).

42. George S. Odiorne, *Management by Objectives* (New York: Pitman, 1965), 77–79.

43. E. Locke and G. Latham, *A Theory of Goal Setting and Task Performance* (Englewood Cliffs, N.J.: Prentice-Hall, 1990).

44. Robert D. Pritchard, Philip L. Roth, Steven D. Jones, Patricia J. Galgay, and Margaret D. Watson, "Designing a Goal-Setting System to Enhance Performance: A Practical Guide," *Organizational Dynamics* 17, no. 1 (Summer 1988): 70. See also Albert Schrader and Taylor G. Seward, "MBO Makes Dollar Sense," *Personnel Journal* 68, no. 7 (July 1989): 32–37.

45. Dennis Daley, "Performance Appraisal and Organizational Success: Public Employee Perceptions in an MBO-Based Appraisal System," *Review of Public Personnel Administration* 9, no. 1 (Fall 1988): 17–27. Also see David Halpern and Stephen Osfsky, "A Dissenting View of MBO," *Public Personnel Management* 19, no. 3 (Fall 1990): 321–30.

46. Blackburn and Rosen, "Total Quality and Human Resources Management." For another example of how TQM and MBO can be combined, see Bernard Stein, "Management by Quality Objectives," *Quality Progress* 24, no. 7 (July 1991): 78–80. For a dissenting view on linking MBO and TQM, see Ronald Starcher, "Mismatched Management Techniques," *Quality Progress* 25, no. 12 (December 1992): 49–52.

47. For an example of how Roberts Express has integrated its MBO system with TQM and customer requirements, see Jack Pickard, "Motivate Employees to Delight Customers," *Transportation and Distribution* 34, no. 7 (July 1993): 48. See also Jim M. Graber, Roger E. Breisch, and Walter E. Breisch, "Performance Appraisal and Deming: A Misunderstanding?" *Quality Progress* 25, no. 6 (June 1992): 59–62; Dennis M. Daley, "Pay for Performance, Performance Appraisal, and Total Quality," *Public Productivity & Management Review* 16, no. 1 (Fall 1992): 39–51.

48. Luis R. Gomez-Mejia, "Evaluating Employee Performance: Does the Appraisal Instrument Make a Difference?" *Journal of Organizational Behavior Management* 9, no. 2 (Fall 1988): 155–72.

49. Dennis M. Daley, "Great Expectations, or a Tale of Two Systems: Employee Attitudes toward Graphic Rating Scales and MBO-Based Performance Appraisal," *Public Administration Quarterly* 15, no. 2 (Summer 1991): 188–209.

50. Aharon Tziner and Gary P. Latham, "The Effects of Appraisal Instrument, Feedback and Goal-Setting on Worker Satisfaction and Commitment," *Journal of Organizational Behavior* 10, no. 2 (April 1989): 145–53.

51. Norman R. F. Maier, *The Appraisal Interview* (New York: John Wiley & Sons, 1958); Maier, *The Appraisal Interview—Three Basic Approaches* (San Diego: University Associates, 1976).

52. Howard J. Klein and Scott A. Snell, "The Impact of Interview Process and Context on Performance Appraisal Interview Effectiveness," *Journal of Managerial Issues* 6, no. 2 (Summer 1994): 160–75. See also Howard J. Klein, Scott A. Snell, and Kenneth N. Wexley, "Systems Model of the Performance Appraisal Interview Process," *Industrial Relations* 26, no. 3 (Fall 1987): 267–79; James McAlister, "Appraisal Do's and Don'ts," *Supervisory Management* 38, no. 4 (April 1993): 12.

53. W. Giles and K. Mossholder, "Employee Reactions to Contextual and Session Components of Performance Appraisal," *Journal of Applied Psychology* 75 (1990):

371–77. See also Klein and Snell, "Impact of Interview Process"; Theodore J. Krein, "Performance Reviews That Rate an 'A,'" *Personnel* 67, no. 5 (May 1990): 38–40; Sandler, "Two-Sided Performance Reviews."

54. Andrew S. Grove, "Criticism: Giving It Effectively," *Working Woman* 18, no. 6 (June 1993): 20–73.

55. George S. Odiorne, "The Trend toward the Quarterly Performance Review," *Business Horizons* 33, no. 4 (July/August 1990): 38–41.

56. Scott A. Snell and Kenneth N. Wexley, "Performance Diagnosis: Identifying the Causes of Poor Performance," *Personnel Administrator* 30, no. 4 (April 1985): 117–27.

57. Dorri Jacobs, "Coaching to Reverse Poor Performance," *Supervisory Management* 10, no. 2 (July 1989): 21–28.

Part 4

Implementing Compensation and Security

The four chapters in Part 4 focus on employee compensation and security issues. Chapter 10 deals with evaluating organizational jobs and establishing monetary rates for these jobs based on both internal and external influences. Also discussed in this chapter are the legal requirements of compensation management. Chapter 11 looks at incentive payment plans for nonmanagerial, managerial, and executive employees. Chapter 12 completes the discussion of compensation administration by reviewing the myriad of benefit programs offered by organizations to their employees. Included here is a relevant discussion of employee benefit costs and various cost-containment programs. Chapter 13 is concerned with the issues pertaining to employee safety and health. It contains discussions related to employee workplace stress, alcoholism, and substance abuse. When managers pay attention to the compensation and security needs of employees, they provide a work environment that contributes to both employee job satisfaction and organizational success.

Chapter

Managing Compensation

After studying this chapter you should be able to

one
objective

Explain employer concerns in developing the compensation program.

two
objective

Identify the various factors that influence the setting of wages.

three
objective

Discuss the mechanics of each of the major job evaluation systems.

four
objective

Explain the purpose of a wage survey.

five
objective

Define the wage curve, pay grades, and rate ranges as parts of the compensation structure.

six
objective

Identify the major provisions of the federal laws affecting compensation.

seven
objective

Discuss the current issues of equal pay for comparable worth, pay compression, and two-tier wage structures.

An extensive review of the literature indicates that important work-related variables leading to job satisfaction include challenging work, interesting job assignments, equitable rewards, competent supervision, and rewarding careers.[1] In Chapter 2 we emphasized that employees currently in the workforce are more concerned than their predecessors with the quality of their work life and with the psychological rewards to be derived from their employment. It is doubtful, however, whether many of them would continue working were it not for the money they earn. Employees desire compensation systems that they perceive as being fair and commensurate with their skills and expectations. Pay, therefore, is a major consideration in HRM because it provides employees with a tangible reward for their services, as well as a source of recognition and livelihood. Employee compensation includes all forms of pay and rewards received by employees for the performance of their jobs. Direct compensation encompasses employee wages and salaries, incentives, bonuses, and commissions. Indirect compensation comprises the many benefits supplied by employers, and nonfinancial compensation includes employee recognition programs, rewarding jobs, and flexible work hours to accommodate personal needs.

Both HR professionals and scholars agree that the way compensation is allocated among employees sends a message about what management believes is important and the types of activities it encourages. Furthermore, for an employer, the payroll constitutes a sizable operating cost. In manufacturing firms compensation is seldom as low as 20 percent of total expenditures, and in service enterprises it often exceeds 80 percent.[2] A sound compensation program, therefore, is essential so that pay can serve to motivate employee production sufficiently to keep labor costs at an acceptable level. This chapter will be concerned with the management of a compensation program, job evaluation systems, and pay structures for determining compensation payments. Included will be a discussion of federal regulations that affect wage and salary rates. Chapter 11 will review financial incentive plans for employees. Employee benefits that are part of the total compensation package are then discussed in Chapter 12.

objective

The Compensation Program

A significant interaction occurs between compensation management and the other functions of the HR program. For example, in the recruitment of new employees, the rate of pay for jobs can increase or limit the supply of applicants. Many fast-food restaurants, traditionally low-wage employers, have needed to raise their starting wages to attract a sufficient number of job applicants to meet staffing requirements. If rates of pay are high, creating a large applicant pool, then organizations may choose to raise their selection standards and hire better-qualified employees. This in turn can reduce employer training costs. When employees perform at exceptional levels, their performance appraisals may justify an increased pay rate. For these reasons and others, an organization should develop a formal HR program to manage employee compensation. This program should establish its intended objectives, the policies for determining compensation payments, and the methods by which the payments will be disbursed. Included as part of the program should be the communication of information concerning wages and benefits to employees.

Compensation Objectives and Policies

Compensation objectives should facilitate the effective utilization and management of an organization's human resources, while also contributing to the overall objectives of the organization. A compensation program, therefore, must be tailored to the needs of an organization and its employees.[3]

It is not uncommon for organizations to establish very specific goals for their compensation program.[4] Formalized compensation goals serve as guidelines for managers to ensure that wage and benefit policies achieve their intended purpose. The more common goals of compensation policy include:

1. To reward employees' past performance
2. To remain competitive in the labor market
3. To maintain salary equity among employees
4. To motivate employees' future performance
5. To maintain the budget
6. To attract new employees
7. To reduce unnecessary turnover

To achieve these goals, policies must be established to guide management in making decisions. Formal statements of compensation policies typically include the following:

1. The rate of pay within the organization and whether it is to be above, below, or at the prevailing community rate
2. The ability of the pay program to gain employee acceptance while motivating employees to perform to the best of their abilities
3. The pay level at which employees may be recruited and the pay differential between new and more senior employees
4. The intervals at which pay raises are to be granted and the extent to which merit and/or seniority will influence the raises
5. The pay levels needed to facilitate the achievement of a sound financial position in relation to the products or services offered

The Pay-for-Performance Standard

To raise productivity and lower labor costs in today's competitive economic environment, organizations are increasingly setting compensation objectives based on a **pay-for-performance standard**.[5] It is agreed that managers must tie at least some reward to employee effort and performance. Without this standard, motivation to perform with greater effort will be low, resulting in higher wage costs to the organization.[6]

The term "pay-for-performance" refers to a wide range of compensation options, including merit pay, cash bonuses, incentive pay, and various gainsharing plans. (Gainsharing plans are discussed in Chapter 11.) Each of these compensation systems seeks to differentiate between the pay of average and outstanding performers. When Peoples Natural Gas Company of Pittsburgh revamped its compensation program, it had as its goals, "to clarify job expectations, to provide communication and feedback, and to provide recognition and rewards for meeting or exceeding performance expectations."[7] Interestingly, productivity studies show that employees will increase their output by 15 to 35 percent when an organization installs a pay-for-performance program.[8]

Unfortunately, designing a sound pay-for-performance system is not easy. Considerations must be given to how employee performance will be measured, the monies to be allocated for compensation increases, which employees to cover, the payout method, and the periods when payments will be made. A critical issue concerns the size of the monetary increase and its perceived value to employees. The American Compensation Association reports that annual salary budgets have only risen between 5 and 5.4 percent since 1987.[9] These percentages only slightly exceed yearly increases in the cost of living. While differences exist as to how large a wage or salary increase must be before it is perceived as meaningful, a pay-for-performance program will lack its full potential when pay increases only approximate rises in the cost of living.

The Motivating Value of Compensation

Pay constitutes a quantitative measure of an employee's relative worth. For most employees, pay has a direct bearing not only on their standard of living, but also on the status and recognition they may be able to achieve both on and off the job. Since pay represents a reward received in exchange for an employee's contributions, it is essential, according to the equity theory discussed in Chapter 14, that the pay be equitable in terms of those contributions. It is essential also that an employee's pay be equitable in terms of what other employees are receiving for their contributions.[10]

Pay Equity

Equity can be defined as anything of value earned through the investment of something of value. Marc Wallace and Charles Fay report that "fairness is achieved when the return on equity is equivalent to the investment made."[11] For employees, **pay equity** is achieved when the compensation received is equal to the value of the work performed.

E. A. Savinelli, founder and chairman/CEO of Aquatec Chemical International Inc., realizes that the perception of internal pay equity is important to employee performance. According to Savinelli:

> Internal equity is especially important in an organization where teamwork is critical to success. In our type of operation, which focuses on high-tech services to customers that requires a cross-section of skills and talents and interdisciplinary teamwork, coworkers need confidence in themselves and their colleagues. An important part of creating an environment in which teamwork is effective, is a pay policy that reflects the true value of work to the overall organization, and helps all members of the team respect one another's contribution and role.[12]

Not only must pay be equitable, it must also be perceived as such by employees. Research clearly demonstrates that employees' perceptions of pay equity, or inequity, can have dramatic effects on their motivation for both work behavior and productivity. Managers must therefore develop pay practices that are both internally and externally equitable. Employees must believe that wage rates for jobs within the organization approximate the job's worth to the organization.

Pay equity

An employee's perception that compensation received is equal to the value of the work performed

Also, the employer's wage rates must correspond closely to prevailing market rates for the employee's occupation.

Pay Expectancy

The expectancy theory of motivation predicts that one's level of motivation depends on the attractiveness of the reward sought. (See Chapter 14.) The theory therefore holds that employees should exert greater work effort if they have reason to expect that it will result in a reward that is valued.[13] To motivate this effort, the value of any monetary reward should be attractive. Employees also must believe that good performance is valued by their employer and will result in their receiving the expected reward.

Figure 10–1 illustrates the relationship between pay-for-performance and the expectancy theory of motivation. The model predicts that high effort will lead to high performance (expectancy), and high performance in turn will lead to monetary rewards that are appreciated (valued). Since we previously stated that pay-for-performance leads to a feeling of pay satisfaction, this feeling should reinforce one's high level of effort.

Thus, how employees view compensation can be an important factor in determining the motivational value of compensation. Furthermore, the effective communication of pay information together with an organizational environment that elicits employee trust in management can contribute to employees having more accurate perceptions of their pay. The perceptions employees develop concerning their pay are influenced by the accuracy of their knowledge and understanding of the compensation program.

Pay Secrecy

Misperceptions by employees concerning the equity of their pay and its relationship to performance can be created by secrecy about the pay that others receive. There is reason to believe that secrecy can generate distrust in the compensation system, reduce employee motivation, and inhibit organizational effectiveness. Yet pay secrecy seems to be an accepted practice in many organizations in both the private and the public sector.

Managers may justify secrecy on the grounds that most employees prefer to have their own pay kept secret. Probably one of the reasons for pay secrecy that managers may be unwilling to admit is that it gives them greater freedom in compensation management, since pay decisions are not disclosed and there is no need to justify or defend them. Employees who are not supposed to know what others are being paid have no objective base for pursuing grievances about their own pay. Secrecy also serves to cover up inequities existing within the pay structure. Furthermore, secrecy surrounding compensation decisions may lead employees to believe that there is no direct relationship between pay and performance.

Hourly or day work
Work paid on an hourly basis

The Bases for Compensation

Work performed in most private, public, and not-for-profit organizations has traditionally been compensated on an hourly basis. It is referred to as **hourly or day**

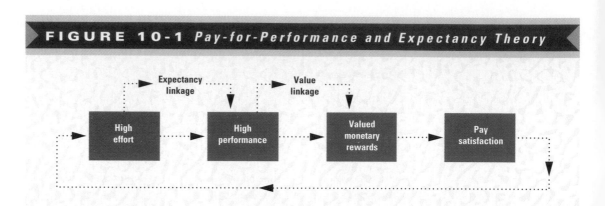

FIGURE 10-1 *Pay-for-Performance and Expectancy Theory*

Piecework

Work paid according to the number of units produced

work, in contrast to **piecework,** in which employees are paid according to the number of units they produce. Hourly work, however, is far more prevalent than piecework as a basis for compensating employees.

Employees compensated on an hourly basis are classified as *hourly employees,* or wage earners. Those whose compensation is computed on the basis of weekly, biweekly, or monthly pay periods are classified as *salaried employees.* Hourly employees are normally paid only for the time they work. Salaried employees, by contrast, are generally paid the same for each pay period, even though they occasionally may work more hours or fewer than the regular number of hours in a period. They also usually receive certain benefits not provided to hourly employees.

Another basis for compensation centers on whether employees are classified as either *nonexempt* or *exempt* under the Fair Labor Standards Act (FLSA). **Nonexempt employees** are covered by the act and must be paid at a rate of 1½ times their *regular* pay rate for time worked in excess of forty hours in their workweek. Most hourly workers employed in interstate commerce are considered nonexempt workers under the FLSA. Employees not covered by the overtime provision of the FLSA are classified as **exempt employees.** Managers and supervisors as well as a large number of white-collar employees are in the exempt category. The U.S. Department of Labor (DOL) imposes a narrow definition of exempt status, and employers wishing to classify employees as exempt must convince the DOL that the job is exempt on the basis of the independent judgment of the jobholder and other criteria. Therefore employers should check the exact terms and conditions of exemption before classifying employees as either exempt or nonexempt. (See Exemptions under the Act later in this chapter.)

Nonexempt employees

Employees covered by the overtime provisions of the Fair Labor Standards Act

Exempt employees

Employees not covered by the overtime provisions of the Fair Labor Standards Act

objective

Components of the Wage Mix

A combination of *external* and *internal* factors can influence, directly or indirectly, the rates at which employees are paid. Through their interaction these factors constitute the wage mix, as shown in Figure 10–2. For example, the area wage rate for administrative assistants might be $8.50 per hour. However, one employer may elect to pay its administrative assistants $10.25 per hour because of their excellent performance. The influence of government legislation on the wage mix will be discussed later in the chapter.

FIGURE 10-2 *Factors Affecting the Wage Mix*

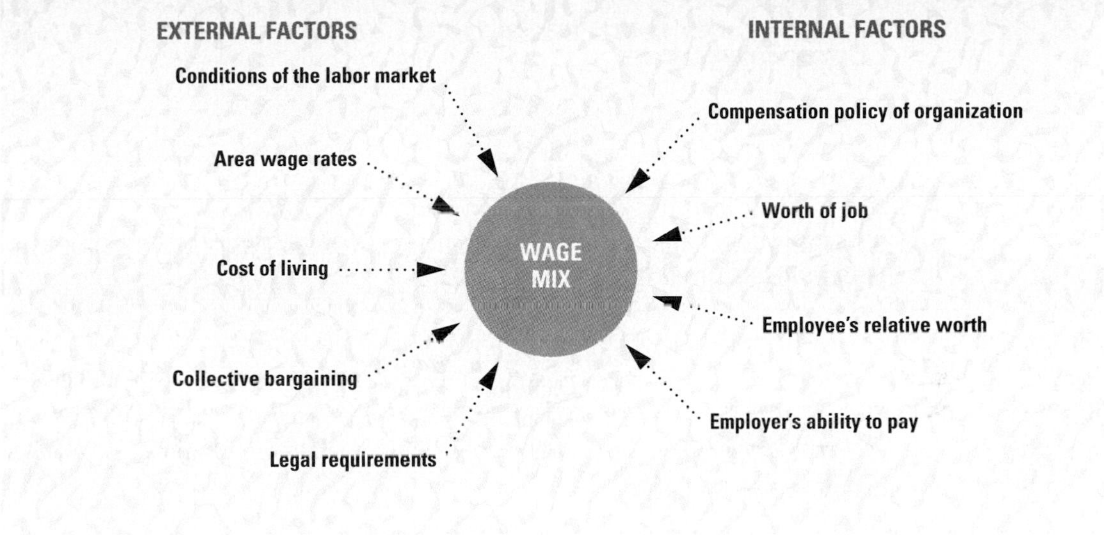

External Factors

The major external factors that influence wage rates include labor market conditions, area wage rates, cost of living, legal requirements, and collective bargaining if the employer is unionized.

Labor Market Conditions

The labor market reflects the forces of supply and demand for qualified labor within an area. These forces help to influence the wage rates required to recruit or retain competent employees. It must be recognized, however, that counterforces can reduce the full impact of supply and demand on the labor market. The economic power of unions, for example, may prevent employers from lowering wage rates even when unemployment is high among union members. Government regulations also may prevent an employer from paying at a market rate less than an established minimum.

Area Wage Rates

A formal wage structure should provide rates that are in line with those being paid by other employers for comparable jobs within the area. Data pertaining to area wage rates may be obtained from local wage surveys. For example, the Arizona Department of Economic Security conducts an annual wage survey for both large and small employers in various cities throughout the state. Wage-survey data also may be obtained from a variety of sources, including the American Management Association, Administrative Management Society, U.S. Department of Labor, and Federal Reserve Banks. Highlights in HRM 1 shows the April 1993 hourly earnings for selected jobs in Riverside–San Bernardino, California, published by the Bureau of Labor Statistics. Smaller employers such as the

HIGHLIGHTS IN HRM

1 WAGE-SURVEY DATA FROM THE BUREAU OF LABOR STATISTICS

WEEKLY HOURS AND EARNINGS OF PROFESSIONAL AND ADMINISTRATIVE OCCUPATIONS, RIVERSIDE–SAN BERNARDINO, CA, APRIL 1993

Occupation and level	Number of workers	Average weekly hours (std.)	Mean	Median	Middle range		
(professional occupations)							
Accountants							
Level II	222	40.0	$ 626	$ 610	$ 576	—	$ 685
Private industry	123	40.0	588	596	542	—	630
Goods producing	62	40.0	598	—	—	—	—
Service producing	61	39.9	579	—	—	—	—
State and local government . . .	99	40.0	672	699	605	—	739
Level III	329	40.0	741	719	665	—	808
Private industry	189	40.0	743	712	668	—	800
Goods producing	59	40.0	732	—	—	—	—
Manufacturing	57	40.0	724	—	—	—	—
Service producing	130	40.0	749	697	642	—	806
State and local government . . .	140	40.0	738	733	658	—	808
Level IV	207	40.0	944	949	839	—	1,040
Private industry	102	40.0	987	950	931	—	1,040
Goods producing	62	40.0	1,004	—	—	—	—
Manufacturing	58	40.0	998	—	—	—	—
State and local government . . .	105	40.0	902	865	795	—	1,029
Attorneys							
Level III:							
State and local government . . .	31	40.0	1,265	—	—	—	—
Level IV	78	40.0	1,599	—	—	—	—
State and local government . . .	66	40.0	1,523	1,494	1,494	—	1,494
Engineers							
Level II	240	40.0	799	808	738	—	867
Private industry	76	40.0	729	—	—	—	—
Goods producing	62	40.0	721	—	—	—	—
State and local government . . .	164	40.0	831	837	786	—	925

Occupation and level	Number of workers	Average weekly hours (std.)	Weekly earnings (in dollars)			
			Mean	Median	Middle range	
(professional occupations)						
Level III...................	1,031	40.0	$ 889	$ 884	$ 793 —	$ 967
Private industry	374	40.0	842	829	770 —	897
Goods producing...........	331	40.0	839	825	764 —	897
Manufacturing............	323	40.0	838	824	764 —	897
State and local government ...	657	40.0	916	907	811 —	1,056
Level IV...................	839	40.0	1,028	1,018	913 —	1,120
Private industry	442	40.0	969	947	867 —	1,066
Goods producing...........	417	40.0	967	937	867 —	1,065
Manufacturing............	409	40.0	961	935	866 —	1,056
State and local government ...	397	40.0	1,093	1,058	956 —	1,254
Level V	461	40.0	1,200	1,188	1,078 —	1,324
Private industry	293	40.0	1,160	1,128	1,039 —	1,243
Goods producing...........	280	40.0	1,155	1,122	1,035 —	1,236
Manufacturing............	280	40.0	1,155	1,122	1,035 —	1,236
State and local government ...	168	40.0	1,268	1,273	1,147 —	1,392

Source: *Occupational Compensation Survey:* Riverside–San Bernardino, California, Bureau of Labor Statistics.

Woodsmith Corporation and Golden State Container, Inc., use government surveys to establish rates of pay for new or senior employees. Many organizations, like the City of Atlanta, Northwest Airlines, and Wang Laboratories, conduct their own surveys. Others engage in a cooperative exchange of wage information or rely on various professional associations for these data. A high percentage of wage data is inexpensive—under $100—and is therefore available to all employers, regardless of size.

Data from area wage surveys can be used to prevent the rates for certain jobs from drifting too far above or below those of other employers in the region. When rates rise above existing area levels, an employer's labor costs may become excessive. Conversely, if they drop too far below area levels, it may be difficult to recruit and retain competent personnel. Wage-survey data must also take into account indirect wages paid in the form of benefits.

Escalator clauses
Clauses in labor agreements that provide for quarterly cost-of-living adjustments in wages, basing the adjustments upon changes in the consumer price index

Consumer price index (CPI)
Measure of the average change in prices over time in a fixed "market basket" of goods and services

Cost of Living

Because of inflation, compensation rates have had to be adjusted upward periodically to help employees maintain their purchasing power. This can be achieved through **escalator clauses** found in various labor agreements. These clauses provide for quarterly cost-of-living adjustments (COLA) in wages based on changes in the **consumer price index (CPI)**. The CPI is a measure of the average change in prices over time in a fixed "market basket" of goods and services.[14] The most common adjustments are 1 cent per hour for each 0.3- or 0.4-point change in the CPI.

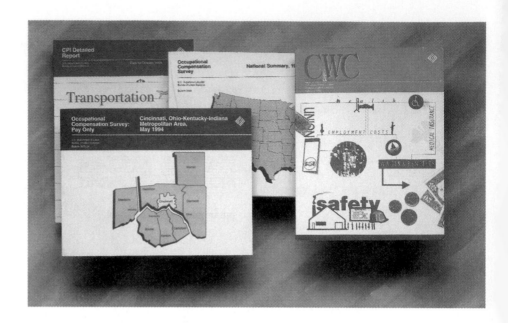

The CPI is calculated each month using price information collected by the Bureau of Labor Statistics.

The CPI is largely used to set wages. The index is based on prices of food, clothing, shelter, and fuels; transportation fares; charges for medical services; and prices of other goods and services that people buy for day-to-day living. The Bureau of Labor Statistics collects price information on a monthly basis and calculates the CPI for the nation as a whole and various U.S. city averages. Separate indexes are also published by size of city and by region of the country. Employers in a number of communities monitor changes in the CPI as a basis for compensation decisions.

Changes in the CPI can have important effects on pay rates. Granting wage increases solely on the basis of the CPI helps to compress pay rates within a pay structure, thereby creating inequities among those who receive the wage increase. Inequities also result from the fact that adjustments are made on a cent-per-hour rather than a percentage basis. For example, a cost-of-living adjustment of 50 cents represents a 10 percent increase for an employee earning $5 per hour, but only a 5 percent increase for one earning $10 per hour. Unless adjustments are made periodically in employee base rates, the desired differential between higher- and lower-paying jobs will gradually be reduced. The incentive to accept more-demanding jobs will also be reduced.

Collective Bargaining

Real wages
Wage increases larger than rises in the consumer price index; that is, the real earning power of wages

One of the primary functions of a labor union, as emphasized in Chapter 17, is to bargain collectively over conditions of employment, the most important of which is compensation. The union's goal in each new agreement is to achieve increases in **real wages**—wage increases larger than the increase in the CPI—thereby improving the purchasing power and standard of living of its members. This goal includes gaining wage settlements that equal if not exceed the pattern established by other unions within the area.

The agreements negotiated by unions tend to establish rate patterns within the labor market. As a result, wages are generally higher in areas where organized labor is strong. To recruit and retain competent personnel and avoid unionization, nonunion employers must either meet or exceed these rates. The "union scale" also becomes the prevailing rate that all employers must pay for work performed under government contract. The impact of collective bargaining therefore extends beyond that segment of the labor force that is unionized.

Internal Factors

The internal factors that influence wage rates are the employer's compensation policy, the worth of a job, an employee's relative worth in meeting job requirements, and an employer's ability to pay.

Employer's Compensation Policy

Highlights in HRM 2 illustrates the compensation objectives of two organizations, Astra-Merck and Hewlett-Packard. The pay objective of Hewlett-Packard is to be an industry pay leader, while Astra-Merck seeks to be wage-competitive by paying employees at the seventy-fifth percentile of their competitors' wages. Both employers strive to promote a compensation policy that is fair and competitive.

Astra-Merck and Hewlett-Packard, like other employers, will establish numerous compensation objectives that affect the pay employees receive. As a minimum, both large and small employers should set pay policies reflecting (1) the internal wage relationship among jobs and skill levels, (2) the external competition or an employer's pay position relative to what competitors are paying, (3) a policy of rewarding employee performance, and (4) administrative decisions concerning elements of the pay system such as overtime premiums, payment periods, and short-term or long-term incentives.[15]

Worth of a Job

Organizations without a formal compensation program generally base the worth of jobs on the subjective opinions of people familiar with the jobs.[16] In such instances, pay rates may be influenced heavily by the labor market or, in the case of unionized employers, by collective bargaining. Organizations with formal compensation programs, however, are more likely to rely on a system of *job evaluation* to aid in rate determination. Even when rates are subject to collective bargaining, job evaluation can assist the organization in maintaining some degree of control over its wage structure.

The use of job evaluation is widespread in both the public and the private sector. The cities of Chicago and Miami use job evaluation in establishing wage structures, as do Levi Strauss and J. C. Penney. The jobs covered most frequently by job evaluation comprise clerical, technical, and various blue-collar groups, whereas those jobs covered least frequently are managerial and top-executive positions.

2 COMPENSATION OBJECTIVES AT ASTRA-MERCK AND HEWLETT-PACKARD

Astra-Merck

- Share commitment and responsibility; foster teamwork
- Balance immediate and strategic interests
- Celebrate performance
- Promote fairness
- Achieve simplicity
- Be market-competitive: pay at the 75th percentile of competitors

Hewlett-Packard

- Help H-P continue to attract creative and enthusiastic people who contribute to its success
- Pay among the leaders
- Reflect sustained relative contribution of unit, division, and H-P
- Be open and understandable
- Ensure fair treatment
- Be innovative, competitive, and equitable

Source: George T. Milkovich and Jerry M. Newman, *Compensation,* 4th ed. (Homewood, Ill.: Irwin, 1993). Used with permission.

Employee's Relative Worth

It is common practice in some industries, notably construction, for unions to negotiate a single rate for jobs in a particular occupation. This egalitarian practice is based on the argument that employees who possess the same qualifications should receive the same rate of pay. Furthermore, the itinerant nature of work in the construction industry usually prevents the accumulation of employment seniority on which pay differentials might be based. Even so, it is not uncommon for employers in the trades to seek to retain their most competent employees by paying them more than the union scale.

In industrial and office jobs, differences in employee performance can be recognized and rewarded through promotion and with various incentive systems. (The incentive systems used most often will be discussed in the next chapter.) Superior performance can also be rewarded by granting merit raises on the basis of steps within a rate range established for a job class. If merit raises are to have their intended value, however, they must be determined by an effective performance appraisal system that differentiates between those employees who deserve the raises and those who do not.[17] This system, moreover, must provide a visible and credible relationship between performance and any raises received. Unfo

"A raise just isn't feasible at this time, Osgood, but we're going to give you the 'wave.'"

Copyright 1994. Reprinted courtesy of Bunny Hoest and *Parade Magazine*.

tunately, too many so-called merit systems provide for raises to be granted automatically. As a result, employees tend to be rewarded more for merely being present than for being productive on the job.

Employer's Ability to Pay

In the public sector, the amount of pay and benefits employees can receive is limited by the funds budgeted for this purpose and by the willingness of taxpayers to provide them. In the private sector, pay levels are limited by profits and other financial resources available to employers. Thus an organization's ability to pay is determined in part by the productivity of its employees. This productivity is a result not only of their performance, but also of the amount of capital the organization has invested in labor-saving equipment. Generally, increases in capital investment reduce the number of employees required to perform the work and increase an employer's ability to provide higher pay for those it employs.

Economic conditions and competition faced by employers can also significantly affect the rates they are able to pay. Competition and recessions can force prices down and reduce the income from which compensation payments are derived. In such situations, employers have little choice but to reduce wages and/or lay off employees, or, even worse, to go out of business. Employers and workers in the trucking and airline industries, for example, can attest to the competitive effects of deregulation and its influence on wage levels and job security. Likewise, companies such as Ford, USX (formerly U.S. Steel), Goodyear, and Phelps Dodge have had their ability to pay large wage increases severely limited by growing competition from the international market.

Job Evaluation Systems

objective

Job evaluation

Systematic process of determining the relative worth of jobs in order to establish which jobs should be paid more than others within an organization

As we discussed earlier, one important component of the wage mix is the worth of the job. Organizations formally determine the value of jobs through the process of job evaluation. **Job evaluation** is the systematic process of determining the *relative* worth of jobs in order to establish which jobs should be paid more than others within the organization. Job evaluation helps to establish internal equity between various jobs. The relative worth of a job may be determined by comparing it with others within the organization or by comparing it with a scale that has been constructed for this purpose. Each method of comparison, furthermore, may be made on the basis of the jobs as a whole or on the basis of the parts that constitute the jobs.

Four methods of comparison are shown in Figure 10–3. They provide the basis for the principal systems of job evaluation. We will begin by discussing the simpler, nonquantitative approaches and conclude by reviewing the more popular, quantitative systems. Regardless of the methodology used, it is important to remember that all job evaluation methods require varying degrees of managerial judgment.[18]

Job Ranking System

Job ranking system

Simplest and oldest system of job evaluation by which jobs are arrayed on the basis of their relative worth

The simplest and oldest system of job evaluation is the **job ranking system,** which arrays jobs on the basis of their relative worth. One technique used to rank jobs consists of having the raters arrange cards listing the duties and responsibilities of each job in order of the importance of the jobs. Job ranking can be done by a single individual knowledgable of all jobs or by a committee composed of management and employee representatives.

Another common approach to job ranking is the paired-comparison method. Raters compare each job with all other jobs by means of a paired-comparison ranking table that lists the jobs in both rows and columns, as shown in Figure 10–4. To use the table, raters compare a job from a row with the jobs from each of the columns. If the row job is ranked higher than a column job, an X is placed in the appropriate cell. After all the jobs have been compared, raters total the Xs for row jobs. The total number of Xs for a row job will establish its worth relative to other jobs.[19] Differences in rankings should then be reconciled

---

FIGURE 10-3 *Different Job Evaluation Systems*

BASIS FOR COMPARISON	SCOPE OF COMPARISON	
	JOB AS A WHOLE (NONQUANTITATIVE)	JOB PARTS OR FACTORS (QUANTITATIVE)
Job vs. job	Job ranking system	Factor comparison system
Job vs. scale	Job classification system	Point system

> **FIGURE 10-4** *Paired-Comparison Job Ranking Table*

Column Jobs / Row Jobs	Senior Administrative Secretary	Data-Entry Operator	Data Processing Director	File Clerk	Systems Analyst	Programmer	Total
Senior Administrative Secretary	—	X		X		X	3
Data-Entry Operator		—		X			1
Data Processing Director	X	X	—	X	X	X	5
File Clerk				—			0
Systems Analyst	X	X		X		X	4
Programmer		X		X		—	2

Directions: Place an X in cell where the value of a row job is higher than that of a column job.

into a single rating for all jobs. After jobs are evaluated, wage rates can be assigned to them through use of the salary survey discussed later in the chapter.

The basic weakness of the job ranking system is that it does not provide a very refined measure of each job's worth. Since the comparisons are normally made on the basis of the job as a whole, it is quite easy for one or more of the factors of a job to bias the ranking given to a job, particularly if the job is complex. This drawback can be partially eliminated by having the raters—prior to the evaluation process—agree on one or two important factors with which to evaluate jobs and the weights to be assigned these factors. Another disadvantage of the job ranking system is that the final ranking of jobs merely indicates the relative importance of the jobs, not the differences in the degree of importance that may exist between jobs. A final limitation of the job ranking method is that it can only be used with a small number of jobs, probably no more than fifteen. Its simplicity, however, makes it ideal for use by smaller employers.

Job classification system

System of job evaluation by which jobs are classified and grouped according to a series of predetermined wage grades

Job Classification System

Grade

In the **job classification system,** jobs are classified and grouped according to a series of predetermined grades. Successive grades require increasing amounts of job responsibility, skill, knowledge, ability, or other factors selected to compare jobs. For example, Grade GS-1 from the federal government grade descriptions reads as follows:

> GS-1 includes those classes of positions the duties of which are to perform, under immediate supervision, with little or no latitude for the exercise of independent judgment (A) the simplest routine work in office, business, or fiscal operations; or (B) elementary work of a subordinate technical character in a professional, scientific, or technical field.

The descriptions of each of the job classes constitute the scale against which the specifications for the various jobs are compared. Managers then evaluate jobs by comparing job descriptions with the different wage grades in order to "slot" the job into the appropriate grade. While this system has the advantage of simplicity, it is less precise than the point and factor comparison systems (discussed in the next sections) because the job is evaluated as a whole. The federal civil service job classification system is probably the best-known system of this type. The job classification system is widely used by municipal and state governments.[20]

Point System

Point system

Quantitative job evaluation procedure that determines the relative value of a job by the total points assigned to it

Considered most valid

The **point system** is a quantitative job evaluation procedure that determines a job's relative value by calculating the total points assigned to it. It has been successfully used by high-visibility organizations such as Digital Equipment Company, TRW, Johnson Wax Company, Boeing, TransAmerica, and many other public and private organizations, both large and small. Although point systems are rather complicated to establish, once in place they are relatively simple to understand and use. The principal advantage of the point system is that it provides a more refined basis for making judgments than either the ranking or classification systems and thereby can produce results that are more valid and less easy to manipulate.

The point system permits jobs to be evaluated quantitatively on the basis of factors or elements—commonly called *compensable factors*—that constitute the job. The skills, efforts, responsibilities, and working conditions that a job usually entails are the more common major compensable factors that serve to rank one job as more or less important than another.[21] The number of compensable factors an organization uses depends on the nature of the organization and the jobs to be evaluated. Once selected, compensable factors will be assigned weights according to their relative importance to the organization. For example, if responsibility is considered extremely important to the organization, it could be assigned a weight of 40 percent. Next, each factor will be divided into a number of degrees. Degrees represent different levels of difficulty associated with each factor.

The point system requires the use of a *point manual*. The point manual is, in effect, a handbook that contains a description of the compensable factors and the degrees to which these factors may exist within the jobs. A manual also will indicate—usually by means of a table (see Highlights in HRM 3)—the number of points allocated to each factor and to each of the degrees into which these factors are divided. The point value assigned to a job represents the sum of the numerical degree values of each compensable factor that the job possesses.

Developing a Point Manual

A variety of point manuals have been developed by organizations, trade associations, and management consultants. An organization that seeks to use one of these existing manuals should make certain that the manual is suited to its particular jobs and conditions of operation. If necessary, the organization should modify the manual or develop its own to suit its needs.

The job factors that are illustrated in Highlights in HRM 3 represent those covered by the American Association of Industrial Management point manual. Each of the factors listed in this manual has been divided into five degrees. The number of degrees into which the factors in a manual are to be divided, however, can be greater or smaller than this number, depending on the relative weight assigned to each factor and the ease with which the individual degrees can be defined or distinguished.[22]

After the job factors in the point manual have been divided into degrees, a statement must be prepared defining each of these degrees, as well as each factor as a whole. The definitions should be concise and yet distinguish the factors and each of their degrees. Highlights in HRM 4 represents another portion of the point manual used by the American Association of Industrial Management to describe each of the degrees for the job knowledge factor. These descriptions enable those conducting a job evaluation to determine the degree to which the factors exist in each job being evaluated.

The final step in developing a point manual is to determine the number of points to be assigned to each factor and to each degree within these factors. Although the total number of points is arbitrary, 500 points is often the maximum.

Using the Point Manual

Job evaluation under the point system is accomplished by comparing the job descriptions and job specifications, factor by factor, against the various factor-degree descriptions contained in the manual. Each factor within the job being evaluated is then assigned the number of points specified in the manual. When the points for each factor have been determined from the manual, the total point value for the job as a whole can be calculated. The relative worth of the job is then determined from the total points that have been assigned to that job.[23]

Factor Comparison System

Factor comparison system

Job evaluation system that permits the evaluation process to be accomplished on a factor-by-factor basis by developing a factor comparison scale

The **factor comparison system,** like the point system, permits the job evaluation process to be accomplished on a factor-by-factor basis. It differs from the point system, however, in that the compensable factors of the jobs to be evaluated are compared against the compensable factors of *key jobs* within the organization that serve as the job evaluation scale. Thus, instead of beginning with an established point scale, the factor comparison system requires a scale to be developed as part of the job evaluation process.[24]

Developing a Factor Comparison Scale

There are four basic steps in developing and using a factor comparison scale: (1) selecting and ranking key jobs, (2) allocating wage rates for key jobs across compensable factors, (3) setting up the factor comparison scale, and (4) evaluating nonkey jobs.

3 POINT VALUES FOR JOB FACTORS OF THE AMERICAN ASSOCIATION OF INDUSTRIAL MANAGEMENT

FACTORS	1ST DEGREE	2ND DEGREE	3RD DEGREE	4TH DEGREE	5TH DEGREE
Skill					
1. Job knowledge	14	28	42	56	70
2. Experience	22	44	66	88	110
3. Initiative and ingenuity	14	28	42	56	70
Effort					
4. Physical demand	10	20	30	40	50
5. Mental or visual demand	5	10	15	20	25
Responsibility					
6. Equipment or process	5	10	15	20	25
7. Material or product	5	10	15	20	25
8. Safety of others	5	10	15	20	25
9. Work of others	5	10	15	20	25
Job Conditions					
10. Working conditions	10	20	30	40	50
11. Hazards	5	10	15	20	25

Source: Developed by the National Metal Trades Association. Reproduced with permission of the American Association of Industrial Management, Springfield, Mass.

Step 1. Select and rank key jobs on the basis of compensable factors. *Key jobs* can be defined as those jobs that are important for wage-setting purposes and are widely known in the labor market. Key jobs have the following characteristics:

1. They are important to employees and the organization.
2. They vary in terms of job requirements.
3. They have relatively stable job content.
4. They are used in salary surveys for wage determination.

HIGHLIGHTS IN HRM

4   DESCRIPTION OF JOB KNOWLEDGE FACTOR AND DEGREES OF THE AMERICAN ASSOCIATION OF INDUSTRIAL MANAGEMENT

highlights

1. Job Knowledge

This factor measures the knowledge or equivalent training required to perform the position duties.

1st Degree   Use of reading and writing, adding and subtracting of whole numbers; following of instructions; use of fixed gauges, direct reading instruments, and similar devices where interpretation is not required.

2nd Degree   Use of addition, subtraction, multiplication, and division of numbers including decimals and fractions; simple use of formulas, charts, tables, drawings, specifications, schedules, wiring diagrams; use of adjustable measuring instruments; checking of reports, forms, records, and comparable data where interpretation is required.

3rd Degree   Use of mathematics together with the use of complicated drawings, specifications, charts, tables; various types of precision measuring instruments. Equivalent to one to three years applied trades training in a particular or specialized occupation.

4th Degree   Use of advanced trades mathematics, together with the use of complicated drawings, specifications, charts, tables, handbook formulas; all varieties of precision measuring instruments. Equivalent to complete accredited apprenticeship in a recognized trade, craft or occupation; or equivalent to a two-year technical college education.

5th Degree   Use of higher mathematics involved in the application of engineering principles and their performance of related practical operations, together with a comprehensive knowledge of the theories and practices of mechanical, electrical, chemical, civil, or like engineering field. Equivalent to complete four years of technical college or university education.

Source: Developed by the National Metal Trades Association. Reproduced with permission of the American Association of Industrial Management, Springfield, Mass.

Key jobs are normally ranked against five factors—skill, mental effort, physical effort, responsibility, and working conditions. It is normal for the ranking of each key job to be different because of the different requirements of jobs. The ranking of three key jobs is shown in Figure 10–5, although usually fifteen to twenty key jobs will constitute a factor comparison scale.

FIGURE 10-5 *Ranking Key Jobs by Compensable Factors*

JOB	SKILL	MENTAL EFFORT	PHYSICAL EFFORT	RESPON-SIBILITY	WORKING CONDITIONS
Machinist planner	1	1	3	1	3
Punch press operator	2	2	1	3	2
Storekeeper	3	3	2	2	1

Step 2. Next, determine the proportion of the current wage being paid on a key job to each of the factors composing the job. Thus the proportion of a key job's wage rate allocated to the skill factor will depend on the importance of skill in comparison with mental effort, physical effort, responsibility, and working conditions. It is important that the factor rankings in step 1 be consistent with the wage-apportionment rankings in step 2. Figure 10–6 illustrates how the rate for three key jobs has been allocated according to the relative importance of the basic factors that make up these jobs.

Step 3. After the wages for each key job have been apportioned across the factors, the data are displayed on a factor comparison scale, which is shown in Figure 10–7 on page 364. The location of the key jobs on the scale and the compensable factors for these jobs provide the benchmarks against which other jobs are evaluated.

Step 4. We are now ready to compare the nonkey jobs against the key jobs in the columns of Figure 10–7. As an example of how the scale is used, let's assume that the job of screw machine operator is to be evaluated through the use of the factor comparison scale. By comparing the skill factor for screw machine operator with the skill factors of the key jobs on the table, it is decided that the skill demand of the job places it about halfway between those of storekeeper and punch press operator. The job is therefore placed at the $5.55 point on the scale. The same procedure is used to place the job at the appropriate point on the scale for the remaining factors.

Using the Factor Comparison Scale

The evaluated worth of the jobs added to the scale is computed by adding up the money values for each factor as determined by where the job has been placed on the scale for each factor. Thus the evaluated worth of the screw machine operator at $9.72 would be determined by totaling the monetary value for each factor as follows:

FIGURE 10-6 *Wage Apportionment for Each Factor*

JOB	TOTAL	SKILL	MENTAL EFFORT	PHYSICAL EFFORT	RESPON-SIBILITY	WORKING CONDITIONS
Machinist planner	$13.00	$6.50 (1)	$3.50 (1)	$0.50 (3)	$1.60 (1)	$0.90 (3)
Punch press operator	11.30	6.20 (2)	1.60 (2)	1.00 (1)	0.80 (3)	1.70 (2)
Storekeeper	9.85	4.90 (3)	1.30 (3)	0.70 (2)	1.20 (2)	1.75 (1)

Skill	$5.55
Mental effort	1.35
Physical effort	0.82
Responsibility	0.60
Working conditions	1.40
	$9.72

Job Evaluation for Management Positions

Because management positions are more difficult to evaluate and involve certain demands not found in jobs at the lower levels, some organizations do not attempt to include them in their job evaluation programs. Those employers that do evaluate these positions, however, may extend their regular system of evaluation to include such positions, or they may develop a separate evaluation system for management positions.

Several systems have been developed especially for the evaluation of executive, managerial, and professional positions. One of the better-known is the **Hay profile method,** developed by Edward N. Hay. The three broad factors that constitute the evaluation in the "profile" include knowledge (or know-how), mental activity (or problem solving), and accountability.[25] The Hay method uses only three factors because it is assumed that these factors represent the most important aspects of all executive and managerial positions. The profile for each position is developed by determining the percentage value to be assigned to each of the three factors. Jobs are then ranked on the basis of each factor, and point values that make up the profile are assigned to each job on the basis of the percentage-value level at which the job is ranked.

Hay profile method

Job evaluation technique using three factors—knowledge, mental activity, and accountability —to evaluate executive and managerial positions

The Compensation Structure

Job evaluation systems provide for internal equity and serve as the basis for wage-rate determination. They do not in themselves determine the wage rate. The evaluated worth of each job in terms of its rank, class, points, or monetary worth must be converted into an hourly, daily, weekly, or monthly wage rate. The compensation tool used to help set wages is the wage and salary survey.

FIGURE 10-7 *Factor Comparison Scale*

HOURLY RATE	SKILL	MENTAL EFFORT	PHYSICAL EFFORT	RESPON-SIBILITY	WORKING CONDITIONS
6.50	• Machinist planner				
6.25					
6.00	• Punch press operator				
5.75					
5.50	• *Screw mach. operator*				
5.25					
5.00	• Storekeeper				
4.75					
4.50					
4.25					
4.00					
3.75					
3.50		• Machinist planner			
3.25					
3.00					
2.75					
2.50					
2.25					
2.00					
1.75					• Storekeeper • Punch press operator
1.50		• Punch press operator • *Screw mach. operator*		• Machinist planner	• *Screw mach. operator*
1.25		• Storekeeper		• Storekeeper	• Machinist planner
1.00			• Punch press operator • *Screw mach. operator*	• Punch press operator	
0.75			• Storekeeper	• *Screw mach. operator*	
0.50			• Machinist planner		

Note: If this scale contained the fifteen to twenty key jobs that typically constitute a factor comparison scale, the gaps between jobs on the scale would be reduced substantially.

objective

Wage and salary survey

Survey of the wages paid to employees of other employers in the surveying organization's relevant labor market

Wage and Salary Surveys

The **wage and salary survey** is a survey of the wages paid by employers in an organization's relevant labor market—local, regional, or national, depending on the job. The labor market is frequently defined as that area from which employers obtain certain types of workers. The labor market for office personnel would be local, whereas the labor market for engineers would be national. It is the wage and salary survey that permits an organization to maintain external equity, that is, to pay its employees wages equivalent to the wages similar employees earn in other establishments. Although surveys are primarily conducted to gather competitive wage data, they can also collect information on employee benefits or organizational pay practices (e.g., overtime rates or shift differentials).

Collecting Survey Data

While many organizations conduct their own wage and salary surveys, a variety of "preconducted" pay surveys are available to satisfy the requirements of most public and not-for-profit or private employers. The Bureau of Labor Statistics (BLS) is the major publisher of wage and salary data, putting out three major surveys: area wage surveys, industry wage surveys, and the National Survey of Professional, Administrative, Technical, and Clerical Pay (PATC). The BLS also publishes the Employee Benefits Survey and the Employment Cost Index (ECI), which reports changes in employee compensation costs. Employers use the ECI as a cross-check on other compensation surveys and to track geographical differentials for various nonexempt jobs.[26] For example, wages paid to welders in Los Angeles and to welders in Orlando, Florida, can be compared through the ECI.

Many states conduct surveys on either a municipal or county basis and make them available to employers. Besides these government surveys, trade groups such as the Dallas Personnel Association, the Administrative Management Society, the Society for Human Resource Management, the American Management Association, the National Society of Professional Engineers, and the Financial Executive Institute conduct special surveys tailored to their members' needs. Employers with global operations can purchase international surveys through large consulting firms. The overseas compensation survey offered by TPF&C reports on the payment practices in twenty countries. While all of these third-party surveys provide certain benefits to their users, they also have various limitations. Two problems with all published surveys are that (1) they are not always compatible with the user's jobs and (2) the user cannot specify what specific data to collect. To overcome these problems, organizations may collect their own compensation data.

Employer-Initiated Surveys

Employers wishing to conduct their own wage and salary survey must first select the jobs to be used in the survey and identify the organizations with whom they actually compete for employees.[27] Since it is not feasible to survey all the jobs in an organization, normally only key jobs are used. The survey of key jobs will usually be sent to ten or fifteen organizations that represent a valid sample of other employers likely to compete for the employees of the surveying organization. A diversity of organizations should be selected—large and small, public and private, new and established, and union and nonunion—since each classification of employer is likely to pay different wage rates for surveyed jobs.

After the key jobs and the employers to be surveyed have been identified, the surveying organization must decide what information to gather on wages, benefit types, and pay policies. For example, when requesting pay data, it is important to specify whether hourly, daily, or weekly pay figures are needed. In addition, those conducting surveys must state if the wage data are needed for new hires or for senior employees. Precisely defining the compensation data needed will greatly increase the accuracy of the information received and the number of purposes for which it can be used. Once the survey data are tabulated, the compensation structure can be completed.

objective

Wage curve
Curve in a scattergram representing the relationship between relative worth of jobs and wage rates

The Wage Curve

The relationship between the relative worth of jobs and their wage rates can be represented by means of a **wage curve.** This curve may indicate the rates currently paid for jobs within an organization, the new rates resulting from job evaluation, or the rates for similar jobs currently being paid by other organizations within the labor market. A curve may be constructed graphically by preparing a scattergram consisting of a series of dots that represent the current wage rates. As shown in Figure 10–8, a freehand curve is then drawn through

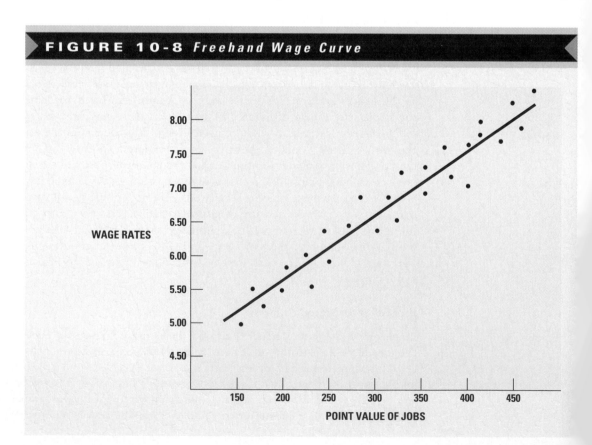

FIGURE 10-8 *Freehand Wage Curve*

the cluster of dots in such a manner as to leave approximately an equal number of dots above and below the curve. The wage curve can be relatively straight or curved. This curve can then be used to determine the relationship between the value of a job and its wage rate at any given point on the line.

Pay Grades

Pay grades

Groups of jobs within a particular class that are paid the same rate or rate range

From an administrative standpoint, it is generally preferable to group jobs into **pay grades** and to pay all jobs within a particular grade the same rate or rate range. When the classification system of job evaluation is used, jobs are grouped into grades as part of the evaluation process. When the point and factor comparison systems are used, however, pay grades must be established at selected intervals that represent either the point or the evaluated monetary value of these jobs. The graph in Figure 10–9 illustrates a series of pay grades designated along the horizontal axis at fifty-point intervals.

The grades within a wage structure may vary in number. The number is determined by such factors as the slope of the wage curve, the number and distribution of the jobs within the structure, and the organization's wage administration

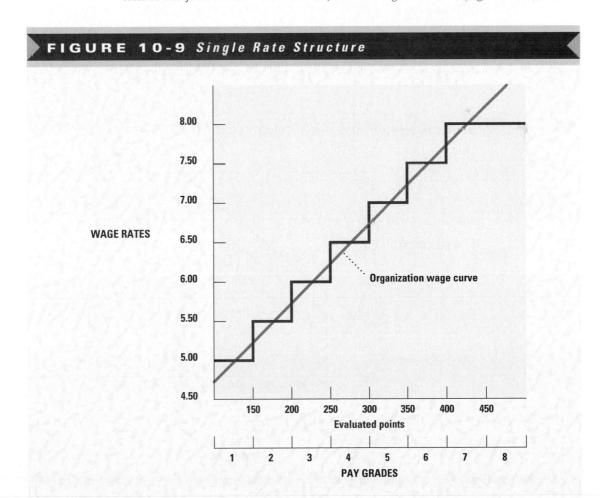

FIGURE 10-9 *Single Rate Structure*

and promotion policies. The number utilized should be sufficient to permit difficulty levels to be distinguished, but not so great as to make the distinction between two adjoining grades insignificant.

Rate Ranges

Although a single rate may be created for each pay grade, as shown in Figure 10–9, it is more common to provide a range of rates for each pay grade. The rate ranges may be the same for each grade or proportionately greater for each successive grade, as shown in Figure 10–10. Rate ranges constructed on the latter basis provide a greater incentive for employees to accept a promotion to a job in a higher grade.

Rate ranges generally are divided into a series of steps that permit employees to receive increases up to the maximum rate for the range on the basis of merit or seniority or a combination of the two. Most salary structures provide for the ranges of adjoining pay grades to overlap. The purpose of the overlap is to permit

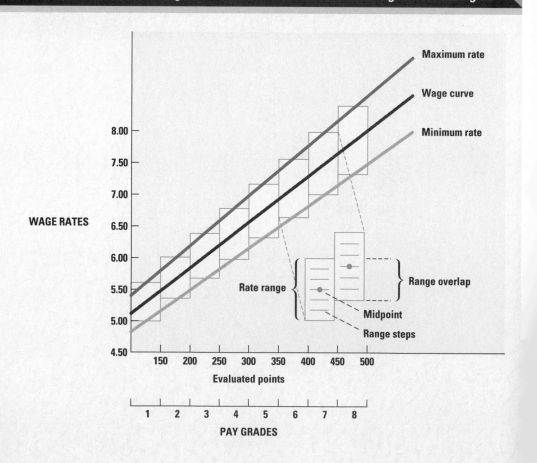

FIGURE 10-10 *Wage Structure with Increasing Rate Ranges*

an employee with experience to earn as much as or more than a person with less experience in the next-higher job classification.

Classification of Jobs

The final step in setting up a wage structure is to determine the appropriate pay grade into which each job should be placed on the basis of its evaluated worth. Traditionally, this worth is determined on the basis of job requirements without regard to the performance of the person in that job. Under this system, the performance of those who exceed the requirements of a job may be acknowledged by merit increases within the grade range or by promotion to a job in the next-higher pay grade.

Unfortunately, such a system often fails to reward employees for the skills or knowledge they possess or to encourage them to learn new job-related skills. It tends to consider employees as jobholders rather than as individuals. To correct these weaknesses, organizations such as General Mills, Frito-Lay, Northern Telecom, Sherwin-Williams, and Honeywell have introduced **skill-based pay** plans.[28] Also referred to as multiskill-based, knowledge-based, or pay-for-knowledge plans, these programs compensate employees for the skills and knowledge they possess rather than for the jobs they hold in a designated job category.

Although the types of skill-based plans are sometimes thought to be interchangeable, there are important differences between them. Organizations using skill-based pay systems compensate employees for the number of different skills they learn and can apply to different jobs in the organization. Skill-based pay plans are frequently used where employees are part of autonomous work groups or employee teams. As one research study noted, skill-based pay reinforces employee-involvement practices. It increases employee flexibility, which broadens employees' perspective on the overall production or service-delivery system. Rewards for learning multiple jobs may also facilitate job rotation and cross-training, which are essential to self-managing team designs.[29]

Skill-based pay plans are particularly attractive to organizations looking for greater job-staffing flexibility. Unfortunately, these plans may bring some long-term difficulties. Some plans limit the amount of compensation employees can earn, regardless of the new skills or knowledge they acquire. Thus, after achieving the top wage, employees may be reluctant to continue their educational training. Furthermore, employees can become discouraged when they acquire new abilities but find there are no higher-rated jobs to which they can transfer. Finally, unless all employees have the opportunity to increase their pay through the attainment of new skills, employees who are not given this opportunity may feel disgruntled.

Skill-based pay
Pay based on how many skills employees have or how many jobs they can perform

Governmental Regulation of Compensation

Compensation management, like the other areas of HRM, is subject to state and federal regulations. A majority of states have minimum wage laws or wage boards that fix minimum wage rates on an industry-by-industry basis. Most states also regulate hours of work and overtime payments.

The three principal federal laws affecting wages are the Davis-Bacon Act, the Walsh-Healy Act, and the Fair Labor Standards Act. These laws were enacted during the 1930s to prevent the payment of abnormally low wage rates and to encourage the spreading of work among a greater number of workers. The latter objective was accomplished by forcing organizations to pay a premium rate for overtime work (all hours worked in excess of a prescribed number).

Davis-Bacon Act of 1931

The Davis-Bacon Act, also referred to as the Prevailing Wage Law, was passed in 1931 and is the oldest of the three federal wage laws. It requires that the minimum wage rates paid to persons employed on federal public works projects worth more than $2,000 be at least equal to the prevailing rates and that overtime be paid at $1\frac{1}{2}$ times this rate.

There have been efforts in Congress to repeal the Davis-Bacon Act on the grounds that the situation it was designed to alleviate at the time of its passage no longer exists. The act is also criticized for contributing to inflation because the minimum pay can be based on the rate paid to only 30 percent of the workers in an area. This "30 percent rule" usually results in forcing contractors on federal construction projects to pay rates negotiated by unions (union scale), as long as their workers represent at least 30 percent of workers within the area. These rates are often higher than the average rate prevailing within the area. Failing to have the act repealed, its opponents have sought to eliminate the 30 percent rule as a basis for establishing the prevailing rate on federal public works projects.

Walsh-Healy Act of 1936

The Walsh-Healy Act, which is officially called the Public Contracts Act, was passed in 1936 and covers workers employed on government contract work for supplies, equipment, and materials worth in excess of $10,000. The act requires contractors to pay employees at least the prevailing wage rates established by the Secretary of Labor for the area, and overtime of $1\frac{1}{2}$ times the regular rate for all work performed in excess of eight hours in one day or forty hours in one week, depending on which basis provides the larger premium. For example, an employee working four days of twelve hours each during a given week would be entitled to receive sixteen hours of overtime and thirty-two hours of regular time for the week. In computing overtime payments under the Walsh-Healy Act, as under the Fair Labor Standards Act, the wage rate used must include any bonuses or incentive payments that may be a part of the employee's total earnings. The Walsh-Healy Act also contains restrictions covering the use of child and convict labor.

Fair Labor Standards Act of 1938 (as Amended)

The Fair Labor Standards Act (FLSA), commonly referred to as the Wage and Hour Act, was passed in 1938 and since then has been amended many times. It covers those employees who are engaged in the production of goods for interstate and foreign commerce, including those whose work is closely related to or essential to such production. The act also covers agricultural workers, as well as em-

Young workers in a Carolina cotton mill before child labor was illegal (circa 1908).

ployees of certain retail and service establishments whose sales volume exceeds a prescribed amount. The major provisions of the FLSA are concerned with minimum wage rates and overtime payments, child labor, and equal rights.[30]

Wage and Hour Provisions

The minimum wage prescribed by federal law has been raised many times, from an original figure of 25 cents per hour to $4.25 per hour in April 1991. (See Highlights in HRM 5 for the federal minimum wage poster that employers are required to display.) This minimum rate applies to the actual earning rate before any overtime premiums have been added. An overtime rate of 1½ times the base rate must be paid for all hours worked in excess of forty during a given week. The base wage rate from which the overtime rate is computed must include incentive payments or bonuses that are received during the period. For example, if a person employed at a base rate of $6 an hour works a total of forty-five hours in a given week and receives a bonus of $90, that person is actually working at the rate of $8 an hour. (The $90 bonus divided by the forty-five hours required to earn it equals $2 per hour, which, when added to the base rate of $6 per hour, increases the employee's earning rate to $8 per hour for the week.) Earnings for the week would total $380, computed as follows:

Regular time   40 × $8 = $320
Overtime   5 × $12 =   60
Total earnings $380

If the bonus is paid on a monthly or quarterly basis, earnings for the period must be recalculated to include this bonus in the hourly rate for overtime payments. When employees are given time off in return for overtime work, it must

HIGHLIGHTS IN HRM

highlights

5   THE FEDERAL MINIMUM WAGE POSTER

YOUR RIGHTS
UNDER THE FAIR LABOR STANDARDS ACT

Federal Minimum Wage

$4.25

Minimum Wage of at least $4.25 per hour beginning April 1, 1991.

Certain full-time students, student learners, apprentices, and workers with disabilities may be paid less than the minimum wage under special certificates issued by the Department of Labor.

Tip credit — The tip credit which an employer may claim with respect to "Tipped Employees" is 50 percent of the applicable minimum wage.

Overtime Pay

At least 1½ times your regular rate of pay for all hours worked over 40 in a workweek.

Child Labor

An employee must be at least **16** years old to work in most non-farm jobs and at least **18** to work in non-farm jobs declared hazardous by the Secretary of Labor. Youths **14** and **15** years old may work outside school hours in various non-manufacturing, non-mining, non-hazardous jobs under the following conditions:

No more than —

- **3** hours on a school day or **18** hours in a school week;
- **8** hours on a non-school day or **40** hours in a non-school week.

Also, work may not begin before 7 a.m. or end after 7 p.m., except from June 1 through Labor Day, when evening hours are extended to 9 p.m. Different rules apply in agricultural employment.

Training Wage

A training wage of at least 85 percent of the applicable minimum wage, or $3.35 per hour, whichever is greater, may be paid to most employees under 20 years of age for up to 90 days under certain conditions. Individuals may be employed at a training wage for a second 90-day period by a different employer if certain additional requirements are met. No individual may be employed at a training wage, in any number of jobs, for more than a total of 180 days. Employers may not displace regular employees in order to hire those eligible for a training wage. **The training wage provisions expire March 31, 1993.** Note to Employers: The requirements for use of a training wage are very specific. If you need assistance, you should contact the nearest Wage and Hour office.

ENFORCEMENT

The Department of Labor may recover back wages either administratively or through court action, for the employees that have been underpaid in violation of the law. Violations may result in civil or criminal action.

Fines of up to $10,000 per minor may be assessed against employers who violate the child labor provisions of the law and up to $1,000 per violation against employers who willfully or repeatedly violate the minimum wage or overtime pay provisions. This law prohibits discriminating against or discharging workers who file a complaint or participate in any proceedings under the Act.

Note:
- Certain occupations and establishments are exempt from the minimum wage and/or overtime pay provisions.
- Special provisions apply to workers in Puerto Rico and American Samoa.
- Where state law requires a higher minimum wage, the higher standard applies.

FOR ADDITIONAL INFORMATION, CONTACT the Wage and Hour Division office nearest you — listed in your telephone directory under United States Government, Labor Department.

The law requires employers to display this poster where employees can readily see it.

U.S. Department of Labor
Employment Standards Administration
Wage and Hour Division
Washington, D.C. 20210

WH Publication 1088
Revised April 1991

*U.S. Government Printing Office: 1991 — 300-512

be granted at 1½ times the number of hours that were worked as overtime. Employees who are paid on a piece-rate basis also must receive a premium for overtime work. The hourly rate on which overtime is to be based is computed by dividing earnings from piecework by the total number of hours of work required to earn this amount. For example, if an employee produced 1,250 units of work at 20 cents per unit during a fifty-hour week, the earning rate would be $5 per hour, computed as follows:

$$\frac{1,250 \text{ units} \times 20 \text{ cents}}{50 \text{ hours}} = \$5 \text{ per hour}$$

Since the ten hours in excess of a forty-hour week constitute overtime at 1½ times the regular rate, total earnings for the week would be $275, computed as follows:

Regular time   40 × $5.00 = $200
Overtime   10 × $7.50 =   75
Total earnings $275

Furthermore, under the FLSA, an employer must pay an employee for whatever work the employer "suffers or permits" the employee to perform, even if the work is done away from the workplace and even if it is not specifically expected or requested. Accordingly, under the FLSA it doesn't matter that the supervisor never asked the employee to work extra time; all that matters is that the supervisor knew the employee was putting in the time and did nothing to prevent it. This rule, as well as the overtime and bonus rules discussed earlier, applies only to nonexempt employees.

Some argue that the "floor" imposed by the minimum wage makes it more difficult for high school students and young adults to find jobs. Many employers who might otherwise be willing to hire these individuals are unwilling to pay them the same rate as adults because of their lack of experience. In addition, civil rights advocates point out that the minimum wage particularly harms black youth, who traditionally have a higher unemployment rate as compared with white youth.

Child Labor Provisions

The FLSA forbids the employment of minors between 16 and 18 years of age in hazardous occupations such as mining, logging, woodworking, meatpacking, and certain types of manufacturing. Minors under 16 cannot be employed in any work destined for interstate commerce except that which is performed in a nonhazardous occupation for a parent or guardian or for an employer under a temporary work permit issued by the Department of Labor.

Exemptions under the Act

The feature of the FLSA that perhaps creates the most confusion is the exemption of certain groups of employees from coverage by the act or from coverage by certain of its provisions. The act now provides more than forty separate exemptions, some of which apply only to a certain group of personnel or to certain provisions of the act, such as those relating to child labor and to overtime. One of the most common exemptions concerns the overtime provisions of the act. Four employee groups—executives, administrators, professionals, and outside salespersons—are specifically excluded from the overtime provisions. However, persons performing jobs in these groups must meet specific job requirements as stated under the law. For example, a manager is defined as someone whose *primary* duty is the direction of two or more other employees. "Primary duty" means that the manager generally devotes more than 50 percent of his or her time to supervising others. Because exemptions are generally narrowly defined under FLSA, an employer should carefully check the exact terms and conditions for each. Detailed information is available from local wage-hour offices.[31]

Equal Rights Provisions

One of the most significant amendments to the FLSA was the Equal Pay Act passed in 1963. (See Chapter 3.) The federal Age Discrimination Act of 1967, as amended, extends the equal rights provisions by forbidding wage discrimination based on age for employees 40 years of age and older. Neither of these acts, however, prohibits wage differentials based on factors other than age or sex. Seniority, merit, and individual incentive plans, for instance, are not affected.

In spite of the Equal Pay Act, the achievement of parity by women in the labor market has been slow in coming. In 1993, the median earnings level of all women workers in the United States was 75.5 percent of the median for all working men. This figure is about 13 percentage points higher than in 1980, with little change since 1990.[32] Fortunately, the 1993 median earnings of young women (ages 16 to 24) are 95 percent of those of similar-age men—up from 78 percent in 1980. If this trend toward greater comparability in earnings continues as these women become older, this age group may set the stage for more equitable treatment in the future. However, it is still important to remember that young women, and young men as well, typically work in low-paying, entry-level jobs. For women, these are often clerical or sales positions.

Because of the continued differences in pay for women and men, some HR professionals are suggesting that the wage differences could be reduced if women were paid on the basis of equal pay for comparable work, which will be discussed in the next section.

objective

Significant Compensation Issues

As with other HR activities, compensation management operates in a dynamic environment. For example, as managers strive to reward employees in a fair manner, they must consider controls over labor costs, legal issues regarding male and female wage payments, and internal pay equity concerns. Each of these concerns is highlighted in three important compensation issues: equal pay for comparable worth, wage-rate compression, and two-tier wage systems.

The Issue of Equal Pay for Comparable Worth

Comparable worth

The concept that male and female jobs that are dissimilar, but equal in terms of value or worth to the employer, should be paid the same

One of the most important gender issues in compensation is equal pay for comparable worth. The issue stems from the fact that jobs performed predominantly by women are paid less than those performed by men. This practice results in what critics term *institutionalized sex discrimination,* causing women to receive less pay for jobs that may be different from but comparable in worth to those performed by men. The issue of **comparable worth** goes beyond providing equal pay for jobs that involve the same duties for women as for men. It is not concerned with whether a female secretary should receive the same pay as a male secretary. Rather, the argument for comparable worth is that jobs held by women are not compensated the same as those held by men, even though both job types may contribute equally to organizational success.[33]

Problem of Measuring Comparability

Advocates of comparable worth argue that the difference in wage rates for predominantly male and female occupations rests in the undervaluing of traditional female occupations. To remedy this situation, they propose that wages should be equal for jobs that are "somehow" equivalent in total worth or compensation to the organization. Unfortunately, there is no consensus on a comparable worth standard by which to evaluate jobs, nor is there agreement on the ability of present job evaluation techniques to remedy the problem.[34] Indeed, organizations may dodge the comparable worth issue by using one job evaluation system for clerical and secretarial jobs and another system for other jobs. Furthermore, the advocates of comparable worth argue that current job evaluation techniques simply serve to continue the differences in pay between the sexes.

The argument over comparable worth is likely to remain an important HR issue for many years to come. Unanswered questions such as the following will serve to keep the issue alive:

1. If comparable worth is adopted, who will determine the worth of jobs, and by what means?
2. How much would comparable worth cost employers?
3. Would comparable worth reduce the wage gap between men and women caused by labor market supply-and-demand forces?
4. Would comparable worth reduce the number of employment opportunities for women?

Position of Congress and the Courts

When the Equal Pay Act was being debated, proponents of comparable worth attempted to have equal pay based on this criterion rather than on equal work. A majority in Congress, however, deliberately chose to avoid using the comparable worth criterion. Thus, as Supreme Court Justice Rehnquist concluded in a dissenting opinion involving a suit by matrons working at the county jail in Washington County, Oregon, "Congress realized that the adoption of the comparable worth doctrine would ignore the economic relations of supply and demand, and would involve both government agencies and the courts in the impossible task of ascertaining the worth of comparable work in an area in which they have little expertise."[35]

In the Oregon case, however, the majority opinion held that the jail matrons who performed similar but not identical work to that performed by male jailers could sue for equal pay. (The county settled out of court by paying each matron $3,500, after which it abolished the job of jail matron.) This leading court case and others, such as *AFSCME v State of Washington*, have given encouragement to supporters of comparable worth.[36] Nevertheless, court decisions are traditionally extremely slow in effecting sweeping changes. In addition, some believe that comparable worth is a societal problem, not just a legal one.[37] Nonjudicial determination of comparable worth through collective bargaining and pressure-group action may be a better way to achieve gender-based pay equity. Currently, organizations like Tektronix and Motorola are adhering closely to internal comparisons, as are BankAmerica Corporation and Northwestern Bell Telephone. These organizations are showing corporate responsibility by providing a positive response to a societal concern.

Finally, organizations implementing comparable worth policies have raised women's wages. In one public-sector study of the impact of comparable worth on men's and women's earnings, the researcher concluded that when comparable worth is implemented through special wage increases, public-sector wages move ahead of local prevailing wage standards and the male/female pay differentials are greatly reduced.[38] The compensation gap between men and women will not disappear overnight, but the persistence of comparable worth advocates will help shrink it.

The Issue of Wage-Rate Compression

Wage-rate compression

Compression of differentials between job classes, particularly the differential between hourly workers and their managers

Earlier, when we discussed the compensation structure, it was noted that the primary purpose of the pay differentials between the wage classes is to provide an incentive for employees to prepare for and accept more-demanding jobs. Unfortunately, this incentive is being significantly reduced by **wage-rate compression**—the reduction of differences between job classes. Wage-rate compression is largely an internal pay-equity concern. The problem occurs when employees perceive that there is too narrow a difference between their compensation and that of colleagues in lower-rated jobs.

HR professionals acknowledge that wage-rate compression is a widespread organizational problem affecting diverse occupational groups: white-collar and blue-collar workers, technical and professional employees, and managerial personnel. It can cause low employee morale, leading to issues of reduced employee performance, higher absenteeism and turnover, and even delinquent behavior such as employee theft.

There is no single cause of wage-rate compression.[39] For example, it can occur when unions negotiate across-the-board increases for hourly employees but managerial personnel are not granted corresponding wage differentials. Such increases can result in part from COLAs provided for in labor agreements. Other inequities have resulted from the scarcity of applicants in computers, engineering, and other professional and technical fields. Job applicants in these fields frequently have been offered starting salaries not far below those paid to employees with considerable experience and seniority. Wage-rate compression often occurs when organizations grant pay adjustments for lower-rated jobs without providing commensurate adjustments for occupations at the top of the job hierarchy.

Identifying wage-rate compression and its causes is far simpler than implementing organizational policies to alleviate its effect. Organizations wishing to minimize the problem may incorporate the following ideas into their pay policies:

Two-tier wage system

Wage system where newly hired employees performing the same jobs as senior employees receive lower rates of pay

1. Give larger compensation increases to more senior employees.
2. Emphasize pay-for-performance and reward merit-worthy employees.
3. Limit the hiring of new applicants seeking exorbitant salaries.
4. Design the pay structure to allow a wide spread between hourly and supervisory jobs or between new hires and senior employees.
5. Provide equity adjustments for selected employees hardest hit by pay compression.

The Issue of Two-Tier Wage Systems

Many organizations affected by deregulation, foreign competition, and aggressive nonunionized competitors implement two-tier wage systems as a means of lowering their labor costs. A **two-tier wage system** is a compensation plan that pays newly hired employees less than present employees performing the same or similar jobs. With some two-tier wage systems, new employees may receive reduced benefit packages. Two-tier wage systems are popular in the airline, aerospace, trucking, retail food, copper, and automobile industries.

There are two basic types of two-tier wage systems. In a permanent system, the wages of new hires, "B-scalers," never merge with the wages of senior employees. In a temporary system, B-scale wages will eventually catch up to A-scale wages after a specified period of time. For example, employees on the B-scale at American Airlines achieve pay parity with senior employees after ten years of service. Unfortunately, lower-paid employees can have feelings of pay inequity when working under either of these wage systems. There is a perceived lack of fairness when new hires and senior employees perform the same job but receive different wages. Feelings of inequity can, in turn, lead

Under a two-tier wage system, a new employee will have to work perhaps ten years before earning the same wages as this senior airline mechanic.

to low levels of job commitment, work attendance problems, reduced productivity, and employee resentment.

Whether two-tier wage systems will continue as a method of labor cost control seems uncertain. Recent reports show that employers are phasing out these programs because of high employee turnover and morale problems.[40] Therefore the gap in employee wages caused by these pay plans will likely decline. If this trend continues, employers are likely to implement other cost-cutting pay strategies such as incentive pay plans, the subject of Chapter 11.

SUMMARY

Establishing compensation programs requires both large and small organizations to consider specific goals—employee retention, compensation distribution, and adherence to a budget, for instance. Compensation must reward employees for past efforts (pay-for-performance) while serving to motivate employees' future performance. Internal and external equity of the pay program affects employees' concepts of fairness. Organizations must balance each of these concerns while still remaining competitive. The ability to attract qualified employees while controlling labor costs are major factors in allowing organizations to remain viable in the domestic or international markets.

The basis on which compensation payments are determined, and the way they are administered, can significantly affect employee productivity and the achievement of organizational goals. External factors influencing wage rates include labor market conditions, area wage rates, cost of living, legal requirements, and the outcomes of collective bargaining. Internal influences include the employer's compensation policy, the worth of the job, performance of the employee, and the employer's ability to pay.

Organizations use one of four basic job evaluation techniques to determine the relative worth of jobs. The job ranking system arranges jobs in numerical order on the basis of the importance of the job's duties and responsibilities to the organization. The job classification system slots jobs into preestablished grades. Higher-rated grades will require more responsibilities, working conditions, and job duties. The point system of job evaluation uses a point scheme based upon the compensable job factors of skill, effort, responsibility, and working conditions. The more of a compensable factor a job possesses, the more points are assigned to it. Jobs with higher accumulated points are considered more valuable to the organization. The factor comparison system evaluates jobs on a factor-by-factor basis against key jobs in the organization.

Wage surveys determine the external equity of jobs. Data obtained from surveys will facilitate establishing the organization's wage policy while ensuring that the employer does not pay more, or less, than needed for jobs in the relevant labor market.

objective

objective

objective

The wage structure is composed of the wage curve, pay grades, and rate ranges. The wage curve depicts graphically the pay rates assigned to jobs within each pay grade. Pay grades represent the grouping of similar jobs on the basis of their relative worth. Each pay grade will include a rate range. Rate ranges will have a midpoint and minimum and maximum pay rates for all jobs in the pay grade.

Both the Davis-Bacon Act and the Walsh-Healy Act are prevailing wage statutes. These laws require government contractors to pay wages normally based on the union scale in the employer's operating area. The Walsh-Healy Act also requires payment of 1½ the regular pay for hours over eight per day or forty per week. The Fair Labor Standards Act contains provisions covering the federal minimum wage, hours worked, and child labor.

The concept of comparable worth seeks to overcome the fact that jobs held by women are compensated at a lower rate than those performed by men. This happens even though both types of jobs may contribute equally to organizational productivity. Wage-rate compression largely affects managerial and senior employees as the pay given to new employees or the wage increases gained through union agreements erode the pay differences between these groups. Employers wishing to lower labor costs will establish two-tier systems, paying junior and senior employees performing the same job from separate pay schedules.

KEY TERMS

comparable worth

consumer price index (CPI)

escalator clauses

exempt employees

factor comparison system

Hay profile method

hourly or day work

job classification system

job evaluation

job ranking system

nonexempt employees

pay equity

pay-for-performance standard

pay grades

piecework

point system

real wages

skill-based pay

two-tier wage system

wage and salary survey

wage curve

wage-rate compression

1. What are the disadvantages of pay secrecy? Despite its disadvantages, why do some managers prefer pay secrecy?
2. Since employees may differ in terms of their job performance, would it not be more feasible to determine the wage rate for each employee on the basis of his or her relative worth to the organization?
3. What are some of the criticisms being raised concerning COLA and the CPI on which COLA is based?
4. During collective bargaining, unions have sometimes responded to a company claim of inability to pay with the statement that the union should not be expected to subsidize inefficient management. To what extent do you feel that a response of this type has or does not have merit?
5. Describe the basic steps in conducting a wage and salary survey. What are some factors to consider?
6. One of the objections to granting wage increases on a percentage basis is that the lowest-paid employees, who are having the most trouble making ends meet, get the smallest increase, while the highest-paid employees get the largest increase. Is this objection a valid one?
7. An employee covered by the FLSA earns $5 per hour, works fifty hours during a given week, and receives a production bonus of $20. What are this employee's gross earnings for the week?
8. What are some of the problems of developing a pay system based on equal pay for comparable work?

CASE STUDY: Pay Decisions at Performance Sports

Katie Perkins' career objective while attending Rockford State College was to obtain a degree in small business management and upon graduation to start her own business. Her ultimate desire was to combine her love of sports and a strong interest in marketing to start a mail-order golf equipment business aimed specifically at beginning golfers.

In February 1991, after extensive development of a strategic business plan and a loan in the amount of $75,000 from the Small Business Administration, Performance Sports was begun. Based on a marketing plan that stressed fast delivery, error-free customer service, and large discount pricing, Performance Sports grew rapidly. At present the company employs sixteen people: eight customer service representatives earning between $6.75 and $8.25 per hour; four shipping and receiving associates paid between $5.50 and $6.50 per hour; two clerical employees, each earning $5.75 per hour; an assistant manager earning

$9.10 per hour, and a general manager with a wage of $10.25 per hour. Both the manager and assistant manager are former customer service representatives.

Perkins intends to create a new managerial position, purchasing agent, to handle the complex duties of purchasing golf equipment from the company's numerous equipment manufacturers. Also, the mail-order catalogue from Performance Sports will be expanded to handle a complete line of tennis equipment. Since the position of purchasing agent is new, Perkins isn't sure how much to pay this person. She wants to employ an experienced individual with between five and eight years of experience in sports equipment purchasing.

While attending an equipment manufacturers' convention in Las Vegas, Nevada, Perkins learns that a competitor, East Valley Sports, pays its customer service representatives on a pay-for-performance basis. Intrigued by this compensation philosophy, Perkins asks her assistant manager, George Balkin, to research the pros and cons of this payment strategy. This request has become a priority since only last week two customer service representatives expressed dissatisfaction with their hourly wage. Both complained that they felt underpaid relative to the large amount of sales revenue each generates for the company.

Questions

1. What factors should Perkins consider when setting the wage for the purchasing agent position? What resources are available for her to consult when establishing this wage?
2. Suggest advantages and disadvantages of a pay-for-performance policy for Performance Sports.
3. Suggest a new payment plan for the customer service representatives.

NOTES AND REFERENCES

1. Robert Kreitner and Angelo Kinicki, *Organizational Behavior*, 3d ed. (Homewood, Ill.: BPI/Irwin, 1995), Chapter 15.
2. Howard W. Risher, "Strategic Salary Planning," *Compensation and Benefits Review* 25, no. 1 (January-February 1993): 46–50. See also Milton L. Rock and Lance A. Berger, *The Compensation Handbook*, 3d ed. (New York: McGraw-Hill, 1991).
3. Luis R. Gomez-Mejia and David B. Balkin, *Compensation, Organizational Strategy, and Firm Performance* (Cincinnati: South-Western Publishing, 1992), Chapter 2. See also Peter V. Leblanc, "Pay for Work: Reviving an Old Idea for the New Customer Focus," *Compensation and Benefits Review* 26, no. 4 (July-August 1994): 5–14; Caroline L. Weber and Sara L. Rymes, "Effects of Compensation Strategy on

Job Pay Decision," *Academy of Management Journal* 34, no. 1 (March 1991): 86–109.
4. Edward E. Lawler III, *Strategic Pay: Aligning Organizational Strategies and Pay Systems* (San Francisco: Jossey-Bass, 1990).
5. Jay R. Schuster and Patricia K. Zingheim, *Linking Employee and Organizational Performance* (Lexington, Mass.: Lexington Books, 1992); see also Peter R. Eyes, "Realignment Ties Pay to Performance," *Personnel Journal* 72, no. 1 (January 1993): 74–77; James P. Guthrie and Edward P. Cunningham, "Pay for Performance for Hourly Workers: The Quaker Oats Alternative," *Compensation and Benefits Review* 24, no. 2 (March-April 1992): 18–23.
6. Arturo R. Thomann, "Flex-Base Addresses Pay Problems," *Personnel Journal* 71, no. 2 (February 1992): 51–55.

7. Kathleen A. Guinn and Robert J. Corona, "Putting a Price on Performance," *Personnel Journal* 10, no. 6 (May 1991): 72.

8. George Milkovich and Carolyn Milkovich, "Strengthening the Pay-Performance Relationship: The Research," *Compensation and Benefits Review* 24, no. 6 (November-December 1992): 53; see also Edward E. Lawler III, "Pay-for-Performance: A Strategic Analysis," in *Compensation and Benefits*, ed. Luis R. Gomez-Mejia (Washington, D.C.: American Society for Personnel Administration/Bureau of National Affairs, 1989): 3–16.

9. Joel M. Stern and G. Bennett Stewart III, "Pay-for-Performance: Only the Theory is Easy," *HR Magazine* 38, no. 6 (June 1993): 48–49.

10. R. Bradley Hill, "A Two-Component Approach to Compensation," *Personnel Journal* 72, no. 5 (May 1993): 154.

11. Marc J. Wallace, Jr., and Charles H. Fay, *Compensation Theory and Practice*, 2d ed. (Boston: PWS-Kent, 1988): 14.

12. Mary A. Hopkinson, "After the Merger: Paying for Keeps," *Personnel Journal* 70, no. 8 (August 1991): 29–31. See also Anne M. Saunier and Elizabeth J. Hawk, "Realizing the Potential of Teams Through Team-Based Rewards," *Compensation and Benefits Review* 26, no. 4 (July-August 1994): 24–33.

13. Jeffrey A. Bradt, "Pay for Impact," *Personnel Journal* 10, no. 6 (May 1991): 76.

14. *CPI Detailed Report March 1993* (U.S. Department of Labor, Bureau of Labor Statistics, March 1993): 96.

15. George T. Milkovich and Jerry M. Newman, *Compensation*, 4th ed. (Homewood, Ill.: Irwin, 1993), 10–12.

16. Robert J. Greene, "Determinants of Occupational Worth," *Personnel Administrator* 34, no. 8 (August 1989): 78–82.

17. Laurent Dufetel, "Job Evaluation: Still at the Frontier," *Compensation and Benefits Review* 23, no. 4 (July-August 1991): 53–67.

18. Sandra M. Emerson, "Job Evaluation: A Barrier to Excellence?" *Compensation and Benefits Review* 23, no. 1 (January-February 1991): 39–51.

19. Frederick S. Hills, *Compensation Decision Making*, 2d ed. (Chicago: Dryden Press, 1994).

20. *Modernizing Federal Classification: An Opportunity for Excellence* (Washington, D.C.: National Academy of Public Administration, 1991).

21. Howard W. Risher, "Job Evaluation: Validity and Reliability," *Compensation and Benefits Review* 21, no. 1 (January/February 1989): 32–33.

22. Kermit Davis, Jr., and William Sauser, Jr., "Effects of Alternative Weighting Methods in a Policy-Capturing Approach to Job Evaluation," *Personnel Psychology* 44, no. 1 (Spring 1991): 85–127; see also Leonard R. Burgess, *Compensation Administration*,

2d ed. (Columbus, Ohio: Merrill, 1989): 166.

23. Kermit R. Davis, Jr. and William I. Sauer, Jr., "A Comparison of Factor Weighting Methods in Job Evaluation: Implications for Compensation Systems," *Public Personnel Management* 22, no. 1 (Spring 1993): 91–103.

24. For an expanded discussion of both the point system and the factor comparison system, see Milkovich and Newman, *Compensation*, Chapter 4.

25. Richard I. Henderson, *Compensation Management*, 6th ed. (Reston, Va.: Reston Publishing, 1993).

26. Linda S. Hartenian and Nancy Brown Johnson, "Establishing the Reliability and Validity of Wage Surveys," *Public Personnel Management* 20, no. 3 (Fall 1991): 367–78.

27. Robert J. Sahl, "Job-Content Salary Surveys: Survey Design and Selection Features," *Compensation and Benefits Review* 23, no. 3 (May-June 1991): 14–21.

28. Gerald E. Ledford, Jr., "Three Case Studies on Skill-Based Pay: An Overview," *Compensation and Benefits Review* 23, no. 2 (March-April 1991): 11–23; see also Richard L. Bunning, "Models for Skill-Based Pay Plans," *HR Magazine* 37, no. 2 (February 1992): 62–64; Fred Luthans and Marilyn L. Fox, "Update on Skill-Based Pay," *Personnel* 66, no. 3 (March 1989): 26–31.

29. Edward E. Lawler III, Gerald E. Ledford, Jr., and Lei Chang, "Who Uses Skill-Based Pay and Why?" *Compensation and Benefits Review* 25, no. 2 (March-April 1993): 22–26; see also Dale Fever, "Paying for Knowledge," *Training* 24, no. 5 (May 1987): 58.

30. Because the FLSA is always subject to future amendments, an employer should consult the appropriate publications of one of the labor services previously mentioned or the Wage and Hour Division of the U.S. Department of Labor in order to obtain the latest information regarding its current provisions, particularly the minimum wage rate.

31. The U.S. Department of Labor has several pamphlets that highlight the provisions of the FLSA. These include *Employers Guide to the Fair Labor Standards Act, Handy Reference Guide to the Fair Labor Standards Act*, and *A Look at Hours Worked under the Fair Labor Standards Act*. Pamphlets are available upon request from the Wage and Hour Division Office, U.S. Labor Department in your vicinity.

32. *Employment and Earnings*, Bureau of Labor Statistics, U.S. Department of Labor, Tables 73, 79. See also Dorothy J. Gaiter, "Black Women's Gains in Corporate America Outstrip Black Men's," *The Wall Street Journal* (March 8, 1994): A6.

33. Mary V. Moore and Yohannan T. Abraham, "Comparable Worth: Is It a Moot Issue?" *Public*

Personnel Management 21, no. 4 (Winter 1992): 455–68.

34. Richard W. Scholl and Elizabeth Cooper, "The Use of Job Evaluation to Eliminate Gender Based Pay Differentials," *Public Personnel Management* 20, no. 1 (Spring 1991): 1–17.

35. *Washington County v Gunther*, 101 Sup. Ct. 2242 (1981), 452 U.S. 161.

36. *AFSCME v State of Washington*, 578 F. Supp. 846 (W.D. Wash. 1983).

37. Jerald Greenberg and Claire L. McCarty, "Comparable Worth: A Matter of Justice," in K. M. Rowland and G. R. Ferris, *Research in Personnel and Human Resources Management*, 8th ed. (Greenwich, Conn.: JAL Press, 1990); see also Larry S. Luton and Suzanne Thompson, "Progress in Comparable Worth: Moving toward Non-Judicial Determination—Problems and Prospects," *Review of*

Public Personnel Administration 9, no. 2 (Spring 1989): 78–85.

38. Greg Hundley, "The Effects of Comparable Worth in the Public Sector on Public/Private Occupational Relative Wages," *Journal of Human Resources* 28, no. 2 (Spring 1993): 319–40; see also Elaine Sorensen, "Effect of Comparable Worth Policies on Earnings," *Industrial Relations* 26, no. 3 (Fall 1987): 227–39.

39. Thomas J. Bergmann, Marilyn A. Bergmann, Desiree Roff, and Vida Scarpello, "Salary Compression: Causes and Solutions," *Compensation and Benefits Review* 23, no. 6 (November-December 1991): 7–16.

40. Edward J. Wasilewski, Jr., "Collective Bargaining in 1992. Contract Talks and Other Activity," *Monthly Labor Review* 115, no. 1 (January 1992): 14.

Chapter

Incentive Compensation

objective one

Discuss the basic requirements for successful implementation of incentive programs.

objective two

List the types of, and reasons for implementing, incentive plans for nonmanagement employees.

objective three

Explain why merit raises may fail to motivate employees adequately and discuss ways to increase their motivational value.

objective four

State and identify the advantage of each of the principal methods used to compensate salespersons.

objective five

Describe the different methods by which executive bonuses may be determined and paid.

objective six

Explain what profit-sharing plans are and the advantages and disadvantages of these programs.

objective seven

Differentiate how gains may be shared with employees under the Scanlon, Rucker, and Improshare gainsharing systems.

I*n the previous chapter we emphasized that the worth of a job is a significant factor in determining the pay rate for that job. However, pay based solely on this measure may fail to motivate employees to perform to their full capacity. Unmotivated employees are likely to meet only minimum performance standards. Recognizing this fact, organizations such as BFGoodrich, Continental Bank, and American Barrick offer some form of incentive to workers.[1] These organizations are attempting to get more motivational mileage out of employee compensation by tying it more clearly to employee performance. Managers at Magma Copper Company note that incentive linked with output "causes workers to more fully apply their skills and knowledge to their jobs while encouraging them to work together as a team." Marshall Campbell, vice president of human resources, remarked, "If we increase production of ore extraction, and tie output to employee compensation, we operate with lower costs and that makes us more competitive in the national and international marketplace."[2] In their attempt to raise productivity, managers are focusing on the many variables that help to determine the effectiveness of pay as a motivator. Financial incentive plans are being developed—on the basis of knowledge acquired by researchers and HR practitioners—to meet the needs of both employees and employers more satisfactorily.[3]*

In this chapter we will discuss incentive plans in terms of the objectives they hope to achieve and the various factors that may affect their success. We will also attempt to identify the plans that are most effective in motivating different categories of employees to achieve these objectives. For discussion purposes, incentive plans have been grouped into two broad categories, individual incentive plans and group incentive plans, as shown in Figure 11–1.

objective

Reasons and Requirements for Incentive Plans

Reasons for Adopting an Incentive Plan

A clear trend in compensation management is the growth of incentive plans, also called variable pay programs, for employees below the executive level. Incentive plans emphasize a shared focus on organizational success by broadening

---

FIGURE 11-1 *Types of Incentive Plans*

INDIVIDUAL		GROUP
Hourly:	*Sales Personnel:*	*Hourly and Managerial:*
Piecework	Sales incentive plans	Scanlon Plan
Bonuses	*Professional:*	Rucker Plan
Standard hour plan	Maturity curves	Improshare
Managerial:	*Executive:*	Profit sharing
Merit raises	Bonuses	
	Stock options	

the opportunities for incentives to nontraditional groups while operating outside the merit (base pay) increase system.[4] Incentive plans create an operating environment that champions a philosophy of shared commitment through the belief that every individual contributes to organizational success.

Over the years, organizations have implemented incentive plans for a variety of reasons: high labor costs, competitive product markets, slow technological advances, and high potential for production bottlenecks.[5] While these reasons are still cited, contemporary arguments for incentive plans focus on pay-for-performance and improved organizational productivity.[6] By linking compensation to employee effort, organizations believe that employees will improve their job performance. Incentives are designed to encourage employees to put out more effort to complete their job tasks—effort they might not be motivated to expend under hourly and/or seniority-based compensation systems. Financial incentives are therefore offered to improve or maintain high levels of productivity and quality, which in turn improves the market for U.S. goods and services in a global economy. Figure 11–2 summarizes the major advantages of incentive pay programs as noted by researchers and HR professionals.

Do incentive plans work? Various studies have demonstrated a measurable relationship between incentive plans and improved organizational performance. In a survey of organizations with more than 500 employees, conducted by the New York Stock Exchange, 70 percent of organizations with gainsharing programs stated that those programs improved productivity.[7] In the area of manufacturing, productivity will often improve by as much as 20 percent after the adoption of incentive plans.[8] Improvements, however, are not limited to goods-producing industries. Service organizations, not-for-profit, and government agencies also show productivity gains when incentives are linked to organizational goals. For example, after beginning an incentive pay program, Viking Freight Systems boosted on-time service performance and reduced customer damage claims, and Taco Bell Corporation reduced food costs and improved customer service scores after it began an employee bonus program in 1991.[9]

FIGURE 11-2   *Advantages of Incentive Pay Programs*

- Incentives focus employee efforts on specific performance targets. They provide real motivation that produces important employee and organizational gains.

- Incentive payouts are variable costs linked to the achievement of results. Base salaries are fixed costs largely unrelated to output.

- Incentive compensation is directly related to operating performance. If performance objectives (quantity and/or quality) are met, incentives are paid. If objectives are not achieved, incentives are withheld.

- Incentives foster teamwork and unit cohesiveness when payments to individuals are based on team results.

- Incentives are a way to distribute success among those responsible for producing that success.

Because of the benefits organizations have derived from incentive pay programs, these programs are predicted to increase in popularity. Highlights in HRM 1 shows the results of one national survey that assessed the level of awareness and the projected use of one incentive compensation plan—gainsharing. Interestingly, respondents in each standard industrial code (SIC), the basis upon which the respondents were grouped, were highly aware of gainsharing plans, with increased usage predicted for each employer classification.[10]

However, for two main reasons, incentive plans have not always led to organizational improvement. First, incentive plans sometimes fail to satisfy employee needs. Second, management may have failed to give adequate attention to the design and implementation of the plan.[11] Furthermore, the success of an incentive plan will depend on the environment that exists within an organization. A plan is more likely to work in an organization where morale is high, employees believe they are being treated fairly, and there is harmony between employees and management.

Requirements for a Successful Incentive Plan

For an incentive plan to succeed, employees must have some desire for the plan. This desire can be influenced in part by how successful management is in introducing the plan and convincing employees of its benefits. Encouraging employees to participate in administering the plan is likely to increase their willingness to accept it.

Employees must be able to see a clear connection between the incentive payments they receive and their job performance. This connection is more visible if there are objective quality or quantity standards by which they can judge their performance. Commitment by employees to meet these standards is also essential for incentive plans to succeed. This requires mutual trust and understanding between employees and their supervisors, which can only be achieved through open, two-way channels of communication. Management should never allow incentive payments to be seen as an *entitlement*.[12] Instead, these payments should be viewed as a reward that must be earned through effort. This perception can be strengthened if the incentive money is distributed to employees in a separate check.

Setting Performance Measures

Measurement is key to the success of incentive plans because it communicates the importance of established organizational goals. What gets measured and rewarded gets attention. For example, if the organization desires to be a leader in quality, then performance indexes may focus on customer satisfaction, timeliness, or being error-free. If being a low-priced producer is the goal, then emphasis should be on cost reduction or increased productivity with lower acceptable levels of quality. While a variety of performance options are available, most focus on quality, cost control, or productivity.

One authority on incentive plans notes that the failure of most incentive plans can be traced to the choice of performance measures.[13] Therefore measures

1   AWARENESS OF GAINSHARING PROGRAMS ACROSS SIC GROUPS COMPARED WITH CONSIDERATION OF INSTALLING GAINSHARING

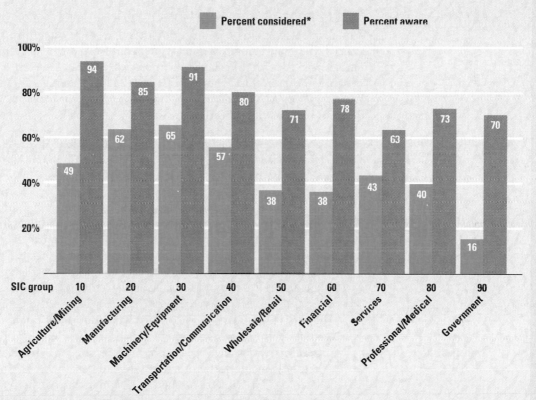

* The percent who considered gainsharing is based on the percent of those who were aware of it.

Note: This national study of gainsharing programs was based on returns from 1,639 HR managers, directors, and vice presidents.

Source: Steven E. Markham, K. Dow Scott, and Beverly L. Little, "National Gainsharing Study: The Importance of Industry Differences," *Compensation and Benefits Review* 24, no. 1 (January-February 1992): 34–45. Reprinted by permission of the publisher, American Management Association, New York.

that are quantitative, simple, and structured to show a clear relationship to improved performance are best. Overly quantitative, complex measures are to be avoided. Also, when selecting a performance measure, it is necessary to evaluate the extent to which the employees involved can actually influence the measurement. Finally, employers must guard against "ratcheting-up" performance goals by continually trying to exceed previous results. This eventually leads to employee frustration and employee perception that the standards are unattainable. The result will be a mistrust of management and a backlash against the entire incentive program.

Administering Incentive Plans

While incentive plans based on productivity can reduce direct labor costs, to achieve their full benefit they must be carefully thought out, implemented, and maintained. A cardinal rule is that thorough planning must be combined with a "proceed with caution" approach. Compensation managers repeatedly stress a number of points related to the effective administration of incentive plans. Three of the more important points are, by consensus:

1. Incentive systems are effective only when managers are willing to grant incentives based on differences in individual performance. Allowing incentive payments to become pay guarantees defeats the motivational intent of the incentive. The primary purpose of an incentive compensation plan is not to pay off under almost all circumstances, but rather to motivate performance. Thus, if the plan is to succeed, poor performance must go unrewarded.

2. Annual salary budgets must be large enough to reward and reinforce exceptional performance. When compensation budgets are set to ensure that pay increases do not exceed certain limits (often established as a percentage of payroll or sales), these constraints may prohibit rewarding outstanding individual or group performance.

3. The overhead costs associated with plan implementation and administration must be determined. These may include the cost of establishing performance standards and the added cost of record keeping. The time consumed in communicating the plan to employees, answering questions, and resolving any complaints about it must also be included in these costs.

objective

Incentives for Nonmanagement Employees

Many factors influence the design of incentive plans for nonmanagement employees. For example, incentive plans for this group are designed with consideration for the type of work these employees do and the technology they use. Also, when employees work in teams, a team incentive plan may be preferred since individual effort may not be distinguishable from team effort.[14] Organizations ma also use team incentives in cases where some employees are likely to try to maximize their output at the expense of their co-workers. One report stated that team incentives may reduce rivalry and promote cooperation and concern for the unit's overall performance.[15] In addition, in highly competitive industries such as foods and retailing, low profit margins will affect the availability of monies for incentive payouts. All these considerations suggest that tradition and philosophy, as well as economics and technology, help to govern the design of nonmanagement incentive systems. The various gainsharing plans discussed later in the chapter are typically offered to both nonmanagement and management employees.

Incentives for Hourly Employees

Incentive payments for hourly employees may be determined by the number of units produced, by the achievement of specific performance goals, or by productivity improvements in the organization as a whole. In the majority of incentive plans, incentive payments serve to supplement the employee's basic wage.

Piecework

Straight piecework
Incentive plan under which employees receive a certain rate for each unit produced

Differential piece rate
Compensation rate under which employees whose production exceeds the standard amount of output receive a higher rate for all of their work than the rate paid to those who do not exceed the standard amount

One of the oldest incentive plans is based on piecework. Under **straight piecework,** employees receive a certain rate for each unit produced. Their compensation is determined by the number of units they produce during a pay period. At Steelcase, an office furniture maker, employees can earn more than their base pay, often as much as 35 percent more, through piecework for each slab of metal they cut or chair they upholster. Under a **differential piece rate,** employees whose production exceeds the standard output receive a higher rate for *all* of their work than the rate paid to those who do not exceed the standard.

Employers will include piecework in their compensation strategy for several reasons. The wage payment for each employee is simple to compute, and the plan permits an organization to predict its labor costs with considerable accuracy, since these costs are the same for each unit of output. The piecework system is more likely to succeed when units of output can be measured readily, when the quality of the product is less critical, when the job is fairly standardized, and when a constant flow of work can be maintained.

Under the piecework system, employees normally are not paid for the time they are idle unless the idleness is due to conditions for which the organization is responsible, such as delays in work flow, defective materials, inoperative equipment, or power failures. When the delay is not the fault of employees, they are paid for the time they are idle.

Computing the piece rate.   Although time standards establish the time required to perform a given amount of work, they do not by themselves determine what the incentive rate should be. The incentive rates must be based on hourly wage rates that would otherwise be paid for the type of work being performed. Say, for example, the standard time for producing one unit of work in a job paying

$6.50 per hour was set at twelve minutes. The piece rate would be $1.30 per unit, computed as follows:

$$\frac{60 \text{ (minutes per hour)}}{12 \text{ (standard time per unit)}} = 5 \text{ units per hour}$$

$$\frac{\$6.50 \text{ (hourly rate)}}{5 \text{ (units per hour)}} = \$1.30 \text{ per unit}$$

Limited use of piecework.   In spite of its incentive value, the use of piecework is limited. One reason is that production standards on which piecework must be based can be difficult to develop for many types of jobs. In some instances the cost of determining and maintaining this standard may exceed the benefits gained from the system. Jobs in which individual contributions are difficult to distinguish or measure, or in which the work is mechanized to the point that the employee exercises very little control over output, also may be unsuited to piecework. The same is true of jobs in which employees are learning the work or in which high standards of quality are paramount.

One of the most significant weaknesses of piecework, as well as of other incentive plans based on individual effort, is that it may not always be an effective motivator. If employees believe that an increase in their output will provoke disapproval from fellow workers, they may avoid exerting maximum effort because their desire for peer approval outweighs their desire for more money.[16] Over a period of time, the standards on which piece rates are based tend to loosen, either because of peer pressure to relax the standards or because employees discover ways to do the work in less than standard time. In either case, employees are not required to exert as much effort to receive the same amount of incentive pay, so the incentive value is reduced.[17]

Piecework incentive programs have been used for many years in the garment industry.

Negative reaction to piecework.   Despite the opportunity to earn additional pay, employees, especially those belonging to unions, have negative attitudes toward piecework plans. Some union leaders have feared that management will use piecework or similar systems to try to speed up production, getting more work from employees for the same amount of money. Another fear is that the system may induce employees to compete against one another, thereby taking jobs away from workers who are shown to be less productive. There is also the belief that the system will cause some employees to lose their jobs as productivity increases or will cause craft standards of workmanship to suffer.

Individual Bonuses

A **bonus** is an incentive payment that is supplemental to the basic wage. It has the advantage of providing employees with more pay for exerting greater effort, while at the same time they still have the security of a basic wage. A bonus payment may be based on the number of units that an individual produces, as in the case of piecework. For example, at the basic wage rate of $7 an hour plus a bonus of 15 cents per unit, an employee who produces 100 units during an eight-hour period is paid $71, computed as follows:

(Hours × wage rate) + (number of units × unit rate) = Wages

(8   × $7   ) + (100   ×   15¢   ) = $71

Bonuses may also be determined on the basis of cost reduction, quality improvement, or performance criteria established by the organization.

Team Bonuses

Team bonuses, as Highlights in HRM 2 illustrates, are most desirable to use when the contributions of individual employees either are difficult to distinguish or depend on group cooperation.[18] Thus, as production has become more automated, as teamwork and coordination among workers have become more important, and as the contribution of those engaged indirectly in production work has increased, team bonuses have grown more popular. Most team bonus plans developed in recent years base incentive payments on such factors as improvements in efficiency, product quality, or reductions in labor costs. Organizations can support group planning and problem solving, thereby building a "team culture."

Team bonuses, unlike incentive plans based solely on output, can broaden the scope of the contributions that employees are motivated to make. For example, if labor costs represent 30 percent of an organization's sales dollars and the organization is willing to pay a bonus to employees, then whenever employee labor costs represent less than 30 percent of sales dollars, those savings are put into a bonus pool for employees. Information on the status of the pool is reported to employees on a weekly or monthly basis, explaining why a bonus was or was not earned. The team bonus may be distributed to employees equally, in proportion to their base pay, or on the basis of their relative contribution to the team.

Bonus
Incentive payment that is supplemental to the base wage

HIGHLIGHTS IN HRM

highlights

2   COMPUTING THE TEAM BONUS AT BF GOODRICH

The BFGoodrich Terre Haute plant links team performance and rewards with plant goals. The Performance Lets Us Share (PLUS) program encourages higher levels of team performance through employee involvement. The PLUS program works in the following ways:

- Base levels of performance are set for specific measurement areas—quality, productivity, cost, and customer service. Base levels are reviewed annually, and they are affected by historical performance and improvements.
- Separate financial pools are used to reward gains in each measurement area.
- Savings generated are shared by the organization and employees. The percentage employees receive depends on the pool, but it ranges from 10 to 50 percent of the gain. The more important an item, and the more control employees have over the item, the higher the percentage.
- Employees receive 50 percent of savings distributed in monthly bonus checks paid separately from the employee's regular paycheck. Each employee's amount is a percentage of the employee's earnings for hours worked during the month.
- The employees' remaining share of 50 percent is placed in a monthly accumulating reserve account. Where monthly performance falls below the baseline, the employees' share of the loss is deducted from the reserve account. Year-end excesses are paid to employees; losses are absorbed by the company.

Source: Adapted, by permission of publisher, from Robert L. Masternak and Timothy L. Ross, "A Bonus Plan or Employee Involvement?" *Compensation and Benefits Review* 24, no. 1 (January–February 1992): 46–54. American Management Association. All rights reserved.

Standard Hour Plan

**Standard
hour plan**

Incentive plan that
sets rates based upon
the completion of a job
in a predetermined
standard time

Another common incentive technique is the **standard hour plan,** which sets incentive rates based on a predetermined "standard time" for completing a job. If employees finish the work in less than the expected time, their pay is still based on the standard time for the job multiplied by their hourly rate. For example, if the standard time to install an engine in a half-ton truck is five hours and the mechanic completes the job in four and a half hours, the payment would be the mechanic's hourly rate times five hours. Standard hour plans are particularly suited to long-cycle operations or those jobs or tasks that are nonrepetitive and require a variety of skills.[19]

The Wood Products Southern Division of Potlatch Corporation has successfully used a standard hour plan for the production of numerous wood products. The incentive payment is based on the standard hours calculated to produce and package 1,000 feet of wood paneling. If employees can produce the paneling in less time than the standard, incentives are paid on the basis of the percentage improvement. Thus, with a 1,000-hour standard and completion of the wood paneling in 900 hours, a 10 percent incentive is paid. Each employee's base hourly wage is increased by 10 percent and then multiplied by the hours worked.

While standard hour plans can motivate employees to produce more, employers must ensure that equipment maintenance and product quality does not suffer as employees strive to do their work faster to earn additional income.

Incentives for Management Employees

Merit raises constitute one of the financial incentive systems used most commonly for managerial employees. Most recent studies of pay practices indicate that as many as 90 percent of large public- and private-sector organizations have merit pay programs for one or more of their employee groups.[20] Incentive pay may also be provided through different types of bonuses. Like those for hourly employees, these bonuses may be based on a variety of criteria involving either individual or group performance. As stated earlier, managerial employees are also usually included in the different types of gainsharing plans. Although they may not technically manage employees, sales employees and professional employees will also be discussed in this section.

Merit Raises

Merit raises can serve to motivate managerial, sales, and professional employees if they perceive the raises to be related to the performance required to earn them. Furthermore, theories of motivation, in addition to behavioral science research, provide justification for merit pay plans as well as other pay-for-performance programs.[21] For employees to see the link between pay and performance, however, their performance must be evaluated in light of objective criteria. If this evaluation also includes the use of subjective judgment by their superiors, employees must have confidence in the validity of this judgment. Most important, any increases granted on the basis of merit should be distinguishable from employees' regular pay and from any cost-of-living or other general increases. Where merit increases are based on pay-for-performance, merit pay should be withheld when performance is seen to decline.[22]

objective

Problems with Merit Raises

Merit raises may not always achieve their intended purpose. Unlike a bonus, a merit raise may be perpetuated year after year even when performance declines. When this happens, employees come to expect the increase and see it as being unrelated to their performance. Furthermore, employees in some organizations are opposed to merit raises because, among other reasons, they do not really trust management. What are referred to as merit raises often turn out to be increases based on seniority or favoritism, or raises to accommodate increases in cost of living or in area wage rates.[23] Even when merit raises are determined by performance, the employee's gains may be offset by inflation and higher income taxes. Compensation specialists also recognize the following problems with merit pay plans:

1. Money available for merit increases may be inadequate to satisfactorily raise employees' base pay.
2. Managers may have no guidance in how to define and measure performance; there may be vagueness regarding merit award criteria.
3. Employees may not believe that their compensation is tied to effort and performance; they may be unable to differentiate between merit pay and other types of pay increases.
4. Employees may believe that organizational politics plays a significant factor in merit pay decisions, despite the presence of a formal merit pay system.
5. There may be a lack of honesty and cooperation between management and employees.
6. It has been shown that "overall" merit pay plans do not motivate higher levels of employee performance.[24]

Probably one of the major weaknesses of merit raises lies in the performance appraisal system on which the increases are based. Even with an effective system, performance may be difficult to measure. Furthermore, any deficiencies in the performance appraisal program (these were discussed in Chapter 9) can impair the operation of a merit pay plan. Moreover, the performance appraisal objectives of employees and their superiors are often at odds. Employees typically want to maximize their pay increases, whereas superiors may seek to reward employees in an equitable manner on the basis of their performance. In some instances, employee pressures for pay increases actually may have a harmful effect on their performance appraisal.

Merit guidelines

Guidelines for awarding merit raises that are tied to performance objectives

While there are no easy solutions to these problems, organizations using a true merit pay plan often base the percentage pay raise on **merit guidelines** tied to performance appraisals. For example, Figure 11–3 illustrates a guideline chart

FIGURE 11-3 *Merit Guideline Chart*

	RATING				
	OUTSTANDING	ABOVE AVERAGE	GOOD	ADEQUATE	UNACCEPTABLE
Percentage increase	14-12	11-9	8-6	5-3	0

Note: Percentage may change on the basis of such factors as annual inflation rate, profitability or ability to pay, job market rates, and/or compensation policy.

for awarding merit raises. The percentages may change each year, depending on various internal or external concerns such as profit levels or national economic conditions as indicated by changes in the consumer price index. Under the illustrated merit plan, to prevent all employees from being rated outstanding or above average, managers may be required to distribute the performance rating according to some preestablished formula (e.g., only 10 percent can be rated outstanding). Additionally, when setting merit percentage guidelines, organizations should consider individual performance along with such factors as training, experience, and current earnings.

Lump-Sum Merit Pay

Lump-sum merit program

Program under which employees receive a year-end merit payment, which is not added to their base pay

To make merit increases more flexible and visible, organizations such as Boeing, Timex, and Westinghouse have implemented a **lump-sum merit program.** Under this type of plan, employees receive a single lump-sum increase at the time of their review, an increase that is not added to their base salary. Unless management takes further steps to compensate employees, their base salary is essentially frozen until they receive a promotion.[25]

Lump-sum merit programs offer several advantages. For employers, this innovative approach provides financial control by maintaining annual salary expenses. Merit increases granted on a lump sum basis do not contribute to escalating base salary levels. In addition, organizations can contain employee benefit costs, since the levels of benefits are normally calculated from current salary levels. For employees, an advantage is that receiving a single lump-sum merit payment can provide a clear link between pay and performance. For example, a 6 percent merit increase granted to an employee earning $25,000 a year translates into a weekly increase of $28.84—a figure that looks small compared with a lump-sum payment of $1,500.

Organizations using a lump-sum merit program will want to adjust base salaries upward after a certain period of time. This can be done yearly or after several years. These adjustments should keep pace with the rising cost of living and increases in the general market wage.

Incentives for Sales Employees

The enthusiasm and drive required in most types of sales work demand that sales employees be highly motivated. This fact, as well as the competitive nature of selling, explains why financial incentives for salespeople are widely used. These incentive plans must provide a source of motivation that will elicit cooperation and trust. Motivation is particularly important for employees away from the office who cannot be supervised closely and who, as a result, must exercise a high degree of self-discipline.

Unique Needs of Sales Incentive Plans

Incentive systems for salespeople are complicated by the wide differences in the types of sales jobs. These range from department store clerks who ring up customer purchases to industrial salespersons from McGraw-Edison who provide consultation and other highly technical services. Salespersons' performance may be measured by the dollar volume of their sales and by their ability to establish new accounts. Other measures are the ability to promote new products or services and to provide various forms of customer service and assistance that do not produce immediate sales revenues.

Performance standards for sales employees are difficult to develop, however, because their performance is often affected by external factors beyond their control.[26] Economic and seasonal fluctuations, sales competition, changes in demand, and the nature of the sales territory can all affect an individual's sales record. Sales volume alone therefore may not be an accurate indicator of the effort salespeople have expended.

In developing incentive plans for salespeople, managers are also confronted with the problem of how to reward extra sales effort and at the same time compensate for activities that do not contribute directly or immediately to sales. Furthermore, sales employees must be able to enjoy some degree of income stability.

Types of Sales Incentive Plans

Compensation plans for sales employees may consist of a straight salary plan, a straight commission plan, or a combination salary and commission plan.[27] A **straight salary plan** permits salespeople to be paid for performing various duties not reflected immediately in their sales volume. It enables them to devote more time to providing services and building up the goodwill of customers without jeopardizing their income. The principal limitation of the straight salary plan is that it may not motivate salespeople to exert sufficient effort in maximizing their sales volume.

On the other hand, the **straight commission plan,** based on a percentage of sales, provides maximum incentive and is easy to compute and understand. For example, organizations that pay a straight commission based on total volume may use the following simple formulas:

$$\text{Total cash compensation} \ = \ 2\% \times \text{total volume}$$

or

$$\text{Total cash compensation} \ = \ 2\% \times \text{total volume up to quota}$$
$$+ \ 4\% \times \text{volume over quota}$$

However, the straight commission plan is limited by the following disadvantages:

1. Emphasis is on sales volume rather than on profits (except in those rare cases where the commission rate is a percentage of the profit on the sale).
2. Territories tend to be milked rather than worked.
3. Customer service after the sale is likely to be neglected.
4. Earnings tend to fluctuate widely between good and poor periods of business, and turnover of trained sales employees tends to increase in poor periods.
5. Salespeople are tempted to grant price concessions.
6. Salespeople are tempted to overload their wholesale customers with inventory.

Straight salary plan
Compensation plan that permits salespeople to be paid for performing various duties that are not reflected immediately in their sales volume

Straight commission plan
Compensation plan based upon a percentage of sales

When a **combined salary and commission plan** is used, the percentage of cash compensation paid out in commissions (i.e., incentives) is called *leverage*. Leverage is usually expressed as a ratio of base salary to commission. For example, a salesperson working under a 70/30 combination plan would receive total cash compensation paid out as 70 percent base salary and 30 percent commission. The amount of leverage will be determined after considering the constraining factors affecting performance discussed earlier and the sales objectives of the organization. The following advantages indicate why the combination salary and commission plan is so widely used:

1. The right kind of incentive compensation, if linked to salary in the right proportion, has most of the advantages of both the straight salary and the straight commission forms of compensation.
2. A salary-plus-incentive compensation plan offers greater design flexibility and can therefore be more readily set up to help maximize company profits.
3. The plan can develop the most favorable ratio of selling expense to sales.
4. The field sales force can be motivated to achieve specific company marketing objectives in addition to sales volume.

Incentives for Professional Employees

Like other salaried workers, professional employees—engineers, scientists, and attorneys, for example—may be motivated through bonuses and merit increases. In some organizations, unfortunately, professional employees cannot advance beyond a certain point in the salary structure unless they are willing to take an administrative assignment. When they are promoted, their professional talents are no longer utilized fully. In the process, the organization may lose a good professional employee and gain a poor administrator. To avoid this situation, some organizations have extended the salary range for professional positions to equal or nearly equal that for administrative positions. The extension of this range provides a double-track wage system, as illustrated in Chapter 8, whereby professionals who do not aspire to become administrators still have an opportunity to earn comparable salaries.

Organizations also use **career curves** or **maturity curves** as a basis for providing salary increases to professional employees. These curves, such as the ones shown in Figure 11–4, provide for the annual salary rate to be based on experience and performance. Separate curves are established to reflect different levels of performance and to provide for annual increases. The curves representing higher levels of performance tend to rise to a higher level and at a faster rate than the curves representing lower performance levels.

Professional employees can receive compensation beyond base pay. For example, scientists and engineers employed by high-tech firms are included in performance-base incentive programs such as profit sharing or stock ownership. These plans encourage greater levels of individual performance. Cash bonuses can be awarded to those who complete projects on or before deadline dates. Payments may also be given to individuals elected to professional societies, granted patents, or meeting professional licensing standards.[28]

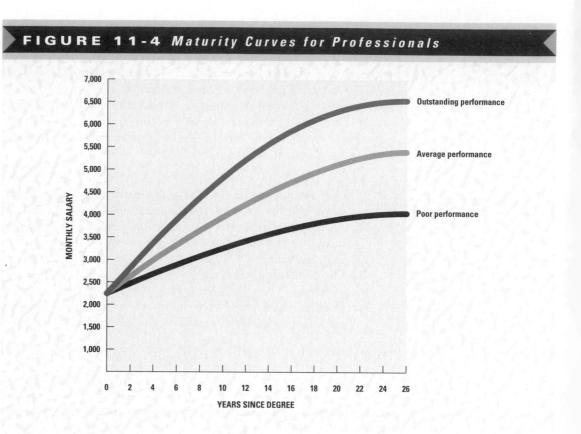

FIGURE 11-4 *Maturity Curves for Professionals*

Outstanding performance

Average performance

Poor performance

MONTHLY SALARY

7,000
6,500
6,000
5,500
5,000
4,500
4,000
3,500
3,000
2,500
2,000
1,500
1,000

0 2 4 6 8 10 12 14 16 18 20 22 24 26

YEARS SINCE DEGREE

five

objective

Incentives for Executive Employees

A major function of incentive plans for executives is to motivate them to develop and use their abilities and contribute their energies to the fullest possible extent. Incentive plans should also facilitate the recruitment and retention of competent executive employees. This can be accomplished with plans that will enable them to accumulate a financial estate and to shelter a portion of their compensation from current income taxes.

Components of Executive Compensation

Organizations commonly have more than one compensation strategy for executives in order to meet various organizational goals and executive needs. For example, chief executive officers (CEOs) may have their compensation packages heavily weighted toward long-term incentives, because CEOs should be more concerned about the long-term impact of their decisions than the short-term implications. Group vice presidents, on the other hand, may receive more short-term incentives since their decisions affect operations on a six- to twelve-month basis. Regardless of the mix, executive compensation plans consist of four basic components: (1) base salary, (2) short-term incentives or bonuses, (3) long-term

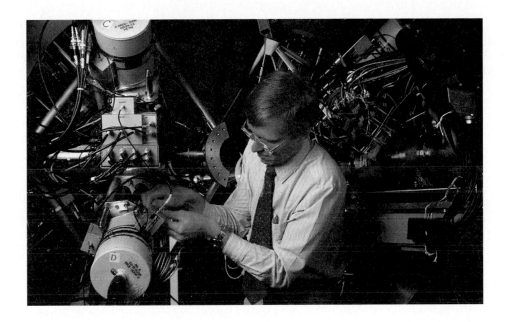

An engineer working on high-tech projects like this gamma ray detector could expect to be part of a performance-based incentive program.

incentives or stock plans, and (4) perquisites.[29] Another important element in compensation strategy is the compensation mix to be paid to managers and executives accepting overseas assignments.

Bases for Executive Salaries

The levels of competitive salaries in the job market exert perhaps the greatest influence on executive base salaries. An organization's compensation committee—normally members of the board of directors—will order a salary survey to find out what executives earn in comparable enterprises.[30] Comparisons may be based on organization size, sales volume, or industry grouping. By analyzing the survey data, the committee can determine the equity of the compensation package outside the organization.[31]

Job evaluation will allow the organization to establish internal equity between top managers and executives. For executives, the Hay profile method (see Chapter 10) is probably the most widely used method of job evaluation. Finally, base pay will be influenced by the performance of the executive. Most organizations evaluate their executives according to a set of predetermined goals or objectives.

Bases for Executive Short-Term Incentives

Incentive bonuses for executives should be based on the contribution the individual makes to the organization. A variety of formulas have been developed for this purpose. Incentive bonuses may be based on a percentage of a company's total profits or a percentage of profits in excess of a specific return on stockholders' investments. In other instances the payments may be tied to an annual profit plan whereby the amount is determined by the extent to which an agreed-upon profit level is exceeded. Payments may also be based on performance ratings or the achievement of specific objectives established with the agreement of executives and the board of directors. Objectives influencing the creation of shareholder value include sales, operating margin, cost of capital, and service and quality measures.[32]

Top corporate executives have the opportunity to earn large sums of money. Frequently, a significant part of their total compensation comes from incentive bonuses. When long-term compensation is added to annual base salary increases and bonuses, the total compensation of some executives may well reach into the millions of dollars. Highlights in HRM 3 shows the compensation received by the nation's twenty highest-paid executives in 1993.

Pros and cons of executive bonuses.   Are top executives worth the salaries and bonuses they receive? The answer may depend largely on whom you ask.[33] Corporate compensation committees justify big bonuses as a way to reward superior performance. Other reasons for defending high levels of compensation include the following:

1. Executives are responsible for large amounts of capital.
2. Business competition is pressure-filled and demanding.
3. Good executive talent is in great demand.
4. Effective executives create shareholder value.

Others justify high compensation as a "fact of business life" reflecting market compensation trends.[34]

Nevertheless, strong criticism is heard regarding high salaries and bonuses awarded to senior executives.[35] Some critics attack the size of incentive bonuses and the often vague criteria on which bonuses are based. Others point out that some executives receive record bonuses while their organizations are in financial trouble and employees are asked to make wage and benefits concessions. Large bonuses can also serve to raise prices, ultimately leading to inflation and higher unemployment.

Another criticism of some executive incentive plans is that the time period for which executive performance is measured is often too short and the rewards are too large. This encourages executives to focus on short-term items such as quarterly earnings growth and to neglect longer-term items such as research and development and market share.[36] In the long run, therefore, stockholders may not receive a return equal to what they might have earned from other investments, and they might look for a better investment with a different organization.

Form of bonus payment.   A bonus payment may take the form of cash or stock. Also, the timing of the payment may vary. Payment can be immediate (which is frequently the case), deferred for a short term, or deferred until retirement.

Most organizations pay their short-term incentive bonuses in cash (in the form of a supplemental check), in keeping with their pay-for-performance strategy. By providing a reward soon after the performance, and thus linking it to the effort on which it is based, they can use cash bonuses as a significant motivator. Cash payment also best serves those executives who must satisfy immediate financial needs. If the money is not needed right away, the executive can invest it elsewhere and receive a greater return than would otherwise be earned in a deferred plan.

HIGHLIGHTS IN HRM

highlights

3   THE 20 HIGHEST PAID CHIEF EXECUTIVES

PAY RANK	CEO/COMPANY	IN THOUSANDS			VALUE OF LONG TERM INCENTIVES AND STOCK GRANTS	TOTAL
		SALARY	BONUS	OTHER		
1	SANFORD I. WEILL Travelers Inc.	$1,019	$3,030	$245	$41,367	$45,660
2	GEORGE M. C. FISHER Eastman Kodak	331	154	5,000	19,908	25,392
3	GERALD M. LEVIN Time Warner	1,050	4,000	244	15,870	21,164
4	JAMES R. MELLOR General Dynamics	670	1,350	12,879	5,380	20,279
5	JAMES E. CAYNE Bear Stearns	200	8,137	0	7,578	15,915
6	LOUIS V. GERSTNER International Business Machines	1,500	1,125	5,085	7,542	15,252
7	JOHN S. REED Citicorp	1,150	3,000	69	8,906	13,125
8	REUBEN MARK Colgate-Palmolive	901	1,264	94	10,658	12,916
9	HARVEY GOLUB American Express	777	1,850	335	8,878	11,840
10	ALSTON D. CORNELL Georgia-Pacific	817	550	667	9,625	11,659
11	RICHARD B. FISHER Morgan Stanley Group	475	4,438	24	5,628	10,565
12	RICHARD K. EAMER National Medical Enterprises	974	0	8,040	1,547	10,561
13	DANIEL P. TULLY Merrill Lynch	500	6,200	161	3,605	10,466
14	ROBERT B. PALMER Digital Equipment	738	0	9	9,473	10,220
15	CHARLES S. SANFORD JR. Bankers Trust New York Corp.	750	8,116	301	1,013	10,180
16	JOHN F. WELCH JR. General Electric	1,750	2,200	441	5,414	9,805
17	DONALD B. MARRON Paine Webber Group	600	6,300	534	2,213	9,647

(continued)

HIGHLIGHTS IN HRM (continued)

PAY RANK	CEO/COMPANY	IN THOUSANDS			VALUE OF LONG-TERM INCENTIVES AND STOCK GRANTS	TOTAL
		SALARY	BONUS	OTHER		
18	CHARLES F. KNIGHT					
	Emerson Electric	$ 800	$1,100	$ 45	$7,593	$9,538
19	KENNETH L. LAY					
	Enron	960	1,040	1,512	5,912	9,424
20	WILLIAM J. ALLEY					
	American Brands	1,054	862	5,263	1,708	8,887

Source: Brian Dumaine, "A Knockout Year for CEO Pay," *FORTUNE* 130, no. 3 (July 25, 1994): 95. Used with permission.

Use of deferred bonuses. A deferred bonus can be used to provide the sole source of retirement benefits or to supplement a regular pension plan. If they are in a lower tax bracket when the deferred benefits are ultimately received—which is not always the case—executives can realize income tax savings. In addition, interest on the deferred amount can allow it to appreciate without being taxed until it is received. To the organization's advantage, deferred bonuses are not subject to the reporting requirement of the Employee Retirement Income Security Act (ERISA). Moreover, the organization can have the use of the money during this period. However, deferred income funds also become a part of the company's indebtedness, a part or all of which might be lost should the company become insolvent. If these funds do not appreciate with inflation, participants also stand to suffer a loss from inflation.

Bases for Executive Long-Term Incentives

Short-term incentive bonuses are criticized for causing top executives to focus on quarterly profit goals to the detriment of long-term survival and growth objectives. Emhart Corporation faced this problem when deciding whether to update and expand a profitable facility that manufactured industrial hardware. At one time, Emhart would have opted not to expand, since the executives making this decision received their incentive bonuses primarily on the basis of profit growth. Expansion of the hardware plant would not increase short-term profit growth and thus would cut into their bonuses. But Emhart revamped its compensation plan, deciding to link executive bonuses with the long-term price of stock. Consequently, according to Emhart chairman T. Mitchell Ford, the company okayed the expansion. "The plan lets us manage with a long-term view of the business," said Sherman B. Carpenter, vice president for administration.[37]

Sears, Combustion Engineering, and Borden, like Emhart, have adopted compensation strategies that tie executive pay to long-term performance measures. Each of these organizations recognizes that, while incentive payments for executives may be based on the achievement of specific goals relating to their positions, the plans must also take into account the performance of the organization as a whole. Important to stockholders are such performance results as growth in earnings per share, return on stockholders' equity, and, ultimately, stock price appreciation. A variety of incentive plans, therefore, has been developed to tie rewards to these performance results, particularly over the long term.

Stock options are the primary long-term incentive offered to executives. The basic principle behind stock options is that executives should have a stake in the business so that they have the same perspective as the owners—i.e., stockholders.[38] The major long-term incentives fall into three broad categories:

1. Stock price appreciation grants
2. Restricted stock and restricted cash grants
3. Performance-based grants

Each of these broad categories includes various stock grants or cash incentives for the payment of executive performance. See Figure 11–5 for definitions of the different grant types. Often, as one observer notes, organizations combine stock options with tandem stock appreciation rights plus performance-based grants to balance market performance and internal, strategic performance.[39] The granting of stock options contributes substantially to executives' million-dollar compensation packages, as Highlights in HRM 3 demonstrates.

Executive Perquisites

Perquisites
Special benefits given to executives; often referred to as perks

In addition to incentive programs, executive employees are often given special benefits and perquisites. **Perquisites,** or "perks," are a means of demonstrating the executives' importance to the organization while giving them an incentive to improve their performance. Furthermore, perks serve as a status symbol both inside and outside the organization. Perquisites can also provide a tax saving to executives, since some are not taxed as income. Some of the more common perquisites include assigned chauffeurs, country club memberships, special vacation policies, executive physical exams, use of an executive dining room, car phones, liability insurance, and financial counseling.[40]

A country club membership is a common executive perk

Compensation in a Global Environment

With the growth of multinational organizations, HR managers have had to develop compensation packages for managers and executives involved in overseas assignments.[41] While those assigned to foreign positions may still participate in the traditional pay practices of their organizations—merit raises, bonuses, and stock options—they may also receive compensation payments unique to a position overseas.[42] For example, managers and executives asked to go abroad are sometimes given a financial incentive to accept these assignments, to compensate them for any reluctance to relocate.[43] Furthermore, they may be provided with supplemental living allowances to

FIGURE 11-5 *Types of Long-Term Incentive Plans*

STOCK PRICE APPRECIATION PLANS

Stock options	Rights granted to executives to purchase shares of their organization's stock at an established price for a fixed period of time. Stock price is usually set at market value at the time the option is granted.
Stock appreciation rights (SARs)	Cash or stock award determined by increase in stock price during any time chosen by the executive in the option period; does not require executive financing.
Stock purchase	Opportunities for executives to purchase shares of their organization's stock valued at full market or a discount price, often with the organization providing financial assistance.
Phantom stock	Grant of units equal in value to the fair market value or book value of a share of stock; on a specified date the executive will be paid the appreciation in the value of the units up to that time.

RESTRICTED STOCK/CASH PLANS

Restricted stock	Grant of stock or stock units at a reduced price with the condition that the stock not be transferred or sold (by risk of forfeiture) before a specified employment date.
Restricted cash	Grant of fixed-dollar amounts subject to transfer or forfeiture restrictions before a specified employment date.

PERFORMANCE-BASED PLANS

Performance units	Grants analogous to annual bonuses except that the measurement period exceeds one year. The value of the grant can be expressed as a flat dollar amount or converted to a number of "units" of equivalent aggregate value.
Performance shares	Grants of actual stock or phantom stock units. Value is contingent both on predetermined performance objectives over a specified period of time and the stock market.
Formula-value grants	Rights to receive units or the gain in value of units determined by a formula (such as book value or an earnings multiplier) rather than changes in market price.
Dividend units	Rights to receive an amount equal to the dividends paid on a specified number of shares; typically granted in conjunction with other grant types, such as performance shares.

compensate for the additional living expenses. In addition, they are often provided with financial assistance covering such items as moving costs, storage payments, and children's educational expenses.[44] Because of the importance of compensation to international HRM, we will elaborate on this topic in Chapter 19.

Challenges for Executive Compensation

Executive compensation is today a highly publicized topic.[45] With the large compensation packages given to senior managers and top-level executives, cries for performance accountability and openness abound. For example, to justify the $2.1 million paid Joseph E. Antonini, chief executive officer of Kmart, the compensation committee of the board of directors hired an independent consultant to offer an "outside perspective" on the compensation received.[46] During the years ahead, compensation professionals note several challenges facing executive compensation:[47]

1. Performance measurement techniques must be refined to reflect individual contributions. The measurement and rewarding of executive performance will require creative compensation approaches.
2. Organizations will need to comply with increased government regulation of executive compensation. The Securities and Exchange Commission (SEC) now permits stockholders to propose and vote to limit executive compensation. Additionally, the SEC requires companies to value stock option grants and report these values in proxy statements. Proxies now require companies to compare their stock's five-year performance with a broad market index and a peer group. These rules changes signal closer scrutiny of all components of executive compensation.
3. Organizations will need to continually fend off general attacks on high executive compensation while gaining the acceptance of innovative variable pay strategies by potentially hostile shareholder groups.
4. Executive compensation practices will need to support global value-creating strategies with well-considered incentive pay programs. Hard questions to be answered include: "What exactly are the implications of global competitiveness and the corresponding strategies required to improve U.S. corporations' effectiveness?" and "How do these new strategies affect organizations and their compensation systems?"[48]

Gainsharing Incentive Plans

Gainsharing plans
Programs under which both employees and the organization share the financial gains according to a predetermined formula that reflects improved productivity and profitability

The emphasis on total-quality management has led many organizations to implement a variety of gainsharing plans.[49] **Gainsharing plans** enable employees to share in the benefits of improved efficiency realized by the organization or major units within it. Many of these plans cover managers and executives as well as hourly workers. The plans encourage teamwork among all employees and reward them for their total contribution to the organization. Such features are particularly desirable when working conditions make individual performance difficult if not impossible to measure.

The basic principle of gainsharing, according to some authorities on productivity and incentives, is to establish effective structures and processes of employee involvement and a fair means of rewarding system-wide performance improvement.[50] At its root, gainsharing is an organizational program designed to increase productivity or decrease labor costs and share monetary gains with employees.[51]

Inherent in gainsharing is the idea that involved employees will improve productivity through more effective use of labor, capital, and raw materials and share the financial gains according to a formula that reflects improved productivity and profitability. The more common gainsharing plans include profit-sharing plans, the Scanlon and Rucker plans, Improshare, and employee stock ownership plans (ESOPs). Highlights in HRM 4 shows the usage of different gainsharing plans according to one study of 1,639 organizations.

objective

Profit sharing

Any procedure by which an employer pays, or makes available to all regular employees, in addition to base pay, special current or deferred sums based upon the profits of the enterprise

Profit-Sharing Plans

Probably no incentive plan has been the subject of more widespread interest, attention, and misunderstanding than profit sharing. **Profit sharing** is any procedure by which an employer pays, or makes available to all regular employees, special current or deferred sums based on the organization's profits. As defined here, profit sharing represents cash payments made to eligible employees at designated time periods, as distinct from profit sharing in the form of contributions to employee pension funds.[52]

Profit-sharing plans are intended to give employees the opportunity to increase their earnings by contributing to the growth of their organization's profits. These contributions may be directed toward improving product quality, reducing operating costs, improving work methods, and building goodwill rather than just increasing rates of production. Profit sharing can help to stimulate employees to think and feel more like partners in the enterprise and thus to concern themselves with the welfare of the organization as a whole. Its purpose therefore is to motivate a total commitment from employees rather than simply to have them contribute in specific areas.

A popular example of a highly successful profit-sharing plan is the one in use at Lincoln Electric Company, a manufacturer of arc welding equipment and supplies. This plan was started in 1934 by J. F. Lincoln, president of the company. Each year the company distributes a large percentage of its profits to employees in accordance with their salary level and merit ratings. In recent years the annual bonus has ranged from a low of 55 percent to a high of 115 percent of annual wages. In addition, Lincoln's program includes a piecework plan with a guarantee, cash awards for employee suggestions, a guarantee of employment for thirty hours of the forty-hour workweek, and an employee stock purchase plan.

The success of Lincoln Electric's incentive system depends on a high level of contribution by each employee. The performance evaluations employees receive twice a year are based on four factors—dependability, quality, output, and ideas and cooperation. There is a high degree of respect among employees and management for Lincoln's organizational goals and for the profit-sharing program.[53]

4   TYPES OF GAINSHARING PROGRAMS ACROSS SIC GROUPS

highlights

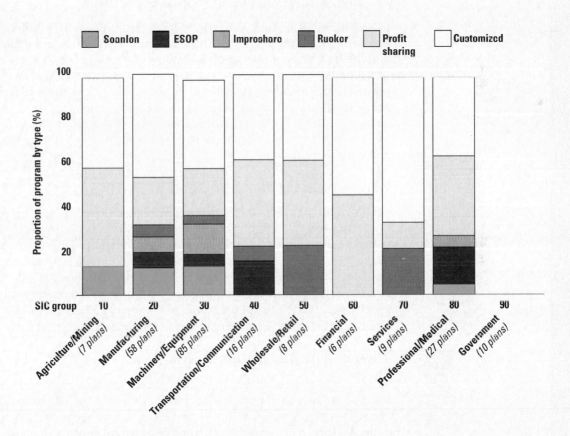

Legend: Scanlon · ESOP · Improshare · Rucker · Profit sharing · Customized

* This national study of gainsharing programs was based on returns from 1,639 HR managers, directors, and vice presidents.

Source: Steven E. Markham, K. Dow Scott, and Beverly L. Little, "National Gainsharing Study: The Importance of Industry Differences," *Compensation and Benefits Review* 24, no. 1 (January-February 1992): 34–45. Reprinted with permission of the publisher, American Management Association, New York.

Variations in Profit-sharing Plans

Profit-sharing plans differ in the proportion of profits shared with employees and in the distribution and form of payment. The amount shared with employees may range from 5 to 50 percent of the net profit. In most plans, however, about 20 to 25 percent of the net profit is shared. Profit distributions may be made to all employees on an equal basis, or they may be based on regular salaries or some formula that takes into account seniority and/or merit. The payments may be disbursed in cash, deferred, or made on the basis of combining the two forms of payment.

Requirements for Successful Profit-Sharing Plans

Most authorities in the field agree that to have a successful profit-sharing program, an organization must first have a sound HR program, good labor relations, and the trust and confidence of its employees. Profit sharing thus is a refinement of a good HR program and a supplement to an adequate wage scale rather than a substitute for either one. As with all incentive plans, it is the underlying philosophy of management, rather than the mechanics of the plan, that may determine its success. Particularly important to the success of a profit-sharing plan are the provisions that enable employees to participate in decisions affecting their jobs and their performance.

Weaknesses of Profit-Sharing Plans

In spite of their potential advantages, profit-sharing plans are also prone to certain weaknesses. The profits shared with employees may be the result of inventory speculation, climatic factors, economic conditions, national emergencies, or other factors over which employees have no control. Conversely, losses may occur during years when employee contributions have been at a maximum. The fact that profit-sharing payments are made only once a year or deferred until retirement may reduce their motivational value. If a plan fails to pay off for several years in a row, this can have an adverse effect on productivity and employee morale.

Three Unique Bonus Plans

objective

To provide employees with bonuses that encourage maximum effort and cooperation but are not tied to profit fluctuation, three unique plans have been developed. Two plans, which bear the names of their originators, Joe Scanlon and Alan W. Rucker, are similar in their philosophy. Both plans emphasize participative management. Both encourage cost reduction by sharing with employees any savings resulting from these reductions. The formulas on which the bonuses are based, however, are somewhat different. The third plan, Improshare, is a gainsharing program based on the number of finished goods that employee work teams complete in an established period.

The Scanlon Plan

The philosophy behind the **Scanlon Plan** is that employees should offer ideas and suggestions to improve productivity and, in turn, be rewarded for their construc-

Scanlon Plan

Bonus incentive plan using employee and management committees to gain cost-reduction improvements

. . . .

tive efforts. The plan requires good management, leadership, trust and respect between employees and managers, and a workforce dedicated to responsible decision making. When correctly implemented, the Scanlon Plan can result in improved efficiency and profitability for the organization and steady employment and high compensation for employees.

According to Scanlon's proponents, effective employee participation, which includes the use of committees on which employees are represented, is the most significant feature of the Scanlon Plan.[54] This gives employees the opportunity to communicate their ideas and opinions and to exercise some degree of influence over decisions affecting their work and their welfare within the organization. Employees have an opportunity to become managers of their time and energy, equipment usage, the quality and quantity of their production, and other factors relating to their work. They accept changes in production methods more readily and volunteer new ideas. The Scanlon Plan encourages greater teamwork and sharing of knowledge at the lower levels. It demands more efficient management and better planning as workers try to reduce overtime and to work smarter rather than harder or faster.

The primary mechanisms for employee participation in the Scanlon Plan are the shop committees established in each department. (See Figure 11–6 for an illustration of the Scanlon Plan suggestion process.) These committees consider production problems and make suggestions for improvement within their respective departments to an organization-wide screening committee. The function of the screening committee is to oversee the operation of the plan, to act on suggestions received from the shop committees, and to review the data on which monthly bonuses are to be based. The screening committee is also responsible for consulting with and advising top management, which retains decision-making authority. Both the shop committees and the screening committee are composed of equal numbers of employees and managers.

Financial incentives under the Scanlon Plan are ordinarily offered to all employees (a significant feature of the plan) on the basis of an established formula. This formula is based on increases in employee productivity as determined by a norm that has been established for labor costs. The norm, which is subject to review, reflects the relationship between labor costs and the sales value of production (SVOP). The SVOP includes sales revenue and the value of goods in inventory. Figure 11–7 illustrates how the two figures are used to determine the Scanlon Plan incentive bonus.

The plan also provides for the establishment of a reserve fund into which 25 percent of any earned bonus is paid to cover deficits during the months when labor costs exceed the norm. After the reserve portion has been deducted, the remainder of the bonus is distributed, with 25 percent going to the organization and 75 percent to the employees. At the end of the year, any surplus that has been accumulated in the reserve fund is distributed to employees according to the same formula.

The Scanlon Plan (and variations of it) has become a fundamental way of managing, if not a way of life, in organizations such as American Valve Company, TRW, and Weyerhaeuser. The Xaloy Corporation, a major manufacturer of

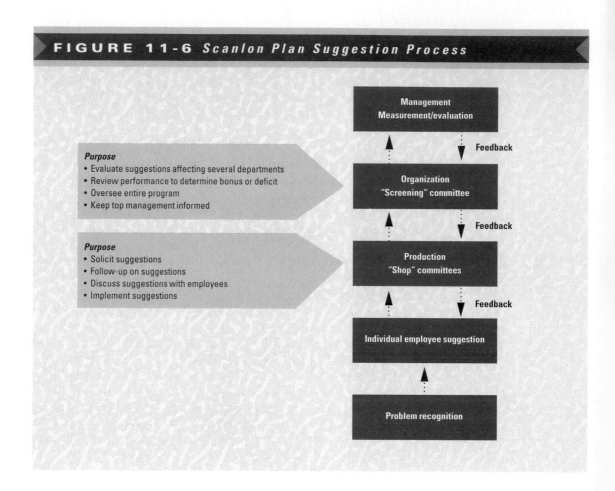

FIGURE 11-6 *Scanlon Plan Suggestion Process*

Purpose
- Evaluate suggestions affecting several departments
- Review performance to determine bonus or deficit
- Oversee entire program
- Keep top management informed

Purpose
- Solicit suggestions
- Follow-up on suggestions
- Discuss suggestions with employees
- Implement suggestions

Management
Measurement/evaluation

Feedback

Organization
"Screening" committee

Feedback

Production
"Shop" committees

Feedback

Individual employee suggestion

Problem recognition

bimetallic cylinders, uses a modified Scanlon program based on the following four principles:

Identity	Employee involvement is linked to the company's mission and purpose statement.
Competence	A high level of competence is expected from employees.
Participation	A suggestion process taps into employee ideas.
Equity	Organizational success is based upon a partnership forged among employees, customers, and investors.[55]

Rucker Plan
Bonus incentive plan based on the historic relationship between the total earnings of hourly employees and the production value created by the employees

The Rucker Plan

The share of production plan (SOP), or **Rucker Plan,** normally covers just production workers but may be expanded to cover all employees. As with the Scanlon Plan, committees are formed to elicit and evaluate employee suggestions. The Rucker Plan, however, uses a far less elaborate participatory structure. As one authority noted, "It commonly represents a type of program that is used as

> # FIGURE 11-7 *Determining the Scanlon Plan Incentive Bonus*

1994 ANNUAL BASE YEAR FIGURES

Sales value of production (SVOP)	=	$15,000,000					
Total wage bill	=	$ 4,750,000					
$\frac{\text{Total wage bill}}{\text{SVOP}}$	(Norm)	=	$\frac{4,750,000}{15,000,000}$	=	0.316	=	31.6%

CURRENT PRODUCTION MONTH

SVOP		$ 1,600,000
Allowable wage bill	.316 x $1,600,000 =	$ 505,600
Monthly wage bill		$ 450,000
Labor cost savings		$ 55,600
Scanlon Plan bonus available for distribution		$ 55,600

Source: Adapted from George T. Milkovich and Jerry M. Newman, *Compensation* (Homewood, Ill.: Irwin, 1993), 366. Used with permission.

an alternative to the Scanlon Plan in firms attempting to move from a traditional style of management toward a higher level of employee involvement."[56]

The financial incentive of the Rucker Plan is based on the historic relationship between the total earnings of hourly employees and the production value that employees create. The bonus is based on any improvement in this relationship that employees are able to realize. Thus, for every 1 percent increase in production value that is achieved, workers receive a bonus of 1 percent of their total payroll costs.[57]

Lessons from the Scanlon and Rucker Plans

Perhaps the most important lesson to be learned from the Scanlon and Rucker plans is that any management expecting to gain the cooperation of its employees in improving efficiency must permit them to become involved psychologically as well as financially in the organization. If employees are to contribute maximum effort, they must have a feeling of involvement and identification with their organization, which does not come out of the traditional manager-subordinate relationship. Consequently, it is important for organizations to realize that while employee cooperation is essential to the successful administration of the Scanlon and Rucker plans, the plans themselves do not necessarily stimulate this cooperation.

The attitude of management is of paramount importance to the success of either plan. For example, where managers show little confidence and trust in their employees, the plans tend to fail. Managers further note that Scanlon and Rucker plans are successful only when the following are true:

- Bonus formulas are clearly understood and can be reviewed by employees.
- Management is highly committed to making the plan succeed.
- Adequate training is given to both employees and supervisors.
- Adequate potential exists for employee rewards.

Like any other incentive plan, the Scanlon and Rucker plans are no better than the organizational environment in which they are used.

Improshare

Improshare Gainsharing program under which bonuses are based upon the overall productivity of the work team

Improshare—improved productivity through sharing—is a gainsharing program developed by Mitchell Fain, an industrial engineer with experience in traditional individual incentive systems. Whereas individual production bonuses are typically based on how much an employee produces above some standard amount, Improshare bonuses are based on the overall productivity of the *work team*. Improshare output is measured by the number of finished products that a work team produces in a given period. Both production (direct) employees and nonproduction (indirect) employees are included in the determination of the bonus.[58] Since a cooperative environment benefits all, Improshare promotes increased interaction and support between employees and management.

The bonus is based not on dollar savings, as in the Scanlon and Rucker plans, but on productivity gains that result from reducing the time it takes to produce a finished product. Bonuses are determined monthly by calculating the difference between standard hours (Improshare hours) and actual hours, and dividing the result by actual hours. The employees and the company each receive payment for 50 percent of the improvement. Companies such as Hinderliter Energy Equipment Corporation pay the bonus as a separate check to emphasize that it is extra income.

Stock Ownership

Stock ownership plans for employees have existed in some organizations for many years. These programs are sometimes implemented as part of an employee benefit plan. However, organizations that offer stock ownership programs to employees do so with the belief that there is some incentive value to the systems. By allowing employees to purchase stock, the organization hopes they will increase their productivity and thus cause the stock price to rise.

Not uncommon are plans for purchasing stock on an installment basis through payroll deductions and without the payment of brokerage fees. Over the years, the stock of some of the larger blue-chip companies such as Sears, General Telephone and Electronic, Warner Communications, and Ralston Purina has proved to be a good investment for their employees. Furthermore, stock ownership programs have become a popular way to salvage a failing organization, thereby saving employee jobs.

. . . .

Employee Stock Ownership Plans (ESOPs)

Employee stock ownership plans (ESOPs) have grown significantly during the past ten years, adding 600 to 800 plans annually that covered a total of 500,000 to 1 million employees.[59] The Chicago Tribune Company, Southwest Airlines, Roadway Services, and Cincinnati Bell are organizations with established ESOPs. Companies such as Weirton Steel and Hyatt Clark Industries have been rescued by ESOP-financed employee buyouts, and Polaroid and Chevron have used ESOPs to fight hostile takeover bids. ESOPs can be used to generate funds to purchase an organization's stock otherwise available to outside raiders.[60] Continental Bank decided that employee stock ownership was an effective and innovative way to give employees a share in Continental's success.[61]

Employee stock ownership plans take two primary forms: a stock bonus plan and a leveraged plan. With either plan, the public or private employer establishes an ESOP trust that qualifies as a tax-exempt employee trust under Section 401(a) of the Internal Revenue Code. With a stock bonus plan, each year the organization gives stock to the ESOP or gives cash to the ESOP to buy outstanding stock. The ESOP holds the stock for employees, and they are routinely informed of the value of their accounts. Stock allocations can be based on employee wages or seniority. When employees leave the organization or retire, they can sell their stock back to the organization, or they can sell it on the open market if it is traded publicly. Leveraged ESOPs work in much the same way as do stock bonus plans, except that the ESOP borrows money from a bank or other financial institution to purchase stock. The organization then makes annual tax-deductible payments to the ESOP, which in turn repays the lending institution. Organizations may also use the stock placed in an ESOP trust as collateral for a bank loan. As the loan is repaid, the stock used as collateral is allocated to employee accounts. Payments of both the principal and interest can be deducted from the organization's income tax liability.

Advantages of ESOPs

Encouraged by favorable federal income tax provisions, employers utilize ESOPs as a means of providing retirement benefits for their employees. Favorable tax incentives permit a portion of earnings to be excluded from taxation if that portion is assigned to employees in the form of shares of stock. Employers can therefore provide retirement benefits for their employees at relatively low cost, because stock contributions are in effect subsidized by the federal government. ESOPs can also increase employees' pride of ownership in the organization, providing an incentive for them to increase productivity and help the organization prosper and grow. Enthusiastic promoters of ESOPs go so far as to claim that these plans will make U.S. organizations more competitive in world markets. The plans, they maintain, will increase productivity, improve employee-management relations, and promote economic justice.[62]

Problems with ESOPs

Generally, ESOPs are more likely to serve their intended purposes in publicly held companies than in closely held ones. A major problem with the closely held company is its potential inability to buy back the stock of employees when they retire. Unfortunately, these employees do not have the alternative of disposing of their stock on the open market. Requiring organizations to establish a sinking fund to be used exclusively for repurchasing stock could eliminate this problem.

Another criticism of ESOPs is that they cost the country a tremendous amount in lost taxes. If Congress determines that employers are abusing ESOP advantages, or if national budget pressures intensify, it could change the tax rules. A growing problem with ESOPs is that as more retirement income comes from these plans, the more dependent a pensioner becomes on the price of company stock. Future retirees are vulnerable to stock market fluctuations as well as to management mistakes. Finally, although studies show that productivity improves when ESOPs are implemented, these gains are not guaranteed. ESOPs help little unless managers are willing to involve employees in organizational decision making. Unfortunately, ESOPs are sometimes set up in ways that restrict employee decision making and expose the ESOP to risk, though providing investors with large potential gains.

SUMMARY

The success of an incentive pay plan depends on the organizational climate in which it must operate, employee confidence in it, and its suitability to employee and organizational needs. Importantly, employees must view their incentive pay as being equitable and related to their performance. Performance measures should be quantifiable, easily understood, and bear a demonstrated relationship to organizational performance.

Piecework plans pay employees a given rate for each unit satisfactorily completed. Employers implement these plans when output is easily measured and when the production process is fairly standardized. Bonuses are incentive payments above base wages paid on either an individual or team basis. A bonus is offered to encourage employees to exert greater effort. Standard hour plans establish a standard time for job completion. An incentive is paid for finishing the job in less than the preestablished time. These plans are popular for jobs with a fixed time for completion.

Merit raises will not serve to motivate employees when they are seen as entitlements, which occurs when these raises are given yearly without regard to changes in employee performance. Merit raises are not motivational when they are given because of seniority or favoritism or when merit budgets are inadequate to sufficiently reward employee performance. To be motivational, merit raises must be such that employees see a clear relationship between pay and performance and the salary increase must be large enough to exceed inflation and higher income taxes.

Salespersons may be compensated by a straight salary, a combination of salary and commission, or a commission only. Paying employees a straight salary allows them to focus on tasks other than sales, such as service and customer goodwill. A straight commission plan causes employees to emphasize sales goals. A combination of salary and commission provides the advantages of both the straight salary and the straight commission form of payments.

objective

Executive bonuses are tied to agreed-upon criteria of organizational performance. Performance objectives might include profit levels; return on capital or operating indexes covering sales, market share, service, and quality measures; or operating margins. A bonus can be received as either cash or stock, and the timing of the payment may vary. Immediate, short-term, and long-term (deferred until retirement) are typical payout periods. Executive compensation will normally also include different types of stock plans as well as other desirable perquisites.

objective

Profit-sharing plans pay to employees sums of money based on the organization's profits. Cash payments are made to eligible employees at specified times, normally yearly. The primary purpose of profit sharing is to provide employees with additional income through their participation in organizational achievement. Employee commitment to improved productivity, quality, and customer service will contribute to organizational success and, in turn, to their compensation. Profit-sharing plans may not achieve their stated gains when employee performance is unrelated to organizational success or failure. This may occur because of economic conditions, other competition, or environmental conditions. Profit-sharing plans can have a negative effect on employee morale when plans fail to consistently reward employees.

objective

The Scanlon, Rucker, and Improshare gainshare plans pay bonuses to employees unrelated to profit levels. Each of these plans encourages employees to maximize their performance and cooperation through suggestions offered to improve organizational performance. The Scanlon Plan pays an employee a bonus based on saved labor cost measured against the organization's sales value of production. The bonus under the Rucker Plan is based on any improvement in the relationship between the total earnings of hourly employees and the value of production that employees create. The Improshare bonus is paid when employees increase production output above a given target level.

KEY TERMS

bonus	perquisites
career curves (maturity curves)	profit sharing
combination salary and commission plan	Rucker Plan
differential piece rate	Scanlon Plan
employee stock ownership plans (ESOPs)	standard hour plan
gainsharing plans	straight commission plan
Improshare	straight piecework
lump-sum merit program	straight salary plan
merit guidelines	

1. A company that paid its production employees entirely on a piece-rate system pointed with pride to the fact that it permitted its employees "to go into business for themselves." To what extent do you feel this claim is true or untrue?
2. The standard time for producing one unit of a product is four minutes. What would the piece rate per unit be if the rate for this particular type of work was $6 an hour?
3. Suggest ways in which the motivating value of merit raises may be increased.
4. What are the reasons for the different payment methods for sales employees?
5. What are some of the primary objectives of financial incentive plans for managers, and how do these plans differ from those for nonmanagement employees?
6. What are some of the advantages and disadvantages to employees of a deferred, as opposed to a cash, bonus plan?
7. What are the reasons for the success of the Scanlon and Rucker plans?
8. What are some of the reasons for the rapid growth of ESOPs? Cite some of the potential problems concerning their use.

CASE STUDY: Incentive Pay: Success at Viking Freight

Federal deregulation of the trucking industry created a fiercely competitive market force among freight companies. Trucking firms learned that superior employee performance and productivity were a main factor in maintaining a competitive edge. At Viking Freight Systems, Inc., one key to developing an effective workforce was to compensate employees for superior performance through an incentive pay program measured against the achievement of corporate objectives. Under the Viking Performance Earnings Plan (VPEP), hourly employees can earn a maximum of 7.5 percent of their gross pay for a four-week accounting period, supervisors can earn up to 11.2 percent, salespeople 12.5 percent, department managers 15 percent, and terminal managers as much as 20 percent when company objectives are met.

At each of Viking's forty-seven freight terminals, employees are divided into distinct groups that share common goals and performance criteria. VPEP objectives are set for groups such as truck drivers, claims administrators, salespersons, and maintenance employees. A customized VPEP is therefore established for each group at each terminal. Measurable performance standards are set by Viking's executive committee and the performance engineering group to sustain or improve key quality or cost-related areas. Individual performance and market conditions are considered when objectives are set. In order to obtain maximum incentive payout, objectives are established that require employees to stretch their performance. Incentive payouts are based entirely upon the company's operating ratio. This ratio is defined as operating expenses divided by revenues before interest and taxes. If Viking's operating ratio for the four-week period isn't less than 95 percent, then no payouts are made, regardless of performance levels.

Terminal performance data is gathered weekly and distributed to individual groups each Monday. Data are presented in easy-to-read bar charts showing particular performance objectives. Employees can quickly identify areas needing improvement. Additionally, regular employee meetings are held, allowing employees to share ideas about how to improve their terminal's performance.

Terry Stambaugh, vice president of human resources, identifies seven factors as contributing to the plan's success:

1. All employees are included in the plan, generating company-wide cooperation and support.
2. Objectives reflect the company's critical performance areas, are controllable by employees, and are easily measured.
3. The incentive program is tied to the company's bottom line; payments aren't made unless the company is profitable.
4. Communication is at the base of everything.
5. Payments are kept separate from base wages for greater visibility.
6. Employees are listened to.
7. The program is regularly reviewed and is revised as necessary to ensure that it continues to meet company objectives.

Source: Adapted from Terry Stambaugh, "An Incentive Pay Success Story," *Personnel Journal* 74, No. 4 (April 1992): 48–54.

Questions
1. Suggest different objectives by which terminal performance could be measured.
2. Discuss ways to keep employees motivated under an incentive pay plan such as Viking's.
3. Recommend other methods by which Viking Freight might elicit performance improvement from employees.

NOTES AND REFERENCES

1. Robert L. Masternak, "Gainsharing Boosts Quality and Productivity at a BFGoodrich Plant," *National Productivity Review* 12, no. 2 (Spring 1993): 225–38; see also "A Gold Standard in Mining Operations," *Business Week* (July 19, 1993): 68. Paul Britton and Christian M. Ellis, "Designing and Implementing Reward Programs: Finding a Better Way," *Compensation and Benefits Review* 26, no. 4 (July-August 1994): 39–46.
2. Personal interview with one of the authors, Tucson, Arizona, August 27, 1993.
3. Richard L. Bunning, "Rewarding a Job Well Done," *Personnel Administrator* 34, no. 1 (January 1989): 60–63.

4. Steven E. Gross and Jeffrey P. Bacher, "The New Variable Pay Programs: How Some Succeed, Why Some Don't," *Compensation and Benefits Review* 25, no. 1 (January-February 1993): 51.

5. Susan Reynolds Baine, "Incentives for the Masses: A Variable Pay Program," *Compensation and Benefits Review* 22, no. 6 (November-December 1990): 50–58.

6. Robert L. Masternak and Timothy L. Ross, "Gainsharing: A Bonus Plan or Employee Involvement?" *Compensation and Benefits Review* 24, no. 1 (January-February 1992): 46–54.

7. David Beck, "Implementing a Gainsharing Plan: What Companies Need to Know," *Compensation and Benefits Review* 24, no. 1 (January-February 1992): 23.

8. Gary W. Florkowski, "Analyzing Group Incentive Plans," *HR Magazine* 35, no. 1 (January 1990): 36–38.

9. Terry Stambaugh, "An Incentive Pay Success Story," *Personnel Journal* 71, no. 4 (April 1992): 48–54; Shari Caudron, "Variable-Pay Program Increases Taco Bell's Profits," *Personnel Journal* 72, no. 6 (June 1993): 64G.

10. Steven E. Markham, K. Dow Scott, and Beverly L. Little, "National Gainsharing Study: The Importance of Industry Differences," *Compensation and Benefits Review* 24, no. 1 (January-February 1992): 34–45.

11. Jay R. Schuster and Patricia K. Zingheim, "The New Variable Pay: Key Design Issues," *Compensation and Benefits Review* 25, no. 2 (March-April 1993): 27–34.

12. Baine, "Incentives for the Masses," 57.

13. Beck, "Implementing a Gainsharing Plan," 26.

14. Theresa M. Welbourne and Luis R. Gomez-Mejia, "Team Incentives in the Workplace," in Milton L. Rock and Lance A. Berger, *The Compensation Handbook*, 3d ed. (New York: McGraw-Hill, 1991): 237–47.

15. Robert D. Pritchard, Philip L. Roth, Patricia Galgay Roth, Margaret D. Watson, and Steven D. Jones, "Incentive Systems: Success by Design," *Personnel* 66, no. 5 (May 1989): 63–68.

16. George T. Milkovich and Jerry M. Newman, *Compensation*, 4th ed. (Homewood, Ill.: Irwin, 1993): 352–54.

17. Thomas B. Wilson, "Is It Time to Eliminate the Piece Rate Incentive System?" *Compensation and Benefits Review* 24, no. 2 (March-April 1992): 43–49.

18. David W. Belcher and Thomas J. Atchinson, *Compensation Administration*, 2d ed. (Englewood Cliffs, N.J.: Prentice-Hall, 1987): 285; see also James E. Nickel and Sandra O'Neal, "Small Group Incentives: Gain Sharing in the Microcosm," *Compensation and Benefits Review* 22, no. 2 (March-April 1990): 22–29.

19. Milkovich and Newman, *Compensation*: 360.

20. Jerry M. Newman and Daniel J. Fisher, "Strategic Impact Merit Pay," *Compensation and Benefits Review* 24, no. 4 (July-August 1992): 38; see also Dale A. Arahood, *How to Design and Install Management Incentive Compensation* (Nashville, Tenn.: Incentive Compensation Publications, 1993).

21. Jeffrey A. Bradt, "Pay for Impact," *Personnel Journal* 70, no. 5 (May 1991): 76–79.

22. Barry L. Wisdom, "Before Implementing a Merit System...Know the Environment and Situations That Demand Caution," *Personnel Administrator* 34, no. 10 (October 1989): 46–49.

23. Glenn Bassett, "Merit Pay Increases Are a Mistake," *Compensation and Benefits Review* 26, no. 2 (March-April 1994): 20–25. See also Lena B. Prewitt, J. Donald Phillips, and Khalad Yasin, "Merit Pay in Academia: Perceptions from the School of Business," *Public Personnel Management* 20, no. 4 (Winter 1991): 409–16.

24. J. Edward Kellough and Haoran Lu, "The Paradox of Merit Pay in the Public Sector: Persistence of a Problematic Procedure," *Public Personnel Administration* 13, no. 2 (Spring 1993): 45–61; see also Herbert G. Heneman and I. Phillip Young, "Assessment of a Merit Pay Program for School District Administrators," *Public Personnel Management* 20, no. 1 (Spring 1991): 35–46.

25. R. Bradley Hill, "A Two-Component Approach to Compensation," *Personnel Journal* 72, no. 5 (May 1993): 154–61.

26. John K. Moynahan, *The Sales Compensation Handbook* (New York: Amacom, 1991).

27. To promote higher sales efforts, organizations may also offer special cash incentives and noncash incentives such as merchandize, travel awards, and status and recognition awards. One study showed that the majority of responding organizations use noncash incentives in addition to their standard compensation plan. See Alfred J. Candrilli, "Success through a Quality-Based Sales Incentive Program," *Compensation and Benefits Review* 22, no. 5 (September-October 1990): 54–59; Jerry McAdams, "Rewarding Sales and Marketing Performance," *Personnel* 64, no. 10 (October 1987): 8–16.

28. George T. Milkovich, "Compensation Systems in High Technology Companies," in *New Perspectives on Compensation*, David B. Balkin and Luis R. Gomez-Mejia, eds. (Englewood Cliffs, N.J.: Prentice-Hall, 1987): 247–81.

29. John D. McMillan, "Executive Pay a New Way," *HR Magazine* 37, no. 6 (June 1992): 46–48.

30. Lawrence M. Baytos, "Board Compensation Committees: Collaboration or Confrontation?" *Compensation and Benefits Review* 23, no. 3 (May-June 1991): 33–38.

31. William L. White, "Managing the Board Review of Executive Pay," *Compensation and Benefits Review* 24, no. 6 (November-December 1992): 35.

32. William L. White and Raymond W. Fife, "New Challenges for Executive Compensation in the

1990's," *Compensation and Benefits Review* 25, no. 1 (January-February 1993): 27–35.

33. Charles F. Schultz and N. Elizabeth Fried, "Fending Off Unreasonable Compensation Attacks," *HR Magazine* 37, no. 6 (June 1992): 49–54.

34. Nandini Rajagopalah and John E. Prescott, "Determinants of Top Management Compensation: Explaining the Impact of Economic, Behavioral, and Strategic Constructs and the Moderating Effects of Industry," *Journal of Management* 16, no. 3 (1990): 515–38.

35. Graef S. Crystal, "Why CEO Compensation Is So High," *California Management Review* 34, no. 1 (Fall 1991): 9.

36. "It's Not How Much You Pay CEOs: But How," *The Wall Street Journal* (May 17, 1990): A16.

37. Jeffrey M. Kanter and Matthew P. Ward, "Long Term Incentives for Managers, Part 4: Performance Plans," *Compensation and Benefits Review* 22, no. 1 (January-February 1990): 36–49.

38. Frederick W. Cook, "How Much Stock Should Management Own?" *Compensation and Benefits Review* 22, no. 5 (September-October 1990): 20–28; see also John D. England, "Don't Be Afraid of Phantom Stock," *Compensation and Benefits Review* 24, no. 5 (September-October 1992): 39–46.

39. Ira T. Kay, "Beyond Stock Options: Emerging Practices in Executive Incentive Programs," *Compensation and Benefits Review* 23, no. 6 (November-December 1991): 18–29.

40. "Labor Letter," *The Wall Street Journal* (September 22, 1992): A1.

41. Douglas J. Carey and Paul D. Howes, "Developing a Global Pay Program," *Journal of International Compensation and Benefits* (July 1992).

42. Ranae M. Hyer, "Executive Compensation in the International Arena: Back to the Basics," *Compensation and Benefits Review* 25, no. 2 (March-April 1993): 49–54.

43. Luis R. Gomez-Mejia and Theresa Welbourne, "Compensation Strategies in a Global Context," *Human Resource Planning* 14, no. 1 (1991): 29–41.

44. Lin P. Crandall and Mark I. Phelps, "Pay for a Global Work Force," *Personnel Journal* 70, no. 2 (February 1991): 28–33.

45. Andrew E. Serwer, "Payday! Payday!" *Fortune* (June 14, 1993): 102–111; see also Mark D. Fefer, "Your CEO Will Get Paid," *Fortune* (October 3, 1994): 18.

46. "Executive Pay: The Party Ain't Over Yet," *Business Week* (April 26, 1993): 56–64.

47. Peter Chingos, "Executive Compensation in the 1990s: The Challenges Ahead," *Compensation and Benefits Review* 22, no. 6 (November-December 1990): 20–30.

48. White, "Managing the Board Review," 27.

49. John G. Belcher, Jr., *Gainsharing: The New Path to Profits and Productivity* (Houston, Texas: Gulf Publishing Company, 1991); see also Robert J. Doyle and Paul I. Doyle, *Gainmanagement: A System for Building Teamwork, Productivity and Profitability Throughout Your Organization* (New York: AMACOM, 1992).

50. Denis Collins, Larry Hatcher, and Timothy L. Ross, "The Decision to Implement Gainsharing: The Role of Work Climate, Expected Outcomes, and Union Status," *Personnel Psychology* 46, no. 1 (Spring 1993): 79.

51. Markham, Scott, and Little, "National Gainsharing Study," 34.

52. Thomas H. Patten and Mark G. Damico, "Survey Details Profit-Sharing Plans: Is Revealing Allocation Formulas a Performance Incentive?" *National Productivity Review* 12, no. 3 (Summer 1993): 383–94.

53. Harry C. Handlin, "The Company Built upon the Golden Rule: Lincoln Electric," *Journal of Organizational Behavior* 12, no. 1 (January 1992): 151–63.

54. Steven E. Markham, K. Dow Scott, and Walter G. Cox, Jr., "The Evolutionary Development of a Scanlon Plan," *Compensation and Benefits Review* 24, no. 2 (March-April 1992): 50–56.

55. Markham, Scott, and Cox, "Evolutionary Development," 51.

56. Edward Ost, "Gain Sharing's Potential," *Personnel Administrator* 34, no. 7 (July 1989): 94.

57. The Rucker Plan uses a somewhat more complex formula for determining employee bonuses. For a detailed example of the Rucker bonus, see Milkovich and Newman, *Compensation:* 366.

58. The standard of Improshare's measurement system is the base productivity factor (BPF), which is the ratio of standard direct labor hours produced to total actual hours worked in a base period. The productivity of subsequent periods is then measured by enlarging standard direct labor hours earned by the BPF ratio to establish Improshare hours (IH). The IH is then compared with actual hours worked in the same period. If earned hours exceed actual hours, 50 percent of the gain is divided by actual hours worked in order to establish a bonus percentage for all employees in the plan.

59. Ronald Farella and Barry M. Subhow, "ESOPs Fables," *PA CPA Journal* 60, no. 4 (Spring 1990): 42–45.

60. "How to Keep Raiders at Bay—On the Cheap," *Business Week* (January 29, 1990): 59.

61. Dennis J. Nirtaut, "ESOP Design and Communication Issues: A Case Study at Continental Bank," *Compensation and Benefits Review* 22, no. 5 (September-October 1990): 48–53.

62. William Smith, Harold Lazarus, and Harold Murray Kalkstein, "Employee Stock Ownership Plans: Motivation and Morale Issues," *Compensation and Benefits Review* 22, no. 5 (September-October 1990): 37–47.

Chapter

Employee Benefits

12

. . . .

In the previous chapter we discussed the different types of incentive compensation plans that organizations use to motivate employees. As we noted, some of those plans provide for deferred payment of compensation, thereby serving as a source of retirement income. Because this deferment reduces the incentive value of these compensation plans, some companies classify profit sharing, stock ownership, and similar deferred incentive plans as employee benefits plans. Whether or not they offer these particular plans, virtually all employers provide a variety of benefits to supplement the cash wages or salaries paid to their employees. These benefits, some of which are required by law, must be considered a part of their total compensation.

In this chapter we examine the characteristics of employee benefits programs. We will study the types of benefits required by law, the major discretionary benefits that employers offer, the employee services provided, and the retirement programs in use.

objective

Employee Benefits Programs

Employee benefits constitute an indirect form of compensation that is intended to improve the quality of work life for employees. In return, employers generally expect employees to be loyal to the organization and to be productive. Since employees have come to expect an increasing number of benefits, the motivational value of these benefits depends on how the benefits program is designed and communicated. Once viewed as a gift from the employer, benefits are now considered rights to which all employees are entitled, and they have become one of the fastest-growing areas of employment law and litigation. Many employers now have a professionally staffed division in the HR department to develop and manage a wide variety of benefits and services.

Growth of Employee Benefits

Not until the 1920s were employee benefits offered by more than just a few employers. Because these benefits were supplemental to the paycheck and were of minor value, they were referred to initially as *fringe benefits*. From this rather meager beginning, benefits programs have expanded in terms of both the types of benefits offered and their cost.

Initially, employee benefits were introduced to promote and reward employee loyalty and to discourage unionization. As unions acquired power during the 1930s, their leaders were able to use collective bargaining to obtain additional benefits, along with higher wages. During World War II, a wage freeze further stimulated the growth of benefits. Wishing to retain their employees but prohibited by the freeze from raising wages, employers provided special inducements in the form of nonwage supplements such as pensions, paid vacations, sick leave, and health and life insurance. Interpretations by the National Labor Relations Board and the Supreme Court to the effect that employers were obligated to bargain for pensions were also major factors stimulating the growth of these particular benefits. Demands for supplemental unemployment insurance, company-paid medical insurance, and other benefits were soon to follow. Another factor in the growth of employee benefits was the exemption from personal income tax on benefits paid for by the employer.

Health benefits must be compatible with the needs of an organization's employees.

Requirements for a Sound Benefits Program

Too often a particular benefit is provided because other employers are doing it, because someone in authority believes it is a good idea, or because there is union pressure. However, the contributions that benefits will make to the HR program depend on how much attention is paid to certain basic considerations.

Establishing Specific Objectives

Like any other component of the HR program, an employee benefits program should be based on specific objectives. The objectives an organization establishes will depend on many factors, including the size of the firm; its location, degree of unionization, and profitability; and industry patterns. Most important, these aims must be compatible with the philosophy and policies of the organization. The chief objectives of most benefits programs are to improve employee satisfaction, to meet employee health and security requirements, to attract and motivate employees, to reduce turnover, to keep the union out, and to maintain a favorable competitive position. Further, these objectives must be considered within the framework of cost containment—a major issue in today's programs.[1]

Unless an organization has a flexible benefits plan (to be discussed later), a uniform package of benefits should be developed. This involves careful consideration of the various benefits that can be offered, the relative preference shown for each benefit by management and the employees, the estimated cost of each benefit, and the total amount of money available for the entire benefits package.

Allowing for Employee Input

Before a new benefit is introduced, the need for it should first be determined through consultation with employees. Many organizations establish committees composed of managers and employees to administer, interpret, and oversee their benefits policies. Opinion surveys are also used to obtain employee input. Having employees participate in designing benefits programs helps to ensure that management is moving in the direction of satisfying employee wants. Pitney Bowes, Quaker Oats, Nike, and Solomon Brothers ask employees to help them improve benefit plans. The companies then ask teams to design a new benefit package that offers more choices without raising costs.[2]

Modifying Employee Benefits

To serve their intended purpose, employee benefits programs must reflect the changes that are continually occurring within our society. Particularly significant are changes in the composition and lifestyles of the workforce. These changes make it necessary to develop new types of benefits to meet shifting needs.[3] For example, as we indicated in Chapter 2, the number of women in the workforce is continuing to grow. Which benefits are most valuable to them (and to men) will be determined largely by whether they have dependent children and whether they have a spouse who has benefit coverage.

Many benefits plans create an environment of disincentives for the young and single, limiting the organization's ability to attract and retain such employees. For example, many employers provide extra compensation in the form of dependent coverage to their workers with families, but the principle of equal pay for equal work suggests that all employees doing the same job should receive the same total compensation, regardless of family status. Similarly, the employer's contribution to the pension plan for a 30-year-old employee is approximately one-fourth the contribution for a 50-year-old employee for the same amount of pension commencing at age 65. This difference in funds spent on older workers in effect discriminates against the younger worker, although legally it is not regarded as discriminatory.[4] These examples illustrate the need for benefits programs that take into account the differing needs of a variety of workers in order to attract a highly capable workforce.

Providing for Flexibility

Flexible benefits plans (cafeteria plans)
Benefit plans that enable individual employees to choose the benefits that are best suited to their particular needs

To accommodate the individual needs of employees, there is a trend toward **flexible benefits plans,** also known as **cafeteria plans.** These plans enable individual employees to choose the benefits that are best suited to their particular needs. They also prevent certain benefits from being wasted on employees who have no need for them. Typically, employees are offered a basic or core benefits package of life and health insurance, sick leave, and vacation, plus a specified number of credits they may use to "buy" whatever other benefits they need.

Benefits programs must be flexible enough to accommodate the constant flow of new legislation and IRS regulations that affect them. A number of benefits-consulting firms are available to help managers keep up with changes in all phases of the programs they oversee. There is also an abundance of computer software for processing employee benefits records that incorporates the latest legislative and regulatory changes.

Communicating Employee Benefits Information

The true measure of a successful benefits program is the degree of trust, understanding, and appreciation it earns from the employees. Employers should carefully communicate information about complicated insurance and pension plans so that there will be no misunderstanding about what the plans will and will not provide.

The communication of employee benefits information improved significantly with passage of the Employee Retirement Income Security Act (ERISA) in 1974. The act requires that employees be informed about their pension and certain other benefits in a manner calculated to be understood by the average employee. A widely used method of communication is in-house publications, including employee benefits handbooks and organization newsletters. To ensure that employees are familiar with the benefits program, managers should be allowed sufficient time in new-hire orientation and other training classes to present information regarding benefits and to answer questions.

In addition to having general information, it is important for each employee to have a current statement of the status of her or his benefits. The usual means is the personalized computer-generated statement of benefits. As Highlights in HRM 1 shows, this statement prepared by Godwins Booke & Dickenson can be one of the best ways of slicing through a maze of benefit technicalities to provide concise data to employees about the status of their personal benefits.[5]

Coopers & Lybrand offers a Benefits Information Line that allows employers to provide employees with instant access to a wide variety of benefits and HR information from any touch-tone telephone. Individual account information is available upon entering a personal identification number. Some employers summarize benefit information on a paycheck stub as a reminder to employees of their total compensation.

Computerized data also enable management to keep accurate records of the cost of each benefit. To assist employers with the administrative and communication functions, the International Foundation of Employee Benefit Plans in Brookfield, Wisconsin, maintains an extensive library of employee benefits publications. It also prepares publications on this subject. The foundation has an on-line database that members can use to get immediate, comprehensive responses to questions about employee benefits. In cooperation with the Wharton School at the University of Pennsylvania and with Dalhousie University in Canada, the foundation offers a college-level program leading to the Certified Employee Benefit Specialist (CEBS) designation.[6]

Concerns of Management

Managing an employee benefits program requires close attention to the many forces that must be kept in balance if the program is to succeed. Management must consider union demands, the benefits other employers are offering, tax consequences, rising costs, and legal ramifications. We will briefly examine the last two concerns.

HIGHLIGHTS IN HRM

1 A PERSONALIZED STATEMENT OF BENEFITS

Highlights of Your Neles-Jamesbury, Inc. Benefits Program

This report is based on various Company records as of January 1, 1990. Please notify Human Resources if any of the following data is incorrect:

Date of Birth: 1/16/51
Date of Hire: 12/12/83
Social Security Number: 123-45-6789

Individually prepared for:

J. J. DOE
NELES-JAMESBURY
640 LINCOLN STREET
WORCESTER, MA   01615

Dear Neles-Jamesbury Employee:

It is our pleasure to provide you with this personalized 1990 statement of benefits.

Neles-Jamesbury's benefit plans are an important part of your total compensation. They help provide for the financial security of you and your family both now and in the future.

After reading this statement, we hope you will better understand and appreciate the importance of your benefits package, and that you will share this information with your family.

You are an important part of Neles-Jamesbury. Our benefits program is just one more way in which we can express our appreciation for your continuing contributions toward the goals of our company.

Sincerely,

Daniel L. DeSantis
President and Chief Executive Officer

Health Care

Hospital Benefits
All of our medical plans pay the following benefits for you and your family:

100% of eligible expenses for semi-private room and board, hospital expenses and covered physicians' services.

100% of eligible maternity benefits including covered physicians' services for normal delivery, Caesarian section, or miscarriage.

Please consult your medical plan comparison booklet for more details on the Health Care options available to you and the services they provide.

After retirement, at age 65, you may choose personal coverage for yourself under Medex III or the Fallon Senior Plan.

Non-Hospital Benefits
100% of eligible office visits, laboratory, and x-ray services, minus $2 to $5 co-pay charges.

100% of eligible outpatient psychiatric services, minus $2 to $5 co-pay charges up to a maximum of $500 per person per calendar year.

100% of eligible therapy visits, minus $2 to $25 co-pay charges.

100% of eligible prescription drugs, minus $1 to $4 co-pay charges.

YOU HAVE FAMILY COVERAGE
WITH BLUE CROSS/BLUE SHIELD.

Dental Insurance
The Plan pays 70% of expenses for covered services up to a $750 calendar year maximum for employees.

Survivors' Security

Lump Sum Benefits
In the event of your death while an active employee, your beneficiaries may receive the following payments:

$50,000 Basic Group Life Insurance
N/A Supplemental Life Insurance
$13,855 Thrift-Investment Plan
$255 Social Security for an eligible dependent

In addition, if death were due to an accident, your beneficiaries might also receive:

$50,000 Basic Accident Insurance
N/A Supplemental Accident Insurance

If death should occur as a result of an accident while traveling on Company business, your survivors may also receive an additional amount of Business Travel Accident Insurance.

Are your beneficiary designations up to date?

Monthly Income Payments
Social Security survivors' benefits are payable to unmarried dependent children under 18, surviving spouses caring for children under 16, and widows or widowers over age 60. Presently, these benefits are estimated to be:

$682 for each eligible child under 18
$682 for a spouse caring for children under 16
$650 for a spouse, age 60
$1,592 is the maximum monthly benefit per family

Post Retirement Benefits
After you retire from the Company, $2,000 of Life Insurance Coverage is continued at no cost to you.

Dependent Life and Accident Insurance

YOU HAVE $50,000 LIFE COVERAGE
FOR YOUR SPOUSE.

IF YOU PURCHASE SUPPLEMENTAL ACCIDENT IN-
SURANCE, YOU MAY ALSO INSURE YOUR SPOUSE
AND CHILDREN BY ELECTING THE FAMILY PLAN.

Sickness and Disability Benefits

Short Term Disability

IF YOU ARE ILL OR INJURED AND UNABLE TO WORK, YOU ARE ELIGIBLE FOR FULL PAY FOR UP TO 13 WEEKS. IF YOU ARE STILL UNABLE TO WORK AFTER 13 WEEKS, YOU WILL BE PAID 75% OF YOUR REGULAR PAY FOR UP TO 13 ADDITIONAL WEEKS.

Long Term Disability

If you remain disabled beyond 26 weeks, you will be eligible to receive $2,777 monthly from the Long Term Disability Plan until you are able to return to work in some capacity or to age 65, whichever occurs first.

This benefit would be reduced by the amount of other sources of income for which you are eligible such as Social Security.

In the event of your total disability you would be eligible to receive the balance of your Thrift-Investment Account in a lump sum.

Employee Thrift-Investment Plan

You are eligible to participate in the Thrift-Investment Plan on the first day of the month following your date of employment.

You may elect to contribute from 1%–15% of your base pay to the Thrift-Investment Plan allowing you to save for your short or long term goals.

Tax Savings Account

Contributions to the Tax Savings Account are limited to 1%–12% of your base pay and are made with pre-tax dollars. These contributions will reduce your current taxable income while providing for long term savings. (Withdrawals from this account are not allowed until age 59½.)

Thrift Account

Contributions to the Thrift Account are limited to 1%–12% of your base pay and are made with after-tax dollars. Withdrawals from this account can be made at the end of any quarter. Distribution takes place approximately 6 to 8 weeks after the end of each quarter.

Matching Company Contributions

The Company adds $.50 to your account for every $1 you save up to the first 6% of your pay.

As of January 1, 1990 $13,855 is the value of your Thrift-Investment Account.

Please refer to your quarterly Thrift-Investment statements for a more detailed explanation of your account.

Your Future Security

Projected Retirement Income

Your Normal Retirement Date (at age 65) is   02/01/2016.

At that time, based on your current salary and assuming continuous service until retirement, you would be eligible for an estimated monthly income of:

$3,394	from the Retirement Plan
$850	from Social Security
$4,244	estimated total monthly retirement income at age 65

If you choose to retire earlier (at age 62) we estimate the following payments:

$2,279	from the Retirement Plan
$877	from Social Security
$3,156	estimated total monthly retirement income at age 62

Vesting

Effective December 1, 1989, participants in the Retirement Plan will become vested after 5 years of service. Prior to this amendment, the service requirement for vesting was ten years.

Social Security

In addition to your benefit shown to the left, your spouse may also qualify for monthly Social Security based on either his or her own working career, or for being your dependent. This estimated benefit would be $425 starting at age 65.

Employee Thrift-Investment Plan

If you are a participant in the Thrift-Investment Plan, you may receive your account balance at retirement in either a lump sum or installments. If you elect the installment method, we will assist you in arranging a tax-deferred annuity.

Your Benefits Cost

In addition to the benefits described above, there are other valuable benefits you enjoy as an employee of Neles-Jamesbury, such as paid Vacation and Holidays, Sick/Emergency pay, Bereavement pay, Workers' Compensation, Unemployment Insurance, Bonus Plan, Tuition Reimbursement/Advancement, and Recreational programs.

You and your family have available the security and protection provided by the benefits described above:

$13,544	is the total estimated annual cost of your benefits program.
$2,270	is your cost including $2,088 for Social Security.
$11,274	is the balance paid by Neles-Jamesbury to provide these benefits.

Note: The complete statement also includes the following sections: Important Retirement Information, Financial Planner, Determination of Net Worth, and explanatory comments about the benefits statement.

Source: Godwins Booke & Dickenson. Reproduced with permission.

Rising Costs

According to a 1994 U.S. Chamber of Commerce study of 1,057 companies, the costs of employee benefits in that year averaged 41.3 percent of payroll, as shown in Figure 12–1. The average distribution of these benefits was $14,807 per employee per year. Costs of benefits were higher in manufacturing than in nonmanufacturing industries. Study Figure 12–1 to obtain an overview of the types of benefits to be discussed in this chapter.[7]

Since many benefits represent a fixed rather than a variable cost, management must decide whether or not it can afford this cost under less favorable economic conditions. If an organization is forced to discontinue a benefit, the negative effects of cutting it may outweigh any positive effects that may have accrued from providing it.

To minimize negative effects and avoid unnecessary expense, many employers enlist the cooperation of employees in evaluating the importance of particular benefits. Increasingly, employers are requiring employees to pay part of the costs of certain benefits, especially medical coverage. At all times, benefit plan administrators are expected to select vendors of benefit services who have the most to offer for the cost.

Besides the actual costs of employee benefits, there are costs of administering them. The federal reporting requirements under ERISA require a considerable amount of paperwork for employers. In addition, new requirements, such as those mandated by the *Consolidated Omnibus Budget Reconciliation Act of 1986* (COBRA), now require employers to make health coverage—at the same rate

---

FIGURE 12-1 *Employee Benefits, by Type of Benefit*

TYPE OF BENEFIT	TOTAL, ALL COMPANIES	TOTAL, ALL MANU-FACTURING	TOTAL, ALL NONMANU-FACTURING
Total employee benefits as percent of payroll	41.3	40.3	41.7
1. Legally required payments (employer's share only)	8.7	9.2	8.6
a. Old-Age, Survivors, Disability, and Health Insurance (employer FICA taxes) and Railroad Retirement Tax	6.9	6.8	6.9
b. Unemployment compensation	0.6	0.8	0.6
c. Workers' compensation (including estimated cost ot self-insured)	1.2	1.5	1.0
d. State sickness benefit insurance	0.0	0.0	0.0
2. Retirement and savings plan payments (employer's share only)	6.6	5.2	7.1
a. Defined benefit pension plan contributions	3.1	1.5	3.7
b. Defined contribution plan payments (401K type)	1.8	1.8	1.8
c. Profit sharing	0.4	0.7	0.3
d. Stock bonus and employee stock ownership plans (ESOP)	0.3	0.6	0.2
e. Pension plan premiums (net) under insurance and annuity contracts (insured and trusted)	0.4	0.0	0.6
f. Administrative and other costs	0.6	0.6	0.6
3. Life insurance and death benefit payments (employer's share only)	0.6	0.8	0.5

TYPE OF BENEFIT	TOTAL, ALL COMPANIES	TOTAL, ALL MANU- FACTURING	TOTAL, ALL NONMANU- FACTURING
4. Medical & medically related benefit payments (employer's share only)	11.1	11.3	11.1
a. Hospital, surgical, medical, and major medical insurance premiums (net)	8.0	8.4	7.8
b. Retiree (payments for retired employees) hospital, surgical, medical, and major medical insurance premiums (net)	1.4	1.4	1.4
c. Short-term disability, sickness or accident insurance (company plan or insured plan)	0.4	0.3	0.5
d. Long-term disability or wage continuation (insured, self-administered, or trusts)	0.2	0.1	0.2
e. Dental insurance premiums	0.5	0.6	0.5
f. Other (vision care, physical and mental fitness benefits for former employees)	0.6	0.5	0.6
5. Paid rest periods, coffee breaks, lunch periods, wash-up time, travel time, clothes-change time, get ready time, etc.	2.3	2.0	2.4
6. Payments for time not worked	10.4	10.4	10.4
a. Payment for or in lieu of vacations	5.6	6.1	5.5
b. Payment for or in lieu of holidays	3.1	3.1	3.1
c. Sick leave pay	1.3	0.8	1.4
d. Parental leave (maternity and paternity leave payments)	0.0	0.0	0.0
e. Other	0.4	0.4	0.4
7. Miscellaneous benefit payments	1.6	1.6	1.6
a. Discounts on goods and services purchased from company by employees	0.2	0.1	0.3
b. Employee meals furnished by company	1.1	0.0	0.1
c. Employee education expenditures	0.2	0.2	0.3
d. Child care	0.0	0.0	0.0
e. Other	1.0	1.3	0.9
Total employee benefits as cents per hour	715.7	748.7	704.8
Total employee benefits as dollars per year per employee	$14,807	$15,839	$14,476

Source: Reprinted, with permission, from the Chamber of Commerce of the United States, from the 1994 edition of *Employee Benefits. Employee Benefits* may be ordered from the Chamber by calling 1-800-638-6582.

the employer would pay—available to employees, their spouses, and their dependents upon termination of employment, death, or divorce.[8] Thus former employees and their families benefit by paying a lower premium for health coverage than is available to individual policyholders. While the former employee pays the premiums, employers have to establish procedures to collect premiums and to keep track of former employees and their dependents.

The cost of health care benefits is a concern to all employers. Private health insurance premiums increase every year. Saving money on health care is important, but employers must be careful to recognize the importance of health care plans to their workers. According to one consultant, "Employees are willing to go on strike rather than have their health benefits reduced."

Legal Concerns

Benefits can become a source of union grievances, employee complaints, even legal actions. Food services, parking, and similar facilities can become a magnet for complaints. An extreme example may be lawsuits by employees over injuries in organization-sponsored recreational activities and during or following organizational social functions where alcohol is served.

three
objective

Employee Benefits Required by Law

Legally required employee benefits constitute nearly a quarter of the benefits package that employers provide. These benefits include employer contributions to Social Security, unemployment insurance, workers' compensation insurance, and state disability insurance. We will discuss all but the last of these benefits.

Social Security Insurance

Passed in 1935, the Social Security Act provides an insurance plan designed to protect covered individuals against loss of earnings resulting from various causes. These causes may include retirement, unemployment, disability, or, in the case of dependents, the death of the worker supporting them. Thus, as with any type of casualty insurance, Social Security does not pay off except in the case where a loss of income is actually incurred through loss of employment.

To be eligible for old-age and survivors' insurance (OASI) as well as disability and unemployment insurance under the Social Security Act, an individual must have been engaged in employment covered by the act. Most employment in private enterprise, most types of self-employment, active military service after 1956, and employment in certain nonprofit organizations and governmental agencies are subject to coverage under the act.[9] Railroad workers and civil service employees who are covered by their own systems and some occupational groups, under certain conditions, are exempted from the act.[10]

The Social Security program is supported by means of a tax levied against an employee's earnings that must be matched by the employer in each pay period. The tax revenues are used to pay three major types of benefits: (1) old-age insurance benefits, (2) disability benefits, and (3) survivors' insurance benefits. Because of the continual changes that result from legislation and administrative rulings, as well as the complexities of making determinations of an individual's rights under Social Security, we will describe these benefits only in general terms.

To qualify for old-age insurance benefits, a person must have reached retirement age and be fully insured. A *fully insured person* has earned forty credits—a maximum of four credits a year for ten years, based on annual earnings of $2,360 (a figure adjusted annually) or more. Having enough credits to be fully insured makes one eligible for retirement benefits, but it does not determine the amount. The amount of monthly Social Security retirement benefits is based on earnings, adjusted for inflation, over the years an individual is covered by Social Security.[11]

To receive old-age insurance benefits, covered individuals must also meet the *retirement earnings test*. Persons under 70 years of age cannot be earning more than the established annual exempt amount through gainful employment without a reduction in benefits. This limitation on earnings does not include income from sources other than gainful employment, such as investments or pensions.

Social Security retirement benefits consist of those benefits that individuals are entitled to receive in their own behalf, called the primary insurance amount, plus supplemental benefits for eligible dependents. There are also both minimum and maximum limits to the amount that individuals and their dependents can receive.

The Social Security program provides disability benefits to workers too severely disabled to engage in "substantial gainful work." To be eligible for such benefits, however, an individual's disability must have existed for at least six months and must be expected to continue for at least twelve months or be expected to result in death. After receiving disability payments for twenty-four months, a disabled person receives Medicare protection. Those eligible for disability benefits, furthermore, must have worked under Social Security long enough and recently enough before becoming disabled. Disability benefits, which include auxiliary benefits for dependents, are computed on the same basis as retirement benefits and are converted to retirement benefits when the individual reaches the age of 65.

Survivors' insurance benefits represent a form of life insurance paid to members of a deceased person's family who meet the eligibility requirements. As with life insurance, the benefits that the survivors of a covered individual receive may greatly exceed their cost to this individual. Survivors' benefits can be paid only if the deceased worker had credit for a certain amount of time spent in work covered by Social Security. The exact amount of work credit needed depends on the worker's age at death. Generally, older workers need more years of Social Security work credit than younger workers, but never more than forty credits. As with other benefits discussed earlier, the *amount* of benefit survivors receive is based on the worker's lifetime earnings in work covered by Social Security.

The United States has agreements with fourteen other countries to coordinate Social Security protection for people who work or have worked in those countries as well as in the United States. It helps those who, without an agreement, would not be eligible for Social Security benefits in one or both countries. It also helps people who would otherwise have to pay Social Security taxes to both countries on the same earnings. The agreements eliminate the double coverage so that taxes are paid to only one system. Agreements cover Social Security taxes and retirement, disability, and survivor insurance benefits. They do not cover benefits under the U.S. Medicare program or the Supplemental Security Income (SSI) Program.[12]

Unemployment Insurance

Employees who have been working in employment covered by the Social Security Act and who are laid off may be eligible for up to twenty-six weeks of unemployment insurance benefits during their unemployment. Eligible persons must submit an application for unemployment compensation with their state employment agency, register for available work, and be willing to accept any suitable employment that may be offered to them. However, the term "suitable" gives individuals considerable discretion in accepting or rejecting job offers.

The amount of compensation that workers are eligible to receive, which varies among states, is determined by their previous wage rate and previous period of employment. Funds for unemployment compensation are derived from a federal payroll tax based on the wages paid to each employee, up to an established maximum. The major portion of this tax is refunded to the individual states, which in turn operate their unemployment compensation programs in accordance with minimum standards prescribed by the federal government.

Workers' Compensation Insurance

Both state and federal **workers' compensation insurance** is based on the theory that the cost of work-related accidents and illnesses should be considered one of the costs of doing business and should ultimately be passed on to the consumer. Individual employees should not be required to bear the cost of their treatment or loss of income, nor should they be subjected to complicated, delaying, and expensive legal procedures.

In all states, except New Jersey, South Carolina, and Texas, workers' compensation insurance is compulsory. When compulsory, every employer subject to it is required to comply with the law's provisions for the compensation of work-related injuries. The law is compulsory for the employee also. In the three states where it is elective, employers have the option of either accepting or rejecting the law. If they reject it, and suits are filed against them, they lose the customary common-law defenses: (1) assumed risk of employment, (2) negligence of a fellow employee, and (3) contributory negligence.[13]

Three methods of providing for workers' compensation coverage are commonly used. One method is for the state to operate an insurance system that employers may join—in some states, are *required* to join. A second method is for the states to permit employers to insure with private companies. Third, in some states, employers may be certified by the commission handling workers' compensation to handle their own coverage without any type of insurance.

Workers' compensation laws typically provide that employees will be paid a disability benefit based on a percentage of their wages. Each state also specifies the length of the period of payment and usually indicates a maximum amount that may be paid. Benefits, which vary from state to state, are generally provided for four types of disability: (1) permanent partial disability, (2) permanent total disability, (3) temporary partial disability, and (4) temporary total disability.[14] Disabilities may result from injuries or accidents, as well as from occupational diseases such as black lung, radiation illness, and asbestosis. Before any workers' compensation claim will be allowed, though, the work relatedness of the disability must be established. Also, the evaluation of the claimant by a physician trained in occupational medicine is an essential part of the claim process.

In addition to the disability benefits, provision is made for payment of medical and hospitalization expenses up to certain limits, and in all states, death benefits are paid to survivors of the employee. Commissions are established to resolve claims at little or no legal expense to the claimant.

Workers' compensation costs have skyrocketed to the point where some employers say they have laid off or postponed new hiring and expansion specifically because of "comp costs." The average cost of a compensation claim tripled in the period from 1982 to 1992. More recently, the direct cost of claims to U.S. businesses has been around $70 billion annually. A *Fortune* 500 company can easily pay out $50 million to $100 million a year in comp claims. Swelling medical costs and benefits paid to workers are the major factors. In addition, there are more disorders today that are harder to assess objectively, such as back pain. Then too, claims are sometimes made for ailments that may have little to do with the workplace, such as hearing loss, stress, and cancer.[15]

Insurance companies are making every effort to cut workers' comp costs. Travelers, for example, hired more compensation claims employees in order to reduce caseloads. They also added several hundred nurses to review claims. Orion Capital employs nurses, attorneys, and investigators to determine whether a prospective client—i.e., an employer—is committed to reducing costs. Continental Insurance uses ergonomists (see Chapter 4) to review tasks at businesses it insures and recommend changes to reduce work-related injuries. Efforts to reduce the fraudulent cases, which are estimated to compose 20 percent of all claims, have also increased.[16]

Steps that the HR department can take to control workers' comp costs include the following:

1. Perform an audit to assess high-risk areas within a workplace.
2. Prevent injuries by proper ergonomic design of the job, effective assessment of job candidates, and worker training.
3. Provide quality medical care to injured employees by physicians with experience and preferably with training in occupational health.
4. Reduce litigation by effective communication between the employer and the injured worker.
5. Manage the care of an injured worker from time of injury until return to work. Keep a partially recovered employee at the worksite.[17]

To this point the discussion has focused on what is important to the employer and the insurance carrier. Managers and HR staff personnel should recognize that a workplace injury presents several problems to the injured worker—medical, financial, insurance, and employment security, and possibly legal problems. Injured employees are likely to feel isolated, and complain when they receive insufficient information about their rights and obligations. Coworkers and supervisors often fail to understand that many disabilities, such as back pain, do not show. There is also a tendency to "blame the victim." This can range from simple accusations of malingering, laziness, or dishonesty to suggestions of a mental disorder. An important step in developing a smoothly functioning system for comp cases is for managers and professionals to consider the perspective of the injured worker and to provide the information and assistance needed in a positive, supportive manner.[18]

Leaves without Pay

Most employers grant leaves of absence to their employees for personal reasons. These leaves are usually taken without pay, but also without loss of seniority or benefits. An unpaid leave may be granted for a variety of reasons, including extended illness, illness in the family, pregnancy, the birth or adoption of a child, educational or political activities, and social service activities.

As growing numbers of women entered the workforce and remained there after having children, the issue of leaves became increasingly important. Several states granted pregnant employees preferential treatment, while other states enacted laws mandating that employees be given leaves for any type of disability. Other states have enacted laws that require employers to grant leaves for paternity, child adoption, or serious illness in the family.[19] The *Family and Medical Leave Act (FMLA)* was passed and became effective on August 5, 1993.[20] The federal legislation preempts state laws only if the state law is less generous to employees. More generous state requirements remain intact.

The FMLA applies to employers having fifty or more employees during twenty or more calendar workweeks in the current or preceding year. It requires the employer to provide up to twelve weeks of unpaid, job-protected leave to eligible employees for certain family and medical reasons. The specific reasons for taking leave are listed on the federally required poster reproduced in Highlights in HRM 2. In studying the poster, note the other important stipulations, such as enforcement and unlawful acts, which are of direct concern to managers.

Like many laws pertaining to HRM, the FMLA is simple in principle but requires revising policies and procedures for compliance. This law affects an organization's benefits program in several of its provisions: It mandates continuation of medical coverage, it prohibits loss of accrued benefits, it provides for restoration of benefits after leave, it permits substitution of paid leave and vacation during leave, it makes communication and notice compulsory, and it prohibits waiver of benefits.[21]

It is apparent that employees as a group will benefit from FMLA at critical times in their lives. Supporters say that it will especially help today's "sandwich generation"—baby boomers born from 1946 to 1964—as they enter middle age and rear children while simultaneously caring for aging parents.[22] Temporary-help firms expect to profit from FLMA by providing workers to fill in for permanent employees who take time off to care for relatives. The temp agencies are prepared to provide temporary managers and executives as well as clerical help.[23]

Discretionary Major Employee Benefits

Employee benefits may be categorized in different ways. In Figure 12–1 we saw the categories of benefits that have been used by the U.S. Chamber of Commerce in studies of benefits since 1951. In the discussion that follows, we will use a somewhat different but compatible grouping of benefits to highlight the important issues and trends in managing an employee benefits program.

Health Care Benefits

The benefits that receive the most attention from employers today because of sharply rising costs and employee concern are health care benefits. In the past, health insurance plans covered only medical, surgical, and hospital expenses. Today employers are under pressure to include prescription drugs as well as dental, optical, and mental health care benefits in the package they offer their workers.

....

HIGHLIGHTS IN HRM

highlights

2   "YOUR RIGHTS": ANOTHER FEDERALLY REQUIRED POSTER

Your Rights
Under The
Family and Medical Leave Act of 1993

FMLA requires covered employers to provide up to 12 weeks of unpaid, job-protected leave to "eligible" employees for certain family and medical reasons. Employees are eligible if they have worked for a covered employer for at least one year, and for 1,250 hours over the previous 12 months, and if there are at least 50 employees within 75 miles.

Reasons For Taking Leave:

Unpaid leave must be granted for *any* of the following reasons:

- to care for the employee's child after birth, or placement for adoption or foster care;
- to care for the employee's spouse, son or daughter, or parent, who has a serious health condition; or
- for a serious health condition that makes the employee unable to perform the employee's job.

At the employee's or employer's option, certain kinds of *paid leave* may be substituted for unpaid leave.

Advance Notice and Medical Certification:

The employee may be required to provide advance leave notice and medical certification. Taking of leave may be denied if requirements are not met.

- The employee ordinarily must provide 30 days advance notice when the leave is "foreseeable."
- An employer may require medical certification to support a request for leave because of a serious health condition, and may require second or third opinions (at the employer's expense) and a fitness for duty report to return to work.

Job Benefits and Protection:

- For the duration of FMLA leave, the employer must maintain the employee's health coverage under any "group health plan."

- Upon return from FMLA leave, most employees must be restored to their original or equivalent positions with equivalent pay, benefits, and other employment terms.
- The use of FMLA leave cannot result in the loss of any employment benefit that accrued prior to the start of an employee's leave.

Unlawful Acts By Employers:

FMLA makes it unlawful for any employer to:

- interfere with, restrain, or deny the exercise of any right provided under FMLA;
- discharge or discriminate against any person for opposing any practice made unlawful by FMLA or for involvement in any proceeding under or relating to FMLA.

Enforcement:

- The U.S. Department of Labor is authorized to investigate and resolve complaints of violations.
- An eligible employee may bring a civil action against an employer for violations.

FMLA does not affect any Federal or State law prohibiting discrimination, or supersede any State or local law or collective bargaining agreement which provides greater family or medical leave rights.

For Additional Information:

Contact the nearest office of the Wage and Hour Division, listed in most telephone directories under U.S. Government, Department of Labor.

U.S. Department of Labor
Employment Standards Administration
Wage and Hour Division
Washington, D.C. 20210

WH Publication 1420
June 1993

GPO : 1993 O – 355-556

Note: Other federally required posters are reproduced in Chapters 3, 6, 10, and 13.

Escalating Costs

According to a U.S. Chamber of Commerce study, medical and medically related benefit costs (employer's share) average 11.1 percent of payroll costs. The Chamber reports that from 1980 to 1993 the employer cost of providing medical and dental insurance increased by 254 percent. The main reason for the increase is that the cost of medical care has risen more than twice the increase in CPI for all items. Health insurance premiums paid by employers increased more than 50 percent faster than medical care costs, compounding the problems facing employers.[24]

The growth in health care costs is attributed to a number of factors, including federal legislation, changes in Medicare pricing, the greater need for health care by an aging population, the costs of technological advances in medicine, skyrocketing malpractice insurance rates, rising costs of health care labor, and overuse of costly health care services.

objective

Cost Containment

The approaches used to contain the costs of health care benefits include reductions in coverage, increased deductibles or copayments, and increased coordination of benefits to make sure the same expense is not paid by more than one insurance reimbursement. Other cost-containment efforts involve alternatives to traditional medical care: the use of health maintenance organizations and preferred providers, incentives for outpatient surgery and testing, and mandatory second opinions for surgical procedures. Employee assistance programs and wellness programs may also allow an organization to cut the costs of its health care benefits.

Health maintenance organizations (HMOs) are organizations of physicians and other health care professionals that provide a wide range of services to subscribers and their dependents on a prepaid basis. As a result of the federal HMO Act of 1973, most employers with health insurance plans must offer an HMO as a voluntary option. At first HMO premiums were higher than traditional plans, but traditional medical insurance premiums have increased so much that HMOs are now used as a way to contain the costs of employee health care. Because they must provide all covered services for a fixed dollar amount, HMOs generally emphasize preventive care and early intervention. Most of the approximately 700 HMOs in the United States are patterned after the one first established in California by industrialist Henry Kaiser, which bears his name.

Preferred provider organizations have also helped to contain costs. The **preferred provider organization (PPO)** is a hospital or group of physicians who establish an organization that guarantees lower costs to the employer. The employer reciprocates by steering workers to the PPO. In an effort to have more control over medical costs, many insurance companies have become active in organizing PPOs. Since employees and the federal government will continue to push for improved health care, employers will find it necessary to have an active program for cost containment.[25]

Health maintenance organizations (HMOs)
Organizations of physicians and health care professionals that provide a wide range of services to subscribers and dependents on a prepaid basis

Preferred provider organization (PPO)
A hospital or group of physicians who establish an organization that guarantees lower health care costs to the employer

"You'll hate it here. The pay is low, conditions are fairly chaotic, and I myself am quite impossible. Nevertheless, we have a pretty good dental plan."

Reprinted with permission of J. B. Handelsman and the *Harvard Business Review*.

Other Health Benefits

Dental care insurance as an employee benefit has grown very rapidly in the past two decades. Dental plans are designed to help pay for dental care costs and to encourage employees to receive regular dental attention. Like medical plans, dental care plans may be operated by insurance companies, dental service corporations, those administering Blue Cross/Blue Shield plans, HMOs, and groups of dental care providers. Typically, the insurance pays a portion of the charges, and the subscriber pays the remainder.

Optical care insurance is another, relatively new benefit that many employers are offering. Coverage can include visual examinations and a percentage of the costs of lenses and frames.

Payment for Time Not Worked

The "payment for time not worked" category of benefits includes paid vacations, bonuses given in lieu of paid vacations, payments for holidays not worked, paid sick leave, military and jury duty, and payments for absence due to a death in the family or other personal reasons.[26] As Figure 12–1 showed, these benefits account for the largest portion of payroll costs—10.4 percent.

Vacations with Pay

It is generally agreed that vacations are essential to the well-being of an employee. Eligibility for vacations varies by industry, locale, and organization size. To qualify for longer vacations of three, four, or five weeks, one may expect to work for seven, fifteen, and twenty years, respectively.

As shown in Figure 12–2, European professional and managerial personnel tend to receive more vacation time than do their U.S., Canadian, and Japanese counterparts. Although most countries have government mandates for employers to guarantee vacation time to workers, the United States and United Kingdom do not.

Paid Holidays

Both hourly and salaried workers can usually expect to be paid for ten holidays a year. The type of business tends to influence both the number and observance of holidays. Virtually all employers in the United States, however, observe and pay their employees for New Year's Day, Memorial Day, Independence Day, Labor Day, Thanksgiving Day, and Christmas Day. Many employers give workers an additional two or three personal days off.

Sick Leave

There are several ways in which employees may be compensated during periods when they are unable to work because of illness or injury. Most public employees, as well as many in private firms, particularly in white-collar jobs, receive a set

FIGURE 12-2 Vacation Days: A Global Look

COUNTRY	LEGAL MINIMUM	TYPICAL PRACTICE	PUBLIC HOLIDAYS
Brazil	22	22	11
Canada	10	20	11
France	25	25–30	13
Germany	18	30–33	13
Hong Kong	7	20–30	17
Japan	19	20	14
Mexico	14	15–20	19
Sweden	30	30–32	10
United Kingdom	0	25–30	9
United States	0	20	10

Source: William M. Mercer, Inc. Reprinted with permission. Data are for professional and managerial personnel.

number of sick-leave days each year to cover such absences. Where permitted, sick leave that employees do not use can be accumulated to cover prolonged absences. Accumulated vacation leave may sometimes be used as a source of income when sick-leave benefits have been exhausted. Group insurance that provides income protection during a long-term disability is also becoming more common. As discussed earlier in the chapter, income lost during absences resulting from job-related injuries may be reimbursed, at least partially, through workers' compensation insurance.

Severance Pay

A one-time payment is sometimes given to employees who are being terminated. Known as *severance pay*, it may cover only a few days' wages or wages for several months, usually depending on the employee's length of service. Employers that are downsizing often use severance pay as a means of lessening the negative effects of unexpected termination on employees.

Supplemental Unemployment Benefits

Supplemental unemployment benefits (SUBs)

A plan that enables an employee who is laid off to draw, in addition to state unemployment compensation, weekly benefits from the employer that are paid from a fund created for this purpose

While *not* required by law, in some industries unemployment compensation is augmented by **supplemental unemployment benefits (SUBs),** which are financed by the employer. These plans enable an employee who is laid off to draw, in addition to state unemployment compensation, weekly benefits from the employer that are paid from a fund created for this purpose. Many SUB plans in recent years have been liberalized to permit employees to receive weekly benefits when the length of their workweek is reduced and to receive a lump-sum payment if their employment is terminated permanently. The amount of benefits is determined by length of service and wage rate. Employer liability under the plan is limited to the amount of money accumulated within the fund from employer contributions based on the total hours of work performed by employees.

Life Insurance

One of the oldest and most popular employee benefits is group term life insurance, which provides death benefits to beneficiaries and may also provide accidental death and dismemberment benefits. It is nearly universal in the United States, with over $4.24 trillion worth of employee and dependent coverage under group life insurance in force at the end of 1992. Group protection amounted to forty percent of life insurance in force in the United States at the end of 1992.[27]

objective

Retirement Programs

Retirement is an important part of life and requires sufficient and careful preparation. In convincing job applicants that theirs is a good organization to work for, employers usually emphasize the retirement benefits that can be expected after a certain number of years of employment. As we observed earlier in the chapter, each employee is typically given a annual personalized statement of benefits that contains information about projected retirement income from pensions, Social Security, and employee investment plans.

A fulfilling life after retirement requires careful planning.

Retirement Policies

Prior to 1979, employers were permitted to determine the age (usually 65) at which their employees would be required to retire. A 1978 amendment to the Age Discrimination in Employment Act of 1967 prohibited mandatory retirement under the age of 70 in private employment and at any age in federal employment. A 1986 amendment removed the ceiling age of 70 and prohibits age-based employment discrimination for *ages 40 and older.* Despite the law's provision for continued employment, there have not been an overwhelming number of older persons who remain on the job. In fact, a growing number of workers are retiring before age 65. Others choose partial retirement or work part-time for a period preceding complete retirement.

To avoid layoffs, particularly of more recently hired members of protected classes, and to reduce salary and benefit costs, employers often encourage early retirement. Encouragement comes in the form of increased pension benefits for several years or cash bonuses, sometimes referred to as the **silver handshake.** The cost of these retirement incentives can frequently be offset by the lower compensation paid to replacements and/or by a reduction in the workforce.

The major factors affecting the decision to retire early are the individual's personal financial condition and health and the extent to which he or she receives satisfaction from the work. Attractive pension benefits, possibilities of future layoffs, and inability to meet the demands of their jobs are also among the reasons workers choose to retire early.

Preretirement Programs

While most people eagerly anticipate retirement, many are bitterly disappointed once they reach this stage of life. Employers may offer preretirement planning programs to help make employees aware of the kinds of adjustments they may

Silver handshake
An early-retirement incentive in the form of increased pension benefits for several years or a cash bonus

need to make when they retire. These adjustments may include learning to live on a reduced, fixed income and having to cope with the problems of lost prestige, family problems, and idleness that retirement may create.

Preretirement programs typically include seminars and workshops that include lectures, videos, and printed materials. Topics covered include pension plans, health insurance coverage, Social Security and Medicare, personal financial planning, wellness and lifestyles, and adjustment to retirement. The numerous publications of the American Association of Retired Persons (AARP), including its popular magazine, *Modern Maturity,* are valuable sources of information.

The National Council on Aging has developed a retirement planning program for employers. Atlantic Richfield, Travelers Insurance, and Alcoa are among the more than seventy-five organizations using this program. In many communities, hospitals are developing resource centers for health and retirement planning. To help older workers get used to the idea of retirement, some organizations experiment with retirement rehearsal. Polaroid, for example, offers employees an opportunity to try out retirement through an unpaid three-month leave program. They also offer a program that permits employees to gradually cut their hours before retirement. Employees are paid only for hours worked, but they receive full medical insurance and prorated pension credits. Most experts agree that pre-retirement planning is a much-needed, cost-effective employee benefit.[28]

Pension Plans

Originally, pensions were based on a *reward philosophy,* which viewed pensions primarily as a way to retain personnel by rewarding them for staying with the organization until they retired. Those employees who quit or who were terminated before retirement were not considered deserving of such rewards. Because of the vesting requirements negotiated into most union contracts and more recently required by law, pensions are now based on an *earnings philosophy.* This philosophy regards a pension as deferred income that employees accumulate during their working lives and that belongs to them after a specified number of years of service, whether or not they remain with the employer until retirement.

Since the passage of the Social Security Act in 1935, pension plans have been used to supplement the floor of protection provided by Social Security. The majority of private pension plans and a significant number of public plans integrate their benefits with Social Security benefits.

The decision whether or not to offer a pension plan is up to the employer. In 1950, 25 percent of the nation's privately employed, full-time workers were covered by traditional employer-financed pension plans. Today 47 percent of the workforce is covered by traditional pensions, 401(k) plans, and other savings plans. There has been a decrease in the percentage of men with pension plans because of corporate downsizings and fewer unionized manufacturing jobs. However, because so many more women are working today, the share of women with their own coverage has increased greatly.[29]

Types of Pension Plans

There are two major ways to categorize pension plans: (1) according to contributions made by the employer and (2) according to the amount of pension benefits

Contributory plan

A pension plan where contributions are made jointly by employees and employers

Noncontributory plan

A pension plan where contributions are made solely by the employer

Defined-benefit plan

A pension plan in which the amount an employee is to receive upon retirement is specifically set forth

Defined- contribution plan

A pension plan that establishes the basis on which an employer will contribute to the pension fund

to be paid. In a **contributory plan,** contributions to a pension plan are made jointly by employees and employers. In a **noncontributory plan,** the contributions are made solely by the employer. Most of the plans existing in privately held organizations are noncontributory, whereas those in government are contributory plans.

When pension plans are classified by the amount of pension benefits to be paid, there are two basic types: the defined-benefit plan and the defined-contribution plan. Under a **defined-benefit plan,** the amount an employee is to receive upon retirement is specifically set forth. This amount is usually based on the employee's years of service, average earnings during a specific period of time, and age at time of retirement. While a variety of formulas exist for determining pension benefits, the one used most often is based on the employee's average earnings (usually over a three- to five-year period immediately preceding retirement), multiplied by the number of years of service with the organization. A deduction is then made for each year the retiree is under age 65. As noted earlier, pension benefits are usually integrated with Social Security benefits.

A **defined-contribution plan** establishes the basis on which an employer will contribute to the pension fund. The contributions may be made through profit sharing, thrift plans, matches of employee contributions, employer-sponsored Individual Retirement Accounts (IRAs), and various other means. The amount of benefits employees receive on retirement is determined by the funds accumulated in their account at the time of retirement and what retirement benefits (usually an annuity) these funds will purchase. These plans do not offer the benefit-security predictability of a defined-benefit plan. However, even under defined-benefit plans, retirees may not receive the benefits promised them if the plan is not adequately funded.

The use of traditional defined-benefit plans, with their fixed payouts, is in decline. Defined-benefit plans are less popular with employers because they cost more and because they require compliance with complicated government rules.[30] Some experts, however, believe that employers may want to consider returning to defined-benefit plans, which allow for flexibility in plan design such as opening paths for the advancement of younger employees while enabling older workers to retire.[31]

The most significant change in pension coverage is the tremendous growth of tax-deferred 401(k) savings plans, which are named after section 401(k) of the Internal Revenue Code. Today even small firms often offer 401(k) savings plans. Also known as the salary-reduction plan, the 401(k) plan allows employees to save through payroll deduction—and possibly to have their contributions matched by the employer. Employees' current taxable income is reduced by the amount of the contribution, and income taxes on these funds and their earnings are deferred until after retirement.[32] For the majority of such plans, full vesting comes within five years. Once vested, participants who leave the job can roll over their account into a qualified plan such as another employer's 401(k) plan or an Individual Retirement Account (IRA).[33] Highlights in HRM 3 shows how employees can increase their retirement savings using a 401(k) plan.

Federal Regulation of Pension Plans

Private pension plans are subject to federal regulation under the Employee Retirement Income Security Act (ERISA).[34] Although the act does not require em-

HIGHLIGHTS IN HRM

3   MAXIMIZING EMPLOYEE SAVINGS WITH A 401(K) PLAN

highlights

Getting the Most from Saving

The following example demonstrates how employees can maximize their savings with a 401(k) plan. The example assumes the employee is in a 25 percent tax bracket, saving $2,400 each year and earning 10 percent.

	Regular Savings Account	401(k) Plan
Savings	$ 2,400	$ 2,400
Income Tax	(600)	0
Balance to Save	1,800	2,400
10% Interest	180	240
Tax on Interest	(45)	0
Net Investment First Year	1,935	2,640
Accumulation in 20 Years	83,795	151,206*

*Annual savings of $2,400 plus interest.

401(k) funds accumulate tax free until withdrawn and may be eligible for favorable 5-year forward averaging.**

**At age 59.5, individuals may withdraw lump-sum contributions from their 401(k) plans, but the money is subject to taxes. However, IRS gives individuals a tax break by using the 5-year forward averaging formula. Instead of paying taxes for the lump-sum withdrawal, the IRS will average the lump-sum amount over a five-year period, therefore, reducing the taxable amount. Taxes are paid on one year's worth of the tax averaging. Taxes are paid in one year, but computed as if the money were received over a 5-year period.

Source: Donald K. Odermann, "Four Steps to a Successful 401(k) Plan," *HR Magazine* 36, no. 8 (August 1991): 44–46. Reproduced with permission.

ployers to establish a pension plan, it provides certain standards and controls for pension plans. It requires minimum funding standards to ensure that benefits will be available when an employee retires. It also requires that the soundness of the actuarial assumptions on which the funding is based be certified by an actuary at least every three years. Of special concern to the individual employee is the matter of vesting.

Vesting
A guarantee of accrued
benefits to participants
at retirement age,
regardless of their
employment status at
that time

Vesting is a guarantee of accrued benefits to participants at retirement age, regardless of their employment status at that time. Vested benefits that have been earned by an employee cannot be revoked by an employer. Under ERISA, all pension plans must provide that employees will have vested rights in their accrued benefits after certain minimum-years-of-service requirements have been met. However, employers can pay out a departing employee's vested benefits if the present value of the benefit is small.

Three government agencies administer ERISA: the Internal Revenue Service (IRS), the Department of Labor, and the Pension Benefit Guaranty Corporation (PBGC). The IRS is concerned primarily with qualified retirement plans—those that offer employers and employees favorable income tax treatment under a special section of the tax law. The Department of Labor's main responsibility is to protect participants' rights.

About 40 million of the 76 million covered workers have their pensions insured by the federal government's Pension Benefit Guaranty Corporation. Pensions in workplaces with fewer than twenty-five employees are not covered. The PBGC ensures that if a plan is terminated, guaranteed minimum benefits are paid to participants. The PBGC is supported by premiums paid by employers. It has become apparent, however, that employer contributions are inadequate to cover the increased use of Chapter 11 bankruptcy, which passes pension liabilities of firms on to the PBGC.

In 1984 the Retirement Equity Act (REA) amended ERISA.[35] REA is intended to provide greater equity under private pension plans for workers and their spouses by taking into account changes in work patterns, the status of marriage as an economic partnership, and the substantial contributions made by both spouses. All qualified pension plans are affected by the act, which brought major changes in eligibility and vesting provisions, parental leave, spouse survivor benefits, assignments of benefits in divorce cases, and other areas. If an employee declines to elect survivors' benefits, the employer is required to inform prospective beneficiaries of this fact. The Deficit Reduction Act of 1984 has had a significant impact on employee benefits, such as pension and group insurance plans, in determining what is taxable and nontaxable to employees.[36]

Pension Portability

A weakness in most traditional pension plans is that they lack the portability to enable employees who change employment to maintain equity in a single pension. Before ERISA, unions sought to address this problem by encouraging multiple-employer plans that covered the employees of two or more unrelated organizations in accordance with a collective bargaining agreement. Such plans are governed by employer and union representatives who constitute the plan's board of trustees. Multiple-employer plans tend to be found in industries where the typical company has too few employees to justify an individual plan. They are also found more frequently in industries where there is seasonal or irregular employment. Manufacturing industries where these plans exist include apparel, printing, furniture, leather, and metalworking. They are also used in such non-manufacturing industries as mining, construction, transport, entertainment, and private higher education.

Employees also have the opportunity to establish their own IRAs as a source of personal retirement benefits. Originally, Congress encouraged the use of IRAs by permitting an employee to shelter from income tax the amount contributed to an IRA, but the Tax Reform Act of 1986 curtailed or eliminated deductible IRA contributions for most employees covered by employer-sponsored pension plans.

Pension Funds

Pension funds may be administered through either a trusteed or an insured plan. In a trusteed pension plan, pension contributions are placed in a trust fund. The investment and administration of the fund are handled by trustees appointed by the employer or, if the employees are unionized, by either the employer or the union. Contributions to an insured pension plan are used to purchase insurance annuities. The responsibility for administering these funds rests with the insurance company providing the annuities.

Private and public pension funds constitute the largest pool of investment capital in the world, with over $4 trillion in assets. Still, one cannot be complacent about the future. Social Security will be stretched thin as baby boomers age, and some private pensions may be vulnerable to poorly performing investments. It should also be noted that the pension funds of some organizations are not adequate to cover their obligations.[37] Such deficiencies present legal and ethical problems that must be addressed.

Current pension fund difficulties have been caused in part by the fact that the wages on which pension benefits are based today drastically exceed the wages on which pension fund contributions were based in earlier years. Furthermore, those drawing pensions are living beyond the life expectancies on which their pension benefits were calculated.

While fund managers are supposed to invest funds where the return will be most profitable, employees often demand a greater voice in determining where pension funds will be invested. There is also a movement to have more pension funds diverted to investments that employees consider "socially desirable," such as in home mortgages, health centers, child care centers, hospitals, and similar investments in areas where members live. Any policy of investing in socially desirable projects must give consideration to the provisions of ERISA, which requires that fiduciaries (fund managers) act solely in the interest of the participants and beneficiaries for the exclusive purpose of providing benefits. The act does, however, permit a consideration of incidental features of investments, provided they are equal in economic terms.

Employee Services

objective

Employee services provided by employers are generally not included in the benefit cost data compiled by the U.S. Chamber of Commerce. However, services, like other benefits, also represent a cost to the employer. The utility that employees and employers derive from them, however, can far exceed their cost. In recent years new types of services are being offered to make life at work more rewarding and to enhance the well-being of employees.

**Employee
assistance
program (EAP)**

Service provided by
employers to help
workers cope with a
wide variety of problems
that interfere with
the way they perform
their jobs

Employee Assistance Programs

To help workers cope with a wide variety of problems that interfere with the way they perform their jobs, organizations have developed **employee assistance programs.** An employee assistance program (EAP) typically provides diagnosis, counseling, and referral for advice or treatment when necessary for problems related to alcohol or drug abuse, emotional difficulties, and financial or family difficulties. (EAPs will be discussed in detail in Chapter 13.) The main intent is to help employees solve their personal problems or at least to prevent problems from turning into crises that affect their ability to work productively. To handle crises, many EAPs offer twenty-four-hour hot lines.[38]

Counseling Services

An important part of an EAP is the counseling services it provides to employees. While most organizations expect managers to counsel subordinates, some employees may have problems that require the services of professional counselors. Most organizations refer such individuals to outside counseling services such as family counseling services, marriage counselors, and mental health clinics. Some organizations have a clinical psychologist, counselor, or comparable specialist on staff, to whom employees may be referred. The methods used by professionals to counsel employees will be described in detail in Chapter 15. Managers should not only understand these methods but should develop some proficiency in using them.

Educational Assistance Plans

One of the benefits most frequently mentioned in literature for employees is the educational assistance plan. The primary purpose of this plan is to help employees

A wide variety of
personal problems may
force employees to seek
counseling through
employee assistance
programs.

keep up to date with advances in their fields and to help them get ahead in the organization. Usually the employer covers the costs of tuition and fees, while the employee is required to pay for books, meals, transportation, and other expenses.

Child Care

The increased employment of women with dependent children has created an unprecedented demand for child care arrangements. In the past, working parents had to make their own arrangements with sitters or with nursery schools for pre-school children. Today benefits may include financial assistance, alternative work schedules, family leave, and on-site child care centers. On-site or near-site child centers are the most visible, prestigious, and desired solution.[39]

Hoffman-LaRoche has a center only one block from its Nutley, New Jersey, plant. The facility has several classrooms and uses innovative teaching methods. Among other companies that offer child care at the work site are Fel-Pro, Merck, Syntex, Baptist Hospital of Miami, and Ben & Jerry's Homemade Ice Cream.[40] According to Beth Wallace of B&J's, many employee-parents have expressed the importance of having their children near them with quality child care. B&J bases its fee schedules on family income, with a specified cap on the charges.[41]

The most common child care benefit offered by employers is the dependent-care spending account. With this account, a portion of a worker's pay before taxes is set aside for caring for a dependent. Child care is "the new benefit of the 1990s," according to the president of America West Airlines. "It is a critical need that companies that can afford it will meet because it is the right thing to do. Even companies that have limited means may be forced to support child care from a competitive standpoint, to attract, retain, and motivate personnel."[42]

Elder Care

Responsibility for the care of aging parents and other relatives is another fact of life for increasing numbers of employees. The term **elder care,** as used in the context of employment, refers to the circumstance where an employee provides care to an elderly relative while remaining actively at work. The majority of care-givers are women.

Many experts believe the worries and distractions caused by elder care can be more damaging to productivity than child care problems. It is estimated that caregivers typically are absent 1.5 times more often than other employees who do not have this responsibility. But only 43 percent of 1,026 employers surveyed by Hewitt Associates (benefits consultants in Lincolnshire, Illinois) offer elder care benefits compared with 74 percent offering some kind of child care assistance.[43]

Some of the organizations that were among the first to provide elder care assistance are Marriott Corporation, American Security Bank, Pepsi, Pitney Bowes, Florida Power & Light, and Mobil Corporation. Elder care counseling, educational fairs and seminars, and distribution of printed resource material are the types of assistance offered in their programs.[44] More recently employers have banded together for better elder care. The Partnership for Elder Care—a consortium of American Express Company, J. P. Morgan, and Philip Morris Company—and other companies use the resources of the New York City Department of

Aging, a public information and aging support agency. Corporate funding helps tailor programs to employee needs.

AT&T has given grants to community organizations to recruit, train, and manage elder care volunteers where its employees live and work. Travelers Corporation is part of a consortium of Connecticut employers that trains family care workers and shares with employees the cost of three days' in-home care for family emergencies.[45] Interest in and demand for elder care programs will increase dramatically when baby boomers are in their early fifties, when they will be managing organizations and experiencing elder care problems with their own parents.[46]

Other Services

The variety of benefits and services that employers offer today could not have been imagined a few years ago. Some are fairly standard, and we will cover them briefly. Some are unique and obviously grew out of specific concerns, needs, and interests. Among the more unique benefits are $3 haircuts at Worthington Industries, $2,000 for earning a college degree at H. B. Fuller, four tickets to every game for employees of the Los Angeles Dodgers, and unlimited paid sick leave at Leo Burnett and Syntex. These examples represent only a few of the possibilities for benefits that go beyond those typically offered.[47]

Food Services

Vending machines represent the most prevalent form of food service program (87 percent of organizations), with cafeterias second (57 percent), according to a survey of organizational subscribers to *Personnel Journal*. Coffee trucks and lunch wagons rank third (15 percent). A few companies—Hewitt Associates, J. P. Morgan, and Northwestern Mutual Life even provide a free lunch.[48] Most employers (81 percent) contract with an outside firm. Although $4.5 billion is spent on employee food service, only 51 percent of the organizations indicated that a manager was employed to oversee this function. The HR department manages the program in 43 percent of the organizations; in 32 percent of the organizations, it has the responsibility for one or more decisions in this area.[49]

The HR staff's participation in food service arrangements would appear to provide it with an excellent opportunity to upgrade the quality of food service. A major problem with vending machines is that they often do not include the most nutritious types of foods. Quality nutrition is a key component of an organization's wellness program, a topic to be discussed in the next chapter.

On-Site Health Services

Most of the larger organizations provide some form of on-site health services. The extent of these services varies considerably, but they are generally designed to handle minor illnesses and injuries. They may also include alcohol- and drug-abuse referral services, in-house counseling programs, and wellness clinics. We will discuss these and related programs in detail in the next chapter.

Legal Services

One of the fastest-growing employee benefits is the prepaid legal service plan. There are two general types: access plans and comprehensive plans. Access plans provide free telephone or office consultation, document review, and discounts on legal fees for more complex matters. Comprehensive plans cover other services such as representation in divorce cases, real estate transactions, and civil and criminal trials.

Financial Planning

One of the newer benefits is financial planning. As yet offered primarily to executives and middle-level managers, it is likely to become available to more employees through flexible benefits programs. Such programs cover investments, tax planning and management, estate planning, and related topics.

Housing and Moving Expenses

The days of "company houses" are now past, except in mining or logging operations, construction projects in remote areas, and the armed forces. However, a variety of housing services is usually provided in nearly all organizations that move employees from one office or plant to another in connection with a transfer or plant relocation. These services may include helping employees find living quarters, paying for travel and moving expenses, and protecting transferred employees from loss when selling their homes.

Transportation Pooling

Daily transportation to and from work is often a major concern of employees. The result may be considerable time and energy devoted to organizing car pools and scrambling for parking spaces. Many employers, like the Arizona Public Service Company and RCA in Bloomington, Indiana, attempt to ease conditions by offering transportation in vans. Employer-organized van pooling is common among private and public organizations with operations in metropolitan areas. Many employers report that tardiness and absenteeism are reduced by van pooling.

Purchasing Assistance

Organizations may use various methods to assist their employees in purchasing merchandise more conveniently and at a discount. Retailers often offer their employees a discount on purchases made at the store. Most firms sell their own products at a discount to their employees, and in some instances they procure certain items from other manufacturers that they then offer to employees at a discount.

Credit Unions

Credit unions exist in many organizations to serve the financial needs of employees. They offer a variety of deposits as well as other banking services and make loans to their members. Although the employer may provide office space and a payroll deduction service, credit unions are operated by the employees under federal and state legislation and supervision. At the end of October 1994 there were 12,619 credit unions in the United States with 66.9 million members and combined assets of $300 billion. In almost all credit unions, deposits are insured up to $100,000 per account by the National Credit Union Share Insurance Fund, a U.S. government agency.[50]

Recreational and Social Services

Many organizations offer some type of sports program in which personnel may participate on a voluntary basis. Bowling, softball, golf, baseball, and tennis are quite often included in an intramural program. In addition to intramurals, many organizations have teams that represent them in competitions with other local organizations. Memberships or discount on membership fees at health clubs and fitness centers are also popular offerings. (See Chapter 13.)

Many social functions are organized for employees and their families. Employees should have a major part in planning if these functions are to be successful. However, the employer should retain control of all events associated with the organization because of possible legal liability. For example, in Florida and California employers may be held liable for injuries to third persons caused by an employee's actions arising *within the course and scope of employment.* Thus accidents occurring while an employee is driving to or from an employer-sponsored event that the employee was encouraged to attend could trigger liability for an employer.[51]

Awards

Awards are often used to recognize productivity, special contributions, and service to an organization. Typically they are presented by top management at special meetings, banquets, and other functions where the honored employees will receive wide recognition. While cash awards are usually given for cost-saving suggestions from employees, a noncash gift is often a more appropriate way to recognize special achievement. For example, travel has emerged as an important part of many sales incentive programs. An all-expense-paid trip for two to Paris is likely to be a unique and more memorable experience than a cash gift. An extensive discussion of awards is included in Chapter 14.[52]

SUMMARY

objective

Since the 1930s benefit programs have expanded in terms of types of benefits offered and their costs, so that today's employees receive a sizable portion of their compensation in the form of benefits. Initially, employers offered benefits to discourage unionization, but as the unions became stronger they were able to obtain additional benefits. Prohibited from raising wages during and after

World War II, employers found that they could retain their employees by providing benefits. Now benefits are an established and integral part of the total compensation package. In order to have a sound benefits program there are certain basic considerations. It is essential that a program be based on specific objectives that are compatible with organizational philosophy and policies as well as affordable. Through committees and surveys a benefit package can be developed to meet employees' needs. Through the use of flexible benefit plans, employees are able to choose those benefits that are best suited for their individual needs. An important factor in how employees view the program is the full communication of benefits information through meetings, printed material, and annual personalized statements of benefits.

According to a 1994 study, the costs of employee benefits in that year averaged 41.3 per cent of payroll or $14,807 per employee. Since many of the benefits represent a fixed cost, management must pay close attention in assuming more benefit expense. Increasingly, employers are requiring employees to pay part of the costs of certain benefits. Employers also shop for benefit services that are competitively priced.

Nearly a quarter of the benefits package that employers provide is legally required. These benefits include employer contributions to Social Security, unemployment insurance, workers' compensation insurance, and state disability insurance. Social Security taxes collected from employers and employees are used to pay three major types of benefits: (1) old-age insurance benefits, (2) disability benefits, and (3) survivors' insurance benefits.

The cost of health care programs has become the major concern in the area of employee benefits. Several approaches are used to contain health care costs, including reduction in coverage, increased coordination of benefits, increased deductible or copayments, use of health maintenance and preferred provider organizations, incentives for outpatient surgery and testing, and mandatory second opinions where surgery is indicated. Employee assistance programs and wellness programs may also contribute to cutting the costs of health care benefits.

Included in the category of benefits that involve payments for time not worked are vacations with pay, paid holidays, sick leave, and severance pay. In most countries, other than the United States and the United Kingdom, the government mandates that the employer guarantee vacation time to workers. The typical practice in the United States is to give twenty days' vacation leave and ten holidays. In addition to vacation time, most employees, particularly in white-collar jobs, receive a set number of sick-leave days. A one-time payment of severance pay may be given to employees who are being terminated.

Prior to 1979 employers were permitted to determine the age (usually 65) at which their employees would be required to retire. While there is now no ceiling, a growing number of workers choose to retire before age 65. Many employers provide incentives for early retirement in the form of increased pension benefits or cash bonuses. Some organizations provide preretirement programs that may include seminars, workshops, and informational materials. The National Council on Aging, the American Association of Retired Persons, and many other organizations are available to assist both employers and employees in preretirement activities.

objective

Whether or not to offer a pension plan is the employers' prerogative. However, once a plan is established it is then subject to federal regulation under ERISA to ensure that benefits will be available when an employee retires. While there are two types of plans available—defined benefit and defined contribution—most employers now opt for the latter. The amount an employee receives upon retirement is based on years of service, average earnings, and age at time of retirement. Pension benefits are typically integrated with Social Security benefits. One of the most significant trends is the growth of 401(k) salary reduction plans. Pension funds may be administered through either a trusteed or an insurance plan. While ERISA requires that funds be invested where the return will be the greatest, employees often demand a voice in determining where funds will be invested.

objective

The types of service benefits that employers typically provide include employee assistance programs, counseling services, educational assistance plans, child care, and elder care. Other benefits are food services, on-site health services, prepaid legal services, financial planning, housing and moving, transportation pooling, purchase assistance, credit unions, social and recreational services, and awards.

KEY TERMS

contributory plan

defined-benefit plan

defined-contribution plan

elder care

employee assistance program (EAP)

flexible benefits plans (cafeteria plans, self-designated plans, or employee choice plans)

health maintenance organizations (HMOs)

noncontributory plan

preferred provider organization (PPO)

silver handshake

supplemental unemployment benefits (SUBs)

vesting

workers' compensation insurance

DISCUSSION QUESTIONS

1. Many organizations are concerned about the rising cost of employee benefits and question their value to the organization and to the employees.
    a. In your opinion, what benefits are of greatest value to employees? To the organization? Why?

   b. What can management do to increase the value to the organization of the benefits provided to employees?

  2. Employee benefits were found to cost over $14,807 a year per employee in organizations surveyed by the U.S. Chamber of Commerce.

    a. What would you think of a plan that called for removing all benefits, except those required by law, and giving the employees this amount in cash as part of wages?

    b. Discuss the advantages and disadvantages of such a plan.

  3. What are some of the reasons for the greater attention organizations are devoting to the communication of benefits information to employees?

  4. Some organizations offer their employees a choice of certain benefits in a self-designated benefits plan. What are the advantages and disadvantages of this type of plan to the employee? To the employer?

  5. What effect is further government intrusion in the area of employee benefits likely to have on benefits programs?

  6. How can the HR program affect employee health?

  7. We observed that prior to 1979, all employers could prescribe a mandatory retirement age—usually 65 years. What would you think are the advantages and disadvantages of a mandatory retirement age?

  8. What factors may affect an individual's decision to retire at a particular time, and what factors may affect his or her ability to adjust to retirement?

CASE STUDY: Keeping the Corporate Connection

Various community organizations recruit retirees as volunteers and promote and coordinate volunteer activities, but company-sponsored programs have proven to be uniquely productive. There was a time when retirees were completely separated from their former employers except for a monthly pension check. But this is no longer the case. A company-sponsored retiree volunteer program provides a valuable link between a retiree and the company that benefits the community in which both reside. A company knows its retirees, how to reach them, and something about what they can do. It also provides the retiree with a comfortable environment—familiar faces and past shared experiences, an esprit de corps, and extension of the workplace that is so important to many retirees. Community organizations do not have this advantage.

An outstanding example of company/retiree partnership is the highly successful Honeywell Retiree Volunteer Project (HRVP), the first formally organized corporate retiree volunteer program in the Twin Cities area, and possibly in the nation. Honeywell initiated this organization in 1979 as part of a program to expand its role with the Minneapolis-St. Paul area nonprofit community service agencies. Since then, HRVP has placed more than 1,600 retirees in responsible volunteer positions at more than 335 volunteer and nonprofit agencies. It is estimated that in 1990 these active seniors contributed more than 350,000 hours to the community. At a nominal $6 an hour, this would be about $2.1 million in-kind contributions.

Although the program has top Honeywell support, it is managed entirely by the retirees themselves, who even share the management responsibilities. Each retiree manager contributes one or two days a week to the project—recruiting volunteers, talking with the various community nonprofit agencies, and managing the day-to-day routine of the project. In addition, each day manager is responsible for certain ongoing projects and interest areas and for referring matters concerning other special projects to the responsible day manager. When a special project becomes too large to be handled as part of the daily routine, a project manager is appointed to oversee its activities and growth. The status of these projects is reviewed at monthly staff meetings.

Every attempt is made to involve retirees in community work that is rewarding, interesting, and challenging. An important step in this process is HRVP's one-on-one interview of each new prospective retiree volunteer to determine individual interest, ability, desire, and motivation. These are then matched, as closely as possible, to a nonprofit agency's needs according to their job descriptions. The prospective volunteer is then interviewed by the agency so that both parties can determine if a match can be made. As a result of this careful interviewing and matching, the turnover rate of HRVP's volunteers after placement is only 6 percent.

Most volunteers work on their own terms, ranging from half a day a week to as much as five days a week. Honeywell retirees are engaged in a variety of community activities: youth and adult educational programs, technical services, rehabilitation services, health services, and recreation and civic organizational projects. These diverse activities meet the needs of the retirees and also of the company and the community. According to Elmer Frykman, HRVP's first manager, "The volunteers like the work because they keep up with their skills and feel useful, and because they maintain the camaraderie established during their working years."

Source: Bernard L. Mooney, manager, promotional projects, Honeywell Retiree Volunteer Project, July 14, 1994. Prepared especially for this text and reproduced with permission.

Questions
1. How does a volunteer program like this one benefit the company?
2. In what ways can an HR department assist the staff that manages the program?
3. Why would some retirees choose to serve as volunteers rather than seek employment in the community?

NOTES AND REFERENCES

1. William E. Wymer, George Faulkner, and Joseph A. Parente, "Achieving Benefit Program Objectives," *HR Magazine* 37, no. 3 (March 1992): 55–62; see also Charles R. Sundermeyer, "Employee Benefit Planning for Small Businesses," *Benefits Quarterly* 9, no. 4 (Fourth Quarter 1993): 78–84. See also Lesley

Alderman, "Smart Ways to Maximize Your Company Benefits," *Money* 24, no. 11 (November 1994): 183–96.

2. Marlene L. Morgenstern, "Compensation and Benefits Challenges for the 1990s: The Board Speaks Out," *Compensation and Benefits Review* 25, no. 1 (January-February 1993): 22–26; see also Joyce E. Santora, "Employee Team Designs Flexible Benefits Program," *Personnel Journal* 73, no. 4 (April 1994): 30–39; "The Changing Role of Flexible Benefit Plans," *HR Focus* 71, no. 3 (March 1994): 16.

3. William J. Wiatrowski, "Family-Related Benefits in the Workplace," *Monthly Labor Review* 13, no. 3 (March 1990): 28–33; see also Lisa Jenner, "Issues and Options for Childless Employees," *HR Focus* 71, no. 3 (March 1994): 22–23; Joy E. Hitchcock, "Southwest Airlines Renovates Benefits System," *HR Magazine* 37, no. 7 (July 1992): 54–56; Jennifer J. Laabs, "Unmarried…with Benefits," *Personnel Journal* 70, no. 12 (December 1991): 62–70.

4. Wymer et al., "Achieving Benefit Program Objectives." See also David E. Bowen and Christopher A. Wadley, "Designing a Strategic Benefits Program," *Compensation and Benefits Review* 21, no. 5 (September-October 1989): 44–56; John S. Rybka, "Outsourcing Employee Benefits: How to Tell If It's Right for Your Organization," *Employee Benefits Journal* 18, no. 4 (December 1993): 2–8.

5. Detailed recommendations for preparing benefits statements are presented in the following articles by James F. White of the benefits-consulting firm of Godwins Booke & Dickenson: "Preparing Benefits Statements," *Personnel* 63, no. 5 (May 1986): 13–18; "Scope of Personalized Communication Is Expanding," *Journal of Compensation and Benefits* 21, no. 5 (September-October 1989): 118–19; and "Communicating Employee Benefits," in press 1995.

6. For over forty years benefit professionals have relied on the International Foundation of Employee Benefit Plans for education and information about employee benefits. Total membership consists of 35,000 individuals who represent more than 7,400 trust funds, corporations, professional firms, and public employee funds throughout the United States, Canada, and overseas. The headquarters address is P.O. Box 69, Brookfield, Wisc. 53008-0069. One of their many publications is a valuable reference book: *Employee Benefit Plans: A Glossary of Terms*, 8th ed. (Brookfield, Wisc.: International Foundation of Employee Benefit Plans, 1993).

7. *Employee Benefits, 1994* (Washington, D.C.: U.S. Chamber of Commerce, 1994); Chester Levine, "Employee Benefits: Growing in Diversity and Cost," *Occupational Outlook Quarterly* 37, no. 4 (Winter 1993–1994): 39–42.

8. COBRA: April 7, 1986, P.L. 99-272, 100 Stat. 82.

9. Active military service completed between 1940 and 1956 inclusive was granted Social Security credit based on monthly earnings of $160 per month. Since the Social Security Act is continually subject to amendment, readers should refer to the literature provided by the nearest Social Security office for the most current details pertaining to the tax rates and benefit provisions of the act. The 1993 editions of these publications were used as the basis for this discussion.

10. For a more detailed account of exempted groups, see the current edition of *Labor Course* or *Tax Course* (Englewood Cliffs, N.J.: Prentice-Hall).

11. U.S. Department of Health and Human Services, *Social Security Handbook*, 11th ed. (Washington, D.C.: U.S. Government Printing Office, 1993): ¶212. The amount changes annually and is published in the November issue of the *Federal Register*.

12. See the *Social Security Handbook* for details on the international agreements and for a list of the participating countries.

13. (1) The doctrine of the assumption of risk holds that when employees accept a job, they assume the ordinary risks of the job. (2) The fellow-servant rule provides that if the employee is injured as a result of the negligence of a fellow employee, the employer is not liable for the injury. (3) The doctrine of contributory negligence states that the employer is not liable if the injury of the employee is due wholly or in part to negligence.

14. Darien A. McWhirter, *Your Rights at Work*, 2d ed. (New York: Wiley, 1993); Charles A. Barreth, "Workers' Compensation Laws: Significant Changes in 1993," *Monthly Labor Review* 117, no. 1 (January 1994): 53–69.

15. Mark D. Fefer, "What to Do about Workers' Comp," *Fortune* (June 29, 1992): 80–82; see also Mark D. Fefer, "Taking Control of Your Workers' Comp Costs," *Fortune* (October 3, 1994): 131–36; Phillip M. Perry, "Twelve Ways to Cut Workers' Comp Costs," *HR Focus* 71, no. 10 (October 1994): 12–13.

16. Chris Roush, "Making Workers' Comp Work," *Business Week* (October 25, 1993): 114; see also Roger Thompson, "Workers' Comp Costs: Out of Control," *Nation's Business* (July 1992): 22–30.

17. Robert J. McCunney and Cheryl Barbanel, "Auditing Workers' Compensation Claims Targets Expensive Injuries, Job Tasks," *Occupational Health and Safety* 32, no. 10 (October 1993): 75–84; Geoffrey Leavenworth, "Setting Standards for Workers' Comp," *Business & Health* 12, no. 10 (October 1994): 49–54.

18. Karen Roberts and Sandra E. Gleason, "What Employees Want from Workers' Comp," *HR Magazine* 36, no. 12 (December 1991): 49–52.

19. Robert J. Nobile, "Leaving No Doubt about Employee Leaves," *Personnel* 67, no. 5 (May 1990): 54–60.

20. FMLA: February 5, 1993, P.L. 103-3, 107 Stat. 6.

21. Joseph A. Brislin, "The Effect of Federal Family and Medical Leave Act upon Employee Benefits," *Employee Benefits Journal* 18, no. 3 (September 1993): 2–7; Elliott H. Shaller and Mary K. Qualiana, "The Family and Medical Leave Act—Key Provisions and Potential Problems," *Employee Relations Labor Journal* 19, no. 1 (Summer 1993): 5–20; see also "Sure, 'Unpaid Leave' Sounds Simple, but . . ." *Business Week* (August 9, 1993): 32.

22. William H. Carlile, "Family-Leave Law to Usher in New Era," *Arizona Republic* (July 31, 1993): 1; Michelle N. Martinex, "FMLA: Headache or Opportunity?" *HR Magazine* 39, no. 2 (February 1994): 42–45.

23. Rhonda Richards, "Family Leave Means Work for Temps," *USA Today* (February 11, 1993): B1.

24. *Employee Benefits 1994*, 12, 38.

25. Linda Thornburg, "What To Do Now About Health-Care Costs," *HR Magazine* 39, no. 1 (January 1994): 44–47 and Shari Caudron, "Health-Care Reform: Act Now or Pay Later," *Personnel Journal* 73, no. 3 (March 1994): 57–67.

26. Bill Leonard, "The Employee's Favorite, Employer's Quandary," *HR Magazine* 39, no. 11 (November 1994): 53–54.

27. *Life Insurance Fact Book Update* (Washington, D.C.: American Council of Life Insurance, 1993): 14.

28. Catherine D. Fyock, "Crafting Secure Retirements," *HR Magazine* 35, no. 7 (July 1990): 30–33; Samuel Greengard, "HR Teaches the Retirement Game," *Personnel Journal* 73, no. 11 (November 1994): 38–44.

29. Data provided by the Employee Benefit Research Institute in Washington, D.C.; see also Aaron Bernstein, "In Search of the Vanishing Nest Egg," *Business Week* (July 30, 1990): 46; Mary Howland, "Pension Options for Small Firms, *Nation's Business* 82, no. 3 (March 1994): 25–27.

30. Larry Light, "The Power of the Pension Funds," *Business Week* (November 6, 1989): 154–58.

31. Donald J. Segal and Howard J. Small, "Are Defined Benefit Pension Plans about to Come Out of Retirement?" *Compensation and Benefits Review* (May-June 1993): 22–26.

32. Dallas L. Salisbury, "Pension Tax Expenditures: What Do They Buy?" *Benefits Quarterly* 9, no. 4 (Fourth Quarter 1993): 66–77.

33. Donald K. Odermann, "Four Steps to a Successful 401(k) Plan," *HR Magazine* 36, no. 8 (August 1991): 44–46; see also Bill Leonard, "Pension Investment Management Shifts to Employee," *HR Magazine* 39,

no. 3 (March 1994): 61–62; "Workers Face Pensionless Futures," *Arizona Republic* (May 13, 1993): A7.

34. ERISA: September 2, 1974, P.L. 93-406, 88 Stat. 829.

35. REA: August 23, 1984, P.L. 98-397, 98 Stat. 1426.

36. Deficit Reduction Act of 1984: July 18, 1984, P.L. 98-369, 98 Stat. 494.

37. Ellen E. Schultz, "Underfunded Pension Plan? Don't Panic Yet," *The Wall Street Journal* (December 3, 1993): C1.

38. Eileen G. Settineri, "Effectively Measuring the Costs of EAPs," *HR Magazine* 36, no. 4 (April 1991): 53–56. See also Ellen E. Schultz, "If You Use Firm's Counselors, Remember Your Secrets Could be Used against You," *The Wall Street Journal* (May 26, 1994): C1.

39. Elanna Yalow, "Corporate Child Care Helps Recruit and Retain Workers," *Personnel Journal* 69, no. 6 (June 1990): 48–55; Jennifer Haupt, "Employee Action Prompts Management to Respond to Work-and-Family Needs," *Personnel Journal* 72, no. 2 (February 1993): 96–107.

40. Robert Levering and Milton Moskowitz, *The 100 Best Companies to Work For in America* (New York: Doubleday, 1993): 126.

41. Telephone interview with Beth Wallace, November 24, 1993.

42. Karen Woodford, "Child Care Soars at America West," *Personnel Journal* 69, no. 2 (December 1990): 46–47; Yalow, "Corporate Child Care." See also Haupt, "Employee Action Prompts Management"; Charlene M. Solomon, "Work/Family's Failing Grade: Why Today's Initiatives Aren't Enough," *Personnel Journal* 73, no. 5 (May 1994): 72–87.

43. Sue Shellenbarger, "Employers Try New Ways to Help with Child Care," *The Wall Street Journal* (May 19, 1993): B1.

44. Kathleen Glynn, "Providing for Our Aging Society," *Personnel Administrator* 33, no. 11 (November 1988): 56–59.

45. Sue Shellenbarger, "Firms Try Harder, but Often Fail, to Help Workers Cope with Elder-Care Problems," *The Wall Street Journal* (June 23, 1993): B1.

46. Sue Shellenbarger, "The Aging of America Is Making Elder Care a Big Workplace Issue," *The Wall Street Journal* (February 16, 1994): A1. See also Shellenbarger, "With Elder Care Comes a Professional and Personal Crisis, *The Wall Street Journal* (November 9, 1994): B1.

47. Levering and Moskowitz, *The 100 Best Companies*, 107.

48. Levering and Moskowitz, *The 100 Best Companies*, 18

49. Morton E. Grossman and Margaret Magnus, "Order Up Food Services," *Personnel Journal* 68, no. 3 (March 1989): 70–72.

50. Data obtained December 16, 1994, from Jerry Karbon of the Credit Union National Association, P.O. Box 431, Madison, Wisc. 53701.

51. "Employer Liable for Actions of Drunk Employee," *The California Labor Letter* V, no. 1 (January 1994): 3.

52. William H. Wagel, "Make Their Day—the Noncash Way," *Personnel* 67, no. 5 (May 1990): 41–44.

Chapter

Safety and Health

13

After studying this chapter you should be able to

one
objective

Summarize the general provisions of the Occupational Safety and Health Act (OSHA).

two
objective

Describe what management can do to create a safe work environment.

three
objective

Cite the measures that should be taken to control and eliminate health hazards.

four
objective

Describe the organizational services and programs for building better health.

five
objective

Explain the role of employee assistance programs in HRM.

six
objective

Describe the employer's role in the management of stress.

. . . .

I*n the preceding chapters we examined the various compensation and benefit programs that are designed to meet the needs of employees for economic security. Their needs for physical and emotional security demand equal attention. Employers are required by law to provide working conditions that do not impair the safety or health of their employees. Therefore employers must ensure a work environment that protects employees from physical hazards, unhealthy conditions, and unsafe acts of other personnel. Through effective safety and health programs, the physical and emotional well-being, as well as the economic security, of employees may be preserved and even enhanced.*

While the laws safeguarding employees' physical and emotional well-being are certainly an incentive, many employers are motivated to provide desirable working conditions by virtue of their sensitivity to human needs and rights. The more cost-oriented employer recognizes the importance of avoiding accidents and illnesses wherever possible. Costs associated with sick leave, disability payments, replacement of employees who are injured or killed, and workers' compensation far exceed the costs of maintaining a safety and health program. Accidents and illnesses attributable to the workplace may also have pronounced effects on employee morale and on the goodwill that the organization enjoys in the community and in the business world.

In today's litigious environment, an organization must be able to document how diligently its management makes an attempt at, and succeeds in, protecting employees on the job. The HR department is generally responsible for coordinating efforts and communicating crucial information on safety and health issues as well as maintaining records needed for documentation.[1]

After discussing the legal requirements for safety and health, we shall focus in the rest of this chapter on the creation of a safe and healthy work environment and on the management of stress.

objective

Legal Requirements for Safety and Health

In the late 1960s, Congress became increasingly concerned that each year, job-related accidents were accounting for more than 14,000 worker deaths and nearly 2.5 million worker disabilities. Also in the late 1960s, estimated new cases of occupational diseases totaled 300,000 annually. As a result of lost productivity and wages, medical expenses, and disability compensation, the burden on the nation's commerce was staggering. There was no way to calculate human suffering. These conditions led to the passage of the Occupational Safety and Health Act (OSHA) in 1970. The act, which was designed "to assure so far as possible every working man and woman in the Nation safe and healthful working conditions and to preserve our human resources," has been very effective in reducing the number of injuries resulting in lost work time, as well as the number of job-related deaths.[2] A comparison of the late 1960s with the early 1990s reveals the improvement that has taken place in occupational safety. In 1993, with almost twice as many workers as in the 1960s, there were 9,100 fatalities and 3.2 million disabling injuries *on the job*. Highway accidents are the leading cause of work-related deaths, followed by assaults and violent acts by persons—a topic discussed in Chapters 6 and 16. In terms of parts of the body affected by accidents, injuries to the back occur most frequently followed by leg, arm, and finger injuries, as

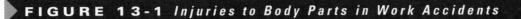

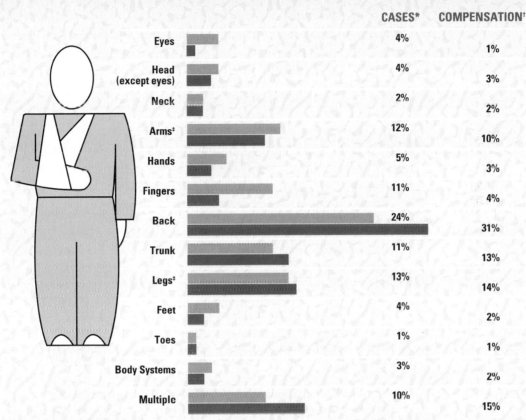

FIGURE 13-1 *Injuries to Body Parts in Work Accidents*

	CASES*	COMPENSATION†
Eyes	4%	1%
Head (except eyes)	4%	3%
Neck	2%	2%
Arms‡	12%	10%
Hands	5%	3%
Fingers	11%	4%
Back	24%	31%
Trunk	11%	13%
Legs‡	13%	14%
Feet	4%	2%
Toes	1%	1%
Body Systems	3%	2%
Multiple	10%	15%

*Cases reported from 23 states.
†Workers' compensation reported from 10 states.
‡Includes multiple or NEC (not elsewhere classified) extremity injuries amounting to less than 2% of the total cases and compensation.

Source: National Safety Council (1994). *Accident Facts, 1994 Edition* (Itasca, Ill.: National Safety Council).

shown in Figure 13–1.[3] In addition to listing the percentage of cases involving each designated body part, the figure shows the percentage of cases involving workers' compensation.

It is more difficult to make simple comparisons in regard to occupational illnesses reported today and in the early 1960s. It is important to note, however, that of 457,000 cases of occupational illnesses recognized or diagnosed in 1992, disorders associated with repeated trauma were the most common illness with 281,800 cases, followed by skin disorders (62,900) and respiratory conditions due to toxic agents (23,500).[4]

OSHA's Coverage

In general, the act extends to all employers and their employees, with only a few exceptions, which include the federal government and any state or political subdivision of a state. Each federal agency, however, is required to establish and maintain a safety and health program that is monitored by the Occupational Safety and Health Administration. Likewise, a state seeking OSHA approval of its safety and health program for the private sector must provide a similar program that covers its state and local government employees and is at least as effective as its program for private employers. Where state programs for the private sector have been approved by the federal government as meeting federal standards, the state carries out the enforcement functions that would otherwise be performed by the federal government. Approximately one-half of the states currently have their own OSHA-approved programs.[5]

OSHA Standards

One of the responsibilities of the Occupational Safety and Health Administration is to develop and enforce mandatory job safety and health standards. OSHA standards fall into four major categories: general industry, maritime, construction, and agriculture. These standards cover the workplace, machinery and equipment, material, power sources, processing, protective clothing, first aid, and administrative requirements. It is the responsibility of employers to become familiar with those standards that are applicable to their establishments and to ensure that their employees use personal protective gear and equipment when required for safety. The *Federal Register* is the principal source of information on proposed, adopted, amended, and deleted OSHA standards. Large employers usually subscribe to it and/or the OSHA Subscription Service.[6]

The Occupational Safety and Health Administration can begin standards-setting procedures on its own initiative or on petition from other parties, including the Secretary of Health and Human Services (HHS) and the National Institute for Occupational Safety and Health (NIOSH). Other bodies that may also initiate standards-setting procedures are state and local governments and any nationally recognized standards-producing organization, employer, or labor representative. NIOSH, however, is the major source of standards. As an agency of the Department of Health and Human Services, it is responsible for conducting research on various safety and health problems, including the psychological factors involved.[7]

Employer Compliance with OSHA

The Secretary of Labor is authorized by the Occupational Safety and Health Act to conduct workplace inspections, to issue citations, and to impose penalties on employers. Inspections have been delegated to the Occupational Safety and Health Administration of the U.S. Department of Labor.

Workplace Inspections

Under the act, "upon presenting appropriate credentials to the owner, operator, or agent in charge," an OSHA compliance officer is authorized to do the following:

- Enter without delay and at reasonable times any factory, plant, establishment, construction site or other areas, workplace, or environment where work is performed by an employee of an employer; and to
- Inspect and investigate during regular working hours, and at other reasonable times, and within reasonable limits and in a reasonable manner, any such place of employment and all pertinent conditions, structures, machines, apparatus, devices, equipment and materials therein, and to question privately any such employer, owner, operator, agent, or employee.[8]

Typically, OSHA inspectors will arrive at a work site unannounced and ask for a meeting with a representative of the employer. At the meeting the inspectors will explain the purpose of the visit, describe the procedure for the inspection, and ask to review the employer's safety and health records. An employer may either agree voluntarily to the inspection or require the inspectors to obtain a search warrant.

The act gives both the employer and the employees the right to accompany inspectors on their tour of the work site. After the tour the OSHA officials will conduct a closing conference to inform the employer and employee representatives, if any, of the results of their inspection. They will point out conditions or practices that appear to be hazardous and issue a written citation if warranted.[9]

Obviously, not all of the 6 million workplaces covered by the act can be inspected at the same time. The worst situations need attention first. Therefore OSHA has established a system of inspection priorities, listed in Figure 13–2.

Citations and Penalties

Citations may be issued immediately following the inspection or later by mail. Citations tell the employer and employees which regulations and standards are alleged to have been violated and the amount of time allowed for their correction. The employer must post a copy of each citation at or near the place the

---

FIGURE 13-2 *OSHA Priorities for Workplace Inspections*

1. Inspection of imminent-danger situations
2. Investigation of catastrophes, fatalities, and accidents resulting in hospitalization of five or more employees
3. Investigation of valid employee complaints of alleged violation of standards or of unsafe or unhealthful working conditions
4. Special-emphasis inspections aimed at specific high-hazard industries, occupations, or substances that are injurious to health
5. Follow-up inspections to determine if previously cited violations have been corrected

Source: U.S. Department of Labor, Occupational Safety and Health Administration, *All about OSHA,* rev. ed. (Washington, D.C.: U.S. Department of Labor, 1992), 17–19.

violation occurred for three days or until the violation is abated, whichever is longer.

OSHA has a wide range of penalties for violations. Fines of as much as $7,000 are imposed for serious violations, including violations of posting requirements. For willful or repeated violations, OSHA can assess penalties of up to $70,000 for each violation, or if a willful violation results in the death of an employee, a fine of up to $250,000 for an individual or $500,000 for a corporation plus imprisonment of up to six months or both. The law provides for appeal by employers and by employees under specified circumstances.[10]

On-site Consultation

OSHA provides a free on-site consultation service. Consultants from the state government or private contractors help employers identify hazardous conditions and determine corrective measures. No citations are issued in connection with a consultation, and the consultant's files cannot be used to trigger an OSHA inspection.

Voluntary Protection Programs

Voluntary protection programs (VPPs)
Programs that encourage employers to go beyond the minimum requirements of OSHA

The **voluntary protection programs (VPPs)** represent one component of OSHA's effort to extend worker protection beyond the minimum required by OSHA standards. There are three specific VPPs—Star, Merit, and Demonstration—which are designed to do the following:

1. Recognize outstanding achievement of those who have successfully incorporated comprehensive safety and health programs into their total management system
2. Motivate others to achieve excellent safety and health results in the same outstanding way
3. Establish a relationship among employers, employees, and OSHA that is based on cooperation rather than coercion.

Once it has been approved for a VPP, an organization is then taken off OSHA's list for routine inspections.[11]

Training and Education

OSHA's area offices provide a variety of informational services to employers. The OSHA Training Institute in Des Plaines, Illinois, provides basic and advanced training in safety and health. Over sixty courses are available. OSHA also provides funds to nonprofit organizations to conduct workplace training.

two objective

Responsibilities and Rights under OSHA

Both employers and employees have certain responsibilities and rights under OSHA. We will discuss only those that relate directly to the management of human resources.

Employers' Responsibilities and Rights

In addition to providing a hazard-free workplace and complying with the applicable standards, employers must inform all of their employees about the safety and health requirements of OSHA. Employers are also required to display the OSHA poster that lists employees' rights and responsibilities (see Highlights in HRM 1), to keep certain records, and to compile and post an annual summary of work-related injuries and illnesses. It is the employer's responsibility to make sure employees use protective equipment when necessary. Employers must therefore engage in safety training and be prepared to discipline employees for failing to comply with safety rules.

Employers must not discriminate against employees who exercise their rights under the act by filing complaints. Employers are afforded many rights under the law, most of which pertain to receiving information, applying for variances in standards, and contesting citations.[12]

Employees' Responsibilities and Rights

Employees are required to comply with all applicable OSHA standards, to report hazardous conditions, and to follow all employer safety and health rules and regulations, including those prescribing the use of protective equipment. Workers have a right to demand safe and healthy conditions on the job without fear of punishment. They also have many rights that pertain to requesting and receiving information about safety and health conditions.[13]

Right-to-Know Laws

While the preamble to the original OSHA standards specified that the rights of workers or their designated representatives would include broad access to relevant environmental exposure and medical records, failure of the federal government in this area led to the passage of **employee right-to-know laws** in several states. These statutes address such issues as the definition of toxic and hazardous substances, the duties of employers and manufacturers to provide health-risk information to employees, trade-secret protection, and enforcement provisions.

Eventually, OSHA published the federal worker "right-to-know" regulation, known as the Hazard Communication Standard (HCS), which applies to all employers and preempts state worker right-to-know laws. The HCS prescribes a system for communicating data on health hazards to employees. It includes a format for **Material Safety Data Sheets (MSDSs).** MSDSs should include the chemical name of a hazardous substance; all of the risks involved in using it, including potential health risks; safe handling practices; personal protective equipment needed; first aid in the event of an accident; and information identifying the manufacturer.

Enforcement Efforts

As with any law, enforcement efforts will vary from one administration to the next. Under the Reagan administration OSHA enforcement efforts were seen as virtually nonexistent; the Bush administration has been described as striking a balance between regulatory zealousness and a hands-off approach; and the Clinton administration is pursuing a more active regulatory position. Still, unions and safety groups continue to worry that OSHA is lax in monitoring its agreements with organizations, and they prefer mandatory standards instead of volun

Employee right-to-know laws

Laws that require employers to advise employees of job hazards

Material Safety Data Sheets (MSDSs)

Documents that contain vital information about hazardous substances

HIGHLIGHTS IN HRM

highlights

1   JOB SAFETY AND HEALTH PROTECTION POSTER

JOB SAFETY & HEALTH PROTECTION

The Occupational Safety and Health Act of 1970 provides job safety and health protection for workers by promoting safe and healthful working conditions throughout the Nation. Provisions of the Act include the following:

Employers

All employers must furnish to employees employment and a place of employment free from recognized hazards that are causing or are likely to cause death or serious harm to employees. Employers must comply with occupational safety and health standards issued under the Act.

Employees

Employees must comply with all occupational safety and health standards, rules, regulations and orders issued under the Act that apply to their own actions and conduct on the job.

The Occupational Safety and Health Administration (OSHA) of the U.S. Department of Labor has the primary responsibility for administering the Act. OSHA issues occupational safety and health standards, and its Compliance Safety and Health Officers conduct jobsite inspections to help ensure compliance with the Act.

Inspection

The Act requires that a representative of the employer and a representative authorized by the employees be given an opportunity to accompany the OSHA inspector for the purpose of aiding the inspection.

Where there is no authorized employee representative, the OSHA Compliance Officer must consult with a reasonable number of employees concerning safety and health conditions in the workplace.

Complaint

Employees or their representatives have the right to file a complaint with the nearest OSHA office requesting an inspection if they believe unsafe or unhealthful conditions exist in their workplace. OSHA will withhold, on request, names of employees complaining.

The Act provides that employees may not be discharged or discriminated against in any way for filing safety and health complaints or for otherwise exercising their rights under the Act.

Employees who believe they have been discriminated against may file a complaint with their nearest OSHA office within 30 days of the alleged discriminatory action.

Citation

If upon inspection OSHA believes an employer has violated the Act, a citation alleging such violations will be issued to the employer. Each citation will specify a time period within which the alleged violation must be corrected.

The OSHA citation must be prominently displayed at or near the place of alleged violation for three days, or until it is corrected, whichever is later, to warn employees of dangers that may exist there.

Proposed Penalty

The Act provides for mandatory civil penalties against employers of up to $7,000 for each serious violation and for optional penalties of up to $7,000 for each nonserious violation. Penalties of up to $7,000 per day may be proposed for failure to correct violations within the proposed time period and for each day the violation continues beyond the prescribed abatement date. Also, any employer who willfully or repeatedly violates the Act may be assessed penalties of up to $70,000 for each such violation. A minimum penalty of $5,000 may be imposed for each willful violation. A violation of posting requirements can bring a penalty of up to $7,000.

There are also provisions for criminal penalties. Any willful violation resulting in the death of any employee, upon conviction, is punishable by a fine of up to $250,000 (or $500,000 if the employer is a corporation), or by imprisonment for up to six months, or both. A second conviction of an employer doubles the possible term of imprisonment. Falsifying records, reports, or applications is punishable by a fine of $10,000 or up to six months in jail or both.

Voluntary Activity

While providing penalties for violations, the Act also encourages efforts by labor and management, before an OSHA inspection, to reduce workplace hazards voluntarily and to develop and improve safety and health programs in all workplaces and industries. OSHA's Voluntary Protection Programs recognize outstanding efforts of this nature.

OSHA has published Safety and Health Program Management Guidelines to assist employers in establishing or perfecting programs to prevent or control employee exposure to workplace hazards. There are many public and private organizations that can provide information and assistance in this effort, if requested. Also, your local OSHA office can provide considerable help and advice on solving safety and health problems or can refer you to other sources for help such as training.

Consultation

Free assistance in identifying and correcting hazards and in improving safety and health management is available to employers, without citation or penalty, through OSHA-supported programs in each State. These programs are usually administered by the State Labor or Health department or a State university.

Posting Instructions

Employers in States operating OSHA approved State Plans should obtain and post the State's equivalent poster.

Under provisions of Title 29, Code of Federal Regulations, Part 1903.2(a)(1) employers must post this notice (or facsimile) in a conspicuous place where notices to employees are customarily posted.

More Information

Additional information and copies of the Act, specific OSHA safety and health standards, and other applicable regulations may be obtained from your employer or from the nearest OSHA Regional Office in the following locations:

Atlanta, GA — (404) 347-3573
Boston, MA — (617) 565-7164
Chicago, IL — (312) 353-2220
Dallas, TX — (214) 767-4731
Denver, CO — (303) 844-3061
Kansas City, MO — (816) 426-5861
New York, NY — (212) 337-2378
Philadelphia, PA — (215) 596-1201
San Francisco, CA — (415) 744-6670
Seattle, WA — (206) 553-5930

Washington, DC
1992 (Reprinted)
OSHA 2203

Robert B. Reich, Secretary of Labor

U.S. Department of Labor
Occupational Safety and Health Administration

To report suspected fire hazards, imminent danger safety and health hazards in the workplace, or other job safety and health emergencies, such as toxic waste in the workplace, call OSHA's 24-hour hotline: 1-800-321-OSHA.

This information will be made available to sensory impaired individuals upon request.
Voice phone: (202) 219-8615; TDD message referral phone: 1-800-326-2577

GPO : 1993 0 – 355-763 QL

....

tary guidelines for problems such as injuries related to jobs involving repetitive motion—a topic to be considered later in this chapter.

In recent years OSHA has imposed more-substantial fines for safety, health, and record-keeping violations. The OSHA leadership favors legislation that would stiffen criminal penalties to as much as ten years in prison for violations that lead to a worker's death. New York's state court of appeals has also ruled that the federal act does not preempt criminal actions against employers that put the safety and health of their workers at risk. In the case where this ruling was made, the defendants face up to fifteen years in prison.[14]

Creating a Safe Work Environment

two
objective

We have seen that employers are required by law to provide safe working conditions for their employees. To achieve this objective, the majority of employers have a formal safety program. Typically, the HR department or the industrial relations department is responsible for the safety program. While the success of a safety program depends largely on managers and supervisors of operating departments, the HR department typically coordinates the safety communication and training programs, maintains safety records required by OSHA, and works closely with managers and supervisors in a cooperative effort to make the program a success.

Organizations with formal safety programs generally have an employee-management safety committee that includes representatives from management, each department or manufacturing/service unit, and employee representatives. Committees are typically involved in investigating accidents and helping to publicize the importance of safety rules and their enforcement.[15]

Safety Motivation and Knowledge

Probably the most important role of a safety program is motivating managers, supervisors, and subordinates to be aware of safety considerations. If managers and supervisors fail to demonstrate this awareness, their subordinates can hardly be expected to do so. Unfortunately, most managers and supervisors wear their "safety hats" far less often than their "production, quality control, and methods improvement hats." Just as important as safety motivation are a knowledge of safety and an understanding of where to place safety efforts. Training can help personnel on all levels understand the organization's policy on safety, its safety procedures, and its system of establishing accountability.[16]

Safety Awareness Programs

Most organizations have a safety awareness program that entails the use of several different media. Safety lectures, commercially produced films, specially developed videocassettes, and other media such as pamphlets are useful for teaching and motivating employees to follow safe work procedures. A page from one of these pamphlets is shown in Highlights in HRM 2. Posters have been found to be very effective because they can be displayed in strategic locations where workers will be sure to see them. For example, a shipyard found that placing posters at the

2 PAGE FROM A SAFETY AWARENESS PAMPHLET

Ask your supervisor which of the following personal protective equipment is required for the equipment, operation or process you work with.

Head Protection
- ☐ Wear a safety hard hat and add other head protection as needed, such as a face shield, goggles or hood.
- ☐ Make sure your hard hat fits securely.
- ☐ Check the hat for gouges and cracks. Look for straps or sweatbands that are frayed or broken.
- ☐ Clean the shell of your hard hat to remove oil, grease and chemicals.

Eye Protection
- ☐ Wear industry-rated eye protection.
- ☐ Get medical help as soon as possible if your eye is injured.
- ☐ Contact lenses alone won't protect your eyes. Add safety goggles or safety glasses.
- ☐ Don't wear contact lenses if you're exposed to chemicals, vapors, splashes, radiant or intensive heat, or suspended particles.

Source: National Safety Council. Reproduced with permission.

work site helped reduce accidents by making employees more conscious of the hazards of using scaffolds.[17]

Safety awareness efforts are usually coordinated by a safety director whose primary function is to enlist the interest and cooperation of all personnel. However, the safety director depends a great deal on managerial and supervisory personnel for the success of the program. It is essential that these personnel set safety goals and provide subordinates with feedback concerning their department's performance in meeting these goals.

Communication Role of the Supervisor

One of a supervisor's major responsibilities is to communicate to an employee the need to work safely. Beginning with new employee orientation, safety should be emphasized continually. Proper work procedures, the use of protective clothing and devices, and potential hazards should be explained thoroughly. Furthermore, employees' understanding of all these considerations should be verified during training sessions, and employees should be encouraged to take some initiative in maintaining a concern for safety.[18] Since training by itself does not ensure continual adherence to safe work practices, supervisors must observe employees at work and reinforce safe practices. Where unsafe acts are detected, supervisors should take immediate action to find the cause. Supervisors should also foster a team spirit of safety among the work group.

Safety Training Programs

The safety training programs found in many organizations cover first aid, defensive driving, accident prevention techniques, handling of hazardous equipment, and emergency procedures. These programs emphasize the use of emergency first-aid equipment and personal safety equipment. The most common types of personal safety equipment are safety glasses and goggles, face protectors, safety shoes, hard hats, hair protectors, and safety belts. There is also a variety of devices used in many jobs to protect hearing and respiration. Furthermore, many organizations provide training in off-the-job safety—at home, on the highway, etc.—as well as in first aid. Injuries and fatalities away from the job occur much more frequently than do those on the job and are reflected in employer costs for insurance premiums, wage continuation, and interrupted production.

Safety Incentives

For safety training programs to reach their objectives, special attention must be given to the incentives that managers and supervisors use to motivate safe behavior in their subordinates. The goal of every safety incentive program is to reduce accidents and make the workplace safer. Too often, however, an incentive program is based more on penalties and punishments than rewards. Two researchers recently looked at twenty-four studies where positive reinforcement and feedback were used to reinforce safe behavior. In all of the studies, they found these incentives successful in improving safety conditions or reducing accidents. The incentives included praise, public recognition, cash awards, and certificates that could be exchanged for company products. Every study emphasized the use of feedback.[19]

Safety Campaigns

In addition to organizing the regular safety training programs, safety directors often plan special safety campaigns. These campaigns typically emphasize competition among departments or plants, with the department or plant having the best safety record receiving some type of award or trophy. In some organizations, cash bonuses are given to employees who have outstanding safety records.

Enforcement of Safety Rules

Specific rules and regulations concerning safety are communicated through supervisors, bulletin-board notices, employee handbooks, and signs attached to equipment. Safety rules are also emphasized in regular safety meetings, at new employee orientations, and in manuals of standard operating procedures. Such rules typically refer to the following types of employee behaviors:

- Using proper safety devices
- Using proper work procedures
- Following good housekeeping practices
- Complying with accident-and-injury reporting procedures
- Wearing required safety clothing and equipment
- Avoiding carelessness and horseplay

Penalties for violation of safety rules are usually stated in the employee handbook. In a large percentage of organizations, the penalties imposed on violators are the same as those for violations of other rules. They include an oral or written warning for the first violation, suspension for repeated violations, and, as a last resort, dismissal. However, for serious violations—such as smoking around volatile substances—even the first offense may be cause for termination.

Accident Investigations and Records

Every accident, even those considered minor, should be investigated by the supervisor and a member of the safety committee. Such an investigation may determine the factors contributing to the accident and may reveal what corrections are needed to prevent it from happening again. Correction may require rearranging workstations, installing safety guards or controls, or, more often, giving employees additional safety training and reassessing their motivation for safety.

OSHA requires that a Log and Summary of Occupational Injuries and Illnesses (OSHA Form 200) be maintained by the organization. All recordable cases are to be entered in the log. A **recordable case** is any occupational death, occupational illness, or occupational injury (except those involving only first aid).[20] Each year the Summary portion of the log is to be posted for one month where employee notices are customarily posted. For every recordable case written in the log, a Supplementary Record of Occupational Injuries and Illnesses (OSHA Form 101) is to be completed. OSHA Form 101 requires answers to questions about the case.

Recordable case
Any occupational death, illness, or injury to be recorded in the log (OSHA Form 200)

three
objective

Creating a Healthy Work Environment

From its title alone, the Occupational Safety and Health Act was clearly designed to protect the health, as well as the safety, of employees. Because of the dramatic impact of workplace accidents, however, managers and employees alike may pay more attention to these kinds of immediate safety concerns than to job conditions that are dangerous to their health. It is essential, therefore, that health hazards be identified and controlled. Attention should also be given to nonwork-related illnesses and injuries and their impact on the organization and its members. Special health programs may also be developed to provide assistance to employees with health problems.

Largely because of the growing public awareness of the efforts of environmentalists, factors in the work environment affecting health are receiving greater attention. Air and water pollution on an unprecedented scale throughout the world has made all of us more conscious of the immediate environment in which we live and work. Articles about workers who have been exposed to potential dangers at work can frequently be found in the newspapers. Pressure from the federal government and unions, as well as increased public concern, has given employers a definite incentive to provide the safest and healthiest work environment possible.

Health Hazards and Issues

At one time health hazards were associated primarily with jobs found in industrial processing operations. In recent years, however, hazards in jobs outside the plant, such as in offices, health care facilities, and airports, have been recognized and preventive methods adopted. Substituting materials, altering processes, enclosing or isolating a process, issuing protective equipment, and improving ventilation are some of the common preventions. General conditions of health with respect to sanitation, housekeeping, cleanliness, ventilation, water supply, pest control, and food handling are also important to monitor.

Proliferating Chemicals

It is estimated that there are more than 65,000 different chemicals currently in use in the United States with which humans may come into contact. No toxicity data are available for about 80 percent of those used commercially.[21] Many of these chemicals are harmful, lurking for years in the body with no outward symptoms until the disease they cause is well established. Cancer, for example, may develop twenty to forty years after the original exposure to a carcinogen. This time-bomb effect can embroil government, industry, labor, and ultimately the public in controversy over how to care for victims of past exposure and how to develop preventive controls. Specialists in HRM inevitably must participate in helping to solve many specific problems that arise as a result of this controversy.

The Toxic Substances Control Act of 1976 requires that the 700-plus new chemicals that are marketed each year must be pretested for safety. Since 1977,

OSHA has been giving greater attention to setting standards for toxic conditions created by hazardous chemicals. Until that time, toxic substances had been a neglected area, despite the fact that their effects showed up in OSHA statistics. As of 1992, skin diseases and disorders (62,900 cases) and respiratory conditions due to toxic agents (23,500 cases) were outnumbered only by disorders associated with repeated trauma to the wrists and arms (281,800).[22] Of increasing concern are the reproductive health hazards faced by employees.

Employers must make the workplace as safe as possible and should warn employees—male and female—of possible hazards. However, some employers, including at least fifteen major corporations, have gone beyond warnings to the adoption of *fetal protection* policies in some of their plants. Among those having such policies are General Motors, DuPont, Olin, Monsanto, and BFGoodrich. While fetal protection policies appear to many to provide reasonable precautions to fetal injury, they have often been viewed as an excuse for denying women equal employment opportunities.

In 1982 Johnson Controls, Inc., the largest maker of automobile batteries, instituted a policy that excluded all women capable of bearing children from its battery factories because they could be exposed to lead—a known danger to a developing fetus. A lawsuit filed by women working in the Johnson Controls plant in Fullerton, California, finally resulted in a U.S. Supreme Court decision (6 to 3 vote). In *International Union v Johnson Controls,* the Court ruled in 1991 that employers may not bar women of childbearing age from certain jobs because of potential risk to their fetuses. The Court said that such policies are a form of sex bias that is prohibited by federal civil rights law. The decision will make it important for employers to inform and to warn women workers about fetal health risks on the job.[23]

Indoor Air Quality

As a consequence of the energy crisis of the 1970s, commercial and some residential construction techniques have been changed to increase energy efficiency of heating, ventilating, and air-conditioning systems. This has included sealing windows, reducing outside air, and in general "buttoning up" buildings—thus resulting in the "sick building" phenomenon that gives rise to such employee complaints as headaches, dizziness, disorientation, fatigue, and eye, ear, and throat irritation. In addition to these complaints are others documented by research reprinted by the National Safety Council.[24]

According to the American Lung Association, four basic ways to overcome polluted buildings are to (1) eliminate tobacco smoke, (2) provide adequate ventilation, (3) maintain the ventilating system, and (4) remove sources of pollution. Figure 13–3 shows the common sources of pollutants in the typical office building. Study the figure carefully in order to have a better understanding of the sources of irritants that can affect the well-being and job performance of the building occupants.[25]

It should be noted that carpeting made from synthetic fibers is a major source of problems. The Environmental Protection Agency (EPA) became interested after a 1987 incident at their offices during which more than 10 percent of the employees reported symptoms after exposure to new carpeting.[26]

FIGURE 13-3 *Air Pollution in the Office Building*

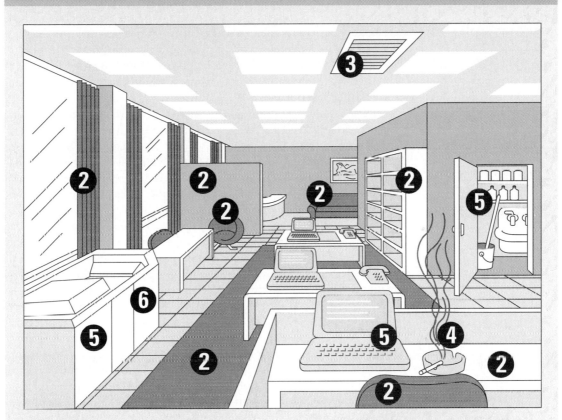

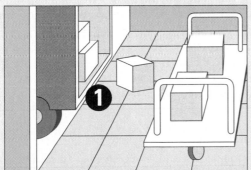

1. **CARBON MONOXIDE**
   Garages, motor vehicles, loading docks

2. **FORMALDEHYDE**
   Glues, partitions, carpet, drapery fabric, particleboard furniture, upholstery fabric

3. **BIOLOGICAL AGENTS**
   Humidifiers, air conditioners, dehumidifiers, washrooms, ventilation pipes and ducts

4. **TOBACCO SMOKE**
   Cigarettes, cigars, pipes

5. **VOLATILE ORGANIC COMPOUNDS**
   Felt-tip markers and pens, cleaning compounds, paint, copy machines, solvents

6. **OZONE**
   Copy machines

Source: Reprinted from "Indoor Air Pollution in the Office," copyright 1993, by the American Lung Association. Reproduced with permission.

Tobacco smoke. Probably the most heated workplace health issue of the 1990s is smoking. Nonsmokers, fueled by studies linking "passive smoking" (inhaling other people's smoke) with disease and death and irritated by smoke getting in their eyes, noses, throats, and clothes, have been extremely vocal in demanding a smoke-free environment. At least forty-two states and the District of Columbia, as well as numerous cities, towns, and counties, have passed laws restricting smoking in offices and other public places. Often, as in California, the local ordinances are broader and more stringent than the state law and frequently mandate stiffer fines for violators.

The number of organizations restricting smoking in the workplace rose from 16 percent in 1980 to 60 percent in 1991. Those banning smoking on the premises rose from 14 percent in 1988 to 56 percent by 1993. Kiplinger predicts that most employers will ban smoking and thus avoid worrying about future lawsuits or being forced into installing ventilation for smokers.[27] Virtually all of the larger organizations and many of the smaller ones have instituted smoking policies. (See Highlights in HRM 3.)

In developing smoking policies it is advisable to have the involvement of both smokers and nonsmokers. At Vanderbilt University Medical Center, for example, a steering committee deliberated for a year before deciding on a policy for the entire medical center. Other organizations emphasizing employee involvement include GTE Northwest, Michigan Bell, Merck, and Comerica, Inc.[28] Currently there are no OSHA regulations on smoking in the workplace, although the issue is under study by the Indoor Air Quality division of both OSHA and the EPA and many experts in the field expect action in the future.[29]

Efforts to help employees quit smoking are being promoted by many employers. The two most popular steps taken are to distribute "quit-smoking" literature and to sponsor employee wellness programs that encourage workers to stop smoking. Employer-sponsored quit-smoking clinics are found in such organizations as Sandia Laboratories in Albuquerque, the Iowa Methodist Medical Center, Alcoa, and Control Data Corporation, as well as in Johnson & Johnson's Live for Life Program.[30]

Because of documented higher health care costs for smokers, some employers are charging smokers more for health insurance or are reducing their benefits. Many employers, however, prefer positive reinforcement through wellness programs to encourage their employees to stop smoking.[31]

Video Display Terminals

The expanding use of computers and video display terminals (VDTs) in the workplace has generated intense debate over the possible hazards to which VDT users may be exposed. Many fears about VDT use have been shown to be unfounded, but serious health complaints remain an issue, drawing attention to the need for more information, education, and positive action. Problems that managers have to confront in this area fall into four major groups:[32]

1. *Visual difficulties.* VDT operators frequently complain of blurred vision, sore eyes, burning and itching eyes, and glare.
2. *Radiation hazards.* Cataract formation and reproductive problems, including miscarriages and birth defects, have been attributed to

3   HALLMARKERS PREPARE FOR SMOKE-FREE WORKPLACE

Kicking the smoking habit has become a priority for many Hallmarkers. In March, about 40 Hallmarkers began attending smoking cessation classes. Another session gets under way next month.

The classes, offered by Hallmark through St. Luke's Hospital, are designed to help smokers adopt healthy lifestyle habits and become non-smokers. Classes focus on breaking the smoking habit, mastering smoking urges, and developing strategies and support systems for maintaining a smoke-free commitment. They also include counseling in nutrition, stress management and weight control.

The cost of the class is $100. Hallmark pays $50 of the fee when you enroll. You may use payroll deductions. If you complete the program and do not smoke for a year, the company will reimburse the $50 you paid.

The classes are being offered as part of our company commitment to health and wellness. They are a resource that Hallmark smokers can use to prepare for the implementation of a smoke-free workplace in Hallmark facilities at headquarters and in the Crown Center complex.

"We want to assist Hallmarkers in making this change," says Jack Gabriel, director of Employee Relations. "The decision was made to go smoke-free because of Hallmarkers' concern about their health and well-being."

- The U.S. Surgeon General, in his 1986 report, "The Health Effects of Involuntary Smoking," concluded that "involuntary smoking is a cause of disease, including lung cancer, in healthy non-smokers. The simple separation of smokers and non-smokers within the same air space can reduce, but does not eliminate, the exposure of non-smokers to environmental tobacco smoke."
- About 350,000 Americans die prematurely each year from diseases related to cigarette smoking.
- A survey of 1,800 headquarters Hallmarkers showed that nearly 60 percent favored a smoke-free environment.

To sign up for a smoking cessation class, contact Diane Murdock in the Medical department at ext. 5520.

Source: Hallmark Cards, Inc. Reproduced with permission.

VDT use. The risks of exposure to VDT radiation have yet to be determined.

3. *Muscular aches and pains.* Pains in the back, neck, and shoulders are common complaints of VDT operators.

4. *Job stress.* Eye strain, postural problems, noise, insufficient training, excessive workloads, and monotonous work are complaints reported by three-quarters of VDT users.[33]

Managers must balance the benefits of computers with the health of employees.

To capitalize on the benefits of VDTs while safeguarding employee health, organizations are advised to consider several strategies. These include educating employees in proper use of VDTs, involving employees in system design, encouraging open-door communication with management so that concerns may be voiced and solutions found, using rest periods and job rotation, using ergonomically designed equipment, and ensuring that workstations have appropriate lighting.

Cumulative Trauma Disorders

Cumulative trauma disorders (CTDs)

Injuries involving tendons of the fingers, hands, and arms that become inflamed from repeated stresses and strains

Meat cutters, fish filleters, cooks, dental hygienists, textile workers, violinists, flight attendants, office workers at computer terminals, and others whose jobs require repetitive motion of the fingers, hands, or arms are reporting injuries in growing percentages. Known as **cumulative trauma disorders (CTDs),** these injuries involve tendons that become inflamed from repeated stresses and strains. One of the more common conditions is *carpal tunnel syndrome*, which is characterized by tingling or numbness in the fingers occurring when a tunnel of bones and ligaments in the wrist narrows and pinches nerves that reach the fingers and base of the thumb. To prevent *repetitive motion injuries*, minibreaks involving exercises, properly designed workstations, the changing of positions, and improvement in tool design have been found helpful. These kinds of injuries often go away if they are caught early. If they are not, they may require months or years of treatment or even surgical correction.

Cumulative trauma disorders make up nearly half of all recordable workplace injuries, and it is estimated that 5 million Americans suffer from them annually. These injuries cost business nearly $27 billion when considering lost earnings and medical costs.[34] Recognizing that the problem is growing, OSHA is attacking it aggressively. The levying of OSHA fines has prompted employers to take action to prevent these injuries.

Unfortunately, many physicians do not see a connection between employees' symptoms and their work environments, and they tell patients that the problem is psychosomatic. Such reports lead employers to believe that workers are malingering. Gradually, however, more physicians are realizing that work is the origin for these disorders.[35] While managers are not expected to play the role of doctor, they should be alert to injuries that occur among employees who perform similar tasks under similar conditions, and they should assume a proactive role in reducing these injuries.

AIDS

In recent years, few workplace issues have received as much attention as AIDS (Acquired Immune Deficiency Syndrome). Many legal and medical questions have arisen that have made it imperative for employers to provide answers to everyone concerned.

As we observed in Chapter 3, AIDS is a disability covered by federal, state, and local protective statutes. Employers subject to statutes under which AIDS victims are likely to be considered disabled are required to hire or retain an AIDS victim qualified to perform the essential functions of his or her job. The federal Rehabilitation Act, the Americans with Disabilities Act, and statutes of several states also require employers to give reasonable accommodation to the person through such adjustments as job restructuring, modified work schedules, and less rigid physical requirements.[36]

While there is still no evidence that AIDS can be spread through casual contact in the typical workplace, one of the major problems employers face is the concern that many people have about contracting it. Employers have found it important to have programs to educate managers about the transmission of AIDS and to educate the entire workforce through newsletters, posters, and seminars.[37] The manager's job of obtaining AIDS information has been assisted by various organizations including the Centers for Disease Control, which has a special office to assist employers and labor organizations.[38]

U.S. employers have generally taken a low-key approach to dealing with AIDS. BankAmerica and Wells Fargo were among the first to establish policy guidelines. BankAmerica's policy may be found in Chapter 3, Highlights in HRM 1. (It would be a good idea to review this policy now. Note that it refers to assisting employees with any life-threatening illness, including AIDS.) In 1987 Polaroid initiated a comprehensive AIDS plan and made it company policy that AIDS was to be treated like any other long-term, life-threatening disease. At Polaroid employees with AIDS are entitled to the full range of benefits, to work accommodations, and to continued employment.[39]

Because of the controversial nature of AIDS, employers have found that managers and HR personnel must be carefully briefed on all aspects of the issue so they may act in the best interests of all concerned. HR journals, as well as health journals, have published numerous articles in the past several years that can be useful in developing reading files for the HR staff and for managerial and supervisory personnel.

Building Better Health

Along with improving working conditions that are hazardous to employee health, many employers provide health services and have programs that encourage employees to improve their health habits. It is recognized that better health not only benefits the individual, but also pays off for the organization in reduced absenteeism, increased efficiency, better morale, and other savings. An increased understanding of the close relationship between physical and emotional health and job performance has made broad health-building programs attractive to employers as well as to employees.

Health Services

The type of health services employers provide is primarily related to the size of the organization and the importance of such services. Small organizations have only limited facilities, such as those needed to handle first-aid cases, while many *Fortune* 500 firms offer complete diagnostic, treatment, and emergency surgical services. Since employers are required to provide medical services after an injury, the larger firms usually have nurses and physicians on full-time duty. Medium-sized and smaller organizations have one or more physicians on call.

In order to get a tighter grip on health care costs more of the larger employers are opening their own primary care clinics for employees, dependents, and retirees. These clinics go far beyond the occupational health clinics staffed for handing work-related injuries. In Highlights in HRM 4 the services offered by six different companies and the charge to employees are presented as a sampling of in-house corporate clinics.[40]

We noted in Chapter 6 that about one-half of all employers give preemployment medical examinations to prospective employees. Generally, these examinations are required to assure employers that the health of applicants is adequate for the job. The preemployment examination should include a medical history with special reference to previous hazardous exposures. Exposure to hazards whose effects may be cumulative, such as noise, lead, and radiation, are especially relevant. For jobs involving unusual physical demands, the applicant's muscular development, flexibility, agility, range of motion, and cardiac and respiratory functions should be evaluated. The preemployment medical examination that includes laboratory analyses can help screen those applicants who abuse drugs. Many organizations also give periodic examinations on either a required or a voluntary basis. Such examinations are useful in determining the effects of potential hazards in the workplace as well as in detecting any health problems to which an employee's particular lifestyle or health habits may contribute.

Alternative Approaches

In a discussion of health services as well as health benefits it should be emphasized that there are many nontraditional approaches to better health. These are typically referred to as *alternative approaches*. According to the *New England Journal of Medicine* (Jan. 28, 1993) approximately one-third of all Americans use them. Many of the approaches differ from traditional medicine in that they empower the patient by enlisting patient participation in health care decisions and

HIGHLIGHTS IN HRM

highlights

4   A SAMPLING OF IN-HOUSE CORPORATE CLINICS

Parent Company Clinic Location	Services	Charge Per Visit
GATES CORP. Denver rubber plant	Internal medicine with visiting specialists ranging from dermatologists to oncologists, ear and eye exams, fitness center, dietitian, on-site chemotherapy, open 24 hours	$10
UNION-CAMP CORP. Savannah, Ga., paper mill	Minor surgery and emergencies, stress testing, immunizations, well-patient care, various specialized procedures	$10
SOUTHERN CALIF. EDISON CO. Eight California clinics	Primary medicine, physicals, eye and hearing exams, sports medicine, dermatology, orthopedics, ophthalmology	10% of bill
GILLETTE CO. Three Boston-area facilities	Primary care, physicals, stress testing, electrocardiograms, endoscopy, open 24 hours	No charge
ADOLPH COORS CO. Golden, Colo., headquarters and brewery	Primary care, minor surgery, physicals, respiratory testing, electrocardiograms, physical rehabilitation	$5
QUAD/GRAPHICS INC. Pewaukee, Wis., headquarters and plant	Family and internal medicine, general surgery, pediatrics, obstetrics and gynecology, mental health, and drug and alcohol counseling	No charge

Source: *The Wall Street Journal* (March 23, 1993), B1. Reprinted by permission of *The Wall Street Journal,* © 1993 Dow Jones & Company, Inc. All rights reserved worldwide.

are less invasive. According to Jane Heimlich, author of *What the Doctor Won't Tell You*, a former U.S. Air Force flight surgeon once told her, "I got tired of doling out pills and never having anyone get well."[41]

Relaxation techniques, chiropractic, therapeutic massage, acupuncture, homeopathy, megavitamin and herbal therapy, special diets, and many other alternative approaches are used to treat a wide variety of health problems. These and other approaches are examined in Heimlich's book and in Linda Rector-Page's *Healthy Healing.*[42] Interest in these alternative approaches influences employee concern about health plan coverage.

This jogger is encouraged to exercise by her employer.

According to Virginia M. Gibson, president of the MG Group, a Baltimore-based consulting firm specializing in employee benefits, consumers are sending a definite message to their benefits managers that cannot be ignored. She writes: "The fact that consumers are accessing and utilizing alternative therapies on such a grand scale must be acknowledged and incorporated into any assessment [of health plans.]"[43]

Wellness Programs

Many organizations have developed programs that emphasize regular exercise, proper nutrition, weight control, and avoidance of substances harmful to health. For example, the employee health management program at Xerox includes cardiovascular fitness through aerobic exercises such as jogging, skipping rope, and racquet sports. The company gives its employees a *Fitbook* that provides instructions and illustrations for a variety of exercises. The book also includes chapters on the hazards of smoking and the effects of alcohol and drug abuse, facts on nutrition and weight control, and guidelines for managing stress and learning to relax.[44] Smaller organizations may distribute booklets available from services specializing in employee health educational and motivational materials.

Tenneco, with headquarters in Houston, has one of the finest fitness centers in corporate America. It includes racquetball courts, exercise rooms, saunas, and a one-fifth-mile indoor jogging track. The center has its own computer program to help employees monitor their progress. Employees of ROLM Corporation in California's Silicon Valley enjoy a million-dollar recreation facility, where in midafternoon it is common to see them swimming, playing racquetball, or working out in an aerobics class. The DuPont Company has a comprehensive multisite employee health management program with over 100 locations.

Research shows that companies with occupational medicine departments are less likely than those without such departments to adopt health-related innovations. This may occur because health management programs are based on a disease prevention, health promotion plan rather than on the traditional medical model.[45]

Focus on Nutrition

There is mounting evidence to support the link between certain nutritional deficiencies and various physiological and psychological disorders, including alcoholism, depression, nervousness, low energy level, perceptual inaccuracy, and lack of reasonability. In fact, a person's mental and emotional states are affected by the foods he or she consumes, hence the wisdom of such sayings as "You are what you eat" and "What you eat today you walk and talk tomorrow." Proponents suggest that the potential return on a minimal investment in a sound nutritional plan is great, in terms of both dollars and morale, because human behavior might b

"Yes, you have to eat your vegetables!
We're vegetarians!"

From *The Wall Street Journal*—Permission, Cartoon Features Syndicate

more easily and quickly modified by dietary changes than by more sophisticated modification techniques.[46]

Many employers provide their employees the opportunity to participate in special programs, such as those offered by the Longevity Research Center of Santa Monica, California, and Miami Beach, Florida. These programs provide training in proper *diet* and *exercise,* primarily walking. The late Nathan Pritikin and his colleagues developed a plan known as the "2100 Program" that has been successful in helping people overcome degenerative diseases. The basis for the diet is given in Pritikin's books, which are now considered classics.[47]

five
objective

Employee Assistance Programs

A broad view of health includes the emotional, as well as the physical, aspects of one's life. While emotional problems, personal crises, alcoholism, and drug abuse are considered to be personal matters, they become organizational problems when they affect behavior at work and interfere with job performance. To be able to handle such problems, 87 percent of all employers with 5,000 or more workers offer an employee assistance program (EAP).[48] Typically, such a program refers employees in need of assistance to in-house counselors or outside professionals. Supervisors are often given training and policy guidance in the type of help they can offer their subordinates. In contracting with professional counselors outside the organization, the HR department needs to give special attention to their credentials, cost, accountability, and service capabilities.

Personal Crises

The most prevalent problems among employees are personal crises involving marital, family, financial, or legal matters. Such problems often come to a supervisor's attention. In most instances, the supervisor can usually provide the best help simply by being understanding and supportive and by helping the individual find the type of assistance he or she needs. In many cases, in-house counseling or referral to an outside professional is recommended. In recent years, crisis hot lines have been set up in many communities to provide counseling by telephone for those too distraught to wait for an appointment with a counselor.

Emotional Problems

While personal crises are typically fraught with emotion, most of them are resolved in a reasonable period of time and the troubled individual's equilibrium is restored. There will, however, be a small percentage of employees—roughly 3 percent on average—who have emotional problems serious enough to require professional treatment. Whether such individuals will be able to perform their jobs must be determined on an individual basis. In reviewing such cases, the organization should pay particular attention to workplace safety factors, since there is general agreement that emotional disturbances are primary or secondary factors in a large proportion of industrial accidents.

Clinical ecology
Study of an individual's reactions to substances in the work environment, such as inhaled chemicals and fumes, that adversely affect the behavior of some workers

Managers should also be aware that the behavior of some individuals is adversely affected by substances in the workplace that apparently do not affect others, or at least not as severely. Such individuals are, in fact, allergic to these substances. They may simply need to be reassigned to a different work environment rather than sent to a physician. Physicians who work in this area, called **clinical ecology,** report numerous cases of individuals whose behavior on and off the job is affected by petrochemicals, molds, cleaning substances, cosmetics and toiletries, plastics, tobacco smoke—in fact, virtually anything that can be found in the environment. (See Figure 13-3 on page 475.)

Those who are allergic to such items may exhibit behavioral symptoms, ranging from severe depression to extreme hyperactivity, that interfere with job performance. Remove the substance, or get the individuals away from the substance, and the symptoms disappear. Dr. Theron Randolph, a Chicago allergist, was among the first to write about the importance of environmental chemicals, in addition to foods, as the cause of many physical and emotional illnesses. His work has stimulated other allergists, as well as mental health practitioners, to study the phenomenon further. Among them is Dr. W. J. Rea of the Environmental Health Center of Dallas.[49]

Alcoholism

Business and industry lose an estimated $20.6 billion each year because of alcoholism, according to the Conference Board. The National Council for Alcoholism reports that in this country alone there are more than 10.5 million alcoholics. Alcoholism affects workers in every occupational category—blue-collar, white-collar, and managerial.[50]

In confronting the problem, employers must recognize that alcoholism is a disease that follows a rather predictable course. Thus they can take specific actions to deal with employees showing symptoms of the disease at particular stages of its progression. Alcoholism typically begins with social drinking getting out of control. As the disease progresses, the alcoholic loses control over how much to drink and eventually cannot keep from drinking, even at inappro priate times. The person uses denial to avoid facing the problems created by the abuse of alcohol and often blames others for these problems. A U.S. Air Force counselor states that the first step in helping the alcoholic is to awaken the person to the reality of his or her situation.[51]

To identify alcoholism as early as possible, it is essential that supervisors monitor the performance of all personnel regularly and systematically. A supervisor should carefully document evidence of declining performance on the job and then confront the employee with unequivocal proof that the job is suffering. The employee should be assured that help will be made available without penalty. Since the evaluations are made solely in terms of lagging job performance, a supervisor can avoid any mention of alcoholism and allow such employees to seek aid as they would for any other problem. Disciplinary action may be taken against employees who refuse to take advantage of such assistance or whose performance does not improve with repeated warnings. Between 70 and 80 percent of the employees accept the offer to get help and resolve their problems. It is important for employers to recognize, however, that in discharge cases brought by alcoholic employees, arbitrators look at on-the-job alcoholism as a sickness, not as a disciplinary matter.

EAPs typically provide assistance to the alcoholic employee. Rehabilitation is generally conducted by referral agencies. A large percentage of medical insurance now covers part of the treatment costs for alcoholism, making it possible to receive treatment at reasonable costs.

Abuse of Illegal Drugs

The abuse of drugs by employees is one of the major employment issues today. Once confined to a small segment of the population, drug abuse is now a national problem that has spread to every industry and occupation as well as employee level. Executives and federal officials say that the use of cocaine and crack in the workplace is growing rapidly. Estimates of the costs of substance abuse by employees vary considerably. The federal government estimates in one report that alcohol and drug abuse cost the economy $177 billion a year, including $99 billion for lost productivity.[52] In addition to lost productivity, there are the costs of increased numbers of accidents and injuries, higher medical insurance costs, and rising rates of employee theft. The costs of substance abuse are having a dramatic impact on the bottom line.

In the past, most efforts to curb workplace drug abuse have been voluntary actions on the part of management. Now, however, a wide range of employers, including federal contractors and private and public transportation firms, are subject to regulations aimed at eliminating the use of illegal drugs on the job. The federal antidrug initiatives include the following:

1. Drug-Free Workplace Act of 1988, which requires federal contractors and recipients of federal grants to take specific steps to ensure a drug-free work environment. One of the main provisions of the act is the preparation and distribution of an antidrug policy statement, a sample of which is shown in Highlights in HRM 5.

NOTICE TO APPLICANTS

We are proud to be a
DRUG-FREE
WORKPLACE

Screening tests for illegal drug use are required as a condition of employment.

A poster such as this is usually found in the employment office.

HIGHLIGHTS IN HRM

5 KINKO'S POLICIES AND PROCEDURES FOR A DRUG-FREE WORKPLACE

Policy Statement:

To ensure a safe, productive work environment and to protect all co-workers and Kinko's property, the use, sale, transfer or possession of alcohol, drugs, or controlled substances when on the job, on company property, or in company vehicles is grounds for immediate dismissal, regardless of the length of employment of the co-worker. In addition, any co-worker under the influence of alcohol, drugs, or a controlled substance while on the job or on company premises is subject to immediate dismissal. Co-workers who are considered to be unable to perform work in a safe and productive manner, who are in a physical or mental condition which creates a risk to the safety or well-being of the co-worker, the public or company property, will be deemed to be under the influence.

Procedure:

Co-worker infractions of this policy are defined as misconduct. When infractions occur, the supervisor will refer to the Human Resources Policy on Termination of Employment.

Note:

Any co-worker who is taking a drug or other medication, whether or not prescribed by a physician for a medical condition, which is known or advertised as possibly affecting or impairing judgment, coordination or senses, or which may adversely affect the co-worker's ability to perform work in a safe and productive manner, must notify his/her supervisor prior to starting work. The supervisor will decide if the co-worker can remain at work or on the company premises or what work restrictions, if any, are deemed necessary.

Source: Kinko's Service Corporation. Reproduced with permission.

2. Department of Defense (DOD) contract rules, which specify that employers entering into contracts with the DOD must agree to a clause certifying their intention to maintain a drug-free workplace.
3. Department of Transportation (DOT) regulations, which require that employees whose jobs include safety- or security-related duties be tested for illegal drug use under DOT rules.

We observed in Chapter 6 that a number of employers test for substance abuse in the final stages of the employee selection process. At this point it is often easy to screen out applicants who may become problem employees. Once an applicant is accepted, however, the employer is faced with the problem of controlling drug abuse. For this reason, an increasing number of employers are instituting drug-testing programs.

As noted earlier, employers operating under the federal requirements are required to test for drug use under certain specified conditions. However, employers that are exempt from the federal requirement may operate under state or local laws restricting or prohibiting drug tests. Issues related to drug testing under state or local laws are discussed in Chapter 16 in the context of employee rights.

Abuse of Legal Drugs

While attention is usually focused on the abuse of illegal drugs, it should be noted that the abuse of legal drugs can also pose a problem for employers. Employees who abuse legal drugs—i.e., those prescribed by physicians—often do not realize they have become addicted or how their behavior has changed as a result of their addiction. Often such individuals have prescriptions from more than one physician and may be cross-medicating with drugs that fall under the general headings of sedatives, narcotics, and stimulants. Others may not have advised their physician of their drug dependency even if they are aware of it. Also, managers should be aware that some employees may be taking legal sedatives or stimulants as part of their medical treatment and that their behavior at work may be affected by their use of these drugs.[53] A standard reference book of legal drugs is the *Physicians' Desk Reference (PDR)*.[54] Available in all libraries and most bookstores, it should be included in the HR department library. The side effects from the many legal drugs available are contained in the narrative for each drug.

Various approaches are used in EAPs to assist individuals with a chemical dependency, ranging from outpatient treatment to an extended stay in a specialized hospital unit. One approach that has proved successful and less expensive is known as a day treatment program. Participants report each day for a structured program that avoids the costs of a residential program with bed and board. Employees prefer this form of treatment because it enables them to stay in touch with their job and to avoid painful separation from their families while receiving treatment.

objective

The Management of Stress

Many jobs require employees to adjust to conditions that place unusual demands on them. In time these demands create stresses that can affect the health of employees as well as their productivity and satisfaction. Fortunately, increasing attention is being given to ways of identifying and preventing undue stress on the job. Even greater attention must be given to identifying and removing sources of stress to protect the well-being of employees and to reduce the costs to organizations. The costs of stress in health insurance claims, disability claims, and lost productivity alone are between $50 billion and $150 billion per year. During the mid-1990s and beyond, NIOSH has predicted a need for greater emphasis on ways to reduce stress in the workplace.[55]

What Is Stress?

Stress
Any adjustive demand caused by physical, mental, or emotional factors that requires coping behavior

Eustress
Positive stress that accompanies achievement and exhilaration

Distress
Harmful stress characterized by a loss of feelings of security and adequacy

Alarm reaction
Response to stress that basically involves an elevated heart rate, increased respiration, elevated levels of adrenaline in the blood, and increased blood pressure

Stress is any demand on the individual that requires coping behavior. Stress comes from two basic sources: physical activity and mental or emotional activity. The physical reaction of the body to both types of stress is the same. According to the late Hans Selye, human beings thrive on stress because "stress is the spice of life."[56] Selye uses two separate terms to distinguish between positive and negative life consequences of stress for the individual, even though reactions to the two forms of stress are the same biochemically. **Eustress** is positive stress that accompanies achievement and exhilaration. Eustress is the stress of meeting challenges such as those found in a managerial, technical, or public contact job. Selye regards eustress as a beneficial force that helps us to forge ahead against obstacles. He is of the opinion that what is harmful is **distress**. Stress becomes distress when we begin to sense a loss of our feelings of security and adequacy. Helplessness, desperation, and disappointment turn stress into distress.

The stress reaction is a coordinated chemical mobilization of the entire body to meet the requirements of fight-or-flight in a situation perceived to be stressful. The sympathetic nervous system activates the secretion of hormones from the endocrine glands that places the body on a "war footing." This response, commonly referred to as the **alarm reaction,** basically involves an elevated heart rate, increased respiration, elevated levels of adrenaline in the blood, and increased blood pressure. It persists until one's estimate of the relative threat to well-being has been reevaluated. While the alarm reaction may have made life safer for our ancestors who were confronted daily with physical peril, it lacks value for most of the invisible enemies of contemporary life.

If distress persists long enough, it can result in fatigue, exhaustion, and even physical and/or emotional breakdown. When Selye first published his experimental findings, many medical practitioners failed to recognize the role of stress in a wide range of illnesses for which there is no specific cause. Some research has suggested a link between stress and heart disease. A number of important studies have shown a connection between chronic stress and hypertension (high blood pressure). High blood pressure, the most common cause of strokes, contributes to heart disease.[57]

Job-related Stress

Although the body experiences a certain degree of stress (either eustress or distress) in all situations, here we are primarily concerned with the stress related to the work setting. It is in this setting that management can use some preventive approaches.

Sources of Job-related Stress

Disagreements with supervisors or fellow employees are a common cause of distress. A myriad of other events may also prove distressful. One individual, for example, remembers the time in the armed forces when he was made to rewrite a letter thirteen times. "I couldn't walk off the job," he recalls, "so I went to the men's room and hit the wall so hard my co-workers came in to see what was wrong." Feeling trapped in a job for which a person is ill-suited can be equally distressing. An airline attendant said that she was sick of "smiling when I don't

A surgeon finds a quiet
spot to relieve his stress.

want to smile" and "making excuses for the airline to furious passengers," but she
did not consider herself qualified for other jobs with similar pay and benefits.

Many minor irritations can also be sources of distress. Lack of privacy in offices, unappealing music, excessive noise, and other conditions can be distressful
to one person or another. There are even more serious conditions related to the
management of personnel. Potentially distressful factors include having little to
say about how a job is performed, overspecialization, lack of communication on
the job, and lack of recognition for a job well done.

Burnout

Most severe stage of
distress, manifesting
itself in depression,
frustration, and loss of
productivity

Burnout is the most severe stage of distress. Career burnout generally occurs
when a person begins questioning his or her own personal values. Quite simply,
one no longer feels that what he or she is doing is important. Depression, frustration, and a loss of productivity are all symptoms of burnout. Burnout is due primarily to a lack of personal fulfillment in the job or a lack of positive feedback
about performance.[58]

objective

Employer Responsibility for Job-related Distress

The issue of stress on the job has received considerable publicity in the various
media. As a result, employees have begun to recognize that stress may have
caused them psychological harm and have responded by striking back in the
courts. Employers that once gave minimal attention to stress on the job are now
required to take positive steps to identify specific sources of organizational stressors and to take corrective action.

In the past decade the number of mental-stress workers' compensation
claims have mushroomed because of (1) the growing number of employees in service jobs where the work is more mental than manual, (2) the repetitive nature
of tasks, (3) the trend toward seeking compensation for mental as well as physical
injuries, and (4) the receptivity of the courts to such cases.

Awareness of the legal implications of workplace stressors will help managers to initiate preventive programs. Citing landmark cases that have provided

compensation for psychological injuries resulting from emotional stress, several experts recommend the following five-step program:

1. Formulate a preventive legal strategy through analysis and forecasting of trends that indicate the direction of new legislation.
2. Develop a stress diagnostic system to increase awareness and sensitivity to employee concerns.
3. Involve top-level management in developing priorities and procedures for correcting problem areas.
4. Evaluate current programs by determining if stress-related problems still remain.
5. Document what has been done to correct situations that result in stress, and be prepared to take further corrective action.[59]

Training managers to recognize the symptoms of stress, to refer employees who may need professional help, and to implement programs for monitoring and treating problems is an important responsibility of the HR department. It is generally agreed that stress-management programs usually result in a net savings rather than a cost.

Stress-Management Programs

Many employers have developed stress-management programs to teach employees how to minimize the negative effects of job-related stress. A typical program might include instruction in relaxation techniques, coping skills, listening skills, methods of dealing with difficult people, time management, and assertiveness. All of these techniques are designed to break the pattern of tension that accompanies stress situations and to help participants achieve greater control of their lives. Organizational techniques, such as clarifying the employee's work role, redesigning and enriching jobs, correcting physical factors in the environment, and effectively handling interpersonal factors, should not be overlooked in the process of teaching employees how to handle stress. A review of research on work-site stress-management programs reveals that organizational stressors have not received the attention they should. There has been too much emphasis on helping individuals adjust to undesirable working conditions rather than on changing the conditions themselves.[60]

Even though the number and severity of organizational stressors can be reduced, everyone encounters situations that may be described as distressful. Those in good physical health are generally better able to cope with the stressors they encounter.

Employees should be made aware that some of the popular rituals that are supposed to relieve stress, such as the "coffee break," may be counterproductive if they lead to overconsumption of beverages containing caffeine. Many individuals develop anxiety symptoms from overdoses of caffeine. Their condition, which is often misdiagnosed as a psychological ailment, may well affect their behavior and their productivity on the job. Instead of coffee breaks, many organizations are encouraging their employees to take exercise breaks.

While sabbatical leaves have been a long tradition in colleges and universities, it is only recently that other types of organizations have introduced them i the form of personal-growth leaves. The benefits-consulting firm Hewitt Associates has found them helpful to their professionals who work long and stressful hours. High-tech firms such as Apple Computer and Tandem Computer are among firms that have introduced these leaves. The expected payoffs to the firm are productivity and retention.[61]

Before concluding this discussion, we should observe that stress that is harmful to some employees may be healthy for others. Most executives learn to handle distress effectively and find that it actually stimulates better performance. However, there will always be those who are unable to handle stress and need assistance in learning to cope with it. The increased interest of young and old alike in developing habits that will enable them to lead happier and more productive lives will undoubtedly be beneficial to them as individuals, to the organizations where they work, and to a society where people are becoming more and more interdependent.

SUMMARY

The Occupational Safety and Health Act was designed to assure, so far as possible, safe and healthful working conditions to every working person. In general, the act extends to all employers and employees. OSHA administration involves setting standards, ensuring employer and employee compliance, and providing safety and health consultation and training where needed. Both employers and employees have certain responsibilities and rights under OSHA. Employers are not only required to provide a hazard-free work environment but must keep employees informed about OSHA requirements and require their employees to use protective equipment when necessary. Under the "right to know" regulations, employers are required to keep employees informed of hazardous substances and instruct them in avoiding the dangers presented. Employees, in turn, are required to comply with OSHA standards, to report hazardous conditions, and to follow all employer safety and health regulations.

In order to provide safe working conditions for their employees, employers typically establish a formal program that, in a large percentage of organizations, is under the direction of the HR manager. The program may have many facets, including providing safety knowledge and motivating employees to use it, making employees aware of the need for safety, and rewarding them for safe behavior. Such incentives as praise, public recognition, and awards are used to involve employees in the safety program. Maintenance of required records from accident investigations provides a basis for information that can be used to create a safer work environment.

Job conditions that are dangerous to the health of employees are now receiving much greater attention than in the past. There is special concern for toxic chemicals that proliferate at a rapid rate and may lurk in the body for years without outward symptoms. Concern for health hazards other than those found in industrial processing operations—indoor air pollution, video display terminals, and cumulative trauma disorders—present special problems that must be addressed. Today tobacco smoke is rarely tolerated in the work environment. While there is no evidence that AIDS can be spread through casual contact in the workplace, employers have found that it is important to educate managers and employees about AIDS and to assist those who are afflicted.

objective

Along with providing safer and healthier work environments, many employers establish programs that encourage employees to improve their health habits. Some of the larger employers have opened primary care clinics for employees and their dependents to provide better health care service and to reduce costs. Wellness programs that emphasize exercise, nutrition, weight control, and avoidance of harmful substances serve employees at all organizational levels.

objective

Virtually all of the larger organizations and many of the smaller ones have found that an employee assistance program is beneficial to all concerned. While emotional problems, personal crises, alcoholism, and drug abuse are often viewed as personal matters, it is apparent that they affect behavior at work and interfere with job performance. An employee assistance program typically provides professional assistance by in-house counselors or outside professionals where needed. In contracting with professional persons outside the organization, the HR department should give special attention to their credentials.

objective

An important dimension to health and safety is stress that comes from physical activity and mental or emotional activity. While stress is an integral part of being alive, when it turns into distress it becomes harmful. We have seen that there are many sources of stress that are job-related. In recognizing the need for reducing stress, employers can develop stress-management programs to assist employees in acquiring techniques for coping with stress. In addition, organizations need to take action to redesign and enrich jobs, to clarify the employee's work role, to correct physical factors in the environment, and to take any other actions that will help reduce stress on the job.

KEY TERMS

alarm reaction

burnout

clinical ecology

cumulative trauma disorders (CTDs)

distress

employee right-to-know laws

eustress

Material Safety Data Sheets (MSDSs)

recordable case

stress

voluntary protection programs (VPPs)

DISCUSSION QUESTIONS

1. When OSHA was enacted in 1970, it was heralded as the most important new source of protection for the American worker in this half of the twentieth century. What opinions about the effectiveness or the ineffectiveness of the act or its implementation have you heard from acquaintances who have been affected by it?

2. What steps should be taken by management to increase motivation for safety?

3. Many occupational health hazards that once existed no longer do. However, industry has to remain vigilant to the possibility of new hazards.
   a. What are some of the occupational health hazards that were once common but are seldom found today? What factors contributed to their elimination?
   b. What are some possible present and future hazards that did not exist in the past?
   c. What role should periodic medical examinations play in the detection and elimination of occupational hazards?

4. What approaches can be used to provide work areas free from tobacco smoke? How far should management go in restricting smoking at work?

5. What value would periodic consultations with a professional counselor have for an executive? Who should pay for this service?

6. We observed that the field of clinical ecology relates directly to work situations.
   a. Have you noticed any chemicals that appear to affect how you feel or your behavior?
   b. On what jobs are these chemicals likely to be found?
   c. How can specialists in HRM use this information?

7. In several states employers can require an employee to take a drug test only if there is a "reasonable cause" for testing. What are some behaviors that would indicate that a worker may be under the influence of drugs?

8. Identify the sources of stress in an organization.
   a. In what ways do they affect the individual employee? The organization?
   b. What can managers and supervisors do to make the workplace less stressful?

CASE STUDY: Violence Prevention in the Postal Service

Not rain, nor sleet nor snow can stop postal workers from doing their jobs. But bullets can, and indeed have. During the past decade, nearly three dozen postal workers have been killed on the job, gunned down by fellow employees.

Statistically speaking, the Postal Service isn't any more dangerous than other businesses. Research by the National Institute for Occupational Safety and Health (NIOSH) indicates that the average annual rate of occupational-injury death in the Postal Service is less than half the rate for all occupations combined. However, it also shows that co-workers appear to be disproportionately responsible for homicides that occur in the Postal Service. Between 1983 and 1989, for example, 57 percent of work-related homicides at the Postal Service were committed by co-workers or former co-workers. Only 4 percent of work-related homicides industrywide in 1992 were committed by this group.

These facts prompted the Postal Service to re-examine its work practices in regard to employee safety. Its examination has led to the development of a six-strategy violence prevention program, coordinated through the agency's national employee relations function. The strategies are:

1. *Selection.* The goal of the Postal Service is to hire selectively, ensuring it gets the right people in the jobs in the first place. Its pre-screening process includes performing competency tests and contracting with an outside firm to do thorough background checks.

2. *Security.* "To protect people from homicide and other violence, a certain amount of security is necessary," says Ann Wright, manager for safety and health, who, until August 20 when the agency brought in a full-time coordinator, managed the program. What that amount is varies from location to location. The Postal Service has 47,000 facilities that range from one-person post offices to 24-hour plants employing 4,000 people. Some facilities rely on awareness programs and training on such issues as how to report incidents. Others employ security guards, attach surveillance cameras on the premises or require access badges. Management at each location assesses the measures that should be taken with the Postal Inspection Service—the law-enforcement arm of the Postal Service.

3. *Policy.* "We're trying to promote a clear, direct, absolute and well-known policy related to violence," Wright says. That includes a prohibition of any kind of weapon on postal property, including parking lots, a no-tolerance philosophy towards threats of any kind and a protocol to intervene early. "There's no minor incident of violence," says Wright. "We want to take action even if there's just pushing, yelling or cussing on the floor so that we can preclude those incidents from escalating into something bigger." For this reason, the policy also includes reporting all incidents.

4. *Climate.* A healthy workplace is a safe workplace, so the Postal Service has an intense initiative to improve the agency's environment. It's putting managers and supervisors through a series of training sessions that deal with such issues as employee empowerment, conflict resolution and positive reinforcement. It's also working with its unions to improve the grievance process. Some regions are testing intervention teams, comprising cross-functional groups of employees and managers, to intervene when their facility's climate isn't conducive to a good work environment. And, the agency has

instituted an employee-opinion survey that measures employee
satisfaction and promotes better interaction between managers and
employees.

5. *Employee Support.* The Postal Service has beefed up its employee
   assistance program (EAP) in the last year and a half and currently is
   conducting training with supervisors and managers on how best to use
   the EAP and how to educate employees on how to use it. The agency
   also has implemented an orientation program for all the employees
   explaining the program. And in addition to the EAP, the Postal
   Service has installed a 24-hour, toll-free hot-line that employees can
   call to report threats or concerns. "We are trying to catch problems
   that individuals might have early enough so that we can deal with
   them before they get to the point at which somebody loses control,"
   Wright says. "We're also trying to make the point with our managers
   and supervisors that firing people doesn't necessarily solve the
   problem. Quite a few of our most violent incidents have been by
   terminated employees who come back and shoot people. So that's part
   of the support system that we're trying to build."

6. *Separation.* Because termination does become necessary at times, the
   agency currently is creating policies and procedures for terminating
   employees in the most effective way. It's also evaluating methods for
   making assessments on whether the people being dismissed may be
   dangerous. Because this is a recent initiative, no specific strategies
   have been developed yet.

Source: Dawn Anfuso, "Deflecting Workplace Violence," *Personnel Journal* 73, no. 10 (October 1994):
66–77. Reproduced with permission.

Questions

1. In his October 1994 Letter to Readers, Allan Halcrow, editor-in-chief of
    Personnel Journal, states that murder on the job was rare enough to make
    headlines in 1992. Today, however, an average of 15 people are killed on
    the job each week. How do you account for this change?

2. In his Letter to Readers, Editor Halcrow reminds us that there are
    invisible victims: families and loved ones. What do you see as
    management's responsibility to them?

3. While all six strategies used by the Postal Service are important, which
    ones do you believe deserve the highest priority? Why?

NOTES AND REFERENCES

1. Matthew P. Weinstock, "Rewarding Safety,"
   Occupational Hazards 56, no. 3 (March 1994): 73–76;
   Christopher J. Bachler, "Workers Take Leave of Job
   Stress," *Personnel Journal* 74, no. 1 (January 1995):
   38–44. See also Cecily A. Waterman and Karen H.
   Peteros, "Health Safety Concerns Knock on HR
   Doors," *HR Magazine* 37, no. 7 (July 1992): 89–91;
   Daniel R. Ilgen, "Health Issues at Work:

Opportunities for Industrial/Organizational Psychology," *American Psychologist* 45, no. 2 (February 1990): 273–83.

2. U.S. Department of Labor, Occupational Safety and Health Administration, *All about OSHA*, rev. ed. (Washington, D.C.: U.S. Government Printing Office, 1992), 1.

3. *Accident Facts—1994 Edition* (Chicago: National Safety Council, 1994), 36–38; John R. Hollenback, Daniel R. Ilgen, and Suzanne M. Crampton, "Lower Back Disability in Occupational Settings: A Review of the Literature from A Human Resources Management View," *Personnel Psychology* 45, no. 2 (Summer 1992): 247–77. See also Melissa Levy, "Data on Occupational Deaths May Spur U.S. to Renew Push for Seat-Belt Use," *The Wall Street Journal* (October 4, 1993): B6; Stephenie Overman, "Driving the Safety Message Home," *HR Magazine* 39, no. 3 (March 1994): 58–59.

4. *Accident Facts*, 52.

5. *All about OSHA*, 5, 43–45. The states with OSHA-approved state programs are Alaska, Arizona, California, Connecticut, Hawaii, Indiana, Iowa, Kentucky, Maryland, Michigan, Minnesota, Nevada, New Mexico, New York, North Carolina, Oregon, South Carolina, Tennessee, Utah, Vermont, Virginia, Washington, and Wyoming as well as Puerto Rico and the Virgin Islands. Programs in Connecticut and New York cover public employees only.

6. *All about OSHA*, 5, 6.

7. *All about OSHA*, 6, 7.

8. *All about OSHA*, 16.

9. *All about OSHA*, 19–23.

10. *All about OSHA*, 24–27.

11. *All about OSHA*, 31–33.

12. *All about OSHA*, 34–35.

13. *All about OSHA*, 37–40.

14. Susan B. Garland, "A New Chief Has OSHA Growling Again," *Business Week* (August 20, 1990): 57; Amy Dockser Marcus and Jose de Cordoba, "Employers Can Be Charged in Injury Cases," *The Wall Street Journal* (October 17, 1990): B7; "Scannell Brings New Look to OSHA," *Occupational Health and Safety* 59, no. 1 (January 1990): 18–20, 34.

15. Thomas W. Planek and Devin T. Fearn, "Reevaluating Occupational Safety Priorities: 1967 to 1992," *Professional Safety* (October 1993): 17–21; see also Thomas W. Planek, "Perception Equals Reality," *Public Risk* (January 1994): 15–16.

16. Dan Petersen, *Safety Management—A Human Approach*, 2d ed. (Rivervale, N.J.: Aloray, 1988), 33–36.

17. Kaija Leena Saarela, "A Poster Campaign for Improving Safety on Shipyard Scaffolds," *Journal of Safety Research* 20 (1989): 177–85; see also Charles D. Spielberger and Robert G. Frank, "Injury Control: A Promising Field for Psychologists," *American Psychologist* 47, no. 8 (August 1992): 1029–30.

18. John A. Jenkins, "Self-Directed Work Force Promotes Safety," *HR Magazine* 35, no. 2 (February 1990): 177–85; see also Robert F. Scherer, James D. Brodzinski, and Elaine A. Crable, "The Human Factor," *HR Magazine* 38, no. 4 (April 1993): 92–97.

19. R. Bruce McAffee and Ashley R. Winn, "The Use of Incentives/Feedback to Enhance Work Place Safety: A Critique of the Literature," *Journal of Safety Research* 20 (1989): 7–19; see also Thomas R. Krause, John H. Hidley, and Stanley J. Hodson, "Broad-Based Changes in Behavior Key to Improving Safety Culture," *Occupational Health and Safety* 59, no. 7 (July 1990): 31–37, 50; Matthew P. Weinstock, "Rewarding Safety," *Occupational Hazards* 56, no. 3 (March 1994): 73–76.

20. OSHA defines an *occupational injury* as any injury, such as a cut, fracture, sprain, or amputation, that results from a work accident or from an exposure involving a single accident in the work environment. An *occupational illness* is any abnormal condition or disorder, other than one resulting from an occupational injury, caused by exposure to environmental factors associated with employment. This category includes acute and chronic illnesses or diseases that may be caused by inhalation, absorption, ingestion, or direct contact. Not recordable are first-aid cases that involve one-time treatment and subsequent observation of minor scratches, cuts, burns, splinters, etc., that do not ordinarily require medical care, even though such treatment is provided by a physician or registered professional personnel.

21. Tina Adler, "Experts Urge Control of Aerospace Toxics," *APA Monitor* (American Psychological Association, May 1989): 1. For coverage of other health issues, see David H. Wegman and Lawrence J. Fine, "Occupational Health in the 1990s," *Annual Review of Public Health* (Palo Alto, Calif.: Annual Reviews, May 1990).

22. *Accident Facts*, 52; Christine Zielinski, "The Toxic Trap," *Personnel Journal* 69, no. 2 (February 1990): 40–49.

23. Stephen Wermiel, "Justices Bar 'Fetal Protection' Policies," *The Wall Street Journal* (March 21, 1991): B1. The Supreme Court decision in *International Union v Johnson Controls* may be found in 59 *U.S. Law Week* 4029.

24. Zack Mansdorf, "Indoor Air Quality: A Modern-Day Dilemma," *Occupational Hazards* 55, no. 3 (March 1993): 11–14; *Accident Facts*, 42.

25. *Indoor Air Pollution in the Office* (New York: American Lung Association, 1993). Available from local offices.

26. Debra Lynn Dadd, *The Nontoxic Home & Office* (Los Angeles, Calif.: Tarcher, 1992), 179 and Chapters 10–13. See also John Bower, *The Healthy House* (New York: Carol Publishing, 1991).

27. Jeffrey S. Harris, "Clearing the Air," *HR Magazine* 38, no. 2 (February 1993): 72–79; Jennifer J. Laabs, "Companies Kick the Smoking Habit," *Personnel Journal* 73, no. 1 (January 1994): 38–48.

28. Harris, "Clearing the Air," 74.

29. Greg LeBar, "Will OSHA Bar the Door to Workplace Smoking?" *Occupational Hazards* 55, no. 7 (July 1993): 27–31.

30. BNA *Policy and Practice Series—Personnel Management* (1989), 347.72–74.

31. Ron Winslow, "Some Firms Put a Price on Smoking," *The Wall Street Journal* (March 6, 1990): B1; Junda Woo, "Employers Fume over New Legislation Barring Discrimination against Smokers," *The Wall Street Journal* (June 4, 1993): B1; Laabs, "Companies Kick the Smoking Habit," 38–48.

32. J. A. Savage, "Are Computer Terminals Zapping Workers' Health?" *Business and Society Review*, no. 84 (Winter 1993): 41–43.

33. BNA *Policy and Practice Series—Personnel Management* (Washington, D.C.: Bureau of National Affairs, 1988), 247.164.

34. Susan Zeloznicki, "Make the Office Work for You," *HR Magazine* 37, no. 9 (September 1992): 65–67; see also Barbara Goldoftas, "Wince While You Work: Repetitive Motion Injuries," *Business & Society Review* no. 77 (Spring 1991): 46–52.

35. Howard M. Sandler, "Are We Ready to Regulate Cumulative Trauma Disorders?" *Occupational Hazards* 55, no. 6 (June 1993): 51–53; see also Marilyn Joyce and Ulrika Wallersteiner, *Ergonomics—Humanizing the Automated Office* (Cincinnati: South-Western, 1989), 85.

36. Linda C. Kramer, "Legal and Ethical Issues Affect Conduct toward AIDS Sufferers," *Occupational Health and Safety* 59, no. 1 (January 1990): 49–50, 57.

37. I. MacAllister Booth, "Corporations That Confront the Scourge of AIDS," *Business & Society Review* no. 85 (Spring 1993): 21–23.

38. CDC Business and Labor Responds to AIDs, P.O. Box 6003, Rockville, Maryland 20849. 1-800-458-5231.

39. Booth, "Corporations That Confront . . . ," 22.

40. Robert Tomsho, "Frustrated Firms Open Their Own Clinics and Try to Control Workers' Medical Costs," *The Wall Street Journal* (March 23, 1993): B1; see also George Lesmes, "Long-Term Strategy Keeps Health Costs Down," *HR Magazine* 38, no. 4 (April 1993): 76–80.

41. Jane Heimlich, *What Your Doctor Won't Tell You* (New York: Harper Collins, 1990), 1–5. A monthly newsletter, *Alternatives—for the Health Conscious Individual*, is published by Mountain Home Publishing Company, P.O. Box 829, Ingram, TX 78025.

42. Linda G. Rector-Page, *Healthy Healing—An Alternative Healing Reference*, 9th ed. (Sonora, Calif.: Healthy Healing Publications, 1994).

43. Virginia M. Gibson, "Alternative Treatments: Assess Risks and Benefits for Plans," *HR Focus* 70, no. 9 (September 1993): 5.

44. Shari Caudron, "Are Health Incentives Disincentives?" *Personnel Journal* 71, no. 8 (August 1992): 34–40.

45. Richard A. Wolfe and Donald F. Parker, "Employee Health Management: Challenges and Opportunities," *The Academy of Management Executive* VIII, no. 2 (May 1994): 22–31.

46. John A. McDougall, *The McDougall Program—12 Days to Dynamic Health* (New York: Penguin Books, Plume Edition, 1991), Part 1. See also Jonathan Dahl, "The Business Traveler's Menu: Fat, Fat, Fat," *The Wall Street Journal* (September 8, 1994): B1; Allan Halcrow, "For Your Information: A Nutritious Plan for Improved Productivity," *Personnel Journal* 64, no. 8 (August 1985): 17; Linus Pauling, *How To Live Longer and Feel Better* (New York: W. H. Freeman, 1986). This book by the two-time Nobel laureate (Chemistry and Peace) contains sound advice on good nutrition and health maintenance. For a stimulating and informative book based on her own experiences with weight control see Susan Powter, *Food* (New York: Simon & Schuster, 1995).

47. The "2100 Program" is described in Robert Pritikin, *The New Pritikin Program* (New York: Simon and Schuster, 1990). See also two classics: Nathan Pritikin with Patrick M. McGrady, Jr., *The Pritikin Program for Diet and Exercise* (New York: Grosset & Dunlap, 1979); Nathan Pritikin, *The Pritikin Promise: 28 Days to a Longer, Healthier Life* (New York: Simon & Schuster, 1983). For an interesting biography of Nathan Pritikin see Tom Monte with Ilene Pritikin, *Pritikin: The Man Who Healed America's Heart* (Emmaus, PA.: Rodale Press, 1988).

48. *BNA Bulletin to Management* 40, no. 6 (February 9, 1989): 44; see also Ellen E. Schultz, "If You Use Firm's Counselors, Remember Your Secrets Could Be Used against You," *The Wall Street Journal* (May 26, 1994): C1; Jerry Beilinson, "Are EAPs the Answer?" *Personnel* 68, no. 1 (January 1991): 3–4.

49. The following books are classics in the field of environmental allergies: Theron G. Randolph, *Human Ecology and Susceptibility to the Chemical Environment* (Springfield, Ill.: Charles C. Thomas,

1962); and Theron G. Randolph and Ralph W. Moss, *An Alternative Approach to Allergies* (New York: Lippincott & Crowell, 1980). See also David Rousseau, W. J. Rea, M.D., and Jean Enwright, *Your Home, Your Health, and Well-Being* (Berkeley, Calif.: Ten Speed Press, 1990); Carolyn P. Gorman, *Less-Toxic Living,* 6th ed. (Dallas, Texas: Environmental Health Center, 1993). This latter publication may be obtained from the American Environmental Health Foundation, Inc., 8345 Walnut Hill Lane, Suite 225, Dallas, Texas 75231-4262. The AEHF is a nonprofit organization designed to further the practice of environmental medicine and dedicated to the study and treatment of adverse environmental effects on the individual.

50. Jim Castelli, "Addiction," *HR Magazine* 35, no. 4 (April 1990): 55–58; see also Alan R. Sell and Richard G. Newman, "Alcohol Abuse in the Workplace: A Management Dilemma," *Business Horizons* 35, no. 6 (November/December 1992): 64–71.

51. Delores A. Rumpel, "Motivating Alcoholic Workers to Seek Help," *Management Review* 78, no. 7 (July 1989): 37–39. See also Dianna L. Stone and Debra A. Kotch, "Individuals' Attitudes toward Organizational Drug Testing Policies and Practices," *Journal of Applied Psychology* 74, no. 3 (June 1989), 518–21; Joseph G. Rosse, Deborah F. Crown, and Howard D. Feldman, "Alternative Solutions to the Workplace Drug Problem: Results of a Survey of Personnel Managers," *Journal of Employment Counseling* 27, no. 2 (June 1990): 60–75.

52. "Corporate America Declares War on Drugs," *Personnel* 68, no. 8 (August 1991): 1, 8; see also Edward J. Miller, "Investing in a Drug-Free Workplace," *HR Magazine* 36, no. 5 (May 1991): 48–51.

53. Michael E. Cavanagh, "Abuse of Legal Drugs," *Personnel Journal* 69, no. 3 (March 1990): 124–28; Helene Cooper, "Warning: Americans Overuse Over-the-Counter Drugs," *The Wall Street Journal*

(January 11, 1994): B1. For details on one company's drug rehabilitation program, see Cheryl Thieme, "Better-Bilt Building a Substance Abuse Program That Works," *Personnel Journal* 69, no. 8 (August 1990): 52–58.

54. The *Physicians' Desk Reference* is published annually. The 1995 edition is the forty-ninth edition.

55. Mark O. Hatfield, "Stress and the American Worker," *American Psychologist* 45, no. 10 (October 1990): 1162–64; see also Timothy Newton, Jocelyn Handy, and Stephen Fineman, *Managing Stress* (Thousand Oaks, Calif.: Sage Publications, 1995); Charlene Marmer Solomon, "Working Smarter: How HR Can Help," *Personnel Journal* 72, no. 6 (June 1993): 54–64; James Campbell Quick, Lawrence R. Murphy, and Joseph J. Hurrell, Jr., *Stress and Well-Being at Work: Assessment and Intervention for Occupational Mental Health* (Washington, D.C.: American Psychological Association, 1992); John M. Ivancevich, Michael T. Matteson, Sara M. Freedman, and James F. Phillips, "Work-Site Stress Management Interventions," *American Psychologist* 45, no. 2 (February 1990): 252–61.

56. Hans Selye, *Stress without Distress* (Philadelphia: Lippincott, 1974; Signet Books Reprint, 1975), 83. This book, and others by Dr. Selye, are considered classics in this field of study.

57. *USA Today* (April 11, 1990): 1A.

58. Cynthia L. Cordes and Thomas W. Dougherty, "A Review and Integration of Research on Job Burnout," *The Academy of Management Review* 18, no. 4 (October 1993): 621–56.

59. John M. Ivancevich, Michael T. Matteson, and Edward P. Richards III, "Who's Liable for Stress on the Job?" *Harvard Business Review* 85, no. 2 (March-April 1985): 60–72.

60. Ivancevich, Matteson, Freedman, and Phillips, "Work-Site Stress Management," 258.

61. "Sabbaticals Being Tried for Stressed Employees," *The Arizona Republic* (May 3, 1993): E6.

Part 5

Creating a Productive Work Environment

Part 5 deals with issues pertaining to the direct supervision of employees. In Chapter 14 the important topics of employee motivation and leadership are discussed. Chapter 15 discusses employee-management communication, highlighting the role played by the HR department in communicating with employees. Chapter 16 is concerned with issues of employee rights and the corresponding responsibilities of managers to provide employees with workplace justice. This chapter concludes with a discussion of disciplinary practices used by managers when employees disregard organizational rules. When these HR activities are performed correctly, employees and managers interact in a productive manner based on mutual understanding and respect.

Chapter

Motivation and Leadership

14

$\mathbf{M}$any managers believe they can increase productivity by adding robots, introducing information systems, or modifying production procedures. Managers know, however, that productivity and the achievement of total-quality management are not only a matter of computers and production systems but of people. Proactive managers understand that human resources and the motivation of people through effective leadership makes the difference between mediocrity and excellence.

Recent data suggest that some industrialized countries, particularly the United States, have fallen far behind other nations in one measure of productivity, output per hour. (See Figure 14–1.) One way to address productivity problems is to focus on the impact of HR practices—selection, performance appraisal, and compensation, for instance—on productivity. A corresponding approach is to value employees, at all levels, as necessary contributors to organizational success. According to U.S. Labor Secretary Robert Reich, total-quality management flourishes where (1) there is an unusual reliance on front-line workers; (2) workers are treated as assets to be developed, not costs to be cut; (3) new forms of worker-management collaboration break down adversarial barriers; and (4) technology and work are integrated in such ways that machines serve human beings, not vice versa.[1] This chapter addresses the conditions that Reich sets forth.

Before managers can address problems of organizational productivity, they must first understand the motivational bases of performance as well as the leadership skills required to motivate employees to increase their output. In this chapter we will examine selected approaches to motivation and leadership that research and practice suggest can help man-

FIGURE 14-1 *Annual Index of Manufacturing Productivity, 1991*

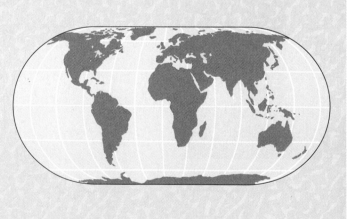

COUNTRY	OUTPUT/HOUR*
United Kingdom	149.8
Japan	146.5
Italy	145.2
Belgium	137.0
Norway	133.5
France	129.1
Netherlands	128.6
United States	128.1
Germany	125.4
Sweden	122.4
Canada	121.7
Denmark	109.3

* 1982 = 100

Source: *Monthly Labor Review* 116, No. 7 (July 1993): 112.

agers improve employee productivity. We begin by discussing motivation, including rewards systems, perceptions of equity, various employee involvement programs, and goal setting. Later we will focus on various theories of leadership, including trait leadership, situational leadership, self-leadership, and transformational leadership.

Using Rewards to Motivate

Managers have numerous choices in motivating employees to be productive. Quite often, a combination of strategies works best. Employee needs and organizational objectives will often determine which motivational technique to use.

Rewards: The Key to Performance

Rewards are an increasingly important motivational tool for any organization. According to a poll of 179 companies conducted by *Total Quality and the Service Edge Newsletter,* 94 percent reported having a reward and recognition program.[2] Although rewards may include a wide range of incentives—paychecks, productivity bonuses, five-year pins, certificates, special vacations—rewards are not always effectively used to enhance productivity. For example, if pay raises are given simply for "showing up" for work rather than for increasing output, they will do little to motivate employees to work harder. In the language of the behavioral scientist, rewards such as these are not "performance-contingent."[3]

According to two noted experts in this field, Fred Luthans and Robert Kreitner, whether employees maintain high productivity depends on how they perceive the consequences of their efforts. If they believe high productivity will be rewarded, they will be more likely to work to achieve it. For this reason, organizations should place considerable emphasis on rewards that employees perceive as desirable.[4]

Using Pay as a Reward

One rather obvious reward for performance is pay and the various forms of incentive pay systems that we discussed in Chapter 11. Since pay can be a powerful incentive, those whose job includes establishing pay systems need to understand the effect of pay on motivation. Managers who understand this relationship are in a much better position to implement effective pay-for-performance systems.

Foremost, pay is something that employees value, and its value may be best understood in terms of the different needs employees have. Abraham Maslow developed the **hierarchy of needs,** a theory of motivation that arranges five universal needs in order of priority: (1) *physiological* needs for food, water, etc.; (2) *safety* needs for physical and psychological security; (3) *belongingness* needs for love and inclusion; (4) *esteem* needs for self-respect; and (5) *self-actualization* needs, or the need to reach one's potential.[5] Pay is an important reward in part because it may satisfy several of these needs. It provides employees with the means to purchase food to satisfy their physiological needs; it allows them to afford shelter to satisfy their need for safety; and it enables them to meet their esteem needs, since pay is one measure of relative worth.[6]

Hierarchy of needs A motivational model that assumes human needs are arranged in a hierarchy of importance

In addition, there are four other important reasons for managers to implement effective pay-for-performance systems. First, pay serves to differentiate among employees. High-performing employees usually resent systems that reward everyone equally, and they may feel that there is no reason to stay with an organization that allows the less competent to "beat the system" by receiving the same reward with less effort or ability. By serving to differentiate among employees, pay strengthens feelings of equity, a topic discussed later in the chapter.

Second, using pay as a reward makes the formal performance appraisal a significant event. Where there is no link between pay and performance, employees may see appraisals as nothing more than a perfunctory requirement of the HR department. Where pay is clearly based on performance, however, it is seen as an important consequence of effective performance, thus underscoring the importance of the appraisal process.

Third, pay-for-performance can be an important means of allocating scarce compensation dollars. Even in difficult financial circumstances, organizations are well advised to retain merit pay for their high-performing employees. Not only will rewarding outstanding performance help retain the superior employees, it may also encourage the poorer-performing employees to leave the organization.

Fourth, pay-for-performance can be used to encourage a culture of high productivity in the organization. Transforming an apathetic culture into one where productivity is highly valued can be a very difficult task. Effective motivational strategies, including using pay as a performance reward, can help to move the organizational culture in the direction of better performance. After all, pay affects every employee in the organization, so it has considerable potential to change the entire culture, one employee at a time.[7]

For example, Northern Telecom changed its organizational culture from one based on the job's sophistication to one in which employees were paid on the basis of the number of skills they possessed. (See Chapter 10 for a more complete description of skill-based pay.) Employees were thus rewarded for acquiring a greater variety of skills, the plant gained flexibility in assigning work to employees, performance improved, and supervision requirements decreased because workers were more knowledgeable about their jobs.[8]

Using Other Rewards

There are a variety of other rewards that are very important to employees and quite useful as a means of motivating performance. Simple feedback from managers serves as a valued reward. A survey conducted for the Council of Communication Management indicated that recognition for a job well done is the top motivator of employee performance.[9] For feedback to be most effective, however, it should be face to face and it should be immediate rather than delayed. Also it should be positive. A high amount of feedback is better than a low amount, since a low amount of feedback conveys low confidence in the subordinate and may even anger the employee.[10]

Positive feedback follows the principles advocated in **reinforcement theory,** which states that behavior is contingent upon reinforcement. In other words, when reinforcement (rewards) follows performance, performance improves. The process of influencing behavior through reinforcement is known as *operant conditioning.*[11] There is general agreement among behaviorists that positive reinforce-

Reinforcement theory
Motivation theory that states that behavior is contingent upon rewards received

"My advice to you, Hawkins, is to take the pins
out of the map and stick them into the salesmen."

Reprinted with permission of Chon Day

ment is the most effective way to motivate and modify behavior. It is an especially useful approach in organizations where a wide variety of positive reinforcers are available to managers and supervisors. Several forms of positive reinforcement are discussed below.

Using Awards Programs to Motivate

What do organizations such as Whitestone Products, Delta Machinery, the City of Atlanta, and Diamond International Corporation all have in common?[12] Each has one or more successful employee awards programs. An example of such a program is provided in Highlights in HRM 1. These programs can include many different awards, such as certificates or gifts of jewelry, crystal, or blazers. Besides these traditional awards, novel and unexpected rewards can be offered. For example, some organizations may find the following useful for encouraging higher levels of performance:

- Workplace visits by top executives to high-performing employees
- Surprise announcements of afternoons or days off
- Trophies, wall plaques, certificates, or pins for exceptional performance

HIGHLIGHTS IN HRM

1   RECOGNITION AT ROSS LABORATORIES

"You did a great job" are words most people enjoy hearing. Usually, employers say them to employees. At Columbus, Ohio-based Ross Laboratories, however, employees are saying these words to each other through a company-wide recognition program. Ross Laboratories, a division of 101-year-old, Chicago-based Abbott Laboratories Corp., manufactures pediatric, pharmaceutical, and nutrition products, including Similac infant formula, Murine eye-care products, Selsun Blue dandruff shampoo, and the Exceed sports nutrition line.

Inspired by the slogan "At Ross, You're in the Company of Excellence," President Dick Gast decided that the company needed a recognition program to enhance its tradition of superior products and services. Because "excellence" is a subjective term, Gast decided that an effective way to put it into more concrete terms—while avoiding standards by which companies usually measure excellence, such as perfect attendance or twenty-five-year tenure—was to allow employees to participate in the process of defining and recognizing excellence. Gast specified that the program should be open to all 4,100 employees, from line workers to executives, and should be completely employee-driven. All company employees should participate in selecting winners and in turn should be eligible to win. At each facility, the program is administered according to the number of people and their particular preferences. Any full-time Ross employee may nominate another full-time employee, whether subordinate or supervisor, for an award. Employees may even nominate themselves. Area committees consider all nominations and select the most deserving people to be voted on by employees in their area.

The award of excellence program allows employees many chances for recognition. Level I area winners are announced at a general meeting, during which they receive a two-ounce silver ingot engraved with the Ross award of excellence logo on the front and the original Ross milk-truck logo on the back.

Each quarter, area employees then vote to select four level II winners from among level I winners. Those four winners receive a five-ounce silver ingot with the same level I award imprints, but this time it's in the shape of an Olympic-style medal, complete with a ribbon. Level II winners also receive a letter of congratulations from the division president. At the end of the year, a recognition dinner is held at each Ross location for all level II winners. At the end of the fourth quarter, an election is held to select level III winners from among the level II winners. Recently, all level III winners congregated in Columbus for a three-day celebration of their achievements. Activities included a visit to the company's headquarters for a president-hosted reception, a double-decker bus tour around the city, and a free afternoon to plan on their own. A president's gala celebration dinner was held in honor of the winners. Each level III winner was awarded a Waterford crystal decanter set.

One interesting outcome of the program is that committee members learn to recognize others' ideas of what excellence is and learn to compromise. Ultimately, each group learns to define excellence in its own terms and recognize it within the company accordingly. One goal of the recognition program at Ross is to encourage other employees to strive for the same kind of excellence as those who are recognized. Recognition by one's co-workers encourages employees to aspire to other personal and professional goals, thereby contributing to company goals.

Source: Adapted from Jennifer J. Koch, "Ross Employees Are in the Company of Excellence," *Personnel Journal* 68, no. 9 (June 1990): 108–10. Reprinted with the permission of *Personnel Journal,* Costa Mesa, California. All rights reserved.

- Letters to the spouse commending the employee's performance
- Personal handwritten notes of thanks accompanying paychecks
- Invitations to lunch by managers
- Achievement decals for hats or cloth badges for jackets
- Small cash awards
- Telephone calls by top executives to employees at home[13]

It should be remembered that, if awards are to be effective, they must be given only to those employees who have performed well. In other words, they must differentiate the mediocre performer from the high performer. Furthermore, to be effective, such programs must ensure that the award is valued by the employee. Research shows awards have less effect when they are given as part of a regular meeting or sandwiched between departmental activities. Special occasions—annual dinners and award meetings—are required if awards are to be perceived as anything more than an afterthought.[14] Figure 14–2 provides additional suggestions for ensuring an effective award system.

FIGURE 14-2 *Making Awards Count for Employees*

1. Tie awards to employees' needs. Managers must get to know their employees well enough to understand their needs.

2. Make sure an award is large enough to have symbolic value. A $25 increase in the monthly paycheck may go unnoticed. A $300 bonus check is more likely to get an employee's attention.

3. Proper timing is important. Schedule the presentation of the award close to the time the award was announced.

4. Attend the awards presentation. The manager's presence shows the importance of an awards ceremony and thus of the awards themselves.

5. Talk up the value of an award. Pointing out the benefits of the award helps to make it more meaningful.

6. Make certain the presenter is someone the employees respect.

7. Use a public forum for the presentation. Schedule a special event to highlight the importance of the award.

8. Set high standards for the awards, and make them contingent upon meeting or exceeding those standards.

9. Increase the exclusiveness of an award. Awards received by fewer employees are valued more highly.

10. Do not oversell the award. Attempting to make a weekly sales bonus seem tremendously valuable only makes the award look meaningless.

11. Clearly establish the goals you want to achieve with the awards program and make sure those goals coincide with your overall objectives.

Equity Theory and Motivation

Equity theory

Motivation theory
that states that the
presence of feelings of
inequity will motivate
an individual to reduce
that inequity

A basic principle in HR management is equity. Employees expect that what they give to the organization will be equivalent to what they receive from it. When things are out of balance, employees will take actions to bring them back into balance. **Equity theory** is the motivation theory that explains how employees respond to situations in which they feel they have received less or more than they deserve. The theory states that feelings of inequity will motivate a person to reduce inequity.[15]

Theory of Inequity

Adams's version of equity theory is perhaps the most extensive and explicit.[16] It is a general theory of social inequity. Central to the theory is the role of perception in motivation and the fact that individuals make comparisons. It states that individuals form a ratio of their inputs in a situation to their outcomes in that situation. They then compare the value of that ratio with the value of the input/outcome ratio for other individuals in a similar class of jobs. If the value of their ratio equals the value of another's, they perceive the situation as equitable and no tension exists. However, if they perceive their input/outcome ratio as inequitable relative to others', this creates tension and motivates them to eliminate or reduce the inequity. The strength of their motivation is proportional to the magnitude of the perceived inequity.

Perceived Inequity

Employees may develop feelings of inequity for a variety of reasons, the most obvious of which is pay. If employees believe they give more effort, but know they are paid less than the person with whom they compare themselves, they will feel that the organization is treating them inequitably. Older, more experienced employees who believe that younger employees are receiving more than their fair share of compensation will feel that they are being treated inequitably. An employee who believes it is her turn to have the day off may resent it and perceive inequity when the day off is given to another employee.

Reactions to Inequity

When faced with perceptions of inequity, employees handle it in a variety of ways. They may behave in one or more of the following ways:

- Sabotage the work process
- Reduce the amount of effort they put into their work
- Seek more pay to achieve equity because of their perceived larger contribution
- Quit their job or increase their absenteeism, thereby avoiding the situation or the person that is the source of their feelings of inequity
- Try to persuade their fellow employees to reduce their effort
- Cognitively reevaluate original estimates of inputs and outcomes

Employees may also decide to compare themselves with yet another person, thus reducing the perceived inequity of the earlier comparison. Some of these means of reducing inequity can be particularly damaging to an organization.

One way for an employer to minimize feelings of inequity in its employees is through a fair compensation plan. Such plans are discussed in detail in Chapter 10 on compensation.

Managing Equity

That inequity can lead to productivity problems for the organization is ample reason for managers to address perceptions of inequity and unfairness, beyond the usual compensation plans. Recognizing the need to address unfairness in a variety of managerial settings, one senior vice president of a *Fortune* 500 firm stated, "What's fair is whatever the workers think is fair. My job is to convince them that what's good for the company is fair for them as individuals." Common techniques managers use to ensure equity in the workplace include (1) announcing all pay raises and promotions, (2) explaining how pay raises are determined, (3) allowing workers to participate in decisions, and (4) explaining why work assignments are made. Other means of addressing inequity and unfairness include the following:

- Emphasizing equitable rewards for employees
- Recognizing that the basis for perceived inequity is comparison with others
- Listening carefully to employees to understand the basis of comparisons
- Responding to employees individually
- Letting employees know of the contributions of others
- Describing employees' current accomplishments in relation to their earlier accomplishments
- Accurately describing the outcomes for specific levels of performance
- Using public meetings to recognize employees[17]

three
objective

Expectancy theory

Motivation theory that states that motivational force is a function of the expectancies that individuals have concerning future outcomes times the value they place on those outcomes

Expectancy Theory and Motivation

Expectancy theory of motivation has developed from the work of psychologists who consider humans as thinking, reasoning persons who have beliefs and anticipations concerning future life events. This theory argues that the motivational force to perform (effort) is a function of the expectancies that individuals have concerning future outcomes times the value (valence) they place on these outcomes. Victor Vroom defines an *expectancy* as a "momentary belief concerning the likelihood that a particular act will be followed by a particular outcome."[18] Thus beliefs that "hard work will lead to desired promotions" and "studying hard will result in good grades" are expectancies. *Valences* are the positive or negative values people place on outcomes. One application of expectancy theory is in predicting behavior in situations where choices are made. For example, it can be used to predict whether to expect large or minimal effort on a task and whether to expect an employee to quit or stay.

Vroom's work has been extended by two organizational behaviorists, Lyman W. Porter and Edward Lawler. Their theoretical model is illustrated in Figure 14–3. According to their theory, the amount of effort or energy expended by

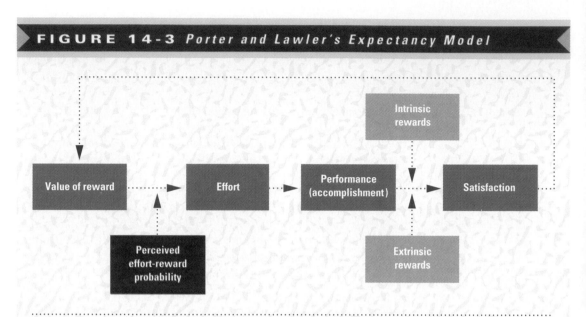

FIGURE 14-3 *Porter and Lawler's Expectancy Model*

Source: Adapted from Porter and Lawler's original model as published in L.W. Porter and Edward E. Lawler, *Managerial Attitudes and Performance* (Homewood, Ill.: Irwin-Dorsey, 1965). Used with permission.

an employee is determined by two key factors: (1) the value (valence) or attractiveness of the reward and (2) the degree to which the employee believes that increased effort will lead to the attainment of these rewards. Porter and Lawler recognize that abilities and traits set the upper limits for performance and that the employee's perception of his or her job role also affects performance. Porter and Lawler also recognize that intrinsic rewards are more closely connected with good performance than are extrinsic rewards. Whether or not the rewards received lead to satisfaction is dependent upon the employee's perception of how equitable they are.

Expectancy theory has several important implications for managers. First, managers can enhance the effort-performance expectancies of employees by helping employees attain their performance goals. This might be accomplished by making sure an employee has needed resources or by encouraging the application of an employee's unique abilities. Second, managers need to identify good performance in order that appropriate behavior can be rewarded. Finally, managers need to determine what employees value and then provide those valued rewards, ensuring that inequities do not exist. Rewards should be large enough to motivate high effort.

objective

Designing Work for Employee Involvement

Providing rewards based on performance and equitably distributing the rewards are only two of the important tools organizations can use to elicit high perfor-

A sales position requires unique rewards to motivate exceptional performance.

Employee involvement

Motivation technique to enhance the quality of decision making while satisfying employee needs for job involvement

mance from their employees. Another is enhancing **employee involvement.** Increased employee involvement in organizations has become the charge of many managers and the hope of numerous self-motivated employees. Although a variety of programs have been developed to involve employees more fully in their organizations, all of these programs have one common ingredient: participation. They increase the degree to which employees participate in making critical job or organizational decisions.

Increased employee participation in decision making offers a number of advantages, including stronger commitment to the organization's goals, better understanding of the decisions made in the organization, and improvement in the quality of the decisions themselves. A more extensive list of the advantages of greater employee participation is provided in Figure 14–4. To achieve these advantages, three general ways to increase employee involvement and participation are proposed: (1) adopting suggestion systems, including employee involvement groups; (2) fostering job involvement through work teams; and (3) building individual commitment to the organization through employee improvement.[19]

Adopting Suggestion Systems

The oldest and still most widely used employee involvement system is the suggestion system, which can take various forms, as shown in Highlights in HRM 2. The traditional suggestion system, to be discussed in Chapter 15, is one of the ways to ensure upward communication in organizations. However, suggestion systems are also an important means of motivating employees by involving them in the decision-making and reward systems of the organization, assuming that management takes its employees' suggestions seriously.[20]

Gainsharing Suggestion Systems

Programs that reward employees for their suggestions are a part of organizational gainsharing systems, so called because employees share in the gains that result

FIGURE 14-4 *Benefits Gained through Employee Participation*

1. Fosters consensus decision making
2. Creates a greater knowledge base from which to gain ideas or resolve organizational problems
3. Develops a team approach to complete workplace tasks
4. Encourages self-training for workgroup members
5. Improves understanding and acceptance of group decisions
6. Improves QWL by meeting employee needs for involvement, achievement, and acceptance
7. Creates greater commitment to the organization's vision and mission
8. Ensures employee criticism with a constructive orientation

from their suggestions. Such systems can have considerable impact on organizational productivity. In its pursuit of market leadership, Herman Miller, Inc., a manufacturer of office furniture, realized $36 million in productivity gains and cost savings from its gainsharing suggestion system.[21] Gainsharing plans are discussed fully in Chapter 11.

Employee Involvement Groups

Employee involvement groups (EIs)

Groups of employees who meet to resolve problems or offer suggestions for organizational improvement

Groups of five to ten employees doing similar or related work who meet together regularly to identify, analyze, and suggest solutions to shared problems are often referred to as **employee involvement groups (EIs).** Also widely known as quality circles (QCs), EIs are used principally as a means of involving employees in the larger goals of the organization through their suggestions for improving product or service quality and cutting costs.[22] Generally, EIs recommend their solutions to management, which decides whether or not to implement them.

The employee involvement group process, illustrated in Figure 14–5, begins with EI members brainstorming job-related problems or concerns and gathering data about these issues. The process continues through the generation of solutions and recommendations that are then communicated to management. If the solutions are implemented, results are measured, and the EI and its members are usually recognized for the contributions they have made. EIs typically meet four or more hours per month, and the meetings are chaired by a group leader chosen from the group. The leader does not hold an authority position but instead serves as a discussion facilitator.

Organizations must do considerable planning to ensure the effective performance of employee involvement groups. Implementing the EI process usually requires the appointment of a project manager. Though this role is sometimes filled by an outside consultant, a better choice may be an insider from the HR department who understands the organizational culture and knows which employees are good candidates for membership in the group. Successful users of EIs have also found it necessary to appoint an advisory committee, composed of

HRM

HIGHLIGHTS IN HRM

2   ORGANIZATION OF A SUGGESTION PROGRAM

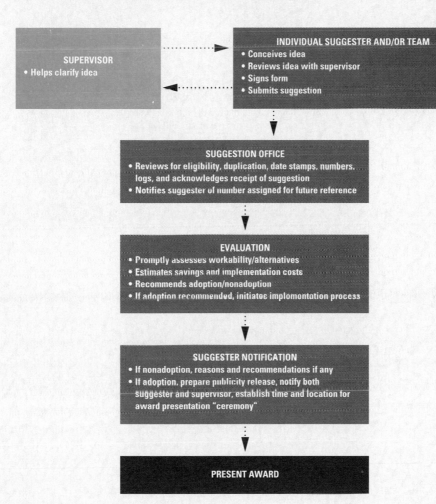

SUPERVISOR
• Helps clarify idea

INDIVIDUAL SUGGESTER AND/OR TEAM
• Conceives idea
• Reviews idea with supervisor
• Signs form
• Submits suggestion

SUGGESTION OFFICE
• Reviews for eligibility, duplication, date stamps, numbers, logs, and acknowledges receipt of suggestion
• Notifies suggester of number assigned for future reference

EVALUATION
• Promptly assesses workability/alternatives
• Estimates savings and implementation costs
• Recommends adoption/nonadoption
• If adoption recommended, initiates implementation process

SUGGESTER NOTIFICATION
• If nonadoption, reasons and recommendations if any
• If adoption, prepare publicity release, notify both suggester and supervisor, establish time and location for award presentation "ceremony"

PRESENT AWARD

Source: David G. Carnevale and Brett S. Sharp, "The Old Suggestion Box: An Undervalued Force for Productivity Improvement," *Review of Public Personnel Administration* 13, no. 2 (Spring 1993): 85. Copyright 1993 by the Institute of Public Affairs, University of South Carolina. All rights reserved.

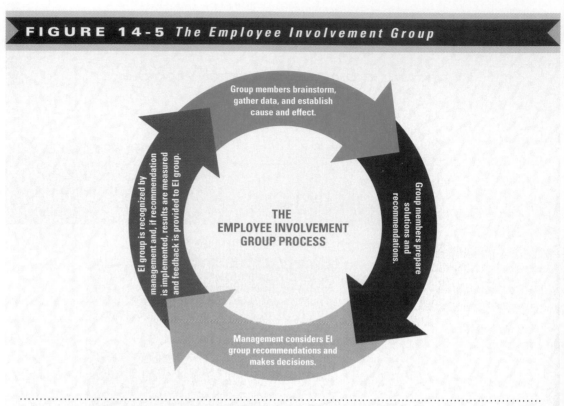

FIGURE 14-5 *The Employee Involvement Group*

Group members brainstorm, gather data, and establish cause and effect.

Group members prepare solutions and recommendations.

THE EMPLOYEE INVOLVEMENT GROUP PROCESS

Management considers EI group recommendations and makes decisions.

EI group is recognized by management and, if recommendation is implemented, results are measured and feedback is provided to EI group.

Source: The Family and Relationship Center, 7946 Ivanhoe Ave., Suite 201, La Jolla, Calif., 92037.

managers, to coordinate the EI process across departments, evaluate recommendations, manage implementation of contributions, and recognize employees and EIs that have made successful contributions. In addition to the advisory committee, EI support staff (usually from the HR department) must provide training to EI members in problem solving, statistical quality control, and group processes.

Although EIs have become an important organizational suggestion system, they are not without their problems and their critics. For example, EIs can go stale. Several ways have been suggested to keep EIs fresh and to revive them when necessary. First, managers should recognize the group when a recommendation is made, regardless of whether the recommendation is adopted. This approach encourages the group to continue coming up with ideas even when they are not all implemented by management. Second, periodic recesses should be planned. After a group has spent weeks wrestling with a particularly complex and difficult problem, its members can be exhausted. A recess is needed to rejuvenate the group. In some cases this break can be used for retraining. Third, field trips can allow a group to visit other parts of the organization, learning how problems are dealt with there and gaining new insight into old problems the group faces in its own area.

Organizations have often modified the traditional EI process to fit their own particular organizational needs. For example, some organizations have found that voluntary EIs have not always proven successful. They have found that the EI process is most successful when natural work groups are used rather than bringing together employees from different work groups. Other organizations have found that EIs run out of ideas, and management must feed them ideas to keep the process going. Still other objections to EIs come from their basic design. Some critics argue that EIs do not fundamentally change the organization in which they are established. As a form of suggestion system, they may work well, but they do not alter organizational culture. Therefore, these critics argue, employees who participate may realize the benefits of participation, but most employees, who are not included in EIs, are unaffected by their efforts. Furthermore, employers may not achieve all of the benefits attributed to EIs. In one study, employees participating in EIs had no more positive attitudes over time than those involved in a control group.[23]

Fostering Job Involvement

Job involvement, another means of designing work for employee involvement, is the degree of identification employees have with their jobs and the degree of importance they place on their jobs. Among the approaches used to increase job involvement are job redesign and the use of work teams.

Job Redesign

The aim of job redesign is to enrich a job so that the employee is more motivated to do the work. This approach usually builds increased autonomy and feedback into the job, adds tasks to the job, and increases the number of skills required to complete the work. One of the earliest theories associated with such job redesign was Herzberg's **two-factor theory,** which identified two sets of factors in organizations: extrinsic factors like pay and working conditions, which Herzberg called *hygiene factors,* and intrinsic factors like job challenge and responsibility, which he called *motivators.*[24] Herzberg's motivators have a parallel in Maslow's self-actualization needs, and it is these factors that bring about the kind of improvement in performance that management seeks. Despite lingering questions about the validity of the two-factor theory, it is still the stimulus for considerable concern with job design, discussed fully in Chapter 4.[25]

Work Teams

Another approach to increasing employee job involvement—the **work team**—focuses on the work group as the primary unit of involvement. It creates group goals, and it compensates employees, at least in part, on the basis of group accomplishment of these goals. The approach also seeks to make all members of the work group share responsibility for the group's performance. Furthermore, decisions are decentralized to the level of the work team.[26] For example, a work team at a Procter & Gamble manufacturing plant may be partly responsible for deciding how many units to produce, making decisions about assignment of tasks, setting prices if working as a product team, making its own quality-control checks,

---

Two-factor theory
A theory that suggests that job satisfaction is a two-dimensional construct, one dimension stressing motivation factors, the other affected by hygiene factors

Work team
A job involvement technique whereby jobs are structured for groups rather than for individuals and team members are given discretion in matters traditionally considered management prerogatives, such as work scheduling, individual work assignments, and/or performance reviews

and also setting inventory levels. In contrast with gainsharing and EIs, work teams involve changes in job design and organizational design, thereby affecting more employees and making a longer-lasting impact on the organizational culture and the employees.

Work teams are based on sociotechnical systems theory that advocates jointly combining the social and technical components of the work environment. Employee training and skill enhancement emphasize both technical knowledge (e.g., task performance) and social skills (e.g., interpersonal relations, communication). The group, rather than the individual, becomes the focus for performing the job. Inherent in work teams is the notion that the group is the logical work unit to apply resources to resolve organizational problems and concerns. Work teams are championed to improve organizational productivity while simultaneously enhancing the quality of work life for employees.[27]

A description of the use of work teams in provided in Highlights in HRM 3. At General Foods, as well as Procter & Gamble, Steelcase Inc., Federal Express, and others, the benefits of work teams have included more integration of individual skills, better performance in terms of quantity and quality, reduced turnover and absenteeism, and a growing sense of confidence and accomplishment among team members.[28]

Despite successes in the use of work teams, there are difficulties, including substantial start-up costs. In some cases, whole plants must be built from scratch or significantly redesigned for the efficient use of the work-team approach. Furthermore, the technology of the organization may make the use of work teams very difficult or even impossible. For successful implementation of this approach, the work should be of the kind that no one individual can do alone or do as well as a team. For example, teams are appropriate in process production facilities such as chemical plants, and they are appropriate to some activities in service areas such as airlines or customer service operations.

In adopting the work-team concept, organizations must address several issues that could present obstacles to effective team function, including expectations, compensation, continuity, career movement, and power. For example, new team members must be retrained to work outside their primary functional areas, and compensation systems must be constructed to reward individuals for team accomplishments. Because of the integration of the team members, continuity in membership is critical. Thus employees may be asked to make a three- to five-year commitment before joining a team, or team members may be chosen from older, less mobile employees. Since team membership demands more-general skills and since it moves an employee out of the historical career path, new career paths to general management must be created from team experience. Finally, as the team members become capable of carrying out functions such as strategic planning that were previously restricted to higher levels of management, managers must be prepared to utilize their newfound expertise.

Another difficulty with work teams is that they alter the traditional manager-employee relationship. Managers often find it hard to adapt to the role of leader rather than supervisor and sometimes feel threatened by the growing power of the team and the reduced power of management. Furthermore, some employees may also have difficulty adapting to a role that includes traditional supervisory responsibilities. A difficulty with work teams is that they must be incorporated into the organization's strategic planning process. Since work teams

HIGHLIGHTS IN HRM

3 PEAK PERFORMANCE THROUGH TEAMWORK AT GENERAL FOODS

General Foods has adopted work teams as a strategic approach to maximizing productivity and promoting high performance among its employees. The groups are called "interfunctional work teams." Achieving peak performance is based on (1) a strong commitment to high levels of performance, (2) collaboration and support among group members, and (3) a strong sense of ownership and responsibility for the results of the team effort. Team members are expected to go beyond the functional contribution they normally make as accountants, marketing specialists, etc. For example, the financial member of the Minute Rice team is expected to contribute to advertising, strategic planning, package design, product quality, and financial structure of the product.

General Foods has sought to emphasize five elements in achieving peak performance:

1. *Goals.* Team members must collaborate to set clear goals, which are to be based on the mission of the strategic business unit.
2. *Roles.* Individuals bring diverse roles to the group, but interdependence is essential; team members must develop a common vision of the expected accomplishments of the team.
3. *Leadership.* The team leader must retain a multifunctional outlook, establish a positive working climate for team members, and obtain resources for the team.
4. *Team relations.* Team members must openly communicate their expectations of each other; interpersonal team processes must be frequently addressed.
5. *Rewards.* Rewards are provided for team members as a group, and the team is encouraged to celebrate its accomplishments during the life of the project.

do alter the organization structurally, they must be taken into account when organizational strategies and tactics are being established. HR managers can play an active role in the strategic planning for work-team implementation by incorporating work-team changes into managerial career ladders, introducing relevant organizational development tactics, and planning for necessary managerial and team-member training.

Finally, empirical studies of work teams suggest that teams are greater contributors to organizational performance when they operate under open and unrestricted access to information, when team membership represents diverse job functions, and when a team has a sufficient number of members to accomplish its effectiveness.[29] Team members achieve their greatest value when participation is valued and viewed as important to success

(2) goals regulate effort (e.g., they motivate us to act); (3) goals increase our persistence in expending effort over extended periods of time; and (4) goals encourage us to develop strategies and action plans.[32] Furthermore, setting goals is an employee involvement technique and is therefore compatible with employee involvement groups, work teams, and empowerment.

Goal-setting theory is generally associated with Edward Locke, who has demonstrated the effect of goal setting on individual performance. His major proposition, which has been supported experimentally, is that those employees who set or accept harder goals perform at levels higher than those who set or accept easier goals. Goal setting provides the foundation for management by objectives (MBO), a technique for managing the goal-setting process in organizations. (MBO is discussed in Chapter 9.)

Edward Locke and Gary Latham have demonstrated that the most reliable effect of goal setting is to raise productivity or improve work quality. But there are a variety of other benefits from goal setting, including the clarification of objectives, the stimulation of competition, relief from boredom, employee satisfaction with performance, pride in achievement, and increased willingness to accept future challenges. In comparing goal setting with other motivational techniques, Locke and Latham conclude that "any given technique will be effective to the degree that it generates or is associated with the setting of specific, challenging goals and/or the degree to which it enhances commitment to those goals."[33]

Motivation through Effective Leadership

It is appropriate to discuss motivation and leadership together since leadership is a key variable in achieving employee motivation. And motivation, in turn, is related to leadership styles. It is the combination of leadership and motivation that produces a productive work environment.

Leadership has been defined in numerous ways, but it is usually seen as the influence exerted by one individual on a group of persons to accomplish some goal.[34] In organizations, leadership is usually associated with the influence that a manager exerts in the accomplishment of goals associated with the productivity of the organization. Thus effective leadership in managers may be viewed as a means of motivating employees to improve their performance. Since a major concern of managers is to improve employee performance, it is not surprising that the study of leadership has been of such interest to them.[35]

objective

Traits of leaders
Qualities that
differentiate effective
leaders from nonleaders

Identification of Effective Leadership Traits

In the first half of this century, more than 100 studies attempted to identify **traits of leaders.** These studies undertook to verify the belief that certain characteristics possessed by leaders are not possessed by nonleaders. Such research has held great interest for HR professionals, since identification of specific leadership traits could facilitate the selection and training functions of HRM. Managers could be selected who possessed certain leadership traits, or managers lacking such traits might be able to develop them.

Early research studied such traits as intelligence, initiative, persistence, self-confidence, and desire for control. In his 1948 review of these studies, Ralph Stogdill found a consistent pattern of support for only five traits: (1) intelligence, (2) scholarship, (3) dependability, (4) social participation, and (5) socioeconomic status. Therefore, he concluded, "A person does not become a leader by virtue of the possession of some combination of traits."[36]

Despite the failure of early studies to identify a consistent set of traits that effective leaders possess, the research has continued. However, behavioral scientists today use a greater variety of measurement procedures and focus more directly on organizational managers rather than on other types of leaders, such as military leaders. Furthermore, today's research looks at traits of leaders in terms of the process of leading.

Cadbury Schweppes, a long-time user of assessment centers, has developed a trait profile of the competent manager for its operations. The traits include vision, drive, sociability, persuasive skills, delegation skills, teamwork skills, analytical ability, organizing skills, and personal factors such as integrity and ambition. Interestingly, social science research has provided results that are somewhat consistent with Cadbury's experience. In fact, social scientists have identified four traits—emotional stability, action orientation, interpersonal skills, and cognitive skills as consistently associated with organizational leaders. These research findings, as well as Cadbury's experience, provide considerable opportunity for HR professionals. For example, this information may be used as a starting point in any organization for developing an organization-specific leader profile that can be used as a basis for selection, training, and employee appraisal.

Finally, the single trait *charisma* is increasingly discussed as a characteristic of effective leaders.[37] Charismatic leaders are heralded as business heroes—reviving failing companies, starting new enterprises, or instilling a spirit of renewal into stagnant organizations. Charismatic leaders are typically able to inspire extraordinary performance in followers as well as to build trust and faith in themselves as leaders. They often achieve success by incorporating their followers' dreams and aspirations in their own vision of success. As noted by two authors, charismatic leaders "develop creative, critical thinking in their followers, provide opportunities for them to develop, welcome positive and negative feedback, recognize the contributions of others, share information with followers, and have moral standards that emphasize collective interest."[38]

McClelland's Managerial Motivation

One modern approach to explaining the traits of leaders has focused on the motivations that managers must possess to be successful. This research has used the *Thematic Apperception Test* (TAT), a projective test, to reveal the strength of three motivations, or needs, in particular: **needs for achievement, power, and affiliation.**[39]

The need for achievement is prominent among successful executives. These individuals generally perceive themselves to be hard-working persons who need solid accomplishments in order to feel satisfied. Executive positions typically give them the challenge they need. Some of the characteristics of those with high achievement motivation are preference for moderate risk, persistence, as-

Needs for achievement, power, and affiliation

David McClelland's theory of leader motivation that differentiates people according to what motivates them

sumption of personal responsibility for performance, need for performance feedback, and innovativeness.[40] Studies have shown that achievement-motivated people prefer tasks of moderate levels of difficulty. Thus a supervisor must structure jobs and assign them to people who see their odds of acceptable performance as neither too low nor too high.

Needs for power and affiliation also characterize those who are successful managers. The need for power is important to managers since they must exercise control and influence over their subordinates, peers, and superiors. McClelland has been careful to describe the need for power among leaders as a need that must be constrained. That is, the need for power must be such that it is satisfied through accomplishments associated with reaching organizational goals. Thus, power is important for leaders as a means of achievement rather than as an end in itself. The need for affiliation must also be constrained. A moderate need for affiliation will enable managers to socialize sufficiently to accomplish their tasks, and it will orient them toward the needs of their subordinates, thereby facilitating the motivation of employees.

Identification of Leadership Behavior

objective

Despite some recent success with the trait approach to leadership studies, early dissatisfaction with it had led instead to the analysis of the behavior of managers. Rather than focusing on the traits of successful managers, this approach emphasized the behavior that facilitates effective interaction of work-group members.

Employee-Centered and Production-Centered Leadership

In the late 1940s, the Survey Research Center of the University of Michigan embarked on a program to determine how leader behavior affected work-group performance and employee satisfaction. One of the major findings of these early studies was that production-centered supervisors, those concerned primarily with production, are less effective in terms of measurable productivity than employee-centered supervisors, those who give their attention to the people who do the work. Even in these early studies, it was found that employee-centered supervisors were production-centered as well, exhibiting concern for high performance goals and enthusiasm for achieving them. The third type of leadership under investigation by the Michigan researchers was participative leadership. In early studies at the university, subordinates who had participative leaders exhibited higher work-related satisfaction and performance.[41]

Consideration and Structure

Consideration
Dimension of supervisory behavior that encourages mutual trust, respect, and a certain warmth and rapport between the supervisor and the group.

At the same time the Michigan studies were underway, researchers at Ohio State University were studying two major dimensions of supervisory behavior—consideration and initiating structure. **Consideration,** like employee orientation in the Michigan research, includes leader behaviors that encourage mutual trust, respect, and warmth between leaders and their work-group members. Initiating

Structure
A cluster of leader behaviors that stresses task orientation, production, and organizing activities

structure, like production orientation in the Michigan studies, includes leader behaviors such as organizing activities, defining the role of work-group members, and assigning tasks to get the work done.

Considerable research has examined the effect of the task and relationship orientations of leaders. Results of questionnaire-based as well as case-based research have demonstrated that at least a moderate degree of *both* orientations is desirable in a leader. It is therefore important in developing more satisfied and productive employees that managers focus on training that encourages both behavioral dimensions of leadership.

The Leadership Grid.   Perhaps the most prominent behavioral-styles model of leadership is the Managerial Grid (renamed the Leadership Grid in 1991). This model has been very popular as a basis for training managers and supervisors.[42] The grid, shown in Figure 14–6, expresses the relationship between concern for people and concern for production. By referring to the grid and identifying their own behavior in the two areas of concern, managers and supervisors are better able to understand the approach they use with their subordinates. Developers of the grid, Robert Blake and Jane Srygley Mouton, emphasize that the 9,9 style of leadership (Team Management) is the best, regardless of the situation. The grid itself, however, only provides the conceptual framework. It must be implemented through participation in seminars if it is to be effective. In the seminars, managers and supervisors learn to identify personal and organizational changes that are necessary and to become more effective in their interpersonal relationships and their work groups.

Situation-Based Theories of Leadership

Despite some support for the revised leadership-trait approach and the leadership-behavior approach, the research has proved inconsistent and inadequate. While leaders may possess certain traits such as achievement motivation and may be more successful if they have both a production-centered and an employee-centered orientation, there was a growing realization that successful leaders behaved differently according to the demands of the situation. From this realization, several situation-based theories of leadership have emerged.

Path-Goal Theory

Path-goal theory
A situation-based leadership theory that states that leaders can achieve organizational success by helping employees satisfy their needs while simultaneously accomplishing organizational requirements

Path-goal theory views the leader's role as being to motivate the employee by increasing the employee's payoffs for achieving work-related goals. The payoffs include a variety of rewards that we discussed earlier in the chapter. The leader acts to increase an employee's payoffs or rewards by clarifying work-related goals, reducing roadblocks to the goals, and increasing the degree of personal satisfaction that the subordinate feels about accomplishing the goals.[43]

Path-goal theory is based on the expectancy theory of motivation, discussed earlier in the chapter. According to the theory, an employee decides how much effort to invest in a task on the basis of the likelihood that the effort will accomplish the task and the likelihood that accomplishment will lead to some

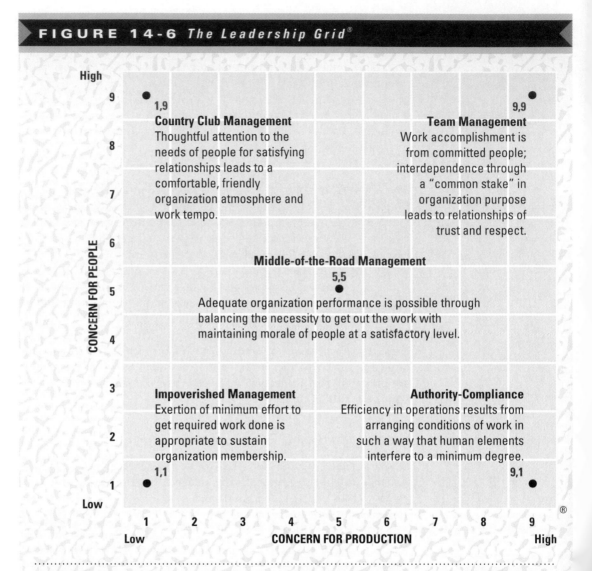

FIGURE 14-6 *The Leadership Grid®*

Source: Robert R. Blake and Anne Adams McCanse, *Leadership Dilemmas—Grid Solutions* (Houston: Gulf Publishing Company, 1991), 29. (First published as the Managerial Grid Figure by Robert R. Blake and Jane S. Mouton). Reproduced with permission.

desired reward. Thus bank tellers are likely to put effort into pleasing customers if they believe that customers can be pleased and if they believe they are likely to be rewarded for pleasing customers. In this example, the path-goal theory of leadership views the supervisor's role as ensuring that customers are not annoyed by other aspects of their banking experience, that tellers clearly understand that customer satisfaction is desired, and that the teller who pleases customers is rewarded.

Research supporting path-goal theory has found that more directive leaders can increase employee satisfaction when employees are faced with unstructured and ambiguous tasks such as those found in customer service positions. In addition, supportive behavior from a leader increases the clarity of job requirements in unstructured tasks. Finally, the path-goal theory of leadership has been instrumental in drawing attention to the variations in leader behavior that different situations require.

Situational Leadership Theory

Situational leadership theory

A situational theory that proposes that leader behavior is based on followers' skill level and maturity

Paul Hersey and Kenneth Blanchard developed another situation-based approach to leadership that they called simply **situational leadership theory.**[44] Like path-goal theory, situational leadership theory assumes that leaders vary their behaviors depending on what the situation demands. However, in Hersey and Blanchard's theory, the leader behavior is broadly defined in terms of relationship behavior and task behavior, and the situation is defined in terms of follower readiness. "Follower readiness" refers to both the skill level and the self-confidence possessed by the subordinate; both affect the behavior of the leader. For example, as employee readiness increases, the leader's task behavior decreases. (See Figure 14–7.) In other words, employees with greater self-confidence and better skills require less supervision from their manager. The contribution the situational leadership theory makes to management is that it recognizes the complexity of the manager's situation.

Emerging Theories of Leadership

eight
objective

Leadership is such a complex phenomenon that no single approach has offered managers a full understanding of what is required to lead employees to higher levels of productivity. Studies such as those associated with McClelland's managerial motivation theory or leader-behavior theory or the situational theories provide managers with some practical advice. Unfortunately, as these theories become more complex in order to address the phenomenon of leadership thoroughly, they become more difficult to test. Growing out of somewhat limited success with these theories are newer views of leadership.

Self-leadership Theory

Self-leadership theory

A leadership theory espousing an approach that encourages subordinates to become self-directed and exercise leadership for themselves

Self-leadership theory focuses on encouraging subordinates to exercise leadership for themselves.[45] The successful manager leads by example (i.e., by modeling self-leadership), by giving rewards for self-leadership among subordinates, and by assisting with employee goal setting, a topic discussed earlier. In these ways, the leader teaches employees to act as their own leaders. Thus the successful leader does not appear to lead by influencing, directing, coercing, or punishing subordinates. Instead, the successful leader is one who encourages others to be self-directed and who offers rewards to subordinates who establish a pattern of self-direction.[46]

Changes in the workforce appear to support the potential of self-leadership theory. As we noted in Chapter 2, there are growing numbers of better-educated and more independent employees in the workforce, and they should be capable

FIGURE 14-7 *Situational Leadership*

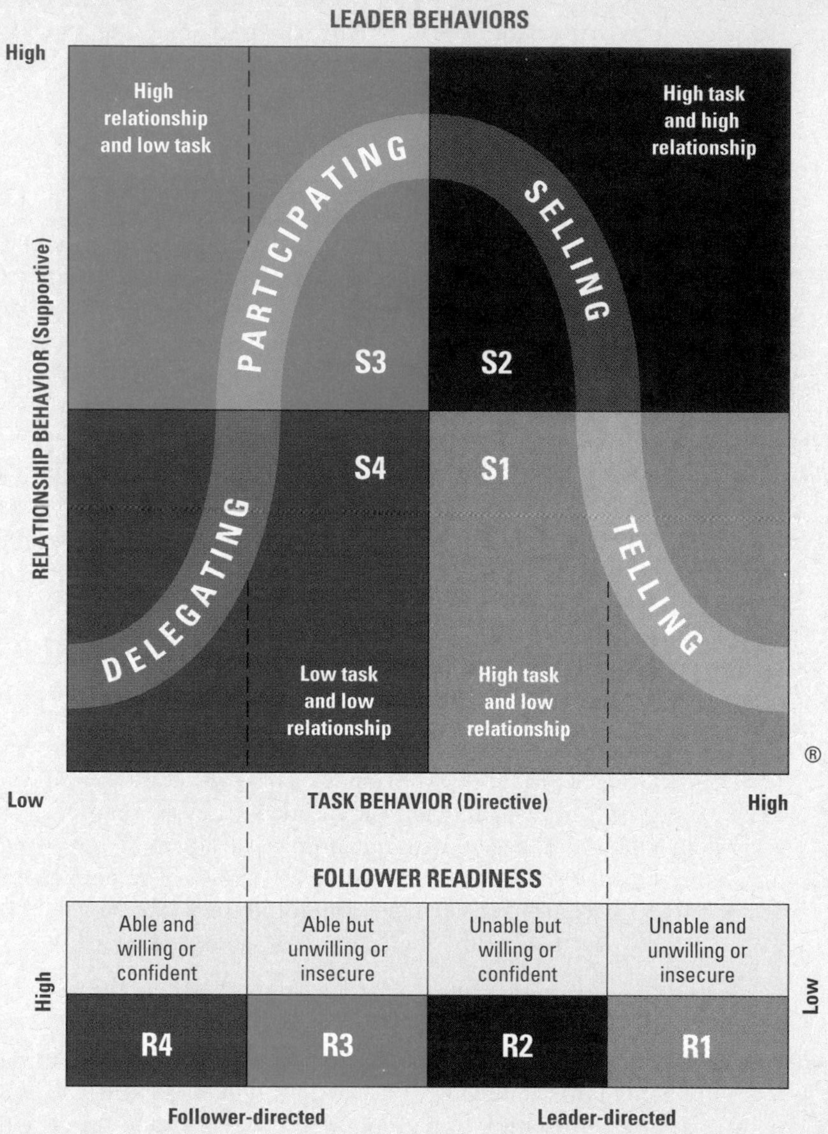
LEADER BEHAVIORS
High
High relationship and low task
High task and high relationship
PARTICIPATING
SELLING
S3
S2
S4
S1
DELEGATING
TELLING
Low task and low relationship
High task and low relationship
RELATIONSHIP BEHAVIOR (Supportive)
Low
TASK BEHAVIOR (Directive)
High
FOLLOWER READINESS
Able and willing or confident
Able but unwilling or insecure
Unable but willing or confident
Unable and unwilling or insecure
High
Low
R4
R3
R2
R1
Follower-directed
Leader-directed

Source: Copyrighted by Center for Leadership Studies. All rights reserved. Used by permission.

of self-leadership. Furthermore, there are a growing number of service organizations, such as community mental health agencies, whose employees perform their tasks largely outside the view of their supervisors. In addition, more-sophisticated information systems permit decentralization of decision making. Where employees act on their own, encouraging self-leadership seems to be the most effective means of ensuring that their behavior is consistent with the organization's mission and goals. Even in the more structured and traditional organizational setting, self-leadership may have merit in that it allows employees autonomy and responsibility for their own performance and satisfaction. Because the workforce is so diverse, managers should recognize that some employees may be better suited to self-leadership than others.

Transformational Leadership

Transformational leadership

Leadership exhibited by those who provide enthusiasm and commitment to a vision and who possess charisma

With the success of such leaders as John Sculley at Apple Computers, Jack Welch at General Electric, and Leslie Wexner at The Limited, public attention has been drawn to the transformational leader. **Transformational leadership** refers to a leader's success in changing an organization by building enthusiasm and commitment to the leader's vision of the organizational mission. The role of the transformational leader may be described in the following way: "The transformational leader motivates followers to do more than originally expected. Such transformation can be achieved by (a) raising an awareness of the importance and value of designated outcomes, (b) getting followers to transcend their own self-interests, or (c) altering or expanding followers' needs on Maslow's hierarchy of needs."[47]

Transformational leaders do not abandon traditional leader behaviors such as providing appropriate rewards or controlling the actions of subordinates in

The success of a clothing store like The Limited stems from the vision of its leadership and the enthusiasm of its staff.

order to accomplish goals. Rather, they go beyond these traditional leader behaviors, sensing what is important and communicating that vision in the form of an organizational mission. They also stimulate the development of individuals by assigning projects and coaching employees in a way that recognizes the individual's capabilities. Finally, transformational leaders provide intellectual stimulation by encouraging followers to think in new ways.[48]

Behavioral science research concerning transformational leadership is encouraging. First, it appears that transformational leaders may be found in a variety of organizational levels, not just at the top. Second, transformational leadership produces positive responses from followers, and it appears to make a difference in their performance. Third, and perhaps its greatest contribution, transformational leadership helps to improve the culture of an organization. Transformational leaders develop a vision for a more successful, higher-performing organization. They then develop commitment for that vision by implementing strategies for institutionalizing the vision among employees as well as in external constituencies of the organization.[49]

SUMMARY

one objective

More organizations are looking at their HRM activities as a key means to improve organizational productivity. Among those activities is the use of appropriate and novel rewards. Rewards serve to recognize past accomplishments while reinforcing positive employee behaviors. Pay is a particularly important reward that is used as a performance-contingent means of enhancing performance.

two objective

Perceptions of equity concern a person's evaluation of whether he or she receives adequate rewards to compensate for contributive inputs. Central to equity theory is that people perform these evaluations by comparing the inputs they bring to the work environment and the rewards they receive from it against a comparison individual. When comparisons of perceived inputs and outputs are not in balance, inequity exists and the person is likely to show unfavorable behavior such as absenteeism and/or low productivity.

three objective

Expectancy theory of motivation is based on our beliefs regarding the effort we put into doing a task combined with the value we place on the outcome of that task. For example, if I study extensively for an exam, I expect to earn a grade of A. And, if I value an A, my motivation to study is high. Managers can use this theory of motivation with employees by learning what employees value. Once employee values are known, then managers should increase employee expectancies that high effort will lead to success and the achievement of things valued.

four objective

Employee involvement groups are groups of employees working in a similar area or performing a similar function who meet regularly to discuss improvement of work performance. By analyzing problems and offering suggestions they seek to improve efficiency, cut costs, and/or address product or service issues.

objective

objective

objective

objective

Managers can empower their employees by including them in tasks and decisions that affect their jobs. Employees become empowered when they are asked to think in innovative ways and to assume more accountability and control over their work functions.

The study of leadership traits has identified literally hundreds of characteristics thought to contribute to leader effectiveness. While it is probably impossible to identify all the traits associated with successful leaders, cognitive skills, interpersonal skills, drive, vision, analytical ability, communication skills, concern, and charisma are frequently associated with today's successful leaders.

Behavioral theories of leadership focus on specific leader behaviors that facilitate work-group performance. The Ohio State and Michigan studies identified two components of leader behavior—consideration and initiating structure—as behaviors that direct good managers. The situational theories emphasize that a manager's behavior (e.g., style of leadership) is contingent upon the environment facing the manager and the types and maturity of employees supervised.

Two emerging theories of leadership are self-leadership and transformational leadership. Self-leadership emphasizes that subordinates exercise leadership for themselves. Self-leadership is enhanced when managers become mentors to their subordinates and reward subordinates when the desired behavior is shown. Transformational leadership is based on a set of abilities that allows the leader to recognize a need for change, to champion a vision for change, and to execute the change effectively. Transformational leaders are frequently characterized as charismatic leaders.

KEY TERMS

consideration

employee empowerment

employee involvement

employee involvement groups (EIs)

equity theory

expectancy theory

hierarchy of needs

needs for achievement, power, and affiliation

path-goal theory

reinforcement theory

self-leadership theory

situational leadership theory

structure

traits of leaders

transformational leadership

two-factor theory

work team

> ### DISCUSSION QUESTIONS

1. How can rewards be used effectively to increase employee performance? What role can organizational award programs play in motivating performance?
2. Why is equity theory a theory of motivation? In what ways can managers strive to create an equitable environment for employees?
3. Describe the relationship of employee involvement groups to suggestion systems, and explain the limitations of employee involvement groups in obtaining employee commitment.
4. How could you increase the empowerment of employees working for you?
5. What is it about goal setting that is motivational? What do you think are effective goal-setting techniques?
6. Which of the theories of leadership discussed in the chapter do you feel would be the most useful in the management of human resources? Why does it appeal to you?
7. How are self-leadership theory and transformational leadership theory inconsistent with one another? What relationship does transformational leadership theory have with the behavioral theories?
8. Consider the approaches to motivation used by different instructors under whom you have studied. Which approaches were most and least effective? Why?

CASE STUDY: Quality: The Goal at Pepsi

Among more than 200 bottlers in the United States, the Pepsi-Cola plant in Springfield, Missouri, is particularly proud of its performance, and justifiably so: It has won the award for highest quality among Pepsi bottlers for ten consecutive years. In addition to its outstanding record of quality, this Missouri bottler has other characteristics worth noting. Turnover is almost nonexistent, with most employees having worked there for fifteen years; no one has worked there for less than eight years. Employees exhibit a high degree of loyalty and pride in their organization. There is a sense of family, with everyone calling each other by their first names.

Several factors seem to make the difference at this bottling plant. One of the most important is its adherence to standards of quality that exceed Pepsi's own corporate standards. Springfield performs all of Pepsi's required tests, but it does so more frequently than other bottlers. If any employee notices any problem on the line, production is halted immediately until management determines that the problem has been solved. In one instance, employees discovered that a shipment of bottles had tiny black specks embedded in the plastic, although the bottles were still entirely sanitary. This discovery was made after 300 cases had already been filled with the imperfect bottles. Nevertheless, all 300 cases were poured out. Customers expect the product to appear exactly as promised, and Springfield employees will not renege on that promise.

In addition, there are no time constraints on quality tests. If repeated tests are required, they are performed until the employee conducting the test is satisfied with the results. Records of the performance of route salespersons are kept on a daily basis, and these workers are given daily feedback on their performance and are recognized for outstanding performance.

Every manager started out as a member of the production line or as a route salesperson. On reaching the managerial level, each manager is expected to know the various jobs in the organization and to be capable of taking over not only a production or route job but other managerial jobs as well.

Managers are expected to lead and motivate by example, and a great deal of emphasis is placed on teamwork. General staff meetings discuss all aspects of the business, including production, finance, and marketing. Managers are expected to communicate regularly with employees and with managers in other departments. Thus the sales manager is expected to work closely with the comptroller concerning sales expectations.

Source: Adapted from D. Keith Denton, "Quality Is Pepsi's Challenge," *Personnel Journal* 67, no. 6 (June 1988): 143–47. Reprinted with the permission of *Personnel Journal*, Costa Mesa, Calif. All rights reserved.

Questions

1. Explain how the Springfield Pepsi bottler is successful in terms of the various motivation theories discussed in this chapter.
2. How does this organization virtually eliminate turnover, and what role does the low turnover play in the overall strategy for motivating employees in this organization?

NOTES AND REFERENCES

1. "Forecasting the Future of the American Workplace," *American Workplace* 1, no. 1, U.S. Department of Labor (September 1993): 1.
2. Peggy Stuart, "Fresh Ideas Energize Reward Programs," *Personnel Journal* 71, no. 1 (January 1992): 102.
3. Dawn Gunsch, "Award Programs That Work," *Personnel Journal* 70, no. 9 (September 1991): 85–89.
4. A leading reference in this field is Fred Luthans and Robert Kreitner, *Organizational Behavior Modification and Beyond: An Operant and Social Learning Approach* (Glenview, Ill.: Scott, Foresman, 1985).
5. These needs are adapted from Abraham H. Maslow, *Motivation and Personality*, 2d ed. (New York: Harper and Brothers, 1970); see also John A. Wagner and John R. Hollenbeck, *Management of Organizational Behavior* (Englewood Cliffs, N.J.: Prentice-Hall, 1992), 205–07.
6. Linda Thornburg, "Pay-for-Performance: What Should You Know," *HR Magazine* 37, no. 6 (June 1992): 58–61.
7. These four reasons for instituting pay-for-performance systems are included in a list of pros and cons for developing such systems by Thomas Rollins, "Pay for Performance: Is It Worth the Trouble?" *Personnel Administrator* 33, no. 5 (May 1988): 42–46; see also Jerry M. Newman and Daniel J. Fisher, "Strategic Impact Pay," *Compensation and Benefits Review* 24, no. 4 (July-August 1992): 38–45.
8. Gerald E. Ledford, Jr., "Three Case Studies on Skill-Based Pay: An Overview," *Compensation and Benefits Review* 23, no. 2 (March-April 1991): 11–23.

9. Stuart, "Fresh Ideas," 102. See also Jennifer Koch, "Perpetual Thanks: Its Assets," *Personnel Journal* 69, no. 1 (January 1990): 72–73.

10. Robert A. Luke, Jr., "Meaningful Praise Makes a Difference," *Supervisory Management* 36, no. 2 (February 1991): 3.

11. Robert Kreitner and Angelo Kinicki, *Organizational Behavior*, 3d ed. (Chicago: Irwin, 1995), Chapter 8. For an interesting discussion of operant conditioning and the scientist whose research transformed our understanding of the learning process, see Iver H. Iverson, "Skinner's Early Research: From Reflexology to Operant Conditioning," *American Psychologist* 47, no. 1 (November 1992): 1318–28. This special issue is entitled *Reflections on B. F. Skinner and Psychology* and was edited by Kennon B. Lattal.

12. Daniel C. Boyle, "Employee Motivation That Works," *HR Magazine* 37, no. 10 (October 1992): 83–89.

13. Jay T. Knippen and Thad B. Green, "Reinforcing the Right Behavior," *Supervisory Management* 35, no. 4 (April 1990): 7; see also Rosalie A. Steele, "Awards Energize a Suggestion Program," *Personnel Journal* 71, no. 10 (October 1992): 96–99.

14. David J. Cherrington, "Follow Through on Award Programs," *HR Magazine* 37, no. 4 (April 1992): 52–55.

15. Gregory Moorhead and Ricky W. Griffin, *Organizational Behavior*, 3d ed. (Boston: Houghton Mifflin, 1992): 155–60.

16. J. Stacey Adams, "Inequity in Social Exchange," in *Advances in Experimental Social Psychology*, ed. L. Berkowitz (New York: Academic Press, 1965), 276–99.

17. There are a variety of practical, work-related and nonwork-related suggestions for managing equity and ensuring fairness in Richard C. Huseman and John D. Hatfield, *Managing the Equity Factor: After All I've Done for You . . .* (Boston: Houghton Mifflin, 1989), 99–100.

18. Victor H. Vroom, *Work and Motivation* (San Francisco: Jossey-Bass, 1994). This landmark book, originally published in 1964, integrates the work of hundreds of researchers seeking to explain choice of work, job satisfaction, and job performance.

19. These three ways are adapted from Professor Lawler's three approaches to employee involvement: (1) parallel suggestions involvement, (2) job involvement, and (3) high involvement. For more information about his three approaches, see Edward E. Lawler, "Choosing an Involvement Strategy," *Academy of Management Executive* 2, no. 3 (August 1988): 197–204. For a landmark work on motivation, see Edward E. Lawler III, *Motivation in Work Organizations* (San Fransisco: Jossey-Bass, 1994).

20. Yuzo Yasuda, *40 Years, 20 Million Ideas: The Toyota Suggestion System* (Cambridge, Mass.: Productivity Press, 1991); see also Michael Michalko, "Bright Idea," *Training and Development Journal* 48, no. 6 (June 1994): 44–47.

21. "HRM Updates," *Personnel Administrator* 34, no. 8 (August 1989): 20.

22. Robert E. Cole, Paul Bacdayan, and B. Joseph White, "Quality, Participation, and Competitiveness," *California Management Review* 35, no. 3 (Spring 1993): 68–81; see also Richard J. Magjuka, "The 10 Dimensions of Employee Involvement," *Training and Development* 47, no. 4 (April 1993): 61–67.

23. Everett E. Adams, Jr., "Quality Circle Performance," *Journal of Management* 17, no. 1 (March 1991): 25–39.

24. Among the classic references to the work of Herzberg and his colleagues are the following: Frederick Herzberg, Bernard Mausner, and Barbara B. Snyderman, *The Motivation to Work*, 2d ed. (New York: Wiley, 1959): 113–14; Frederic Herzberg, *Work and the Nature of Man* (Cleveland: World, 1966).

25. Michael A. Champion and Carol L. McClelland, "Follow-up and Extension of the Interdisciplinary Costs and Benefits of Enlarged Jobs," *Journal of Applied Psychology* 78, no. 3 (June 1993): 339–51; Ricky W. Griffin, "Effects of Work Redesign on Employee Perceptions, Attitudes, and Behaviors: A Long-Term Investigation," *Academy of Management Journal* 34, no. 2 (June 1991): 425–35.

26. Charles C. Manz and Henry P. Sims, Jr., *Business without Bosses* (New York: Wiley, 1993); see also Kevin Goldman, "Avrett Free Staffers Form Teams That Leap the Generation Gap," *The Wall Street Journal* (December 21, 1994): B4; W. Alan Randolph and Barry Z. Posner, *Getting the Job Done: Managing Project Teams and Task Forces for Success* (Englewood Cliffs, N.J.: Prentice-Hall, 1992).

27. Charles C. Manz, "Self-Leading Work Teams: Moving beyond Self-Managing Myths," *Human Relations* 45, no. 11 (November 1992): 1119–40; see also Jeanne M. Wilson, Jill George, Richard S. Wellins, and William C. Byham, *Leadership Trapeze: Strategies for Leadership in Team-Based Organizations* (San Francisco: Jossey-Bass, 1994).

28. Jana Schilder, "Work Teams Boost Productivity," *Personnel Journal* 71, no. 2 (February 1992): 67; see also Sam T. Johnson, "Work Teams: What's Ahead in Work Design and Rewards Management," *Compensation and Benefits Review* 25, no. 2 (March-April 1993): 35–41.

29. Richard J. Magjuka and Timothy T. Baldwin, "Team-Based Employee Involvement Programs: Effects of Design and Administration," *Personnel Psychology* 44, no. 4 (Winter 1991): 793–811; see also Anthony R. Montebello and Victor R. Buzzotta, "Work Teams That Work," *Training and Development* 47, no. 3 (March 1993): 59–64.

30. "Forecasting the Future of the American Workplace," 2.

31. John H. Dobbs, "The Empowerment Environment," *Training and Development* 47, no. 2 (February 1993): 55–57.

32. Kreitner and Kinicki, *Organizational Behavior*, 220.

33. Edward A. Locke and Gary P. Latham, *Goal Setting—A Motivational Technique That Works* (Englewood Cliffs, N.J.: Prentice-Hall, 1984), 121.

34. Although one of the classic references on leadership is Ralph M. Stogdill, *Handbook of Leadership: A Survey of the Literature* (New York: Free Press, 1974), readers may also wish to consult Bernard M. Bass and Ralph M. Stogdill, *Bass and Stogdill's Handbook of Leadership: Theory, Research, and Managerial Applications*, 3d ed. (New York: Free Press, 1990).

35. Peter Koestenbaum, *Leadership: The Inner Side of Greatness* (San Francisco: Jossey-Bass, 1991).

36. Stogdill is considered a pioneer of research in leadership traits. For those interested in his original work, see Ralph M. Stogdill, "Personal Factors Associated with Leadership: A Survey of the Literature," *Journal of Psychology* 25 (1948).

37. Robert J. Richardson and S. Katharine Thayer, *The Charisma Factor: How to Develop Your Natural Leadership Ability* (Englewood Cliffs, N.J.: Prentice-Hall, 1993).

38. Jane M. Howell and Bruce J. Avolio, "The Ethics of Charismatic Leadership: Submission or Liberation?" *Academy of Management Executive* 6, no. 2 (May 1992): 43–53.

39. John J. Hudy, "The Motivation Trap," *HR Magazine* 37, no. 12 (December 1992): 63–67.

40. David C. McClelland, *Human Motivation* (Glenview, Ill.: Scott, Foresman, 1985), 595–96.

41. The results of the University of Michigan studies were summarized in two books by Rensis Likert: *New Patterns of Management* (New York: McGraw-Hill, 1961) and *The Human Organization: Its Management and Value* (New York: McGraw-Hill, 1967).

42. Robert R. Blake and Jane S. Mouton, *The Versatile Manager* (Homewood, Ill.: Irwin, 1981). Earlier books about the grid by these authors were published in 1964 and 1978.

43. The path-goal theory of leadership was originally published in Robert J. House, "A Path-Goal Theory of Leader Effectiveness," *Administrative Science Quarterly* 16, no. 3 (September 1971): 321–39.

44. Paul Hersey and Kenneth H. Blanchard, *Management of Organizational Behavior*, 6th ed. (Englewood Cliffs, N.J.: Prentice-Hall, 1993).

45. Charles C. Manz, "Developing Self-Leaders through Super Leadership," *Supervisory Management* 36, no. 9 (September 1991): 3; Charles C. Manz, *Mastering Self-Leadership: Empowering Yourself for Personal Excellence* (Englewood Cliffs, N.J.: Prentice-Hall, 1991).

46. Marshall Whitmire and Philip R. Nienstedt, "Lead Leaders into the 90s," *Personnel Journal* 70, no. 5 (May 1991): 80–85.

47. David A. Nadler and Michael L. Tushman, "Beyond the Charismatic Leader: Leadership and Organizational Change," *California Management Review* 32 (Winter 1990): 77.

48. Robert T. Keller, "Transformational Leadership and the Performance of Research and Development Project Groups," *Journal of Management* 18, no. 13 (September 1992): 489–501.

49. Noel M. Tichy and Mary Ann Devannag, *The Transformational Leader* (New York: Wiley, 1986).

Chapter

The Role of Communication in HRM

After studying this chapter you should be able to

Explain the nature of communication and the barriers that reduce communication effectiveness.

Identify effective downward communication systems.

Provide examples of various upward communication systems.

Discuss the informal communication system and its role in spreading information.

Explain how to improve managerial communication competency.

Define the problems of communicating with diverse groups.

Explain the counseling process and the major techniques used in counseling.

N*o aspect of HRM is so pervasive as communication. Communication provides the means of gathering and disseminating information in the employee selection process. Through communication, managers give feedback and counsel to employees in the performance appraisal process. Compensation programs depend on the communication skills of those who gather information for setting wage rates; labor relations are affected by negotiation skills, counseling skills, and presentation skills; and successful training programs depend on how effectively trainers, videotapes, and written materials communicate. Moreover, HR managers are frequently charged with ensuring that the organization has an effective program of organizational communication. Managers must therefore understand how to manage communication as well as how to communicate effectively with employees at all levels of the organization.[1]*

In this chapter we address each of these communication responsibilities. We will list the communication skills that effective managers need and discuss the communication systems that must be managed by HR departments. Finally, we will devote special attention to the communication skills required for counseling, a technique widely used by managers in disciplining and appraising, as well as assisting their employees.

The Importance of Communication

A manager's day is consumed with communicating—with subordinates, with other managers, with supervisors, with consumers, with regulators. Authorities in business communication note that more than 75 percent of a manager's time is spent communicating.[2] Managers spend the largest amount of their communication time (45 percent) communicating with subordinates. About 25 percent of communicating time is spent talking with persons outside the organization, and the remaining 30 percent is divided about equally between communicating with their superiors and with others within the organization. Not surprisingly, managers use face-to-face communication as the predominant medium. In fact, when one-on-one communication is considered together with meetings, more than 80 percent of managers' communication may be classified as face-to-face as opposed to written or telephone communication.[3]

Effective managers are effective communicators.[4] Their communication skills can affect the satisfaction of those who work for them, the effectiveness of the work unit, and their subordinates' understanding of their duties. One management consultant described the relationship of communication to managing this way: "We all learn in school that management is supposed to link levels vertically and departments horizontally through planning, leadership, organizing, and controlling. In practice, these things cannot be done without constant attention to good communication. It isn't an adjunct to the manager's job, it is the manager's job."[5]

The Nature of Communication

Managers must first understand the process of communication before they can successfully address any problems that result from poor communication. Communication is a process in which a sender and a receiver of a message interact in order to give the message meaning. (See Figure 15–1.) This complex process has often been oversimplified in traditional communication models: A sender delivers a message that is captured by a receiver, who in turn provides feedback to the sender, indicating that the message has been received. This simplistic model of communication ignores communication difficulties created by an interaction process that relies on individual perceptions of complex verbal and nonverbal messages along with other barriers to communication.

Communicating with Symbols

Verbal symbols
Words that stand for objects and abstractions

We are able to communicate with one another because we can manipulate a broad range of **verbal symbols** that stand for objects and abstractions. For example, if we tell someone to "lay the pen on the table," selecting symbols (i.e., words) such as "table" and "pen" to communicate our message, we only have to agree with that person on the general meaning of the symbols for the communication to succeed. However, in the complex world of organizational communication, a variety of words can be used to refer to the same object, practice, or idea, so the choice of a particular word often implies bias in communicators' evaluations and perceptions.[6] For example, managers may choose to call those who report to them subordinates, workers, supervisees, staff, crew, the gang, or my people. Employees will perceive a certain kind of relationship with their manager depending on which word is used to describe them. Managers therefore face the challenge of choosing the right words to communicate with employees, since this choice can have a significant influence on their relationship.

Furthermore, the words a manager chooses when communicating convey a message themselves about the manager, about the person the manager is communicating with, and about the situation. Words can be loaded weapons: When used improperly, they can be dangerous. For example, certain words can convey racial or sex bias on the part of the communicator, and managers must recognize this danger if they are to communicate effectively with diverse groups of employees.

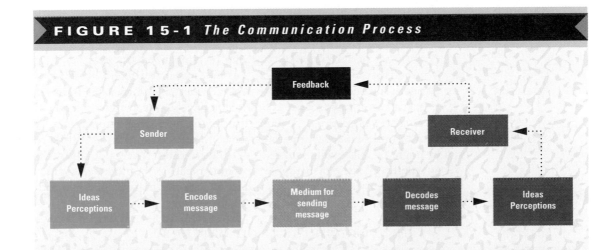

FIGURE 15-1 *The Communication Process*

Nonverbal symbols

Bodily actions such as gestures, facial expressions, posture, and tone of voice that influence the communication between individuals

Nonverbal symbols affect communication outcomes and occur simultaneously with the communication of verbal symbols. In face-to-face communication, the parties are responding to facial expressions, gestures, bodily positions, and voice tones that are just as important to the communication process as the words that are being spoken.[7] These expressions, gestures, and bodily positions together constitute our *body language,* which conveys to others our attitudes and feelings. Whenever the meaning of a nonverbal symbol conflicts with that of the verbal, the receiver is likely to find the nonverbal more believable.

Problems of False Assumptions

The effective communicator must also recognize the role that assumptions play in communication. The perceptions of communicators are based on certain assumptions they have about one another, about the situation, and about other persons and places they have in common. Whenever senders and receivers have conflicting assumptions, the quality of their communication deteriorates. Highlights in HRM 1 provides an illustration of the effect of different perceived assumptions in manager-employee communication. This account demonstrates why managers must take the time to adapt their messages to the intended receiver. We can list some of the assumptions that led to the communication problem:

- The use of a written medium for the initial message when an oral or less formal medium would have conveyed more information
- The lack of openness and honesty between the two managers
- The usual reluctance of subordinates to communicate their negative reactions and feelings to their managers
- The failure of the manager to solicit the subordinate's reactions and feelings
- The failure of the manager to communicate her own reactions and feelings about the subordinate's messages

One method used to minimize the problems of false assumptions is to separate facts from inferences. A fact is a verifiable statement to which many people can agree. An **inference** is a conclusion that is based on fact but depends on the assumptions that are made. An example of an inference may be seen in the illustration in Highlights in HRM 1: Watson *inferred* that Alvarez was displeased with her performance because she recommended the new managerial training program. Communication can be improved by differentiating facts from inferences. By training oneself to separate factual information from the inferences made from those facts, it is possible to develop an awareness of the distinction in a variety of settings. A supervisor might infer, for example, that the employee who works late every day is extremely interested in the job. While this inference might be reasonably sound, it is still just an inference, not a fact. Both facts and inferences are indispensable to communication, but managers must take care to remember that one person's inference may not be the same as another's, despite their being derived from the same set of facts.

Inference

Conclusions based on facts but colored by assumptions made by observers

Other Communication Barriers

The grouping of people into a complex organization imposes conditions affecting human relations that may become potential barriers to communication. In order

HIGHLIGHTS IN HRM

HRM highlights

1   A PROBLEM IN COMMUNICATION

Laura Alvarez had moved from California to east Tennessee as the first training director for a division of a large electronic manufacturing company. As the director she developed a relatively large training staff that provided three types of training: (1) technical training, (2) managerial training, and (3) remedial, basic education. These three areas were headed by unit managers who reported to Alvarez. Sharon Watson now headed the managerial training unit. Alvarez had hired Watson as a trainer when the division had first opened, and her satisfaction with Watson's performance and demonstrated potential had led her to promote Watson to manager of the managerial training unit.

One day Alvarez received a report from her counterpart at the home office in California. The report described impressive improvements in productivity that could be attributed to a new concept that had been introduced in the California office's managerial training program. Alvarez hastily scribbled a note to Watson—"Why aren't we doing this?"—and, attaching her note to the report, she gave it to her new secretary to forward to Watson. Rather than send the handwritten note, however, the secretary typed it before sending it on. Knowing Alvarez's preference for "no secrets" in the training area, the secretary also sent a copy of the note and report to the other unit directors in training, but she failed to list them as copy recipients on the typed memorandum.

When Watson received the memorandum, she was surprised at the curtness of the note and its unusual formality. Why, she wondered, had Alvarez sent the report? Was she implying that Watson was unable to implement training programs that really made a difference? She was also annoyed at Alvarez's having blind-copied the memorandum and report.

Watson requested a meeting with Alvarez, unusual in itself since they generally met informally rather than at scheduled meetings. The meeting went poorly. Watson had assumed, prior to receiving Alvarez's memorandum, that she was an excellent manager and a favorite of Alvarez's. Alvarez, prior to this meeting, assumed that Watson thought well of her and trusted her. Not understanding the purpose of the meeting and immediately noticing Watson's cool demeanor, Alvarez felt herself becoming defensive. Watson was anxious and spoke rather stiffly as she showed Alvarez the report and asked what her expectations were. When Alvarez suggested, defensively, that her expectations were that Watson would read the material and use it, Watson replied, "Then you don't think we're doing all we can in my area?" Again not really understanding, Alvarez responded, "Of course I don't think we're doing all we can. There are always new ways to do things."

By now, Watson assumed that Alvarez was disappointed in her and was looking for someone new to manage her unit. Alvarez, too, was revising her assumptions about Watson, seeing her as unpredictable and more difficult to work with than she had earlier thought.

From that point on, the relationship deteriorated. Alvarez found it increasingly difficult to talk with Watson; she noticed that Watson avoided her and that Watson's contributions at staff meetings were minimal. It was only a few weeks before she received Watson's notice that she was leaving the company.

for communication to be effective, it is essential for managers to recognize these potential barriers and to plan communication so that these barriers may be eliminated or at least minimized.

Differences in Perception

One result of prior experiences is that each employee brings to the job a unique way of looking at things, or, in other words, a personal frame of reference. This frame of reference determines the way in which whatever is seen or heard will be interpreted. If, for example, a manager is perceived as a "parent figure," an employee may accept or reject what the manager says, depending upon his or her own personal experience. Similarly, employees who have been "let down" by previous managers are likely to view a new manager as someone not to be trusted. Managers and supervisors should therefore learn enough about each individual to know what meaning may be applied to their messages and what emotional overtones will be inferred.

Differences in Interpretation (Semantics)

Words, like gestures, can be interpreted in various ways, thus creating a barrier to communication. Since there is not necessarily a connection between a symbol (the word) and what is being symbolized (the meaning), the communication may be received quite differently from what was intended. For example, the word "cool" can be interpreted as being cold or being "with it." Thus, in selecting words, the communicator should consider the audience and its likely interpretation of the words being used.

Bias

Bias may be a barrier in face-to-face as well as in written communication. In one study, for example, the same article was read by several persons. For some of the readers, the article was accompanied by a picture of an attractive female, who was designated as its author. For other readers, the article was accompanied by a picture of an unattractive female. The article written by the attractive "author" was evaluated by both male and female readers as being higher in quality than that written by the unattractive "author."[8] Likewise, personal bias may enter any form of communication, including letters, speeches, personal conversations, or reports.

Downward Communication Systems

HR professionals have a responsibility to be effective communicators. In addition, they are often responsible for developing effective communication systems for the organization, many of which are designed to convey information from management to employees. This type of communication is usually referred to as **downward communication.**

    The success of downward communication systems is affected by the general communication philosophy and policy of the organization.[9] Thus organizations such as Eaton Corporation, First Investment Company, and Blockbuster Enter-

Downward communication
Communication flowing from managers to employees

tainment have developed strong policies that encourage management to communicate with employees. These policies emanate from general philosophies of how employees should be treated and the ideal relationship that should exist between employees and management.

Employee Handbooks and Policy Manuals

One of the important means of training and socializing new employees is the employee handbook. It provides information about organizational benefits; it describes the rights and responsibilities of employees; and it often explains the organization's disciplinary system. Employers know that a well-written handbook is a good defense against employee lawsuits and discrimination charges.[10] Smaller employers who lack the resources to develop a handbook can obtain help from available computer software programs.[11]

Managers today have also become concerned with developing a limited set of policies that are critical to the functioning of the organization and consistent with the philosophy and culture of senior management. These policies are frequently compiled in a formal document called a "policy manual." Policy manuals help to ensure that policies are enforced. Written but unenforced policies have been the basis of many court actions by employees against present or former employers, and employers have thus been given an incentive to make their actions correspond to their policies. Figure 15–2 lists several important guidelines for effectively communicating organizational policies.

Organizations must constantly update policy manuals to cover changes in benefits, social concerns, and employee rights, as well as the adoption of new programs such as employee involvement groups and flextime. To make policy

FIGURE 15-2 *Guidelines for Communicating Policies*

1. Policies should be written in a manner that will communicate the organization's culture and philosophy.
2. There should be no policy proliferation. Only those areas where employees and managers need guidance should be addressed.
3. Policies should be complete and sufficiently detailed to cover the topic — no more, no less.
4. Because policy manuals have sometimes been held to be a binding contract between the organization and the employee, the manual should include statements to the effect that it does not constitute a binding contract between the parties.
5. The wording of the manual should be sensitive to the language, cultural, and gender differences of the workforce.
6. Policies must be communicated by means other than just the policy manual (e.g., group meetings, orientation programs, special bulletins).
7. Policies should be reviewed on a regular basis and outdated ones should be revised or removed.
8. Policies must not violate laws or inadvertently contradict one another.

manuals a useful addition to their downward communication systems, organizations must communicate policy or legal changes through several channels, including HR-developed training programs. (See Highlights in HRM 2.)

The U.S. District Court ruling in *Kalwecz v AM International, Inc.*, made it clear that employees must receive proper notice of changes in policy manuals and the employee handbook.[12] Kalwecz, an employee of AM International, was awarded $130,000 as a result of the company's failure to notify him properly of a disclaimer in the employee handbook. The disclaimer concerned a previous policy of finding another position in the company for employees of ten years or longer tenure whose jobs were being eliminated. (Figure 15–2 provides suggestions for clearly communicating policies to employees.)

Organizational Newspapers

Organizational newspapers serve a variety of purposes for management. First, they provide a convenient means for announcing changes in organizational policy and procedure. Second, they may be used to publish notices of job openings for the organization's in-house job posting program. Third, they are a way to convey the organization's mission and long-term goals, and fourth, they offer management a means of responding to questions. Some organizations have also found that they can use their newspapers to encourage *upward communication* (see below) by running a routine column that encourages employees to ask questions. In providing answers to these questions, organizations satisfy employees' need to know and contribute to the general knowledge that employees have about the organization.

Bulletin Boards

Bulletin boards are used for a variety of types of messages that must be communicated to a broad audience. Job openings are posted there, as well as safety information and announcements of a broad range of organization- or department-wide events, including meetings, picnics, and sporting events.

Using bulletin boards effectively means placing them where employees are likely to pause in the course of their day—for example, near water fountains, time clocks, or reception areas. Getting employees to read posted messages requires that the bulletin boards be routinely monitored, with notices arranged neatly for easy reading and dated postings removed. Many organizations that are geographically dispersed use fax machines to provide their employees with timely notices for their bulletin boards.

One of the newest approaches to handling notices is the electronic bulletin board. Ciba-Geigy uses a computerized job posting system instead of tacking up its monthly list of job openings on bulletin boards. This system allows the company to list jobs immediately when they open up and to delete them as soon as they are filled. Organizations that use electronic mail heavily have three additional electronic options for posting announcements. First, notices can be flashed on videotext screens as users sign onto the electronic mail system, forcing the employee to at least "pass by" the notices. Second, special electronic bulletin systems can be designed to enable users to access a special screen for current notices. A third option is the ability of some systems to flash notices to each of the videotext screens currently being used in conjunction with the electronic mail system.

> ## HIGHLIGHTS IN HRM

highlights

2   COMMUNICATING POLICY CHANGES AT CENTINELA HOSPITAL MEDICAL CENTER

When Centinela Hospital Medical Center in Los Angeles felt the strain of revised labor laws, it took innovative action. Legislation affecting employee termination, union activity, and workers' compensation claims had all been changed over the last several years, resulting in confusion for many managers and supervisors whose jobs required them to understand the issues, enforce them, and abide by them.

Centinela's solution was the development of a six-hour class called Employee Relations for Managers. Participants continue to find that one of the most innovative and enjoyable parts of the class discussion session is the Employee Relations Board Game. The stated object of the game is to reach "Finish" on the board before the other players, but the underlying goal is to communicate hospital policy and legal changes affecting employee relations.

The game uses several different kinds of cards. Players pick the cards and try their hands at answering the questions printed thereon. Their progress along the game board is based on their answers.

Any organization can use the same game format and plug in questions related to its own communication needs. The format works well for any type of communication that is detail-oriented and factual and that deals with situations in which an employee must have a strong knowledge base in order to consider alternatives and make effective decisions. For example, it might work well for training in accounting principles, cash management, and procurement practices.

Instructions for the Employee Relations Board Game

Welcome to the Employee Relations Board Game. Please read all the instructions before playing. The object is to choose the correct answers to the questions and be the first team to reach "Finish."

Preparing for the game. Each player chooses a partner. For example, in a group of six players, there will be three teams consisting of two people each. Each team selects a playing piece and places it on the board in the space marked "Start." The teams take turns rolling the die. The high scorer starts the game, the second highest plays next, and so on.

Playing the game. Game play proceeds as outlined below.

1. The first team chooses a Knowledge card; an opposing team reads the question aloud. Members of the first team attempt to answer the question within the one-minute time limit. If the first team answers correctly, its members move their playing piece forward by one space and get to take another turn. A roving coach settles all disputes.
2. The first time a team answers a question incorrectly, members receive their first written warning (a blue card). If they miss another question, they receive a second written warning (a yellow card) and must draw a penalty card. The penalty card directs the team to a "Consequence Station" on the board. A marker is placed on the space from which the team's playing piece was moved.

(*continued*)

HIGHLIGHTS IN HRM (*continued*)

3. About halfway through the game, players will begin to reach squares that direct them to draw Situation cards. These questions are more complicated; answering them will probably require assistance from the roving coach. The opposing team is responsible for scoring the answer, with the coach's help. The coach listens to the team members' input, allows the responding team to defend its answer, oversees the decision, and settles disputes. The coach should encourage players to air their views; Situation cards are designed to provoke discussion and learning.

Winning the game. The first team to reach the space marked "Finish" is the winner.

Source: Adapted from Ellen A. Ensher and Jeanne Hartley, "The Employee Relations Game," *Training and Development* 46, no. 11 (December 1992): 21–24. Reprinted with permission of the American Society for Training and Development. All rights reserved.

Videos

The potential for using video messages in organizations is unlimited. So far the most frequent uses have been for orientation programs, specialized training programs, safety instructions, and special messages from senior executives. Organizations may also use video messages to describe benefits such as medical plans or retirement options or to provide realistic job previews, mentioned earlier in Chapter 5 and illustrated here in Highlights in HRM 3. The advantages of video include employees' familiarity with the medium, the medium's ability to demonstrate something visually, and the savings associated with videos when training must be repeated many times or provided in distant locations.

One variation on videos that is becoming increasingly useful to organizations is the interactive video.[13] Interactive videos combine the use of computers, video images, and touch-sensitive screens. They allow employees to ask questions and receive information geared specifically to the topic of immediate interest. For example, employees contemplating retirement can examine the long-term results of various retirement plans offered by the organization. The interactive format allows retirement information to be adapted to the employee in terms of the individual's age, time with the company, and projected income. Other possible topics for interactive videos include medical benefits, managerial training, organizational history, current news from senior management, and information about special events such as parties or stress-management classes.

UNNUM, a Maine-based life insurance company, has gone one step further in its use of interactive video technology. The company created a video game for workers to learn about employee benefits. The game challenges employees to test their knowledge of their benefits. As a series of questions is asked, the users

HIGHLIGHTS IN HRM

3   USING VIDEO-RECORDED MESSAGES FOR THE REALISTIC JOB PREVIEW

highlights

The use of video-recorded messages in realistic job previews (RJPs) is receiving more and more attention from HR professionals. RJPs are designed to give recruits organizational information that is likely to be dissatisfying when discovered and may therefore result in turnover. The Canadian armed forces use short, five-minute videos for each of their military specialities (rifleman, tank crew member, etc.). Each video highlights critical issues that may lead to dissatisfaction on the job.

Businesses have found that RJPs can save them from 6 to 12 percent of their replacement costs, depending on their turnover rates. To realize these savings, organizations must develop effective RJPs, which may include written documents, the selection interview, and, of course, the video version. For the video to be effective, it must have the following characteristics:

1. The people used in the video should be real employees, not actors.
2. The employees in the video should go beyond merely describing aspects of the organization; they must express their opinions. For example, in discussing the realities of working in a public accounting firm, the employees in the video should mention the unpleasant aspects of having to rearrange family schedules to meet a client's unexpected request.
3. An effective RJP video provides negative information, but the degree of negativity is moderate rather than high. Topics of moderate negativity might include hours of work required, lack of opportunity for praise, or having to stand long hours while working. Topics of high negativity, such as the possibility of serious injury or exposure to potential health hazards, should not be given too much attention.

Source: Adapted from John P. Wanous, "Installing a Realistic Job Preview: Ten Tough Choices," *Personnel Psychology* 42, no. 1 (Spring 1989): 117–34. Reprinted with permission.

watch as Flex, a cartoon character, attempts to lift a pair of dumbbells; Flex succeeds if the worker responds correctly to the question. Employees report that the game is fun, and UNNUM's HR staff has concluded that employees learn a great deal about the benefits program.[14]

Meetings

None of us likes to attend useless meetings, particularly those where we have to sit quietly while the speaker drones on about an uninteresting topic. Yet there are times when the most expedient way to communicate information is at one time to a group of employees. Such meetings are a worthwhile part of the organization's downward communication program. In fact, failure to hold informational meetings will probably lead employees to feel alienated from the organization.

In these meetings the division head, the departmental manager, or another senior manager typically gives an overview of some major change in the organization's long-term goals. For example, USAA, a major life insurance firm for military officers and their dependents, has found that large employee meetings have been especially helpful in obtaining employees' commitment to its goals. Another, somewhat different use of large meetings is to announce reductions in the workforce. Managers have found that negative information, such as layoff announcements, should be communicated promptly and openly.[15] Reporting bad news quickly will help the organization get past difficult times in a shorter period by letting employees vent their anger and frustration. Furthermore, it will reduce the amount of time employees spend needlessly discussing partially accurate information, and because it is honest communication, it will gain the respect of employees.

Through periodic conferences to which individuals in certain positions are invited, department managers, including HR managers, can communicate information and ideas and obtain feedback from the participants. In the larger organizations, where operations are widely separated, conferences that utilize telephone circuits, known as teleconferences, may be held. Teleconferences may be restricted to voice transmission or may include videoconferencing. Teleconferencing facilitates the interaction of participants and avoids the inconvenience and expense associated with travel.

James McElwain, vice president for HR services at NCR Corporation, and his staff have developed S-Net, a satellite network with 140 downlinks to 90 percent of NCR's employees. S-Net's interactive video format permits NCR's employees to meet by teleconference. In fact, NCR publishes a weekly program guide listing about thirty hours of weekly programming. With increased attention given to autonomous work teams and self-leadership (see Chapter 14), teleconferencing serves as a substitute for on-premise leadership.[16]

Whatever form the informational meeting takes, its success will depend on the skills of the manager who makes the presentation. Effective presentations require audience analysis, careful preparation, and a positive, employee-oriented attitude. Figure 15–3 presents several useful suggestions for developing an effective presentation.[17]

In making a presentation, the presenter should consider the value that can be derived from appropriate visuals. Studies have clearly shown that visuals increase the effectiveness of presentations. One study demonstrated that employee attention can be increased by about 10 percent with visuals and the persuasive impact can be increased by about 43 percent. When using visuals, however, these guidelines should be followed:

1. Convey only one idea per visual.
2. Use only one illustration per visual.
3. Present no more than six or seven lines per visual.
4. Use no more than seven words per line.
5. Hold lettering sizes to three or fewer different sizes per visual.
6. Include no more than four colors.[18]

FIGURE 15-3 *Making Effective Presentations*

1. Prepare an outline of the presentation, listing the most important ideas to be communicated.

2. Understand the purpose and motives for making the presentation. Answer the question, "What is the purpose of this talk?"

3. Anticipate your audience's point of view and try to understand their needs, attitudes, and biases.

4. Early in the presentation, state the purpose of the talk and how the information received will benefit the audience.

5. Prepare attractive visuals that will allow the audience to grasp your message more easily.

6. Set realistic time limits; consider the content of the presentation (detailed versus factual), disposition of audience, and time of day.

7. Present yourself in a professional manner and avoid being overly casual, defensive, or autocratic.

8. Talk directly to your audience.

9. Practice your presentation by reading it aloud before a small audience if possible.

10. Listen carefully to audience comments and questions and respond to both the emotion and content of a participant's remarks.

11. Be available after the presentation to talk with individuals on an informal basis.

12. Enjoy making the presentation. Your enthusiasm will be relayed to the audience.

Upward Communication Systems

three
objective

Upward communication

Communication flowing from employees to managers or supervisors

Through **upward communication,** organizations such as Lands' End, Nordstrom, Foot Locker, and British Petroleum obtain useful ideas, resolve problems, and motivate and encourage organizational commitment.[19] Fortunately, both managers and employees agree that the upward flow of information is important for organizational success. Unfortunately, they often disagree on how much opportunity there is for this type of communication.

One survey of employees found that 40 percent believed they had no opportunity for upward communication.[20] However, these same employees identified three ways that managers can promote upward communication. First, managers should venture out and meet employees to give employees a chance to communicate face to face. Second, management can give employees the opportunity to participate in decisions affecting their own jobs. Third, managers can use feedback systems so that employees know their messages are being heard. These systems can include a forum for questions and answers in the organizational newspaper and special meetings in which the employees ask questions and managers respond. Furthermore, employees must feel free from reprisal for communicating negative information; some upward communication systems must guarantee anonymity to senders of this sort of message.

This special meeting allows an employee to communicate with his manager face to face.

Complaint Procedures

No matter how hard managers try to manage effectively, problems will come up that lead to employee complaints about supervisors, the job, or the organization. As a result, a growing number of organizations have gone beyond the traditional upward communication systems and have introduced whistle-blowing policies and investigative procedures to allow employees to report wrongdoing before harm comes to the organization.[21] Problems are magnified when supervisors are not receptive to the problems their employees face, and sometimes the supervisors themselves can be the source of the problem. When this happens, employees need to be able to communicate their complaints or observations of wrongdoing to management anonymously. In response to these needs, organizations have developed a variety of complaint systems that are usually managed by the HR department. Some use voice-mail technology, enabling employees to dial into a computerized telephone system and describe problems or make complaints. Others use special counselors or ombudsmen within the HR department. (See Chapter 16.) Other complaint systems use specially designed forms on which employees can write a complaint and submit it to management. Only the administrator of the program knows the identity of the writer. By serving as a focal point, the administrator can direct an employee's question or concern to an appropriate executive and obtain a written, confidential response, which is then given to the employee.

Suggestion Programs

The suggestion program is a type of upward communication that is widely used to stimulate participation by rewarding employees for their suggestions. The suggestions may cover such areas as work methods and procedures, equipment

design, safety devices, and other matters related to the effectiveness of the organization. For the program to succeed, it must have the support of managers and
supervisors. Supervisors, however, sometimes feel that such programs infringe on
their time, and they fear adverse effects if employees make suggestions they
themselves should have proposed.

Today suggestion programs encourage employees to submit ideas that will
contribute to increased productivity, quality, safety, and other important
outcomes.[22] Most firms pay employees a percentage of the net savings, up to a
maximum amount, that result from their suggestions. In 1992, the more than
1,000-member organizations of the National Association of Suggestion Systems
(NASS) adopted over 325,000 suggestions, resulting in a total savings of approximately $2 billion.[23] Along with cost-cutting advantages are intangible benefits
such as improved communication between employees and managers; increased
team spirit; and involved employees who are thinking about productivity, product quality, and workplace safety.

Attitude Surveys

The employee attitude survey is another method designed to help employees
communicate with management. The survey is best accomplished through the
use of questionnaires that are completed anonymously. From responses to the
questionnaires, management can learn how employees view their jobs, their supervisors, their wages and benefits, their working conditions, and other aspects
of their employment.[24] Among the newest versions of the attitude survey is the
computerized employee opinion survey. It is faster, more flexible, and easier to
analyze than traditional surveys and is preferred by employees. Regardless of
the format used, HR professionals recognize that the best employee surveys are
organization-specific, investigating areas of particular concern to managers and
employees.[25] Highlights in HRM 4 shows a company-specific survey developed
by AT&T Call Servicing.

Before conducting a survey, an organization should be able to answer yes to
three specific questions:

1. Is the organization willing to invest the time and money to conduct
   the survey properly?
2. Is management willing to report the major findings of the survey to
   employees?
3. Is management willing to take action on the basis of the survey's
   results?

The support of top management for the survey needs to be conveyed
through a cover letter to all employees, signed by the CEO or president. Steps
should be taken to assure employees that the anonymity of their responses will
be preserved and that the survey results will be acted on. The organization must
enlist the participation of as many employees as possible to ensure an accurate
assessment of their attitudes. Also, management must report the survey results to
employees even when those results are negative or show the organization in an
unfavorable light.[26] Finally, management must work to develop an action plan for
dealing with the responses it receives from the survey.[27] At ARCO Transportation

HIGHLIGHTS IN HRM

4 AT&T CALL SERVICING: SAMPLE FEEDBACK INSTRUMENT

To what extent does the manager...	ALMOST ALWAYS	OFTEN	SOMETIMES	SELDOM	ALMOST NEVER	DO NOT KNOW
Planning						
1. Develop plans that accurately anticipate future needs.	6	5	4	3	2	1
2. Communicate a consistent and clear direction for the team.	6	5	4	3	2	1
3. Take actions that place the team above the individual.	6	5	4	3	2	1
Communication						
4. Communicate business issues in an understandable way.	6	5	4	3	2	1
5. Tell the truth about business issues and their effect on the team.	6	5	4	3	2	1
6. Help you and others understand your importance to overall business success.	6	5	4	3	2	1
Problem Solving						
7. Involve you and others when making decisions.	6	5	4	3	2	1
8. Address business problems in new and creative ways.	6	5	4	3	2	1
9. Use facts and measures as the basis for solving problems.	6	5	4	3	2	1
10. Identify problems completely before moving to solutions.	6	5	4	3	2	1

Source: Milan Moravec, "A 21st Century Communication Tool," *HR Magazine* 38, no. 7 (July 1993): 79. Reprinted with permission of *HR Magazine,* published by the Society for Human Resource Management, Alexandria, Va.

one of the action plans that came from an attitude survey was the creation of an anonymous employee feedback system in which a third party, a "processor," solicits feedback from the manager's subordinates and shares the results with the manager, thus preserving the anonymity of the subordinates.[28] More information about attitude surveys is found in Chapter 20.

Committees

Although committees may be used to make decisions, provide suggestions, and represent other employees, their primary purpose is to facilitate upward communication. This role becomes clear from the variety of assignments that organizations give to their committees—evaluating employee suggestions, resolving grievances, evaluating jobs and employee performance, selecting candidates for promotion, and investigating safety infractions and accidents. Some organizations also use committees to consider compensation issues as well as employment policies and work practices.[29]

Electronic Mail

Electronic mail (e-mail) is becoming an increasingly useful tool for upward communication. Organizations with electronic mail systems usually make "address lists" of all users available to any employee with access to the system. Communicating with the CEO or the vice president for human resources is thus as easy as communicating with a colleague. Furthermore, messages from all employees, whether managers or not, appear in similar form. Rapid access and the greater volume of messages have encouraged the use of electronic mail as a means of upward communication.

Organizations with global operations find electronic mail an attractive way to avoid the hassle of time zones. All worldwide users of electronic mail are able to communicate during their normal working hours.[30]

Organizations that successfully use electronic mail have identified certain qualities that contribute to its growing use.[31] One is access to the system by nearly all employees. Another is wide acceptance and usage of electronic mail by managers. A third quality is the responsiveness of managers to employees' messages. When senior managers respond quickly to messages, employees are encouraged to send additional messages.

The Informal Communication System

Grapevine
Channel of communication that fans out through the organization without regard to formal channels

In addition to the formal systems of upward and downward communication in organizations, there is also an informal system. Sometimes called the **grapevine,** this system can convey messages upward, downward, laterally, and externally. It can foster employee motivation, encourage commitment, and create job and organizational satisfaction. Unfortunately, it can also distort information, create resentment, and work against management plans and objectives. Communication experts note that the grapevine is a generally accurate means of communication and that employees rely on it more heavily when they feel threatened or

Informal meetings like this one provide managers with access to the grapevine.

insecure.[32] Recently, electronic transmission of messages by facsimile (fax) and electronic mail have added to the speed with which the grapevine functions.[33]

Patterns of Informal Communication

Although the grapevine's structure may be influenced by formal organizational relationships, it is more likely to be influenced by a variety of other factors, such as the setup of the workplace. The placement of building entrances, partitions, elevators, even restrooms affects employees' ability to exchange information. Lunches and coffee breaks provide time for talking with co-workers or friends. Friendships at work lead to after-hours get-togethers at the health club or local hangout. These opportunities and relationships serve to facilitate communication across work groups and lines of management.[34]

Using the Informal Communication System

The informal communication system provides a great deal of useful information to employees. Because employees value it and because it grows out of such natural relationships as friendships between co-workers, this network cannot be controlled or eliminated by management, nor should it be. Attempts by management to control the informal communication of employees will only create resentment and will probably not succeed anyway.

Since they cannot control the grapevine, managers must learn to accept it and use it effectively. For example, managers know that the grapevine can transmit accurate information much faster than the formal communication system. Therefore, those willing to listen to the grapevine will be able to identify employee concerns or organizational problems more quickly. The grapevine can also provide meaningful additional information to employee feedback from attitude surveys.

Besides using the grapevine as a source of information, managers can also use it to communicate information to employees, though this requires some knowledge of how the grapevine works. In particular, it is helpful for managers to know which employees have the widest range of contacts in the organization.[35]

Despite the grapevine's numerous advantages, some managers object strongly to it. Their objections may arise in part because of the system's tendency to distort information or convey it before it is complete. However, the realities of the grapevine will not change, and management must accept this. What can change is how the organization deals with this system of communication. Also, if management takes steps to ensure open, candid communication, the formal system will carry most of the same messages as the informal system. With an open system of communication, therefore, there will be less need for managers and employees to rely on the grapevine.

Improving Organizational Communication

Experience has shown that putting upward and downward communication systems into place and managing the grapevine effectively will not solve all of an organization's communication problems, nor will it guarantee effective communication. HR managers must champion communication as their responsibility and, at the same time, as the responsibility of all organizational managers. In describing the challenges for management at Levi Strauss, Donna Goya, senior vice president for personnel, focused almost exclusively on the single issue of communication: The challenges ahead for managers, she said, are "to communicate with their employees, to give regular feedback, not just once-a-year appraisals, so there are no surprises. To give recognition, not just when merit increase time rolls around but to continually say thank you, and have some fun and make people feel appreciated. To allow diverse opinions and not to be so control-oriented as to deny you don't have all the answers."[36]

A study of the communication behavior of leaders confirms the accuracy of these remarks. Managers who are effective leaders provide task information so employees are aware of job requirements and performance information so employees know how well they are doing. In addition to these types of communication, the study also identified two other specific types that are important for effective leadership. First, day-to-day, nontask-related communication such as personal greetings and inquiries about the employee's well-being helps to establish a basis for a good working relationship between manager and employee. Second, communication about the career development of the employee is also critical.[37]

Communication Competency

Managers can improve their ability to provide task-related, performance-related, career-related, and personal communication by focusing on specific communication skills or competencies that are known to affect managerial performance. **Communication competency** refers to a manager's oral communication skills (speaking and listening), written communication skills (reading and writing), and ability to choose the appropriate medium for communication.[38]

Speaking and Listening Skills

Managers must be able to deliver an oral message competently, and they must have good listening skills. Interestingly, research studies also show that the delivery of our spoken message influences how we are perceived as leaders, particularly if we are seen by employees as a charismatic leader.[39] There are a variety of options for improving a manager's skill at speaking. Community colleges and universities offer courses in communication, and most cities have Toastmasters Clubs for assistance in developing oral presentation skills. For managers who are particularly apprehensive about speaking, special programs are available that focus on reducing public speaking anxiety.[40]

Despite a willingness to improve their speaking skills, too frequently managers have the feeling that there is little that can be done to improve listening skills. In fact, trainers also teach listening skills. Moreover, there are a variety of things managers can do on their own to improve their listening skills.

First, managers can force themselves to talk less and listen more during conversations with employees. By doing so, they can focus on what they can learn from a discussion, and talking less will encourage them to search for new information.

Second, managers can learn to listen attentively. They should look directly at the speaker and give him or her their complete attention. Third, listening is improved when we listen objectively. We should be careful not to tune out the speaker whose ideas and biases differ from our own.

Reading and Writing Skills

The performance of managers is directly related to their competency in handling written communication, including message-writing ability and reading comprehension.[41] HR departments can help to improve the reading and writing skills of managers by suggesting communications courses offered at local colleges, as well as through training programs developed by the department itself. Often the first step in improving written communication competency is an HR-department-sponsored evaluation of managers. The link between this competency and managerial performance provides a sound argument for such evaluation.

Media Sensitivity

Media sensitivity
The ability to select the appropriate medium for sending a message

Another important communication skill is **media sensitivity,** the ability to select an appropriate medium for sending a message. It will come as no surprise that higher-performing managers have greater media sensitivity.[42] Among the choices of media are the face-to-face meeting, the telephone, the electronic mail system, and the written memorandum. Some of these media are "richer" than others in that they can convey more information. Face-to-face communication is the richest medium: It permits immediate feedback, it includes both verbal and nonverbal messages, and it is the most personal. The written letter or memorandum is much less rich: Feedback is slow, the medium is strictly visual, and it is formal and impersonal. Other media such as the telephone or electronic mail have a richness somewhere between these two extremes.[43]

Communicating with Diverse Groups

As we discussed in early chapters of this book, the workforce in the United States, Canada, and elsewhere is undergoing tremendous changes as a result of immigration, increased numbers of working women, and greater opportunities for minorities. While just over 50 percent of the U.S. workforce is currently made up of minorities and women, demographers predict that this will rise to 80 percent by the year 2000. Further adding to the demands of communicating with diverse and multicultural workers are the changes that are occurring internationally. As we will discuss in Chapter 19, the internationalization of business makes U.S. managers more likely to find themselves interacting with managers from Europe, Asia, Africa, and Latin America. At the same time, American businesses wishing to stay competitive are likely to increase their activities in international markets. The internationalization of business and changes in the demography of the labor pool will increase the cross-cultural communication demands on managers. By necessity they will have to communicate effectively with very diverse cultural groups.[44]

Communication between Men and Women

Behavioral scientists have identified some differences in the communication styles of men and women. For example, masculine rhetoric is often viewed as decisive, direct, rational, authoritative, logical, and impersonal while female rhetoric is judged to be cautious, receptive, indirect, emotional, conciliatory, and polite.[45] Furthermore, the fact that the workplace has been traditionally dominated by men has meant that the language found there is more reflective of the way men communicate. It does not mean, however, that there is some inherent reason that this should be the preferred form of business communication. With increased use of employee involvement projects, team building, and employee empowerment, women may be better able to facilitate group involvement, a needed element in these workplace techniques.

Some research studies have shown that women tend to use tentative speech more often than men in groups of men and women.[46] A "tag question" such as "This is the way we do it, isn't it?" is one example of tentative speech. While this is an accepted form of speech, unfortunately it makes the user—according to the studies, it is generally a woman—seem indecisive.[47] Also, some research has documented that men's speech is less grammatical than women's, which may lead to the perception that women are more formal than men. While there is some disagreement among social scientists about these and other research findings, researchers do conclude that there are real differences between the communication styles of men and women.[48]

Language Differences

Special communication problems also originate from cultural and language differences. Consider the following hypothetical instruction: "Before vacating the work site at the end of the workday, the excavation crew supervisor must make sure that workers put up the orange safety cones."

To most English-speaking employees, this statement means that the safety cones are to be placed at the excavation site and remain there overnight. For speakers of Southern Midland English (much of Georgia and Alabama), this instruction can be interpreted to mean that workers should put the cones back on the truck after work. For many southern employees, "putting up" means "putting away," as in "Put up your own tools; others aren't expected to pick up after you."[49]

While geographical language differences are evident, the problem becomes more or less acute when foreign workers are employed by U.S. organizations. For example, European managers working in the United States, Canada, and Latin America usually make a relatively easy transition to the languages found there. Asian and Middle Eastern managers, however, often face a more considerable language barrier in the Americas, because of the fundamentally greater differences in the languages.[50] All managers in cross-cultural positions therefore need to be sensitive to the language difficulties they and their foreign counterparts are likely to encounter.

American slang, jargon, and cliches present communication difficulties to foreign-born employees. When foreigners learn English, they normally learn a version of formal English. When American managers use slang or idioms like "Let's get rolling" or "I'm all ears," the foreign-born employee can become confused. A literal translation of these phrases can be perplexing to a nonnative speaker. Furthermore, sayings such as "first among equals" and "last but not least" appear illogical and contradictory and are sometimes untranslatable into a foreign worker's native tongue.[51] Figure 15–4 presents excellent tips for managers who communicate with foreign-born employees.

Although less troublesome than language differences, unfamiliar accents can sometimes create communication difficulties. A manager whose subordinate is not a native English speaker, for example, must be careful to distinguish the person's ability to do the job from his or her ability to use English fluently. Though communicating with such employees may be difficult, managers should not let this influence their judgment of an employee's other capabilities.

Nonverbal Cultural Differences

Cross-cultural communication difficulties go beyond language. They also include differences in nonverbal communication. For example, in appraisal interviews and in work-group meetings, foreign-born employees may not openly communicate their perceptions and ideas. These employees may be reluctant to express their thoughts for fear of showing their limited language skills. Or their culture may have taught them to respect authority even when they believe that the authority is wrong. Addressing these and other communication problems that come from managing a multicultural and diverse workforce requires the attention of the HR department. Managerial training in communication and cultural differences is needed in all types of organizations.[52]

Counseling

In a discussion of organizational communication that focuses on HRM, the role of counseling in the achievement of individual and organizational objectives

> ### FIGURE 15-4 *Communicating with Foreign-Born Employees*

The following tips will assist managers who communicate with someone whose English skills are minimal, to assess how well the individual has understood what has been said and to understand better what employees whose native language isn't English are saying.

When communicating with people for whom English is a second language,

- Construct your sentences carefully and precisely.
- Speak slowly and distinctly.
- Emphasize key words.
- Allow pauses.
- Let the worker read your lips.
- Organize your thoughts.
- Use handouts.
- Use nonverbal signals (cautiously).
- Be aware of your tone of voice.
- Use familiar words.
- Repeat and recap frequently.
- Take care not to patronize.
- Check often for understanding.
- Don't give too much information at one time.
- Be careful when translating.
- Use bilingual group leaders.

When assessing how well you've been understood,

- Watch for nonverbal signs that indicate confusion or embarrassment.
- Notice a lack of interruptions.
- Notice any effort to change the subject.
- Notice the complete absence of questions.
- Notice inappropriate laughter.

- Invite questions in private and in writing.
- Allow enough time for questions to be formulated.
- Be alert to the yes that means "Yes, I hear your question" as opposed to the yes that means "Yes, I understand."
- Be alert to a positive response to a negative question.
- Be alert to a qualified yes in response to the question, "Do you understand?"
- Have the listener repeat what you have said.
- Observe behavior of employees and inspect production.

To understand people who are learning English,

- Share the responsibility for poor communication.
- Invite the speaker to speak more slowly.
- Repeat what the speaker has said.
- Encourage the worker to write.
- Allow the worker to spell difficult words.
- Read the speaker's lips.
- Give the speaker plenty of time in which to communicate.
- Listen to all that the speaker has to say before assuming that you don't understand.
- Observe body language.
- Remember to listen and expect to understand.

Source: Adapted from Charlene Marmer Solomon, "Managing Today's Immigrants," *Personnel Journal* 72, no. 2 (February 1993): 62. Used with permission of *Personnel Journal,* Costa Mesa, CA. All rights reserved.

deserves special attention. Managers and supervisors, HR department personnel, those responsible for various employee assistance programs, and other staff members find that their job responsibilities require them to serve in a counseling role. Depending on their position, the amount of time they must spend in this activity will vary.

Counseling becomes an even more important HR function because of the increase of violence and terrorism in the workplace. Consider these facts: The Bureau of Labor Statistics (BLS), collecting data from thirty-one states and New York City for 1991, counted 769 assaults, violent acts, self-inflicted injuries, and assaults by animals that resulted in death. Of the 769 fatalities, 533 were shootings; 58 were stabbings; 29 were hitting, kicking, or other assaults; 85 were suicides; 18 were death by animal; and the remainder, other causes. According to the National Institute for Occupational Safety and Health (NIOSH) figures for 1980–1988, at least 750 people die every year as a result of occupational homicides.[53]

When violent incidents, such as the death of a co-worker, occur at work, employees can experience shock, guilt, anger, grief, apathy, resentment, increased cravings for drugs and alcohol, cynicism, and a host of other emotions.[54] Jim Martin, an employee assistance program professional with the Detroit Fire Department, notes that after an incident of violence, employees become frightened and they may not want to return to work.[55] Such incidents require crisis intervention through positive counseling techniques.

The Counseling Process

Counseling

Process involving a dynamic relationship between two parties in which one is free to discuss needs, feelings, and problems of concern for the purpose of obtaining help

Unlike an interview, which is often restricted to obtaining and giving information, **counseling** is a process involving a dynamic relationship between two parties in which a person is free to discuss needs, feelings, and problems of concern for the purpose of obtaining help. As shown in Figure 15–5, it involves many variables on the side of the helper as well as the helpee. The relationship is the chief means of meshing the helpee's problems with the counsel of the helper.[56] The relationship is constantly changing at verbal and nonverbal levels. It typically involves an expression of emotions and feelings that goes beyond that of the ordinary interview.

Purpose of Counseling

The purpose of counseling is to allow the person seeking help to achieve four kinds of outcomes. A counseling session, if successful, is likely to result in a combination of these outcomes.

1. *Changes in feeling states,* especially negative feeling states, including frustration, depression, anger, and jealousy. This outcome can be accomplished by helping a person clarify underlying values and assumptions.
2. *Increased understanding.* The type of understanding that is lacking is usually understanding about oneself, others, and circumstances.

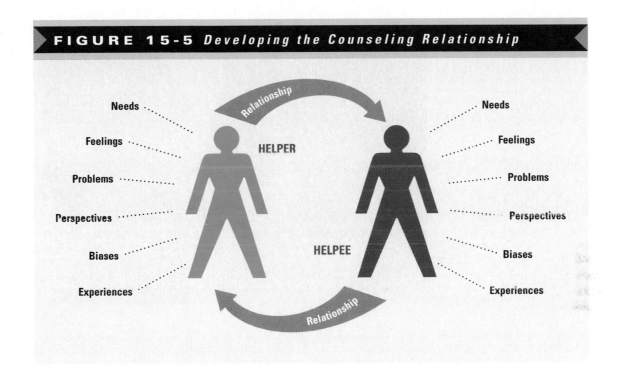

FIGURE 15-5 *Developing the Counseling Relationship*

It can be caused by incomplete or inaccurate information and misperception.

3. *Coming to a decision.* Helping people to clarify their concerns and assisting them in learning decision-making skills are important uses of counseling.

4. *Implementing a decision.* Helping to plan action necessary to carry through with what one has decided is another critical function of counseling.

Nature of the Relationship

Counseling does not take place in a vacuum. The basic relationship between the two parties is the context in which counseling occurs. Whether an employee is counseled by a supervisor, a career counselor, a psychologist in the HR department, or a professional outside the organization, the context will affect the counseling relationship. In organizations, authority affects the nature of the relationship between the two parties. An employee, for example, is not free to ignore a supervisor's help in matters related to the job. Another factor in the counseling relationship is confidentiality. Generally, what takes place in a counseling relationship is expected *not* to go beyond the two parties involved. There are times, however, when it is necessary to report certain types of information that may result in serious harm to others if not reported. Another

This counselor listens to his colleague without interruption.

factor that can affect the relationship is the counselor's degree of commitment to be of assistance.

The Counselor's Attitude

The counselor's attitude toward the counselee is a major factor in determining the outcomes of counseling. It is essential that the counselor convey acceptance of the counselee as a person and of the counselee's statements. Acceptance does not imply agreement, but rather accepting the counselee's right to have opinions and feelings. Certainly, a desire to help and to provide whatever information, assistance, or reassurance is necessary is basic and should be conveyed both verbally and nonverbally to the counselee.

Counseling techniques. Like other communication skills, counseling techniques can be learned. At first these techniques often seem strange, but with experience they become a comfortable and customary way of interacting with others in a counseling situation.

All of us have a natural tendency to judge, to evaluate, to approve or disapprove. Sometimes we engage in these judgments prematurely on the basis of our preconceived assumptions, thereby reducing our ability to communicate effectively. One way to limit these premature judgments is through a counseling technique called **active listening.** Active listening involves trying to understand what the other person is thinking by allowing this person to explain his or her perspective more fully without interruptions, questions, or introduction of new topics. The counselor should maintain eye contact and should be relaxed and attentive to what the counselee says or is trying to say.

Active listening
Process of trying to understand what the speaker is saying by paying close attention and focusing responses on what is said

While active listening is important in all circumstances, it is absolutely essential when:

1. We do not understand how the other person feels and we need to understand the person's perspective
2. We believe that what is being said is not as important as what is *not* being said
3. The other person is so confused that a clear message cannot be communicated

In addition to active listening, a counselor will use a technique known as **reflecting feelings.** This technique involves expressing, in somewhat different words, the counselee's feelings, either stated or implied. The goal is to focus on feelings rather than content, to bring vaguely expressed feelings into clearer focus, and to assist the person in talking about his or her feelings.

Reflecting feelings

A technique of focusing on a counselee's feelings and expressing them in the counselor's own words

Examples of this technique include the use of expressions such as "You resent the way the boss treats you," and "You feel that you deserve more recognition from the company." The technique of reflecting feelings is especially useful in the early stages of counseling to bring out the counselee's feelings. It is the standard procedure in nondirective counseling, a type of counseling to be discussed later.

Very often a counselee is confused and needs assistance in determining what the problem really is. Rather than trying to make a diagnosis or questioning the counselee like a trial lawyer, the professional counselor uses techniques to assist the counselee in identifying the problem. One approach is *restatement*. By restating in their own words what the counselee has said, counselors provide feedback that helps to clarify the problem. *Paraphrasing*, in which counselors restate in their own words what the counselee has said, is another clarification technique.

Another way to assist the counselee is to ask questions that will help that person understand his or her problem. Generally, they should be *open-ended questions*, i.e., those that cannot be answered with a yes or no—"Tell me more about your experiences with Mr. Jones." They should be questions that lead to clarification for the counselee rather than information for the counselor. Open-ended questions leave the counselee free to take the interview in the direction that will do the most for him or her.

Counseling Approaches

In attempting to help an employee who has a problem, a variety of counseling approaches are used. All of these approaches, however, depend on active listening. Sometimes the mere furnishing of information or advice may be the solution to what at first appeared to be a knotty problem. More frequently, however, the problem cannot be solved easily because of frustrations or conflicts that are accompanied by strong feelings such as fear, confusion, or hostility. A counselor, therefore, needs to learn to use whatever approach appears to be suitable at the time. Because counseling is a dynamic process, the effective counselor is one who is *flexible* in the use of approaches.

Directive Counseling

**Directive
counseling**

Counseling in which the
counselor tries to
control the topics about
which the counselee
speaks, describes the
choices available to the
counselee, and/or
advises the counselee
what to do

In **directive counseling,** the counselor attempts to control, directly or indirectly, the topics the counselee is talking about, describes the choices the counselee faces, and/or advises the counselee what to do. While directive counseling has its place in the practice of trained professionals, it is not recommended as an approach to be used indiscriminately by the layperson. There are many instances in job counseling and contacts when it is appropriate to furnish information and advice in areas where the counselor is knowledgeable and experienced, especially where information and/or advice is sought. However, where there are choices to be made and frustration and/or conflict are apparent, the use of the directive approach is to be avoided.

Nondirective Counseling

**Nondirective
counseling**

Counseling in which the
counselee is permitted
to have maximum
freedom in determining
the course of the
interview

In **nondirective counseling,** the counselee is permitted to have maximum freedom in determining the course of the interview. The importance of nonevaluative listening as a communication skill was described earlier. It is also a primary technique used in nondirective counseling. Fundamentally, the approach is to listen, with understanding and without criticism or appraisal, to the problem as it is described by the counselee. The counselee is encouraged, through the counselor's attitude and reaction to what is said or not said, to express feelings without fear of shame, embarrassment, or reprisal.

As the counseling session progresses, the counselor should strive to reflect the counselee's feelings by restating them. For example, if the counselee has discussed several situations that indicate feelings of being treated unfairly, the counselor would probably summarize the situation by saying, "You feel that you have been treated unfairly." While questions may be used at appropriate places in the counseling session, the counselor should use general questions that stimulate the counselee to pursue those areas that are troublesome. Questions that call for yes or no answers by the counselee should be avoided.

The free expression that is encouraged in the nondirective approach tends to reduce tensions and frustrations. The counselee who has had an opportunity to release pent-up feelings is usually in a better position to view the problem more objectively and with a problem-solving attitude. The permissive atmosphere allows the counselee to try to work through the entanglements of the problem and to see it in a clearer perspective, often to reach a more desirable solution. There are times, however, when a directive approach will be more suitable, such as when counselees ask for specific information or when it is essential that counselors express their opinions or inform counselees of rules that may have been violated.

Participative Counseling

The directive and nondirective approaches that have just been described are obviously at the extremes of a continuum. While a particular professional counselor may tend to be at one end of the continuum or the other, most counselors vary their approach during the course of a session and/or in subsequent sessions. Many choose to emphasize a middle-of-the-road approach in which both parties work together in planning how a particular problem will be analyzed and solved. This approach, which may be thought of as **participative counseling,** is particularly suitable for use in work organizations.

> **Participative counseling**
>
> Counseling in which both parties work together in planning how a particular problem will be analyzed and solved

Many of the problems that managers and supervisors are concerned with require not only that the subordinates' feelings be recognized, but also that subordinates be made aware of and adhere to management's expectations for them to be productive, responsible, and cooperative. On the other side of the coin, most people with problems would prefer to be actively involved in the solution once they see that there is a positive course of action available. In many of the work situations where counseling will be used, the participative approach is recommended in working with an individual over a period of time. To repeat, at different times, however, in the course of a single session, it may be advisable to be both directive and nondirective.

Success and Failure in Counseling

Counseling as a helping relationship has been discussed in order to present techniques that facilitate communication and help solve problems that affect the well-being of employees and the organization. It should be recognized, however, that counseling by managers will not always be successful in achieving this goal. Nevertheless, some progress can often be made by using counseling techniques where this type of action is appropriate. In cases where counseling apparently fails to yield results, it will often be necessary to take other measures, such as discipline or a transfer.

Since a manager or supervisor may not have the skill or time to handle the more complex personal problems of employees, there should be an established system for making referrals to trained counselors. Sometimes the problem area is one over which the supervisor has little or no influence, such as an employee's family relationships. Then it may be advisable for the supervisor to recommend the employee see a professional counselor. Usually the HR department has the responsibility for handling referrals to professionals who are competent and licensed to perform such services.

SUMMARY

Communication is a complex interaction that takes place between a sender and receiver of a message. Communication messages are subject to various distortions, including those embedded in the ideas and perceptions of the communicators and/or in the medium for sending the message. Nonverbal symbols such as voice tone or gestures also serve to either help or hinder the processing of information. Barriers to effective communication include the problems of false assumptions, differences in the past experiences of communicators (e.g., differences in perceptions), and semantic differences regarding the different meanings given to a single word. Personal bias is a particularly difficult communication barrier because biases often work to the disadvantage of different groups of employees.

 When upper-level managers wish to communicate with employees, they engage in downward communication. Downward communication systems include employee handbooks and policy manuals, organizational newspapers, bulletin boards, videos, and meetings.

 Managers realize that upward communication from employees to management is vital for organizational success. This upward flow of information can contribute to improving product or service quality as well as informing managers of employee concerns. Various employee complaint procedures, suggestion programs, attitude surveys, committees, and electronic mail compose different upward communication systems.

 The grapevine is an extremely effective means of transmitting messages upward, downward, and laterally throughout the organization as well as externally to interested constituents. Unfortunately, messages transmitted through it can distort information, create resentment, and work against the plans and goals of management. Managers need to be aware of how the grapevine works, its influential leaders, and the messages it carries.

 Communication competency refers to the oral skills (speaking and listening) and written skills (reading and writing) of managers. Organizations may offer various training classes to improve different communication deficiencies; college classes, seminars, and correspondence courses are external sources available to improve communication skills.

 With the growth of diverse groups in the workforce, managers face additional challenges to their oral and written communication. Research has shown that men and women possess different speech patterns, which can possibly lead to false assumptions. Geographical language differences, either in the United States or across national boundaries, create problems of misinterpretation and faulty understanding. Slang, jargon, and cliches create communication barriers for foreign workers or others when terms are untranslatable or difficult to understand.

 Counseling is a process for providing help to employees with problems. It involves a frank and open discussion of the needs, feelings, and concerns of employees. When managers assume the role of counselor they have available to them a host of techniques to achieve understanding. Active listening is very important since it involves attempting to understand what another person is saying and the reasons and motives behind the thoughts and behavior of another individual. Reflecting the feelings of an employee is a technique that serves to help the employee obtain a clearer perspective of the problem. Additionally, the counseling technique of paraphrasing can help to clarify the thoughts of the counselee. Each of these techniques can be used in the different counseling approaches, whether directive, nondirective, or participative.

KEY TERMS

active listening

communication competency

counseling

directive counseling

downward communication

grapevine

inference

media sensitivity

nondirective counseling

nonverbal symbols

participative counseling

reflecting feelings

upward communication

verbal symbols

DISCUSSION QUESTIONS

1. Explain why effective communication is so critical to HRM.
2. In our everyday language, especially when we talk about people, we use labels such as "businessman," "union leader," "good-looking secretary," and "blue-collar worker." What effect does the use of such labels have on communication? Does the use of these labels facilitate or hinder communication? Explain.
3. Many people are not good listeners.
   a. How do you account for this fact?
   b. What effect may this deficiency have on an individual's progress in a job and in other areas of life?
   c. How can listening ability be improved?
4. What problems have you experienced in your attempts to communicate with individuals who are younger or older than you? Have you been able to make any improvement in such communication? What approaches have you used?
5. We observed that suggestion programs in which cash awards are paid are used to improve efficiency and safety and to reduce costs.
   a. In your opinion, what procedures should be followed in soliciting and processing suggestions?
   b. What role should supervisors have in a suggestion program?
   c. What problems can arise in the administration of a suggestion program?
   d. In what ways can a suggestion program contribute to the objectives of the HR program?

6. What are the advantages of conducting periodic employee attitude surveys? What problems are likely to arise in conducting a survey? Explain.
7. What are the major differences among the three counseling approaches described in the chapter? How should one decide which approach to use at a particular time and with a particular counselee?
8. How is the internal communication of an organization related to its communication with customers and the community?

CASE STUDY: Working through
                   Cultural Differences

Tran Song, a Vietnamese-born employee, has been an effective employee in the produce warehouse of a large grocery chain in Seattle, Washington. Song, who is 29 years old, immigrated to the United States in 1993. While living in Da Nang, he attended college for two years while working part-time for an equipment distributor.

Song's managers have noticed his skills, his ability to work with others (especially persons of Asian and Mexican origin), and his willingness to put extra effort into his work. He is currently enrolled at a community college, taking both oral and written communication classes. As a result of encouragement from those around him, he has applied for the position of supervisor.

Sandra Westfield, the human resources specialist in charge of recruitment, has read Song's resume and was favorably impressed. She also received excellent references from several people who have worked with him. She calls Song to her office for an interview. When she asks him to elaborate on his work experience and his education, he has little to say, though he does point out to her that all of this information is stated on his resume. Furthermore, during the interview Song is deferential to Westfield, offering little additional information to her questions and assuming a passive role in the interview. Westfield is surprised by his reluctance and concludes that he must lack confidence in his abilities. After all, he should be willing to describe his strengths. Since a supervisor is a leadership position, Westfield expects Song to show a more "take charge" approach in the interview setting.

Westfield is also surprised by the thickness of Song's accent. He is difficult to understand and several times he asked for clarification to questions that Westfield felt were very straightforward. Once when Westfield asked Song to "weigh the pros and cons of supervision," he became confused and asked what she meant. Since English skills are essential for the position, Westfield begins to question Song's language skills and his ability to effectively communicate with those he would supervise. As a result of the interview, Westfield decides to recommend another applicant for the position of supervisor.

Questions
1. For what possible reasons would Song be reluctant to describe his own strengths?

2. How can managers do an effective job of assessing the qualifications of foreign-born applicants?

NOTES AND REFERENCES

1. A description of an organization's communication system is available in Leslie Lamkin and Emily W. Carmain, "Crisis Communication at Georgia Power," *Personnel Journal* 70, no. 1 (January 1991): 35–37.

2. Larry Smeltzer, John Waltman, and Donald Leonard, *Managerial Communication: A Strategic Approach*, 2d ed. (Needham Heights, Mass.: Ginn Press, 1991), 3.

3. Fred Luthans and Janet K. Larsen, "How Managers Really Communicate," *Human Relations* 39, no. 2 (February 1986): 161–78.

4. Jay A. Conger, "Inspiring Others: The Language of Leadership," *Academy of Management Executive* 5, no. 1 (February 1991): 31–44.

5. Len Sandler, "Rules for Management Communication," *Personnel Journal* 67, no. 9 (September 1988): 40.

6. Elmore R. Alexander III, Larry E. Penley, and I. Edward Jernigan, "The Relationship of Basic Decoding Skills to Managerial Effectiveness," *Management Communication Quarterly* 6, no. 1 (August 1992): 58–71.

7. Gerald H. Graham, Jeanne Unruh, and Paul Jennings, "The Impact of Nonverbal Communication in Organizations—A Survey of Perceptions," *The Journal of Business Communication* 28, no. 1 (Winter 1991): 45–61.

8. Beverly Sherman, "Evaluation of Articles Based on the Physical Attractiveness and Biographical Descriptions of Female Authors" (master's thesis, California State University, Sacramento, 1978), 35–36.

9. Patrice M. Johnson, "Corporate Communications," *Training and Development Journal* 46, no. 11 (December 1992): 19–21.

10. Janie Magruder, "Worker Handbook Helps the Boss," *Arizona Business Gazette* (April 29, 1993): 3.

11. Advertisements for employee handbook computer programs are found in HR professional journals such as *HR Magazine* and *Personnel Journal*.

12. N. C. Baker, "The Need for Caution in Handbook Changes," *Resources* 7, no. 12 (December 1988): 6.

13. Elizabeth Minich, Michael A. DiBattista, and Brian Raila, "Are You Game for Video Information?" *Personnel Journal* 67, no. 4 (April 1988): 57–63.

14. Minich, DiBattista, and Raila, "Are You Game...?" 57–59.

15. David M. Schweiger and Angelo S. Denisi, "Communication with Employees Following a Merger: A Longitudinal Field Experiment," *Academy of Management Journal* 34, no. 1 (March 1991): 110–35.

16. Larry R. Smeltzer, "Supervisory-Subordinate Communication When Mediated by Audio-Graphics Teleconferencing," *The Journal of Business Communication* 29, no. 2 (Spring 1992): 161–75.

17. Donna Ferrier, "How to Make the Most of Your Meeting," *Training and Development Journal* 46, no. 10 (October 1992): 70–75.

18. Virginia Johnson, "Picture-Perfect Presentations," *Training and Development Journal* 43, no. 5 (May 1989): 45–47.

19. Milan Moravec, "A 21st Century Communication Tool," *HR Magazine* 38, no. 7 (July 1993): 77–79.

20. Valorie A. McClelland, "Upward Communication: Is Anyone Listening?" *Personnel Journal* 67, no. 6 (June 1988): 51–55.

21. Timothy R. Barnett and Daniel S. Cochran, "Making Room for the Whistleblower," *HR Magazine* 36, no. 1 (January 1991): 58–61.

22. Thomas F. O'Boyle, "A Manufacturer Grows Efficient by Soliciting Ideas from Employees," *The Wall Street Journal* (June 5, 1993). A-1.

23. The Employee Involvement Association provided the 1992 data in a telephone conversation on October 14, 1993.

24. Scott Warrick, "Supervisor Review Sheds Light on Blind Spots," *HR Magazine* 37, no. 6 (June 1992): 111–14.

25. Robert J. Sahl, "Develop Company-Specific Employee Attitude Surveys," *Personnel Journal* 69, no. 5 (May 1990): 46–51.

26. Catherine M. Perrini, "Another Look at Employee Surveys," *Training and Development* 47, no. 7 (July 1993): 15–18.

27. Stephen L. Guinn, "Surveys Capture Untold Story," *HR Magazine* 35, no. 9 (September 1990): 64–66.

28. "HRM Update," *Personnel Administrator* 34, no. 7 (July 1989): 19.

29. For information on committee management, see Dave Day, "Make the Most of Meetings," *Personnel Journal* 69, no. 3 (March 1990): 34–39.

30. Lorraine Parker, "Collecting Data the E-Mail Way," *Training and Development* 46, no. 7 (July 1992): 52–54.

31. Susan H. Komsky, "A Profile of Users of Electronic Mail in a University," *Management Communication Quarterly* 4, no. 3 (February 1991): 310–33.

32. For one of the classic articles on the grapevine, see Keith Davis, "Management Communication and the Grapevine," *Harvard Business Review* 31, no. 5 (September-October 1953): 43–49.

33. Both authorized intended use and unintended use of facsimiles are discussed in Jerry Jakubovics, "Companies Hop Aboard the Fax Express," *Supervisory Management* 35, no. 2 (February 1990): 53.

34. William C. Himstreet, Wayne Marlin Baty, and Carol M. Lehman, *Business Communications,* 10th ed. (Belmont, Calif.: Wadsworth, 1993), 15–17.

35. David B. Freeland, "Turning Communication into Influence," *HR Magazine* 38, no. 9 (September 1993): 93–96; see also James L. Garnett, "Coping with Rumors and Grapevines: Tactics for Public Personnel Management," *Review of Public Personnel Management* 12, no. 3 (May-August 1992): 42–48.

36. Holly Rawlinson, "Homegrown for HRM," *Personnel Administrator* 34, no. 8 (August 1989): 53.

37. Larry E. Penley and Brian Hawkins, "Studying Interpersonal Communication in Organizations: A Leadership Approach," *Academy of Management Journal* 28, no. 2 (June 1985): 309–26.

38. Several studies have investigated the relationship between aspects of communication competence and managerial performance. One study examined the relationship of communication competence to upward mobility; see Beverly D. Sypher and Theodore E. Zorn, "Communication-Related Abilities and Upward Mobility: A Longitudinal Investigation," *Human Communication Research* 12, no. 3 (September 1986): 420–31. Another study examined the relationship of various oral and written skills to managerial performance; see Larry E. Penley, Elmore R. Alexander, I. Edward Jernigan, and Katherine Henwood, "Communication Abilities of Managers: The Relationship to Performance," *Journal of Management* 17, no. 1 (March 1991): 57–73.

39. Sherry J. Holladay, "Communicating Vision: An Exploration of the Role of Delivery in the Creation of Leader Charisma," *Management Communication Quarterly* 6, no. 4 (May 1993): 405–25.

40. Lynne Kelly, "Implementing a Skills Training Program for Reticent Communication," *Communication Education* 38, no. 2 (April 1989): 85–101.

41. Thomas D. Clark, *Power Communications* (Cincinnati: South-Western, 1994), 134–41; see also Joseph T. Straub, "Memos and Reports: Write Them Right the First Time," *Supervisory Management* 36, no. 7 (July 1991): 6.

42. James B. Stiff, *Pervasive Communication* (New York: Guilford Press, 1993); see also Janet Fulk and Brian Boyd, "Emerging Theories of Communication in Organizations," *Journal of Management* 17, no. 2 (June 1991): 407–40.

43. Ronald E. Rice, Shan-Ju Chang, and Jack Torobin, "Communicator Style, Media Use, Organizational Level, and Use and Evaluation of Electronic Messaging," *Management Communication Quarterly* 6, no. 1 (August 1992): 3–29; see also Gail S. Russ, Richard L. Daft, and Robert H. Lengel, "Media Selection and Managerial Characteristics in Organizational Communications," *Management Communication Quarterly* 4, no. 2 (November 1990): 151–73.

44. Catherine M. Petrini, "The Language of Diversity," *Training and Development* 47, no. 4 (April 1993): 35–37.

45. Margaret Ann Baker, "Gender and Verbal Communication in Professional Settings," *Management Communication Quarterly* 5, no. 1 (August 1991): 36–63.

46. Tina Adler, "Competence Determined by Status Characteristics," *Monitor* (April 1993): 18.

47. Terri R. Lituchy and Wendy J. Wiswall, "The Role of Masculine and Feminine Speech Patterns in Proposal Acceptance," *Management Communication Quarterly* 4, no. 4 (May 1991): 450–63; see also Laura MacLeod, Jolene Scriven, and F. Stanford Wayne, "Gender and Management Level Differences in the Oral Communication Patterns of Bank Managers," *The Journal of Business Communication* 29, no. 4 (Fall 1992): 343–63.

48. Christopher J. Zajn, "The Bases for Differing Evaluations of Male and Female Speech: Evidence from Ratings of Transcribed Conversation," *Communication Monographs* 56, no. 1 (March 1989): 59–74.

49. Don Rubin, "Cultural Bias Undermines Assessment," *Personnel Journal* 71, no. 5 (May 1992): 48; see also George P. Rimalower, "Translation, Please," *Training and Development* 46, no. 2 (February 1992): 71–76.

50. Sondra Thiederman, "Overcoming Cultural and Language Barriers," *Personnel Journal* 67, no. 12 (December 1988): 35–40; see also Charlene Marmer Solomon, "Managing Today's Immigrants," *Personnel Journal* 72, no. 2 (February 1993): 57–65.

51. Ronald E. Dulek, John S. Fielden, and John S. Hill, "International Communication: An Executive Primer," *Business Horizons* 34, no. 1 (January-February 1991): 21–25.

52. Linda Beamer, "Learning Intercultural Communication Competence," *The Journal of Business Communication* 29, no. 3 (Summer 1992): 285–303.

53. Jenny C. McCune, "Companies Grapple with Workplace Violence," *Management Review* (March 1994): 52–57; see also Linda Thornburg, "When Violence Hits Business," *HR Magazine* 38, no. 7 (July 1993): 40–45.

54. Henlen Frank Bensimon, "Violence in the Workplace," *Training and Development Journal* 5

(January 1994): 27–32; see also Marianne L. McManus, "When a Co-Worker Dies on Duty," *EAP Digest* 12, no. 4 (May-June 1992): 39.

55. Thornburg, "When Violence Hits Business," 44.

56. Lawrence M. Brammer, *The Helping Relationship: Process and Skills*, 5th ed. (Boston: Allyn and Bacon, 1993). For an expanded discussion of counseling techniques, see Brammer, *Therapeutic Psychology*, 5th ed. (Englewood Cliffs, N.J.: Prentice-Hall, 1989).

Chapter

Employee Rights and Discipline

16

Explain due process, the employment-at-will principle, and the implied contract.

Identify the job expectancy rights of employees.

Explain the process of establishing disciplinary policies, including the proper implementation of organizational rules.

Discuss the meaning of discipline and how to investigate a disciplinary problem.

Explain two approaches to disciplinary action.

Identify the different types of alternative dispute-resolution procedures.

Understand the symptoms of employee complaints and their major causes.

. . . .

In this chapter we discuss employee rights, workplace privacy, and employee discipline. HR managers note that these topics have a major influence on the activities of both employees and supervisors. Eric H. Joss, a corporate attorney, states that employee rights and workplace privacy are "the hottest employment law topics of the 1990s."[1] Managers are discovering that the right to discipline and discharge employees—a traditional responsibility of management—is more difficult to exercise in light of the growing attention to employee rights. Furthermore, disciplining employees is a difficult and unpleasant task for most managers and supervisors; many of them report that taking disciplinary action against an employee is the most stressful duty they perform. Balancing employee rights and employee discipline may not be easy, but it is a universal requirement and a critical aspect of good management.

Because the growth of employee rights issues has led to an increase in the number of lawsuits filed by employees, we conclude this chapter with a discussion of alternative dispute resolution as a way to foster organizational justice. Since disciplinary actions are subject to challenge and possible reversal through governmental agencies or the courts, management should make a positive effort to prevent the need for such action. When disciplinary action becomes impossible to avoid, however, that action should be taken in accordance with carefully developed HR policies and practices.

Employee Rights

Various antidiscrimination laws, wage and hour statutes, and safety and health legislation have secured basic employee rights and brought numerous job improvements to the workplace. Now employee rights litigation is shifting to such workplace issues as an employee's right to protest unfair disciplinary action, to refuse to take a drug test, to have access to their personnel files, to challenge employer searches and surveillance, and to receive advance notice of a plant closing.[2]

Employee rights

Guarantees of fair treatment from employers, particularly regarding an employee's right to privacy

The current emphasis on employee rights is a natural result of the evolution of societal, business, and employee interests. **Employee rights** can be defined as the guarantees of fair treatment that employees expect in protection of their employment status.[3] These expectations become rights when they are granted to employees by the courts, legislatures, or employers. Employee rights frequently involve an employer's alleged invasion of an employee's right to privacy. Unfortunately, the difference between an employee's legal right to privacy and the moral or personal right to privacy is not always clear. The confusion is due to the lack of a comprehensive and consistent body of privacy protection, whether from laws or from court decisions.

Balanced against employee rights is the employer's responsibility to provide a safe workplace for employees while guaranteeing safe, quality goods and services to consumers. An employee who uses drugs may exercise his or her privacy right and refuse to submit to a drug test. But should that employee produce a faulty product as a result of drug impairment, the employer can be held liable for any harm caused by that product. Employers must therefore exercise *reasonable care* in the hiring, training, and assignment of employees to jobs. Without the exercise of reasonable care, employers can be held negligent by outside parties or other employees injured by a dishonest, unfit, or incompetent employee.[4] In law, **negligence** is the failure to use a reasonable amount of care where such failure results in injury to another person.

Negligence

Failure to provide reasonable care where such failure results in injury to consumers or other employees

It is here that employee rights and employer responsibilities can come most pointedly into conflict. The failure of employers to honor employee rights can result in costly lawsuits, damage the organization's reputation, and hurt employee morale. But failure to protect the safety and welfare of employees or consumer interests can invite litigation from both groups. In the remainder of this section we will discuss various rights employees have come to expect from their employers.

Employment Protection Rights

It is not surprising that employees should regard their jobs as an established right—a right that should not be taken away without just cause.[5] This line of reasoning has led to the emergence of three legal considerations regarding the security of one's job: Due process, the employment-at-will principle, and the concept of the implied contract.

Due Process

Due process

An employee's right to present his or her position during a disciplinary action

Management has traditionally possessed the right to direct employees and to take corrective action when needed. Nevertheless, many individuals also believe that a job is the property right of an employee and that the loss of employment has such serious consequences that employees should not lose their jobs without the protection of due process. HR managers normally define **due process** as the employee's right to be heard through the use of the employer's organizational complaint procedure.[6] However, proactive employers will additionally incorporate the following principles—or rights—in their interpretation of due process:

1. The right to know job expectations and the consequences of not fulfilling those expectations
2. The right to consistent and predictable management action for the violation of rules
3. The right to fair discipline based on facts, the right to question those facts, and the right to present a defense
4. The right to appeal disciplinary action
5. The right to progressive discipline

In general, the concept of due process does *not* guarantee employees a permanent right to their jobs. It does, however, obligate management to act in a consistent manner that is fair and equitable to all employees.[7]

Employment-at-Will

Employment-at-will principle

The right of an employer to fire an employee without giving a reason and the right of an employee to quit when he or she chooses

The employment relationship has traditionally followed the common-law doctrine of employment-at-will. The **employment-at-will principle** assumes that an employee has a right to sever the employment relationship for a better job opportunity or for other personal reasons. Employers, likewise, are free to terminate the employment relationship at any time—and without notice—for any reason, no reason, or even a bad reason.[8] In essence, employees are said to work "at the will" of the employer.

The employment-at-will relationship is created when an employee agrees to work for an employer for an unspecified period of time. Since the employment is of an indefinite duration, it can, in general, be terminated at the whim of either party. This freedom includes the right of management to unilaterally determine the conditions of employment and to make personnel decisions. In 1908, the Supreme Court upheld the employment-at-will doctrine in *Adair v United States,* and this principle continues to be the basic rule governing the private-sector employment relationship.[9]

Public-sector employees have additional constitutional protection of their employment rights under the Fifth and Fourteenth Amendments to the Constitution. One author writes that these amendments have "acted to limit the methods and reasons that may be utilized to dismiss an incumbent employee in the public sector."[10] The clauses of the Fifth Amendment that prohibit denial of either life, liberty, or property without due process of law, as well as the Fourteenth Amendment, provide the principal constitutional protection afforded public-sector employees.

Wrongful Discharge

Estimates of the American workforce subject to arbitrary discharge under the employment-at-will doctrine range from 55 million to 65 million employees. Approximately 2 million workers are discharged each year. Estimates of unfair employee dismissals range from 50,000 to 200,000 a year.[11] In recent years, a substantial number of these employees have sued their former employers for "wrongful or unjust discharge." One study shows that the typical jury verdict in such suits awarded damages averaging $800,000 and that the employees were victorious in 70 percent of the jury trials.[12]

The significance of these suits is that they challenge the employer's right under the employment-at-will concept to unilaterally discharge employees. Various state courts now recognize the following three important exceptions to the employment-at-will doctrine:

1. *Violation of public policy.* This exception occurs in instances where an employee is terminated for refusing to commit a crime; for reporting criminal activity to government authorities; for disclosing illegal, unethical, or unsafe practices of the employer; or for exercising employment rights.[13] (See Figure 16–1 for examples of public policy violations.)
2. *Implied contract.* This exception occurs when employees are discharged despite the employer's promise (expressed or implied) of job security or contrary to established termination procedures. An employer's oral or written statements may constitute a contractual obligation if they are communicated to employees and employees rely on them as conditions of employment.
3. *Implied covenant.* This exception occurs where a lack of good faith and fair dealing by the employer has been suggested. By inflicting harm without justification, the employer violates the implied covenant. Discharged employees may seek tort damages for mental distress or defamation.

At the present time the confusion and conflict between the traditional right of employers to terminate at will and the right of employees to be protected

> ### FIGURE 16-1 *Discharges That Violate Public Policy*

An employer may *not* terminate an employee for:

- Refusing to commit perjury in court on the employer's behalf
- Cooperating with a government agency in the investigation of a charge or giving testimony
- Refusing to violate a professional code of conduct
- Reporting Occupational Safety and Health Administration (OSHA) infractions
- Refusing to support a law or political candidate favored by the employer
- "Whistle-blowing," or reporting illegal conduct by the employer
- Informing a customer that the employer has stolen property from the customer
- Complying with summons to jury duty

from unjust discharges are far from resolved. However, some important principles for the employment-at-will doctrine were established by *Foley v Interactive Data Corporation*.[14] In this landmark California case, the court endorsed violations of public policy, breach of implied contract, and breach of covenant of good faith and fair dealing as exceptions to the employment-at-will doctrine. The court held, however, that costly tort remedies were generally not available to employees suing for breach of implied covenant. The Foley decision can help employees prove their wrongful discharge claims, since the court ruled that an implied covenant of good faith and fair dealing constitutes a part of every employment relationship as a matter of contract law.[15] The decision also provides relief to employers by eliminating most tort actions, punitive damages, and costly jury trials.[16] Employees can generally seek only compensatory damages, such as lost wages, when suing their employer for wrongful discharge.

Implied Contract

Although it is estimated that 70 percent of employees in the United States work without benefit of an employment contract, under certain conditions these employees may be granted contractual employment rights. This can occur when an implied promise by the employer suggests some form of job security to the employee. These implied contractual rights can be based on either oral or written statements made during the preemployment process or subsequent to hiring. Often these promises are contained in employee handbooks, HR manuals, or employment applications or are made during the selection interview. Once these explicit or implicit promises of job security have been made, courts have generally prohibited the employer from terminating the employee without first exhausting the conditions of the contract. For example, a leading case, *Toussaint v Blue Cross and Blue Shield of Michigan*, found an employee handbook enforceable as a unilateral contract.[17] The following are some examples of how an implied contract may become binding:

- Telling employees their jobs are secure as long as they perform satisfactorily and are loyal to the organization
- Stating in the employee handbook that employees will not be terminated without the right of defense or access to an appeal procedure—that is, due process
- Urging an employee to leave another organization by promising higher wages and benefits, then denying those promises after the person has been hired

Fortunately, employers may lessen their vulnerability to implied contract lawsuits by prudent managerial practices, training, and HR policies. HR experts recommend the following approaches:

1. Training supervisors and managers not to imply contract benefits in conversations with new or present employees.
2. Including in employment offers a statement that an employee may voluntarily terminate employment with proper notice and the employee may be dismissed by the employer at any time and for a justified reason. The language in this statement must be appropriate, clear, and easily understood.
3. Including employment-at-will statements in all employment documents—for example, employee handbooks, employment applications, and letters of employment. (See Highlights in HRM 1.)
4. Having written proof that employees have read and understood the employment-at-will disclaimers.

objective

Job Expectancy Rights

Once hired, employees expect certain rights associated with fair and equitable employment. Employee rights on the job include those regarding substance abuse and drug testing, privacy, plant closing notification, and just-cause disciplinary and discharge procedures.

Substance Abuse and Drug Testing

The impact on employers of employee drug abuse is staggering. Drug abuse by employees costs U.S. employers an estimated $120 billion each year.[18] In a recent year, illegal drug use among its employees cost Motorola—in lost time, impaired productivity, health care, and workers' compensation claims—$190 million, or nearly 40 percent of the company's net profits. This amount is equivalent to the yearly salary of 8,000 of Motorola's domestic workers.[19] Motorola's new drug policy states simply, "No use of illegal drugs; no use of legal drugs illegally."[20]

In these litigious times, the failure of an employer to ensure a safe and drug-free workplace can result in astronomical liability claims when consumers are injured because of a negligent employee or faulty product.[21] The Bureau of Labor Statistics reports that, in response to the workplace drug problem, 67 percent of all companies with 5,000 or more employees have some kind of drug-testing policy.[22]

HIGHLIGHTS IN HRM

1   EXAMPLES OF EMPLOYMENT-AT-WILL STATEMENTS

highlights

Employment-at-will statements are classified as strong, moderate, and soft on the basis of the *extent* and *intensity* by which an employee can assert the at-will nature of the employment relationship.

A *strong* statement would read as follows:

I understand that if I am employed by XYZ Company my employment and compensation can be terminated, with or without cause and with or without notice, at any time at the option of either the company or myself. I also understand that neither this application for employment nor any present or future employee handbook or personnel policy manual is an employment agreement, either expressed or implied, and that no employee or manager of XYZ Company except the vice president of human resources has any authority to enter into any agreement for employment for any specified period of time or to make any agreement contrary to the foregoing.

I understand that my employment and compensation can be terminated, with or without cause and with or without notice, at any time at the option of either the employer or myself. I further understand that no representative of the employer other than the employer's president has any authority to enter into any agreement of employment for any specified period or to make any agreement contrary to the foregoing.

A *moderate* statement might read as follows:

I understand that my employment is not governed by any written or oral contract and is considered an at-will arrangement. This means that I am free, as is the company, to terminate the employment relationship at any time for any reason, so long as there is no violation of applicable federal or state law.

In the event of employment, I understand that my employment is not for any definite period or succession of periods and is considered an at-will arrangement. That means I am free to terminate my employment at any time for any reason, as is the company, so long as there is no violation of applicable federal or state law.

A *soft* statement might be phrased as follows:

I understand that, if employed, I may end my employment at any time and that the employer has the same right with any employees. I understand my employment is at-will, as it is not the practice of the company to enter into employment contracts, express or implied.

I understand that no representative of the company is authorized to state or imply that a contract for permanent employment shall exist between the company and me.

Source: Raymond L. Hilgert, "Employers Protected by At-Will Statements," *HR Magazine* 36, no. 3 (March 1991): 59. Reprinted with the permission of *HR Magazine,* published by the Society for Human Resource Management, Alexandria, Va.

Drug testing is most prevalent among employees in sensitive positions within the public sector, in organizations doing business with the federal government, and in public and private transportation concerns.[23] While the definition of *sensitive position* is still being formulated by the courts, employees holding positions requiring top-secret national security clearance (*Harmon v Thornburgh*), those working in the interdiction of dangerous drugs (*Treasury Employees Union v Von Raab*), uniformed police officers and firefighters (*City of Annapolis v United Food and Commercial Workers Local 400*), and employees in transportation safety positions (*Skinner v Railway Labor Executives Association*) can be required to submit to a drug test even without an "individualized suspicion" of drug usage.[24] The Federal Aviation Administration (FAA) mandatory drug testing program for flight crew members, flight attendants, air traffic controllers, maintenance personnel, aircraft dispatchers, and aviation security was upheld in *Bluestein v Skinner*.[25]

The courts in these cases have held that an employer's interest in maintaining a drug-free workplace outweighs any privacy interest the employee may have. At the federal level, the Drug-Free Workplace Act of 1988 requires, among other things, that organizations with government contracts of $25,000 or more publish and furnish to employees a policy statement prohibiting drug usage at work, establish awareness programs, and notify the federal contracting agency of any employees who have been convicted of a drug-related criminal offense. (See Chapter 13 for a sample policy statement.)

Legislation on drug testing in the private sector is still in the formative stage. Unless state or local laws either restrict or prohibit drug testing, private employers have a right to require employees to submit to a urinalysis or blood test where *reasonable suspicion* or *probable cause* exists.[26] Probable cause could include observable safety, conduct, or performance problems; excessive absenteeism or tardiness; or increased difficulty in working cooperatively with supervisors or co-workers.[27] Employers who want to implement mandatory or random drug testing programs may face more stringent state court restrictions.[28]

Urinalysis is the most common form of drug testing, although other more nonintrusive methods such as hair analysis and video-based testing are available.[29] (See Highlights in HRM 2.) The National Institute on Drug Abuse, an agency of the U.S. Department of Health and Human Services, has focused federal testing on five drug classes, which include seven drugs: marijuana, cocaine, the opiates (morphine and codeine), phencyclidine, and the amphetamines (amphetamine and methamphetamine).[30]

Some of the sharpest criticism of drug testing concerns the technology and standards with which the tests are conducted. Drug testing involves a number of different steps in which human error can occur. Testing equipment can be miscalibrated or insufficiently cleaned, samples can become contaminated, and chain-of-custody problems can occur. (*Chain-of-custody* documentation accounts for the integrity of each urine specimen by tracking its handling and storage from point of collection to final disposition.) Any of these difficulties can cause a *false positive* test result in which a particular drug is mistakenly identified in a specimen. To overcome these problems, employers are establishing drug testing standards, such as the two-step process of an immunoassay screen followed by a gas chromatography/mass spectrometry confirmation. Many large organizations are now using a medical review officer as a safeguard in the testing procedure.

HIGHLIGHTS IN HRM

HRM

highlights

2   ALTERNATIVES TO BODY-FLUID TESTING

Pupillary-Reaction Test

A trained professional may determine if a subject is under the influence of drugs or alcohol by examining the subject's eyes. The pupil will react differently to light (a flashlight is used) if the subject is under the influence of drugs. Follow-up tests of body fluids are needed to confirm results.

Positive features: Is noninvasive.

Negative features: Must be administered by trained professional; some medical conditions may give a false positive result; follow-up tests are necessary.

Hair Analysis

Hair samples are examined using radioimmunoassay, then confirmed by gas chromatography or mass spectrometry. The same techniques are used to test urine samples. Chemicals—drugs, legal or illegal—are left behind in hair as it grows and provide a record of past drug use. Type of drug and frequency and duration of use can be determined. Because hair grows about half an inch per month, a relatively small sample can provide a long record of drug use.

Positive features: Accepted by courts in criminal trials; yields detailed record of past drug use; cannot be avoided as easily as urinalysis; is less awkward than urinalysis.

Negative features: Is highly invasive; judges lifestyle rather than readiness for work.

Video-Based Eye-Hand Coordination Test

Video-based tests of eye-hand coordination are self-administered and quickly completed. These tests determine only impairment, and the employees are tested against their own normal performance. Lack of sleep, illness, stress, or drug or alcohol use could cause an individual to fail the test.

Positive features: Can be used on site, immediately before employee begins work; is noninvasive; determines readiness to work rather than judging lifestyle; is self-administered; involves low cost.

Negative features: Follow-up tests are necessary.

Environmental Testing

In place of testing employees, the workplace is scanned and tested with vapor-detection instruments to determine the presence of Class A narcotics—cocaine, heroin, and methamphetamine. To protect individual employees, the company offering the service requires employers to sign an agreement indicating they will not use the test to incriminate specific individuals.

Positive features: Is noninvasive.

Negative features: Follow-up tests are necessary.

Source: Jonathan A. Segal, "To Test or Not to Test," *HR Magazine* 37, no. 4 (April 1992): 42. Reprinted with permission of *HR Magazine* (formerly *Personnel Administrator*) published by the Society for Human Resource Management, Alexandria, Va.

TWA and 3M believe that medical review officers help both managers and employees to understand the complexities of drug testing.[31]

Employee Searches and Surveillance

The U.S. Chamber of Commerce estimates that employee theft costs U.S. businesses $40 billion annually.[32] Estimates are that 33 percent of workers steal from their employers and approximately 20 percent of all businesses fail (more than 16,000 U.S. firms annually) because of internal theft.[33] To help fight these employee crimes, the courts have allowed random searches of lockers, desks, suitcases, toolboxes, and general work areas where adequate justification exists and employees have received proper notification beforehand. Employees have no reasonable expectation of privacy in places where work rules that provide for inspections have been put into effect. They must comply with probable-cause searches by employers. And they can be appropriately disciplined, normally for insubordination, for refusing to comply with search requests. Albert Pendergast, senior vice president for human resources for MasterCard International, says, "We've taken the position that we want a clean company and that we aren't going to tolerate white-collar crime."[34]

Managers must be diligent when conducting employee searches. Improper searches can lead to employee lawsuits charging the employer with invasion of privacy, defamation of character, and negligent infliction of emotional distress. Employers are advised to develop an HR search policy based on the following guidelines:

1. The search policy should be widely publicized and should advocate a probable or compelling reason for the search.
2. The search policy should be applied in a reasonable, evenhanded manner.
3. Where possible, searches should be conducted in private.
4. The employer should attempt to obtain the employee's consent prior to the search.
5. The search should be conducted in a humane and discreet manner to avoid infliction of emotional distress.[35]

Nordstrom Department Stores and Continental Bank in Chicago verify information provided on employee applications, check references, conduct FBI checks, and use psychological tests to weed out potentially dishonest employees.

It is not uncommon for employers to monitor the conduct of employees through surveillance techniques. General Electric uses tiny fish-eye lenses installed behind pinholes in walls and ceilings to observe employees suspected of crimes. DuPont employs long-distance cameras to monitor its loading docks. One of the most common means of electronic surveillance by employers is telephone surveillance to ensure that customer requests are handled properly or to prevent theft. Employers have the right to monitor employees, provided they do it for compelling business reasons and employees have been informed that their calls will be monitored.[36] Employees can sue for invasion of privacy, but courts have held that to win damages, an employee must show that the reasonable expectation of privacy outweighs the organization's reason for surveillance.[37]

The loss of manufacturing jobs like those at this truck assembly plant could mean the loss of many other jobs in the community.

Plant Closing Notification

Millions of jobs have been lost in the United States as a result of the closing of large firms. Approximately two-thirds of all employees laid off do not receive advance notice. Plant closings have a tragic impact on the lives of employees and their communities. It is estimated that for every 100 jobs lost from a plant closing, the local community loses 200 to 300 jobs through a ripple effect.[38]

The federal government, several states, and local jurisdictions have passed legislation restricting the unilateral right of employers to close or relocate their facilities. Maine, Wisconsin, Connecticut, and Massachusetts adopted plant closing legislation that includes prenotification or severance provisions. Wisconsin's law requires sixty days' notification for plant closings and major layoffs.[39] In 1989 Congress passed the Workers' Adjustment Retraining and Notification Act (WARN), which requires organizations with more than 100 employees to give employees and their communities sixty days' notice of any closure or layoff affecting fifty or more full-time employees.[40] Notice must be given to collective bargaining representatives, unrepresented employees, the appropriate state dislocated-worker agency, and the highest-elected local official. Terminated employees must be notified individually in writing. The act allows several exemptions, including "unforeseeable circumstances" and "faltering businesses." Failure to comply with the law can subject employers to liability for back pay, fringe benefits, prejudgment interest, and attorney's fees. WARN does not prohibit employer closings, layoffs, or loss of jobs; the law simply seeks to lessen the hardships caused by job loss.

Access to Personnel Files

The information kept in an employee's personnel file can have a significant impact—positive or negative—on career development. The personnel file, typically kept by the HR department, can contain performance appraisals, salary notices, investigatory reports, credit checks, criminal records, test scores, and family data. The Americans with Disabilities Act (discussed in Chapter 3) requires that an employee's medical history must be kept in a file separate from other personnel information. Errors and/or omissions in personnel files, or access to the files by unauthorized persons, can create employment or personal hardships.[41] The growth of HR information systems (HRIS) can create problems by making personnel information more accessible to those with prying eyes or those who might use the information inappropriately. New technology (e-mail, voice mail, fax, phone monitors) creates opportunities for information monitoring and reproduction. High technology creates a critical balance between employee privacy and the employer's need to know.

Legislation at the federal level (see Figure 16–2) and, in several instances, at the state level permits employees to inspect their own personnel files. The states that grant employees this privilege generally provide certain privacy rights:

- The right to know of the existence of one's personnel file
- The right to inspect one's own personnel file
- The right to correct inaccurate data in the file

Even in the absence of specific legislation, most employers give their employees access to their personnel files. According to a study by the Society for

FIGURE 16-2 *Right-to-Privacy Laws*

LAW	EFFECT
Crime Control and Safe Streets Act (1968)	Prohibits employers from intercepting or listening to an employee's confidential communication without the employee's prior consent.
Fair Credit Reporting Act (1970)	Permits job applicants and employees to know of the existence and context of any credit files maintained on them. Employees have the right to know of the existence and nature of an investigative consumer report compiled by the employer.
Privacy Act (1974)	Applies to federal agencies and to organizations supplying goods or services to the federal government; gives individuals the right to examine references regarding employment decisions; allows employees to review their personnel records for accuracy. Employers who willfully violate the act are subject to civil suits.
Family Education Rights and Privacy Act—The Buckley Amendment (1974)	Prohibits educational institutions from supplying information about students without prior consent. Students have the right to inspect their educational records.

Human Resource Management, 96 percent of 520 responding organizations permit such access. Many employer policies, however, include restrictions on access. For example, 92 percent require that a member of the HR department be present during the review; 52 percent either disallow or limit the copying of files; and 49 percent specify designated viewing hours or require appointments.[42]

Employee Conduct Outside the Workplace

Consider the following case. On Monday morning the HR manager of ABC Corporation reads in the newspaper that a company employee has been charged with robbery and assault on a local convenience store owner. The employee has been released pending trial. A phone call to the employee's supervisor reveals that the employee has reported to work. What should the HR manager do?

HR managers generally conclude that the off-duty behavior of employees is not subject to employer disciplinary action. One attorney notes, "There is a developing body of case law that suggests that misconduct outside the workplace may not, in some circumstances, be a lawful justification for employee discipline."[43] Organizations that want to discipline employees for off-duty misconduct must establish a clear relationship between the misconduct and its negative effect on other employees or the organization. This might be established, for example, in cases where off-duty criminal misconduct (e.g., child molestation) creates a disruptive impact on the workplace. Another example might be where the public nature of the employee's job (e.g., police or fire department personnel) creates an image problem for the organization. Generally, however, little of what an employee does outside the workplace bears discipline by the employer.[44]

three
objective

Disciplinary Policies and Procedures

The rights of managers to discipline and discharge employees is increasingly limited. There is thus a great need for managers at all levels to understand discipline procedures. Disciplinary action taken against an employee must be for justifiable reasons, and there must be effective policies and procedures to govern its use. Such policies and procedures serve to assist those responsible for taking disciplinary action and help to ensure that employees will receive fair and constructive treatment. Equally important, these guidelines help to prevent disciplinary action from being voided or from being reversed through the appeal system.

Disciplinary policies and procedures should extend to a number of important areas to ensure thorough coverage. Figure 16–3 presents a disciplinary model that illustrates the areas where provisions should be established. The model also shows the logical sequence in which disciplinary steps must be carried out to ensure enforceable decisions.

A major responsibility of the HR department is to develop, and to have top management approve, its disciplinary policies and procedures. The development, however, must involve the supervisors and managers who are to carry out these policies. Their experience can contribute to more effective coordination and consistency in the use of disciplinary action throughout the organization. The HR department is also responsible for ensuring that disciplinary policies, as well

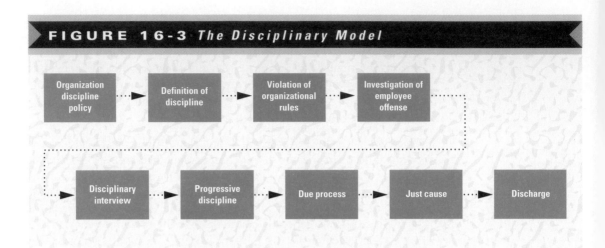

FIGURE 16-3 *The Disciplinary Model*

as any disciplinary actions taken against employees, are consistent with the labor agreement (if one exists) and conform with current law.

The primary responsibility for preventing or correcting disciplinary problems rests with an employee's immediate supervisor. This person is best able to observe evidence of unsatisfactory behavior or performance and to discuss the matter with the employee. Discussion is frequently all that is needed to correct the problem, and disciplinary action becomes unnecessary. However, when disciplinary action is needed, the supervisor should strive to use a problem-solving attitude. Causes underlying the problem are as important as the problem itself, and any attempt to prevent recurrence will require an understanding of them. Admittedly, it is often difficult for supervisors to maintain an objective attitude toward employee infractions. But if supervisors can maintain a problem-solving stance, they are likely to come up with a diagnosis that is nearer the truth than would be possible were they to use the approach of a trial lawyer.

The Results of Inaction

Figure 16–4 lists the more common disciplinary problems identified by managers. Failure to take disciplinary action in any of these areas only serves to aggravate a problem that eventually must be resolved.[45] Failure to act implies that the performance of the employee concerned has been satisfactory. If disciplinary action is eventually taken, the delay will make it more difficult to justify the action if appealed. In defending against such an appeal, the employer is likely to be asked why an employee who had not been performing or behaving satisfactorily was kept on the payroll. Or an even more damaging question might be "Why did that employee receive satisfactory performance ratings (or perhaps even merit raises)?"

Such contradictions in practice can only aid employees in successfully challenging management's corrective actions. Unfortunately, there are supervisors who try to build a case to justify their corrective actions only after they have

FIGURE 16-4 *Common Disciplinary Problems*

ATTENDANCE PROBLEMS
- Unexcused absence
- Chronic absenteeism
- Unexcused/excessive tardiness
- Leaving without permission

DISHONESTY AND RELATED PROBLEMS
- Theft
- Falsifying employment application
- Willfully damaging organizational property
- Punching another employee's time card
- Falsifying work records

WORK PERFORMANCE PROBLEMS
- Failure to complete work assignments
- Producing substandard products or services
- Failure to meet established production requirements

ON-THE-JOB BEHAVIOR PROBLEMS
- Intoxication at work
- Insubordination
- Horseplay
- Smoking in unauthorized places
- Fighting
- Gambling
- Failure to use safety devices
- Failure to report injuries
- Carelessness
- Sleeping on the job
- Using abusive or threatening language with supervisors
- Possession of narcotics or alcohol
- Possession of firearms or other weapons
- Sexual harassment

decided that a particular employee should be discharged. The following are common reasons given by supervisors for their failure to impose a disciplinary penalty:

1. The supervisor had failed to document earlier actions, so no record existed on which to base subsequent disciplinary action.
2. Supervisors believed they would receive little or no support from higher management for the disciplinary action.
3. The supervisor was uncertain of the facts underlying the situation requiring disciplinary action.
4. Failure by the supervisor to discipline employees in the past for a certain infraction caused the supervisor to forgo current disciplinary action in order to appear consistent.
5. The supervisor wanted to be seen as a likable person.

Setting Organizational Rules

The setting of organizational rules is the foundation for an effective disciplinary system. These rules govern the type of behavior expected of employees. Organizations as diverse as Gerber Products, Wal-Mart, Steelcase, and Pitney-Bowes have written policies explaining the type of conduct required of employees.

Wal-Mart is one of many companies that has written policies to govern the conduct of its employees.

Since employee behavior standards are established through the setting of organizational rules and regulations, the following suggestions may help reduce problems in this area:

1. Rules should be widely disseminated and known to all employees. It should not be assumed that employees know all the rules.
2. Rules should be reviewed periodically—perhaps annually—especially those rules critical to work success.
3. The reasons for a rule should always be explained. Acceptance of an organizational rule is greater when employees understand the reasons behind it.
4. Rules should always be written. Ambiguity should be avoided, since this can result in different interpretations of the rules by different supervisors.
5. Rules must be reasonable and relate to the safe and efficient operation of the organization. Rules should not be made simply because of personal likes or dislikes.
6. If management has been lax in the enforcement of a rule, the rule must be restated, along with the consequences for its violation, before disciplinary action can begin.
7. Have employees sign that they have read and understand the organizational rules.

When seeking reasons for unsatisfactory behavior, supervisors must keep in mind that employees may not be aware of certain work rules. Before initiating any disciplinary action, therefore, it is essential that supervisors determine whether they have given their employees careful and thorough orientation in the rules and regulations relating to their jobs. In fact, the proper communication of organizational rules and regulations is so important that labor arbitrators cite *neglect in communicating rules* as a major reason for reversing the disciplinary action taken against an employee.[46]

The Hot-Stove Approach to Rule Enforcement

Hot-stove rule

Rule of discipline that can be compared with a hot stove in that it gives warning, is effective immediately, is enforced consistently, and applies to all employees in an impersonal and unbiased way

Regardless of the reason for the disciplinary action, it should be taken as soon as possible after the infraction has occurred and a complete investigation has been conducted. HR professionals often use the **hot-stove rule** to explain the correct application of discipline. A hot stove gives warning that it should not be touched. Those who ignore the warning and touch it are assured of being burned. The punishment is an immediate and direct consequence of breaking the rule never to touch a hot stove. Likewise, a work rule should apply to all employees and should be enforced consistently and in an impersonal and unbiased way. Employees should know the consequences of violating the rule, so that it has preventive value.

objective

Defining Discipline

Discipline

(1) Treatment that punishes; (2) orderly behavior in an organizational setting; or (3) training that molds and strengthens desirable conduct—or corrects undesirable conduct—and develops self-control

In management seminars conducted by the authors of this text, when managers are asked to define the word "discipline," their most frequent response is that discipline means punishment. Although this answer is not incorrect, it is only one of three possible meanings. As normally defined, **discipline** has these meanings:

1. Treatment that punishes
2. Orderly behavior in an organizational setting
3. Training that molds and strengthens desirable conduct—or corrects undesirable conduct—and encourages development of self-control

To some managers, discipline is synonymous with force. They equate the term with the punishment of employees who violate rules or regulations. Other managers think of discipline as a general state of affairs—a condition of orderliness where employees conduct themselves according to standards of acceptable behavior. Discipline viewed in this manner can be considered positive when employees willingly practice self-control and respect organizational rules.

The third definition considers discipline a management tool used to correct undesirable employee behavior. Discipline is applied as a constructive means of getting employees to conform to acceptable standards of performance. Many organizations, such as Goodyear Aerospace and Arizona State University, define the term "discipline" in their policy manual as "training that corrects, molds, or perfects knowledge, attitudes, behavior, or conduct." Discipline is thus viewed as a way to correct poor employee performance rather than simply as punishment for an offense. As these organizations emphasize, discipline should be seen as a method of training employees to perform better or to improve their job attitudes or work behavior. It is also interesting to note that the word "discipline" is derived from the word "disciple," which means follower or pupil. At least one group of researchers believes that the implication here is that good discipline is based on good supervisory leadership.[47]

When taken against employees, disciplinary action should never be thought of as punishment. Discipline can embody a penalty as a means of obtaining a desired result; however, punishment should not be the intent of disciplinary action. Rather, discipline must have as its goal the improvement of the employee's future behavior. To apply discipline in any other way—as punishment or as a way of getting even with employees—can only invite problems for management, including possible wrongful discharge suits.

objective

Investigating the Disciplinary Problem

It's a rare manager who has a good, intuitive sense of how to investigate employee misconduct. Too frequently investigations are conducted in a haphazard manner; worse, they overlook one or more investigative concerns. In conducting an employee investigation, it is important to be objective and to avoid the assumptions, suppositions, and biases that often surround discipline cases. Figure 16–5 lists seven questions to consider in investigating an employee offense. Attending to each question will help ensure a full and fair investigation while providing reliable information free from personal prejudice.

Documentation of Employee Misconduct

"It's too complicated"; "I just didn't take time to do it"; "I have more important things to do." These are some of the frequent excuses used by managers who have failed to document cases of employee misconduct. The most significant cause of inadequate documentation, however, is that managers have no idea of what constitutes good documentation. Unfortunately, the failure of managers to record employee misconduct accurately can result in the reversal of any subsequent disciplinary action. The maintenance of *accurate* and *complete* work records, therefore, is an essential part of an effective disciplinary system.[48] For documentation to be complete, the following eight items should be included:

1. Date, time, and location of the incident(s)
2. Negative performance or behavior exhibited by the employee—the problem
3. Consequences of that action or behavior on the employee's overall work performance and/or the operation of the employee's work unit
4. Prior discussion(s) with the employee about the problem
5. Disciplinary action to be taken and specific improvement expected
6. Consequences if improvement is not made, and a follow-up date
7. The employee's reaction to the supervisor's attempt to change behavior
8. The names of witnesses to the incident (if appropriate)

When preparing documentation, it is important for a manager to record the incident immediately after the infraction takes place, when the memory of it is still fresh, and to ensure that the record is complete and accurate. Documentation need not be lengthy, but it must include the eight points in the preceding list. Remember, a manager's records of employee misconduct are considered business documents, and as such they are admissible as evidence in arbitration hearings, administrative proceedings, and courts of law.

> **FIGURE 16-5** *Considerations in Disciplinary Investigations*

1. In very specific terms, what is the offense charged?
   - Is management sure it fully understands the charge against the employee?
   - Was the employee really terminated for insubordination, or did the employee merely refuse a request by management?

2. Did the employee know he or she was doing something wrong?
   - What rule or provision was violated?
   - How would the employee know of the existence of the rule?
   - Was the employee warned of the consequence?

3. Is the employee guilty?
   - What are the sources of facts?
   - Is there direct or only indirect evidence of guilt?
   - Has anyone talked to the employee to hear his or her side of the situation?

4. Are there extenuating circumstances?
   - Were conflicting orders given by different supervisors?
   - Does anybody have reason to want to "get" this employee?
   - Was the employee provoked by a manager or another employee?

5. Has the rule been uniformly enforced?
   - Have all managers applied the rule consistently?
   - What punishment have previous offenders received?
   - Were any other employees involved in this offense?

6. Is the offense related to the workplace?
   - Is there evidence that the offense hurt the organization?
   - Is management making a moral judgment or a business judgment?

7. What is the employee's past work record?
   - How many years of service has the employee given the organization?
   - How many years or months has the employee held the present job?
   - What is the employee's personnel record as a whole, especially his or her disciplinary record?

The Investigative Interview

Before any disciplinary action is initiated, an investigative interview should be conducted to make sure employees are fully aware of the offense. This interview is necessary because the supervisor's perceptions of the employee's behavior may not be entirely accurate. The interview should concentrate on how the offense violated the performance and behavior standards of the job. It should avoid

A disciplinary investigation requires accurate and complete documentation.

getting into personalities or areas unrelated to job performance. Most important, the employee must be given a full opportunity to explain his or her side of the issue so that any deficiencies for which the organization may be responsible are revealed.

In the leading case *NLRB v Weingarten, Inc.*, the Supreme Court upheld a National Labor Relations Board ruling in favor of the employee's right to representation during an investigative interview in a unionized organization. The Court reasoned that the presence of a union representative would serve the beneficial purpose of balancing the power between labor and management, since the union representative could aid an employee who was "too fearful or inarticulate to relate accurately the incident being investigated, or too ignorant to raise extenuating factors."[49] In the *Weingarten* case, the Court decided that since the employee had reason to believe that the investigative interview might result in action jeopardizing her job security, she had the right to representation. The *Weingarten* decision does not apply to nonunion employers, however. In the *Sears Roebuck and Company* case, the NLRB decided that when no union is present, an employer is entirely free to choose how it will deal with its employees regarding actual or potential disciplinary action.[50]

It is important to note also that an employee's right to representation in a unionized organization does not extend to all interviews with management. The *Weingarten* case places some carefully defined limits on an employee's representation rights. The rules limiting these rights are as follows:

1. Representation rights apply only to *investigative interviews*, not to run-of-the-mill shop-floor discussions.
2. The rights arise only in incidents where the employee requests representation and where the employee *reasonably believes that discipline may result* from the interview.

3. Management has *no obligation to bargain* with the employee's representative.[51]

Even if employees and management comply with these rules, managers are still not required to hold an investigative interview. The *Weingarten* decision does not guarantee an employee an investigative interview; it only grants the right to representation *if requested*. The law does permit employers to cancel the interview if a representative is requested, and management may then continue the investigation by other appropriate means. Where employers violate the law, however, the NLRB can impose remedies, including cease-and-desist orders, reinstatement and back pay for discharged employees, and the removal of the record of disciplinary action.

five
objective

Approaches to Disciplinary Action

If a thorough investigation shows that an employee has violated some organization rule, disciplinary action must be imposed. Two approaches to disciplinary action are progressive discipline and positive discipline.

Progressive Discipline

Generally, discipline is imposed in a progressive manner. By definition, **progressive discipline** is the application of corrective measures by increasing degrees. Progressive discipline is designed to motivate an employee to correct his or her misconduct voluntarily. The technique is aimed at nipping the problem in the bud, using only enough corrective action to remedy the shortcoming. However, the sequence and severity of the disciplinary action vary with the type of offense and the circumstances surrounding it. Since each situation is unique, a number of factors must be considered in determining how severe a disciplinary action should be. Some of the factors to consider were listed in Figure 16–5.[52]

The typical progressive discipline procedure includes four steps. From an oral warning (or counseling) that subsequent unsatisfactory behavior or performance will not be tolerated, the action may progress to a written warning, to a suspension without pay, and ultimately to discharge. The progressive discipline used by Samaritan Systems is shown in Highlights in HRM 3. The "capital punishment" of discharge is utilized only as a last resort. Organizations normally use lower forms of disciplinary action for less severe performance problems. It is important for managers to remember that three important things occur when progressive discipline is applied properly:

1. Employees always know where they stand regarding offenses.
2. Employees know what improvement is expected of them.
3. Employees understand what will happen next if improvement is not made.

Positive Discipline

Although progressive discipline is the most popular approach to correcting employee misconduct, recently some managers have questioned its logic. They have noted that it has certain flaws, including its intimidating and adversarial nature,

highlights

3   THE SAMARITAN HEALTH SYSTEM CORRECTIVE ACTION PROCESS

When corrective action is necessary, managers should take the lowest-level action possible to correct the problem, even if that means repeating a step previously used. Samaritan believes that a progressive corrective action process is in the best interest of the employee and Samaritan. Progressive corrective action is not intended to be punishment, but rather to impress upon the employee the need for improvement. All facts, including length of service, previous performance, and attendance, will be considered.

An informal counseling with the employee may be all that is necessary to correct performance or attendance problems and should be used before beginning corrective action. This is an opportunity to discuss with the employee the problem, the resources available to him or her, and the ways to resolve the problem.

- *Step 1: Verbal warning.* Discuss the problem with the employee, pointing out what is needed to correct the problem. Be clear with the employee by saying, "This is a verbal warning," and by indicating that a written warning will result if performance or attendance is not improved as expected. This action should be documented and kept in the supervisor's file for future reference. No record of this warning is to be placed in the employee's official personnel record.

- *Step 2: Written warning.* If sufficient improvement is not observed in performance or attendance after issuing the verbal warning, a written warning is to follow. The problem and relevant facts should be described on the corrective action form. The employee must be told that if performance or attendance does not improve, further corrective action will occur in the form of a final written warning or suspension. A record of this warning should be placed in the employee's personnel record.

- *Step 3: Final written warning or suspension.* If sufficient improvement is not observed after the written warning, the supervisor should proceed to a final written warning or suspension. A suspension may be for one to three days and in the progressive action process is always without pay. Employees should be advised that the suspension is the last step before discharge and the time away from work is to be used to decide whether they can correct their performance or attendance problem. As with suspension, employees should be told that a final written warning is the final step before discharge. Suspensions and final written warnings are to be documented with relevant information and the dates of previous corrective action steps on the corrective action form.

- *Step 4: Discharge.* Before making the final decision to terminate, the supervisor should discuss with the employee the issue/incident that has caused the decision to discharge him or her. If the employee gives information that needs to be investigated, the supervisor should take time to do so. If there is no new information, then the human resources department should be consulted prior to discharging the employee. A Notice of Discharge form should be completed at the time the employee is discharged. The statement on the form should document the dates of the verbal, written, and final written warnings and the degree of suspension. It should also address the particular events that have brought about this decision and any other actions that have been taken or suggested to the employee to assist in the correction of the problem.

Immediate Action

Occasionally an infraction is so severe that immediate corrective action, up to and including termination, may appear to be warranted. If it is necessary to remove an employee from the work area, suspend him or her immediately, pending an investigation that should not last for more than a few days. There is no reason to terminate an employee "on the spot." The investigation may reveal that disciplinary action was not appropriate. In such cases the employee will be paid for the days of suspension.

Source: Adapted from *Samaritan Employee Handbook* and *Management Guideline.* Used with permission of Samaritan Health System, Phoenix, Az.

Positive, or nonpunitive, discipline

System of discipline that focuses on the early correction of employee misconduct, with the employee taking total responsibility for correcting the problem

which prevent it from achieving the intended purpose. For these reasons, organizations such as Tampa Electric Company, Ocean Spray, the Texas Department of Mental Health and Mental Retardation, Pennzoil, and Bay Area Rapid Transit are using an approach called **positive, or nonpunitive, discipline.** Positive discipline is based on the concept that employees must assume responsibility for their personal conduct and job performance.[53]

Positive discipline requires a cooperative environment where the employee and the supervisor engage in joint discussion and problem solving to resolve incidents of employee irresponsibility. The approach focuses on the early correction of misconduct, with the employee taking total responsibility for resolving the problem. Nothing is imposed by management; all solutions and affirmations are jointly reached. As James Redeker states, "Nonpunitive discipline replaces threats and punishment with encouragement."[54]

Figure 16–6 illustrates the procedure for implementing positive discipline. While positive discipline appears similar to progressive discipline, its emphasis is on giving employees reminders rather than reprimands as a way to improve performance. The technique is implemented in three steps.[55] The first is a conference between the employee and the supervisor. The purpose of this meeting is to find a solution to the problem through discussion, with oral agreement by the employee to improve his or her performance. The supervisor refrains from reprimanding or threatening the employee with further disciplinary action. Supervisors may document this conference, but a written record of this meeting is not placed in the employee's file unless the misconduct occurs again.

If improvement is not made after this first step, the supervisor holds a second conference with the employee to determine why the solution agreed to in the first conference did not work. At this stage, however, a written reminder is given to the employee. This document states the new or repeated solution to the problem, with an affirmation that improvement is the responsibility of the employee and a condition of continued employment.

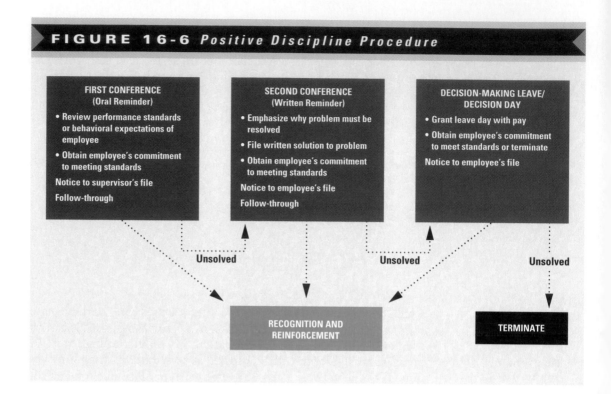

FIGURE 16-6 *Positive Discipline Procedure*

FIRST CONFERENCE
(Oral Reminder)

- Review performance standards or behavioral expectations of employee
- Obtain employee's commitment to meeting standards

Notice to supervisor's file

Follow-through

SECOND CONFERENCE
(Written Reminder)

- Emphasize why problem must be resolved
- File written solution to problem
- Obtain employee's commitment to meeting standards

Notice to employee's file

Follow-through

DECISION-MAKING LEAVE/
DECISION DAY

- Grant leave day with pay
- Obtain employee's commitment to meet standards or terminate

Notice to employee's file

Unsolved   Unsolved   Unsolved

RECOGNITION AND REINFORCEMENT

TERMINATE

When both conferences fail to produce the desired results, the third step is to give the employee a one-day *decision-making leave* (a paid leave). The purpose of this paid leave is for the employee to decide whether he or she wishes to continue working for the organization. The organization pays for this leave to demonstrate its desire to retain the person. Also, paying for the leave eliminates the negative effects for the employee of losing a day's pay. Employees given a decision-making leave are instructed to return the following day with a decision either to make a total commitment to improve performance or to quit the organization. If a commitment is not made, the employee is dismissed with the assumption that he or she lacked responsibility toward the organization.

Compiling a Disciplinary Record

In applying either progressive or positive discipline, it is important for managers to maintain complete records of each step of the procedure. When employees fail to meet the obligation of a disciplinary step, they should be given a warning, and the warning should be documented by their manager. A copy of this warning is usually placed in the employee's personnel file. After an established period—frequently six months—the warning is usually removed, provided that it has served its purpose. Otherwise it remains in the file to serve as evidence should a more severe penalty become necessary later.

An employee's personnel file contains the employee's complete work history. It serves as a basis for determining and supporting disciplinary action and for evaluating the organization's disciplinary policies and procedures. Maintenance of proper records also provides management with valuable information about the soundness of its rules and regulations. Those rules that are violated most frequently should receive particular attention, because the need for them may no longer exist or some change might be required to facilitate their enforcement. If the rule is shown to have little or no value, it should be revised or rescinded. Otherwise, employees are likely to feel they are being restricted unnecessarily.

Discharging Employees

When employees fail to conform to organizational rules and regulations, the final disciplinary action in many cases is discharge. Since discharge has such serious consequences for the employee—and possibly for the organization—it should be undertaken only after a deliberate and thoughtful review of the case.[56] If an employee is fired, he or she may file a wrongful discharge suit claiming the termination was "without just or sufficient cause," implying a lack of fair treatment by management.

If an employee termination is to be upheld for good cause, what constitutes fair employee treatment? This question is not easily answered, but standards governing just cause discharge do exist, in the form of rules developed in the field of labor arbitration.[57] These rules consist of a set of guidelines that are applied by arbitrators to dismissal cases to determine if management had just cause for the termination. These guidelines are normally set forth in the form of questions, provided in Figure 16–7. For example, before discharging an employee, did the manager forewarn the person of possible disciplinary action? A no answer to any of the seven questions in the figure generally means that just cause was not established and that management's decision to terminate was arbitrary, capricious, or discriminatory. The significance of these guidelines is that they are being applied not only by arbitrators in discharge cases, but also by judges in wrongful discharge suits. It is critical that managers at all levels understand the just cause guidelines, including their proper application.[58]

Informing the Employee

Regardless of the reasons for a discharge, it should be done with personal consideration for the employee affected. Every effort should be made to ease the trauma a discharge creates. The employee must be informed honestly, yet tactfully, of the exact reasons for the action. Such candor can help the employee face the problem and adjust to it in a constructive manner.

Managers may wish to discuss, and even rehearse, with their peers the upcoming termination meeting. This practice can ensure that all important points are covered while giving confidence to the manager. While managers agree that there is no single right way to conduct the discharge meeting, the following guidelines will help to make the discussion more effective:

1. Come to the point within the first two or three minutes, and list in a logical order all reasons for the termination.
2. Be straightforward and firm, yet tactful, and remain resolute in your decision.

> ### FIGURE 16-7 *"Just Cause" Discharge Guidelines*
>
> 1. Did the organization forewarn the employee of the possible disciplinary consequences of his or her action?
> 2. Were management's requirements of the employee reasonable in relation to the orderly, efficient, and safe operation of the organization's business?
> 3. Did management, before discharging the employee, make a reasonable effort to establish that the employee's performance was unsatisfactory?
> 4. Was the organization's investigation conducted in a fair and objective manner?
> 5. Did the investigation produce sufficient evidence or proof of guilt as charged?
> 6. Has management treated this employee under its rules, orders, and penalties as it has other employees in similar circumstances?
> 7. Did the discharge fit the misconduct, considering the seriousness of the proven offense, the employee's service record, and any mitigating circumstances?

3. Make the discussion private, businesslike, and fairly brief.

4. Avoid making accusations against the employee and injecting personal feelings into the discussion.

5. Avoid bringing up any personality differences between you and the employee.

6. Provide any information concerning severance pay and the status of benefits and coverage.

7. Explain how you will handle employment inquiries from future employers.

Termination meetings should be held in a neutral location, such as a conference room, so that the manager can leave if the meeting gets out of control. Finally, the prudent manager will have determined, prior to the termination decision, that the dismissal does not violate any legal rights the employee may have.[59] Certain federal and state laws limit an employer's freedom to discharge employees. As we will discuss in Chapter 17, the Taft-Hartley Act makes it illegal for an employer to discharge or otherwise discriminate against employees because of their union activities. As we noted in Chapter 3, state fair employment practice laws, Title VII of the Civil Rights Act, and other statutes prohibit discrimination in personnel decisions on the basis of race, religion, color, sex, national origin, physical or mental disabilities, or age. Also prohibited are reprisals against employees who exercise their rights under these laws. The antidiscrimination laws make it essential that managers review their discharge decisions carefully to ensure that there is no evidence of bias or prejudice on the part of supervisors who have made the decisions.

Providing Outplacement Assistance

Employers often use employment agencies to assist in locating jobs for employees who are being discharged. This assistance is especially likely to be provided for managers of long tenure. Sometimes it is also provided for employees being laid off as a result of organizational rightsizing or restructuring, or because they don't fit a changed corporate identity.[60] Rather than being called a discharge, a termination under such conditions is often referred to as **outplacement.**

Managers note the following reasons for providing outplacement services: Concern for the well-being of the employees, protection against potential age-discrimination and fair employment practice lawsuits, competition from other organizations offering such services, and the psychological effect on remaining employees. Outplacement consultants assist employees being terminated by reducing their anger and grief and helping them regain self-confidence as they begin searching in earnest for a new job. Since many terminated workers have been out of the job market for some time, they may lack the knowledge and skills needed to look for a new job. Outplacement specialists can coach them in how to develop contacts, probe for job openings through systematic letter and telephone campaigns, and handle employment interviews and salary negotiations.

Outplacement

Services provided by organizations to help terminated employees find a new job—and to reduce the stress of job loss

Appealing Disciplinary Actions

With growing frequency, organizations are taking steps to protect employees from arbitrary and inequitable treatment by their supervisors. A particular emphasis is placed on creating a climate in which employees are assured that they can voice their dissatisfaction with their superiors without fear of reprisal. This safeguard can be provided through the implementation of a formal procedure for appealing disciplinary actions.

Alternative Dispute-Resolution Procedures

objective

Alternative dispute resolution (ADR)

Term applied to different types of employee complaint or dispute-resolution procedures

In unionized workplaces, grievance procedures are stated in virtually all labor agreements. In nonunion organizations, however, **alternative dispute resolution (ADR)** procedures are a relatively recent development.[61] The employer's interest stems from the desire to meet employees' expectations for fair treatment in the workplace while guaranteeing them due process—in the hope of minimizing discrimination claims or wrongful discharge suits. ADR procedures received a boost from the U.S. Supreme Court when, in *Gilmer v Interstate/Johnson Lane Corp.*, the Court enforced a private agreement that required the arbitration of an age discrimination claim.[62] Additionally, Section 118 of the Civil Rights Act of 1991 encourages the use of ADR procedures, including arbitration.

Some organizations champion these procedures as an avenue for upward communication for employees and as a way to gauge the temperament of the workforce. Others view these systems as a way to resolve minor problems before they mushroom into major issues, thus leading to improved employee morale and productivity.[63]

The appeal procedures that will be described in this chapter are the step-review system, the peer-review system, the use of a hearing officer, the open-door policy, and the use of an ombudsman.

Step-Review Systems

Step-review system

System for reviewing employee complaints and disputes by successively higher levels of management

As Figure 16–8 illustrates, a **step-review system** is based on a preestablished set of steps—normally four—for the review of an employee complaint by successively higher levels of management. These procedures are patterned after the union grievance systems we will discuss in Chapter 18. For example, they normally require that the employee's complaint be formalized as a written statement. Managers at each step are required to provide a full response to the complaint within a specified time period, perhaps three to five working days.

An employee is sometimes allowed to bypass the meeting with his or her immediate supervisor if the employee fears reprisal from this person. Unlike appeal systems in unionized organizations, however, nonunion appeal procedures ordinarily do not provide for a neutral third party—such as an arbitrator—to serve as the judge of last resort.[64] In most step-review systems, the president, chief executive officer, vice president, or HR director acts as the final authority, and this person's decision is not appealable. Some organizations give employees assistance in preparing their complaint cases. For example, an employee who desires it may be able to get advice and counsel from a designated person in the HR department before discussing the issue with management.

Unfortunately, step-review systems may not yield their intended benefits. Employees may believe that management is slow in responding to complaints and that management's response often does not solve the problem. Furthermore, employees may believe that, regardless of policies forbidding reprisal, supervisors would still hold it against them if they exercised their rights as spelled out in the step-review system. These concerns should not lead to the conclusion that all step-review systems are ineffective, but rather that management must take special precautions to ensure the systems work and provide the benefits intended. We offer the following suggestions to make step-review systems successful:

1. Consult employees when designing the complaint system. Commitment to the process is enhanced when employees participate in its design.
2. Train supervisors in handling complaints.
3. Handle complaints in a timely manner.

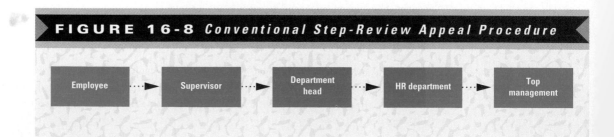

FIGURE 16-8 *Conventional Step-Review Appeal Procedure*

Employee ····▶ Supervisor ····▶ Department head ···▶ HR department ··▶ Top management

4. Make sure that all employees know how to use the complaint procedure and *encourage* them to use the system when they feel aggrieved.

5. Handle cases in a fair manner and assure employees that they need not fear reprisal for filing complaints.

Peer-Review Systems

Peer-review system

System for reviewing employee complaints that utilizes a group composed of equal members of employee representatives and management appointees, which functions as a jury since its members weigh evidence, consider arguments, and after deliberation vote independently to render a final decision

A **peer-review system,** also called a complaint committee, is composed of equal numbers of employee representatives and management appointees. Employee representatives are normally elected by secret ballot by their co-workers for a rotating term, whereas management representatives are assigned, also on a rotating basis. A peer-review system functions as a jury since its members weigh evidence, consider arguments, and, after deliberation, vote independently to render a final decision.[65]

Organizations such as Turner Brothers Trucking, Northrop Corporation, Polaroid, and Citicorp consider one of the benefits of the peer-review system to be the sense of justice that it creates among employees. The peer-review system can be used as the sole method for resolving employee complaints, or it can be used in conjunction with a step-review system. For example, if an employee is not satisfied with management's action at step 1 or 2 in the step-review system, the employee can submit the complaint to the peer-review committee for final resolution.

Use of a Hearing Officer

Hearing officer

Person who holds a full-time position with an organization but assumes a neutral role when deciding cases between the aggrieved employees and management

This procedure is ordinarily confined to large organizations, such as a state government, where employees may be represented by unions. The **hearing officer** holds a full-time position with the organization but assumes a neutral role when deciding cases between an aggrieved employee and management. Hearing officers are employed by the organization; however, they function independently from other managers and occupy a special place in the organizational hierarchy. Their success rests on being perceived as neutral, highly competent, and completely unbiased in handling employee complaints. They hear cases upon request, almost always made by the employee. After considering the evidence and facts presented, they render decisions or awards that are normally final and binding on both sides. Like the peer-review system, the hearing-officer system can be used by itself or as part of a step-review procedure.

Open-Door Policy

Open-door policy

Policy of settling grievances that identifies various levels of management above the immediate supervisor for employee contact

The open-door policy is an old standby for settling employee complaints. In fact, most managers, regardless of whether their organization has adopted a formal open-door policy, profess to maintain one for their employees. The traditional **open-door policy** identifies various levels of management above the immediate supervisor that an aggrieved employee may contact; the levels may extend as high as a vice president, president, or chief executive officer. Typically the person who acts as "the court of last resort" is the HR director or a senior staff official.

The problems with an open-door policy are well documented. Two of its major weaknesses are the unwillingness of managers to listen honestly to employee complaints and worker reluctance to approach managers with their complaints. As an employee once told the authors of this text, "My manager has an open-door policy but the door is only open one inch." Obviously this employee felt he had little opportunity to get through to his manager. Other problems are attributed to this system as well. The open-door policy generally fails to guarantee consistent decision making since what is fair to one manager may seem unfair to another. Higher-level managers tend to support supervisors for fear of undermining authority. And, as a system of justice, open-door policies lack credibility with employees. Still, the open-door policy is often successful where it is supported by all levels of management and where management works to maintain a reputation for being fair and open-minded.

Ombudsman System

Ombudsman

Designated individual from whom employees may seek counsel for the resolution for their complaints

An **ombudsman** is a designated individual from whom employees may seek counsel for the resolution of their complaints.[66] The ombudsman listens to an employee's complaint and attempts to resolve it by mediating a solution between the employee and the supervisor. This individual works cooperatively with both sides to reach a settlement, often employing a clinical approach to problem solving. Since the ombudsman has no authority to finalize a solution to the problem, compromises are highly possible and all concerned tend to feel satisfied with the outcome.

The use of an ombudsman to resolve complaints has received increased acceptance. While ombudsmen are used most commonly to protect individuals from abuses by government agencies, they are also used more in educational and other nonprofit organizations to assist employees in resolving their problems. Ombudsmen are found in some private corporations, too. Xerox and General Electric are examples of two corporations that have had considerable success with them.

To function successfully, ombudsmen must be able to operate in an atmosphere of confidentiality that does not threaten the security of the managers or subordinates who are involved in a complaint. While ombudsmen do not have power to overrule the decision made by an employee's supervisor, they should be able to appeal the decision up the line if they believe an employee is not being treated fairly. Apart from helping to achieve equity for employees, ombudsmen can help to provide management with a check on itself.

Complaint Procedures in Government Organizations

Public organizations have traditionally offered as many as three appeals procedures by which employees can seek redress for their complaints. First, an employee might appeal a disciplinary action to a civil service board or merit commission. A decision by this body may be appealed to the courts. Second, public agencies that have collective bargaining contracts with unions or employee associations have formalized grievance procedures specified in the labor agreement. As a third option, public agencies have implemented ADR procedures for the adjudication of specific employee complaints.

In a study examining ADR procedures in twenty-two public-sector organizations, the predominant method of complaint adjustment was the step-review system used either alone or in combination with a peer-review committee.[67] In a city agency, for example, the step-review procedure preceded the peer-review committee where "the Grievance Committee is a neutral administrative hearing board and shall be composed of four city employees (two supervisory employees and two non-supervisory employees) to be randomly selected. A separate committee will normally be designated for each grievance."[68] Decisions resulting in a tie or based on a majority vote are reviewable by a final agency representative—an agency head, HR officer, or city manager. Interestingly, government agencies are careful to exempt specific issues from the ADR procedure, including employment status, position classification, salaries and benefits, civil service examination and results, and employee performance ratings. Employees with complaints in these areas may use other governmental appeal procedures to seek redress.

objective

Reducing Complaints

The most effective way to reduce complaints is to encourage them to be brought out into the open. Once expressed, they should be resolved quickly in a mutually satisfactory manner. The HR department may uncover evidence of dissatisfaction through the analysis of survey results that it compiles or through its direct communication with employees. However, immediate supervisors who are in continual contact with employees are in a better position to draw out and listen to complaints. For this reason it is important for supervisors to create the type of climate and rapport that will encourage their subordinates to speak up and discuss anything that may be bothering them without fear of provoking resentment.

Symptoms of Complaints

Usually the complaints that are the most difficult for managers to resolve are those that employees are unable or unwilling to express. These complaints may be evidenced by such symptoms as sullenness, moodiness, tardiness, indifference, insubordination, or a decline in quality and quantity of work. The manager who can interpret these symptoms correctly will be more successful in resolving complaints. Such results can be achieved with an approach aimed at diagnosing the causes underlying the symptoms. With many complaints, the symptoms may represent only the tip of the iceberg.

Causes of Complaints

The fact that complaints may be the result of more than one cause can make them difficult to diagnose and handle. Some of the causes of complaints include those relating to the labor agreement, to the employee's job, and to problems of a personal nature.

Causes Relating to the Labor Agreement

Many grievances related to the labor agreement result from omissions or ambiguities in its provisions. (Also see Chapter 18.) The grievances may also result from union attempts to make changes in the agreement that it was unable to win at the bargaining table. At times, union representatives may solicit grievances simply to demonstrate to employees what the union can do for them or to divert the attention of members from union weaknesses or leadership deficiencies. Court decisions, as we have noted, also have made union officers more likely to process grievances that previously might have been dropped.

Causes Relating to the Job

Job-related complaints may stem from the failure of employees either to meet the demands of their jobs or to gain satisfaction from performing them. Employees who are placed in the wrong job or who lack adequate training or supervision are more likely to perform unsatisfactorily. They may become dissatisfied with their employment and be a problem to their supervisors. Job-related complaints, therefore, are often a result of how well individuals are able to meet the demands of their jobs. The supervisor's attitude and behavior toward individual workers may also be a cause for job-related complaints. Supervisors who play favorites, fail to live up to promises, or are too demanding are likely to encounter many complaints from workers.

Causes Relating to Personal Problems

Poor health, drug or alcohol abuse, family concerns, and financial difficulties are typical personal problems that employees may bring with them to the job. The frustration resulting from these problems may cause employees to find fault with their jobs or with others around them. Their expressed complaints thus may not accurately reflect the real cause of their dissatisfactions.

Complaints stemming from personal problems frequently cannot be resolved by changing jobs or employment conditions. Since the cause of these problems is not job-related, corrective action requires making the necessary personal adjustments. Therefore, an important part of every manager's job is to counsel troubled subordinates and to help them to recognize and to work out solutions to their personal problems. This can be done through the counseling process, which was discussed in Chapter 15.

SUMMARY

Both employees and employers have rights and expectations in the employment relationship. The due process right of employees is the right to tell one's views concerning an incident while the employment-at-will doctrine regards the rights of employees and employers to terminate the employment relationship. The implied contract concept is an exception to the employment-at-will doctrine. Under this concept, an employer's oral or written statements may form a contractual obligation that can preclude the automatic termination of employees.

Once employed, employees expect certain privacy rights regarding fair and equitable treatment on the job. These rights extend over such issues as substance abuse and drug testing, searches and surveillance, plant closing notification, and off-duty privacy rights.

The HR department, in combination with other managers, should establish disciplinary policies. This will help achieve both acceptance of policy and its consistent application. To reduce the need for discipline, organizational rules and procedures should be widely known, reviewed on a regular basis, and written and explained to employees. The rules must relate to the safe and efficient operation of the organization. When managers overlook the enforcement of rules, they must reemphasize the rule and its enforcement before disciplining an employee.

The term "discipline" has three meanings—punishment, orderly behavior, and the training of employee conduct. When used with employees, discipline should serve to correct undesirable employee behavior, creating within the employee a desire for self-control. This third definition of discipline can only be achieved when managers conduct a complete and unbiased investigation of employee misconduct. The investigation of employee misconduct begins with the proper documentation of wrongdoing. When managers are investigating employee problems they need to know specifically the infraction of the employee, whether the employee knew of the rule violated, and any extenuating circumstances that might justify the employee's conduct. When employees are to receive discipline, the rule must be uniformly enforced and the past work record of the employee must be considered.

The two approaches to discipline are progressive discipline and positive discipline. Progressive discipline follows a series of steps based upon increasing the degrees of corrective action. The corrective action applied should match the severity of the employee misconduct. Positive discipline, based upon reminders, is a cooperative discipline approach where employees accept responsibility for the desired employee improvement. The focus is on coping with the unsatisfactory performance and dissatisfactions of employees before the problems become major.

Alternative dispute-resolution procedures present ways by which employees exercise their due process rights. The most common forms of ADRs are step-review systems, peer-review systems, hearing officers, the open-door system, and the ombudsman system.

Workplace complaints may be recognized through the behavior of employees. While some employees may simply voice their concerns to managers, others will show such unacceptable behavior as absenteeism, poor attitude, insubordination, or a decline in work performance. When these symptoms are identified, corrections of the unspecified problem can begin. Causes of employee complaints frequently center around personal problems, job-related concerns, or, where one exists, complaints about the labor-management agreement.

KEY TERMS

alternative dispute resolution	ombudsman
discipline	open-door policy
due process	outplacement
employee rights	peer-review system
employment-at-will principle	positive, or nonpunitive, discipline
hearing officer	progressive discipline
hot-stove rule	step-review system
negligence	

▶ DISCUSSION QUESTIONS ◀

1. Define the employment-at-will doctrine. What are the three major court exceptions to the doctrine?
2. What are the legislative and court restrictions on employer drug testing in both the private and the public sector?
3. If you were asked to develop a policy on discipline, what topics would you believe should be covered in the policy?
4. What should be the purpose of an investigative interview, and what approach should be taken in conducting it?
5. Discuss why documentation is so important to the disciplinary process. What constitutes correct documentation?
6. Why do some employers make use of outplacement consultants to assist them with terminations?
7. What do you think would constitute an effective alternative dispute-resolution system? What benefits would you expect from such a system?
8. If you were asked to rule on a discharge case, what facts would you analyze in deciding whether to uphold or reverse the employer's action?

CASE STUDY: The Whistle-Blower's Dilemma

Tom Corbin has worked as a manager at Harbor Electric for eleven years. Shortly after being promoted to director of the electric generator division, he made a discovery that dramatically changed his managerial career. While cleaning out

"I'm sensing confidence, boldness and moral sensibility. You're not going to turn out to be a whistle-blower are you?"

From *The Wall Street Journal*—Permission, Cartoon Features Syndicate

some old files, he stumbled across a seven-year-old report that clearly documented some design flaws in the company's large industrial R-1 electric generator. While these flaws presented no safety hazards, they held the potential to increase construction costs, creating cost overruns for the purchaser. Also, though breakdowns would probably not be immediate, the flaws made the units more susceptible to mechanical failure. If breakdowns occurred after the warranty period had expired, the costly repairs would have to be paid for by the purchasing organization. The R-1 generators were sold mainly to utility companies, so cost overruns or the cost of mechanical failures would ultimately be passed on to consumers.

Corbin was genuinely upset by the report and quickly decided to show it to Robert Medlock, the vice president of manufacturing. Their meeting was brief and to the point. Medlock expressed surprise and dismay at the report but seemed to have no great desire to correct the problems. While not denying the design flaws, Medlock explained that the R-1 generator was basically a well-designed unit that offered an excellent value to purchasers. He further noted that the success of the company rested largely on sales of the generator and to admit any design flaws at this time would be catastrophic to future sales. Public exposure could lead to complaints from consumer groups and government regulators while providing competitors with damaging product information. When Corbin argued that Harbor was essentially "ripping off" utility companies and consumers, he was told to cool down and to forget he ever saw the report. Corbin replied that he couldn't believe Harbor would risk its reputation by selling generators with potentially costly design flaws. He concluded the meeting by saying that he had joined the company because of its honesty and dedication to responsible customer relations, but now he had serious doubts.

Corbin stormed out of Medlock's office. On his way back to the generator division, he considered calling the state utility commission to report the design flaws. He recognized clearly what public knowledge of the problems would do to sales of the R-1 generator. He also considered the consequences of reporting the design flaws on his career with Harbor Electric.

Questions

1. Discuss all the possible consequences of reporting the design flaws to the state utility commission, including the possible consequences for Corbin's career.

2. Suggest a proper course of action for Corbin in correcting the problems surrounding the design flaws in the R-1 generator.

NOTES AND REFERENCES

1. "Is Your Boss Spying on You?" *Business Week* (January 15, 1990): 71. See also Michael B. Bixby, "Was It an Accident or Murder? New Thrusts in Corporate Criminal Liability for Workplace Deaths," *Labor Law Journal* 41, no. 7 (July 1990): 417–24.

2. James W. Hunt and Patricia K. Strongin, *The Law of the Workplace: Rights of Employers and Employees* (Washington, D.C.: Bureau of National Affairs, 1994); see also David S. Hames and Nickie Diersen, "The Common Law Right to Privacy: Another Incursion into Employers' Rights to Manage Their Employees?" *Labor Law Journal* 42, no. 11 (November 1991): 757–65.

3. Alfred G. Feliv, *Primer on Individual Employee Rights* (Rockville, Md.: Bureau of National Affairs, 1992); see also Richard Edwards, *Rights at Work* (Washington, D.C.: Brookings Institution, 1993), Chapter 2.

4. Donald H. Weiss, "How to Avoid Negligent Hiring Law Suits," *Supervisory Management* 36, no. 6 (June 1991): 6.

5. James R. Redeker, *Employee Discipline: Policies and Practices* (Washington, D.C.: Bureau of National Affairs, 1989), 21. This book has an excellent discussion of the rights and responsibilities of employers and employees in the employment relationship; it also provides a comprehensive discussion of employee discipline.

6. Robert S. Seeley, "Corporate Due Process," *HR Magazine* 37, no. 7 (July 1992): 46–49.

7. Redeker, *Employee Discipline*, 25–38.

8. William E. Fulmer and Ann Wallace Casey, "Employment at Will: Options for Managers," *Academy of Management Executive* 4, no. 1 (May 1990): 102–107; see also Robert J. Aalberts and Lorne Seidman, "The Employment at Will Doctrine. Nevada's Struggle Demonstrates the Need for Reform," *Labor Law Journal* 43, no. 10 (October 1991): 651–61.

9. *Adair v United States*, 2078 U.S. 161 (1908).

10. Gary L. Tidwell, "Employment at Will: Limitations in the Public Sector," *Public Personnel Management* 13, no. 3 (Fall 1984): 293–300.

11. Leonard B. Mandelbaum, "Employment-at-Will: Is the Model Termination Act the Answer?" *Labor Law Journal* 44, no. 5 (May 1993): 175–285; see also Paul F. Gerhart and Donald P. Crane, "Wrongful Dismissal: Arbitration and the Law," *Arbitration Journal* 48, no. 2 (June 1993): 56–68.

12. Mandelbaum, "Employment-at-Will," 277.

13. Marcy Mason, "The Curse of Whistle-Blowing," *The Wall Street Journal* (March 14, 1994): A14; see also Tim Barnett, "Overview of State Whistleblower Protection Statutes," *Labor Law Journal* 43, no. 7 (July 1992): 440–48; Timothy R. Barnett, "Will Your Employees Blow the Whistle?" *HR Magazine* 37, no. 7 (July 1992): 76–78; Marcia P. Miceli and Janet P. Near, *Blowing the Whistle: The Organizational and Legal Implications for Companies and Employees* (Lexington, Mass.: Lexington Books, 1992).

14. *Foley v Interactive Data Corporation*, 47 Cal. 3d654, 254 Cal. Rptr. 211 (1988).

15. "Management Attorney Says Foley Will Aid Discharged Employees," *BNA's Employee Relations Weekly* 7 (October 23, 1989): 1323.

16. "Management Attorney," 1323.

17. Raymond L. Hilgert, "Employers Protected by At-Will Statements," *HR Magazine* 36, no. 3 (March 1991): 57–60; see also Lisa Jenner,

"Employment-at-Will Liability: How Protected Are You?" *HR Focus* 71 no. 3 (March 1994): 11; Philip R. Voluck and Michael J. Hanlon, "Contract Disclaimers in Policy Documents," *Personnel Journal* 66, no. 8 (August 1987): 123–31.

18. Rob Brookler, "Industry Standards in Workplace Drug Testing," *Personnel Journal* 71, no. 4 (April 1992): 128–32.

19. Dawn Gunsch, "Training Prepares Workers for Drug Testing," *Personnel Journal* 72, no. 5 (May 1993): 52.

20. Gunsch, "Training Prepares Workers," 54.

21. Edward J. Miller, "Investigating in a Drug-free Workplace," *HR Magazine* 36, no. 5 (May 1991): 48–51.

22. Brookler, "Industry Standards," 128.

23. Stephen A. Liem, "The Fourth Amendment and Drug Testing in the Workplace: Current U.S. Court Decisions," *Labor Law Journal* 43, no. 1 (January 1992): 50–57.

24. *Harmon v Thornburgh*, CA, DC No. 88–5265 (July 30, 1989); *Treasury Employees Union v Von Raab*, US SupCt No. 86-18796 (March 21, 1989); *City of Annapolis v United Food and Commercial Workers Local 400*, Md. CtApp No. 38 (November 6, 1989); *Skinner v Railway Labor Executives Association*, US SupCt No. 87-1555 (March 21, 1989).

25. *Bluestein v Skinner*, 908 F2d. 451 9th CR (1990).

26. Arthur F. Silbergeld and Sarah Galvarro, "Private Sector Drug Testing: Legal Limitations in California," *Employee Relations Law Journal* 16, no. 3 (Winter 1990–91): 347–58.

27. Jonathan A. Segal, "To Test or Not to Test," *HR Magazine* 37, no. 4 (April 1992): 40–43.

28. Robert M. Peter, Jr., "The Impact of Drug Testing," *Labor Law Journal* 40, no. 1 (January 1989): 50–57.

29. Hair analysis tests are based on the fact that drugs from the bloodstream are absorbed into hair follicles as the follicles grow. An analysis of a number of hair strands can reportedly determine the chronology and degree of drug use. Video tests, or performance testing, is a motor-skills test assessing the employee's ability to work. See Cory R. Fine, "Video Tests Are the New Frontier in Drug Detection," *Personnel Journal* 71, no. 6 (June 1992): 149–61; Stephen A. Plass, "Testing Hair Follicles for Drugs: In Search of Privacy, Accuracy, and Reliability," *Labor Law Journal* 42, no. 2 (February 1991): 111–15.

30. Mark D. Uhrich, "Are You Positive the Test Is Positive?" *HR Magazine* 37, no. 4 (April 1992): 44–51.

31. Information on individual state laws can be obtained from *A Guide to State Drug Testing Laws and Legislation*, published annually by the Institute for a Drug-Free Workplace. A free copy of the Institute's *Mandatory Guidelines for Federal Workplace Drug Testing Programs* and its official list of certified laboratories can be obtained by calling the National Clearing House for Alcohol and Drug Information at (800) 729–6686. The American Bar Association's *Model Drug Testing in Employment Statutes* is also useful.

32. Samuel Greengard, "Theft Control Starts with HR Strategies," *Personnel Journal* 72, no. 4 (April 1993): 81–91.

33. Phyllis Gillespie, "Stolen Trust: Employee Theft Costs $320 Billion," *Arizona Republic* (May 4, 1992): Section E.

34. Greengard, "Theft Control," 81.

35. Susan R. Mendelsohn and Kathryn K. Morrison, "Employee Searches," *Personnel* 65, no. 7 (July 1988): 24.

36. Jennifer J. Laabs, "Surveillance: Tool or Trap?" *Personnel Journal* 71, no. 6 (June 1992): 102.

37. Ann K. Bradley, "An Employer's Perception on Monitoring Telemarketing Calls: Invasion of Privacy or Legitimate Business Practice?" *Labor Law Journal* 42, no. 5 (May 1991): 259–73.

38. Denis Collins, "Plant Closings: Establishing Legal Obligations," *Labor Law Journal* 40, no. 2 (February 1989): 67.

39. James F. Fitzpatrick, ed., *WARN Act and State Plant-Closing Handbook* (Rockford, Md.: Bureau of National Affairs, 1993).

40. John F. Meyers, "Notice of Plant Closings and Layoffs—Significant Case Development," *Employee Relations Law Journal* 18, no. 2 (Autumn 1992): 297–308.

41. Bill Leonard, "The Tough Decision to Use Confidential Information," *HR Magazine* 38, no. 7 (July 1993): 72–75.

42. "Most Employers Surveyed Give Employees Restricted Access to Personnel Files," *BNA's Employee Relations Weekly* 7, no. 30 (July 24, 1989): 936.

43. Steve Bergsman, "Employee Conduct outside the Workplace," *HR Magazine* 36, no. 3 (March 1991): 62.

44. Bergsman, "Employee Conduct," 64.

45. "Help for Discipline Dodgers," ed. Catherine M. Petrini, *Training and Development* 47, no. 5 (May 1993): 19–22.

46. Caleb S. Atwood, "Discharge Now, Pay Later? Establishing Reasonable Rules Can Keep You Out of Hot Water," *Personnel Administrator* 34, no. 8 (August 1989): 92–93.

47. Donald C. Mosley, Leon C. Megginson, and Paul H. Pietri, *Supervisory Management: The Art of Developing and Empowering People*, 3d ed. (Cincinnati: South-Western, 1993).

48. Cecily A. Waterman and Teresa A. Maginn, "Investigating Suspect Employees," *HR Magazine* 38, no. 1 (January 1993): 85–87.

49. *NLRB v Weingarten, Inc.*, 95 S. Ct. 959 (1975), 402 U.S. 251, 43 L. Ed. 2nd 171.

50. 274 NLRB No. 55 (February 22, 1985).

51. Christopher J. Martin, "Some Reflections on *Weingarten* and the Free Speech Rights of Union Stewards," *Employee Relations Law Journal* 18, no. 4 (Spring 1993): 647–53.

52. Brian S. Klars and Hoyt N. Wheeler, "Managerial Decision Making about Employee Discipline: A Policy-Capturing Approach," *Personnel Psychology* 43, no. 1 (Spring 1990): 117–34.

53. Readers interested in the pioneering work on positive discipline should see James R. Redeker, "Discipline, Part 1: Progressive Systems Work Only by Accident," *Personnel* 62, no. 10 (October 1985): 8–12; James R. Redeker, "Discipline, Part 2: The Nonpunitive Approach Works by Design," *Personnel* 62, no. 11 (November 1985): 7–14. See also Alan W. Bryant, "Replacing Punitive Discipline with a Positive Approach," *Personnel Administrator* 29, no. 2 (February 1984): 79–87.

54. Mark Sherman and Al Lucia, "Positive Discipline and Labor Arbitration," *Arbitration Journal* 47, no. 2 (June 1992): 56–58.

55. Chimezie A. B. Osigweh, Yg and William R. Hutchison, "Positive Discipline," *Human Resources Management* 28, no. 3 (Fall 1989): 367–83; see also James R. Redeker, *Employee Discipline: Policies and Procedures* (Washington, D.C.: Bureau of National Affairs, 1989).

56. William J. Morin and Lyle Yorks, *Dismissal* (New York: Drake, Beam, Morin, Inc., 1990).

57. Adolph M. Koven and Susan N. Smith, *Just Cause: The Seven Tests*, 2e. (Washington, D.C.: Bureau of National Affairs, Inc., 1992).

58. For an expanded discussion of just cause see Frank Elkouri and Edna Asher Elkouri, *How Arbitration Works*, 4th ed. (Washington, D.C.: Bureau of National Affairs, 1985): 650–54.

59. James G. Frierson, "How to Fire without Getting Burned," *Personnel* 67, no. 9 (September 1990): 44–48.

60. Lewis Newman, "Outplacement the Right Way,"

Personnel Administrator 34, no. 2 (February 1989): 83–86.

61. Stephenie Overman, "Why Grapple with the Cloudy Elephant," *HR Magazine* 38, no. 3 (March 1993): 60–65.

62. *Gilmer v Interstate/Johnson Lane Corp.*, 111 S. Ct. 1647 (1991). For additional discussion of *Gilmer*, see Thomas J. Piskorski and David B. Ross, "Private Arbitration as the Exclusive Means of Resolving Employment-Related Disputes," *Employee Relations Law Journal* 19, no. 2 (Autumn 1993): 205–19; Todd H. Thomas, "Using Arbitration to Avoid Litigation," *Labor Law Journal* 44, no. 1 (January 1993): 3–17.

63. George W. Bohlander and Harold C. White, "Building Bridges: Nonunion Employee Grievance Systems," *Personnel* 65, no. 7 (July 1988): 62–66.

64. Douglas M. McCabe, "Corporate Nonunion Grievance Arbitration Systems: A Procedural Analysis," *Labor Law Journal* 40, no. 7 (July 1989): 432–37.

65. Douglas M. McCabe, *Corporate Nonunion Complaint Procedures and Systems* (New York: Praeger, 1988), 9; see also Dawn Anfuso, "Coors Taps Employee Judgement," *Personnel Journal* 13, no. 2 (February 1994): 50.

66. James T. Ziegehfoss, Mary Rowe, Lee Robbins, and Robert Munzenrider, "Corporate Ombudsman," *Personnel Journal* 68, no. 3 (March 1989): 76–79.

67. George W. Bohlander, "Public Sector Independent Grievance Systems: Methods and Procedures," *Public Personnel Management* 18, no. 3 (Fall 1989): 339–54; see also George W. Bohlander and Ken Behringer, "Public Sector Nonunion Complaint Procedures: Current Research," *Labor Law Journal* 41, no. 8 (August 1990): 563–68; Dennis M. Daley, "Formal Disciplinary Procedures and Conflict Resolution Remedies: Availability and the Effects of Size and City Manager among North Carolina Municipalities," *Public Personnel Management* 22, no. 1 (Spring 1993): 153.

68. Bohlander, "Public Sector Independent Grievance Systems," 349.

Part 6

Enhancing Employee-Management Relations

The two chapters in Part 6 discuss employee representation by labor unions. Chapter 17 focuses on issues involved in the unionization of employees, including the legal statutes governing this very specific area of HR management. Included in Chapter 17 is a discussion of the many challenges that currently face the union movement. Chapter 18 explores the relationship between labor and management once employees elect to unionize and a labor agreement is negotiated between the two parties. Recent trends in collective bargaining are reviewed, as are programs to enhance labor-management cooperation. An understanding of labor relations and its processes will improve the supervisory skills of managers in both union and nonunion enterprises.

Chapter

The Dynamics of Labor Relations

After studying this chapter you should be able to

one
objective

Identify and explain the principal federal laws that provide the framework for labor relations.

two
objective

Cite the reasons why employees join unions.

three
objective

Describe the process by which unions organize employees and gain recognition as their bargaining agent.

four
objective

Describe the overall structure of the labor movement and the functions labor unions perform at the national and local levels.

five
objective

Describe the differences between private-sector and public-sector labor relations.

six
objective

Discuss some of the effects that changing conditions are having on labor organizations.

M*ention the word "union" and most people will have some opinion, positive or negative, regarding U.S. labor organizations. To some, the word evokes images of labor-management unrest—grievances, strikes, picketing, boycotts. To others, the word represents industrial democracy, fairness, opportunity, equal representation. Many think of unions as simply creating an adversarial relationship between employees and managers.*

Regardless of attitudes toward them, since the mid-1800s unions have been an important force shaping organizational practices, legislation, and political thought in the United States. Today unions remain of interest because of their influence on organizational productivity, U.S. competitiveness, the development of labor law, and HR policies and practices. Like business organizations themselves, unions are undergoing changes in both operation and philosophy. Labor-management cooperative programs, company buyouts by unions, and labor's increased interest in global trade are illustrative of labor's new role in society.

In spite of the long history of unions, the intricacies of labor relations are unfamiliar to many individuals. Therefore, this chapter describes government regulation of labor relations, the labor relations process, the reasons why workers join labor organizations, the structure and leadership of labor unions, and contemporary challenges to labor organizations.

Unions and other labor organizations can affect significantly the ability of managers to direct and control the various functions of HRM. For example, union seniority provisions in the labor contract may influence who is selected for job promotions or training programs. Pay rates may be determined through union negotiations, or unions may impose restrictions on management's employee appraisal methods. Therefore, it is essential that managers understand how unions operate and be thoroughly familiar with the growing body of law governing labor relations. Labor relations is a highly specialized function of HRM to which managers must give appropriate consideration.

Government Regulation of Labor Relations

Unions have a long history in America, and the regulations governing labor relations have evolved from labor's historical developments. Prior to 1930, employers strongly opposed union growth, using court injunctions (e.g., court orders forbidding various union activities, such as picketing and strikes) and the "yellow-dog contract." A yellow-dog contract was an employer's antiunion tactic by which employees bound themselves not to join a union while working for the employer's organization. Using strikebreakers, blacklisting employees (e.g., circulating the names of union supporters to other employers), and discriminating against those who favored unionization were other defensive maneuvers of employers.

As unions became stronger under federal laws passed during the 1930s, legislation was passed to curb union abuses of power and to protect the rights of union members from unethical union activities. Today the laws governing labor relations seek to create an environment where both unions and employers can discharge their respective rights and responsibilities. Knowledge of labor relations laws will assist the understanding of how union-management relations operate in the United States. The first federal law pertaining to labor relations was the Railway Labor Act of 1926. Other major laws that affect labor relations in the private sector are the Norris-LaGuardia Act, the Wagner Act, the Taft-Hartley Act, and the Landrum-Griffin Act.

Railway Labor Act

...mary purpose of the Railway Labor Act (RLA) is to avoid service inter-... resulting from disputes between railroads and their operating unions. To ... this end, the RLA contains two extensive procedures to handle these ...anagement disputes. First, the National Mediation Board resolves nego-...impasses by using mediation and/or arbitration. The board is additionally ... with holding secret-ballot elections to determine if employees desire ...ization. Second, the National Railway Adjustment Board functions to ... grievance and arbitration disputes arising during the life of an agreement.

Norris-LaGuardia Act

...Norris-LaGuardia Act, or Anti-Injunction Act, of 1932 severely restricts ...bility of employers to obtain an injunction forbidding a union from engag-...n peaceful picketing, boycotts, or various striking activities. Previously, fed-...court injunctions had been an effective antiunion weapon because they forced unions to either cease such activities or suffer the penalty of being held in contempt of court. Like the RLA, this act promotes collective bargaining and encourages the existence, formation, and effective operation of labor organizations.

Injunctions may still be granted in labor disputes. Before an injunction may be issued, however, employers must show that there were prior efforts to resolve the dispute peaceably, that law enforcement agencies are unable or unwilling to protect the employer's property, and that lack of an injunction will cause greater harm to the employer than to the union. This act also contains provisions that made the yellow-dog contract unenforceable in court.

The Wagner Act

The Wagner Act of 1935 (or National Labor Relations Act) has had by far the most significant impact on union-management relations. It placed the protective power of the federal government firmly behind employee efforts to organize and bargain collectively through representatives of their choice. The Wagner Act created the National Labor Relations Board (NLRB) to govern labor relations in the United States. Although this act was amended by the Taft-Hartley Act, most of its major provisions that protected employee bargaining rights were retained. Section 7 of the law guarantees these rights as follows:

> Employees shall have the right to self-organization, to form, join, or assist labor organizations, to bargain collectively through representatives of their own choosing, and to engage in concerted activities, for the purpose of collective bargaining or other mutual aid or protection, and shall also have the right to refrain from any or all of such activities except to the extent that such right may be affected by an agreement requiring membership in a labor organization as a condition of employment.[1]

Unfair labor practices (ULPs)

Specific employer and union illegal practices that operate to deny employees their rights and benefits under federal labor law

To guarantee employees their Section 7 rights, Congress outlawed specific employer practices that deny employees the benefits of the law. Section 8 of the act lists five **unfair labor practices (ULPs)** of employers. These practices are defined as follows:

1. Interfering with, restraining, or coercing employees in the exercise of their rights guaranteed in Section 7

2. Dominating or interfering with the formation or administration of any labor organization, or contributing financial or other support to it
3. Discriminating in regard to hiring or tenure of employment or any term or condition of employment so as to encourage or discourage membership in any labor organization
4. Discharging or otherwise discriminating against employees because they file charges or give testimony under this act
5. Refusing to bargain collectively with the duly chosen representatives of employees

Many ULPs are either knowingly or unknowingly committed each year by employers. In fiscal year 1993, for example, 33,744 unfair labor practices were filed with the NLRB. Alleged violations of the act by employers were filed in 22,272 cases. The majority of all charges against employers concerned illegal discharge or other discrimination against employees.[2] It is therefore imperative that managers at all levels receive training in employee rights and unfair labor practices. Where employers violate employee rights, the NLRB can "take such affirmative action including reinstatement of employment with or without back pay, as well as effectuate the policies of the Act, and make discriminated employees whole."[3] For example, in 1993 the NLRB ordered Reichhold Chemical Company to pay $1.45 million to 200 workers when the company refused to bargain in regard to determining the bargaining unit under an existing contract, a mandatory issue of bargaining.

The National Labor Relations Board

The agency responsible for administering and enforcing the Wagner Act is the National Labor Relations Board. It serves the public interest by reducing interruptions in production or service caused by labor-management strife. To accomplish this goal the NLRB is given two primary charges: (1) to hold secret-ballot elections to determine whether employees wish to be represented by a union and (2) to prevent and remedy unfair labor practices. The NLRB does not act on its own initiative in either function. It processes only those charges of unfair labor practices and petitions for employee elections that may be filed at one of its regional offices or other smaller field offices.[4]

The Taft-Hartley Act

Because the bargaining power of unions increased significantly after the passage of the Wagner Act, certain restraints on unions were considered necessary. The Taft-Hartley Act of 1947 (also known as the Labor-Management Relations Act) defined the following activities as unfair union practices:

1. Restraint or coercion of employees in the exercise of their rights
2. Restraint or coercion of employers in the selection of the parties to bargain in their behalf
3. Persuasion of employers to discriminate against any of their employees
4. Refusal to bargain collectively with an employer
5. Participation in secondary boycotts and jurisdictional disputes

6. Attempt to force recognition from an employer when another union is already the certified representative
7. Charge of excessive initiation fees and dues
8. "Featherbedding" practices that require payment of wages for services not performed

In short, by passing the Taft-Hartley Act, Congress balanced the rights and duties of labor and management in the collective bargaining arena. No longer could the law be criticized as favoring unions.

Health care employees represent a large and important part of the workforce. In 1974 the Taft-Hartley Act was amended to include coverage of employees working in privately owned hospitals and nursing homes. Because of the critical nature of health care services, the 1974 amendments place special requirements on collective bargaining in this industry. For example, before a union of health care employees can strike, it must give a ten-day notice to the employer. Unions must also notify health care facilities of their intent to renegotiate a labor contract at least ninety days prior to the expiration of the agreement; there is a sixty-day requirement for other industries covered by the act.

The Federal Mediation and Conciliation Service

Because of the high incidence of strikes after World War II, the Taft-Hartley Act created the Federal Mediation and Conciliation Service (FMCS) to help resolve negotiating disputes. The function of this independent agency is to help labor and management reach collective bargaining agreements through the processes of mediation and conciliation. These functions use a neutral party who maintains communications between bargainers in an attempt to gain agreement. Unlike the NLRB, the FMCS has no enforcement powers, nor can it prosecute anyone. Rather, the parties in a negotiating impasse must voluntarily elect to use the service. Once the FMCS is asked to mediate a dispute, however, its involvement in the process can greatly improve labor-management relations while providing a vehicle for the exchange of collective bargaining proposals.[5] According to Larry Babcock, director of operations support of the FMCS, the agency mediates annually between 6,000 and 7,000 collective bargaining disputes.[6] In recent years the FMCS has been highly visible in resolving deadlocks involving the communications, sports, auto, and transportation industries.

The Landrum-Griffin Act

In 1959 Congress passed the Landrum-Griffin Act (also known as the Labor-Management Reporting and Disclosure Act) to safeguard union member rights and prevent racketeering and other unscrupulous practices by employers and union officers. The act also establishes certain ground rules governing the control that national unions may exert over local unions where locals are alleged to have violated member rights.

One of the most important provisions of the Landrum-Griffin Act is the Bill of Rights of Union Members, which requires that every union member must be given the right to (1) nominate candidates for union office, (2) vote in union elections or referendums, (3) attend union meetings, and (4) participate in union meetings and vote on union business. Members who are deprived of these rights are permitted to seek appropriate relief in a federal court. The court's action may include obtaining an appropriate injunction. Union members are also granted the right to examine union accounts and records in order to verify information contained in union reports and to bring suit against union officers as necessary to protect union funds. Moreover, under the act, unions are required to submit a financial report annually to the Secretary of Labor, and employers must report any expenditures that are made in attempting to exercise their bargaining rights.

The Labor Relations Process

Labor relations process

Logical sequence of four events: (1) workers desire collective representation, (2) union begins its organizing campaign, (3) collective negotiations lead to a contract, and (4) the contract is administered

Individually, employees may be able to exercise relatively little power in their relations with employers. The treatment and benefits they receive depend in large part on how their employers view their worth to the organization. Of course, if they believe they are not being treated fairly, they have the option of quitting. However, another way to correct the situation is to organize and bargain with the employer collectively. When employees pursue this direction, the labor relations process begins. As Figure 17–1 illustrates, the **labor relations process** consists of a logical sequence of four events: (1) workers desire collective representation, (2) union begins its organizing campaign, (3) collective negotiations

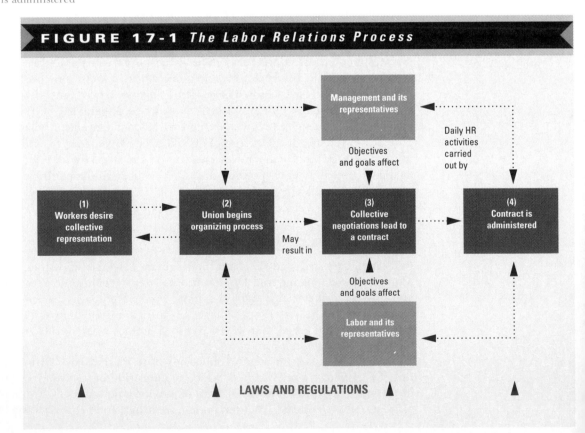

FIGURE 17-1 *The Labor Relations Process*

lead to a contract, and (4) the contract is administered. Laws and administrative rulings influence each of the separate events by granting special privileges to, or imposing defined constraints on, workers, managers, and union officials.[7]

objective

Why Employees Unionize

The majority of research on why employees unionize comes from the study of blue-collar employees in the private sector. These studies generally conclude that employees unionize as a result of economic need, because of a general dissatisfaction with managerial practices, and/or as a way to fulfill social and status needs. In short, employees see unionism as a way to achieve results they cannot achieve acting individually.

It should be pointed out that some employees join unions because of the union-shop provisions of the labor agreement. In states where it is permitted, a **union shop** is a provision of the labor agreement that requires employees to join as a condition of employment. Even when compelled to join, however, many employees accept the concept of unionism once they become involved in the union as a member.

Union shop

Provision of the labor agreement that requires employees to join the union as a requirement for their employment

Economic Needs

Whether or not a union can become the bargaining agent for a group of employees will be influenced by the employees' degree of dissatisfaction, if any, with their employment conditions. It will depend also on whether the employees perceive the union as likely to be effective in improving these conditions.[8] Dissatisfaction with wages, benefits, and working conditions appears to provide the strongest reason to join a union. This point is continually supported by research studies that find that both union members and nonmembers have their highest expectations of union performance regarding the "bread and butter" issues of collective bargaining.[9] It is these traditional issues of wages and benefits on which unions are built.

Dissatisfaction with Management

Employees may seek unionization when they perceive that managerial practices regarding promotion, transfer, shift assignment, or other job-related policies are administered in an unfair or biased manner. Employees cite favoritism shown by managers as a major reason for joining unions. This is particularly true when the favoritism concerns the HR areas of discipline, promotion, and wage increases.

The failure of employers to give employees an opportunity to participate in decisions affecting their welfare may also encourage union membership. It is widely believed that one reason managers begin employee involvement programs and seek to empower their employees is to avoid collective action by employees. In a highly publicized organizing effort by the United Auto Workers at the Nissan plant in Smyrna, Tennessee, the union lost the election because workers were satisfied with the voice in decision making that Nissan's participatory style of management gave them. Nissan's director of HR noted, "We pride ourselves in being a company that functions in a participatory way. The vote was a statement of support for the strongly participatory management at Nissan."[10]

Social and Status Concerns

Employees whose needs for status and recognition are being frustrated may join unions as a means of satisfying these needs. Through their union, they have an opportunity to fraternize with other employees who have similar desires, interests, problems, and gripes. Joining the union also enables them to put leadership talents to use.

The limited studies conducted on employee unionization in the public sector generally find public employees unionizing for reasons similar to those of their private-sector counterparts. For example, higher wages and benefits, job security, and protection against arbitrary and unfair management treatment are primary motives for unionization among public-sector employees. In the final analysis, the extent to which employees perceive that the benefits of joining a union outweigh the costs associated with membership is likely to be the deciding factor.[11]

Gender, Race, and Ethnic Attitudinal Differences toward Unionization

While managers have always been interested in discovering why employees unionize, recent interest and research have focused on those groups of workers who show the greatest propensity to unionize. For example, an important finding of one study showed that white-collar women, representing over half of the female nonunion workforce, are more favorably disposed toward voting for a union than are their male counterparts. Women's prounion sentiments reflect their belief that a union can improve their wages and enable them to participate more favorably in workplace decisions.[12] Supporting this finding are U.S. Department of Labor data showing that the female share of union membership has grown steadily; in 1993 women accounted for two out of every three new union members. Women now compose 39.3 percent of the unionized workforce.[13]

In a study investigating the likely union voting behavior of blacks, Anglos, and Hispanics, blacks were shown to have the most favorable attitudes toward unionization while Hispanics showed the least favorable attitudes. Hispanic attitudes, while lower, were not significantly different from Anglos.[14] The findings of this study are consistent with results from other research regarding the voting behaviors of different race and ethnic groups.[15] The results from all of these studies have important implications for both managers and union officials.

three
objective

Organizing Campaigns

Once employees desire to unionize, a formal organizing campaign may be started either by a union organizer or by employees acting on their own behalf. Contrary to popular belief, most organizing campaigns are begun by employees rather than by union organizers. Large national unions like the United Auto Workers, the United Brotherhood of Carpenters, the United Steelworkers, and the Teamsters, however, have formal organizing departments whose purpose is to identify organizing opportunities and launch organizing campaigns.

Since such campaigns can be expensive, union leaders carefully evaluate their chances of success and the possible benefits to be gained from their efforts. Important in this evaluation is the employer's vulnerability to unionization.[16] Union leaders also consider the effect that allowing an employer to remain nonunion may have on the strength of their union within the area. A nonunion employer can impair a union's efforts to standardize employment conditions within an industry or geographic area, as well as weaken the union's bargaining power with employers it has unionized.

Organizing Steps

Terry Moser, president, Teamster Local 104, once told the authors that the typical organizing campaign follows a series of progressive steps that can lead to employee representation. The organizing process as described by Moser normally includes the following steps:

1. Employee/union contact
2. Initial organizational meeting
3. Formation of in-house organizing committee
4. Election petition and voting preparation
5. Contract negotiations

Step 1. The first step begins when employees and union officials make contact to explore the possibility of unionization. During these discussions, employees will investigate the advantages of labor representation, and union officials will begin to gather information on employee needs, problems, and grievances. Labor organizers will also seek specific information about the employer's financial health, supervisory styles, and organizational policies and practices. To win employee support, labor organizers must build a case *against* the employer and *for* the union.

Step 2. As an organizing campaign gathers momentum, the organizer will schedule an initial union meeting to attract more supporters. The organizer will use the information gathered in step 1 to address employee needs and explain how the union can secure these goals. Two additional purposes of organizational meetings are (1) to identify employees who can help the organizer direct the campaign and (2) to establish communication chains that reach all employees.

Step 3. The third important step in the organizing drive is to form an in-house organizing committee composed of employees willing to provide leadership to the campaign. The committee's role is to interest other employees in joining the union and in supporting its campaign. An important task of the committee is to have employees sign an **authorization card** (see Highlights in HRM 1) indicating their willingness to be represented by a labor union in collective bargaining with their employer. The number of signed authorization cards demonstrates the potential strength of the labor union.[17] At least 30 percent of the employees must sign authorization cards before the National Labor Relations Board will hold a representation election.

Step 4. If a sufficient number of employees support the union drive, the organizer will seek a government-sponsored election. A representation petition will be filed with the NLRB, asking that a secret-ballot election be held to determine if employees actually desire unionization. Before the election, a large publicity campaign will be directed toward employees, seeking their support and election votes. This is a period of intense emotions for the employees, the labor organization, and the employer.

Authorization card

A statement signed by an employee authorizing a union to act as a representative of the employee for purposes of collective bargaining

1 UNITED FOOD & COMMERCIAL WORKERS INTERNATIONAL UNION AUTHORIZATION CARD

United Food & Commercial Workers International Union

Affiliated with AFL-CIO-CLC

AUTHORIZATION FOR REPRESENTATION

I hereby authorize the United Food & Commercial Workers International Union, AFL-CIO-CLC, or its chartered Local Union(s) to represent me for the purpose of collective bargaining.

_____   _____
(Print Name)   (Date)

_____   _____
(Signature)   (Home Phone)

_____   _____
(Home Address)   (City)   (State)   (Zip)

_____   _____
(Employer's Name)   (Address)

_____
(Hire Date)   (Type Work Performed)   (Department)

                           Day   Night   Full   Part-
_____ _____ Shift _____   Shift _____   Time _____   Time _____
(Hourly Rate)   (Day Off)
Would you participate in an organizing committee?   Yes _____   No _____

Step 5. Union organizing is concluded when the union wins the election. The NLRB will "certify" the union as the legal bargaining representative of the employees. Contract negotiations will now begin; these negotiations represent another struggle between the union and employer. During negotiations each side will seek employment conditions favorable to its position. Members of the in-plant organizing committee and the union organizer will attempt to negotiate the employees' first contract. In about one out of four union campaigns, unions are unable to secure a first contract after winning a representation election.[18] Should the union fail to obtain an agreement within one year from winning the election, the Taft-Hartley Act allows the employees to vote the union out through an NLRB "decertification" election.

Employer Tactics

In counteracting a union campaign, employers must not threaten employees with the loss of their jobs or loss or reduction of other employment benefits if they vote to unionize. However, within the limits permitted by the Taft-Hartley Act, employers can express their views about the disadvantages of being represented by a union. When possible, employers will stress the favorable employer-employee relationship they have experienced in the past without a union.[19] Employers may emphasize any advantages in wages, benefits, or working conditions the employees may enjoy in comparison with those provided by organizations that are already unionized.[20] "While you have a right to join a union," the employers may remind their employees, "you also have a right not to join one and to deal directly with the organization free from outside interference."

Employers may also emphasize any unfavorable publicity the organizing union has received with respect to corruption or the abuse of members' legal rights. Employers may use government statistics to show that unions commit large numbers of unfair labor practices. For example, 10,077 unfair labor practices were charged against unions in 1993; the majority (7,824) alleged illegal restraint and coercion of employees.[21]

If the union has engaged in a number of strikes, employers may stress this fact to warn employees about possible work disruption and loss of income.[22] Also, employers will point out to employees the cost of union dues and special assessments, along with any false promises made by the union in the course of its campaign. Furthermore, employers may initiate legal action should union members and/or their leaders engage in any unfair labor practices during the organizing effort.

How Employees Become Unionized

The employees to be organized constitute the bargaining unit to be covered by the labor agreement. The NLRB defines a **bargaining unit** as a group of two or

Bargaining unit
Group of two or more employees who share common employment interests and conditions and may reasonably be grouped together for purposes of collective bargaining

Nurses often have different interests when negotiating their labor agreements.

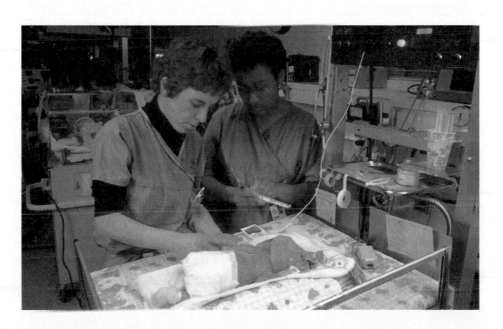

more employees who have common employment interests and conditions and may reasonably be grouped together for purposes of collective bargaining.[23] If an employer and a union cannot agree on who should be in the bargaining unit, an appropriate bargaining unit will be determined by the NLRB on the basis of a similarity of interests (e.g. wages, job duties, training) among employees within the unit. For example, in hospitals, the NLRB has designated separate units for nurses, technicians, doctors, maintenance employees, office clerical personnel, all other nonprofessionals, and guards.[24]

Employer Recognition

If it succeeds in signing up at least 50 percent of employees within the bargaining unit, the union may request recognition by the employer. Typically, evidence is produced in the form of authorization cards signed by employees. If no other union is competing to represent the employees, the employer at this point can simply agree to recognize the union and negotiate an agreement with it.[25] This procedure is referred to as "certification on a card count." Smitty's food stores in Phoenix, Arizona, agreed to recognize the United Food & Commercial Workers (UFCW) as bargaining representatives of store employees when over 70 percent of the employees signed authorization cards. However, if the employer believes that a majority of its employees do not want to belong to the union or if more than one union is attempting to gain recognition, the employer can insist that a representation election be held. This election will determine which union, if any, will represent the employees. The petition to hold representation elections usually is initiated by the union although employers, under certain conditions, have the right to petition for one. (See Highlights in HRM 2.)

Types of NLRB Representation Elections

Consent election
NLRB election option wherein the petition to hold a representation election is not contested by either the employer or the union

Stipulation election
NLRB election option wherein the parties seek settlement of representation questions such as the NLRB's jurisdiction or the appropriate employees to be included in the bargaining unit

The NLRB offers two election options. The first option, called a **consent election,** is used when the petition to hold a representation election is not contested. Here there are no disagreements between the union and the employer. The NLRB sets a date to hold the election, and voting is conducted by secret ballot. Should the request for representation be contested by the employer or should more than one union be seeking recognition, then *preelection hearings* must be held. This second option is called a **stipulation election.** At the preelection hearings several important issues will be discussed, including the NLRB's jurisdiction to hold the election, determination of the bargaining unit (if contested by the parties), and the voting choice(s) to appear on the ballot. The ballot lists the names of the unions that are seeking recognition and also provides for the choice of "no union."

After the election is held, the winning party will be determined on the basis of the number of actual votes, not on the number of members of the bargaining unit. For example, suppose the bargaining unit at XYZ Corporation comprised 100 employees, but only 27 employees voted in the election. The union receiving 14 yes votes among the 27 voting (a majority) would be declared the winner, and the union would bargain for all 100 employees. By law the union would be granted *exclusive representation* over all bargaining unit employees.

HIGHLIGHTS IN HRM

highlights

2   NLRB ELECTION POSTER

NOTICE TO EMPLOYEES

FROM THE
National Labor Relations Board

A PETITION has been filed with this Federal agency seeking an election to determine whether certain employees want to be represented by a union.

The case is being investigated and NO DETERMINATION HAS BEEN MADE AT THIS TIME by the National Labor Relations Board. IF an election is held Notices of Election will be posted giving complete details for voting.

It was suggested that your employer post this notice so the National Labor Relations Board could inform you of your basic rights under the National Labor Relations Act.

YOU HAVE THE RIGHT under Federal Law

- To self-organization
- To form, join, or assist labor organizations
- To bargain collectively through representatives of your own choosing
- To act together for the purposes of collective bargaining or other mutual aid or protection
- To refuse to do any or all of these things unless the union and employer, in a state where such agreements are permitted, enter into a lawful union-security agreement requiring employees to pay periodic dues and initiation fees. Nonmembers who inform the union that they object to the use of their payments for nonrepresentational purposes may be required to pay only their share of the union's costs of representational activities *(such as collective bargaining, contract administration, and grievance adjustments)*.

It is possible that some of you will be voting in an employee representation election as a result of the request for an election having been filed. While NO DETERMINATION HAS BEEN MADE AT THIS TIME, in the event an election is held, the NATIONAL LABOR RELATIONS BOARD wants all eligible voters to be familiar with their rights under the law IF it holds an election.

The Board applies rules that are intended to keep its elections fair and honest and that result in a free choice. If agents of either unions or employers act in such a way as to interfere with your right to a free election, the election can be set aside by the Board. Where appropriate the Board provides other remedies, such as reinstatement for employees fired for exercising their rights, including backpay from the party responsible for their discharge.

NOTE:

The following are examples of conduct that interfere with the rights of employees and may result in the setting aside of the election.

- Threatening loss of jobs or benefits by an employer or a union
- Promising or granting promotions, pay raises, or other benefits to influence an employee's vote by a party capable of carrying out such promises
- An employer firing employees to discourage or encourage union activity or a union causing them to be fired to encourage union activity
- Making campaign speeches to assembled groups of employees on company time within the 24-hour period before the election
- Incitement by either an employer or a union of racial or religious prejudice by inflammatory appeals
- Threatening physical force or violence to employees by a union or an employer to influence their votes

Please be assured that IF AN ELECTION IS HELD every effort will be made to protect your right to a free choice under the law. Improper conduct will not be permitted. All parties are expected to cooperate fully with this Agency in maintaining basic principles of a fair election as required by law. The National Labor Relations Board, as an agency of the United States Government, does not endorse any choice in the election.

NATIONAL LABOR RELATIONS BOARD
an agency of the
UNITED STATES GOVERNMENT

THIS IS AN OFFICIAL GOVERNMENT NOTICE AND MUST NOT BE DEFACED BY ANYONE

FORM NLRB-666 (5-90)   ☆ U.S. Government Printing Office: 1990-270-693/10127

If none of the available choices receives a majority of the votes, a runoff election must be conducted between the two top choices. Unless the majority votes no union, the union that receives a majority of the votes in the initial or the runoff election is the one certified by the NLRB as the bargaining agent for a period of at least a year, or for the duration of the labor agreement. Once the union is certified, the employer is obligated to begin negotiations leading toward a labor agreement.

An important statistic in labor relations is the win/loss record of unions in certification elections. This statistic is often regarded as an indication of the general vitality of the union movement. As Figure 17–2 shows, from 1975 through 1993 unions consistently lost more than 50 percent of elections held by the NLRB. This contrasts sharply with the union win rate of 74.5 percent in 1950 and 60.2 percent in 1965. The conclusion can be drawn from Figure 17–2 that unions have lost much of their ability to unionize employers.[26]

Impact of Unionization on HRM

The unionization of employees can affect HRM in several ways. Perhaps most significant is the effect it can have on the prerogatives exercised by management

FIGURE 17-2 *NLRB Elections, Selected Years*

YEAR	ELECTIONS HELD	UNIONS WON	UNION PERCENTAGE WINS
1950	5,619	4,186	74.5
1955	4,215	2,849	67.6
1965	7,775	4,880	60.2
1975	8,577	4,134	48.2
1985	4,614	1,956	42.4
1986	4,520	1,951	43.2
1987	4,069	1,788	43.9
1988	4,153	1,921	46.3
1989	4,413	2,059	46.7
1990	4,210	1,965	46.7
1991	3,752	1,663	44.3
1992*	3,599	1,673	46.5
1993*	3,586	1,706	47.6

*Data for 1992 and 1993 are preliminary.

Source: Annual Reports of the National Labor Relations Board, U.S. Government Printing Office, Washington, D.C.

in making decisions about employees. Furthermore, unionization restricts the freedom of management to formulate HR policy unilaterally and can challenge the authority of supervisors.

Challenges to Management Prerogatives

Management prerogatives
Decisions regarding organizational operations over which management claims exclusive rights

Unions typically attempt to achieve greater participation in management decisions that affect their members. Specifically, these decisions may involve such issues as the subcontracting of work, productivity standards, and job content. Employers quite naturally seek to claim many of these decisions as their exclusive **management prerogatives**—decisions over which management claims exclusive rights. However, these prerogatives are subject to challenge and erosion by the union. They may be challenged at the bargaining table, through the grievance procedure, and through strikes.

Bilateral Formulation of HR Policies

Some HR policies, such as those covering wages, work hours, work rules, and benefits, must be consistent with the terms of the labor agreement. When formulating these policies, management should consult with the union to gain the union's acceptance of them as well as its cooperation in administering them. Because unions are on the lookout for inconsistencies in the treatment of employees, a more centralized coordination in the enforcement of HR policies may be required. Such coordination provides a greater role for the HR staff.

Possible Dilution of Supervisory Authority

The focal point of the union's impact is at the operating level, where supervisors administer the terms of the labor agreement. These terms can determine what corrective action is to be taken in directing and in disciplining employees. When disciplining employees, supervisors must be certain they can demonstrate *just cause* (see Chapter 16) for their actions, because these actions can be challenged by the union and the supervisor called as defendant during a grievance hearing. If the challenge is upheld, the supervisor's effectiveness in coping with subsequent disciplinary problems may be impaired.

four
objective

Structures, Functions, and Leadership of Labor Unions

Craft unions
Unions that represent skilled craft workers

Industrial unions
Unions that represent all workers—skilled, semiskilled, unskilled—employed along industry lines

Unions that represent skilled craft workers, such as carpenters or masons, are called **craft unions.** Craft unions include the International Association of Iron Workers, the United Brotherhood of Carpenters, and the United Association of Plumbers and Pipefitters. Unions that represent unskilled and semiskilled workers employed along industry lines are known as **industrial unions**. The American Union of Postal Workers is an industrial union, as are the United Auto Workers; the United Steelworkers; the American Federation of State, County, and Municipal Employees; and the Office and Professional Employees International Union. While this distinction still exists, technological changes and

Teachers are often supported as a group by associations rather than unions.

competition among unions for members have helped to reduce it. Today skilled and unskilled workers, white-collar and blue-collar workers, and professional groups are being represented by both types of union.

Besides unions, there are also **employee associations** representing various groups of professional and white-collar employees. Examples of employee associations include the National Education Association, the Michigan State Employees Association, the American Nurses' Association, and the Air Line Pilots Association. In competing with unions, these associations, for all purposes, may function as unions and become just as aggressive as unions in representing members.

Regardless of their type, labor organizations are diverse organizations, each with its own method of governance and objectives. Furthermore, they have their own structures that serve to bind them together. For example, when describing labor organizations, most researchers divide them into three levels: (1) the American Federation of Labor and Congress of Industrial Organizations (AFL-CIO), (2) national unions, and (3) local unions belonging to a parent national union. Each level has its own purpose for existence as well as its own operating policies and procedures.

Employee associations

Labor organizations that represent various groups of professional and white-collar employees in labor-management relations

Structure and Functions of the AFL-CIO

In 1955 the American Federation of Labor—composed largely of craft unions—and the Congress of Industrial Organizations—made up mainly of industrial unions—merged to form the AFL-CIO. The AFL-CIO is a federation of eighty-nine autonomous national and international unions. Because the interests and organizing activities of these autonomous unions in the AFL-CIO do not always coincide, a chief advantage of belonging to the AFL-CIO is a provision that affords protection to member unions against "raiding" by other unions within the federation. A violation of this no-raiding provision can lead to expulsion from the federation.

In effect, the AFL-CIO is the House of Labor that serves to present a united front on behalf of organized labor. Most major unions belong to this federation. The AFL-CIO claims a membership of almost 14 million members, or about 75 percent of all union members.[27] As Figure 17–3 shows, the AFL-CIO is composed of different trades and industrial departments that reflect the diversity of labor's objectives. Specifically, the AFL-CIO serves its members by:

1. Lobbying before legislative bodies on subjects of interest to labor
2. Coordinating organizing efforts among its affiliated unions
3. Publicizing the concerns and benefits of unionization to the public
4. Resolving disputes between different unions as they occur

Besides offering these services, the AFL-CIO maintains an interest in international trade and domestic economic issues as well as foreign policy matters. On the staff of the AFL-CIO are researchers, economists, and quality-of-work-life experts.

The federation is governed by its constitution and various policies set at its biennial conventions. National unions send a number of delegates to the convention according to the size of the unions. Thus larger unions have greater voting power on the resolutions adopted at the convention. Between conventions, the AFL-CIO is run by its executive council. The affiliated unions pay per capita dues (currently 42 cents per member per month) to support federation activities.

Structure and Functions of National Unions

The center of power in the labor movement resides with national and international unions. It is these organizations that set the broad guidelines for governing union members and for formulating collective bargaining goals in dealing with management. The only major difference between a national and an international union is that the international union organizes workers and charters local unions in foreign countries. For example, the United Auto Workers is an international union with locals in Canada.

A national union, through its constitution, establishes the rules and conditions under which the local unions may be chartered. Most national unions have regulations governing dues, initiation fees, and the internal administration of the locals. National unions also may require that certain standard provisions be included in labor agreements with employers. Standard contract terms covering safety or grievance procedures and seniority rights are examples. In return for these controls, they provide professional and financial assistance during organizing drives and strikes and help in the negotiation and administration of labor agreements. Other services provided by national unions include (1) training of union leaders, (2) legal assistance, (3) leadership in political activity, (4) educational and public relations programs, and (5) discipline of union members.

Like the AFL-CIO, national unions hold conventions to pass resolutions, amend their constitutions, and elect officers. This last function is very important to a national union because its president often exerts a large influence—if not control—over the union's policies and direction. Furthermore, many presidents—such as George Becker (United Steelworkers), Gerald McEntee (American Federation of State, County, and Municipal Employees), and Owen Bieber (United Auto Workers)—are highly visible individuals who represent the labor

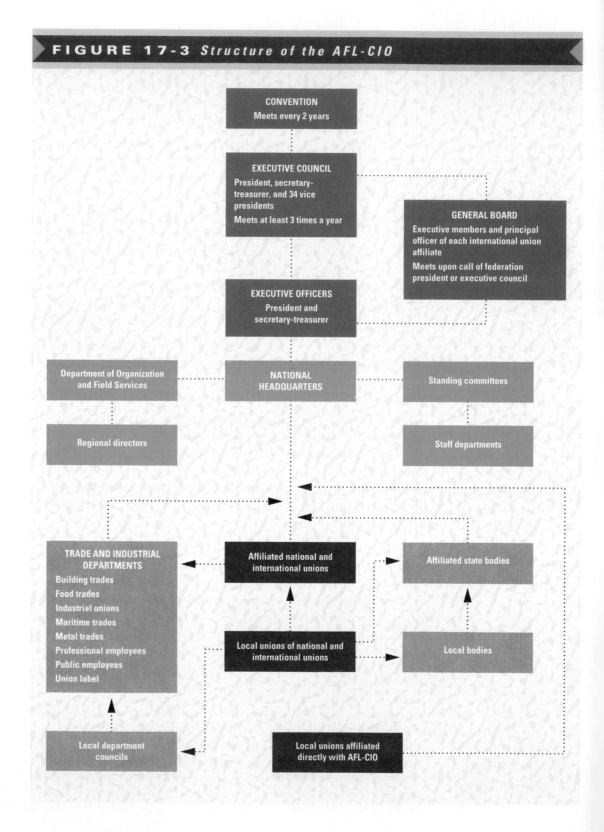

FIGURE 17-3 *Structure of the AFL-CIO*

FIGURE 17-4 *Typical Organization of a National Union*

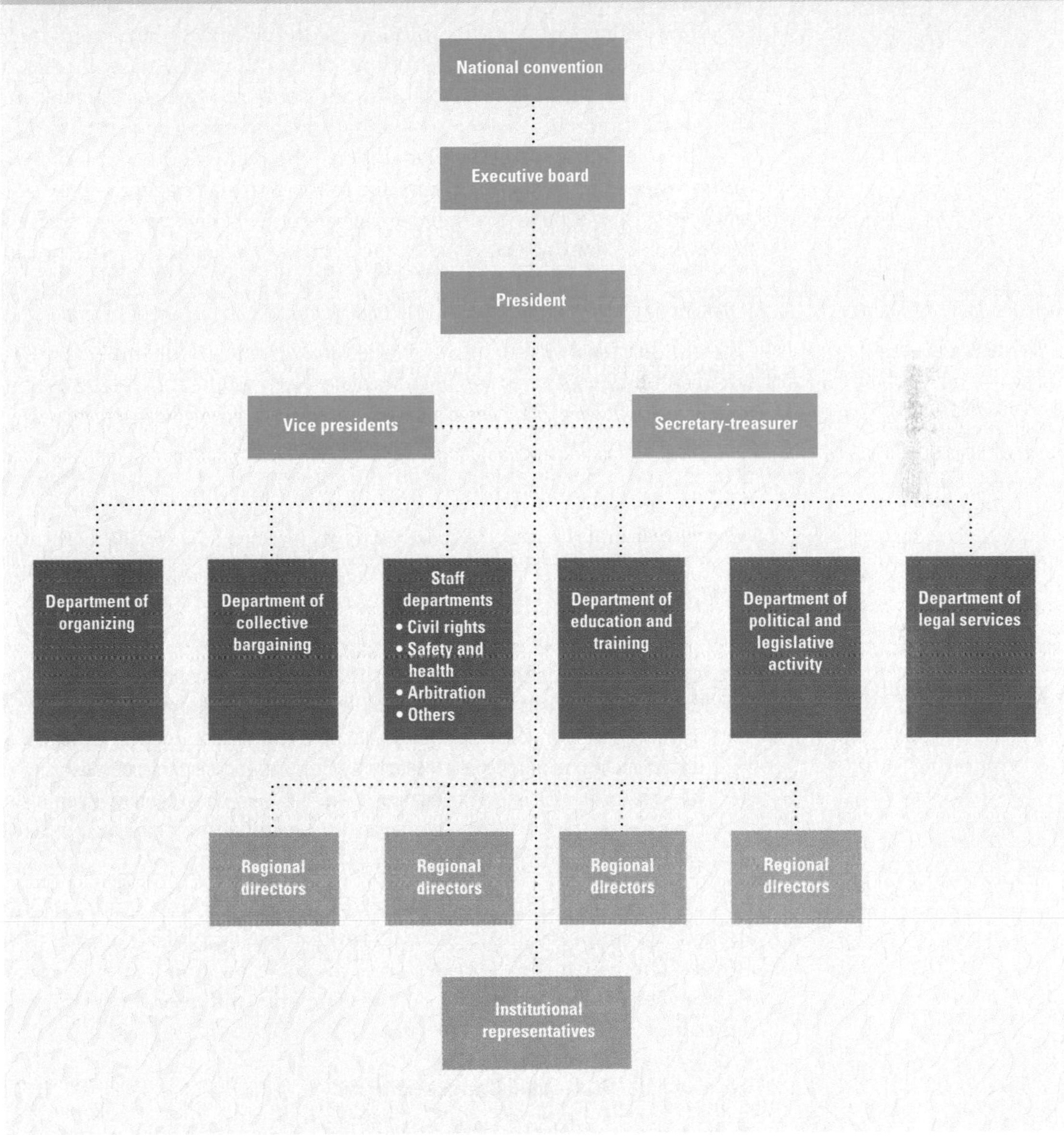

movement to the public. In addition, the president of a national union is responsible for the overall administration of the union and of the different union departments, as shown in Figure 17–4.

Structure and Functions of Local Unions

The officers of a local union are usually responsible for negotiating the local labor agreement and for investigating and processing member grievances. Most important, they assist in preventing the members of the local union from being treated by their employers in ways that run counter to management-established HR policies.[28]

The officers of a local union typically include a president, vice president, secretary-treasurer, business representative, and various committee chairpersons. Depending on the size of the union, one or more of these officers, in addition to the business representative, may be paid by the union to serve on a full-time basis. The remaining officers are members who have regular jobs and who serve the union without pay except perhaps for token gratuities and expense allowances. In many locals, the business representative is the dominant power. In some locals, however, the dominant power is the secretary-treasurer or the president.

Role of the Union Steward

Union steward

Employee who as a nonpaid union official represents the interests of members in their relations with management

The **union steward** represents the interests of union members in their relations with their immediate supervisors and other members of management. Stewards are normally elected by union members within their department and serve without union pay. Since stewards are full-time employees of the organization, they often spend considerable time after working hours investigating and handling member problems. When stewards represent members during grievance meetings on organizational time, their lost earnings are paid by the local union.

In describing the role of a union steward, Al Nash sees a person-in-the-middle, caught between conflicting interests and groups. Nash notes:

> The steward's role as grievance handler and maid-of-all-work for the union thrusts him/her into a number of roles. He/she represents the workers in the internal and external government of the union and in negotiating with management. He/she is an agent of the union leadership within the workplace and, to some extent, a quasi-agent of management in enforcing the collective bargaining agreement and company rules. His/her role-set, then, consists of members of his/her own constituency, some of whom may be non-union members, members of immediate management, and higher union officials with whom he/she must deal.[29]

It is evident from the preceding definition that if stewards perform their tasks effectively, they serve as important links between union members and their employer. Their attitudes and actions can have an important bearing on union-management cooperation and on the efficiency and morale of the employees they represent.[30]

Role of the Business Representative

Business representative

Normally a paid labor official responsible for negotiating and administering the labor agreement and working to resolve union members' problems

Negotiating and administering the labor agreement and working to resolve problems arising in connection with it are major responsibilities of the **business representative.** In performing these duties, business representatives must be all things to all persons within their unions. They frequently are required to assume the role of counselor in helping union members with both personal and job-related problems. They are also expected to dispose satisfactorily of the members' grievances that cannot be settled by the union stewards. Administering the daily affairs of the local union is another significant part of the business representative's job.

Union Leadership Approaches and Philosophies

To evaluate the role of union leaders accurately, one must understand the nature of their backgrounds and ambitions and recognize the political nature of the offices they occupy. The leaders of many national unions have been able to develop political machines that enable them to defeat opposition and to perpetuate themselves in office.[31] Tenure for the leaders of a local union, however, is less secure. In the local union, officers, by federal law, must run for reelection at least every third year. If they are to remain in office, they must be able to convince a majority of the members that they are serving them effectively.

Although it is true that union leaders occupy positions of power within their organizations, rank-and-file members can and often do exercise a very strong influence over these leaders, particularly with respect to the negotiation and administration of the labor agreement. It is important for managers to understand that union officials are elected to office and, like any political officials, must be responsive to the views of their constituency. The union leader who ignores the demands of union members may risk (1) being voted out of office, (2) having members vote the union out as their bargaining agent, (3) having members refuse to ratify the union agreement, or (4) having members engage in wildcat strikes or work stoppages.

Business unionism
Term applied to the goals of U.S. labor organizations, which collectively bargain for improvements in wages, hours, job security, and working conditions

To be effective leaders, labor officials must also pay constant attention to the general goals and philosophies of the labor movement. **Business unionism** is the general label given to the goals of American labor organizations: increased pay and benefits, job security, and improved working conditions. Furthermore, union leaders also know that unions must address the broader social, economic, and legislative issues of concern to members. For example, the United Auto Workers continually lobbies Congress for protective legislation affecting the auto industry. The American Federation of State, County, and Municipal Employees, the International Ladies' Garment Workers' Union, and the Independent Federation of Flight Attendants representing flight attendants at TWA have been active supporters of women's issues at both the state and national levels.

Finally, as part of America's adjustment to increased global competition, union leaders are forced to concentrate on more intangible quality-of-work-life issues while attempting to make their employing industries more competitive. Those traits associated with transformational leaders in business are increasingly important for union leaders. For example, Irving Bluestone of the United Auto Workers and Robert Guadiana of the United Steelworkers exhibit transformational leadership traits. Both union leaders have visions of greater labor-management cooperation. Working closely with managers, they have implemented cooperative programs in organizations where they represent employees.

Rank-and-file members have the power to influence the decisions of union leaders.

Labor Relations in the Public Sector

Collective bargaining among federal, state, and local government employees has been an area of growth for the union movement since the early 1960s.[32] In 1993 slightly over 7 million public workers belonged to unions or employee associations. They constituted about 37 percent of government employees. The latest union membership figures show that the nation's largest labor organization is the National Education Association with 2 million members.[33] As unions and employee associations of teachers, police, firefighters, and state employees have grown in size and political power, they have demanded the same rights to bargain and strike that private-sector employees have.

While public- and private-sector collective bargaining have many features in common, a number of factors differentiate the two sectors. In this section, we will highlight several of the major differences between public-sector and private-sector industrial relations and discuss how these differences affect HRM. Three areas will be explored: (1) legislation governing collective bargaining in the public sector, (2) the political nature of the labor-management relationship, and (3) public-sector strikes.

Public-Sector Legislation

Public-sector legislation affecting HRM includes executive orders, the Civil Service Reform Act of 1978, and state laws.

Executive Orders

Regulations governing labor relations with federal employees have been modeled after those developed for the private sector. However, the rights granted to labor organizations under these regulations are fewer than those accorded by the Taft-Hartley Act.

Issued in 1962 by President Kennedy, Executive Order 10988 contained provisions similar to those in Section 7 of the Taft-Hartley Act. These provisions state that federal employees have the right freely and without fear of penalty or reprisal to form, join, or assist any labor organization or to refrain from such activity.[34] Included in this executive order are provisions for establishing bargaining units within government agencies. Labor organizations also are permitted to bargain collectively with the government in reaching a labor agreement for members.

Issued in 1971 by President Nixon, Executive Order 11491 defined the bargaining rights of federal employees more precisely and provided procedures for safeguarding these rights. This executive order created the Federal Labor Relations Council to hear appeals relating to unfair practices and bargaining issues. A body called the Federal Service Impasses Panel also was established to deal with collective bargaining deadlocks.

The Civil Service Reform Act of 1978

The Civil Service Reform Act of 1978 made the regulation of labor relations in the federal government even more consistent with that contained in the Taft-Hartley Act for the private sector. The Federal Labor Relations Authority

(FLRA), an agency similar to the NLRB, was created to decide on unfair practices and representation cases and to enforce the provisions of the act. An office of general counsel, similar to that provided by the Taft-Hartley Act, also was created to investigate and decide which unfair labor practices and complaints are to be prosecuted.[35]

Even with the Civil Service Reform Act, labor organizations representing federal employees do not have rights equal to those provided by the Taft-Hartley Act. Most important, they lack the legal right to strike to enforce their bargaining demands. Furthermore, management rights in the federal government are accorded greater protection than those of employers in the private sector. Rules, procedures, and area restrictions that govern bargaining further reduce the influence that labor organizations can exercise over employment conditions in federal agencies.[36]

State Legislation

One distinctive characteristic of public-sector collective bargaining at the state level is the great diversity among the various state laws. This occurs because the regulation of public-sector labor-management relations falls within the separate jurisdiction of each state. For example, some states, like Arizona, Utah, and Mississippi, have no collective bargaining laws; other states, like Florida, Hawaii, and New York, have comprehensive laws granting collective bargaining rights to all public employees. Between these extremes are state laws granting collective bargaining rights only to specific employee groups such as teachers and the uniformed services (police and fire). Comprehensive state laws provide for an administrative agency analogous to the NLRB and the Federal Labor Relations Authority.[37] A frequent state restriction concerns the right to negotiate labor agreements. Public employees may have only the right to "meet and confer" with representatives of management for the purpose of developing an agreement, often called "a memorandum of understanding."

Political Nature of the Labor-Management Relationship

Government employees are not able to negotiate with their employers on the same basis as their counterparts in private organizations. It is doubtful that they will ever be able to do so because of inherent differences between the public and private sectors.

One of the significant differences is that labor relations in the private sector has an economic foundation, whereas in government its foundation is political. Since private employers must stay in business in order to sell their goods or services, their employees are not likely to make demands that could bankrupt them. A strike in the private sector is a test of the employer's economic staying power, and usually the employer's customers have alternative sources of supply. Governments, on the other hand, must stay in business because alternative services are usually not available. Nevertheless, unions representing government employees are not reluctant to press for financial gains that will be paid for by the public.

Another difference between the labor-management relationship in the public and private sectors is the source of management authority. In a private organization the authority flows downward from the board of directors and ultimately from the shareholders. In the public sector, however, authority flows upward from the public at large to their elected representatives and to the appointed or elected managers. Therefore public employees can exert influence not only as union members but also as pressure groups and voting citizens.[38]

Strikes in the Public Sector

Strikes by government employees create a problem for lawmakers and for the general public. Because the services that government employees provide are often considered essential to the well-being of the public, public policy is opposed to such strikes. Thus most state legislatures have not granted public employees the right to strike. In those states where striking is permitted, the right is limited to specific groups of employees—normally nonuniformed employees—and the strike cannot endanger the public's health, safety, or welfare. Public-employee unions contend, however, that by denying them the same right to strike as employees in the private sector, their power during collective bargaining is greatly reduced.

Despite the absence of any legal right to do so, public employees do strike. Teachers, sanitation employees, police, transit employees, firefighters, and postal employees have all engaged in strike action. Despite stringent potential strike penalties, public employees have often struck without penalty. To avoid a potentially critical situation, various arbitration methods are used for resolving collective bargaining deadlocks in the public sector. One is **compulsory binding arbitration** for employees such as police officers, firefighters, and others in jobs where strikes cannot be tolerated. Another method is **final-offer arbitration,** under which the arbitrator must select one or the other of the final offers submitted by the disputing parties. With this method, the arbitrator's award is more likely to go to the party whose final bargaining offer has moved the closest toward a reasonable settlement.

Compulsory binding arbitration
Binding method of resolving collective bargaining deadlocks by a neutral third party

Final-offer arbitration
Method of resolving collective bargaining deadlocks whereby the arbitrator has no power to compromise but must select one or another of the final offers submitted by the two parties

objective

Contemporary Challenges to Labor Organizations

Among the changes that pose challenges to labor organizations today are foreign competition and technological advances, a decline in labor's public image, the decrease of union membership, and employers' focus on maintaining nonunion status.

Foreign Competition and Technological Change

The importation of steel, consumer electronics, automobiles, clothing, textiles, and shoes from foreign countries creates a loss of jobs in the United States for workers who produce these products.[39] Furthermore, foreign subsidiaries of American corporations such as Rockwell, Westinghouse, and Xerox have been accused by labor unions of exporting the jobs of American workers. As a result, unions are demanding more government protection against imports. Such protection has spurred lively congressional debate between those who argue that protective trade barriers create higher prices for American consumers and those who seek to protect American jobs from low-cost overseas producers. U.S. unions were highly opposed to passage of the North American Free Trade Agreement (NAFTA), claiming American jobs would be lost to low-wage employers in Mexico.[40]

Coupled with the threat of foreign competition is the challenge to labor brought about by rapid technological advances.[41] Improvements in computer technology and highly automated operating systems have lowered the demand for certain types of employees. Decline in membership in the auto, steel, rubber, and transportation unions illustrates this fact. Technological advances have also diminished the effectiveness of strikes because highly automated organizations are capable of maintaining satisfactory levels of operation with minimum staffing levels during work stoppages.

Decline in Public Image of Labor

Organized labor has suffered a decline in its public image.[42] For example, critics of labor cite wage increases gained by labor unions as a factor that not only contributes to inflation but also helps to drive American products out of the foreign and domestic markets. Union leaders are viewed as overly powerful individuals who frequently act in their own self-interest, appear to be contemptuous of the public, are often dishonest and unethical, and are out of touch with the rank-and-file membership. Moreover, public resentment of strikes by public-employee unions has affected the image of all labor unions.

Well aware of its negative public image, the labor movement has programs under way that are designed to communicate to the American public, and especially to a new generation of workers, the benefits and relevance of organized labor. The AFL-CIO created the Labor Institute for Public Affairs charged with telling "labor's story" to Congress and the public. The labor movement's "Union Yes" advertisements on prime-time television, billboards, and bumper stickers seek to present a positive, upbeat view of unions. The ultimate goal of the campaign is to create a favorable image of unions that will help organizing efforts. At the local level, unions support charitable programs and contribute financially to community service projects. For example, Labor's Community Services Agency, in Phoenix, Arizona, has contributed to the letter carriers' annual food drive; donated services to the housing rehabilitation program for those earning low wages; and volunteered union labor to build family emergency shelters, day-care centers, and homeless housing projects throughout the Phoenix area.

Decrease in Union Membership

A major challenge confronting organized labor is to halt the decline in union membership. The magnitude of the problem is shown in Figure 17–5, which illustrates how union membership has declined in total numbers and as a percentage of the total civilian labor force.[43] The combination of a growing labor force and decreasing union membership dropped organized labor's share of the civilian workforce to a new modern-era low of 15.8 percent in 1993. In the private sector, union membership accounted for approximately 12 percent of all those employed, or about 10 million workers. The loss of union jobs reflects, in part, the decline in U.S. manufacturing jobs, coupled with the failure of unions to draw membership from among the white-collar ranks, where the labor force is growing more rapidly.

FIGURE 17-5 *Union Membership, Selected Years*

YEAR	UNION MEMBERSHIP (IN THOUSANDS)	MEMBERSHIP AS A PERCENTAGE OF CIVILIAN LABOR FORCE
1970	21,248	25.7
1972	21,657	24.9
1974	22,809	24.8
1976	22,662	23.6
1978	22,757	22.3
1980	22,366	20.9
1982	19,763	19.3
1984	17,340	18.8
1985	16,996	18.0
1986	16,975	17.5
1987	16,913	17.0
1988	17,002	16.8
1989	16,900	16.4
1990	16,740	16.1
1991	16,568	16.1
1992	16,390	15.8
1993	16,598	15.8

Source: Courtney D. Gifford, *Directory of U.S. Labor Organizations, 1994-95 Edition.* Copyright 1994.

Efforts to Unionize White-Collar Employees

In past years, white-collar employees tended to identify themselves with owners or managers as a group enjoying certain privileges (e.g., not having to punch a time clock) and socioeconomic status that blue-collar workers did not possess. Improvements in working conditions, for which union members had to make sacrifices, generally were extended to the white-collar group without any need for collective action on their part. The high turnover rate of employees in clerical jobs also increased the difficulty of organizing them. For these reasons, and because union drives to organize white-collar employees were not attuned psychologically to their needs and thinking, white-collar employees have been slow to unionize. In recent years, however, growth in the size of private organizations has tended to depersonalize the work of white-collar groups and to isolate them from management. The lack of job security during layoffs, together with growing difficulties in attempting to resolve grievances, has helped to push white-collar workers toward unionization.

The "Union Yes" campaign strives to establish a positive view of unions.

In response to these changes, unions are stepping up their efforts to organize white-collar workers. Many unions are recruiting employees of small businesses and employees in the so-called pink-collar ghetto, a term describing low-paying clerical and sales positions traditionally held by women. Unions are also capitalizing on new health and safety issues in white-collar jobs, such as the effects of working at video display terminals or working with potentially hazardous substances. Unions active in recruiting white-collar employees include the Service Employees International Union; the International Brotherhood of Teamsters; 9 to 5, the National Association of Working Women; the Office and Professional Employees International Union; the Insurance Workers International Union; the United Auto Workers; and the United Steelworkers of America.

Trend toward Maintaining Nonunion Status

A significant trend in U.S. labor relations during the 1980s and into the 1990s is the growth in union avoidance programs. Managers in all types of organizations are vocal in their desire to maintain a union-free environment. To support this goal, employers are providing wages, benefits, and services designed to make unionism unattractive to employees. In addition, a participative management style, profit-sharing plans, and alternative dispute-resolution procedures are offered to counteract the long-established union goals of improved wages and working conditions. Highlights in HRM 3 lists the key strategies identified by HR specialists as means of avoiding unionization. It is important to recognize that these strategies react to the conditions cited at the beginning of the chapter as the main reasons why workers unionize. Since these conditions are under the direct control of management, they can be changed to help discourage or prevent unionism.

Organizations may even go so far as to provoke strikes in order to hire replacement workers and permanently lay off striking union members. The

HIGHLIGHTS IN HRM

3   UNION AVOIDANCE STRATEGIES

highlights

- Offer competitive wages and benefits based on labor market comparisons and salary and benefit surveys.
- Train supervisors in progressive human relations skills, including employee motivation, job design, and employment law.
- Institute formal procedures to resolve employee complaints and grievances; these may include peer-review committees, step-review complaint systems, or open-door policies.
- Involve employees in work decisions affecting job performance or the quality or quantity of the product or service provided.
- Give attention to employee growth and development needs; recognize that the workforce is growing older, more female, more militant, better educated, less patient, and more demanding.
- Draft HR policies that reflect legal safeguards and that are fair and equitable in employment conditions such as discipline, promotions, training, and layoffs.

president of the North Carolina AFL-CIO notes, "Strikes are now a weapon of management. In a lot of cases, management wants you to go out on strike so they can bust the strike and bust the union."[44] In recent years unionized employees at Holsum Bakery and Phelps Dodge Corporation have lost their jobs after lengthy bitter strikes. It seems clear that a hard-line management approach to employee unionization contributes to the defeat of union organizing efforts.

SUMMARY

The Railway Labor Act (1926) affords collective bargaining rights to workers employed in the railway and airline industries. The Norris-LaGuardia Act (1932) imposes limitations on the granting of injunctions in labor-management disputes. Most private employees are granted representation rights through the Wagner Act (1935), which has helped to protect and encourage union organizing and bargaining activities. The passage of the Taft-Hartley Act (1947) and the Landrum-Griffin Act (1959) has served to establish certain controls over the internal affairs of unions and their relations with employers.

Studies show that workers unionize for different economic, psychological, and social reasons. While some employees may join unions because they are required to do so, most belong to unions because they are convinced that unions help them to improve their wages, benefits, and various working conditions. Employee unionization is largely caused by dissatisfaction with managerial practices and procedures.

A formal union organizing campaign will be used to solicit employee support for the union. Once employees demonstrate their desire to unionize through signing authorization cards, the union will petition the NLRB for a secret-ballot election. If 51 percent of those voting in the election vote for the union, the NLRB will certify the union as the bargaining representative for all employees in the bargaining unit. If employee support for the union is very high, management may avoid the election and recognize the union on the basis of authorization cards.

The U.S. labor movement is composed of three basic units: the AFL-CIO, a federation to which national and international unions can elect to belong; national unions; and local unions chartered by the different national labor organizations. National unions and their locals perform various functions for members which include negotiating the contract, handling grievances, training union officials, offering social functions, and providing legal and political activity.

Legislation governing labor relations in the public and private sectors is vastly different. Public employees are largely denied the right to strike and public unions may be denied, by law, the right to bargain over specific topics such as grievance procedures or certain economic terms of employment. Another difference is that collective bargaining in the private sector has an economic base, whereas in government the base is political. Additionally, in the private sector, authority flows downward; in the public sector, authority flows upward.

Challenges facing union leaders today include a declining membership caused by technological advancements and increased domestic and global competition. The general public has come to view unions in a less favorable light, which affects their efforts to recruit new members. Labor organizations experience less success in organizing when employers establish progressive HR policies or when they take a hard-line approach toward the unionization of their employees.

KEY TERMS

authorization card	final-offer arbitration
bargaining unit	industrial unions
business representative	labor relations process
business unionism	management prerogatives
compulsory binding arbitration	stipulation election
consent election	unfair labor practices (ULPs)
craft unions	union shop
employee associations	union steward

> ### ▶ DISCUSSION QUESTIONS ◀

1. How is the management of an organization's human resources likely to be affected by the unionization of its employees?
2. Contrast the arguments concerning union membership that are likely to be presented by a union with those presented by an employer.
3. What are the functions of the national union and of the local union?
4. Under the provisions of the Taft-Hartley Act, which unfair labor practices apply to both unions and employers?
5. What arguments would public-sector managers put forth in opposition to unionization?
6. What are some of the actions being taken by unions to cope with the contemporary challenges they face?
7. Why have attitudes toward organized labor, on the part of certain segments of our society, become less favorable than they were in the past?

CASE STUDY: The Unfair Labor Practice Charge against Apollo Corporation

Bob Thomas was discharged after nineteen years as a plant maintenance engineer with Apollo Corporation. During that time he had received average, and sometimes below-average, annual performance appraisals. Thomas was known as something of a complainer and troublemaker, and he was highly critical of management. Prior to his termination, his attendance record for the previous five years had been very poor. However, Apollo Corporation had never enforced its attendance policy, and Thomas had never been disciplined for his attendance problems. In fact, until recently, Apollo management had been rather laid-back in its dealings with employees.

Apollo Corporation produces general component parts for the communications industry—an industry beset since 1989 by intense competitive pressures. To meet this competitive challenge, Jean Lipski, HR director, held a series of meetings with managers in which she instructed them to tighten up their supervisory relationship with employees. They were told to enforce HR policies strictly and to begin disciplinary action against employees not conforming to company policy. These changes did not sit well with employees, particularly Bob Thomas. Upon hearing of the new management approach, Thomas became irate and announced, "They can't get away with this. I wrote the book around here." Secretly, Thomas believed his past conduct was catching up with him, and he became concerned about protecting his job.

One night after work, Thomas called a union organizer of the Brotherhood of Machine Engineers and asked that a union drive begin at Apollo. Within a week employees began handing out flyers announcing a union meeting. When Lipski heard of the organizing campaign and Thomas's leadership in it, she decided to terminate his employment. Thomas's termination paper read: "Discharged for poor work performance and unsatisfactory attendance." Thomas was called into Lipski's office and told of the discharge. After leaving her office, Thomas called the union organizer, and they both went to the regional office of the NLRB to file an unfair labor practice charge on Thomas's behalf. The ULP alleged that he was fired for his support of the union and the organizing drive.

Questions

1. What, if any, violation of the law did the Apollo Corporation commit?
2. What arguments will Jean Lipski and Bob Thomas use to support their cases?

NOTES AND REFERENCES

1. *Labor-Management Relations Act*, Public Law 101, 80th Congress, 1947.
2. *Fifty-eighth Annual Report of the National Labor Relations Board—1993* (Washington, D.C.: Government Printing Office, 1994), 6.
3. *Labor-Management Relations Act*, Section 10(c), 1947, as amended.
4. Matthew M. Franckiewicz, "How To Win NLRB Cases: Tips from a Former Insider," *Labor Law Journal* 44, no. 1 (January 1991): 40–48.
5. Robert A. Berun, "Mediation from A to Z," *Dispute Resolution Journal* 49, no. 1 (March 1994): 31. See also Steven Briggs and Daniel J. Koys, "What Makes Labor Mediators Effective?" *Labor Law Journal* 40, no. 8 (August 1989): 517–20.
6. Telephone interview with Larry Babcock, director of operations support, Federal Mediation and Conciliation Service, Washington, D.C., December 1, 1993.
7. For an expanded model of the labor relations process, see John Dunlop, *Industrial Relations Systems* (New York: Henry Holt, 1958), Chapter 1. This book is a classic in the labor relations field. Also, those interested in labor relations may wish to explore in greater detail the historical developments of the U.S. labor movement. Much can be learned about the current operations of labor organizations and the philosophies of labor officials from labor's historical context. A brief but comprehensive history of labor unions can be found in *A Brief History of the American Labor Movement*, U.S. Department of Labor, Bureau of Labor Statistics, Bulletin 1000.
8. Masoud Hemmasi and Lee A. Graf, "Determinants of Faculty Voting Behavior in Union Representation Elections: A Multivariate Model," *Journal of Management* 19, no. 1 (Spring 1993): 13–32.
9. John A. Fossum, *Labor Relations: Development, Structure, Process*, 6th ed. (Homewood, Ill.: Irwin, 1995): 3.
10. Stephenie Overman, "Nissan Sees Union's Loss as Management Style's Win," *Resource* 8, no. 10 (September 1989): 1.
11. Hugh D. Hindman and Charles G. Smith, "Correlates of Union Membership and Joining Intentions in a Unit of Federal Employees," *Journal of Labor Research* 14, no. 4 (Fall 1993): 441.
12. Lisa A. Schur and Douglas L. Kruse, "Gender Differences in Attitudes toward Unions," *Industrial and Labor Relations Review* 46, no. 1 (October 1992): 89–102.
13. *Employment and Earnings* (Washington, D.C.: U.S. Department of Labor, Bureau of Labor Statistics, January 1994), Table 57.
14. Ronnie Silverblatt and Robert J. Amann, "Race, Ethnicity, Union Attitudes, and Voting Predilections," *Industrial Relations* 30, no. 2 (Spring 1991): 271–85.
15. Stephen Hill, "The Attitudes of Union and Nonunion Male Workers toward Union Representation," *Industrial and Labor Relations Review* 38, no. 2 (January 1985): 23–31.
16. For a discussion of union organizers, see Thomas F. Reed, "Profiles of Union Organizers from Manufacturing and Service Unions," *Journal of Labor Research* 11, no. 1 (Winter 1990): 73–80.
17. Robert L. Sauer and Keith E. Voelker, *Labor Relations: Structure and Process*, 2d ed. (New York: Macmillan Publishing, 1993): 171.

18. Thomas F. Reed, "Securing a Union Contract: Impact of the Union Organizer," *Industrial Relations* 32, no. 2 (Spring 1993): 188–203.

19. Richard B. Peterson, Thomas W. Lee, and Barbara Finnegan, "Strategies and Tactics in Union Organizing Campaigns," *Industrial Relations* 31, no. 2 (Spring 1992): 370–81.

20. Charles L. Hughes, *Making Unions Unnecessary*, 2d ed. (New York: Executive Enterprise Publications Co., 1989).

21. *Fifty-eighth Annual Report of the National Labor Relations Board*, 6.

22. Cheryl L. Maranto and Jack Fiorito, "The Effect of Union Characteristics on the Outcome of the NLRB Certification Elections," *Industrial and Labor Relations Review* 40, no. 2 (January 1987): 225–40.

23. For an expanded discussion of the bargaining unit, see Benjamin J. Taylor and Fred Witney, *Labor Relations Law*, 6th ed. (Englewood Cliffs, N.J.: Prentice-Hall, 1992).

24. Clyde Scott and Nicholas A. Beadles, "Unit Placement Decisions in Acute Care Hospitals," *Labor Law Journal* 44, no. 3 (March 1993): 143–52.

25. Michael D. Esposito, "How Much Is Too Much? Primer for Testing the Limits of Lawful Assistance to a Union Organizing Effort," *Labor Law Journal* 43, no. 3 (March 1992): 172–76. If over 50 percent of the employees have signed authorization cards, the union can ask the employer for recognition. A union will not usually make a request for recognition unless a substantial majority—often 60 or 70 percent—of employees sign cards. This large percentage is necessary since the employer will likely question the legitimacy of some cards or the eligibility of some workers to be represented or vote in the election. If the employer does not voluntarily recognize the union, either party can petition for an NLRB certification election to determine whether the union has majority support.

26. A large body of research has explored those factors influencing the ability of unions to win representation elections. Factors studied include size of the bargaining unit, union seeking representation, skill-homogeneity of the bargaining unit, and worker attitudes. See, for example, Rebecca A. Demsetz, "Voting Behavior in Union Representation Elections: The Influence of Skill Homogeneity and Skill Group Size," *Industrial and Labor Relations Review* 47, no. 1 (October 1993): 99–113.

27. Courtney D. Gifford, *Directory of U.S. Labor Organizations: 1994–95 Edition* (Washington, D.C.: Bureau of National Affairs, 1994): 4.

28. E. Kevin Kelloway and Julian Barling, "Members' Participation in Local Union Activities: Measurement, Prediction, and Replication," *Journal of Applied Psychology* 78, no. 2 (April 1993): 262–78.

29. The research of Al Nash on union stewards is considered a major work on these important labor officials. He is frequently cited when the function and power of union stewards is discussed. See Al Nash, *The Union Steward: Duties, Rights, and Status*, Key Issues Series no. 22 (Ithaca, N.Y.: ILR Press, 1983): 11–12.

30. Researchers have discussed the erosion of union steward power in contract administration. The loss of power has been attributed to bureaucratization and centralization of labor relations activity within both unions and management hierarchies. While no one doubts the influence—positive or negative—that stewards can have on labor-management relations, the shifting power of the steward is important in deciding labor-management controversies. See Patricia A. Simpson, "A Preliminary Investigation of Determinants of Local Union Steward Power," *Labor Studies Journal* 18, no. 2 (Summer 1993): 51–67.

31. J. Lawrence French, "The Power and Pay of International Union Officials," *Journal of Labor Research* 13, no. 2 (Spring 1992): 157–71.

32. Donald E. Klinger, "Public Sector Collective Bargaining," *Review of Public Personnel Administration* 13, no. 3 (Summer 1993): 19–27.

33. Gifford, *Directory*, 4–5.

34. CFR (Code of Federal Regulations), 1959–1963 Compilation, 521.

35. George W. Bohlander, "The Federal Labor Relations Authority: A Review and Analysis," *Journal of Collective Bargaining in the Public Sector* 8, no. 4 (1989): 273–88.

36. John Pyne, "What Public Employee Relation Boards and the Courts Are Deciding," *Review of Public Personnel Administration* 13, no. 3 (Summer 1993): 58–69.

37. E. Edward Herman, Joshua L. Schwarz, and Alfred Ruhn, *Collective Bargaining and Labor Relations*, 3d ed. (Englewood Cliffs, N.J.: Prentice-Hall, 1992): 358–59.

38. Harry C. Katz and Thomas A. Kochan, *An Introduction to Collective Bargaining and Industrial Relations* (New York: McGraw-Hill, 1992): 372–73.

39. Mark Partridge, "Technology, International Competitiveness, and Union Behavior," *Journal of Labor Research* 14, no. 2 (Spring 1993): 131–45.

40. David A. Dilts and William H. Walker, Jr., "Labor Standards and North America Free Trade: Economic Dynamic or Dilemma?" *Labor Law Journal* 44, no. 7 (July 1993): 445–48.

41. Yonatan Reshef, "Employees, Unions, and Technological Changes: A Research Agenda," *Journal of Labor Research* 14, no. 2 (Spring 1993): 111–27.

42. Diane E. Schmidt, "Public Opinion and Media

Coverage of Labor Unions," *Journal of Labor Research* 14, no. 2 (Spring 1993): 151–63.

43. Charles McDonald, "U.S. Union Membership in Future Decades: A Trade Unionist's Perspective," *Industrial Relations* 31, no. 1 (Winter 1992): 13–30. See also Michael H. Leroy, "State of the Unions:

Assessment of Elite American Labor Leaders," *Journal of Labor Research* 13, no. 4 (Fall 1992): 371–77.

44. William J. Bizones and Ellen R. Price, "Responding to Union Decertification Elections," *Personnel Administrator* 33, no. 8 (August 1988): 49.

Chapter

Collective Bargaining and
Contract Administration

18

After studying this chapter you should be able to

one
objective
Discuss the bargaining process and the bargaining goals and strategies of a union and an employer.

two
objective
Describe the forms of bargaining power that a union and an employer may utilize to enforce their bargaining demands.

three
objective
Cite the principal methods by which bargaining deadlocks may be resolved.

four
objective
Give examples of current collective bargaining trends.

five
objective
Identify the major provisions of a labor agreement and describe the issue of management rights.

six
objective
Describe a typical union grievance procedure.

seven
objective
Explain the basis for arbitration awards.

made during the previous negotiations while the experience is still current in their minds.

Sources to Consult

Internal data relating to grievances, disciplinary actions, transfers and promotions, layoffs, overtime, former arbitration awards, and wage payments are useful in formulating and supporting the employer's bargaining position. The supervisors and managers who must live with and administer the labor agreement can be very important sources of ideas and suggestions concerning changes that are needed in the *next* agreement. Their contact with union members and representatives provides them with a firsthand knowledge of the changes that union negotiators are likely to propose.

Data obtained from government publications such as the *Monthly Labor Review* and agencies such as the Department of Labor's Bureau of Labor Statistics can help to support the employer's position during negotiations; information from *The Wall Street Journal* and publications of the Bureau of National Affairs and Commerce Clearing House can also be of use. Each of these data sources can provide information on general economic conditions, cost-of-living trends, and geographical wage rates covering a wide range of occupations.

Bargaining Patterns

When unions negotiate provisions covering wages and other benefits, they generally seek to achieve increases at least equal to those provided in other agreements existing within the industry or region. For example, the United Auto Workers would negotiate similar contract provisions for workers at Ford, General Motors, and Chrysler. Employers quite naturally try to minimize these increases by citing other employers who are paying lower wages and benefits. Other negotiated labor agreements can establish a pattern that one side or the other may seek to follow in support of its own bargaining position. This practice is known as **pattern bargaining.** In preparing for negotiations, therefore, it is essential for both the union and the employer to be fully aware of established bargaining patterns within the area or the industry.

Pattern bargaining
Bargaining in which unions negotiate provisions covering wages and other benefits that are similar to those provided in other agreements existing within the industry or region

Academic researchers and managers have widely discussed the decline in pattern bargaining.[7] With periods of low economic growth, combined with increased domestic and global competition, employers have been more willing to resist union demands to "accept the pattern." For employers, profitability and efficiency and comparative labor costs become additional arguments against accepting existing contract terms of other employers. However, pattern bargaining still remains a characteristic of U.S. collective bargaining.[8] Pattern bargaining allows unions to show their members that they are receiving wages and benefits similar to other employees doing like work (a necessity in avoiding union political problems), and employers are assured that their labor costs are comparable with those of their competitors.[9]

Bargaining Strategies

Negotiators for an employer should develop a plan covering their bargaining strategy. To ensure adherence to the employer's course of action, this plan should be prepared as a written document. The plan should consider the proposals that the union is likely to submit, based on the most recent agreements with other employers and the demands that remain unsatisfied from previous negotiations. The plan should also consider the goals the union is striving to achieve and the extent to which it may be willing to make concessions or to resort to strike action in order to achieve these goals.

At a minimum, the employer's bargaining strategy must address these points:

- Likely union proposals and management responses to them
- A listing of management demands, limits of concessions, and anticipated union responses
- Development of a database to support management bargaining proposals and to counteract union demands
- A contingency operating plan should employees strike

Certain elements of strategy are common to both the employer and the union. Generally, the initial demands presented by each side are greater than those it actually may hope to achieve. This is done in order to provide room for concessions. Moreover, each party will usually avoid giving up the maximum it is capable of conceding in order to allow for further concessions that may be needed to break a bargaining deadlock.

Conducting the Negotiations

The economic conditions under which negotiations take place, the experience and personalities of the negotiators on each side, the goals they are seeking to achieve, and the strength of the relative positions are among the factors that tend to make each bargaining situation unique. Some labor agreements can be negotiated informally in a few hours, particularly if the contract is short and the

National Hockey League Players Association President Mike Gartner arriving at NHL headquarters for what would become protracted negotiations with the league on a new collective bargaining agreement.

terms are not overly complex. Other agreements, such as those negotiated with large organizations like the National Hockey League, the City of San Francisco, and the Caterpillar Company, required months before settlements were reached.

Bargaining Teams

The composition and size of bargaining teams are often a reflection of industry practice and bargaining history. Normally, each side will have four to six representatives at the negotiating table. The chief negotiator for management will be the vice president or manager for labor relations; the chief negotiator for the union will be the local union president or union business agent. Others making up management's team may include representatives from accounting or finance, operations, employment, legal, or training. The local union president is likely to be supported by the chief steward, various local union vice presidents, and a representative from the national union.

Many negotiators, over a period of time, acquire the ability "to read their opponents' minds," to anticipate their actions and reactions. Inexperienced negotiators bargaining for the first time, on the other hand, may misinterpret their opponents' actions and statements and unintentionally cause a deadlock. Furthermore, U.S. managers who must bargain with labor officials in a different culture may be unaware of the rules, rituals, and steps to be followed to keep negotiations moving toward a mutually acceptable agreement. In Japan, for example, "saving face" is an important aspect of Japanese culture that often influences the negotiating process.[10]

Opening the Negotiations

The initial meeting of the bargaining teams is a particularly important one because it establishes the climate that will prevail during the negotiations that follow. A cordial attitude, with perhaps the injection of a little humor, can contribute much to a relaxation of tensions and help the negotiations to begin smoothly. This *attitudinal structuring* is done to change the attitudes of the parties toward each other, often with the objective of persuading one side to accept the other side's demands.[11]

The first meeting is usually devoted to establishing the bargaining authority possessed by the representatives of each side and to determining the rules and procedures to be used during negotiations. If the parties have not submitted their proposals in advance, these may be exchanged and clarified at this time.

Analyzing the Proposals

The negotiation of a labor agreement can have some of the characteristics of a poker game, with each side attempting to determine its opponent's position while not revealing its own. Each party will normally try to avoid disclosing the relative importance that it attaches to a proposal so that it will not be forced to pay a higher price than is necessary to have the proposal accepted.[12] As with sellers who will try to get a higher price for their products if they think the prospective buyer strongly desires them, negotiators will try to get greater concessions in return for granting those their opponents want most.

The proposals that each side submits generally may be divided into those it feels it must achieve, those it would like to achieve, and those it is submitting primarily for trading purposes. Proposals submitted for trading purposes, however, must be realistic in terms of the opponent's ability and willingness to concede them. Unrealistic proposals may serve only to antagonize the opponent and cause a deadlock.

Resolving the Proposals

Regardless of its degree of importance, every proposal submitted must be resolved if an agreement is to be finalized.[13] A proposal may be withdrawn, accepted by the other side in its entirety, or accepted in some compromise form.

For each bargaining issue to be resolved satisfactorily, the point at which agreement is reached must be within limits that the union and the employer are willing to accept. In a frequently cited bargaining model, Ross Stagner and Hjalmar Rosen call the area within these two limits the **bargaining zone.** In some bargaining situations, such as the one illustrated in Figure 18–2, the solution desired by one party may exceed the limits of the other party. Thus that solution is outside the bargaining zone. If that party refuses to modify its demands sufficiently to bring them within the bargaining zone or if the opposing party refuses to extend its limit to accommodate the demands of the other party, a bargaining deadlock will result.[14]

For example, when bargaining a wage increase for employees, if the union's lowest limit is a 4 percent increase and management's top limit is 6 percent, an acceptable range—the bargaining zone—is available to both parties. If management's top limit is only 3 percent, however, a bargaining zone is not available to either side and a deadlock is likely to occur. Figure 18–2, which is based on the original model by Stagner and Rosen, shows that as bargaining takes place, several important variables influence the negotiators and their ability to reach agreement within the bargaining zone.

objective

The Union's Power in Collective Bargaining

During negotiations, it is necessary for each party to retreat sufficiently from its original position to permit an agreement to be achieved. If this does not occur, the negotiations will become deadlocked, and the union may resort to the use of economic power to achieve its demands. Otherwise, its only alternative will be to have members continue working without a labor agreement once the old one has expired. The economic power of the union may be exercised by striking, picketing, or boycotting the employer's products and encouraging others to do likewise. As managers know well, the ability to engage or even threaten to engage in such activities also can serve as a form of pressure.

Striking the Employer

A strike is the refusal of a group of employees to perform their jobs. Although strikes account for only a small portion of total workdays lost in industry each year, they are a costly and emotional event for all concerned.[15] Unions usually will seek strike authorization from their members to use as a bargaining ploy to

FIGURE 18-2 *The Bargaining Zone and Negotiation Influences*

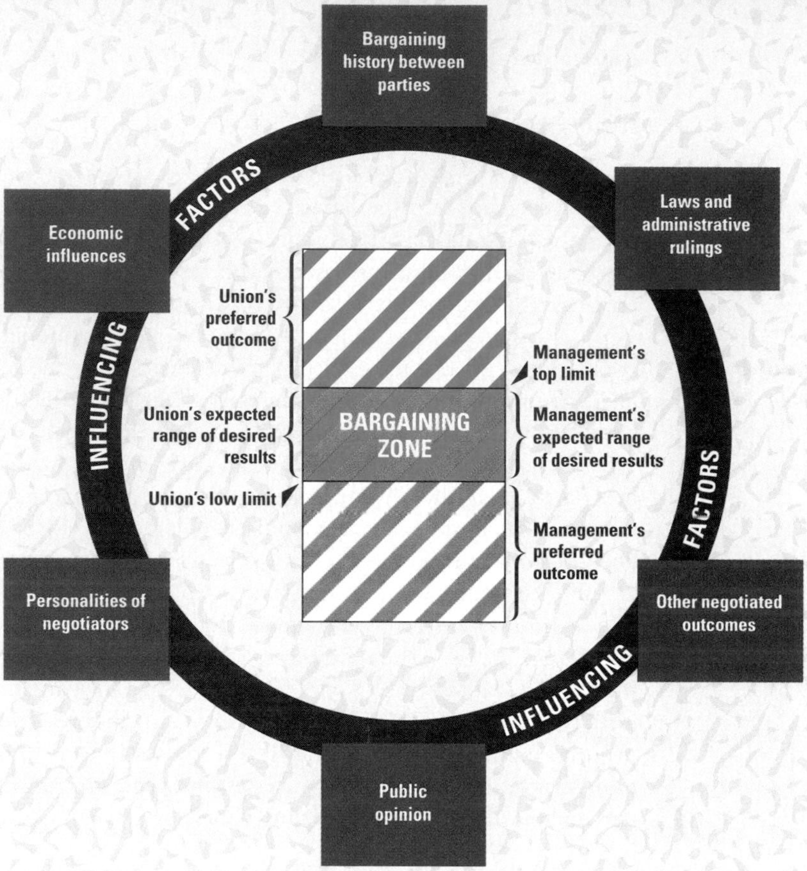

Source: Adapted from Ross Stagner and Hjalmar Rosen, *Psychology of Union-Management Relations* (Belmont, CA: Wadsworth Publishing Company, Inc., 1965), p. 96. Adapted with permission from Brooks/Cole Publishing Co.

gain concessions that will make a strike unnecessary. A strike vote by the members does not mean they actually want or expect to go out on strike. Rather, it is intended as a vote of confidence to strengthen the position of their leaders at the bargaining table.

Since a strike can have serious effects on the union and its members, the prospects for its success must be analyzed carefully by the union. It is most important for the union to estimate the members' willingness to endure the personal hardships resulting from a strike, particularly if it proves to be a long one.[16] Research has shown clear differences between employees willing to strike and those less certain about crossing a picket line. For example, potential strikers

The national union sanctioned the strike of these local union workers.

have more seniority, are better paid, have more years of union membership, and express more support for their union than nonstrikers.[17]

Also of critical importance is the extent, if any, to which the employer will be able to continue operating through the use of supervisory and nonstriking personnel and employees hired to replace the strikers. The greater the ability of the employer to continue operating, the less the union's chances of gaining the demands it is attempting to enforce through the strike.[18] Failure to achieve a desired settlement can result in the employees' voting either the union officers out of office or the union out of the organization in an NLRB-conducted decertification election.

Since 1985 the number of work stoppages in the United States involving 1,000 or more workers has declined to well under 75 each year. In 1993 the Bureau of Labor Statistics reported 35 such stoppages,[19] a figure that contrasts sharply with the number of strikes reported in the 1960s (282 average each year) and 1970s (288 average each year). HRM practitioners conclude that the decline in the use of the strike by unions can be attributed to the increased willingness of employers to hire replacements when employees strike and the increased availability of workers through unemployment. Additionally, both employee support and public tolerance for strikes has lessened.

Picketing the Employer

When a union goes on strike, it will picket the employer by placing persons at business entrances to advertise the dispute and to discourage people from entering or leaving the premises. Even when the strikers represent only a small proportion of the employees within the organization, they can cause the shutdown of an entire organization if a sufficient number of the organization's remaining employees (i.e., sympathy strikers) refuse to cross their picket line. Also, because unions often refuse to cross another union's picket line, the pickets may serve to prevent trucks and railcars from entering the business to deliver and pick up goods. For example, a Teamster truck driver may refuse to deliver produce to a food store whose employees are out on strike with the United Food & Commercial Workers Union.

If a strike fails to stop an employer's operations, the picket line may serve as more than a passive weapon. Employees who attempt to cross the line may be subjected to verbal insults and even physical violence. Mass picketing, in which large groups of pickets try to block the path of people attempting to enter an organization, may also be used. However, the use of picket lines to exert physical pressure and incite violence is illegal and may harm more than help the union cause.

Boycotting the Employer

Boycott

A union tactic to encourage others to refuse to patronize an employer

Another economic weapon of unions is the **boycott,** which is a refusal to patronize the employer. This action can hurt an employer if conducted by a large enough segment of organized labor. In contrast to a strike, a boycott may not end completely with the settlement of the dispute. During the boycott, many former customers may have developed either a bias against the employer's products or a change in buying habits that is not easily reversed.

A *primary boycott* occurs where a union asks its members or customers not to patronize a business where there is a labor dispute; for example, production employees on strike against a hand tool manufacturer might picket a retail store that sells the tool made by the employees. Under most circumstances this type of boycott is legal, provided the union advises consumers to boycott the tools and *not* the neutral store. A union may go a step further, however, and attempt to induce third parties, primarily suppliers of the struck employer, to refrain from business dealings with the employer with whom it has a dispute. A boycott of this type, called a *secondary boycott,* generally is illegal under the Taft-Hartley Act.

The Employer's Power in Collective Bargaining

two
objective

Outsourcing

Act of subcontracting operations to other employers

The employer's power in collective bargaining largely rests in being able to shut down the organization or certain operations within it. The employer can transfer these operations to other locations or can subcontract them to other employers through **outsourcing.** General Motors outsources to foreign manufacturers many parts used in the assembly of American cars. In exercising their economic freedom, however, employers must be careful that their actions are not interpreted by the NLRB to be an attempt to avoid bargaining with the union.

Operating during Strikes

When negotiations become deadlocked, typically it is the union that initiates action and the employer that reacts. In reacting, employers must balance the cost of taking a strike against the long- and short-term costs of agreeing to union demands. They must also consider how long operations might be suspended and the length of time that they and the unions will be able to endure a strike. An employer who chooses to accept a strike must then decide whether or not to continue operating if it is possible to do so.

Organizations today seem to be more willing to face a strike than they were in former years. Several reasons have been advanced to explain this change, including:

1. Union members seem less willing to support strike activity. Thus the union is less able to maintain strike unity among its members.
2. Because organizations are forced to reduce labor costs to meet domestic and global competition, unions have no choice but to accept lower wages and benefits.
3. Technological advances enhance the employer's ability to operate during a strike.
4. Organizations are able to obtain favorable, often concessionary, contracts.

Should employees strike the organization, employers have the right to hire replacement workers. Striking employees have reemployment rights for one year, beginning when they indicate a desire to return to work, should an opening arise. Employers, however, are not obligated to terminate replacement employees to make openings for striking employees.

Using the Lockout

Lockout
Strategy by which the employer denies employees the opportunity to work by closing its operations

Although not often used, a **lockout** occurs when an employer takes the initiative to close its operations. Besides being used in bargaining impasses, lockouts may be used by employers to combat union slowdowns, damage to their property, or violence within the organization that may occur in connection with a labor dispute.

Under NLRB rulings, employers are granted the right to hire temporary replacements during a legitimate lockout. With this right, employers acquire a bargaining weapon equal in force to the union's right to strike. As one observer noted, "The availability of a lockout-with-replacement strategy improves management's ability to battle a union head-on in the way that unions have battled employers for decades." Employers may still be reluctant to resort to a lockout, however, because of their concern that denying work to regular employees might hurt the organization's image.

three
objective

Resolving Bargaining Deadlocks

When a strike or a lockout occurs, both parties are soon affected by it. The employer will suffer a loss of profits and customers, and possibly of public goodwill. The union members suffer a loss of income that is likely to be only partially offset by strike benefits or outside income. The union's leaders risk the possibility of losing members, of being voted out of office, of losing public support, or of having the members vote to decertify the union as their bargaining agent. As the losses to each side mount, the disputing parties usually feel more pressure to achieve a settlement.

Mediation and Arbitration

Mediator
Third party in a labor dispute who meets with one party and then the other in order to suggest compromise solutions or to recommend concessions from each side that will lead to an agreement

When the disputing parties are unable to resolve a deadlock, a third party serving in the capacity of either a mediator or an arbitrator may be called upon to provide assistance. A **mediator** serves primarily as a fact finder and to open up a channel of communication between the parties. Typically, the mediator meets with one party and then the other in order to suggest compromise solutions or to recommend concessions from each side that will lead to an agreement without causing either to lose face. Mediators have no power or authority to force either side toward an agreement. They must use their communication skills and the power of persuasion to help the parties resolve their differences.[20]

An **arbitrator,** on the other hand, assumes the role of a decision maker and determines what the settlement between the two parties should be. In other words, arbitrators write a final contract that the parties *must* accept. Compared with mediation, arbitration is not often used to settle private-sector bargaining disputes. In the public sector, where strikes are largely prohibited, the use of **interest arbitration** is a common method to resolve bargaining deadlocks.[21] Generally, one or both parties are reluctant to give a third party the power to make the settlement for them. Consequently, a mediator typically is used to break a deadlock and assist the parties in reaching an agreement. An arbitrator generally is called upon to resolve disputes arising in connection with the administration of the agreement, called *rights arbitration* or *grievance arbitration,* which will be discussed shortly.

Government Intervention

In some situations, deadlocks may have to be resolved directly or indirectly as the result of government intervention, particularly if the work stoppage is a threat to the national security or to the public welfare. The Taft-Hartley Act provides that the president of the United States may stop a strike in "an entire industry or a substantial part thereof" if the strike would "imperil the national health or safety." Fortunately, the national emergency strike provisions of the Taft-Hartley Act have not often been used. Rather, the federal government is more likely to become involved in labor disputes through the services of the Federal Mediation and Conciliation Service. (See Chapter 17.) The FMCS has been highly successful in resolving bargaining deadlocks.

Arbitrator
Third-party neutral who resolves a labor dispute by issuing a final decision in the disagreement

Interest arbitration
The binding determination of a collective bargaining agreement by an arbitrator

objective

Trends in Collective Bargaining

Managers continue to see the 1990s as a period of great importance to labor-management relations. Advances in technology, management's antiunion posture, and continued competitive pressures have their impact. These conditions affect the attitudes and objectives of both employers and unions in collective bargaining. They also influence the climate in which bargaining occurs and the bargaining power each side is able to exercise.[22]

Changes in Collective Bargaining Relationships

Traditionally, the collective bargaining relationship between an employer and a union has been an adversarial one. The union has held the position that, while the employer has the responsibility for managing the organization, the union has the right to challenge certain actions of management. Unions also have taken the position that the employer has an obligation to operate the organization in a manner that will provide adequate compensation to employees. More-

PEANUTS reprinted by permission of UFS, Inc.

over, unions maintain that their members should not be expected to subsidize poor management by accepting less than their full entitlement.

Most unions, such as the United Steelworkers in bargaining with National, Inland, and Bethlehem steel companies; the Amalgamated Clothing and Textile Workers Union in bargaining with Xerox Corporation; and the Office and Professional Employees International Union in bargaining with Northwest Natural Gas Company, have been sufficiently enlightened to recognize the danger of making bargaining demands that will create economic adversity for employers.[23] This fact, however, has not stopped these unions from bargaining for what they consider to be a fair and equitable agreement for their members. While the goal of organized labor has always been to bargain for improved economic and working conditions, large layoffs caused by economic downturns and domestic and global competition have caused both sides to change their bargaining goals and tactics. We are seeing a gradual movement away from direct conflict and toward more labor-management accommodation.

Facilitating Union-Management Cooperation

Improving union-management cooperation generally requires a restructuring of attitudes by both managers and union officials and members. Robert Frey, president, Cin-Made Corporation, notes, "Key barriers to adopting these new work systems are managers who are more comfortable giving orders with little input and complacent employees who like not having to think. We must understand how difficult the change process is for people and that firm leadership is needed to lead the process."[24]

Furthermore, the crisis of survival has forced unions, their members, and management to make concessions at the bargaining table and to collaborate in finding the solutions that will ensure survival. If cooperation is to continue after the crisis has passed, however, it must rest on a more solid foundation. For example, it has been noted that cooperation lasts only when both sides undertake the endeavor through a systems approach grounded in developmental activities.[25] Also, union-management cooperation programs have a greater chance for success when both parties jointly establish goals and philosophies for mutual gain. Highlights in HRM 1 shows the jointly written statement of principles and philosophy developed for the highly successful Magma Copper Company labor-management partnership.

. . . .

claim in arbitration, this did not preclude the individual from filing a subsequent EEO charge.[45] In *Gilmer v Interstate/Johnson Lane,* however, the Supreme Court held that arbitration is appropriate for the resolution of age discrimination in employment cases.[46] It seems certain that arbitration will increasingly be used to settle employee grievances in union-management cases and under alternative dispute resolution (ADR) procedures.[47]

Expedited Arbitration

Expedited arbitration

A faster, less expensive, and less legalistic way to resolve grievances regarding discipline cases, routine work issues, and cases of insignificant monetary cost to the disputing parties

The steel industry, the U.S. Postal Service, and the maritime industry use **expedited arbitration** as a way of overcoming the high costs, time delays, and legalism of grievance arbitration. While each labor agreement may have its own procedures governing the use of expedited arbitration, the following are typical characteristics of this particular arbitration process:

1. The arbitration hearing is held within ten days from the demand for arbitration.
2. The hearing is completed in one day.
3. Awards must be rendered within five days from the close of the hearing, and only short written awards (one or two pages) are required.
4. Hearings are informal; attorneys, legal briefs, and court reporters are not involved.

Expedited arbitration is an effective way to dispose of disciplinary cases, routine work issues, and cases of insignificant monetary cost to the parties. Complex contract-interpretation cases may not be amenable to the expedited procedures.

SUMMARY

objective

Negotiating a labor agreement is a detailed process. Each side will prepare a list of proposals it wishes to achieve while additionally trying to anticipate those proposals desired by the other side. Bargaining teams must be selected and all proposals must be analyzed to determine their impact on and cost to the organization. Both employer and union negotiators will be sensitive to current bargaining patterns within the industry, general cost-of-living trends, and geographical wage differentials. Managers will establish goals that seek to retain control over operations and to minimize costs. Union negotiators will focus their demands around improved wages, hours, and working conditions. An agreement will be reached when both sides compromise their original positions and final terms fall within the limits of the parties' bargaining zone.

objective

The collective bargaining process includes not only the actual negotiations but also the power tactics used to support negotiating demands. When negotiations become deadlocked, bargaining becomes a power struggle to force from either side the concessions needed to break the deadlock. The union's power in collective bargaining comes from its ability to picket, strike, or boycott the employer. The employer's power during negotiations comes from its ability to lock out employees or to operate during a strike by using managerial or replacement employees.

Mediation is the principal way of resolving negotiating deadlocks. Federal mediators provided by the U.S. Federal Mediation and Conciliation Service seek to assist the negotiators through opening up lines of communication between the parties and offering suggestions to resolve deadlocked proposals. In some situations, interest arbitration is employed to finalize the labor agreement. Interest arbitration is rarely used in the private sector; however, it is used often in the public sector where unions are largely prohibited from striking.

During the decade of the 1990s several trends in labor relations have become evident. These include attempts to develop more cooperative labor-management endeavors and attitudes of less adversarial collective bargaining. Management has used concessionary bargaining to minimize or lower labor costs while improving workplace productivity through the reduction of restrictive work rules. Unions have stressed employee retraining and job security where employer concessions are sought.

The typical labor agreement will contain numerous provisions governing the employment relationship between labor and management. The major areas of interest concern wages (rates of pay, overtime differentials, holiday pay), hours (shift times, days of work), and working conditions (safety issues, performance standards, retraining). To managers the issue of management rights is particularly important. These rights hold that management's authority is supreme for all issues except those shared with the union through the labor agreement.

When differences arise between labor and management they will normally be resolved through the grievance procedure. Grievance procedures are negotiated and thus reflect the needs and desires of the parties. The typical grievance procedure will consist of three, four, or five steps—each step having specific filing and reply times. Higher-level managers and union officials will become involved in disputes at the higher steps of the grievance procedure. The final step of the grievance procedure may be arbitration. Arbitrators will render a final decision to problems not resolved at lower grievance steps.

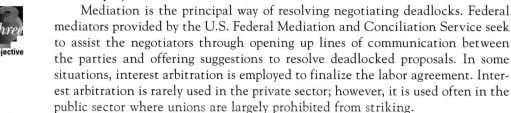

The submission agreement is a statement of the issue to be solved through arbitration. It is simply the problem which the parties wish to have settled. The arbitrator must answer the issue by basing the arbitration award on four factors: the contents of the labor agreement, the submission agreement as written, testimony and evidence obtained at the hearing, and various arbitration standards developed over time to assist in the resolution of different types of labor-management disputes. Arbitration is not an exact science since arbitrators will give varying degrees of importance to the evidence and criteria by which disputes are resolved.

KEY TERMS

arbitration award	grievance procedure
arbitrator	interest arbitration
bargaining zone	lockout
boycott	mediator
collective bargaining process	outsourcing
defined rights	pattern bargaining
expedited arbitration	reserved rights
fair representation doctrine	rights arbitration
grievance mediation	submission agreement

DISCUSSION QUESTIONS

1. Is collective bargaining the same as negotiating? Explain.

2. Of what significance is the "bargaining zone" in the conduct of negotiations? What are some influences affecting negotiated outcomes?

3. What are some of the possible reasons an employer may be willing to face a strike that could result in a loss of customers and profits?

4. How does mediation differ from arbitration, and in what situations is each of these processes most likely to be used?

5. What are some of the bargaining concessions generally sought by employers and unions in return for the concessions they may grant?

6. What are some of the developments that are posing a threat to union security today?

7. At an election conducted among the twenty employees of the Exclusive Jewelry Store, all but two voted in favor of the Jewelry Workers Union, which subsequently was certified as their bargaining agent. In negotiating its first agreement, the union demanded that it be granted a union shop. The two employees who had voted against the union, however, informed the management that they would quit rather than join. Unfortunately for the store, the two employees were skilled gem cutters who were the most valuable of its employees and would be difficult to replace. What position should the store take with regard to the demand for a union shop?

8. What are some of the reasons a union or an employer may allow a weak grievance to go to arbitration?

. . . .

CASE STUDY: Labor-Management Partnership at Magma Copper

Highlights in HRM 1 shows the principles and philosophy statement guiding the labor-management partnership at Magma Copper Company, the fourth largest copper producer in the United States. Its principal products are high-quality copper cathode and rod, which are sold worldwide. The company employs 4,300 workers in Arizona, 75 percent of whom are represented by nine unions. Local 937 of the United Steelworkers, the company's largest local union, represents nearly 1,300 employees at San Manuel, Arizona.

Before 1989, labor relations at Magma were bitterly adversarial. Union and management officials confronted each other with different issues, beliefs, politics, and desired outcomes. Each side brought to their relationship a confrontational behavior forged from a long pattern of hostile interactions. The unions viewed management as an autocratic group that cared little for employees and that demanded numerous "givebacks" through bargaining concessions. Management viewed union leaders as antagonistic and solely interested in preserving the status quo by using threats or pressure politics.

The turnaround in labor relations at Magma Copper began only when both sides realized the significance of their problems and decided to develop a cooperative labor-management partnership based upon mutual respect and joint collaboration. To implement the cooperative process, educational workshops were jointly developed by labor and management teams. These training sessions were presented to groups of fifty employees, equally represented by labor and management participants. Since 1989 the company has spent over $5 million on employee-management training and employee involvement efforts.

The labor-management partnership at Magma Copper becomes effective through the use of Breakthrough Projects. These projects tackle specific business or technical problems by using strategic teams composed of equal numbers of employees, supervisors, and/or managers. Breakthrough Project teams apply learned participative skills and new technological changes to increase productivity and reduce costs. All Breakthrough Projects must demonstrate considerable improvement to operational performance beyond what is presently possible. Breakthrough Projects must have a definable outcome in time and measurement, and they must foster the cooperative labor-management partnership.

The cornerstone of the partnership at Magma is a unique cooperative labor agreement signed in November of 1991. Negotiated through a problem-solving approach to bargaining, this historic labor agreement assures the labor stability needed for a continuous cooperative labor-management environment. Specifically meaningful are clauses related to the union-management partnership. These include:

- A fifteen-year agreement crafted to support cooperative labor relations
- An initial contract period of five years after which new economic conditions may be set for a second period

- A wage agreement containing a variety of features linking employee compensation to the productivity and profitability of the company
- A provision for arbitration on major new economic terms
- A lengthy memorandum of understanding outlining the vision, philosophy, and structure of work redesign methods based on a constructive union-management partnership

Source: Research conducted by George W. Bohlander.

Questions

1. What factors led to the development of a partnership at Magma Copper?
2. Discuss different types of problems/issues that could be addressed through the use of Breakthrough Projects.
3. What do you think are key issues to maintaining the effectiveness of cooperative labor-management programs?

NOTES AND REFERENCES

1. Thomas R. Colosi and Arthur E. Berkeley, *Collective Bargaining: How It Works and Why* (New York: American Arbitration Association, 1992). See also Francisco Hernandez-Senter, Jr., "Closing the Communication Gap in Collective Bargaining," *Labor Law Journal* 41, no. 7 (July 1990): 438–44.
2. Employers who refuse to pay union demands are not legally required to provide financial data to union representatives. The requirement to provide financial data would normally arise where an employer asserts during negotiations that it cannot survive if it agrees to union wage proposals or that it has no operating profit. See Katrina L. Abel, "The Duty to Disclose Relevant Financial Information," *Employee Relations Law Journal* 15, no. 2 (Autumn 1989): 281–89.
3. Michael R. Carrell and Christina Heavrin, *Collective Bargaining and Labor Relations: Cases, Practice, and Law,* 3d ed. (Columbus, Ohio: Merrill, 1992).
4. The National Labor Relations Board offers an excellent book on the National Labor Relations Act. This book discusses good-faith bargaining as well as other important legal issues—for example, employers covered by the law, unfair labor practices, and election procedures. See *A Guide to Basic Law and Procedures under the National Labor Relations Act* (Washington, D.C.: U.S. Government Printing Office, 1991).
5. John Thomas Delaney and Donna Stockell, "The Mandatory-Permissive Distinction and Collective Bargaining Outcomes," *Industrial and Labor Relations Review* 42, no. 4 (July 1989): 566–81.

6. John A. Fossum, *Labor Relations: Development, Structure, Process,* 6th ed. (Homewood, Ill.: BPI-Irwin, 1995): 278.
7. Peter Cappelli, "Is Pattern Bargaining Dead? A Discussion," *Industrial and Labor Relations Review* 44, no. 1 (October 1990): 152–55.
8. John W. Budd, "The Determinants and Extent of UAW Pattern Bargaining," *Industrial and Labor Relations Review* 45, no. 3 (April 1992): 523–37.
9. Daniel Q. Mills, *Labor-Management Relations,* 5th ed. (New York: McGraw-Hill, 1994).
10. Peter H. Corne, "The Complex Art of Negotiation between Different Cultures," *Arbitration Journal* 47, no. 4 (December 1992): 46–50.
11. For the original description of attitudinal structuring, see Richard E. Walton and Robert B. McKersie, *A Behavioral Theory of Labor Negotiations* (New York: McGraw-Hill, 1965). This book is considered a classic in the labor relations field.
12. William Ury, *Getting Past No: Negotiating with Different People* (New York: Bantam Books, 1991).
13. Bruce C. Herniter, Erran Carmel, and Jay F. Nunamaker, Jr., "Computers Improve Efficiency of the Negotiation Process," *Personnel Journal* 72, no. 4 (April 1993): 93–99.
14. Ross Stagner and Hjalmar Rosen, *Psychology of Union-Management Relations* (Belmont, Calif.: Wadsworth, 1965): 95–97.
15. Rajib H. Sanyal, "The Withering Away of the Strike: The Ross-Hartman Analysis Thirty Years Since," *Labor Studies Journal* 15, no. 4 (Winter 1990): 47–68.

16. Jan I. Ondrich and John F. Schnell, "Strike Duration and the Degree of Disagreement," *Industrial Relations* 32, no. 3 (Fall 1993): 412–31.
17. Michael H. LeRoy, "Multivariate Analysis of Unionized Employees' Propensity to Cross Their Union's Picket Line," *Journal of Labor Research* 13, no. 3 (Summer 1992): 285–91.
18. Brenda Paik Sunoo and Jennifer J. Lambs, "Winning Strategies for Outsourcing Contracts," *Personnel Journal* 13, no. 3 (March 1994): 69; see also Bruce E. Kaufman, "Labor's Inequality of Bargaining Power: Changes over Time and Implications for Public Policy," *Journal of Labor Research* 10, no. 3 (Summer 1989): 285–97; John G. Kilgor, "Can Unions Strike Anymore? The Impact of Recent Supreme Court Decisions," *Labor Law Journal* 41, no. 5 (May 1990): 259–69.
19. Bureau of Labor Statistics, *News* (February 10, 1994): 1.
20. Deborah M. Kolb, *When Talk Works: Profiles of Mediators* (San Francisco, Calif.: Jossey-Bass, 1994). See also Sam Kagel and Kathy Kelly, *The Anatomy of Mediation: What Makes It Work* (Washington, D.C.: Bureau of National Affairs, 1989).
21. Homer C. LaRue, "An Historical Overview of Interest Arbitration in the United States," *Arbitration Journal* 42, no. 4 (December 1987): 18–19.
22. Ernest J. Savoie, "Recognition and Revitalization Fundamentals for Sustaining Change," *Labor Law Journal* 44, no. 8 (August 1993): 486–91.
23. For examples of concessionary bargaining and the development of labor-management cooperative programs, see Keith L. Alexander, "It's Time for USX to Take Labor's Outstretched Hand," *Business Week* (August 16, 1993): 30; "Labor Deals That Offer a Break from Us vs. Them," *Business Week* (August 2, 1993): 30; Peggy Stuart, "Labor Unions Become Business Partners," *Personnel Journal* 72, no. 8 (August 1993): 54–63.
24. *American Workplace* 1, no. 1 (September 1993): 2.
25. Jill Kriesky and Edwin Brown, "The Union Role in Labor-Management Cooperation: A Case Study at the Boise Cascade Company's Jackson Mill," *Labor Studies Journal* 18, no. 3 (Fall 1993): 17–32.
26. George W. Bohlander and Marshall H. Campbell, "Forging a Labor-Management Partnership: The Magma Copper Experience," *Labor Studies Journal* 18, no. 4 (Winter 1994): 3–20; George W. Bohlander and Marshall H. Campbell, "Problem-Solving Bargaining and Work Redesign: Magma Copper's Labor-Management Partnership," *National Productivity Review* 12, no. 4 (Autumn 1993): 519–33.
27. Paula B. Voss, "The Influence of Cooperative Programs on Union-Management Relations, Flexibility, and Other Labor Relations Outcomes," *Journal of Labor Research* 10, no. 1 (Winter 1989): 103.
28. Richard B. Peterson and Lane Tracy, "Lessons from Labor-Management Cooperation," *California Management Review* 31, no. 1 (Fall 1988): 41.
29. Jim Armshaw, David Carnevale, and Bruce Waltuck, "Union-Management Partnership in the U.S. Department of Labor," *Review of Public Personnel Administration* 13, no. 3 (Summer 1993): 94–105.
30. David A. Dilts, "Labor-Management Cooperation: Real or Nominal Changes in Collective Bargaining?" *Labor Law Journal* 44, no. 2 (February 1993): 124–28. See also Stephen I. Schlossberg and Miriam B. Reinhart, "*Electromation* and the Future of Labor-Management Cooperation in the U.S.," *Labor Law Journal* 43, no. 9 (September 1992): 608–20.
31. Leslie A. Nay, "The Determinants of Concession Bargaining in the Airline Industry," *Industrial and Labor Relations Review* 44, no. 2 (January 1991): 305–65.
32. Peter Nulty, "Look What the Unions Want Now," *Fortune* (February 1993): 128–35.
33. For an expanded discussion of management's reserved rights, see Paul Prasow and Edward Peters, *Arbitration and Collective Bargaining*, 2d ed. (New York: McGraw-Hill, 1983): 33–34.
34. Labor agreement, Wabash Fibre Box Company and Paperworkers.
35. Judith L. Carter and Edwin L. Brown, "Union Leaders' Perception of the Grievance Procedure," *Labor Studies Journal* 15, no. 1 (Spring 1990): 54–55; see also Frank Elkouri and Edna Asher Elkouri, *How Arbitration Works*, 4th ed. (Washington, D.C.: Bureau of National Affairs, 1985): 153.
36. Jeanette A. Davy and George W. Bohlander, "Recent Findings and Practices in Grievance-Arbitration Procedures," *Labor Law Journal* 43, no. 3 (March 1992): 184–90.
37. George W. Bohlander, "Public-Sector Grievance Arbitration: Structure and Administration," *Journal of Collective Negotiations in the Public Sector* 21, no. 4 (Fall 1992): 278.
38. Michael J. Duane, "To Grieve or Not To Grieve: Why Reduce It to Writing?" *Public Personnel Management* 20, no. 1 (Spring 1991): 83–88.
39. Sylvia Skratek, "Grievance Mediation: How to Make the Process Work for You," *Labor Law Journal* 44, no. 8 (August 1993): 507–11.
40. Edward J. Costello, "Selecting a Neutral," *Arbitration Journal* 48, no. 3 (September 1993): 42–46.
41. Benjamin J. Taylor and Fred Witney, *Labor Relations Law*, 6th ed. (Englewood Cliffs, N.J.: Prentice-Hall, 1992): 224–36. Arbitration awards are not final in all cases. Arbitration awards may be overturned through the judicial process if it can be shown that the arbitrator was prejudiced or failed to render an award based on the essence of the agreement.
42. Some labor agreements call for using arbitration boards to resolve employee grievances. Arbitration boards, which may be either temporary or permanent, are composed of one or more members

chosen by management and an equal number chosen by labor. A neutral member serves as chair. See Peter A. Veglahn, "Grievance Arbitration by Arbitration Boards: A Survey of the Parties," *Arbitration Journal* 42, no. 2 (July 1987): 47–53.

43. For an interesting article on the historical process of labor arbitration, see Daniel F. Jennings and A. Dale Allen, Jr., "How Arbitrators View the Process of Labor Arbitration: A Longitudinal Analysis," *Labor Studies Journal* 17, no. 4 (Winter 1993): 41–48.

44. George W. Bohlander, "Why Arbitrators Overturn Managers in Employee Suspension and Discharge Cases," *Journal of Collective Bargaining in the Public Sector* 23, no. 1 (Spring 1994): 73–89.

45. *Alexander v Gardner-Denver Company,* 415 U.S. 147 (1974).

46. *Gilmer v Interstate/Johnson Lane,* 111 S.Ct. 1647 (1991).

47. David A. Dilts, "The Future for Labor Arbitration," *Arbitration Journal* 48, no. 2 (June 1993): 24–31.

Part 7

International Human Resources Management and HR Audits

Part 7 focuses on the topics of HR in multinational companies and the auditing of specific HR functions. Chapter 19 deals with the challenges faced by multinational enterprises when they staff managers and executives in overseas assignments. Special considerations are given to understanding cultural, social, and legal differences of job assignments in foreign countries. In Chapter 20 the effectiveness of HR programs is examined. Included here are HR audit procedures available to both department supervisors and HR specialists. Auditing the many HR functions and programs is a prerequisite to the effective utilization of both monetary and human resources.

Chapter

International Human Resources
Management

19

After studying this chapter you should be able to

one
objective

Identify the types of organizational forms used for competing internationally.

two
objective

Explain how domestic and international HRM differ.

three
objective

Discuss the staffing process for individuals working internationally.

four
objective

Identify the unique training needs for international assignees.

five
objective

Reconcile the difficulties of home-country and host-country performance appraisals.

six
objective

Identify the characteristics of a good international compensation plan.

seven
objective

Explain the major differences between U.S. and European labor relations.

T*he emphasis throughout this book has been on HRM as it is practiced in organizations in the United States. But many of these firms also engage in international trade. A large percentage carry on their international business with only limited facilities and representation in foreign countries. Others, particularly Fortune 500 corporations, have extensive facilities and personnel in various countries of the world. Managing these resources effectively, and integrating their activities to achieve global advantage, is a challenge to the leadership of these companies.*

We are quickly moving toward a global economy. While estimates vary widely, approximately 70 to 85 percent of the U.S. economy today is affected by international competition. Recent popular books have suggested that many U.S. companies need to reassess their approach to doing business overseas, particularly in the area of managing human resources. To a large degree, the challenge of managing across borders boils down to the philosophies and systems we use for managing people.[1] In this chapter we will observe that much of what is discussed throughout this text can be applied to foreign operations, provided one is sensitive to the requirements of a particular international setting.

The first part of this chapter presents a brief introduction to international business firms. In many important respects, the way a company organizes its international operations influences the type of managerial and human resources issues it faces. In addition, we briefly describe some of the environmental factors that also affect the work of managers in a global setting. Just as with domestic operations, the dimensions of the environment form a context in which HRM decisions are made. A major portion of this chapter deals with the various HR activities involved in the recruitment, selection, development, and compensation of employees who work in an international setting. Throughout the discussion the focus will be on U.S. multinational corporations.

Managing Across Borders

International business operations can take several different forms. Figure 19–1 shows four basic types of organizations and how they differ in the degree to which international activities are *separated* to respond to the local regions and *integrated*

The corporate headquarters of Procter & Gamble.

FIGURE 19-1 *Types of Organizations*

	Low LOCAL RESPONSIVENESS High	
High **GLOBAL EFFICIENCY**	**GLOBAL** Views the world as a single market; operations are controlled centrally from the corporate office.	**TRANSNATIONAL** Specialized facilities permit local responsiveness; complex coordination mechanisms provide global integration.
Low	**INTERNATIONAL** Uses existing capabilities to expand into foreign markets.	**MULTINATIONAL** Several subsidiaries operating as stand-alone business units in multiple countries.

Source: Christopher A. Bartlett and Sumantra Ghoshal, *Managing across Borders: The Transnational Solution* (Boston: Harvard Business School Press, 1991); Arvind V. Phatak, *International Dimensions of Management,* 3d ed. (Boston: PWS-Kent, 1992); Peter J. Dowling and Randall S. Schuler, *International Dimensions of Human Resource Management* (Boston: PWS-Kent, 1990).

International corporation

A domestic firm that uses its existing capabilities to move into overseas markets

Multinational corporation (MNC)

A firm with independent business units operating in multiple countries

Global corporation

A firm that has integrated worldwide operations through a centralized home office

Transnational corporation

A firm that attempts to balance local responsiveness and global scale via a network of specialized operating units

to achieve global efficiencies. The **international corporation** is essentially a domestic firm that builds on its existing capabilities to penetrate overseas markets. Companies such as Honda, General Electric, and Procter & Gamble used this approach to gain access to Europe—they essentially adapted existing products for overseas markets without changing much else about their normal operations.[2]

A **multinational corporation (MNC)** is a more complex form that usually has fully autonomous units operating in multiple countries. Shell, Philips, and ITT are three typical MNCs. These companies have traditionally given their foreign subsidiaries a great deal of latitude to address local issues such as consumer preferences, political pressures, and economic trends in different regions of the world. Frequently these subsidiaries are run as independent companies, without much integration. The **global corporation,** on the other hand, can be viewed as a multinational firm that maintains control of operations back in the home office. Japanese companies such as Matsushita and NEC, for example, tend to treat the world market as a unified whole and try to combine activities in each country to maximize efficiency on a global scale. These companies operate much like a domestic firm, except that they view the whole world as their marketplace.

Finally, a **transnational corporation** attempts to achieve the local responsiveness of an MNC while also achieving the efficiencies of a global firm. To balance this "global/local" dilemma, a transnational uses a network structure that coordinates specialized facilities positioned around the world. By using this flexible structure, a transnational provides autonomy to independent country operations, but brings these separate activities together into an integrated whole. For most companies, the transnational form represents an ideal, rather than a reality. However, companies such as Ford, Unilever, and British Petroleum have made good progress in restructuring operations to function more transnationally.[3]

International Staffing

International management poses many problems in addition to those faced by a domestic operation. Because of geographic distance and a lack of close, day-to-day relationships with headquarters in the home country, problems must often be resolved with little or no counsel or assistance from others. It is essential, therefore, that special attention be given to the staffing practices of overseas units.

There are three sources of employees with whom to staff international operations. First, the company can send people from its home country. These employees are often referred to as **expatriates,** or **home-country nationals.** Second, it can hire **host-country nationals** (natives of the host country) to do the managing. Third, it can hire **third-country nationals,** natives of a country other than the home country or the host country.

Use of each of the three sources of overseas personnel involves certain advantages and disadvantages. Some of the more important advantages are presented in Figure 19–5. Most corporations use all three sources for staffing their multinational operations, although some companies exhibit a distinct bias for one of the three sources.[11] Over the years, and especially as MNCs have evolved, many have steadily shifted to the use of local personnel. There are three reasons for this trend: (1) Hiring local citizens is less costly because the company does not have to worry about the costs of home leaves, transportation, and special schooling allowances. (2) Since local governments usually want good jobs for their citizens, foreign employers may be required to hire them. (3) Using local talent avoids the problem of employees having to adjust to the culture.

At early stages of international expansion, many businesses prefer to use host-country nationals, since these individuals can best help the company respond to local customs and concerns. As the company's international presence grows, home-country managers are frequently expatriated to stabilize operational activities (particularly in less developed countries). At later stages of internationalization, different companies use different staffing strategies; how-

Expatriates (home-country nationals)
Employees from the home country who are sent on international assignment

Host-country nationals
Natives of the host country

Third-country nationals
Natives of a country other than the home country or the host country

---

FIGURE 19-5 *Comparing Sources of Overseas Managers*

HOST-COUNTRY NATIONALS	HOME-COUNTRY NATIONALS (EXPATRIATES)	THIRD-COUNTRY NATIONALS
Less cost	Talent available within company	Broad experience
Preference of host-country governments	Greater control	International outlook
Intimate knowledge of environment and culture	Company experience	Multilingualism
Language facility	Mobility	
	Experience provided to corporate executives	

ever, most employ some combination of host-country, home-country, and third-country nationals in the top management team.

Recently, there has been a trend away from putting expatriates in the top management positions. In many cases, U.S. companies want to be viewed as true international citizens. To avoid the strong influence of the home country, companies frequently change staffing policies to replace U.S. expatriates with local managers.[12] In Honeywell's European Division, for example, twelve of the top executive positions are held by non-Americans.[13] Over the years, U.S.-based companies, in particular, have tended to use more third-country expatriates. For example, when Eastman Kodak recently put together a launch team to market its new Photo-CD line, the team members were based in London, but the leader was from Belgium.

It should be recognized that while top managers may have preferences for one source of employees over another, the host country may place pressures on them that restrict their choices. Such pressure takes the form of sophisticated government persuasion through administrative or legislative decrees to employ host-country individuals.

Recruitment

In general, employee recruitment in other countries is subject to more government regulation than it is in the United States. Regulations range from those that cover procedures for recruiting employees to those that govern the employment of foreign labor or require the employment of the physically disabled, war veterans, or displaced persons.[14] Many Central American countries, for example, have stringent regulations about the number of foreigners that can be employed as a percentage of the total workforce. Virtually all countries have work-permit or visa restrictions that apply to foreigners. A **work permit** or **work certificate** is a document issued by a government granting authority to a foreign individual to seek employment in that government's country.

**Work permit/
work certificate**

Government document granting a foreign individual the right to seek employment

As in the United States, various methods are used to recruit employees from internal and external sources. In any country, but particularly in the developing countries, a disadvantage of using current employees as recruiters is that considerations of family, similar social status, culture, or language are usually more important than qualifications for the vacant position. More than one manager depending on employees as recruiters has filled a plant with relatives or people from the same hometown. In small towns much of the recruiting is done by word of mouth. Thus, having locals involved is critical. Churches, unions, and community groups also play a role.

MNCs tend to use the same kinds of external recruitment sources as are used in their home countries. While unskilled labor is readily available in the developing countries, recruitment of skilled workers is more difficult. Many employers have learned that the best way to find workers in these countries is through radio announcements because many people lack sufficient reading or writing skills. The solution is to have a recruiter who uses local methods within the context of the corporation's culture and needs or to put an expatriate in charge of recruiting.

The laws of almost all countries require the employment of local people if adequate numbers of skilled people are available. Thus, recruiting is limited to a restricted population. Specific exceptions are granted (officially or unofficially) for contrary cases, as for Mexican farmworkers in the United States and for Italian, Spanish, Greek, and Turkish workers in Germany and the Benelux countries (i.e., Belgium, Netherlands, Luxembourg). Foreign workers invited to come to perform needed labor are usually referred to as **guest workers.** The employment of nonnationals may involve lower direct labor costs, but indirect costs— language training, health services, recruitment, transportation, and so on—may be substantial.[15]

Guest workers

Foreign workers invited in to perform needed labor

Selection

American corporations have had a very significant impact on foreign HRM practices. The success of U.S.-based international businesses has caused many local firms and corporations based in other countries to study the methods of the American firms. Employment selection practices in U.S. corporations emphasize merit, with the best-qualified person getting the job. In other countries, firms have tended to hire on the basis of family ties, social status, language, and common origin. The candidate who satisfies these criteria gets the job even if otherwise unqualified. There has been a growing realization among foreign organizations, however, that greater attention must be given to hiring those most qualified.

In the industrialized countries, most businesses follow standard procedures of requesting employee information, including work experiences, in interviews and on application forms. Prospective employees may be given a physical examination and employment tests. In many European countries an employer is forbidden to make unfavorable statements about former employees. In Belgium and France, this prohibition was established by legislation; in Germany, by court decision.[16]

The Selection Process

The selection process should emphasize different employment factors, depending on the extent of contact that one would have with the local culture and the degree to which the foreign environment differs from the home environment. For example, if the job involves extensive contacts with the community, as with a chief executive officer, this factor should be given appropriate weight. The magnitude of differences between the political, legal, socioeconomic, and cultural systems of the host country and those of the home country should also be assessed.

If a candidate for expatriation is willing to live and work in a foreign environment, an indication of his or her tolerance of cultural differences should be obtained. On the other hand, if local nationals have the technical competence to carry out the job successfully, they should be carefully considered for the job before the firm launches a search (at home) for a candidate to fill the job. As stated previously, most corporations realize the advantages to be gained by staffing foreign subsidiaries with host-country nationals wherever possible.[17]

Selecting home-country and third-country nationals requires that more factors be considered than in selecting host-country nationals. While the latter must of course possess managerial abilities and the necessary technical skills, they have the advantage of familiarity with the physical and cultural environment and the language of the host country. The discussion that follows will focus on the selection of expatriate managers from the home country.

Selecting Expatriates

Estimates suggest that by the year 2000, nearly 15 percent of all employee transfers and relocations will be to an international location. Figure 19–6 shows a list of the most common locations for expatriate assignment.

The problem facing many corporations is to find employees who can meet the demands of working in a foreign environment. Unfortunately, the **failure rate** among expatriates has been estimated to range from 25 to 50 percent, with an average cost per failure of $40,000 to $250,000.[18] The most prevalent reasons for failure among expatriates are shown in Highlights in HRM 2. Many of these causes extend beyond technical and managerial capabilities and include personal and social issues as well. Interestingly, one of the biggest causes of failure is a spouse's inability to adjust to his or her new surroundings.[19]

There are no screening devices to identify with certainty who will succeed and who will fail. But there are requirements that one should meet to be considered for a managerial position in an international location. Historically, expatriate selection decisions have been driven by an overriding concern with technical competency. And this is an important criterion for success. However, the ability to adapt to a different type of environment frequently overshadows technical competence in the selection decision. Satisfactory adjustment depends on flexibility, emotional maturity and stability, empathy for the culture, language and communication skills, resourcefulness and initiative, and diplomatic skills. Companies such as Colgate-Palmolive, Whirlpool, and Dow Chemical have identified a set of **core skills** that they view as critical for success abroad and a set of **augmented skills** that help facilitate the efforts of expatriate managers. These skills and their managerial implications are shown in Highlights in HRM 3.[20] It is worth noting that many of these skills are not significantly different from those required for managerial success at home.

Failure rate
Percentage of expatriates who do not perform satisfactorily

Core skills
Skills considered critical in an employee's success abroad

Augmented skills
Skills helpful in facilitating the efforts of expatriate managers

---

FIGURE 19-6 *Top 10 U.S. Expatriate Assignments*

1	England	6	Singapore
2	Belgium	7	Germany
3	Australia	8	Netherlands
4	France	9	Hungary
5	Mexico	10	Japan

Source: From a survey by PHH Homequity, reported in "Rating the International Relocation Hot Spots," *Personnel Journal* (December 1993): 19. Reprinted with permission.

HIGHLIGHTS IN HRM

HRM
highlights

2   RANKING OF CAUSES OF EXPATRIATE FAILURE

	U.S. Managers	Expatriate Managers*	Asian Managers	Australian Managers
1. Manager's inability to adapt	2	1	1	1
2. Spouse's inability to adapt	1	2	2	2
3. Inability to cope with larger responsibilities	5	4	6	3
4. Other family-related matters	3	5	5	4
5. Manager's personality	4	3	3	5
6. Lack of motivation to work overseas	7	7	4	6
7. Lack of technical expertise	6	6	7	7
8. Other	8	8	8	8

* Expatriates were Americans, British, Canadians, French, New Zealanders, or Australians working outside their home countries.

Sources: R. J. Stone, "Expatriate Selection and Failure," *Human Resource Planning* 14, no. 1 (1991): 9–18; R. L. Tung, "Selection and Training Procedures of U.S., European, and Japanese Multinationals," Copyright 1982 by The Regents of the University of California, reprinted from the *California Management Review* 25, no. 1 (1982) by permission of The Regents.

Women Going Abroad

Traditionally, companies have been hesitant to send women on overseas assignments. Executives may either mistakenly assume that women do not want international assignments, or they assume that host-country nationals are prejudiced against women. The reality is that women frequently do want international assignments—at least at a rate equal to that of men. And while locals may be prejudiced against women in their own country, they view women first as foreigners (*gaijin* in Japanese) and only secondly as a women. Therefore, cultural barriers that typically constrain the roles of women in a male-dominated society may not totally apply in the case of expatriates.

Importantly, in those cases where women have been given international assignments, they generally have performed quite well. The success rate of female expatriates has been estimated to be about 97 percent—a rate far superior to that of men.[21] Ironically, women expatriates attribute at least part of their success to the fact that they are women. Because locals are aware of how unusual it is for a women to be given a foreign assignment, they frequently assume that the

HIGHLIGHTS IN HRM

3   PROFILE OF THE 21st-CENTURY EXPATRIATE MANAGER

HRM
highlights

CORE SKILLS	MANAGERIAL IMPLICATIONS
Multidimensional perspective	Extensive multiproduct, multi-industry, multifunctional, multicompany, multicountry, and multienvironment experience
Proficiency in line management	Track record in successfully operating a strategic business unit(s) and/or a series of major overseas projects
Prudent decision-making skills	Competence and proven track record in making the right strategic decisions
Resourcefulness	Skillful in getting himself or herself known and accepted in the host country's political hierarchy
Cultural adaptability	Quick and easy adaptability into the foreign culture—an individual with as much cultural mix, diversity, and experience as possible
Cultural sensitivity	Effective people skills in dealing with a variety of cultures, races, nationalities, genders, religions; also sensitive to cultural difference
Ability as a team builder	Adept in bringing a culturally diverse working group together to accomplish the major mission and objective of the organization
Physical fitness and mental maturity	Endurance for the rigorous demands of an overseas assignment

AUGMENTED SKILLS	MANAGERIAL IMPLICATIONS
Computer literacy	Comfortable exchanging strategic information electronically
Prudent negotiating skills	Proven track record in conducting successful strategic business negotiations in multicultural environment
Ability as a change agent	Proven track record in successfully initiating and implementing strategic organizational changes
Visionary skills	Quick to recognize and respond to strategic business opportunities and potential political and economic upheavals in the host country
Effective delegatory skills	Proven track record in participative management style and ability to delegate

Source: C. G. Howard, "Profile of the 21st-Century Expatriate Manager," *HR Magazine* (June 1992): 93–100. Reprinted with the permission of *HR Magazine,* published by the Society for Human Resource Management, Alexandria, Va.

company would not have sent a woman unless she was the very best. In addition, because women expatriates are novel (particularly in managerial positions), they are very visible and distinctive. In many cases, they may even receive special treatment not given to their male colleagues.[22]

Staffing Transnational Teams

Transnational team
Teams composed of members from multiple nationalities working on projects that span multiple countries

In addition to focusing on individuals, it is also important to note that companies are increasingly using **transnational teams** to conduct international business. Transnational teams are composed of members from multiple nationalities working on projects that span multiple countries.[23] These teams are especially useful for performing tasks that the firm as a whole is not yet designed to accomplish. For example, they may be used to transcend the existing organizational structure to customize a strategy for different geographic regions, transfer technology from one part of the world to another, and communicate between headquarters and subsidiaries in different countries.

The fundamental task in forming a transnational team is assembling the right composition of people who can work together effectively to accomplish the goals of the team. Many companies try to build variety into their teams in order to maximize responsiveness to the special needs of different countries. For example, when Heineken formed a transnational team to consolidate production facilities, it made certain that team members were drawn from each major region within Europe. Team members tended to have specialized skills, and additional members were added only if they offered some unique skill that added value to the team.

Selection Methods

The methods of selection most commonly used by corporations operating internationally are interviews, assessment centers, and tests. While some companies interview only the candidate, others interview both the candidate and the spouse, lending support to the fact that companies are becoming increasingly aware of the significance of the spouse's adjustment to a foreign environment and the spouse's contribution to managerial performance abroad. However, despite the potential value of considering a spouse's adjustment, the influence of such a factor over the selection/expatriation decision raises some interesting issues about validity, fairness, and discrimination. For example, if someone is denied an assignment because of concerns about their spouse, there may be grounds for legal action. This is particularly true now that the Civil Rights Act of 1991 makes it clear that U.S. laws apply to employees working for U.S. companies overseas.

To ensure validity, selection interviews are best conducted by senior executives who have had managerial experience in foreign countries. For example, at Mobil Oil the manager of international placement and staffing and two assistants with foreign experience conduct a four-hour interview with the candidate and the spouse to discuss all phases of the job. Emphasis is placed on the culture and the adaptability demands made on the candidate and the spouse.[24]

Assessment centers typically use individual and group exercises, individual interviews with managers and/or psychologists, and some personality and mental ability tests to evaluate candidates. Exercises that reflect situations characteris-

The Civil Rights Act of 1991 raises issues about the legality of assessing a spouse's adaptability to a foreign environment when making an overseas assignment.

tic of the potential host culture are usually included. The use of assessment centers has been shown to have high face validity and to be an effective tool for selecting from a large pool of international managerial candidates.[25]

A variety of measures, particularly personality inventories, can be used to determine an individual's ability to adapt to a different cultural environment.[26] Such inventories as the *Minnesota Multiphasic Personality Inventory (MMPI)*, the *Guilford-Zimmerman Temperament Survey*, and the *California Test* (the Indirect Scale for Ethnocentrism) are among those generally recommended. This third test is probably the most promising of these measures, since data suggest that high ethnocentrism correlates with overseas job failure.[27]

As noted in Chapter 6, the validity of any selection method is likely to be higher when it is based on a thorough job analysis, and personality tests are no exception to this rule. In using personality inventories and other types of personality tests, it is advisable to employ the services of a licensed psychologist. One New York consulting firm has developed an assessment tool known as the *Overseas Assignment Inventory (OAI)*. Based on twelve years of research involving more than 7,000 cases, the *OAI* helps identify characteristics and attitudes that potential international candidates should have.[28] One test, the *Modern Language Aptitude Test*, predicts with considerable accuracy a person's chances of being able to learn a foreign language. Where it is essential that a person learn a foreign language, employers find that it is important to have some assurance that the prognosis is favorable.[29]

Training and Development

objective

Although companies try to recruit and select the very best people for international work, it is often necessary to provide some type of training to achieve the desired level of performance. Over time, given the velocity of change in an international setting, employees may also need to upgrade their skills as they continue on the job. Such training may be provided within the organization or outside in some type of educational setting.

Skills of the Global Manager

If businesses are to be managed effectively in an international setting, managers need to be educated and trained in global management skills. A recent Korn/Ferry study of 1,500 CEOs and senior managers found that one of the biggest concerns is that by the year 2000, there will be a critical shortage of U.S. managers equipped to run global businesses.[30] In this regard, Levi Strauss has identified the following six attributes of **global managers**: (1) able to seize strategic opportunities, (2) capable of managing highly decentralized organizations, (3) aware of global issues, (4) sensitive to issues of diversity, (5) competent in interpersonal relations, and (6) skilled in building community.[31]

Global managers

Managers equipped to run global businesses

As noted throughout the book, it is particularly important for U.S. managers to learn to work with others in teams.[32] Unlike their counterparts in other parts of the world, U.S. managers are frequently at a disadvantage because they lack experience in working with people from different backgrounds. For transnational teams to perform well, team leaders need to perform three primary roles. First, they must act as an *integrator* of the team, bringing people from different functional backgrounds and cultures together. Second, they must be a *catalyst* for the team, encouraging individual team members to initiate and act on their own ideas, often across dispersed geographical areas. Third, team leaders need to be an external *advocate,* representing the team to persons outside the team and outside the organization.

Corporations that are serious about succeeding in global business are tackling these problems head-on by providing intensive training. Companies such as Amoco, Bechtel, 3M, Hyatt, Honeywell, and others with large international staffs prepare employees for overseas assignments. (These firms and others, including Coca-Cola, Motorola, Chevron, and Mattel, also orient employees who are still located in the United States but who deal in international markets.) The biggest mistake managers can make is to assume that people are the same everywhere. An organization that makes a concerted effort to ensure that its employees understand and respect cultural differences will realize the impact of its effort on its sales, costs, and productivity.[33]

Content of Training Programs

There are at least four essential elements of training and development programs that prepare employees for working internationally: (1) language training, (2) cultural training, (3) career development and mentoring, and (4) managing personal and family life.[34]

Language Training

In Chapter 15 we saw the types of problems that managers face in communicating with people from the same culture who speak the same language. Communication with individuals who have a different language and a different cultural orientation is much more difficult. Most executives agree that it is the biggest problem for the foreign business traveler. Even with an interpreter, much is missed.

While foreign language fluency is important in all aspects of international business, only a small percentage of Americans are skilled in a language other than English. Students who plan careers in international business should start instruction in one or more foreign languages as early as possible.[35] Programs designed to train participants for international business, such as those offered at the American Graduate School of International Management in Glendale, Arizona, and the Global Management Program at the University of South Carolina, provide intensive training in foreign languages.

Fortunately for most Americans, English is almost universally accepted as the primary language for international business. Particularly in cases where there are many people from different countries working together, English is usually the designated language for meetings and formal discourse.[36] Although English is a required subject in many foreign schools, students may not learn to use it effectively. Many companies provide instruction in English for those who are required to use English in their jobs. Where trainers use English to communicate information and instructions about the job, they must recognize the discomfort that foreign trainees may experience. Learning job skills in a second language is usually much more difficult than learning them in one's native tongue. In addition, certain concepts may not even exist in the foreign trainees' culture. The word "achievement," for example, doesn't exist in some Asian and African languages. There is no direct translation for "management" in French.

Several tips for teaching where English is a second language for the trainees are presented in Highlights in HRM 4. Many of the tips may also be applied in interpersonal communication on and off the job with people who have a limited understanding of American English. By placing oneself in the foreigner's position, one can soon learn how far to go in applying the tips.

Learning the language is only part of communicating in another culture. One must also learn how the people think and act in their relations with others. The following list illustrates the complexities of the communication process in international business.

1. In England, to "table" a subject means to put it on the table for present discussion. In the United States, it means to postpone discussion of a subject, perhaps indefinitely.
2. In America, information flows to a manager. In cultures where authority is centralized (Europe and South America), the manager must take the initiative to seek out the information.
3. Getting straight to the point is uniquely Western. Europeans, Arabians, and many others resent American directness in communication.
4. In Japan, there are sixteen ways to avoid saying "no."
5. When something is "inconvenient" to the Chinese, it is most likely downright impossible.

HIGHLIGHTS IN HRM

4   TEACHING TIPS WHEN ENGLISH IS A SECOND LANGUAGE

- Speak slowly and enunciate clearly.
- Do not use idioms, jargon, or slang.
- Repeat important ideas expressed in different ways.
- Use short, simple sentences; stop between sentences.
- Use active, not passive, verbs.
- Use visual reinforcement: charts, gestures, demonstrations.
- Have materials duplicated in the local language.
- Pause frequently and give breaks.
- Summarize periodically.
- Check comprehension by having students reiterate material.
- Encourage and reward, as appropriate to the culture.
- Never criticize or tease.

Source: Lennie Copeland and Lewis Griggs, *Going International* (New York: Random House, 1985), 149. Reproduced with permission.

6. In most foreign countries, expressions of anger are unacceptable; in some places, public display of anger is taboo.

7. The typical American must learn to treat silences as "communication spaces" and not interrupt them.

8. In general, Americans must learn to avoid gesturing with the hand.[37]

We observed in Chapter 15 that to understand the communication process, attention must be given to nonverbal communication. Figure 19–7 illustrates that some of our everyday gestures have very different meanings in other cultures. In summary, when one leaves the United States, it is imperative to remember that perfectly appropriate behavior in one country can lead to an embarrassing situation in another.

Since factors other than language are also important, those working internationally need to know as much as possible about (1) the place where they are going, (2) their own culture, and (3) the history, values, and dynamics of their

FIGURE 19-7 *Nonverbal Communications in Different Cultures*

CALLING A WAITER

In the United States, a common way to call a waiter is to point upward with the forefinger. In Asia, a raised forefinger is used to call a dog or other animal. To get the attention of a Japanese waiter, extend the arm upward, palm down, and flutter the fingers. In Africa, knock on the table. In the Middle East, clap your hands.

INSULTS

In Arab countries, showing the soles of your shoes is an insult. Also, an Arab may insult a person by holding a hand in front of the person's face.

A-OKAY GESTURE

In the United States, using the index finger and the thumb to form an "o" while extending the rest of the fingers is a gesture meaning okay or fine. In Japan, however, the same gesture means money. Nodding your head in agreement if a Japanese uses this sign during your discussion could mean you are expected to give him some cash. And in Brazil the same gesture is considered a seductive sign to a woman and an insult to a man.

EYE CONTACT

In Western and Arab cultures, prolonged eye contact with a person is acceptable. In Japan, on the other hand, holding the gaze of another person is considered rude. The Japanese generally focus on a person's neck or tie knot.

HANDSHAKE AND TOUCHING

In most countries, the handshake is an acceptable form of greeting. In the Middle East and other Islamic countries, however, the left hand is considered the toilet hand and is thought to be unclean. Only the right hand should be used for touching.

SCRATCHING THE HEAD

In most Western countries, scratching the head is interpreted as lack of understanding or non-comprehension. To the Japanese, it indicates anger.

INDICATING "NO"

In most parts of the world, shaking the head left and right is the most common way to say no. But among the Arabs, in parts of Greece, Yugoslavia, Bulgaria, and Turkey, a person says no by tossing the head to the side, sometimes clicking the tongue at the same time. In Japan, no can also be said by moving the right hand back and forth.

AGREEMENT

In addition to saying yes, Africans will hold an open palm perpendicular to the ground and pound it with the other fist to emphasize "agreed." Arabs will clasp their hands together, forefingers pointed outward, to indicate agreement.

Source: S. Hawkins, *International Management* 38, no. 9 (September 1983): 49. Reprinted with permission from *International Management*.

own organization. Highlights in HRM 5 gives an overview of what one needs to study for an international assignment.

Culture Training

Cross-cultural differences represent one of the most elusive aspects of international business. Generally unaware of their own culture-conditioned behavior, most people tend to react negatively to tastes and behavior that deviate from those of their own culture.

Managerial attitudes and behaviors are influenced, in large part, by the society in which managers receive their education and training. Similarly, reactions of employees are the result of cultural conditioning. Each culture has its expectations for the roles of managers and employees. For example, what one culture encourages as participative management another might see as managerial incompetence.[38] Being successful as a manager depends on one's ability to understand the way things are normally done and to recognize that changes cannot be made abruptly without considerable resistance, and possibly antagonism, on the part of local nationals. Some of the areas in which there are often significant variations among the different countries will be examined briefly.

A wealth of data from cross-cultural studies reveals that nations tend to cluster according to similarities in certain cultural dimensions such as work goals, values, needs, and job attitudes. Using data from eight comprehensive studies of cultural differences, Simcha Ronen and Oded Shenkar group countries into the clusters shown in Figure 19–8. Countries having a higher GDP per capita in comparison with other countries are placed close to the center.

Ronen and Shenkar point out that while evidence for the grouping of countries into Anglo, Germanic, Nordic, Latin European, and Latin American clusters appears to be quite strong, clusters encompassing the Far Eastern and Arab countries are ill defined and require further research, as do clusters of countries classified as independent. Many areas, such as Africa, have not been studied much at all.[39] It should also be noted that the clusters presented in Figure 19–8 do not include Russia and the former satellites of what was the Soviet Union.

Studying cultural differences can be helpful to managers in identifying and understanding differences in work attitudes and motivation in other cultures. In Japan, for example, employees are more likely to feel a strong loyalty to their company, although recent reports show that this may be changing. Americans, when compared with the Japanese, may feel little loyalty to their organization. On the other hand, the Latin American tends to work not for a company but for an individual manager. Thus managers in Latin American countries can encourage performance only by using personal influence and working through individual members of a group. In the United States, competition has been the name of the game; in Japan, Taiwan, and other Asian countries, cooperation is more the underlying philosophy.[40]

One of the important dimensions of leadership discussed in Chapter 14 is the degree to which managers invite employee participation in decision making. While it is difficult to find hard data on employee participation in various countries, careful observers report that American managers are about in the middle on a continuum of autocratic to democratic decision-making styles. Scandinavian and Australian managers also appear to be in the middle. South American

5 PREPARING FOR AN INTERNATIONAL ASSIGNMENT

To prepare for an international assignment, study the following subjects:

1. Social and business etiquette
2. History and folklore
3. Current affairs, including relations between the country and the United States
4. The culture's values and priorities
5. Geography, especially the cities
6. Sources of pride: artists, musicians, novelists, sports, great achievements of the culture, including things to see and do
7. Religion and the role of religion in daily life
8. Political structure and current players
9. Practical matters such as currency, transportation, time zones, hours of business
10. The language

Source: Lennie Copeland and Lewis Griggs, *Going International* (New York: Random House, 1985), 216. Reproduced with permission.

and European managers, especially those from France, Germany, and Italy, are toward the autocratic end of the continuum; Japanese managers are at the most participatory end. Because Far Eastern cultures and religions tend to emphasize harmony, group decision making predominates there.[41]

Most research on motivation in work settings is about people in industrially advanced nations. Those studies that have been done in third-world countries reveal that work motivation can be attributed to **culture strength** (beliefs, values, and norms that have not been diluted by other cultures) as well as to the level of industrialization. As Western values influence the culture and as industrialization increases, worker motivation changes.[42] Motivation is a dynamic process and requires continued study in any setting. Understanding work motivation in a particular culture is crucial to the overseas manager.

Culture strength
Beliefs, values, and norms undiluted by cross-cultural influences

Career Development

International assignments provide some definite developmental and career advantages. For example, working abroad tends to increase a person's responsibilities and influence within the corporation. In addition, it provides a person with

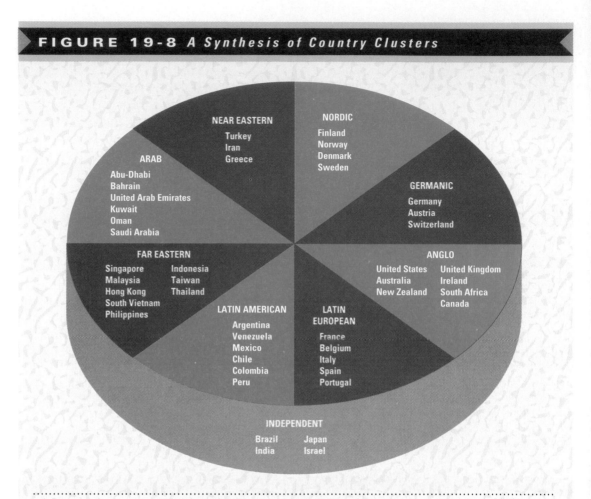

FIGURE 19-8 *A Synthesis of Country Clusters*

NEAR EASTERN
Turkey
Iran
Greece

NORDIC
Finland
Norway
Denmark
Sweden

ARAB
Abu-Dhabi
Bahrain
United Arab Emirates
Kuwait
Oman
Saudi Arabia

GERMANIC
Germany
Austria
Switzerland

FAR EASTERN
Singapore   Indonesia
Malaysia   Taiwan
Hong Kong   Thailand
South Vietnam
Philippines

ANGLO
United States   United Kingdom
Australia   Ireland
New Zealand   South Africa
                Canada

LATIN AMERICAN
Argentina
Venezuela
Mexico
Chile
Colombia
Peru

LATIN EUROPEAN
France
Belgium
Italy
Spain
Portugal

INDEPENDENT
Brazil   Japan
India   Israel

Source: Simcha Ronen and Oded Shenkar, "Clustering Countries on Attitudinal Dimensions: A Review and Synthesis," *Academy of Management Review* 10, no. 3 (July 1985): 435-54. Copyright *Academy of Management Review*. Reprinted with permission of the *Academy of Management Review* and the authors.

a set of experiences that are uniquely beneficial to both the individual and the firm.[43] Most people who accept international assignments do so in order to enhance their understanding of the global marketplace and to work on a project they perceive as important to the organization.[44]

However, in many cases, an overseas assignment is more risky for the average employee than staying with the employer in the United States. Far too often, people who have been assigned abroad return home after a few years to find that there is no position for them in the firm and that they no longer know anyone who can help them. In a surprising number of cases, returning expatriates experience reverse culture shock, and may have even more difficulty adjusting to life at home than they did adjusting to their foreign assignment.[45] Even in those

2

cases where employees are successfully repatriated, their companies often do not fully utilize the knowledge, understanding, and skills they developed in overseas experiences. This hurts the employee, of course, but it may hurt equally the firm's chances of using that learning to gain competitive advantage.

To maximize the career benefits of a foreign assignment, two key questions about the employer should be asked before accepting an overseas post: (1) Do the organization's senior executives view the firm's international business as a critical part of their operation? (2) Within top management, how many executives have a foreign-service assignment in their background, and do they feel it important for one to have overseas experience? At Dow Chemical, for example, fourteen of the firm's twenty-two-member management committee, including the CEO, have had overseas assignments. To ensure appropriate career development, Dow appoints what employees refer to as a "godfather" for those who get overseas assignments. The godfather, usually a high-level manager in the expatriate's particular function, is the stateside contact for information about organizational changes, job opportunities, and anything related to salary and compensation. At Exxon, employees are given a general idea of what they can expect after an overseas assignment even before they leave to assume it. With this orientation, they can make a smooth transition and continue to enhance their careers.[46]

Colgate-Palmolive and Ciba-Geigy make a special effort to keep in touch with expatriates during the period that they are abroad. Colgate's division executives and other corporate staff members make frequent visits to international transferees. Ciba-Geigy provides a full repatriation program for returning employees for the purpose of (1) reversing culture shock for the transferee and his or her family and department, (2) smoothing the return to the home organization, and (3) facilitating the readjustment process so that the company can benefit from the expatriate's knowledge and experience.[47]

Not all companies have career development programs designed specifically for repatriating employees. A study of 175 employers who belong to SHRM International reveals that many U.S.-based companies are not aware of the need for such programs. Only 31 percent of those included in the survey had formal programs. The reasons most frequently mentioned for not having a program were (1) lack of expertise in establishing a program (47 percent), (2) cost of the program (36 percent), and (3) no need perceived by top management for such a program (35 percent). It is interesting to note that HR managers also did not perceive the need for training and thus did not alert top managers to the problem.[48]

Managing Personal and Family Life

As noted previously, one of the most frequent causes of an employee's failure to complete an international assignment is personal and family stress. **Culture shock**—a disorientation that causes perpetual stress—is experienced by people who settle overseas for extended periods. The stress is caused by hundreds of jarring and disorienting incidents such as being unable to communicate, having trouble getting the telephone to work, being unable to read the street signs, and a myriad of other everyday matters that are no problem at home. Soon minor frustrations become catastrophic events, and one feels helpless and drained, emotionally and physically.

Culture shock

Perceptual stress experienced by people who settle overseas

In Chapter 8, we observed that more and more employers are assisting two-career couples in finding suitable employment in the same location. This assistance seems especially warranted when one considers that the U.S. Department of Labor has estimated that 81 percent of all marriages would be dual-career by 1995.[49] To accommodate dual-career partnerships, some employers are providing informal job help to the spouses of international transferees. However, other companies are establishing more formal programs to assist expatriate couples. These include career and life planning counseling, continuing education, intercompany networks to identify job openings in other companies, and job-hunting/fact-finding trips. In some cases, a company may even create a job for the spouse—though this is not widely practiced. The U.S. Chamber of Commerce, the U.S. State Department, and various women's organizations, such as Focus in London and Cairo, have initiated job counseling, networking groups, and assistance programs in several business centers.[50] The available evidence suggests that while a spouse's career may create some problems initially, in the long run it actually may help ease an expatriate's adjustment process.[51]

Training Methods

There are a host of training methods available to prepare an individual for an international assignment. Unfortunately, the overwhelming majority of companies only provide superficial preparation for their employees. Lack of training is one of the principal causes of failure among employees working internationally.

In many cases, the employee and his or her family can learn much about the host country through books, lectures, and videotapes about the culture, geography, social and political history, climate, food, and so on. The content is factual and the knowledge gained will at least help the participants to have a better understanding of their assignments. Such minimal exposure, however, does not fully prepare one for a foreign assignment. Training methods such as sensitivity training, which focuses on learning at the affective level, may well be a powerful technique in the reduction of ethnic prejudices. The Peace Corps, for example, uses sensitivity training supplemented by field experiences. Field experiences may sometimes be obtained in nearby "microcultures" where similarities exist.[52]

Companies often send employees on temporary assignments—lasting, say, a few months—to encourage shared learning. These temporary assignments are probably too brief for completely absorbing the nuances of a culture; however, companies such as Ferro and Dow use them to help employees learn about new ideas and technologies in other regions.[53]

In other instances employees are transferred for a much longer period of time. For example, in 1985 Fuji-Xerox sent fifteen of its most experienced engineers from Tokyo to a Xerox facility in Webster, New York. Over a five-year period, these engineers worked with a team of American engineers to develop the "world" copier. By working together on an extended basis, the U.S. and Japanese employees learned from each other—both the technical as well as the cultural requirements necessary for a continued joint venture.[54]

Developing Local Resources

Apart from developing talent for overseas assignments, most companies have found that good training programs also help them attract needed employees from the host countries. In less developed countries especially, individuals are quite eager to receive the training they need to improve their work skills. Oftentimes, however, a company's human capital investment does not pay off. It is very common, for example, that locally owned firms hire away those workers who have been trained by the foreign-owned organizations. Managers of American subsidiaries in Mexico have been heard to complain that "they must be training half the machinists in Mexico."[55]

Apprenticeship Training

A major source of trained labor in European nations is apprenticeship training programs (described in Chapters 2 and 7). On the whole, apprenticeship training in Europe is superior to that in the United States. In Europe, the dual-track system of education directs a large number of youths into vocational training. The German system of apprenticeship training, one of the best in Europe, provides training for office and shop jobs under a three-way responsibility contract between the apprentice, his or her parents, and the organization. At the conclusion of their training, apprentices can work for any employer but generally receive seniority credit with the training firm if they remain in it.[56]

Management Development

One of the greatest contributions that the United States has made to work organizations is in improving the competence of managers, a fact noted some years ago by Eugene de Facq, an international management consultant. Americans have a facility for reasoning that is part of their lives. They tend to make decisions on a rational basis and to have a better psychological background for decision making. Decisions of European managers, by way of contrast, are sometimes based on engineering-like and short-term thinking.[57]

Foreign nationals have generally welcomed the type of training they have received through management development programs offered by American organizations. Increasingly, companies such as Motorola and Hewlett-Packard have entered into partnerships with university executive education programs to customize training experiences to the specific needs of expatriate managers and foreign nationals.[58]

objective

Performance Appraisal

As we noted earlier, individuals frequently accept international assignments because they know that they can acquire skills and experiences that will make them more valuable to their companies. Unfortunately, one of the biggest problems with managing these individuals is that it is very difficult to evaluate their performance. Even the notion of performance evaluation is indicative of a U.S. management style that focuses on the individual, which can cause problems in other countries. For these reasons, performance appraisal problems may be among the biggest reasons why failure rates among expatriates are so high and why international assignments can actually derail an individual's career rather than enhance it.[59]

Who Should Appraise Performance?

In many cases, an individual working internationally has at least two allegiances: one to his or her home country (the office that made the assignment) and the other to the host country in which the employee is currently working. Superiors in each location frequently have different information about the employee's performance and may also have very different expectations about what constitutes good performance.[60]

Home-Country Evaluations

Domestic managers are frequently unable to understand expatriate experiences, value them, or accurately measure their contribution to the organization. Geographical distances pose severe communication problems for expatriates and home-country managers. Instead of touching base regularly, there is a tendency for both expatriates and domestic managers to work on local issues rather than coordinate across time zones and national borders. Information technology has improved this situation, and it is far easier to communicate globally today than just a few years ago.[61] But even when expatriates contact their home-country offices, it is frequently not to converse with their superiors. More likely they talk with peers and others throughout the organization.

Host-Country Evaluations

Although local management may have the most accurate picture of an expatriate's performance—managers are in the best position to observe effective and ineffective behavior—there are problems with using host-country evaluations. First, local cultures may influence one's perception of how well an individual is performing. As noted earlier in the chapter, participative decision making may be viewed either positively or negatively, depending on the culture. Such cultural biases may not have any bearing on an individual's true level of effectiveness. In addition, local management frequently does not have enough perspective of the entire organization to know how well an individual is truly contributing to the firm as a whole.

Given the pros and cons of home-country and host-country evaluations, most observers agree that performance evaluations should try to balance the two sources of appraisal information.[62] Although host-country employees are in a good position to view day-to-day activities, in many cases the individual is still formally tied to the home office. Promotions, pay, and other administrative decisions are connected there, and as a consequence, the written evaluation is usually handled by the home-country manager. Nevertheless, the appraisal should be completed only after vital input has been gained from the host-country manager. As discussed in Chapter 9, multiple sources of appraisal information can be extremely valuable for providing independent points of view—especially if someone is working as part of a team. If there is much concern about cultural bias, it may be possible to have persons of the same nationality as the expatriate conduct the appraisal.

Adjusting Performance Criteria

As we discussed at the beginning of this chapter, an individual's success or failure is affected by a host of technical and personal factors. (See Highlights in HRM 2.) Many of these factors should be considered in developing a broader set of performance criteria.

Augmenting Job Duties

Obviously the goals and responsibilities inherent in the job assignment are among the most important criteria used to evaluate an individual's performance. However, because of the difficulties in observing, documenting, and interpreting performance information in an international setting, superiors often resort to using "easy" criteria such as productivity, profits, and market share. These criteria may be valid—but deficient—if they do not capture the full range of an 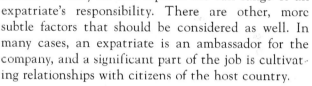 expatriate's responsibility. There are other, more subtle factors that should be considered as well. In many cases, an expatriate is an ambassador for the company, and a significant part of the job is cultivating relationships with citizens of the host country.

Individual Learning

Personnel abroad may require training to teach them how to cultivate relationships with citizens of the host country.

Any foreign assignment involves learning. As one might guess, it is much easier to adjust to similar cultures than to dissimilar ones. An American can usually travel to Australia and work with locals almost immediately. Send that same individual to Malaysia, and the learning curve is less steep. The expatriate's adjustment period may be even longer if the company has not yet established a good base of operations in the region. The first individuals to a country have no one to show them the ropes or to explain local customs. Even relatively simple activities such as navigating the rapid transit system can prove to be problematic. The U.S. State Department and defense forces have developed rating systems that attempt to distinguish whether regional assignments are (1) somewhat more difficult than they would be in the United

States, (2) more difficult than in the United States, and (3) much more diffi-cult than in the United States. These difficulty factors can be built into the ap-praisal system.[63]

Organizational Learning

It is worth noting that bottom-line measures of performance may not fully con-vey the level of learning gained from a foreign assignment. Yet learning may be among the very most important reasons for sending an individual overseas, particularly at early stages of internationalization.[64] Even if superiors do acknowl-edge the level of learning, they frequently use it only as an excuse for less-than-desired performance, rather than treating it as a valuable outcome in itself. What they fail to recognize is that knowledge gained—if shared—can speed the ad-justment process for others. However, if the learning is not shared, then each new employee to a region may have to go through the same cycle of adjustment.

Providing Feedback

One of the most interesting things about performance feedback in an interna-tional setting is that it is clearly a two-way street. Although the home-country and host-country superiors may tell an expatriate how well he or she is doing, it is also important for expatriates to provide feedback regarding the support they are receiving, the obstacles they face, and the suggestions they have about the assignment. More than in most any other job, expatriates are in the very best position to evaluate their own performance.

In addition to ongoing feedback, an expatriate should have a debriefing in-terview immediately upon returning home from an international assignment. These repatriation interviews serve several purposes. First, they help an expatri-ate reestablish old ties with the home organization and may prove to be impor-tant for setting new career paths. Second, the interview can address technical issues related to the job assignment itself. Third, the interview may address gen-eral issues regarding the company's overseas commitments, such as how relation-ships between the home and host countries should be handled. Finally, the interview can be very useful for documenting insights an individual has about the region. These insights can then be incorporated into training programs for future expatriates.

Six
objective

Compensation

One of the most complex areas of international HRM is compensation. Different countries have different norms for employee compensation. Managers should consider carefully the motivational use of incentives and rewards in foreign countries. For Americans, while nonfinancial incentives such as prestige, inde-pendence, and influence may be motivators, money is likely to be the driving force. Other cultures are more likely to emphasize respect, family, job security, a satisfying personal life, social acceptance, advancement, or power. Since there are many alternatives to money, the rule is to match the reward with the values of the culture. For example, Figure 19–9 shows how pay plans can differ on the basis of one cultural dimension: individualism. In individualistic cultures, such as the United States, pay plans often focus on individual performance and achievement. However, in collectively oriented cultures such as Japan and Taiwan, pay plans focus more on internal equity and personal needs.[65]

In general, a guiding philosophy for designing pay systems might be "think globally and act locally." That is, executives should normally try to create a pay plan that supports the overall strategic intent of the organization but provides enough flexibility to customize particular policies and programs to meet the needs of employees in specific locations.[66] After a brief discussion of compensation practices for host country employees and managers, we will focus on the problems of compensating expatriates.

Compensation of Host-Country Employees

Host-country employees are generally paid on the basis of productivity, time spent on the job, or a combination of these factors. In industrialized countries, pay is generally by the hour; in developing countries, by the day. The piece-rate method is quite common. In some countries, including Japan, seniority is an important element in determining employees' pay rates. When companies commence operations in a foreign country, they usually set their wage rates at or slightly higher than the prevailing wage for local companies. Eventually, though, they are urged to conform to local practices to avoid "upsetting" local compensation practices.

Employee benefits in other countries are frequently higher than those in the United States. In France, for example, benefits are about 70 percent of wages and in Italy 92 percent, compared with around 40 percent in the United States. Whereas in the United States most benefits are awarded to employees by employers, in other industrialized countries most of them are legislated or ordered by governments.[67]

In Italy, Japan, and some other countries, it is customary to add semiannual or annual lump-sum payments equal to one or two months' pay. These payments are not considered profit sharing but an integral part of the basic pay package. Profit sharing is legally required for certain categories of industry in Mexico, Peru, Pakistan, India, and Egypt among the developing countries and in France among the industrialized countries.[68] Compensation patterns in eastern Europe are in flux as these countries experiment with more-capitalistic systems.

Compensation of Host-Country Managers

In the past, remuneration of host-country managers has been ruled by local salary levels. However, increased competition among different companies with subsidiaries in the same country has led to a gradual upgrading of host-country managers' salaries. Overall, international firms are moving toward a narrowing of the salary gap between the host-country manager and the expatriate.

FIGURE 19-9 *Individualism and Compensation Strategies*

	DOMINANT VALUES	CORPORATE FEATURES	COMPENSATION STRATEGIES	SAMPLE COUNTRIES
HIGH	• Personal accomplishment • Selfishness • Independence • Individual attributions • Internal locus of control • Belief in creating one's own destiny • Utilitarian relationship with employee	• Organizations not compelled to care for employees' total well-being • Employees look after individual interests • Explicit systems of control necessary to ensure compliance and prevent wide deviation from organizational norms	• Performance-based pay utilized • Individual achievement rewarded • External equity emphasized • Extrinsic rewards are important indicators of personal success • Attempts made to isolate individual contributions (i.e., who did what) • Emphasis on short-term objectives	• United States • Great Britain • Canada • New Zealand
LOW	• Team accomplishment • Sacrifice for others • Dependence on social unit • Group attributions • External locus of control • Belief in the hand of fate • Moral relationship	• Organizations committed to a high level of involvement in worker's personal lives • Loyalty to the firm is critical • Normative, rather than formal, systems of control to ensure compliance	• Group-based performance is important criterion • Seniority-based pay utilized • Intrinsic rewards essential • Internal equity key in guiding pay policies • Personal need (e.g., number of children) affects pay received	• Singapore • South Korea • Indonesia • Japan • Taiwan

(Left axis label: INDIVIDUALISM)

Source: L. R. Gomez-Mejia and T. Welbourne, "Compensation Strategies in a Global Context," *Human Resources Planning* 14, no. 1 (1991): 29-41.

Compensation of Expatriate Managers

Compensation plans for expatriate managers must be competitive, cost-effective, motivating, fair and easy to understand, consistent with international financial management, easy to administer, and simple to communicate. To be effective, an international compensation program must

1. Provide an incentive to leave the United States
2. Allow for maintaining an American standard of living
3. Facilitate reentry into the United States
4. Provide for the education of children
5. Allow for maintaining relationships with family, friends, and business associates[69]

Balance-sheet approach

A compensation system designed to match the purchasing power of a person's home country

Expatriate compensation programs used by most U.S.-based international corporations rest on the **balance-sheet approach,** a system designed to equalize the purchasing power of employees at comparable position levels living overseas and in the home country and to provide incentives to offset qualitative differences between assignment locations. The balance-sheet approach comprises four elements:

1. *Base pay,* which is made essentially equal to pay of domestic counterparts in comparably evaluated jobs
2. *Differentials,* which are given to offset the higher costs of overseas goods, services, housing, and taxes
3. *Incentives,* which compensate the person for separation from family, friends, and domestic support systems, usually 15 percent of base salary
4. *Assistance programs,* which cover added costs such as moving and storage, automobile, and education expenses[70]

The differentials element is intended to correct for the higher costs of overseas goods and services so that in relation to their domestic peers expatriates neither gain purchasing power nor lose it. It involves a myriad of calculations to arrive at a total differential figure. Fortunately, employers do not have to do extensive research to find comparative data. They typically rely on data published quarterly by the U.S. Department of State for use in establishing allowances to compensate American civilian employees for costs and hardships related to assignments abroad.[71]

The costs of utilizing expatriate managers are higher today than ever before. For example, the employer's typical first-year expenses of sending one U.S. executive to Great Britain, as shown in Highlights in HRM 6, are $200,000 above the base salary. Many U.S. corporations are sending fewer managers overseas, often substituting host-country managers. Others are reducing allowances, benefits, and overseas pay incentives.[72] An increasing number of corporations employ foreign graduates from U.S. M.B.A. programs. The many foreign graduate students enrolled in business programs at U.S. universities are a pool of potential managers who combine the training and enculturation of an American M.B.A. with their own native background.

6 THE PRICE OF AN EXPATRIATE

An employer's typical first-year expenses of sending a U.S. executive to Britain, assuming a $100,000 salary and a family of four

Direct compensation costs

Base salary	$100,000
Foreign-service premium	15,000
Goods and services differential	21,000
Housing costs in London	39,000*

Transfer costs

Relocation allowance	$5,000
Air fair to London	2,000
Moving household goods	25,000

Other costs

Company car	$15,000
Schooling (two children)	20,000
Annual home leave (four people)	4,000
U.K. personal income tax	56,000*
TOTAL	**$302,000**

Note: Additional costs often incurred aren't listed above, including language and cross-cultural training for employee and family, and costs of selling home and cars in the U.S. before moving.

---

* Figures take into account payments by employee to company based on hypothetical U.S. income tax and housing costs.

Source: Reprinted by permission of *The Wall Street Journal* © 1989 Dow Jones & Company, Inc. All rights reserved worldwide.

objective

International Organizations and Labor Relations

Labor relations in countries outside the United States differ significantly from those in the United States. Differences exist not only in the collective bargaining process but also in the political and legal conditions. An American who works as an executive or as a manager overseas soon learns the differences and learns how to operate effectively under conditions that are quite different from those at home. These executives also learn that there may be no assistance of value from headquarters and that they must rely heavily on local employees with expertise in labor-management relations.

To acquaint the reader with the nature of labor-management relations in an international setting, we will look at the role of unions in different countries, at international labor organizations, and at the extent of labor participation in management.

The Role of Unions

The role of unions varies from country to country and depends on many factors, such as the level of per capita labor income, mobility between management and labor, homogeneity of labor (racial, religious, social class), and level of employment. These and other factors determine whether the union will have the strength it needs to represent labor effectively. In countries with relatively high unemployment, low pay levels, and no union funds for welfare, the union is driven into alliance with other organizations: political party, church, or government. This is in marked contrast to the United States, where the union selected by the majority of employees bargains only with the employer, not with other institutions.

Even in the major industrial countries one finds national differences are great with respect to (1) the level at which bargaining takes place (national, industry, or workplace), (2) the degree of centralization of union-management relations, (3) the scope of bargaining, (4) the degree to which government intervenes, and (5) the degree of unionization.[73]

Labor relations in Europe differ from those in the United States in certain significant characteristics:

1. In Europe, organizations typically negotiate the agreement with the union at the national level through the employer association representing their particular industry, even when there may be local within-company negotiations as well. This agreement establishes certain minimum conditions of employment which frequently are augmented through negotiations with the union at the company level.

2. Unions in many European countries have more political power than those in the United States, with the result that when employers deal with the union they are, in effect, dealing indirectly with the government. Unions are often allied with a particular political party, although in some countries these alliances are more complex, with unions having predominant but not sole representation with one party.

3. There is a greater tendency in Europe for salaried employees, including those at the management level, to be unionized, quite often in a union of their own.[74]

Like the United States, European countries are facing the reality of a developing global economy. It has been increasingly evident in Europe that workers are less inclined to make constant demands for higher wages. The trend has been to demand compensation in other ways—through a proliferation of benefits, for example, or through greater participation in company decision making.[75] Various approaches to participation will be discussed later.

Collective Bargaining in Other Countries

We saw in Chapter 18 how the collective bargaining process is typically carried out in companies operating in the United States. When we look at other countries, we find that the whole process can vary widely, especially with regard to the role that government plays. In the United Kingdom and France, for example, government intervenes in all aspects of collective bargaining. Government involvement is only natural where parts of industry are nationalized. Also, in countries where there is heavy nationalization there is more likely to be acceptance of government involvement, even in the nonnationalized companies. At Renault, the French government–owned automobile manufacturer, unions make use of political pressures in their bargaining with managers, who are essentially government employees. The resulting terms of agreement then set the standards for other firms. In developing countries it is common for the government to have representatives present during bargaining sessions to make sure that unions with relatively uneducated leaders are not disadvantaged in bargaining with skilled management representatives.

International Labor Organizations

The fact that international corporations can choose the countries in which they wish to establish subsidiaries generally results in the selection of those countries that have the most to offer. Certainly inexpensive labor is a benefit that most strategists consider. By coordinating their resources, including human resources, and their production facilities, companies operate from a position of strength. International unions, such as the United Auto Workers, have found it difficult to achieve a level of influence anywhere near that found within a particular industrial nation. Those that have been successful operate in countries that are similar, such as the United States and Canada.

The most active of the international union organizations has been the International Confederation of Free Trade Unions (ICFTU), which has its headquarters in Brussels. Cooperating with the ICFTU are some twenty International Trade Secretariats (ITSs), which are really international federations of national trade unions operating in the same or related industries. The significance of the ITSs from the point of view of management lies in the fact that behind local unions may be the expertise and resources of an ITS. Another active and influential organization is the International Labor Organization (ILO), a specialized agency of the United Nations. It does considerable research on an international basis and endorses standards for various working conditions, referred to as the *International Labor Code*. At various times and places this code may be quoted to management as international labor standards to which employers are expected to conform.

Labor Participation in Management

In many European countries, provisions for employee representation are established by law. An employer may be legally required to provide for employee representation on safety and hygiene committees, worker councils, or even on boards of directors. While their responsibilities vary from country to country, worker councils basically provide a communication channel between employers and workers. The legal codes that set forth the functions of worker councils in France are very detailed. Councils are generally concerned with grievances, problems of individual employees, internal regulations, and matters affecting employee welfare.

Codetermination

Representation of labor on the board of directors of a company

A higher form of worker participation in management is found in Germany, where representation of labor on the board of directors of a company is required by law. This arrangement is known as **codetermination** and often by its German word *Mitbestimmung*. Power is generally left with the shareholders, and shareholders are generally assured the chairmanship. Other European countries and Japan either have or are considering minority board participation.[76]

Each of these differences makes managing human resources in an international context more challenging. But the crux of the issue in designing HR systems is not choosing one approach that will meet all the demands of international business. Instead, organizations facing global competition must balance multiple approaches and make their policies flexible enough to accommodate differences across national borders. Throughout this book we have noted that different situations call for different approaches to managing people, and nowhere is this point more clearly evident than in international HRM.

SUMMARY

one
objective

There are four basic ways to organize for global competition: (1) The *international* corporation is essentially a domestic firm that has leveraged its existing capabilities to penetrate overseas markets; (2) the *multinational* corporation has fully autonomous units operating in multiple countries in order to address local issues; (3) the *global* corporation has a worldview but controls all international operations from its home office; and (4) the *transnational* corporation uses a network structure to balance global and local concerns.

two
objective

three
objective

International HRM has greater emphasis on a number of responsibilities and functions such as relocation, orientation, and translation services to help employees adapt to a new and different environment outside their own country.

Because of the special demands made on managers in international assignments, many factors must be considered in their selection and development. Though hiring host-country nationals or third-country nationals automatically avoids many potential problems, expatriate managers are preferable in some circumstances. The selection of the latter requires careful evaluation of the personal characteristics of the candidate and his or her spouse.

four
objective

Once an individual is selected, an intensive training and development program is essential to qualify that person for the assignment. Wherever possible, development should extend beyond information and orientation training to include sensitivity training and field experiences that will enable the manager to understand cultural differences better. Those in charge of the international program should provide the help needed to protect managers from career development risks, reentry problems, culture shock, and terrorism.

Although home-country managers frequently have formal responsibility for individuals on foreign assignment, they may not be able to fully understand expatriate experiences because geographical distances pose severe communication problems. Host-country managers may be in the best position to observe day-to-day performance but may be biased by cultural factors and may not have a view of the organization as a whole. To balance the pros and cons of home-country and host-country evaluations, performance evaluations should combine the two sources of appraisal information.

Compensation systems should support the overall strategic intent of the organization but be customized for local conditions. For expatriates, in particular, compensation plans must provide an incentive to leave the United States, enable maintenance of an equivalent standard of living, facilitate repatriation, provide for the education of children, and make it possible to maintain relationships with family, friends, and business associates.

In many European countries—Germany, for one—employee representation is established by law. Organizations typically negotiate the agreement with the union at a national level, frequently with government intervention. Since European unions have been in existence longer than their U.S. counterparts, they have more legitimacy and much more political power. In Europe, it is more likely for salaried employees and managers to be unionized.

KEY TERMS

augmented skills	global manager
balance-sheet approach	guest workers
codetermination	host country
core skills	host-country nationals
cultural environment	international corporation
culture shock	multinational corporation (MNC)
culture strength	third-country nationals
expatriates/home-country nationals	transnational organization
failure rate	transnational team
global corporation	work permit/work certificate

DISCUSSION QUESTIONS

1. Describe the effects that different components of the cultural environment can have on HRM in an international firm.
2. In what ways are American managers likely to experience difficulties in their relationships with employees in foreign operations? How can these difficulties be minimized?
3. This chapter places considerable emphasis on the role of the spouse in the success of an overseas manager. What steps should management take to increase the likelihood of a successful experience for all parties involved?
4. What are the major differences between labor-management relations in Europe and those in the United States?
5. In recent years we have observed an increase in foreign investment in the United States. What effect are joint ventures, such as General Motors–Toyota, likely to have on HRM in the United States?
6. What is codetermination? Do you believe that it will ever become popular in the United States? Explain your position.
7. If you were starting now to plan for a career in international HRM, what steps would you take to prepare yourself for overseas assignments?
8. Talk with a foreign student on your campus; ask about his or her experience with culture shock on first arriving in the United States. What did you learn from your discussion?

CASE STUDY: Teleco's Expansion within the European Union

Teleco Electronics is heavily involved in sales of computer and electronic equipment in Europe. At this time, Teleco's international sales account for 31 percent of its total volume, and almost half of those sales are in the European Union (EU) countries. Because of the large volume of sales in Europe, Teleco has decided to build a manufacturing operation in one of the EU countries. There are a number of advantages that Teleco can derive from this decision. Currently, because the company must work through numerous intermediaries, sales within Europe are very complicated and expenses are high. By building a manufacturing operation, Teleco can reduce some of these sales expenses. Furthermore, Teleco can take advantage of the Single European Act of 1992 by avoiding the taxes associated with imported products if its products are manufactured within one of the EU countries.

The vice president of human resources, Chuck Waldo, has stated that an important part of the decision to expand is determining which EU country would provide the best location for the facility. Labor laws still vary widely among EU member countries, and despite the Single European Act, there is disagreement among member countries over which of the labor laws are to become common across countries. Even with considerable commonality, cultures and languages will still affect labor practices to a great extent. In deciding which country to choose for the manufacturing plant, Waldo has charged his staff with considering several important issues associated with the management of human resources in the EU. Among the issues to be considered are the social policies of the countries.

Germany represents one extreme in the area of social policy. It has very strong labor unions and one of the best-protected labor forces among EU member states. Its workers receive a minimum of 18 days of vacation per year; the maximum hours of work per day are 8, and 48 per week. Spain represents the other extreme in social policy associated with labor protection. Its workforce has much less protection than Germany's in the areas of wages, health, and safety. Unemployment in Spain is about 20 percent, and labor costs are much lower than elsewhere. By contrast with Germany, however, its minimum vacation is longer—2.5 days per month—and while its maximum workday is 9 hours, the maximum per week is 40 hours. Ireland represents still another labor environment. Its per capita income is low and unemployment is high, somewhat like Spain's. However, the educational level of its citizens is very high. Minimum vacation is 3 weeks per year, and there is no maximum on the number of hours that one may work per day or week.

Despite differences among the countries, there is pressure from the labor unions for a common social charter among EU member states. The implementation of common social policy in the form of an EU-mandated social charter has important implications for HR decisions. The charter has the potential for drastically changing the way a firm operates in the EU. A common charter would remove the competitive advantages of a given country. For example, Spain would no longer be able to offer the advantage of cheap labor with the implementation of a common wage and salary structure. The likelihood of these social issues being settled soon is still low despite the Single European Act of 1992, and many observers believe that adoption of a common charter prior to the year 2000 is very unlikely.

Questions

1. What considerations led Teleco to decide to expand its manufacturing to Europe?
2. What considerations should Waldo take into account in choosing among EU member states for the location of the manufacturing plant?
3. Besides those mentioned in the case, are there other labor force factors that Teleco should consider when selecting a country?

NOTES AND REFERENCES

1. A. P. Carnevale, *America and the New Economy*, (San Francisco: Jossey-Bass, 1991); K. Ohmae, *The Borderless World: Power and Strategy in the Interlinked Economy* (New York: Harper Business, 1990).

2. Christopher A. Bartlett and Sumantra Ghoshal, *Managing across Borders: The Transnational Solution* (Boston: Harvard Business School Press, 1991).

3. Charles C. Snow, Sue Canney Davison, Donald C. Hambrick, and Scott A. Snell, *Transnational Teams in Global Network Organizations* (Lexington, Mass.: International Consortium for Executive Development Research, 1993).

4. Arvind V. Phatak, *International Dimensions of Management*, 4th ed. (Cincinnati: South-Western, 1995), Chapter 1. See also Taylor Cox, Jr., "The Multicultural Organization," *Academy of Management Executive* 5, no. 2 (May 1991): 34–47; Noritake Kobayashi, "Comparison of Japanese and Western Multinationals—Part I," *Tokyo Business Today* 58, no. 10 (October 1990): 50.

5. Brian Brooks, Marsh Cameron Haller, Jean Robert Viguie, "EC 92: The Impact on Pay Delivery," *Benefits and Compensation International* 19, no. 8 (February 1990): 20–22. For a comprehensive overview of EC-92 designed to assist managers in planning a strategy for the European market, see Heinz Weihrich, "Europe 1991: What the Future May Hold," *Academy of Management Executive* 4, no. 2 (May 1990): 7–18. See also Robert O'Connor, "Britain Trains to Compete in a Unified Europe," *Personnel Journal* 70, no. 5 (May 1991): 67–70.

6. Stewart J. Black and Lyman W. Porter, "Managerial Behaviors and Job Performance: A Successful Manager in Los Angeles May Not Succeed in Hong Kong," *Journal of International Business Studies* 22, no. 1 (1991): 99–113.

7. Vern Terpstra and Kenneth David, *The Cultural Environment of International Business*, 3d ed. (Cincinnati: South-Western, 1991).

8. Nancy J. Adler and Susan Bartholomew, "Managing Globally Competent People," *Academy of Management Executive* 6, no. 3 (1992): 52–65. See also Nancy J. Adler and Susan Bartholomew, "Academic and Professional Communities of Discourse: Generating Knowledge of Transnational Human Resource Management," *Journal of International Business Studies* 23, no. 3 (1992): 551–69.

9. Ellen Brandt, "Global HR," *Personnel Journal* (March 1991): 38–44; Peter J. Dowling, "International HRM," in *Human Resource Management—Evolving Roles & Responsibilities*, ed. Lee Dyer (Washington, D.C.: Bureau of National Affairs, 1988), 1:228–1:242. See also A. G. Kefalas, *Global Business Strategy—A Systems Approach* (Cincinnati: South-Western, 1990), Chapter 12; Noel Shumsky, "Keeping Track of Global Managers," *Human Resources Professional* 5, no. 4 (Spring 1993): 6–9.

10. Brandt, "Global HR," 38–44.

11. Phatak, *International Dimensions of Management*, Chapter 6.

12. Peter Coy and Neil Gross, "When the Going Gets Tough, Yanks Get Yanked," *Business Week* (April 26, 1993): 30; Daniel Pruzin, "Location. . . and More," *World Trade* 6, no. 9 (October 1993): 84–92.

13. Cecil G. Howard, "Profile of the 21st-Century Expatriate Manager," *HR Magazine* 37, no. 6 (June 1992): 93–100.

14. Herbert J. Chruden and Arthur W. Sherman, Jr., *Personnel Practices of American Companies in Europe* (New York: American Management Association, 1972), 25.

15. Richard D. Robinson, *Internationalization of Business: An Introduction* (New York: Dryden Press, 1984), 104–106.

16. Lennie Copeland, "Cross-Cultural Training: The Competitive Edge," *Training* 22, no. 7 (July 1985): 49–53.

17. Raymond J. Stone, "Expatriate Selection and Failure," *Human Resource Planning* 14, no. 1 (1991): 9–18. See also Rosalie L. Tung, "Selection and Training of Personnel for Overseas Assignments," *Columbia Journal of World Business* 16, no. 1 (Spring 1981): 68–78; Rosalie L. Tung, *The New Expatriates: Managing Human Resources Abroad* (Cambridge, Mass.: Ballinger, 1988).

18. Gary W. Hogan and Jane R. Goodson, "The Key to Expatriate Success," *Training and Development Journal* 44, no. 1 (January 1990): 50–52. See also Allan Bird and Roger Dunbar, "Getting the Job Done over There: Improving Expatriate Productivity," *National Productivity Review* 10, no. 2 (Spring 1991): 145–56.

19. Stone, "Expatriate Selection and Failure," 9–18; Tung, "Selection and Training of Personnel," 68–78.

20. Stewart J. Black and Hal B. Gregersen, "Antecedents to Cross-Cultural Adjustment for Expatriates in Pacific Rim Assignments," *Human Relations* 44, no. 5 (May 1991): 497–515. See also Bruce W. Stening and Mitchell R. Hammer, "Cultural Baggage and the Adaptation of Expatriate American and Japanese Managers," *Management International Review* 32, no. 1 (1992): 77–89.

21. Howard, "Profile of the 21st-Century Expatriate Manager," 93–100.

22. Nancy J. Adler, "Women Managers in a Global Economy," *HR Magazine* 38, no. 9 (September 1993): 52–55. See also Nancy J. Adler, "Pacific Basin Managers: A *Gaijin*, Not a Woman," *Human Resource Management* 26, no. 2 (1987): 169–91; Hilary Harris, "Women in International Management: Opportunity or Threat?" *Women in Management Review* 8, no. 5 (1993): 9–14.

23. Snow et al., *Transnational Teams*.

24. Simcha Ronen, *Comparative and Multinational Management* (New York: Wiley, 1986), 184–86.

25. Ronen, *Comparative and Multinational Management*, 539.

26. R. L. Tung, "Selection and Training Procedures of U.S., European, and Japanese Multinationals," *California Management Review* 25, no. 1 (Fall 1982): 57–71.

27. Tung, "Selection and Training of Personnel," and Ronen, *Comparative and Multinational Management*,

536. See also Robert P. Tett, Douglas N. Jackson, and Mitchell Rothstein, "Personality Measures as Predictors of Job Performance: A Meta-Analytic Review," *Personnel Psychology* 44 (1991): 703–40.

28. Madelyn R. Callahan, "Preparing the New Global Manager," *Training & Development Journal* 43, no. 3 (March 1989): 29–32.

29. Terpstra and David, *Cultural Environment of International Business*, 41.

30. Donald C. Hambrick, James W. Fredrickson, Lester B. Korn, and Richard M. Ferry, "Reinventing the CEO," *21st Century Report* (Korn/Ferry and Columbia Graduate School of Business, 1989).

31. Sheila Rothwell, "Leadership Development and International HRM," *Manager Update* 4, no. 4 (Summer 1993): 20–32. See also Peter Blunt, "Recent Developments in Human Resource Management: The Good, the Bad and the Ugly," *International Journal of Human Resource Management* 1, no. 1 (June 1990): 45–59.

32. Victoria J. Marsick, Ernie Turner, and Lars Cederholm, "International Managers as Team Leaders," *Management Review* 78, no. 3 (March 1989): 46–49; Terpstra and David, *Cultural Environment of International Business*, 5; Spencer Hayden, "Our Foreign Legions Are Faltering," *Personnel* 67, no. 8 (August 1990): 40–44; J. R. Katzenbach and D. K. Smith, *The Wisdom of Teams: Creating the High Performance Team* (Boston: Harvard Business School Press, 1993). See also M. Domsch and B. Lichtenberger, "Managing the Global Manager: Predeparture Training and Development for German Expatriates in China and Brazil," *Journal of Management Development* 10, no. 7 (1991): 41–52.

33. Lennie Copeland, "Cross-Cultural Training: The Competitive Edge," *Training* 22, no. 7 (July 1985): 49–53. See also Mark Mendenhall and Gary Oddou, "The Dimensions of Expatriate Acculturation: A Review," *Academy of Management Review* 19, no. 1 (January 1985): 39–47; "Learning to Accept Cultural Diversity," *The Wall Street Journal* (September 12, 1990); Barry Rubin, "Europeans Value Diversity," *HR Magazine* 36, no. 1 (January 1991): 38–41, 78.

34. Edward Dunbar and Allan Katcher, "Preparing Managers for Foreign Assignments," *Training and Development Journal* 44, no. 9 (September 1990): 45–47. See also Paul R. Sullivan, "Trainings's Role in Global Business," *Executive Excellence* 8, no. 9 (September 1991): 9–10.

35. Lee H. Radebaugh and Janice C. Shields, "A Note on Foreign Language Training and International Business Education in U.S. Colleges and Universities," *Journal of International Business Studies* 15, no. 3 (Winter 1984): 195–99.

36. Snow et al., *Transnational Teams*.

37. Lennie Copeland and Lewis Griggs, *Going International* (New York: Random House, 1985).

38. Dean B. McFarlan, Paul D. Sweeney, and John L. Cotton, "Attitudes toward Employee Participation in Decision-Making: A Comparison of European and American Managers in a United States Multinational Company," *Human Resource Management* 31, no. 4 (Winter 1992): 363–83.

39. Lee Roberts, "HRD in Africa," in Leonard Nadler (ed.), *The Handbook of Human Resource Development*, 2d ed. (New York: Wiley, 1990). See also Merrick L. Jones, "Management Development: An African Focus," in Mark Mendenhall and Gary Oddou (eds.), *Readings and Cases in International Human Resource Management*, 2d ed. (Cincinnati: South-Western, 1995): 250–63.

40. Fred Luthans, Harriette S. McCaul, and Nancy Dodd, "Organizational Commitment: A Comparison of American, Japanese, and Korean Employees," *Academy of Management Journal* 28, no. 1 (March 1985): 213–18. See also Nancy J. Adler, *International Dimensions of Organizational Behavior* (Boston: Kent, 1991).

41. Geert Hofstede, "Cultural Constraints in Management Theories," *Academy of Management Executive* 7, no. 1, (February 1993): 81–94. See also Ronen, *Comparative and Multinational Management*, 184–86.

42. Fons Trompenaars, *Riding the Waves of Culture: Understanding Cultural Diversity in Business* (London: Economist Books, 1993).

43. Gary Oddou and Mark Mendenhall, "Grooming Our Future Business Leaders?" *Business Horizons* 34, no. 1 (January/February 1991): 26–34.

44. Snow et al., *Transnational Teams*.

45. Stewart J. Black, "Returning Expatriates Feel Foreign in Their Native Land," *Personnel* 68, no. 8 (August 1991): 17. See also Hal B. Gregersen, "Commitments to a Parent Company and a Local Work Unit during Repatriation," *Personnel Psychology* 45, no. 1 (Spring 1992): 29–54.

46. Carey W. English, "Weigh the Risks First on That Job Abroad," *U.S. News & World Report* (December 2, 1985): 82. See also Philip R. Harris, "Employees Abroad: Maintain the Corporate Connection," *Personnel Journal* 65, no. 8 (August 1986): 106–110; Paul L. Blocklyn, "Developing the International Executive," *Personnel* 66, no. 3 (March 1989): 44–47; Mark Mendenhall and Gary Oddou, "The Overseas Assignment: A Practical Look," *Business Horizons* 31, no. 5 (September-October 1988): 78–84.

47. Blocklyn, "Developing the International Executive," 47. See also Susan Carey, "Expatriates Find Long Stints Abroad Can Close Doors to Credit at Home," *The Wall Street Journal* (Monday, May 17, 1993): B1.

48. Michael G. Harvey, "Repatriation of Corporate Executives: An Empirical Study," *Journal of International Business Studies* 20, no. 1 (Spring 1989):

131–44; Robert T. Moran, "Corporations Tragically Waste Overseas Experience," *International Management* 43, no. 1 (January 1988): 74.

49. Calvin Reynolds and Rita Bennett, "The Career Couple Challenge," *Personnel Journal* 70, no. 3 (March, 1991): 46–47.

50. Reynolds and Bennett, "Career Couple Challenge."

51. Gregory K. Stephens and Stewart Black, "The Impact of Spouse's Career-Orientation on Managers during International Transfers," *Journal of Management Studies* 28, no. 4 (July 1991): 417–28.

52. Tung, "Selection and Training of Personnel." See also Simcha Ronen, "Training the International Assignee," in *Training and Career Development*, ed. I. Goldstein (San Francisco: Jossey-Bass, 1989), 430; Gary W. Hogan and Jane R. Goodson, "The Key to Expatriate Success," *Training & Development Journal* 44, no. 1 (January 1990): 50–52; J. Stewart Black and Mark Mendenhall, "A Practical But Theory-Based Framework for Selecting Cross-Cultural Training Methods," in Mendenhall and Odou, *International Human Resource Management*, 194–221.

53. Snow et al., *Transnational Teams*.

54. Snow et al., *Transnational Teams*.

55. Donald A. Ball and Wendell H. McCulloch, Jr., *International Business—Introduction and Essentials*, 4th ed. (Plano, Texas: Business Publications, 1990), 628.

56. Chruden and Sherman, *Personnel Practices*, 40–41.

57. Chruden and Sherman, *Personnel Practices*, 7–8.

58. Althea Bloom, "The Wide World of Corporate Training," *Hemispheres* (September 1993): 39–43.

59. Gary Oddou and Mark Mendenhall, "Expatriate Performance Appraisal: Problems and Solutions," in Mendenhall and Oddou, *International Human Resource Management*, 399–410.

60. R. S. Schuler, J. R. Fulkerson, and P. J. Dowling, "Strategic Performance Measurement and Management in Multinational Corporations," *Human Resource Management* 30, no. 3 (Fall 1991): 365–92.

61. S. A. Snell, P. Pedigo, and G. M. Krawiec, "Managing the Impact of Information Technology in Human Resource Management," in G. R. Ferris, D. Rosen, and D. T. Marnum, *Handbook of Human Resources Management* (Oxford, U.K.: Blackwell Publishing, in press).

62. Stewart J. Black and Hal B. Gregersen, "Serving Two Masters: Managing the Dual Allegiance of Expatriate Employees," *Sloan Management Review* 33, no. 4 (Summer 1992): 61–71.

63. Mendenhall and Oddou, *International Human Resource Management*, 406.

64. Bartlett and Ghoshal, *Managing across Borders*, 24–25.

65. Richard M. Hodgetts and Fred Luthans, "U. S. Multinationals' Compensation Strategies for Local Management: Cross Cultural Implications," *Compensation and Benefits Review* 25, no. 2 (March-April 1993): 42–48.

66. Douglas J. Carey and Paul D. Howes, "Developing a Global Pay Program," *Journal of International Compensation and Benefits* (July/August, 1992). See also Mariah E. De Forest, "Thinking of a Plant in Mexico?" *Academy of Management Executive* 8, no. 1 (February 1994): 33–40.

67. Ball and McCulloch, *International Business*, 640.

68. Robinson, *Internationalization of Business*, 108–13. See also Lin P. Crandall and Mark I. Phelps, "Pay for a Global Work Force," *Personnel Journal* 70, no. 2 (February 1991): 28–33.

69. Raymond J. Stone, "Pay and Perks for Overseas Executives," *Personnel Journal* 65, no. 1 (January 1986): 64–69. See also Ranae M. Hyer, "Executive Compensation in the International Arena: Back to the Basics," *Compensation and Benefits Review* 25, no. 2 (March-April 1993): 49–54; Peggy Stuart, "Global Payroll—A Taxing Problem," *Personnel Journal* 70, no. 10 (October 1991): 80–90.

70. Calvin Reynolds, "Compensation of Overseas Personnel," in Joseph J. Famularo (ed.) *Handbook of Human Resources Administration*, 2d ed. (New York: McGraw-Hill, 1986), 56-2, 56-3. See also Crandall and Phelps, "Pay for a Global Work Force," 28–33.

71. *U.S. Department of State Indexes of Living Costs Abroad, Quarters, Allowances, and Hardship Differentials* (Washington, D.C.: Bureau of Labor Statistics, published quarterly).

72. Joann S. Lublin, "Companies Try to Cut Subsidies for Employees," *The Wall Street Journal* (December 11, 1989): B1. See also Neil B. Krupp, "Overseas Staffing for the New Europe," *Personnel* 67, no. 7 (July 1990): 20–24; Kate Gillespie, "U.S. Multinationals and the Foreign MBA," *Columbia Journal of World Business* 24, no. 2 (Summer 1989): 45–51.

73. Robinson, *Internationalization of Business*, 94–97.

74. Chruden and Sherman, *American Companies in Europe*, 116. See also Brooks Tigner, "The Looming Labour Crunch," *International Management* 44, no. 2 (February 1989): 26–31.

75. Reginald Dale, "International Forces Will Prevail, but Will Unions Be Able to Change with New Global Workplace?" *Personnel Administrator* 28, no. 12 (December 1983): 100–104. See also "Looking for Work: In Employment Policy, America and Europe Make a Sharp Contrast," *The Wall Street Journal* (March 14, 1994): A1; "Payroll Policy: Unlike Rest of Europe, Britain Is Creating Jobs, but They Pay Poorly," *The Wall Street Journal* (March 28, 1994): A1.

76. Robinson, *Internationalization of Business*, 86.

Chapter

Auditing the Human Resources
Management Program

After studying this chapter you should be able to

 Discuss the contributions of HR audits to an organization.

 Identify specific HR areas to be audited.

 Identify the major formulas used to evaluate the work environment.

 Describe employee attitude surveys and the information that can be gained from their use.

 Explain how to analyze audit findings.

W*e have completed the discussion of the functions that make up the HR program. Now it seems appropriate to analyze the ways in which the value of this program to an organization may be assessed. Auditing the HR program will be the focus of this chapter.*

Like financial audits, audits of the HR program should be conducted periodically to ensure that its objectives are being accomplished. An HR audit typically involves anlyzing data relative to the HR program, including employee turnover, grievances, absences, accidents, employee attitudes, and job satisfaction. The most effective audit is one that provides the maximum amount of valid information concerning the overall effectiveness of the HR program in contributing to the strategic objectives of the organization.

While it typically focuses on the HR department, an HR audit is not restricted to the activities of that department. It involves a study of the functions of HRM throughout the total organization, including those performed by managerial and supervisory personnel. More emphasis, however, should be placed on judging the effectiveness of the HR department at the operating level because of its impact on employee attitudes and behaviors and its services to managers and employees. The decisions and activities of HR managers influence the effectiveness of the HR function as well as overall human resources, and ultimately, organizational effectiveness.

objective

Contributions of the Human Resources Audit

Current emphasis on productivity improvement, pay-for-performance, employee empowerment, and team building has increased the attention given to human resources and their contributions to the achievement of organizational success. The HR audit is a method of ensuring that the human resource potential of the organization is being fulfilled, while providing an opportunity to:

1. Evaluate the effectiveness of HR functions—compensation, training, recruitment, selection, EEO, safety and health, and so on
2. Benchmark HR activities to ensure continuous improvement
3. Ensure compliance with laws, policies, and regulations
4. Improve the quality of the HR staff
5. Promote change and creativity
6. Focus the HR staff on important issues
7. Bring HR closer to the line functions of the organization[1]

If an organization is to remain competitive, it must undergo continual change. An audit of its HR program can help managers identify variances between actual and expected or desired conditions. The audit becomes a data-based stimulus for change. Not only can the audit expedite change, it can be used as an instrument of change. For example, if it is desirable that an HR manager make changes in the department, an audit can be used as a neutral instrument for the views of superiors, peers, subordinates, and non-HR personnel in the organization. Thus multiple pressures for change are brought upon all managers.

Conducting the Audit

Audits may be conducted by internal or external personnel.[2] There are advantages and disadvantages to each approach. Insiders know more about the organization and are in a better position to determine which aspects require evaluation.

They are also less likely to be viewed as a threat by those being audited. How objective the insiders will be, however, is always a question. External auditors are likely to be more objective and have less ego involvement.

The fact that legal and HR considerations have become so complex makes it appropriate for employers to consider using an external auditor who has substantial experience in both HR and employment law.[3] At the present time, however, only about 3 percent of companies surveyed use outside consultants. Corporate or executive management, corporate HR administration, or the HR research department typically performs the audit.[4]

Steps in the Audit Process

Before discussing the various aspects of the HR program that provide the content for an audit, we will first take a look at the steps typically followed in an organizational audit. HR auditing specialists suggest that the audit process should consist of the following six steps:

1. Introduce the idea of the audit and emphasize the benefits to be derived from it. Obtain commitment of top management.
2. Select personnel with a broad range of skills for the audit team and provide training as needed.
3. Gather data from different levels in the organization.
4. Prepare audit reports for line managers and HR department evaluation.
5. Discuss reports with operating managers who then prepare their own evaluation.
6. Incorporate corrective actions into the regular organization objective-setting process.

Since auditing is a form of research, it is important that the findings be based on objective, reliable, and valid data. HR records of all types are available for use in audits. In addition to analyzing records, interviews are usually

These managers are being briefed on the objectives of their HR audit.

conducted with managers at different levels, the HR manager, the HR staff, and a selected number of supervisors and nonmanagement personnel.

objective

HR Areas to Be Audited

The most important function of the HR audit is to determine the effectiveness with which the objectives of the HR program are being met. Before starting the audit, the objectives and standards of the program should be stated clearly. An audit should include at least three major approaches: (1) measuring HR's compatibility with organizational goals, (2) determining compliance with laws and regulations, and (3) evaluating the performance of specific HR programs and functions.

Measuring Compatibility with Organizational Goals

The process of setting goals requires close coordination with top management. This ensures that the HR policies and procedures are consistent with top management's goals and objectives. The audit provides an opportunity to assess the extent to which objectives are being met and to revise policies and procedures accordingly.

Benchmarking

A continuous and systematic process for comparing some aspect of organizational performance against data from an organization considered to be superior in that area

Once HR objectives are established, the HR staff may benchmark different HR activities or functions in order to identify areas for improvement. **Benchmarking**—a part of the total-quality movement—operates as a systematic process for comparing some aspect of an organization with that of an organization recognized as a leader in the particular area under study. The HR practices of Malcolm Baldrige National Quality Award winners—Cadillac, Globe Metallurgical, and Wallace—provide useful benchmarks for organizations wishing to assess their own HR activities.

For the HR department to use benchmarking successfully, it must benchmark on the basis of clearly defined measures of competency and performance. The measures must objectively define the current situation and identify areas for improvement.[5] Highlights in HRM 1 shows several aspects of training that can be benchmarked against organizations considered superior in the training function. While no single model exists to benchmark exactly, the simplest models are based on the late Edward Deming's classic four-step process. The four-step process advocates that managers:

- *Plan.* Conduct a self-audit to define internal processes and measurements; decide on areas to be benchmarked and choose the comparison organization.
- *Do.* Collect data through surveys, interviews, site visits, and/or historical records.
- *Check.* Analyze data to discover performance gaps and communicate findings and suggested improvements to management.
- *Act.* Establish goals, implement specific changes, monitor progress, and redefine benchmarks as a continuous improvement process.[6]

Like other quality initiatives, benchmarking and its evaluative component should become part of the regular HR audit process.

HIGHLIGHTS IN HRM

highlights

1 BENCHMARKING HR TRAINING

MEASUREMENT NAME	MEASUREMENT TYPE	HOW TO CALCULATE	EXAMPLE
Percent of payroll spent on training	Training activity	Total training expenditures ÷ total payroll	U.S. average = 1.4 percent of payroll spent on training per year.
Training dollars spent per employee	Training activity	Total training expenditures ÷ total employees served	Three Baldrige winners spent $1,100 per employee on training in 1990.
Average training hours per employee	Training activity	Total number of training hours (hours × participants) ÷ total employees served	U.S. average for large firms (100+ employees) = 33 hours per employee in 1990.
Percent of employees trained per year	Training activity	Total number of employees receiving training ÷ total employee population	Three Baldrige winners trained an average of 92.5 percent of their workforces in 1990.
HRD staff per 1,000 employees	Training activity	Number of HRD staff ÷ total employee population × 1,000	Three Baldrige winners had an average of 4.1 HRD staff members per 1,000 employees.
Cost savings as a ratio of training expenses	Training results: Bottom line	Total savings in scrap or waste ÷ dollars invested in training	A Baldrige winner reported saving $30 for every $1 spent on TQM training (for an ROI of 30:1).
Profits per employee per year	Training results: Bottom line	Total yearly gross profits ÷ total number of employees	An electronics firm earned average profits per employee of $21,000 in 1990.
Training costs per student hour	Training efficiency	Total costs of training ÷ total number of hours of training	Three Baldrige winners reported $27 in average training costs per hour of training in 1990.

Source: Adapted from Donald J. Ford, "Benchmarking HRD," *Training and Development* 47, no. 6 (June 1993): 36–41. Copyright 1993 by the American Society for Training and Development. Reprinted with permission. All rights reserved.

. . . .

Determining Compliance with Laws and Regulations

As we have noted throughout this book, the number of laws and regulations affecting HRM has increased dramatically over the years. Organizations typically establish programs and procedures for achieving compliance with them. Top management needs to be aware of the manner in which managers at all levels are complying with the laws and regulations.[7] Equal employment opportunity, safety and health, and pension plans are among the compliance areas often investigated in comprehensive audits.

Employers are required to maintain records for these programs in specified formats for examination by compliance investigators from federal and state agencies. To illustrate the types of demands on employers that government agencies can make, we cite a few items included in one compliance review:

1. A listing by ethnic group of minority promotions in a twelve-month period, giving "from" and "to" position titles, along with effective dates
2. Copies of seniority lists by plant, division, and department, with minority members identified
3. An explanation of how tests were validated, by whom the tests were validated, and the scores used to make employment decisions
4. A listing of craft jobs from the EEO-1 Report, broken down to show totals and minorities by ethnic group
5. Names of those who referred minority candidates, and how many were refused
6. Information on how many employees, by ethnic grouping, were in the summer employment program

It is essential that managers anticipate the types of information that will be required by government agencies and establish systems for maintaining such information in a computer file. The collection of data in advance will avoid last-minute crises in data-gathering requests.

Employers should take a proactive approach to compliance with laws and regulations. It is important not only to establish effective policies and procedures but also to make sure that subordinates understand them thoroughly. Sexual harassment, discussed in Chapter 3, is a good example of a problem area. Problems often arise from lack of knowledge of the specific on-the-job behaviors that constitute sexual harassment under the law. Through a questionnaire it is possible to test employee understanding of what is and is not sexual harassment.

Highlights in HRM 2 is a sampling of items that could be used during a sexual harassment audit. Such an instrument, which is essentially a test, is a valuable tool for determining what employees know and do not know about important areas.

Evaluating Program Performance

Each of the functional areas of HRM should help to meet the overall objectives of an HR program. It is important, therefore, to audit each of these functions to determine how effectively and economically they are being performed. Since it is not possible to discuss in this text all the details involved in the audit of each

HIGHLIGHTS IN HRM

highlights

2   QUESTIONS USED IN AUDITING SEXUAL HARASSMENT

ACTIVITY	IS THIS SEXUAL HARASSMENT?			ARE YOU AWARE OF THIS BEHAVIOR IN THE ORGANIZATION?	
• Employees post cartoons on bulletin boards containing sexually related material.	Yes	No	Uncertain	Yes	No
• A male employee says to a female employee that she has beautiful eyes and hair.	Yes	No	Uncertain	Yes	No
• A male manager habitually calls all female employees "sweetie" or "darling."	Yes	No	Uncertain	Yes	No
• A manager fails to promote a female (male) employee for not granting sexual favors.	Yes	No	Uncertain	Yes	No
• Male employees use vulgar language and tell sexual jokes that are overheard by, but not directed at, female employees.	Yes	No	Uncertain	Yes	No
• A male employee leans and peers over the back of a female employee when she wears a low-cut dress.	Yes	No	Uncertain	Yes	No
• A supervisor gives a female (male) subordinate a nice gift on her (his) birthday.	Yes	No	Uncertain	Yes	No
• Two male employees share a sexually explicit magazine while observed by a female employee.	Yes	No	Uncertain	Yes	No

functional area, we suggest in Figure 20–1 the general types of questions that should be answered in an audit. The sources of in-house information—usually records and reports—that are available for use in the audit are also included in the figure.

Most of the sources of information listed in Figure 20–1 yield statistical data that are readily available in many organizations. Where electronic information systems are being used, such information can be kept current for analysis

---

FIGURE 20-1 *Auditing the Major Functions in HRM*

HUMAN RESOURCES FUNCTION	SOURCES OF INFORMATION
Planning and Recruitment • Do job specifications contain bona fide occupational qualifications? • Are job descriptions accurate, periodically reviewed, and updated? • Are there any human resources that are not being fully utilized? • Is the affirmative action program achieving its goals? • How effective is the recruiting process? • How productive are the recruiters?	• HR budgets • Recruitment cost data • Job descriptions and specifications • Hiring rate
Selection • How valid are selection techniques? • Is there evidence of discrimination in hiring? • Are interviewers familiar with the job requirements? • Do interviewers understand what questions are acceptable and unacceptable to ask of job applicants? • Are tests job-related and free from bias? • How do hiring costs compare with those of other organizations?	• Employment interview records • Applicant rejection records • Transfer requests • EEOC complaints
Training and Development • How effective are training programs in increasing productivity and improving the quality of employee performance? • Are there sufficient opportunities for women and minorities to advance into management positions? • What is the cost of training per person-hour of instruction? • What is the relationship between training costs and accidents?	• Training costs data • Production records • Accident records • Quality-control records
Performance Appraisal • Are the performance standards objective and job-related? • Do the appraisal methods emphasize performance rather than traits? • Are the appraisers adequately trained and thoroughly familiar with the employees' work? • Are the appraisals documented and reviewed with employees? • Are the performance appraisal data assembled in such form that they can be used to validate tests and other selection procedures?	• Performance appraisal records • Production records • Scrap loss records • Appraisal interview records • Attendance records • Disciplinary action records

FIGURE 20-1 *Continued*

HUMAN RESOURCES FUNCTION	SOURCES OF INFORMATION
Compensation • Does the pay system, including incentive plans, attract employees and motivate them to achieve organizational goals? • Do the compensation structure and policies comply with EEO, ERISA, and IRS requirements? • Is the choice of weights and factors in job evaluation sound and properly documented? • Do benefits costs compare favorably with those of similar organizations?	• Wages and benefits data • Wage-survey records • Unemployment compensation insurance • Turnover records • Cost-of-living surveys
Labor Relations • Are supervisors trained to handle grievances effectively? • Is there ongoing preparation for collective bargaining? • What is the record of the number and types of grievances, and what percentage of grievances have gone to arbitration? • What percentage of disciplinary discharges have been challenged?	• Grievance records • Arbitration award records • Work stoppage records • Unfair labor-practice complaint records

and reporting. HR professionals predict even greater use of information systems in carrying out the various HR audit functions. One need only turn to the *Personnel Journal* or *HR Magazine* to find articles with specific recommendations for the use of computers as well as advertisements of companies specializing in software for HR activities.[8]

As valuable as the information sources listed in Figure 20–1 are in measuring the effectiveness of the major HRM functions, overreliance on quantitative measures may yield conclusions that seem objectively valid but fail to assess whether HR clients are really satisfied with the services they receive. This suggests using periodic studies of clients' perception of services rendered. Clients may include line executives and managers, employees, applicants, or even union officers.[9] User reactions may be obtained through attitude surveys, discussions with employees and focus groups, manager and supervisor comments, and similar approaches.

Measuring Human Resources Costs

Management is typically interested in the costs of the activities that are required to meet the HR objectives. Standard cost-accounting procedures can be applied to all of the HRM functions. Cost savings are easily demonstrated in (1) compensation policies and procedures, (2) benefit programs and insurance premiums, (3) personnel taxes (such as unemployment taxes), (4) recruiting, training, and management development, (5) affirmative action, and (6) turnover and outplacement.[10]

In establishing a program for measuring HR costs, it is important to enlist the participation of the HR staff. In addition to gaining understanding and acceptance for the audit process, through participation the staff can identify a large number of measurable activities that can be included in formulas for measuring costs. Costs of orientation, for example, can be computed per employee per department (or HR department orientation expense). The cost of various recruiting and hiring procedures can likewise be computed. For example, the source cost of recruits per hire (SC/H) can be computed by the following formula:

$$SC/H = \frac{AC + AF + RB + NC}{H}$$

where AC = advertising costs, total monthly expenditure (example: $28,000)
AF = agency fees, total for the month (example: $19,000)
RB = referral bonuses, total paid (example: $2,300)
NC = no-cost hires, walk-ins, nonprofit agencies, etc. (example: $0)
H = total hires (example: 119)

Substituting the example numbers in the formula:

$$SC/H = \frac{\$28,000 + \$19,000 + \$2,300 + \$0}{119}$$

$$= \frac{\$49,300}{119}$$

$$= \$414 \text{ (source cost of recruits per hire)}$$

The basic formula can be varied by changing total hires to include only exempt hires (EH) or nonexempt hires (NEH). The example of source costs per hire is only one of many formulas available.

Area-Specific Audits

In addition to reviewing the functional activities of the HR department, area-specific audits can evaluate topics of current importance to managers. Two areas of present concern are cultural audits and the glass ceiling.

Cultural Audits

Cultural audit
Audit of the organizational culture and quality of work life in an organization

Companies such as Syntex, Lotus Development, and Southwest Airlines are identified as organizations having an employee-oriented culture. The **cultural audit** essentially involves discussions among top-level managers of how the organization's culture reveals itself and how the culture may be influenced. It requires a serious examination of such questions as:

- What do employees spend their time doing?
- How do they interact with each other?
- Are employees empowered? (See Chapter 14.)
- What is the predominant leadership style of managers?
- How do employees advance within the organization?

Conducting in-depth interviews and making observations over a period of time are the ways to learn about the culture. With the increased diversity of the U.S. workplace, cultural audits can be used to determine the existence of subcultures. Subcultures within an organization may well have very different views about the nature of work and how work should be done.

Glass Ceiling Audits

Glass ceiling

The invisible, yet real or perceived, attitudinal or organizational barriers that serve to limit the advancement opportunities of minorities and women

The U.S. Department of Labor defines the **glass ceiling** "as those artificial barriers based on attitudinal or organizational bias that prevent qualified individuals from advancing upward in their organizations into management level positions." Glass Ceiling Reviews, also known as Corporate Reviews, are conducted by the Department of Labor. These reviews focus on the culture of the organization, including practices that appear to hinder the upward mobility of qualified minorities and women. The Department of Labor will look for such things as equal access to:

- Upper-level management and executive training
- Rotational assignments
- International assignments
- Opportunities for promotion
- Opportunities for executive development programs at universities
- Desirable compensation packages
- Opportunities to participate on high-profile project teams
- Upper-level "special assignments"[11]

Conducting a glass ceiling self-audit prior to government review can help to avoid fines and externally imposed corrective action. As noted by one HR practitioner, "The audit can document any ceilings and the reasons they exist."[12] It

The advancement of women to upper-level management is often hindered by the glass ceiling.

. . . .

will be increasingly untenable for an organization to have a diverse workforce and a majority male senior management team. Self-audits are one step to tapping the potentials of a diversified workforce.

objective

Indicators in Evaluating the Work Environment

Throughout this book we have emphasized that the work environment can have a significant effect on the motivation, performance, job satisfaction, and morale of employees. It is possible to assess the quality of the environment within an organization by studying certain indicators. These indicators, which may also be used to assess the HR functions, are widely used in all types and sizes of organizations. They include employee turnover rates, absenteeism rates, injury and illness records, and responses from employee attitude surveys.

Employee Turnover Rates

"Employee turnover" refers to the movement of employees in and out of an organization. It is often cited as one of the factors behind the failure of U.S. employee productivity rates to keep pace with those of foreign competitors.

Costs of Turnover

Replacing an employee is time-consuming and expensive. Costs can generally be broken down into three categories: separation costs for the departing employee, replacement costs, and training costs for the new employee. These costs are conservatively estimated at two to three times the monthly salary of the departing employee, and they do not include indirect costs such as low productivity prior to quitting and lower morale and overtime for other employees because of the vacated job. Consequently, reducing turnover could result in significant savings to an organization. Highlights in HRM 3 details one organization's costs associated with the turnover of one computer programmer. Note that the major expense is the cost involved in training a replacement.

Computing the Turnover Rate

Turnover rate
Number of separations during a month divided by the total number of employees at midmonth times 100

The **turnover rate** for a department or an entire organization is an indicator of how employees respond to their work environment. The U.S. Department of Labor suggests the following formula for computing turnover rates:

$$\frac{\textbf{Number of separations during the month}}{\textbf{Total number of employees at midmonth}} \times \textbf{100}$$

Thus, if there were 25 separations during a month and the total number of employees at midmonth was 500, the turnover rate would be:

$$\frac{25}{500} \times 100 = 5 \text{ percent}$$

HIGHLIGHTS IN HRM

highlights

3 COSTS ASSOCIATED WITH THE TURNOVER OF ONE COMPUTER PROGRAMMER

Turnover costs = Separation costs + Replacement costs + Training costs

Separation costs

1. Exit interview = cost for salary and benefits of both interviewer and departing employee during the exit interview = $30 + $30 = $60
2. Administrative and record-keeping action = $30
    Separation costs = $60 + $30 = $90

Replacement costs

1. Advertising for job opening = $2,500
2. Preemployment administrative functions and record-keeping action = $100
3. Selection interview = $250
4. Employment tests = $40
5. Meetings to discuss candidates (salary and benefits of managers while participating in meetings) = $250
    Replacement costs = $2,500 + $100 + $250 + $40 + $250 = $3,140

Training costs

1. Booklets, manuals, and reports = $50
2. Education = $240/day for new employee's salary and benefits × 10 days of workshops, seminars, or courses = $2,400
3. One-to-one coaching = ($240/day/new employee + $240/day/staff coach or job expert) × 20 days of one-to-one coaching = $9,600
4. Salary and benefits of new employee until he or she gets "up to par" = $240/day for salary and benefits × 20 days = $4,800
    Training costs = $50 + $2,400 + $9,600 + $4,800 = $16,850

Total turnover costs = $90 + $3,140 + $16,850 = $20,080

. . . .

Source: Adapted from Michael W. Mercer, *Turning Your Human Resources Department into a Profit Center* (New York: AMACOM, 1993). Copyright 1993 Michael W. Mercer. Reproduced with permission from Michael W. Mercer, Ph.D., Industrial Psychologist, The Mercer Group, Inc., Chicago, Ill.

Turnover rates are computed on a regular basis for more than four out of five organizations responding to a Bureau of National Affairs (BNA) survey. More than three-fourths of them use the data to compare rates among specific groups within the organizations such as departments, divisions, and work groups. In half of these organizations, comparisons are made with data provided by other organizations as well. The BNA's *Quarterly Report on Job Absence and Turnover* is used by the majority as a source of comparative turnover data.[13]

Another method of computing the turnover rate is one in which the rate reflects only the avoidable separations (S). This is accomplished by subtracting unavoidable separations (US), for example, pregnancy, return to school, death, or marriage, from all separations. The formula for this method is as follows:

$$\frac{(S - US)}{M} \times 100 = T \text{ (turnover rate)}$$

where M represents the total number of employees at midmonth. For example, if there were 25 separations during a month, 5 of which were US, and the total number of employees at midmonth (M) was 500, the turnover rate would be

$$\frac{25 - 5}{500} \times 100 = 4 \text{ percent}$$

This method yields what is probably the most significant measure of the effectiveness of the HR program, since it can serve to direct attention to avoidable separations where management has the most opportunity to influence better selection, training, supervisory leadership, improved working conditions, better wages, and opportunities for advancement.

The quantitative rate of turnover is not the only factor to be considered. The quality of personnel who leave an organization is also important.

Determining Causes of Turnover

Exit interview
Interview conducted to determine why employees leave an organization

To determine why employees leave, many organizations conduct an **exit interview** during the employee's final week of employment. One study of a limited number of organizations found that 83 percent of these interviews are conducted by the HR department. In most cases the interviewers are employment recruiters. This is advantageous for two reasons: (1) Employees are likely to be more open when speaking with someone with whom they have had previous contact, and (2) recruiters are usually experienced interviewers.[14] Topics covered in exit interviews are shown in Figure 20–2.

The validity of the reasons for leaving that employees give during the exit interview has to be questioned. Many employees follow the rule of leaving on good terms and may consider frank discussion detrimental to their interests. Standardizing the interview by asking the same questions, advising exiting em-

---

> ## FIGURE 20-2 *Topics Covered during Exit Interviews*
>
> - Reasons for departure
> - Relationships with supervisors
> - Fairness of performance appraisal reviews
> - Evaluation of pay and advancement opportunities
> - Rating of working conditions
> - Things liked best about job/organization
>
> - Things liked least about job/organization
> - Communication from management
> - Evaluation of training received
> - Organizational climate
> - Suggestions

ployees that information will be used in a constructive, not retaliatory, manner, and checking reasons given with supervisory personnel and co-workers can help to improve the reliability and validity of data.

Absenteeism Rates

Absenteeism rate

Number of worker days lost through job absence during a period divided by the average number of employees times the number of workdays, and the result multiplied by 100

How frequently employees are absent from their work—the **absenteeism rate**—may also indicate the state of the work environment and the effectiveness of the HR program. A certain amount of absenteeism is, of course, unavoidable. There will always be some who must be absent from work because of sickness, accidents, serious family problems, and other legitimate reasons.

Costs of Absenteeism

Traditional accounting and personnel information systems often do not generate data that reflect the costs of absenteeism. To call management's attention to the severity of the problem, absenteeism should be translated into dollar costs. A system for computing absenteeism costs for an individual organization is available. Organizations with computerized absence-reporting systems should find this additional information easy and inexpensive to generate. The cost of each person-hour lost to absenteeism is based on the hourly weighted average salary, costs of employee benefits, supervisory costs, and incidental costs.

For example, for a hypothetical company of 1,200 employees with 78,000 person-hours lost to absenteeism, the total absence cost is $560,886. When this figure is divided by 1,200, the cost is $464.41 per employee for the period covered. (In this example the absent workers were paid. If absent workers are not paid, their salary figures are omitted from the computation.)

Computing the Absenteeism Rates

It is advisable for management to determine the seriousness of its absenteeism problem by maintaining individual and departmental attendance records and by computing absenteeism rates. Neither a universally accepted definition of absence nor a standard formula for computing absenteeism rates exists.[15] However, the method of computing absenteeism rates most frequently used is that recommended by the U.S. Department of Labor:

$$\frac{\text{Number of worker days lost through job absence during period}}{\text{Average number of employees} \times \text{number of workdays}} \times 100$$

If 300 worker days are lost through job absence during one month having 25 scheduled working days at an organization that employs 500 workers, the absenteeism rate for that month is:

$$\frac{300}{500 \times 25} \times 100 = 2.4 \text{ percent}$$

The Department of Labor defines job absence as the failure of employees to report to work when their schedules require it, whether or not such failure to report is excused. Scheduled vacations, holidays, and prearranged leaves of absence are not counted as job absence.

Comparing Absenteeism Data

The Bureau of Labor Statistics of the U.S. Department of Labor receives data on job absences from the Current Population Survey of Households conducted by the Bureau of the Census, and analyses of these data are published periodically. These analyses permit the identification of problem areas—those industries, occupations, or groups of workers with the highest incidence of absence or with rapidly increasing rates of absence. Comparison with other organizations may be made by referring to Bureau of Labor Statistics data reported in the *Monthly Labor Review* or by consulting such reporting services as the Bureau of National Affairs, Prentice-Hall, and Commerce Clearing House.[16]

Nearly six out of ten organizations responding to a BNA survey reported that they compute absence rates on a regular basis for at least one employee group. These organizations encouraged their supervisors to compare their department rates with those of other departments and with the company average so that problems could be promptly identified and corrected.

Reducing Absenteeism

While an employer may find that absenteeism rates and costs are within an acceptable range, it is advisable to study the statistics and determine exactly where the numbers are rooted. Rarely does absenteeism spread itself evenly across an organization.[17] A fairly high number of workers may have perfect attendance records, while some may be absent frequently. Effective HRM requires that individual attendance records be monitored by supervisors, that incentives be provided for perfect attendance, and that progressive discipline procedures (see Chapter 16) be used with employees having a record of chronic absenteeism.[18] The direct and continuing involvement of all managers and supervisors is essential.

By establishing a comprehensive absenteeism policy, the Allen-Bradley Company was able to cut absenteeism 83.5 percent in a twenty-five-month period. Part of the company's attendance policy reads:

> "It is important to the successful operation of the Motion Control Division that employees be at work each scheduled workday. Each employee is performing an important set of tasks or activities. Excessive and/or avoidable absenteeism places unfair burdens on co-workers and increases the company's cost of doing business by disruption of work schedules, [creating] inefficiency and waste, delays, costly overtime, job pressures and customer complaints."[19]

Occupational Injuries and Illnesses

We noted in Chapter 13 that employers are required by OSHA to maintain a log and summary of occupational injuries and illnesses and to prepare a supplementary record for every recordable injury or illness. Detailed information about accidents and illnesses provides a starting point for analyzing problem areas, making changes in the working environment, and motivating personnel to promote safety and health.

From the records that are maintained, the Bureau of Labor Statistics and other organizations, such as the National Safety Council, compile data that an employer can use as a basis for comparison. In order to make such comparisons, it is necessary to compute for an individual organization the *incidence rate*, which is the number of injuries and illnesses per 100 full-time employees during a given year. The standard formula for computing the incidence rate is shown by the following equation, where 200,000 equals the base for 100 full-time workers who work 40 hours a week, 50 weeks a year:

$$\text{Incidence rate} = \frac{\text{Number of injuries and illnesses} \times 200{,}000}{\text{Total hours worked by all employees during period covered}}$$

Incidence rates thus provide a basis for making comparisons with other organizations doing similar work. These rates are also useful for making comparisons between work groups, between departments, and between similar units within an organization. Application of this formula to the experience of one organization and the use of a table for comparative purposes are illustrated in the following example.

Shannon's Concrete Company, with an average annual employment of 80 individuals during 1994, experienced 15 recordable injuries and illnesses in that year. The total number of hours worked by all employees during this period was 127,000 (from payroll or other time records):

$$\frac{15 \times 200{,}000}{127{,}000} = 23.6 \text{ incidence rate}$$

Therefore Shannon's Concrete experienced an incidence rate for total recordable cases of 23.6 injuries and illnesses per 100 full-time employees during 1994.

By examining the line marked off in Figure 20–3, which gives data from organizations with 50 to 99 employees, we find that Shannon's incidence rate of 23.6 is higher than the median (15.4) but lower than that in at least one-quarter of other establishments. It should be noted that the same formula can be used to

FIGURE 20-3 *Comparison Data for Injuries and Illnesses*

Occupational injury and illness incidence rates of total recordable cases for construction industries by employment size and quartile distribution, 1987.

Industry, SIC code[1], and employment size	INCIDENCE RATES PER 100 FULL-TIME WORKERS			
	COLUMN A	**COLUMN B**	**COLUMN C**	**COLUMN D**
	Average incidence rates for all establishments: (mean)	One-quarter of the establishments had a rate lower than or equal to: (1st quartile)	One-half of the establishments had a rate lower than or equal to: (median)	Three-fourths of the establishments had a rate lower than or equal to: (3rd quartile)
Special trade contractors Concrete work (SIC 177)				
All sizes	13.2	0.0	0.0	0.0
1 to 19	6.2	0.0	0.0	0.0
20 to 49	15.1	0.0	7.5	24.2
50 to 99	19.6	5.6	15.4	30.9
100 to 249	25.9	11.3	21.2	31.4
250 to 499	22.7	(2)	(2)	(2)
500 to 999	19.3	(2)	(2)	(2)
1,000 to 2,499	19.0	(2)	(2)	(2)

Note: (1) *Standard Industrial Classification Manual,* 1972 edition, 1977 supplement (Washington, D.C.: Office of Management and Budget).

(2) Quartile rates were not derived because fewer than 25 establishment reports were included in the industry employment-size group.

Source: *Evaluating Your Firm's Injury and Illness Record—Construction Industries* (Washington, D.C.: Bureau of Labor Statistics, Report 776, March 1990), 4.

compute incidence rates for (1) the number of workdays lost because of injuries and illnesses, (2) the number of nonfatal injuries and illnesses without lost work-days, and (3) cases involving only injuries or only illnesses.

objective

Employee Attitude Surveys

The influence of attitudes and values on employee productivity is well recognized. In assessing attitudes, employers are typically interested in those attitudes that relate to the job; to effectiveness of supervision; and to communication, compensation, training and development, and special organizational concerns.[20] With such information it is possible to make organizational changes that will, it is hoped, increase productivity and job satisfaction. One of the most objective and economical approaches to obtaining data for use in making organizational changes is through **attitude surveys.** These surveys are usually conducted on an organization-wide or plant-wide basis and usually involve the administration of a questionnaire (or inventory) or the use of interviews.

Organization-Specific Attitude Surveys

Attitude surveys

Employee surveys conducted on an organization-wide or department-wide basis to obtain data for use in making organizational changes

A central reason for developing an organization-specific attitude survey is the recognition that each organization has distinctive characteristics as a place to work. Surveys that include customized questions produce data on key issues such as quality of training or supervision that are critical to current operations.[21] Furthermore, tailormade questionnaires can uncover vital information about the progress of newly implemented HR activities while pointing the way to new or improved HR programs.[22]

Organization-specific surveys are best designed when managers and employees participate with the HR staff to develop survey areas and questions. Top managers can identify overall issues for review while employees provide input in concerns relevant to them.[23] The authors of this text have successfully used manager/employee focus groups to develop surveys for organizations such as Del Webb Communities and Doubletree Hotels.

Organization-specific questionnaires are not readily comparable to industry averages. Fortunately these surveys provide a tool for gauging progress toward attaining an organizational vision. By using your organization as your primary benchmark, surveys can be designed to measure progress toward attaining a specific cultural vision, instilling certain values, or achieving organizational goals.[24] The steps in conducting a questionnaire survey are described in Figure 20–4.

Commercial Questionnaires

Organizations can purchase standard survey instruments from national sources. This practice will save the HR staff from the development, tabulation, and analysis of data. It allows for comparison of responses with related industry groups and is considered an economical way to run an employee survey.

One commercially available questionnaire is the *Campbell Organizational Survey* (COS), published by National Computer Systems, Inc. This survey is

> ┌───┐
> **FIGURE 20-4** *Steps in Conducting an Attitude Survey*

1. **Planning the survey.** A careful planning of the survey is essential to its success. The objectives of the survey should be clearly determined and discussed by representatives of the various groups concerned, namely, managers, supervisors, employees, and the union.

2. **Designing the questionnaire.** The questionnaire or inventory used in a survey should cover all phases of the employment situation that are believed to be related to employee satisfaction and dissatisfaction. Attitude surveys are better accepted by employees when employees at all levels participate in the development of the questionnaire items.

3. **Administering the questionnaire.** The conditions under which the attitude questionnaire is administered are of vital importance to the success of the survey and to the morale of the participants. Employees should be fully oriented so that they understand the purpose of the survey. Prepublicity should be given through newsletters, special bulletins, and mailers. The usual procedure is to administer the questionnaire anonymously to large groups during working hours.

4. **Analyzing the data.** A tabulation of results broken down by departments, male versus female employees, hourly versus managerial personnel, and other meaningful categories is the starting point in analyzing the data. If data are available from previous surveys, comparisons can be made. Comparisons are usually made between departments within the organization.

5. **Taking appropriate action.** Once problems are identified, appropriate action should be taken. Feedback on survey results and follow-up action that management has planned should be given to employees.

designed to collect information about employee feelings of satisfaction, or frustration, about various aspects of the working environment such as supervision, support for innovation, and top leadership.[25] The COS asks for responses to statements about working life such as the following:

> I have a lot of freedom to decide how to do my work.
> Many of my co-workers are under a lot of pressure.
> My supervisor keeps me up-to-date about what is happening.

The forty-four items in the COS cover the thirteen scales listed in Highlights in HRM 4. According to the developer's research, these scales are related to job satisfaction and productivity.

The COS provides not only summary statistics for an entire working group but also a personal profile of each respondent. Thus the COS can serve as both an attitude survey and a job satisfaction questionnaire. The manual for the COS contains considerable information on the reliability and validity of the COS, the use of the instrument for one-on-one counseling and in small group discussions, and the implementation of the results.

Getting the most from the answers obtained in a survey requires careful analysis of the data. (See step 4 in Figure 20–4.) While data on the total population will probably reveal areas of HRM that need improvement, problems of

HIGHLIGHTS IN HRM

highlights

4   CAMPBELL ORGANIZATIONAL SURVEY SCALES

The categories listed compose the thirteen scales used to measure job satisfaction and productivity in the COS.

The work itself	Benefits
Working conditions	Job security
Freedom from stress	Promotional opportunities
Co-workers	Feedback/Communications
Supervision	Organizational planning
Top leadership	Support for innovation
Pay	

Source: David Campbell, *Manual for the Campbell Organizational Survey* (Minneapolis, Minn.: National Computer Systems, 1990), 6. Reproduced with permission.

small critical groups of employees can be lost when ratings of all employees are combined and averaged. Ratings of those who are very dissatisfied will be offset by the ratings of those who are extremely satisfied. To obtain a clear picture of the strengths and weaknesses of the organization and provide a guide to solutions, analysis by groups is essential.

In one survey, conducted by one of the authors, the organization specified that results be tabulated according to departments compared against the organizational average for each survey question. Highlights in HRM 5 illustrates how the data for questions were presented to senior management. Findings from this study clearly indicate that a better understanding of organizational problems can be obtained from a careful analysis of the patterns of ratings for different groups within an organization, however the groups are defined.

Use of Interviews

Another way to learn about employee attitudes is through an interviewing program.[26] Interviewers should make it clear that the object of the interviews is to ascertain how to make the organization a more productive and satisfying place to work. The emphasis is on listening and encouraging participants to speak freely.

highlights

5   ATTITUDE RATINGS, DEPARTMENT AND COMPANY AVERAGES—SELECTED QUESTIONS

DIMENSION	DEPARTMENT AVERAGES*				COMPANY AVERAGE†
	A	B	C	D	
My supervisor gives me timely feedback about my performance.	3.6	3.9	3.8	3.0	3.7
My supervisor is available and willing to discuss issues of concern to me.	4.3	4.2	4.5	3.4	4.2
My supervisor has good human relations skills.	3.5	3.9	3.8	3.3	3.8
I feel well informed about overall company policies and procedures.	3.9	3.3	3.8	3.7	3.5
Communications from managers are complete.	2.5	2.9	3.8	3.3	3.0
Departments cooperate with each other.	3.3	3.3	4.5	3.0	3.3
I believe morale is good in my department.	3.1	3.3	3.7	2.7	3.4
My pay is competitive with other companies within this industry.	2.9	3.2	3.3	3.3	3.4
I am adequately trained to perform my present job.	3.7	4.1	4.3	3.6	4.1
The promotional opportunities in this company are good.	2.3	2.6	3.0	2.4	3.2
This company cares about its employees.	3.3	3.2	4.0	3.3	3.5

* Averages are based on numbers assigned to each scale choice: Very satisfied = 5, Satisfied = 4, Neutral = 3, Dissatisfied = 2, and Very dissatisfied = 1.
† Company average is based on nine department averages.

Source: Results taken from an actual attitude survey conducted by George W. Bohlander.

A list of items requiring action is maintained, and concrete and prompt feedback to employees on the action taken is essential. Organizations such as Xerox, Copperweld, Kraft Foods, and General Electric have found that the upward communication system utilizing interviews has paid off in terms of reduced absenteeism and turnover, less waste and spoilage, improved safety records, increased productivity, and higher profits.

Regardless of the method used to collect employee opinions, to be useful the data must be evaluated against some comparison group. Figure 20–5 identifies different ways to compare survey data.

Using Audit Findings

In the preceding discussion we observed that there are many sources and indicators from which information may be obtained about the overall effectiveness of the HRM program. This information must then be analyzed to identify the types of corrective action needed and the personnel best suited to carry it out.

five
objective

Methods of Analyzing the Findings

Several approaches may be used in analyzing the information gathered from the various sources that have been described. These approaches include the following:

1. Compare HR programs with those of other organizations, especially the successful ones.
2. Base an audit on some source of authority, such as consultant norms, behavioral science findings, or an HRM textbook.
3. Rely on some ratios or averages, such as the ratio of HR staff to total employees.
4. Use a compliance audit to measure whether the activities of managers and staff in HRM comply with policies, procedures, and rules—an internal audit.
5. Manage the HR department by objectives and use a systems type of audit.[27]

George Odiorne recommends approach 5 of the approaches listed above, for when HR department objectives or goals are supportive of the organizational goals, top management is more likely to recognize the value of the department's functions and provide the support it needs. Where the comparison method is used, figures from outside sources are available. We have seen that comparison data may be obtained from government agencies, reporting services, employer associations, industry trade associations, and consulting firms.

Surveys conducted regularly by various organizations provide information that can be used to compare costs of the total program and its parts. Data on the compensation of HR professionals, department budgets, and personnel staff ratios are reported periodically in journals and in reporting services' publications. The Bureau of National Affairs reports data on personnel staff ratios. The **personnel staff ratio** is the number of persons on the personnel staff per 100 employees on the organization payroll. For all organizations reporting in an

Personnel staff ratio

Number of persons on the HR staff per 100 employees on the organization payroll

> **FIGURE 20-5** *Ways to Compare Employee Survey Data*

After data are collected, they must be analyzed—the numbers must be translated into a clear picture. Yet, the meaning of a specific result is not always obvious. For example, if 55 percent of employees say the organization is a good place to work, is this an area of concern? The majority gave favorable ratings, but 45 percent did not. To identify the key strengths and concerns, your data can be compared:

- **Among major topic areas in the survey.** Do employees give very favorable ratings to the benefits but unfavorable ratings to pay? How do ratings of training compare to ratings of advancement and opportunity?

- **Among employee subgroups.** Do senior managers differ from middle managers in their perceptions of the organization? Do hourly employees differ from professionals in their sense of pay equity? How do older employees differ in their view of advancement opportunities?

- **To other organizations.** Consulting firms with expertise in employee opinion surveys typically maintain large databases of employee responses to standard questions. Using this information, you can compare your results to what would be expected from other employers in your industry or geographic area.

- **To past surveys in your organization.** Are employee opinions becoming more or less favorable? As important as it is to know where you stand now, it's equally important to know where you are headed.

- **To corporate objectives.** Some employers take the strategy of attracting and retaining employees through superior pay and advancement opportunities. Others prefer to emphasize a rich benefit program and job security. In both cases, it's important to compare how management wants to position the corporation relative to employee perception.

To understand your results and develop appropriate action plans, management needs to look at the information from each of these perspectives.

Source: William E. Wymer and Jeanne M. Carsten, "Alternative Ways to Gather Opinions," *HR Magazine* 37, no. 4 (April 1992): 71–78. Reprinted with the permission of *HR Magazine,* published by the Society for Human Resource Management, Alexandria, Va.

SHRM-BNA survey, the median personnel staff ratio in 1993 was 1.0 HR department employee for every 100 employees on the payroll. The range was from 0.03 to 7.1.[28] As the size of the workforce increases, the relative size of the HR staff decreases.

Costs of the Program

We noted earlier in the chapter that it is important to translate audit findings into dollar costs wherever possible. Saying that turnover is "expensive" is not enough. When cost data are available, it is possible to make informed decisions about how much should be spent to improve existing programs or institute new ones, such as a program to reduce turnover. HR specialists should take the lead in preparing cost figures for as many of the HR activities as possible. With such

Cost-benefit analysis

A comparison of the monetary costs of a particular function against the nonmonetary benefits received, like improved employee morale

Cost-effectiveness analysis

A comparison of the monetary costs of a particular function against the monetary benefits resulting from increased organizational performance

figures the relationship between costs and benefits, and between costs and effectiveness of the proposed activities can be clearly demonstrated. A **cost-benefit analysis** is the analysis of the costs of a particular function—for example, training—in monetary units as compared with nonmonetary benefits such as attitudes, health, and safety. A **cost-effectiveness analysis** is the analysis of the costs of a particular function in monetary units as compared with monetary benefits resulting from increases in production, reductions in waste and downtime, and so on.

If HR managers are to be effective and valued as part of the management team, they must have a measurement orientation.[29] According to Jac Fitz-cnz, since value in organizations is most often expressed in financial terms, "HR professionals are gradually giving up vague, subjective terms for the more specific, objective language of numbers."[30] Innovative HR departments are increasing their influence within their organizations by moving beyond the traditional administrative role and practicing "human value management"—helping their organizations to achieve important human, production, and financial objectives by using people's skills and talents to the best advantage.

Preparation of Reports and Recommendations

One of the most important activities of the audit team is the preparation of reports of their findings, evaluations, and recommendations. The reports should include everything that is pertinent and will be useful to the recipients. One report is usually prepared for line managers. A special report is prepared for the HR department manager, who also receives a copy of the report given to line managers.

The value to be derived from information obtained from audits lies in the use made of the information to correct deficiencies in the HR program. An analysis of the data may reveal that procedures for carrying out some of the HR functions need to be revised. It is even possible that certain parts of the total program should undergo a thorough revision if they are to meet the objectives that have been established for them. Finally, the policies for each of the various functions should be examined to determine their adequacy as part of the overall HR policy.

HR managers must crunch the numbers to translate audit findings into dollar costs.

SUMMARY

HR audits serve to evaluate various personnel policies, functions, or activities that contribute to organizational success. The audit is a data-based evaluation that can be used to support or change existing HR policies or procedures or to suggest completely new areas for improvement.

objective

objective

objective

objective

Comprehensive HR audits will encompass three areas: assessing the HR department's compatibility with overall organizational goals; assessing organizational compliance with all applicable federal, state, and local laws and regulations; and evaluating the individual HR functions such as recruitment, safety and health, and compensation. Area-specific audits may evaluate topics of current concern to managers such as the culture of the organization or the existence of a glass ceiling.

Various formulas exist for assessing the HR functions. Several of the more common formulas include those that compute employee turnover rates, absenteeism rates, and injury and illness rates.

An employee attitude survey is a means of hearing and understanding what employees think on a variety of issues and reveals employee perceptions of the organization's strengths and weaknesses. An effective survey provides management with feedback on how HR policies and programs are functioning and whether additional attention or changes may be needed. While an organization may collect information on any topic of concern, employee surveys normally ask questions in the areas of supervision, HR policies and programs, job-related factors, communication, and top leadership.

To be meaningful, audit findings should be compared with some accepted measure of performance. This can be done, for example, by benchmarking against other organizations or by comparison with industry norms or different research findings. In the HR field, various studies done by the Bureau of National Affairs, the Society for Human Resource Management, and the Conference Board can be used as evaluative data.

KEY TERMS

absenteeism rate

attitude surveys

benchmarking

cost-benefit analysis

cost-effectiveness analysis

cultural audit

exit interview

glass ceiling

personnel staff ratio

turnover rate

DISCUSSION QUESTIONS

1. Why is it important to audit the HRM program periodically?
2. Some organizations employ specially trained consultants to conduct HR resources audits.
   a. What are the advantages and disadvantages of using consultants for this purpose?

....

    b. Consultants often compare the audit findings from an organization with those of other organizations with which they are familiar. Of what value are such comparisons?

3. Explain how benchmarking contributes to a successful HR audit.
4. Many organizations have found it necessary to be prepared for compliance audits by government agencies.
    a. How can managers best prepare themselves for such an audit?
    b. How much effort should be devoted to preparing for compliance audits?
5. Describe the type of information available in records and reports that can be used in auditing the major HR functions. Give some examples of data that are easily computerized.
6. Why is it important to compute absenteeism rates? What steps can management take to reduce absenteeism?
7. What are the advantages of conducting periodic employee attitude surveys? Are any problems likely to arise over a survey? Explain.

CASE STUDY: Midwest Cannery's Employee Attitude Survey

The management of Midwest Cannery, a firm that employs 1,500 workers to prepare and can baby foods, decided it was time to survey its employees to determine their attitudes toward their jobs and general working conditions. For about two weeks the operations manager, who had had previous experience with surveys, met with representatives of management and employees to develop areas and questions for the survey. A timetable was established for completion of the survey instrument and for conducting the survey. All employees were given details about the purpose of the survey and how it would be conducted.

On the scheduled day, employees assembled in the company auditorium in groups of 200. After a brief orientation by the operations manager, a questionnaire containing about 100 items was administered. The employees answered the items by checking "Agree," "Disagree," or "Undecided." Provision was also made for employees to write their comments on the form. The only identification required on the questionnaire was the individual's crew number.

After all employees had participated and data were tabulated and summarized, reports were prepared for submission to the department heads and the plant manager. The reports were broken down by each major department and by crews. The comments that employees had written on the form were summarized to facilitate their use by those concerned.

The following is an extract from the company report that was sent to the manager of the preparation department. It concerned a crew of forty-five employees (Crew X-31) who prepared meats and vegetables for canning. The crew was under the supervision of a general supervisor who had three lead persons also responsible to him. Crew X-31 employees were paid on the basis of straight time plus incentive bonuses.

Extract of Report

The statistical analysis of the questionnaires for this crew reveals that attitudes toward the company as a whole, top management, and other areas measured are quite favorable. Employee attitudes toward the following areas, however, are quite unfavorable:

- Friendliness and cooperation of fellow employees
- Supervisor and employee interpersonal relations
- Technical competence of supervision

The comments that employees wrote on their answer sheets concerning the three areas viewed unfavorably can be summarized as follows.

- *Friendliness and cooperation of fellow employees.* There are apparently older employees who adopt a bossy and domineering manner regarding those with less seniority. Certain groups in the crew, specifically Asians, Hispanics, and women, feel underutilized and treated in an inferior manner by their employees. Those ordinarily engaged in the preparation of vegetables resent being transferred, when necessary, to the preparation of chicken on the basis that they cannot make a sufficient bonus. They suspect favoritism at such times.
- *Supervisor and employee interpersonal relations.* The general supervisor often bypasses the lead persons in contacts with employees. There are frequent changes in work that come up without warning or explanation, allowing only enough time to give orders to change what is being done and to transfer employees to other types of work where perhaps less bonus is to be made. The lead person, therefore, becomes more often than not the harbinger of bad news rather than the motivator. Scheduling of rest periods is a problem.
- *Technical competence of supervision.* Although there is possibly enough equipment available for the employees to do their jobs, the equipment does not seem to be in the right place at the right time. Food carts are one of the main shortages, and any change in work amplifies this. Employees do their job the same way day after day, but the inspectors can change their minds in interpreting procedure. They then write a note about an employee, giving name and badge number to the plant manager. The employee sometimes gets a written reprimand, and this causes friction. Employees feel that it should be brought to the employee's attention in some other way. There have been times when the employees tried to retaliate by damaging the product.

Questions

1. If you were the manager of the preparation department, what immediate action would you take on the basis of this report? What long-range action would you take?
2. What role should the HR department play in the follow-up of the critical aspects of the attitude survey?

3. Was this survey necessary? Couldn't management obtain the same type of information by just keeping its eyes and ears open? Discuss.

NOTES AND REFERENCES

1. Mark A. Huselid, "Documenting HR's Effect on Company Performance," *HR Magazine* 39, no. 1 (January 1994): 79–85. See also Anne S. Tsui and Luis R. Gomez-Mejia, "Evaluating Human Resource Effectiveness," in *Human Resource Management: Evolving Roles and Responsibilities,* ed. Lee Dyer (Washington, D.C.: Bureau of National Affairs, 1988), 1:187–1:198.
2. Vicki S. David, "Self-Audits: First Step in TQM," *HR Magazine* 37, no. 9 (September 1992): 39–41.
3. Johnathan A. Segal and Mary A. Quinn, "How to Audit Your HR Programs," *Personnel Administrator* 34, no. 5 (May 1989): 67–70.
4. Tsui and Gomez-Mejia, "Evaluating Human Resource Effectiveness," 1:198.
5. Donald J. Ford, "Benchmarking HRD," *Training and Development* 47, no. 6 (June 1993): 36–41. See also Michael J. Spendolini, "The Benchmarking Process," *Compensation and Benefits Review* 24, no. 5 (September-October 1992): 21–29.
6. Ford, "Benchmarking," 38.
7. Ronald L. Adler and Francis T. Coleman, *Employment-Labor Law Audit* (Rockville, Md.: Bureau of National Affairs, 1994).
8. Joanne Wisniewski, "The Needs-Based HRIS Audit," *HR Magazine* 36, no. 9 (September 1991): 61–82.
9. Tsui and Gomez-Mejia, "Evaluating Human Resource Effectiveness," 1:194, 1:195.
10. Wayne F. Cascio, *Costing Human Resources: The Financial Impact of Behavior in Organizations,* 3d ed. (Boston: PWS-Kent, 1991): 8–9. See also Eric G. Flamholtz, *Human Resource Accounting: Advances in Concepts, Methods, and Applications,* 2d ed. (San Francisco: Jossey-Bass, 1985).
11. Cari M. Dominguez, "A Crack in the Glass Ceiling," *HR Magazine* 35, no. 12 (December 1990): 65–66.
12. Patrick Kelly, "Conduct a Glass Ceiling Self-Audit Now," *HR Magazine* 38, no. 10 (October 1993): 76–80.
13. This quarterly report is part of *BNA Bulletin to Management*. For an excellent review of the relationship between performance and voluntary turnover, see Charles R. Williams and Linda

Parrack Livingstone, "Another Look at the Relationship between Performance and Voluntary Turnover," *Academy of Management Journal* 37, no. 2 (April 1994): 269–98.
14. Robert A. Giacalone and Stephen B. Knouse, "Farewell to Fruitless Exit Interviews," *Personnel* 66, no. 9 (September 1989): 60–62. See also Steve Jenkins, "Turnover: Correcting the Causes," *Personnel* 65, no. 12 (December 1988): 43–48.
15. Dan R. Dalton and Debra J. Mesch, "On the Extent and Reduction of Avoidable Absenteeism: An Assessment of Absence Policy Provisions," *Journal of Applied Psychology* 76, no. 6 (December 1991): 810–16.
16. The reader has probably observed that the loose-leaf services of these organizations are sources of invaluable information for the HR professional. As noted in Chapter 1, these services may be found in most libraries containing business reference books.
17. K. Dow Scott and Elizabeth L. McClellan, "Gender Differences in Absenteeism," *Public Personnel Management* 19, no. 2 (Summer 1990): 229–52.
18. Jeff Stinson, "Company Policy Attends to Chronic Absentees," *Personnel Journal* 70, no. 8 (August 1991): 82–85.
19. Allen-Bradley Employee Handbook.
20. Stephen L. Guinn, "Surveys Capture Untold Story," *HR Magazine* 37, no. 9 (September 1990): 64–66.
21. Catherine M. Petrini, "Another Look at Employee Surveys," *Training and Development* 49, no. 7 (July 1993): 15–18.
22. Robert J. Sahl, "Develop Company-Specific Employee Attitude Surveys," *Personnel Journal* 69, no. 5 (May 1990): 46–51.
23. Michael T. Roberson and Eric Sundstrom, "Questionnaire Design, Return Rates, and Response Favorableness in an Employee Attitude Questionnaire," *Journal of Applied Psychology* 75, no. 3 (June 1990): 354–57. See also Thomas Rotondi, "The Anonymity Factor in Questionnaire Surveys," *Personnel Journal* 68, no. 2 (February 1989): 92–101; Leland G. Verheyen, "How to Develop an Employee Attitude Survey," *Training and Development Journal* 42, no. 8 (August 1988): 72–76.

24. David W. Bracken, "Benchmarking Employee Attitudes," *Training and Development* 46, no. 6 (June 1992): 49–53.

25. Information about the *Campbell Organizational Survey* may be obtained from National Computer Systems, 5606 Green Circle Drive, Minneapolis, Minn. 55343.

26. William E. Wymer and Jeanne M. Carsten, "Alternative Ways to Gather Opinions," *HR Magazine* 37, no. 4 (April 1992): 17–78.

27. George S. Odiorne, "Evaluating the Human Resources Program," in Joseph J. Famularo, *Handbook of Human Resources Administration*, 2d ed. (New York: McGraw-Hill, 1986).

28. *BNA Policy and Practices Series—Personnel Management* (Washington, D.C.: Bureau of National Affairs, 1994): 251:161.

29. Cascio, *Costing Human Resources*, 119–21.

30. Jac Fitz-enz, *Human Value Management* (San Francisco: Jossey-Bass, 1990): 311–12.

COMPREHENSIVE CASES

....

CASE 1   Managing Diversity at International Transportation Systems

The widely publicized demographic changes commonly referred to as "Workforce 2000" highlight the inevitable: More minorities, women, and immigrants will enter organizations. Workforce diversity as an organizational concern has gone beyond the stage of recognition to give rise to various proactive measures for integrating a heterogeneous workforce. Yet while diversity is championed as a positive for productivity, questions remain as to its value and as to what groups are to be included under its banner. Additionally, except for a handful of well-publicized examples—Digital Equipment Corporation, US West, Corning, Honeywell—many organizations have yet to conquer the complexities of managing a diverse workforce.

During the fall of 1994, senior managers of International Transportation Systems (ITS) began planning for diversity training for company employees. Far from being a simple discussion of possible training topics and methods, the planning sessions expanded to include individual opinions concerning how to define diversity and how to measure its positive and negative values for ITS. ITS operates in the global market and employs approximately 27,000 workers worldwide. The company develops and manufactures high-speed, high-technology commuter transportation electronic systems. Corporate offices are located in Denver, Colorado.

The following comments of one G. Thomas Ormrod, senior executive for product development, to Angelo Tasca, vice president for operations, represent the thoughts of several ITS managers.

> Angelo, now that we are deep into planning for diversity training, let me share some personal opinions on the subject. In fact, let me play the devil's advocate on this diversity issue. To me, managing diversity seems to be about coping with unassimilated individual differences. It's about managing people who aren't like you and who don't necessarily want to be like you. Diversity seems to be about separate groups wanting to protect their own turf at the expense of assimilation into the workforce. Isn't this against our traditional view of America as a melting pot for the good of all? I'm becoming concerned that teaching diversity might lead to the fragmentation of ITS employees by race, culture, age, gender, or other ways under this new popular concept of "multiculturalism."
>
>   Furthermore, aren't we stirring up something here that hasn't been a problem in the past? By pointing out the differences between separate groups might we only intensify resentments and animosities, driving even deeper the wedge between races and nationalities? We only have to look at our college campuses to see how incidents of diversity training have backfired. Perhaps the best plan would be to continue along as always, letting change take place on a gradual basis. We certainly need all the talented people we can get to operate in a global market, but the slow assimilation of our diverse employees has worked well at ITS; I don't think we should change things.
>
>   Also, isn't managing diversity just another fancy label for EEO? Frankly, several of us think that diversity is nothing more than just more governmental protection. Those pushing diversity are members of groups already covered by antidiscrimination laws. Just another case of push, push, push. ITS has a very good record in equal employment

hiring and promotion. As a government contractor, we've seen our affirmative action program approved by the Office of Federal Contract Compliance Programs.

Furthermore, I am deeply concerned about how ITS intends to define diversity. I mean, exactly who do we propose to include under the diversity label? Since white males will occupy a lower percentage of the workforce in the years ahead, are we included under the diversity banner? We could actually say that every one of us belongs to a diverse group in some way. Isn't diversity about me, whoever I am? If diversity is to include small segments of our workforce, aren't we creating a Pandora's box, leading to further employee fragmentation and raising more special-interests groups? And, as more groups claim to be diverse, won't this create a political backlash? I mean the separate groups could become bitter toward one another as they each strive for the limited benefits of corporate life. We could be creating problems for truly deserving groups with recognized and legitimate problems. Angelo, before we finalize our diversity training program, I believe we need to address these concerns.

Source: The case is known to the authors and represents the concerns of several senior executives of a major organization in the Southwest. All names are fictitious.

Questions

1. Identify and explain the specific arguments against diversity noted by G. Thomas Ormrod.
2. Develop counterarguments to those proposed by Ormrod.
3. List topics that organizations might discuss in diversity training.

CASE 2   Coping with AIDS at Dexter Equipment

It has been two months since that dreadful meeting with Tom Malvern, and Janice Proctor-Murphy still can't think about their discussion without feeling remorse or second-guessing her actions. The fact is, she simply hasn't recovered from the shock she experienced when Malvern revealed to her that he was dying of AIDS. And now this—the threat of a suit hanging over her and the company.

Between May 1989 and June 1993, Tom Malvern had an excellent record as a sales representative under Proctor-Murphy in Dexter Equipment Corporation's (DEC) home office. Over the past six months, however, a series of short illnesses and days off for personal reasons had lowered Malvern's work performance. Proctor-Murphy didn't need a medical degree to know that Malvern simply did not look well. Furthermore, his illness had left him moody and despondent, and his chronic absences were disrupting the work of other sales representatives.

In early October 1993, Proctor-Murphy had finally decided to have a frank talk with Malvern about his absences and his declining productivity. This meeting was unpleasant from the start and, as Proctor-Murphy later related, it ended on a sour note. Malvern denied that he had any major medical problems. He claimed that he was suffering from a lingering virus infection. As for any decline in job performance, he assured Janice that his fourth-quarter sales figures would be strong.

Shortly after this meeting, Vic Lucente, sales supervisor in another unit, had asked Proctor-Murphy about Malvern's health. "It's okay," she'd begun, "Well, really it's not okay but he assures me that nothing is seriously wrong. Why do you ask?" Lucente explained that Linda Keller, a fellow sales representative, had seen Tom enter an establishment known to be frequented by homosexuals, and rumor had it that several of Tom's personal friends were avowed homosexuals. One friend had even died of AIDS.

Over the next six weeks Tom's sick days kept piling up. A common cold turned into acute bronchitis, and there were side effects to Tom's medication that kept him from working for two and three days at a time. Proctor-Murphy, known as a taskmaster among DEC managers, began to lose patience with Malvern's behavior, as did the other sales representatives in the unit. Sales reps were organized into sales teams, each team member contributing to the achievement of established sales goals. Malvern's absences were clearly influencing the team's sales performance. Judith Blanc expressed the feelings of other team members: "Our success depends completely on a team effort," she said. "To meet our sales goals, we're having to carry Tom's load and he's getting credit for our work to meet those goals. There's a real feeling of inequity among all of us."

As Malvern's illness increased, so did the rumor mill. He was often the topic of lunchtime discussions. His supposed sexuality made some co-workers hesitant to interact with him. Eventually, Proctor-Murphy heard that several employees would not use the department water fountain. One employee told her, "I don't know if Tom has AIDS or not, but I'm not going to take any chances."

The problem finally came to a head during a Friday morning sales meeting. With sales figures down from the first quarter, Proctor-Murphy admonished her representatives for their poor performance and what she described as a "lack of cooperation" between team members. Tempers flared and accusations were made. That afternoon Proctor-Murphy called Malvern into her office and explained that if his attendance and his performance didn't improve he risked disciplinary action, including possible discharge. Visibly shaken, Malvern broke down and admitted that he was terminally ill with AIDS.

Late that same Friday afternoon Vic Lucente chanced to see Proctor-Murphy as she was leaving for home. "How's Tom doing these days?" he asked. "I hear he's taking more days off than ever." Proctor-Murphy responded quietly: "I'm just sick, Vic," she said. "Tom just told me he's dying from AIDS. I don't know what to do."

Unfortunately, it didn't take long for Malvern's medical condition to be known throughout DEC. Word even reached several of his clients, who openly expressed their concern about dealing with him and talked of terminating their service contracts with the company. Malvern suddenly experienced noticeable isolation from other employees, and the department began to face serious morale problems. Malvern now faced the reality of dealing not only with his illness but also with less-than-friendly co-workers.

Feeling both physical and mental pressure, Malvern resigned from DEC on January 12, 1994. Proctor-Murphy expressed sympathy but was nevertheless relieved at his voluntary termination. Relief turned to anger and fear, however, when DEC attorneys informed her that Malvern was suing the company for alleged invasion of privacy. He was also charging that the adverse treatment shown him during December 1993 and January 1994 had left him with no alternative but to resign (constructive discharge). The Equal Employment Opportunity Commission informed DEC on February 10, 1994, that Malvern had filed a discrimination charge against them under the Americans with Disabilities Act.

Questions

1. Discuss fully Janice Proctor-Murphy's handling of this incident.
2. Assume that DEC has no policy on life-threatening illnesses; explain what the organization should include in drafting such a policy.
3. What points might Tom Malvern make to support his lawsuit and discrimination charge before the EEOC?

CASE 3   College Recruiting at Landstar

Three months after graduating from Greenview State University's College of Business, John Schroder and David Ludwig met for dinner to discuss their job-hunting experiences and to talk about their newly found jobs. Schroder and Ludwig had met at Greenview while taking a required business statistics class and had become close friends. Schroder's area of specialization was marketing, while Ludwig's interests were in communication and general business management. After college, both graduates were fortunate to have found employment with large national companies in the St. Louis area and were therefore able to continue their friendship.

During the last semester of their senior year, Schroder and Ludwig had registered with University Career Services in order to be interviewed by organizations wishing to recruit graduating seniors. Each had scheduled ten interviews with organizations they were interested in. After these initial campus meetings, Schroder had received invitations to visit four companies, Ludwig three.

On April 19, 1994, both graduating seniors had received plant interviews with Landstar Communications, Inc., a growing telecommunications organization having headquarters in Atlanta and employing approximately 3,200 workers. The letter from Elizabeth Shepard, director of human resources, had advised them that the interviews would take place in Atlanta on May 17, 18, and 19, and that Shepard herself would coordinate their interview schedule and act as host during their stay. The letter to Schroder had said that he was being considered for an opening in the marketing department; the letter to Ludwig had said that he was being interviewed for a first-line supervisory position in the manufacturing department. Both candidates were to make their own transportation and accommodation arrangements and report to the HR office at 9:30 A.M. on May 17 to begin the interview process.

Business students at Greenview State generally considered Landstar an excellent employer. The company had a reputation as a growth organization with good advancement opportunities and was noted for the high starting salaries it paid to college graduates. It also offered its employees an excellent "cafeteria-type" benefits package.

Shortly after their interviews in May, both Schroder and Ludwig had received offers of employment, with starting dates of July 1, 1994. They had met for

. . . .

lunch on June 17, and after a lengthy and involved conversation they had both decided to reject the Landstar offers. Both starting salary offers were well above average, and the jobs appeared to be exciting and personally rewarding. However, it was the three-day interview process and the impression they received from the company visit that had led to their decision to turn down the employment offers.

Listen to Schroder's description of his interviewing experience:

I was really pumped up for the Landstar visit. When I arrived at the human resources office at 9:30, I was surprised to find eleven other college graduates waiting to see Ms. Shepard. Somehow I thought our first meeting would be a little more personal. Her secretary gave each of us an employment application and medical history form to complete, after which she informed us that Ms. Shepard would begin briefing us individually in fifteen-minute time slots starting at 11:00 A.M. The employment forms were very complex, and most of us hadn't brought all of the information needed to complete them. I felt uneasy about the sections I left blank because I didn't want to make a negative impression right off. Since the employment forms could be completed in about one hour, we spent the remaining thirty minutes engaging in nervous conversation to kill time.

My briefing with Ms. Shepard was very structured, and she seemed somewhat aloof. The only purpose of this meeting was to give me my personal preemployment schedule for the three-day visit. My schedule consisted of seven interviews, a physical examination, testing by the HR department, a group interview conducted by top managers from the marketing department, and several management exercises, which I assumed were given to evaluate my managerial and leadership skills.

My first interview that afternoon was with Steven Rayford, director of marketing. The interview was a marathon event lasting almost three hours. He quizzed me about my career goals, marriage and family plans, college classes, extracurricular activities, and how I felt about coming to work for Landstar. He seemed interested in my answers, although our meeting was often halted by phone calls and interruptions by other marketing department personnel. He was always polite to those people, answered their questions, and asked about their families or personal lives. Mr. Rayford seemed friendly to me, but my impression was that he had more important things on his mind than our interview. In fact, I had this impression about many of the marketing people I met with. Furthermore, one manager was late to our interview because of a "personal" meeting with one of his employees. I don't know, perhaps these incidents were simply a characteristic of a busy, growing company.

I was looking forward to my interview on Wednesday morning with Ms. Simpson, sales manager for the East Coast. In fact, I really prepared for our meeting since her department had the opening I was interviewing for. Unfortunately, this interview was very superficial. Ms. Simpson and I mostly discussed her personal likes and dislikes and her travel experiences to Europe and Africa, where Landstar has several clients. She also was very impressed with my Christian youth work and my affiliation with the Young Republican Club at Greenview. Toward the end of our meeting, she asked me some general questions about three of my marketing classes, and that's about all.

We spent the afternoon of May 18 with Ms. Shepard in human resources. She asked four of us to take personality tests and to fill out some forms, which were explained to us as a new method of honesty testing. I felt uneasy that only four of us were required to undergo these employment procedures, but I felt I had no other option but to complete the testing if I wanted the job. If I refused, they might think I was uncooperative or had something to hide. Ms. Shepard then asked all of us to take some general aptitude tests, which she explained were given to all future Landstar employees, regardless of the position applied for. The day ended in the HR medical office where we were required to take a drug-screening test.

My schedule on May 19 consisted of several more short interviews, which I thought went well, except for the one with Gloria Winkler. The interview with Ms. Winkler, director of advertising, was strange, to say the least. After my introduction to her, she simply sat there and let me talk about anything that seemed important to me. Her total involvement in the interview was to gesture approval of my statements and to ask three or four follow-up questions. After thirty minutes I had nothing more to say, and the interview was terminated.

We finished the employment process in Ms. Shepard's office at 3:00 P.M. She was very polite and thanked each of us for coming to Landstar. My impression of this final meeting was that it seemed very canned and perfunctory. After the meeting I asked some of the other applicants if they had had any final questions to ask of Ms. Shepard, and they all said yes, but that the atmosphere just didn't seem right to ask them. At 3:30 I was on the way to the airport for the return trip to Greenview State.

Questions

1. Comment specifically on the interviewing, testing, and overall scheduling procedure used at Landstar.
2. Discuss the interview procedure used by Gloria Winkler. Is this an effective interview method?
3. Develop a successful employment selection system for Landstar Communications that would remove the problems noted in this case.

CASE 4   The Case of the Second Appraisal

Marcus Singh, a naturalized U.S. citizen from India, is a research economist in the City of Rock Falls Office of Research and Evaluation. He is 40 years old and has worked for the City of Rock Falls for the past ten years. During that time, Singh has been perceived by his supervisors as an above-average performer, although no formal personnel evaluations have ever been done in his department. About ten months ago he was transferred from the department's Industrial Development unit to the newly formed Office of Research and Evaluation. Other employees were also transferred as part of an overall reorganization. The organizational chart for the department is depicted in Exhibit 4-1.

Out of concern for equal employment opportunity, the department director, Victor Popelmill, recently issued a directive to all of the unit heads to formally evaluate the performance of their subordinates. Attached to his memorandum was a copy of a new performance appraisal form to be used in conducting the evaluations. Garth Fryer, head of the Office of Research and Evaluation, decided to allow his subordinates to have some input in the appraisal process. (In addi-

EXHIBIT 4-1 *Organizational Chart*

CITY OF ROCK FALLS, OFFICE OF RESEARCH AND EVALUATION

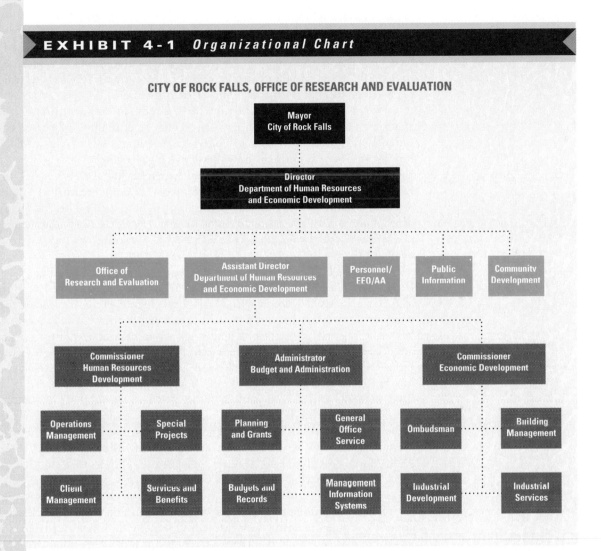

tion to Garth Fryer, the Office of Research and Evaluation comprised Marcus Singh and another research economist, Jason Taft, and one secretary, Connie Millar.) Fryer told each of the researchers to complete both a self-appraisal and a peer appraisal. After reviewing these appraisals, Fryer completed the final and official appraisal of each researcher. Before sending the forms to Popelmill's office, Fryer met with each researcher individually to review and explain his ratings. Each researcher signed his appraisal and indicated agreement with the ratings.

About one week after submitting the appraisals to the department director, Fryer received a memorandum from Popelmill stating that his evaluations were unacceptable. Fryer was not the only unit head to receive this memorandum; in fact, they all received the same note. On examination of the completed appraisal forms from the various departments, the director had noticed that not one employee was appraised in either the "fair" or "satisfactory" category. In fact, the vast majority of the employees were rated as "outstanding" in every category. Popelmill felt that his unit heads were too lenient and asked them to redo the evaluations in a more objective and critical manner.

Garth Fryer explained the director's request to his subordinates and asked them to redo their appraisals with the idea of being more objective this time. Once again, after reviewing his subordinates' appraisals, Fryer formulated his ratings and discussed them individually with each employee.

Marcus Singh was not pleased at all when he found out that his supervisor had rated him one level lower on each category. (Compare Exhibits 4-2 and 4-3.) Although he signed the second appraisal form, he indicated on the form that he did not agree with the evaluation. Jason Taft, the other researcher in the Office of Research and Evaluation, received all "outstanding" ratings on his second evaluation.

Like Singh, Taft has a master's degree in economics, but he has been working for the City of Rock Falls for less than two years and is only 24 years old. Taft had also worked closely with Garth Fryer before being transferred to his new assignment ten months ago. Recently, the mayor of the city had received a letter from the regional director of a major government agency praising Jason Taft's and Garth Fryer's outstanding research. For his part, Marcus Singh's working relationship with Garth Fryer and Jason Taft and with others in the department has been good. On some occasions, though, he has found himself in awkward disagreements with his co-workers in areas where he holds strong opinions.

After Singh and Taft had signed the appraisals, Garth Fryer forwarded them to Popelmill's office, where they were eventually added to the employees' permanent files. When pay raises were awarded in the department three weeks later, Marcus Singh did not receive a merit raise. He was told that it was due to his less-than-outstanding appraisal. He did, however, receive the general increase of $1,000, given to all employees regardless of their performance appraisal.

Singh has refused to speak one word to Garth Fryer since they discussed the appraisal, communicating only through Connie Millar or in writing. Singh has lost all motivation and complains bitterly to his colleagues about his unfair ratings. While he reports to work at 8:00 A.M. sharp and does not leave until 5:00 P.M. each day, he has been observed to spend a lot of time reading newspapers and books while at work.

Questions

1. What is the problem in this case? Who is to blame?
2. How would you have reacted if you were Marcus Singh?
3. Could this problem have been avoided? How?
4. Critically evaluate the rating form used in this case. Suggest specific improvements.
5. What can be done to motivate Marcus Singh?

Source: This case was prepared by James G. Pesek and Joseph P. Grunenwald of Clarion University of Pennsylvania. Reprinted with permission.

....

EXHIBIT 4-2   *Employee Appraisal Form*

Employee Name: Marcus Singh   Date: October 4, 1994

Job Title: Economist/Researcher

Please indicate your evaluation of the employee in each category by placing a check mark (✓) in the appropriate block.

	Outstanding	Good	Satisfactory	Fair	Unsatisfactory
KNOWLEDGE OF JOB Assess overall knowledge of duties and responsibilities of current job.	✓	☐	☐	☐	☐
QUANTITY OF WORK Assess the volume of work under normal conditions.	☐	✓	☐	☐	☐
QUALITY OF WORK Assess the neatness, accuracy, & effectiveness of work.	☐	✓	☐	☐	☐
COOPERATION Assess ability & willingness to work with peers, superiors, & subordinates.	☐	✓	☐	☐	☐
INITIATIVE Assess willingness to seek greater responsibilities & knowledge. Self starting.	☐	✓	☐	☐	☐
ATTENDANCE Assess reliability with respect to attendance habits.	✓	☐	☐	☐	☐
ATTITUDE Assess disposition & level of enthusiasm. Desire to excel.	✓	☐	☐	☐	☐
JUDGMENT Assess ability to make logical decisions.	☐	✓	☐	☐	☐

Comments on ratings: Valuable employee!

_____

Supervisor's signature: *Garth Fryer*   Date: *Oct. 4, 1994*

Department: Office of Research and Evaluation

Employee's signature: *Marcus Singh*

Does the employee agree with this evaluation? ___x___ Yes _____ No

EXHIBIT 4-3 *Employee Appraisal Form*

Employee Name: Marcus Singh   Date: October 18, 1994

Job Title: Economist/Researcher

Please indicate your evaluation of the employee in each category by placing a check mark (✓) in the appropriate block.

	Outstanding	Good	Satisfactory	Fair	Unsatisfactory
KNOWLEDGE OF JOB Assess overall knowledge of duties and responsibilities of current job.	☐	☑	☐	☐	☐
QUANTITY OF WORK Assess the volume of work under normal conditions.	☐	☐	☑	☐	☐
QUALITY OF WORK Assess the neatness, accuracy, & effectiveness of work.	☐	☐	☑	☐	☐
COOPERATION Assess ability & willingness to work with peers, superiors, & subordinates.	☐	☐	☑	☐	☐
INITIATIVE Assess willingness to seek greater responsibilities & knowledge. Self starting.	☐	☐	☑	☐	☐
ATTENDANCE Assess reliability with respect to attendance habits.	☐	☑	☐	☐	☐
ATTITUDE Assess disposition & level of enthusiasm. Desire to excel.	☐	☑	☐	☐	☐
JUDGMENT Assess ability to make logical decisions.	☐	☐	☑	☐	☐

Comments on ratings: Marcus needs to increase the quantity of his work to receive

higher ratings. Also, he should take a greater initiative in his job.

Supervisor's signature: *Garth Fryer*   Date: *Oct. 18, 1994*

Department: Office of Research and Evaluation

Employee's signature: *Marcus Singh*

Does the employee agree with this evaluation? _____ Yes   *x*   No

CASE 5   An ESOP at World International Airlines

The fortunes of World International Airlines (WIA) changed drastically with the deregulation of the airline industry in the early 1980s. Prior to this period, the airline had been regarded by passengers as a high-quality carrier with an excellent service and on-time record. Safety and service complaints filed with the Civil Aeronautics Board were low, and employee morale was high. Employees enjoyed wages, benefits, and work rules on a par with those of employees of other major U.S. domestic and international carriers. Unfortunately, the airline was slow to take advantage of a deregulated environment, and new start-up carriers began to cut into WIA's domestic market. In addition, other major U.S. airlines entered WIA's international markets, further increasing competition.

World International Airlines began losing large sums of money in the early and mid-1980s. In 1985, the airline became the target of a takeover attempt by a corporate raider. After a prolonged and highly publicized battle, the takeover was completed. This occurred shortly before the start of collective bargaining negotiations with the pilots, machinists, and flight attendants. Under the direction of new management, WIA negotiators adopted a hard-line position during bargaining sessions. Union leaders were asked to grant large concessions to the company, mainly through productive work rule changes and large monetary "give-backs." The pilots were asked to reduce their wages by 25 percent, the machinists by 15 percent, and the flight attendants by 22 percent. After difficult bargaining discussions, both the pilots and machinists reached agreement on wages, accepting wage cuts of 25 percent and 15 percent, respectively. Negotiations with the flight attendants, however, were unsuccessful, and in 1986, 6,000 flight attendants struck the airline. Management immediately began hiring permanent replacements under a newly implemented two-tier wage schedule. Under this compensation plan, B-scalers (new hires) were paid $1,000 per month; under the previous labor agreement the lowest pay for a flight attendant had been $1,136. After nine weeks the strike was halted when the union agreed to return to work. Flight attendants returned to their jobs by accepting a 22 percent cut in wages and benefits. The company implemented work rule changes and also increased the flying hours of all flight attendants by ten hours per month.

Shortly after the strike, employee morale dropped dramatically. Senior flight attendants complained of having to fly more hours with less pay. New hires felt inequitably treated since they received B-scale pay while performing job duties identical to those of senior flight attendants. Pilots and machinists were largely unhappy with their lower pay rates and work rule changes.

Since 1986, WIA has reported profits in a few selected quarters. The overall financial position of the airline has, however, continued to decline. To meet operating expenses and service a heavy debt, management sold profitable routes and other valued assets, including planes and a state-of-the-art reservation system. Unfortunately, these measures did not stem the flow of red ink, and in early 1993 an airline analyst predicted that WIA was close to financial disaster.

Senior management continued to seek employee wage concessions, arguing that employees should be willing to "help with" the company's financial burden. Specifically, in 1993 management asked for additional wage and benefit cuts totaling $50 million. This time, however, pilots were reluctant to reduce their earnings. At union meetings, various pilots, machinists, and flight attendants expressed adamant opposition to further wage reductions. The feeling of employees could generally be summed up as "Enough is enough." Management countered by claiming that without these concessions the airline could not survive in its present financial position.

In 1993 senior airline management indicated a willingness to sell WIA if the right buyer could be found. It was generally acknowledged by airline financial analysts, however, that finding a buyer would be difficult because of the carrier's poor financial position. One possible strategy to financially strengthen WIA is an employee buyout of company stock through an employee stock ownership plan (ESOP). The machinists have been leaders in suggesting an ESOP-leveraged buyout. Other employee groups regard an ESOP as preferable to selling the airline to outsiders, who might institute unwelcome changes. Both labor and management are now exploring the feasibility of implementing a leveraged ESOP.

Questions

1. In light of WIA's poor financial position, why are employees reluctant to grant additional concessions to management?
2. What are the apparent advantages to employees of establishing a leveraged ESOP?
3. What risks might employees assume if the ESOP is implemented? How might these risks be minimized?

Source: This case is adapted from an actual experience. The background information is factual. All names are fictitious.

CASE 6 Toxic Substances at Lukens Chemical Industries

With fifty-three plants operating in fifteen countries throughout the world, Lukens Chemical is a multinational corporation and a world leader in the production of standard and specialty chemicals. Highly committed to chemical research and development, Lukens also has nineteen research laboratories worldwide. A partial listing of the company's chemicals includes the following:

Agricultural
Insecticides, herbicides, fungicides, phosphate and nitrogen fertilizer products

Specialty chemicals
Dyes, plastic additives, aerospace and manufacturing chemicals, organic and inorganic paint pigments, and chemicals for residential and commercial water treatment

Consumer
Personal care chemicals, home cleaning and maintenance aids

Medical products
Steroids, antibiotics, vaccines, various pharmaceuticals

Because of the nature of its products and general public criticism of the chemical industry, senior management has adopted a proactive stance toward the handling and distribution of toxic substances. The company has taken extensive efforts to protect the health and safety of its employees while complying with OSHA standards applicable to toxic substances in the chemical industry. Environmentalists have spoken approvingly of company actions to protect both its employees and the environment.

Under the direction of a dynamic president and CEO, Lukens Chemical has experienced a 12 percent annual growth in plants and facilities. Managerial, engineering, technical, and other professional employees needed to staff the company have come largely from competitors and college recruiting. In order to develop its HR personnel, in 1989 the company started a specialized management training program for HR specialists. Individuals selected for this program are rotated every six months through the functional areas of recruitment and selection, compensation administration, training and development, labor relations, and equal employment opportunity. Upon completion of these assignments HR specialists are assigned as plant HR assistants. One or more of these field assignments normally lead to the HR directorship at a major chemical plant.

In early 1994 Paul Chavis was promoted to the position of HR director of the New Orleans plant of Lukens Chemical. During Chavis's interview with Chad Welker, plant manager of the New Orleans facility, he was told that the major HR concerns were a high level of union grievance activity, high turnover, and the need to recruit new engineering and technical personnel. It was not long after assuming his new assignment, however, that a more pressing problem developed. The problem began shortly after a lengthy meeting with Dr. Howard Loy, the plant's health and safety physician. The following is part of the conversation between the two.

Loy: Paul, as you know, our corporate management is always concerned about the problems of employees coming into contact with toxic chemicals. Part of my job is to monitor the facilities here and to report any work-related health problems. Since the lead pigments department is a highly suspect area, I keep a very close watch on this particular facility.

Chavis: I know that it is an important area to us. Besides supplying significant products, the lead pigments department employs over 150 employees.

Loy: My personal study, and those of other researchers, shows a relationship between lead exposure and serious health conditions, especially various female reproductive dangers.

Chavis: Howard, this could be a real problem for us. We have seventeen women between the ages of 23 and 45 working in lead pigments. What medical problems might women encounter from exposure to lead?

Loy: Pregnant women who have been exposed to lead may miscarry or give birth to children with serious defects. The possibility of sterility is another danger. I believe we are running a real risk by continuing to employ women in these jobs.

Additionally troublesome was the fact that the department used a lead chromate pigment process, which can be especially dangerous to women. Furthermore, the problems described by Dr. Loy have been confirmed by the National Institute of Occupational Safety and Health (NIOSH).

Shortly after the meeting with Dr. Loy, Chavis wrote to Dr. Kathryn Long in Houston, recommending that some policy be developed regarding the exposure of women to lead. In July 1994 the company established a policy that only women beyond childbearing years or those surgically sterilized could hold jobs involving exposure to lead. All women in the lead pigments department were told of this policy. Those women not accepting the company's offer of surgical sterilization could transfer to jobs involving no contact with lead. Unfortunately, those jobs were largely in clerical and maintenance positions, jobs paying considerably less than the technical positions in the lead pigments department. Management established this policy with the belief that it was being institutionally responsive to women's health needs.

Shortly after the policy was announced, nine women filed an EEOC sex discrimination charge against the company, alleging that it was forcing them to be surgically sterilized as a condition for retaining their jobs. The complaining employees noted in the charge, "No female should be forced to give up her reproductive rights in order to keep her job." The EEOC suit came as a complete surprise to management, since no women in the lead pigments department had indicated displeasure with the policy, and the company had acted with what it felt was a responsible and humane concern for its female employees.

Questions

1. Given the recommendations of Dr. Loy, what possible courses of action could the company take regarding women's exposure to lead?
2. Evaluate the rights and responsibilities of both the company and the employees in this case.

Source: This case is adapted from an actual experience. The background information is factual. All names are fictitious.

CASE 7   Self-Managed Teams at Lake Superior Paper Company

Lake Superior Paper Company, located in Duluth, Minnesota, near plentiful timber sources, is the largest producer of uncoated, supercalendered groundwood paper in North America. The mill is equipped with state-of-the-art technology and is designed to produce nearly a quarter-million tons of paper a year. It has highly automated facilities, with operations continuously monitored by skilled workers.

When Lake Superior Paper first opened its mill, it formed twenty self-managed teams, among them crews from the wood yard, wood handling laboratory, pulp mill, paper machine, calendering and roll finishing, laboratory, and maintenance areas. There is also a core of team managers in the plant and a design team (consisting of the president and vice presidents) that spearheaded the initial mill design, start-up, and task assignments. A self-managing team system was chosen for the new mill, said one of the mill managers, because "It would have been against the norm in the paper industry if we used a traditional work system in a new start-up operation." Another executive explained, "We had a state-of-the-art mill in terms of technology. We wanted a state-of-the-art social system to go with it, not an old, outdated kind of traditional system."

Since it began operations, the Lake Superior Paper mill has been both highly efficient and productive. The mill has been named as the most successful greenfield site (start-up) in the paper industry.

In the early stages of the mill's start-up operations, management provided specific directions to the work teams. The majority of the workers had no prior experience in the paper industry or with working in a team structure. The development of truly self-managing teams was expected to take from five to eight years. Initially, teams were under the direct leadership of the team manager, with no rotation of member skill roles and responsibilities. Ultimately, it was hoped that teams would find the required skills and abilities within themselves, with members exercising control over their problems and rotating among various coordinating and scheduling roles. Team members are compensated on a pay-for-knowledge basis. As an employee masters new skills, he or she is advanced upward in the nine-point pay scale. Exhibit 7-1 shows the long-term evolutionary plan, with team managers moving from direct supervision (stage 1) to positions of shared authority (stage 2), to boundary managers and leaders (stages 3 and 4).

Despite the success of the mill, the implementation of self-managed teams has not been without problems, and significant challenges remain. These include the following:

1. Reactions to the concept of self-managing teams still range from skepticism to their embrace as a cure-all. Debate continues over whether the mill, with its state-of-the-art technology, would be just as productive with a traditional style of organization.

2. Supervisory positions within the mill are fraught with conflict. Supervisors are often caught in the middle, trying to satisfy the demands of management from above and the expectations of team workers from below. Team managers express the same sentiments. One manager described her primary role as a kind of buffer that "gets it from both ways," resulting in the occasional wish that she could just turn toward one group and say, "All right, you do it."

3. The team manager's role is difficult, since many of the managers obtained their work and supervisory experiences in more traditional organizations where directive modes of leadership were the norm. The transition to a team system calls not only for a new set of roles but for an entirely different managerial philosophy. This creates internal conflicts for team leaders.

4. There is a haunting, if not always stated, fear among some team managers that they risk managing themselves out of a job. If they were to be truly successful, their team would become self-managing and appear to require a team manager no longer.

5. Disgruntled technical team workers also question management's fairness. As more self-managed team workers complete training and are compensated through the pay-for-knowledge policy, salary gaps

EXHIBIT 7-1   *Evolution of the Team Leader's Role*

Stage 1: Start-up Team

Authority   Coordinator
Expert   Team supervisor
Teacher   Mentor
Problem solver

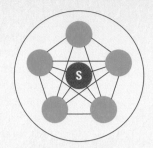

Stage 2: Transitional Team

Shared authority   Teacher
Monitor   Evaluator
Helper   Information provider
Example setter   Link to other teams

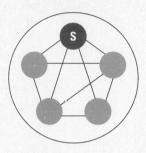

Stage 3: Well-Trained, Experienced Team

Manager of boundary Goal-setting guider
Auditor   Information provider
Expert   Protector/buffer
Resource provider

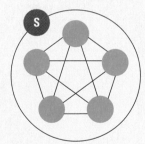

Stage 4: Well-Trained, Mature Team

Boundary leader   Counselor
Shared values   Resource provider
Coach   Supporter
Champion   Shared responsibilities

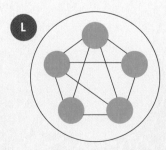

Key: 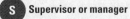 **S** Supervisor or manager   **L** Leader

between technical and nontechnical workers shrink. "Techs" object to the pay-for-knowledge component of the self-managed team system, which rewards workers with weak skills, knowledge, and experience for completing training. Techs have also protested when called upon to do tasks they consider below their status—responsibilities they would escape under a traditional system with narrowly defined job tasks for each level.

At Lake Superior Paper, team members, managers, and top executives realize that self-managing teams are vulnerable entities. Members and leaders stress that they have almost no opportunity to rest on their laurels. One employee stressed that "Working in the system is great, but it can be very fragile." He explained that "One moment a team can be really clicking, with things going really well, and the next moment things can be in turmoil, with people hollering at one another and a lot of hard feelings produced." This merely reflects one element of the organization's mission and philosophy statement, which suggests that though "conflict is inevitable," it must be resolved in a "timely and equitable manner."

Questions

1. Why do you think there is still skepticism at Lake Superior Paper regarding the team structure?
2. One team manager explained his role as being a "kind of psychologist," reacting to the feelings, needs, and interactions of employees. What do you believe he meant by this statement?
3. What might top management do to lessen the concern of team managers?

Source: This case is adapted from "The Good and the Bad of Teams: A Practical Look at Successes and Challenges," Charles C. Manz and Henry P. Sims, Jr., *Business Without Bosses,* copyright 1993, John Wiley and Sons, Inc. Reprinted by permission of the publisher.

CASE 8 Ill-Fated Love at Centrex Electronics

Nancy Miller-Canton never imagined she would lose her job at Centrex Electronics Corporation (CEC), and certainly not under such unpleasant circumstances. Unfortunately, after eleven years of employment, the last two as a senior product engineer in the firm's military/space division in Atlanta, she made a mistake: She fell in love.

Miller-Canton joined Centrex Electronics shortly after graduating from Georgia State University in 1980. At that time she was married to Tom Canton, her college sweetheart. In 1986, Canton died suddenly. As a single parent, his widow became dependent upon her job for the majority of her family's support.

Miller-Canton enjoyed rapid promotions through various engineering positions until reaching her present job as senior product engineer. In 1993, the year before her dismissal, she was awarded the firm's Engineering Distinction Award for her research and development work in metallography. In January 1994, one week after receiving a 14.2 percent raise, she was called on the carpet. The question from the military/space division manager was clear and direct: "Are you dating Mike Domzalski?" Domzalski was a former CEC senior engineer who had changed employment in 1993 to work for International Technologies, a direct competitor of CEC. There was no denying the romance. The two had dated while Domzalski was with CEC, and he still played on CEC's softball team. It was widely known among Miller-Canton's friends that she was "extremely fond" of Domzalski.

Now, chastised for her involvement, Miller-Canton was ordered to forget about Domzalski or be demoted. After the meeting she told a friend, "I was so socialized in CEC culture and so devoted to my job that I thought seriously about breaking up with Mike." As she later testified in court, however, she never got the chance because she was dismissed the day after the meeting with her manager.

Human resources professionals agree that CEC is highly regarded as a quality employer in the electronics industry. It is a multinational corporation with engineering services and production facilities in Spain, Canada, Hong Kong, Mexico, and Germany. With more than 12,000 employees in the United States, the firm has been named as one of the country's top 100 organizations to work for by several studies. Centrex Electronics is known as a top-paying corporation with proactive employee relations policies. Kathryn Garner, vice president of human resources, is credited with establishing many positive employee rights policies, including those covering drug testing, search and surveillance, employee files, and employee smoking. The corporation permits marriage between employees except in cases where "one employee is in a direct reporting relationship with the other."

At the root of Miller-Canton's dismissal is a corporate policy regarding the leakage of confidential product information. The policy seeks to avoid situations where an employee of CEC might be compromised into providing sensitive or confidential information to an employee of a competing organization. Miller-Canton's work in research and development made her subject to the following CEC policy:

> Employees performing jobs where they have access to sensitive or confidential information which could benefit competitors are prohibited from being married to or from having a romantic relationship with individuals employed by competing organizations.

Since Mike Domzalski's work at International Technologies is similar to Miller-Canton's at CEC, the corporation felt their "romantic relationship" made her discharge appropriate.

Feeling aggrieved, Miller-Canton engaged the services of an attorney specializing in employee rights claims. In preparing her wrongful-discharge suit, the attorney told her that, given the nature of her case and the continuous erosion of the employment-at-will doctrine, he believed she could win the lawsuit. Furthermore, while gathering background information for the trial, the attorney discovered something that her former division manager didn't know. Shortly before her discharge, no less an authority than former CEC chairman Joseph M. Torell had declared that "CEC employees are responsible for their own off-the-job behavior. We are concerned with an employee's off-the-job conduct only when it reduces the employee's ability to perform normal job assignments."

. . . .

A jury trial in state court upheld the wrongful-discharge suit and awarded Miller-Canton $425,000 in back pay and punitive damages. Like other trials, however, this one took its toll on the parties involved. "I couldn't function for four or five months after the trial, I was so emotionally upset and drained," Miller-Canton said. She is now employed as an engineer for a computer company; she and Domzalski are no longer dating. "It was a bad experience all around," she says. "There was a real sense of belonging and a feeling of personal job worth at CEC. If I had my way, I'd take my old job back today."

Questions

1. What exceptions to the employment-at-will doctrine would the attorney have used to file the lawsuit?

2. Comment on the confidential information policy adopted by Centrex Electronics. Do you agree with the way it is used?

3. Is dating a "romantic relationship"? How might this term become a problem for the corporation?

. . . .

Source: This case is adapted from an actual situation known to the authors. All names are fictitious.

CASE 9 The Last Straw for Aero Engine

The meeting lasted only ten minutes, since all those present quickly agreed that Tom Kinder should be fired. According to management, Kinder had caused the company numerous problems over the last eighteen months, and the incident on Saturday had been "the straw that broke the camel's back." Plant management believed it had rid itself of a poor employee—one the company knew it had offered numerous opportunities for improvement. It seemed like an airtight case and one the union couldn't win if taken to arbitration.

Tom Kinder had worked for the Aero Engine Company for fourteen years prior to his discharge. He was initially employed as an engine mechanic servicing heavy-duty diesel engines. For his first nine years with Aero Engine, he was considered a model employee by his supervisors and plant management. Kinder was also well liked by his fellow employees. His performance appraisals were always marked "exceptional," and his personnel folder contained many commendation letters from customers and supervisors alike. Supervisor Mark Lee described Kinder as "devoted to his job of building and repairing engines." Through company-sponsored training classes and courses taken at a local trade school, Kinder had acquired the knowledge and experience to build and repair specialty engines used in arctic oil exploration.

The Aero Engine Company, with headquarters in the Midwest, was engaged primarily in the production and maintenance of specialty engines used in drilling, heavy manufacturing, and diesel transportation. The company had experienced very rapid growth in sales volume, number of products produced, and the size of its workforce since 1970. (At the time of Tom Kinder's termination, the company employed about 1,700 employees.) Aero Engine avoided hiring new personnel and then laying them off if they should no longer be needed. Company policy stated that layoffs were to be avoided except in extreme circumstances. When heavy workloads arose, the natural solution to the problem was to schedule large amounts of overtime and to hire temporary employees who could be obtained through one of the local temporary help services.

Tom Kinder's work problems had begun approximately five years ago when he went through a very emotional and difficult divorce. He was a devoted family man, and the divorce was a shock to his values and his way of life. The loss of his children was particularly devastating to his mental well-being. He became sullen, withdrawn, and argumentative with his supervisors. An absenteeism problem developed and continued until his discharge. Over the eighteen months prior to this termination, Tom was absent twenty-seven complete days and nine partial days and was tardy nineteen times. Twelve months ago he was given a written warning that his attendance must improve or he would face further disciplinary action, including possible discharge. Unfortunately his attendance did not improve; however, he received no further disciplinary action until his discharge on Monday, June 13, 1994.

Management had also experienced other problems with Tom Kinder. The quantity and quality of his work had decreased to only an acceptable level of performance. His supervisor had discussed this with him on two occasions, but no disciplinary action was ever instituted. Furthermore, during heavy production periods Kinder either would refuse to work overtime assignments or, once assigned, would often fail to report for work. It was an incident that occurred during a Saturday overtime shift that caused his discharge.

On Saturday, June 11, Kinder was assigned to a high-priority project that required him to build a specialty engine for a large and loyal customer. The big new engine was needed to replace a smaller engine that had exploded on an Alaskan drilling rig. The engine was being built in a newly constructed plant building located one-half mile from the company's main production facilities. At approximately 9:15 A.M. on Saturday, Gordon Thompson, Kinder's supervisor, walked over to the new building to check on the progress of the engine. As Thompson passed by a window, he noticed Kinder sitting at a desk with his feet up reading a magazine. The supervisor decided to observe him from outside the building. After about twenty-five minutes Kinder had not moved, and Thompson returned to the plant to report the incident to Glenn Navarro, the plant production manager. Neither the supervisor nor the production manager confronted Kinder about the incident.

At 8:15 A.M. on Monday morning, supervisor Thompson and production manager Navarro met with the director of human resources to review the total work performance of Tom Kinder. After this short meeting, all those present decided that Tom Kinder should be fired. Tom's discharge notice read, "Terminated for poor work performance, excessive absenteeism, and loafing." At 10:15 that morning Kinder was called into Navarro's office and told of his discharge. Navarro then handed him his final paycheck, which included eight hours of work for Monday.

Questions

1. Comment on the handling of this case by the supervisor, production manager, and director of human resources.

....

2. To what extent were the concepts of good discipline and "just cause" discharge applied?
3. If Tom Kinder's discharge went to arbitration, how would you decide the case? Why? What arguments would labor and management present to support their respective positions?

....

Source: This case is based on an actual arbitration heard by George W. Bohlander. All names are fictitious.

CASE 10   Labor-Management Relations at Palo Verde Mining

The right of employees to strike their employers is an established guarantee under the National Labor Relations Act. Consequently, strikes have long been an accepted part of the labor-management collective bargaining setting. Traditionally, when employees elected to strike, the organization would shut down its operations entirely or continue to operate with a limited complement of supervisory personnel. While this practice continues today, more and more employers are hiring strike replacements to keep facilities running when strike action occurs. The Greyhound Corporation, Trans World Airlines (TWA), Phelps Dodge, Hormel, and the National Football League are recent examples of organizations that were willing to hire replacement workers in order to maintain operations. One labor relations scholar has noted, "No longer can unions expect the strike to provide the force needed to make employers capitulate to union demands. The growing anti-union attitudes of managers, technological advances, and foreign and domestic competition have made the strike weapon largely ineffective in many situations." Unfortunately, with this change has come a new period of labor-management unrest accompanied by violence, threats of strikebreaking, and other hostile labor-management interactions. The following case illustrates these points.

For forty years labor negotiations between the Palo Verde Mining Company and the International Mine Workers Union had concluded without a major incident. While both sides had had their differences, and several short strikes had taken place, negotiations had ended with both labor and management believing that a fair bargain had been reached. This changed dramatically in 1992, when copper prices fell and company management bargained hard to hold down wage increases and obtain productive work rule changes.

In February 1992, shortly before the contract was to expire, tentative agreements had been reached on all important bargaining items except one, contractual arrangements granting employees a cost-of-living allowance (COLA). Management demanded elimination of the COLA wage provision since it caused uncontrollable wage increases and other copper companies had successfully removed this costly wage guarantee from their contracts. Union officials argued that the COLA was needed to keep pace with inflation and maintain employees' purchasing power. During the last week of negotiations no progress was made on the COLA issue and on February 10, 1992, 2,300 union members began striking the company's mining facilities at Queen Creek, Desert City, and the Salt River Basin. The company immediately announced that it would hire strike replacements, an action not taken during previous strikes. With unemployment high and the good wages and benefits available to new hires, the Palo Verde Mining Company was able to return to 80 percent operations within seven weeks.

During the strike, tensions between management, strikers, and strike replacements were extremely high. Violent outbreaks between union strikers and strike replacements were common, as was the destruction of company property by striking employees. The strike received national attention in March when a small child was accidentally shot by an unknown individual. Further violence caused the governor of the state to send in the National Guard and state police to restore order in the mining communities.

Capitalizing on its success in hiring strike replacements, Palo Verde management changed its bargaining agenda in subsequent negotiations to include items not previously discussed. In addition, management negotiators insisted on reopening many of the tentative agreements reached in bargaining during late January and early February. Labor relations experts regarded this action as a way of backing the union into an unacceptable position to resolve the strike. When the bargaining talks broke down, the union immediately filed unfair labor practice charges with the National Labor Relations Board (NLRB). These charges alleged that the company was refusing to bargain in good faith.

Tensions remained hostile between union members, management, and strike replacements during April, May, and June of that year. In July, the Palo Verde Mining Company issued eviction notices to strikers to leave their company-owned homes. (Providing subsidized company housing is a common practice in southwestern mining communities.) As the strike continued, many former employees began to cross the union picket lines, heightening tensions between family members and fellow striking employees.

In March 1993, one year after the strike began, employees of the Palo Verde Mining Company petitioned the NLRB to hold a decertification election. The NLRB held this election on May 14, 1993. An overwhelming number of miners voted to decertify the union. Since decertification of the union the company has operated as a nonunion employer, and recent organizing attempts at Palo Verde have been unsuccessful. While the bitterness of the strike still plagues families in the mining communities, operations at the mines have returned to normal.

Questions

1. Comment specifically on the company's decision to hire strike replacements. What are the advantages and disadvantages of this action to the company?
2. Discuss the effectiveness of the strike in light of today's labor-management environment.
3. How do you think the NLRB might have resolved the unfair labor practice charge filed by the union? What criteria might the NLRB have used to settle the charge?

Source: This case is adapted from an actual experience. The background information is factual. All dates and names are fictitious.

CASE 11   International Training at GE Medical Systems

The Optimas award is presented yearly by the *Personnel Journal* for excellence in international HRM. In 1992, the award was given to the HR department of GE Medical Systems (GEMS) for development of the company's Global Leadership Program (G.L.P.). By recognizing that global outlook in human resources is one of the most important prerequisites for international business success, GEMS is heavily committed to international HR training. Due, in part, to its cross-cultural training background, GEMS' non-U.S. business revenue has increased from 13 percent of total revenue in 1985 to more than 40 percent today.

GEMS, with headquarters in Milwaukee, operates worldwide. The company manufactures, sells, and services diagnostic imaging equipment such as CAT-scanners, magnetic resonance, nuclear medicine, and ultrasound systems. Major manufacturing plants are located in Milwaukee, Paris, and Tokyo, with smaller facilities in Italy and Spain. The company maintains joint ventures in Korea, China, India, and Russia. The company has 17,000 employees; 7,000 of those employees are outside the United States, 3,800 are in Milwaukee.

Though the Global Leadership Program has since been disbanded, it operated for four years and trained more than 200 key managers worldwide. Managers came together to work in teams to develop solutions to various global HR business issues. These issues were real business problems with imposed deadlines. Teams would use interpreters or consultants as needed. Additionally, team members were involved in a recreational team-training exercise—scaling a wall—where members did not speak a common language. Training sessions, which lasted from two to three days over a six month period, were hosted by individual team members in their home countries. This fostered the learning of work and cultural differences. At specific times during the training program, teams were required to present the nature and progress of their projects. At the end of the training session, a two-and-one-half-day meeting took place where each team was given twenty minutes to present conclusions and recommendations regarding its project.

The crux of this program has been incorporated into different global training endeavors. For example, GEMS is heavily involved in the cross-cultural orientation of expatriate employees. Called "expats," these individuals include both American employees going abroad to work or foreign managers coming to work in the United States. Cross-cultural training looks at host-country support services, culture and language training, and an individualized education plan for children. "Repats," managers and families who have returned from an overseas assignment, serve as trainees and mentors to departing families. Upon returning to the United States, all GEMS employees receive a profile questionnaire to complete. Employees indicate their willingness to be involved in cross-cultural orientation and general knowledge of areas in their host country, such as child care, medical facilities, clubs and organizations, employment opportunities, and shopping. The peer mentor program has an overseas counterpart in the region of assignment. This mentor stays close to the new expatriate for several weeks to help with work and social adjustments.

In 1990 GEMS opened a worldwide communication network with global videoconferencing facilities. HR developed a videoconferencing manual that is culture-sensitive and designed to improve communication between employees from various cultures. Users are advised to frequently check for understanding and to avoid the use of slang or idioms. Specific communication suggestions for individual countries are included.

Questions

1. What global HR issues might have been discussed by the G.L.P. team members?
2. As a manager receiving an overseas assignment, what cross-cultural information would you desire for yourself or family members?

Source: Adapted from Peggy Stuart, "Global Outlook Brings Good Things to GE Medical." *Personnel Journal* 71, no. 6 (June 1992): 138–43.

GLOSSARY

Absenteeism rate Number of worker days lost through job absence during a period divided by the average number of employees times the number of workdays, and the result multiplied by 100

Achievement tests Measures of what a person knows or can do right now

Active listening Process of trying to understand what the speaker is saying by paying close attention and focusing responses on what is said

Adverse impact A concept that refers to the rejection of a significantly higher percentage of a protected class for employment, placement, or promotion when compared with the successful, nonprotected class

Affirmative action Policy that goes beyond equal employment opportunity by requiring organizations to comply with the law and correct past discriminatory practices by increasing the numbers of minorities and women in specific positions

Alarm reaction Response to stress that basically involves an elevated heart rate, increased respiration, elevated levels of adrenaline in the blood, and increased blood pressure

Alternative dispute resolution (ADR) Term applied to different types of employee complaint or dispute resolution procedures

Apprenticeship training System of training in which a worker entering the skill trades is given thorough instruction and experience, both on and off the job, in the practical and theoretical aspects of the work

Aptitude tests Measures of a person's capacity to learn or acquire skills

Arbitration award A final and binding award issued by an arbitrator in a labor-management dispute

Arbitrator Third-party neutral who resolves a labor dispute by issuing a final decision in the disagreement

Assessment center Process by which individuals are evaluated as they participate in a series of situations that resemble what they might be called upon to handle on the job

Attitude surveys Employee surveys conducted on an organization-wide or department-wide basis to obtain data for use in making organizational changes

Augmented skills Skills not critical but helpful in facilitating the efforts of expatriate managers

Authorization card A statement signed by an employee authorizing a union to act as a representative of the employee for purposes of collective bargaining

Balance-sheet approach A compensation system designed to match the purchasing power of a person's home country

Bargaining unit Group of two or more employees who share common employment interests and conditions and may reasonably be grouped together for purposes of collective bargaining

Bargaining zone Area within which the union and the employer are willing to concede when bargaining

Behavior modeling (interaction management) Approach that emphasizes the involvement of the supervisory trainees in handling real-life employee problems and receiving immediate feedback on their performance

Behavior modification Technique that operates on the principle that behavior that is rewarded, or positively reinforced, will be exhibited more frequently in the future, whereas behavior that is penalized, or unrewarded, will decrease in frequency

Behavior observation scale (BOS) A behavioral approach to performance appraisal that measures the frequency of observed behavior

Behavioral description interview (BDI) An interview in which an applicant is asked questions about what he or she actually did in a given situation

Behavioral sciences Various disciplines of psychology, sociology, anthropology, social economics, political science, linguistics, and education

Behaviorally anchored rating scale (BARS) A behavioral approach to performance appraisal that consists of a series of vertical scales, one for each important dimension of job performance

Benchmarking   Process of measuring one's own services and practices against the recognized leaders in order to identify areas for improvement

Bona fide occupational qualification (BFOQ)   Suitable defense against a discrimination charge only where age, religion, sex, or national origin is an actual qualification for performing the job

Bonus   Incentive payment that is supplemental to the base wage

Bottom-line concept   Concept that specifies that, though an employer is not required to evaluate each component of the selection process individually, that employer should ensure that the end result of the selection process is predictive of future job performance if adverse impact is present

Boycott   A union tactic to encourage others to refuse to patronize an employer

Burnout   Most severe stage of distress, manifesting itself in depression, frustration, and loss of productivity

Business necessity   Work-related practice that is necessary to the safe and efficient operation of an organization

Business representative   Normally a paid labor official responsible for negotiating and administering the labor agreement and working to resolve union members' problems

Business unionism   Term applied to the goals of U.S. labor organizations, which collectively bargain for improvements in wages, hours, job security, and working conditions

Career counseling   Process of discussing with employees their current job activities and performance, their personal job and career goals, their personal skills, and suitable career development objectives

Career curves (maturity curves)   Experience or performance bases for providing salary increases for professional employees

Career paths   Lines of advancement within an organization in an occupational field

Career plateau   Situation in which for either organizational or personal reasons the probability of moving up the career ladder is low

Certification   Recognition of having met certain professional standards

Charge form   Discrimination complaint filed with the EEOC by employees or job applicants

Clinical ecology   Study of an individual's reactions to substances in the work environment such as inhaled chemicals and fumes that adversely affect the behavior of some workers

Codetermination   Representation of labor on the board of directors of a company

Collective bargaining process   Process of negotiating a labor agreement, including the use of economic pressures by both parties

Combined salary and commission plan   Compensation plan that includes a straight salary and a commission

Communication competency   A manager's skill in speaking and writing effectively, including the ability to select the proper medium for communication

Comparable worth   The concept that male and female jobs that are dissimilar, but equal in terms of value or worth to the employer, should be paid the same

Compensatory model   Selection decision model in which a high score in one area can make up for a low score in another area

Compulsory binding arbitration   Binding method of resolving collective bargaining deadlocks by a neutral third party

Computer-assisted instruction (CAI)   System that delivers instructional material directly through a computer terminal in an interactive format

Computer-managed instruction (CMI)   System normally employed in conjunction with CAI that uses a computer to generate and score tests and to determine the level of training proficiency

Concurrent validity   The extent to which test scores (or other predictor information) match criterion data obtained at about the same time from current employees

Consent election   NLRB election option wherein the petition to hold a representation election is not contested by either the employer or the union

Consideration   A cluster of leader behaviors manifesting mutual trust, respect, and rapport between the superior and the group

Construct validity   The extent to which a selection tool measures a theoretical construct or trait

Consumer price index (CPI)   Measure of the average change in prices over time in a fixed "market basket" of goods and services

Content validity   The extent to which a selection instrument, such as a test, adequately samples the range of knowledge and skills needed to perform a particular job

Contrast error   Performance-rating error in which an employee's evaluation is biased either upward or downward because of comparison with another employee just previously evaluated

Contributory plan   A pension plan where contributions are made jointly by employees and employers

Cooperative training   Training program that combines practical on-the-job experience with formal educational classes

Core skills   Skills considered critical for an employee's success abroad

Cost-benefit analysis   A comparison of the monetary costs of a particular function against the nonmonetary benefits received, like improved employee morale

Cost-effectiveness analysis   A comparison of the monetary costs of a particular function against the monetary benefits resulting from increased organizational performance

Counseling   Process involving a dynamic relationship between two parties in which one is free to discuss needs, feelings, and problems of concern for the purpose of obtaining help

Craft unions   Unions that represent skilled craft workers

Criterion-related validity   The extent to which a selection tool predicts, or significantly correlates with, important elements of work behavior

Critical incident   Unusual event that denotes superior or inferior employee performance in some part of the job

Critical incident method   Job analysis method by which important job tasks are identified for job success

Cross-validation   Verifying the results obtained from a validation study by administering a test or test battery to a different sample (drawn from the same population)

Cultural audit   Audit of the organizational culture and quality of work life in an organization

Cultural environment   The language, religion, values, attitudes, education, social organization, technology, politics, and laws of a country

Culture shock   Perceptual stress experienced by people who settle overseas

Culture strength   Beliefs, values, and norms undiluted by cross-cultural influences

Cumulative trauma disorders (CTDs)   Injuries involving tendons of the fingers, hands, and arms that become inflamed from repeated stresses and strains

Customer appraisal   Performance appraisal, which, like team appraisal, is based on TQM concepts and seeks evaluation from both external and internal customers

Defined-benefit plan   A pension plan in which the amount an employee is to receive upon retirement is specifically set forth

Defined-contribution plan   A pension plan that establishes the basis on which an employer will contribute to the pension fund

Defined rights   Concept that management's authority should be expressly defined and clarified in the collective agreement

Differential piece rate   Compensation rate under which employees whose production exceeds the standard amount of output receive a higher rate for all of their work than the rate paid to those who do not exceed the standard amount

Directive counseling   Counseling in which the counselor tries to control the topics about which the counselee speaks, describes the choices available to the counselee, and/or advises the counselee what to do

Disabled individual   Any person who (1) has a physical or mental impairment that substantially limits one or more of such person's major life activities, (2) has a record of such impairment, or (3) is regarded as having such an impairment

Discipline   (1) Treatment that punishes; (2) orderly behavior in an organizational setting; or (3) training that molds and strengthens desirable conduct—or corrects undesirable conduct—and develops self-control

Disparate treatment   Situation in which protected-class members receive unequal treatment or are evaluated by different standards

Distress   Harmful stress characterized by a loss of feelings of security and adequacy

Downward communication   Communication flowing from managers to employees

Dual-career partnerships   Marriages in which both members follow their own careers and actively support each other's career development

Due process   An employee's right to present his or her position during a disciplinary action

EEO-1 report   An employer information report that must be filed annually by employers of 100 or more employees (except state and local government employers) and government contractors and subcontractors to determine an employer's workforce composition

Elder care   Care provided to an elderly relative by an employee who remains actively at work

Employee assistance program (EAP)   Service provided by employers to help workers cope with a wide variety of problems that interfere with the way they perform their jobs

Employee associations   Labor organizations that represent various groups of professional and white-collar employees in labor-management relations

Employee empowerment   Granting employees power to initiate change, thereby encouraging them to take charge of what they do

Employee involvement   Motivation technique to enhance the quality of decision making while satisfying employee needs for job involvement

Employee involvement groups (EIs)   Groups of employees who meet to resolve problems or offer suggestions for organizational improvement

Employee leasing   Process of dismissing employees who are then hired by a leasing company (that handles all HR-related activities) and then contracting with that company to lease back the employees

Employee rights   Guarantees of fair treatment from employers, particularly regarding an employee's right to privacy

Employee right-to-know laws   Laws that require employers to advise employees of job hazards

Employee stock ownership plans (ESOPs)   Stock plans in which an organization contributes shares of its stock to an established trust for the purpose of stock purchases by its employees

Employee teams   Teams of employees offering production or service suggestions to improve organizational performance

Employment-at-will principle   The right of an employer to fire an employee without giving a reason and the right of an employee to quit when he or she chooses

Entrepreneur   One who starts, organizes, manages, and assumes responsibility for a business or other enterprise

Environment   The conditions, circumstances, and influences that affect the organization's ability to achieve its objectives

Environmental scanning   Analyzing the environment and the changes occurring within it

Equal employment opportunity   The treatment of individuals in all aspects of employment—hiring, promotion, training, etc.—in a fair and nonbiased manner

Equity theory   Motivation theory which states that the presence of feelings of inequity will motivate an individual to reduce that inequity

Error of central tendency   Performance-rating error in which all employees are rated about average

Escalator clauses   Clauses in labor agreements that provide for quarterly cost-of-living adjustments in wages, basing the adjustments upon changes in the consumer price index

Essay method   An approach to performance appraisal that requires the rater to compose a statement describing employee performance

Eustress   Positive stress that accompanies achievement and exhilaration

Exempt employees   Employees not covered by the overtime provisions of the Fair Labor Standards Act

Exit interview   Interview conducted to determine why employees leave an organization

Expatriates (home-country nationals)   Employees from the home country who are sent on international assignment

Expectancy theory   Motivation theory which states that motivational force is a function of the expectancies that individuals have concerning future outcomes times the value they place on those outcomes

Expedited arbitration   A faster, less expensive, and less legalistic way to resolve grievances regarding discipline cases, routine work issues, and cases of insignificant monetary cost to the disputing parties

External environment   The environment that exists outside an organization

Factor comparison system   Job evaluation system that permits the evaluation process to be accomplished on a factor-by-factor basis by developing a factor comparison scale

Failure rate   Percentage of expatriates who do not perform satisfactorily

Fair employment practices (FEPs)   State and local laws governing equal employment opportunity that are often more comprehensive than federal laws

Fair representation doctrine   Doctrine under which unions have a legal obligation to provide assistance to both members and non-members in labor relations matters

Fast-track program   Program that encourages young managers with high potential to remain with an organization by enabling them to advance more rapidly than those with less potential

Final-offer arbitration   Method of resolving collective bargaining deadlocks whereby the arbitrator has no power to compromise but must select one or another of the final offers submitted by the two parties

Flexible benefits plans (cafeteria plans)   Benefit plans that enable individual employees to choose the benefits that are best suited to their particular needs

Flextime   Flexible working hours that permit employees the option of choosing daily starting and quitting times, provided that they work a set number of hours per day or week

Forced-choice method   An approach to performance appraisal that requires the rater to choose from statements designed to distinguish between successful and unsuccessful performance

Four-fifths rule   Rule of thumb followed by the EEOC in determining adverse impact for use in enforcement proceedings

Functional job analysis (FJA)   Quantitative approach to job analysis that utilizes a compiled inventory of the various functions or work activities that can make up any job and that assumes that each job involves three broad worker functions: (1) data, (2) people, and (3) things

Gainsharing plans   Programs under which both employees and the organization share the financial gains according to a predetermined formula that reflects improved productivity and profitability

Glass ceiling   The invisible, yet real or perceived, attitudinal or organizational barriers that serve to limit the advancement opportunities of minorities and women

Global corporation   A firm that has integrated worldwide operations through a centralized home office

Global managers   Managers equipped to run global businesses

Grapevine   Channel of communication that fans out through the organization without regard to formal channels

Graphic rating scale method   A trait approach to performance appraisal whereby each employee is rated according to a scale of characteristics

Grievance mediation   A process where a neutral party assists in the resolution of an employee grievance

Grievance procedure   Formal procedure that provides for the union to represent members and nonmembers in processing a grievance

Guest workers   Foreign workers invited in to perform needed labor

Hawthorne studies   Experiments in the 1920s to determine what effect hours of work, periods of rest, and lighting have upon worker fatigue and productivity

Hay profile method   Job evaluation technique using three factors—knowledge, mental activity, and accountability—to evaluate executive and managerial positions

Health maintenance organizations (HMOs) Organizations of physicians and health care professionals that provide a wide range of services to subscribers and dependents on a prepaid basis

Hearing officer   Person who holds a full-time position with an organization but assumes a neutral role when deciding cases between the aggrieved employees and management

Hierarchy of needs   A motivational model that assumes human needs are arranged in a hierarchy of importance

Host country   The country in which an international corporation operates

Host-country nationals   Natives of the host country

Hot-stove rule   Rule of discipline that can be compared with touching a hot stove in that it gives warning, is effective immediately, is enforced consistently, and applies to all employees in an impersonal and unbiased way

Hourly or day work   Work paid on an hourly basis

HR budget   Financial plan and a control for the expenditure of funds necessary to support the HR program

HR information system (HRIS)   Network of procedures, equipment, information, and personnel to provide data for purposes of control and decision making

HR objectives   Goals to be achieved in the area of HRM

HR policies   Guides to actions required to achieve the HR objectives

HR procedures   Prescribed sequence of steps to be followed in carrying out HR policies

Human engineering   An interdisciplinary approach to designing machines and systems that can be easily and efficiently used by human beings

Human relations movement   Movement that focused attention on individual differences among employees and on the influence that informal groups have upon employee performance and behavior

Human resources management (HRM) Extension of the traditional requirements of personnel management, which recognizes the dynamic interaction of personnel functions with each other and with the strategic and planning objectives of the organization

Human resources planning (HRP)   The process of anticipating and making provision for the movement of people into, within, and out of an organization

Improshare   Gainsharing program under which bonuses are based upon the overall productivity of the work team

In-basket technique   Training method in which trainees are given several documents, each describing some problem or situation the solution of which requires an immediate decision

Industrial engineering   A field of study concerned with analyzing work methods and establishing time standards

Industrial unions   Unions that represent all workers—skilled, semiskilled, unskilled—employed along industry lines

Inference   Conclusions based on facts but colored by assumptions made by the observers

Instructional objectives   Desired outcomes of a training program

Interest arbitration   The binding determination of a collective bargaining agreement by an arbitrator

Internal environment (organizational climate)   The environment that exists within an organization

International corporation A domestic firm that has used its existing capabilities to move into overseas markets

Internship programs Programs jointly sponsored by colleges, universities, and other organizations that offer students the opportunity to gain real-life experience while allowing them to find out how they will perform in work organizations

Intrapreneurs Employees who remain in the organization but are given freedom to create new products, services, and/or production methods

Issues management Process by which managers keep abreast of current issues and bring organizational policies in line with prevailing public opinion

Job A group of related activities and duties

Job analysis Process of obtaining information about jobs by determining what the duties, tasks, or activities of jobs are

Job characteristics model Job design that purports that three psychological states (experiencing meaningfulness of the work performed, responsibility for work outcomes, and knowledge of the results of the work performed) of a jobholder result in improved work performance, internal motivation, and lower absenteeism and turnover

Job classification system System of job evaluation by which jobs are classified and grouped according to a series of predetermined wage grades

Job description Statement of the tasks, duties, and responsibilities of a job to be performed

Job design Outgrowth of job analysis that improves jobs through technological and human considerations in order to enhance organization efficiency and employee job satisfaction

Job enlargement An increase in the number and variety of tasks in a job in order to offer additional variety to the jobholder

Job enrichment Enhancing a job by adding more meaningful tasks and duties to make the work more rewarding or satisfying

Job evaluation Systematic process of determining the relative worth of jobs in order to establish which jobs should be paid more than others within an organization

Job posting and bidding Posting vacancy notices and maintaining lists of employees looking for upgraded positions

Job progressions Hierarchy of jobs a new employee might experience, ranging from a starting job to successive jobs that require more knowledge and/or skill

Job ranking system Simplest and oldest system of job evaluation by which jobs are arrayed on the basis of their relative worth

Job requirements The duties, tasks, and responsibilities that make up a job

Job specification Statement of the needed knowledge, skills, and abilities of the person who is to perform the job

Knowledge workers Employees whose responsibilities include a rich array of activities such as planning, decision making, and problem solving

Labor market The area from which applicants are to be recruited

Labor relations process Logical sequence of four events: (1) workers desire collective representation, (2) union begins its organizing campaign, (3) collective negotiations lead to a contract, and (4) the contract is administered

Leaderless group discussions Assessment-center activities in which trainees are gathered in a conference setting to discuss an assigned topic, either with or without designated group roles

Leniency or strictness error Performance-rating error in which the appraiser tends to give a group of employees either unusually high or unusually low ratings

Lockout Strategy by which the employer denies employees the opportunity to work by closing its operations

Lump-sum merit program Program under which employees receive a year-end merit payment, which is not added to their base pay

Management by objectives (MBO) Philosophy of management that rates performance on the basis of employee achievement of goals set by mutual agreement of employee and manager

Management forecasts   The opinions (judgments) of supervisors, department managers, or others knowledgeable about the organization's future employment needs

Management prerogatives   Decisions regarding organizational operations over which management claims exclusive rights

Manager and/or supervisor appraisal   Performance appraisal done by an employee's manager and often reviewed by a manager one level higher

Markov analysis   A statistical method for tracking the pattern of employee movements through various jobs

Material Safety Data Sheets (MSDSs)   Documents that contain vital information about hazardous substances

Media sensitivity   The ability to select the appropriate medium for sending a message

Mediator   Third party in a labor dispute who meets with one party and then the other in order to suggest compromise solutions or to recommend concessions from each side that will lead to an agreement

Mentoring functions   Functions concerned with the career advancement and psychological aspects of the person being mentored

Mentors   Managers who coach, advise, and encourage individuals of lesser position

Merit guidelines   Guidelines for awarding merit raises that are tied to performance objectives

Mixed standard scale method   A trait approach to performance appraisal similar to other scale methods but based on comparison with (better than, equal to, or worse than) a standard

Multinational corporation (MNC)   A firm with independent business units operating in multiple countries

Multiple cutoff model   Selection decision model that requires an applicant to achieve some minimum level of proficiency on all selection dimensions

Multiple hurdle model   A sequential strategy in which only the applicants with acceptable scores at an initial test stage go on to subsequent stages

Needs for achievement, power, and affiliation   David McClelland's theory of leader motivation that differentiates people according to what motivates them: need for achievement, need for affiliation, or need for power

Negligence   Failure to provide reasonable care where such failure results in injury to consumers or other employees

Nepotism   A preference for hiring relatives of current employees

Noncontributory plan   A pension plan where contributions are made solely by the employer

Nondirective counseling   Counseling in which the counselee is permitted to have maximum freedom in determining the course of the interview

Nondirective interview   An interview in which the applicant is allowed the maximum amount of freedom in determining the course of the discussion, while the interviewer carefully refrains from influencing the applicant's remarks

Nonexempt employees   Employees covered by the overtime provisions of the Fair Labor Standards Act

Nonverbal symbols   Bodily actions such as gestures, facial expressions, posture, and tone of voice that influence the communication between individuals

Ombudsman   Designated individual from whom employees may seek counsel for the resolution of their grievances

On-the-job training (OJT)   Method by which employees are given hands-on experience with instructions from their supervisor or other trainer

Open-door policy   Policy of settling grievances that identifies various levels of management above the immediate supervisor for employee contact

Organizational analysis   Examination of the goals, resources, and environment of the organization to determine where training emphasis should be placed

Organizational capability   The capacity to act and change in pursuit of sustainable competitive advantage

Organizational culture   The shared philosophies, values, assumptions, beliefs, expectations, attitudes, and norms that knit an organization together

Orientation   Formal process of familiarizing new employees with the organization, their job, and their work unit

Outplacement services   Services provided by organizations to help terminated employees get a new job

Outsourcing   Act of subcontracting operations to other employers

Panel interview   An interview in which a board of interviewers questions and evaluates a single candidate

Participative counseling   Counseling in which both parties work together in planning how a particular problem will be analyzed and solved

Participative management   A system of management that enables employees to participate in decisions relating to their work and employment conditions, thereby creating a psychological partnership between management and employees

Path-goal theory   A situation-based leadership theory stating that leaders can achieve organizational success by helping employees satisfy their needs while simultaneously accomplishing organizational requirements

Pattern bargaining   Bargaining in which unions negotiate provisions covering wages and other benefits that are similar to those provided in other agreements existing within the industry or region

Pay equity   An employee's perception that compensation received is equal to the value of the work performed

Pay-for-performance standard   Standard by which managers tie compensation to employee effort and performance

Pay grades   Groups of jobs within a particular class that are paid the same rate or rate range

Peer appraisal   Performance appraisal done by one's fellow employees, generally on forms that are compiled into a single profile for use in the performance interview conducted by the employee's manager

Peer-review system   System for reviewing employee complaints that utilizes a group composed of equal members of employee representatives and management appointees, which functions as a jury since its members weigh evidence, consider arguments, and after deliberation vote independently to render a final decision

Perquisites   Special benefits given to executives; often referred to as perks

Person analysis   Determination of the specific skills, knowledge, and attitudes required of people on the job

Personnel management   Basic functions of selection, training, compensation, etc., in the management of an organization's personnel

Personnel staff ratio   Number of persons on the HR staff per 100 employees on the organization payroll

Piecework   Work paid according to the number of units produced

Point system   Quantitative job evaluation procedure that determines the relative value of a job by the total points assigned to it

Position   The different duties and responsibilities performed by only one employee

Position analysis questionnaire (PAQ)   Questionnaire covering 194 different tasks which, by means of a five-point scale, seeks to determine the degree to which different tasks are involved in performing a particular job

Positive, or nonpunitive, discipline   System of discipline that focuses on the early correction of employee misconduct, with the employee taking total responsibility for correcting the problem

Predictive validity   The extent to which applicants' test scores match criterion data obtained from those applicants/employees after they have been on the job for some indefinite period

Preferred provider organization (PPO)   A hospital or group of physicians who establish an organization that guarantees lower health care costs to the employer

Profit sharing   Any procedure by which an employer pays, or makes available to all regular employees, in addition to base pay, special current or deferred sums based upon the profits of the enterprise

Progressive discipline   Application of corrective measures by increasing degrees

Protected classes   Individuals of a minority race, women, older persons, and those with disabilities who are covered by federal laws on equal employment opportunity

Quality of work life (QWL)   The extent to which work is rewarding, meaningful, and free of anxieties and stresses

Real wages   Wage increases larger than rises in the consumer price index; that is, the real earning power of wages

Realistic job preview (RJP)   Informing applicants about all aspects of the job, including both its desirable and undesirable facets

Reasonable accommodation   Attempt by employers to adjust, without undue hardship, the working conditions or schedules of employees with disabilities or religious preferences

Recency error   Performance-rating error in which the appraisal is based largely on the employee's most recent behavior rather than on behavior throughout the appraisal period

Recordable case   Any occupational death, illness, or injury to be recorded in the log (OSHA Form 200)

Reflecting feelings   A technique in which the counselor focuses on the counselee's stated or strongly implied feelings and expresses them in his/her own words

Reinforcement   Anything that strengthens the trainee's response

Reinforcement theory   A theory that suggests that behavior is a function of its consequences

Reliability   The degree to which interviews, tests, and other selection procedures yield comparable data over time and with alternative measures

Relocation services   Services provided to an employee who is transferred to a new location, which might include help in moving, in selling a home, in orienting to a new culture, or in learning a new language

Replacement charts   Listings of current job-holders and persons who are potential replacements if an opening occurs

Reserved rights   Concept that management's authority is supreme in all matters except those it has expressly conceded to the union in the collective agreement

Reverse discrimination   Act of giving preference to members of protected classes to the extent that unprotected individuals believe they are suffering discrimination

Rights arbitration   Arbitration over interpretation of the meaning of contract terms or employee work grievances

Rucker Plan   Bonus incentive plan based on the historic relationship between the total earnings of hourly employees and the production value created by the employees

Scanlon Plan   Bonus incentive plan using employee and management committees to gain cost-reduction improvements

Scientific management   Using scientific investigation and knowledge in place of individual judgment of either the worker or the manager

Selection   The process of choosing individuals who have relevant qualifications to fill existing or projected job openings

Selection ratio   The number of applicants compared with the number of persons hired

Self-appraisal   Performance appraisal done by the employee being evaluated, generally on an appraisal form completed by the employee prior to the performance interview

Self-leadership theory   A leadership theory espousing an approach that encourages subordinates to become self-directed and exercise leadership for themselves

Sexual harassment   Unwelcome advances, requests for sexual favors, and other verbal or physical conduct of a sexual nature in the working environment

Silver handshake   An early-retirement incentive in the form of increased pension benefits for several years or a cash bonus

Similar-to-me error   Performance-rating error in which an appraiser inflates the evaluation of an employee because of a mutual personal connection

Situational interview An interview in which an applicant is given a hypothetical incident and asked how he or she would respond to it

Situational leadership theory A situational theory that proposes that leader behavior is based on followers' skill level and maturity

Skill-based pay Pay based on how many skills employees have or how many jobs they can perform

Skill inventories Files of education, experience, interests, skills, etc., that allow managers to quickly match job openings with employee backgrounds

Sociotechnical system Environment in which the technical and social systems are integrated so that job design is based on human as well as technological considerations

Staffing tables Pictorial representations of all organizational jobs, along with the numbers of employees currently occupying those jobs and future (monthly or yearly) employment requirements

Standard hour plan Incentive plan that sets rates based upon the completion of a job in a predetermined standard time

Step-review system System for reviewing employee complaints and disputes by successively higher levels of management

Stipulation election NLRB election option wherein the parties seek settlement of representation questions such as the NLRB's jurisdiction or the appropriate employees to be included in the bargaining unit

Straight commission plan Compensation plan based upon a percentage of sales

Straight piecework Incentive plan under which employees receive a certain rate for each unit produced

Straight salary plan Compensation plan that permits salespeople to be paid for performing various duties that are not reflected immediately in their sales volume

Stress Any adjustive demand caused by physical, mental, or emotional factors that requires coping behavior

Structure A cluster of leader behaviors that stresses task orientation, production, and organizing activities

Structured interview An interview in which a set of standardized questions having an established set of answers is used

Submission agreement Formal document that describes the issues to be resolved through arbitration

Subordinate appraisal Performance appraisal of a superior by an employee, which is more appropriate for developmental than for administrative purposes

Succession planning The process of identifying, developing, and tracking key individuals for executive positions

Supplemental unemployment benefits (SUBs) A plan that enables an employee who is laid off to draw, in addition to state unemployment compensation, weekly benefits from the employer that are paid from a fund created for this purpose

Task analysis Process of determining what the content of a training program should be on the basis of a study of the tasks or duties involved in the job

Team appraisal Performance appraisal, based on TQM concepts, that recognizes team accomplishment rather than individual performance

Telecommuting Use of microcomputers, networks, and other communications technology such as fax machines to do work in the home that is traditionally done in the workplace

Third-country nationals Natives of a country other than the home country or the host country

Total-quality management (TQM) A set of principles and practices whose core ideas include doing things right the first time, striving for continuous improvement, and understanding customer needs

Traits of leaders Qualities that differentiate effective leaders from nonleaders, the subject of many studies and still only broadly defined

Transfer Placement of an individual in another job for which the duties, responsibilities, status, and remuneration are approximately equal to those of the previous job

Transfer of training   Effective application of principles learned to what is required on the job

Transformational leadership   Leadership exhibited by those who provide enthusiasm and commitment to a vision and who possess charisma

Transnational corporation   A firm that attempts to balance local responsiveness and global scale via a network of specialized operating units

Transnational team   Teams composed of members from multiple nationalities working on projects that span multiple countries

Trend analysis   A quantitative approach to forecasting labor demand based on an organizational index such as sales

Turnover rate   Number of separations during a month divided by the total number of employees at midmonth times 100

Two-factor theory   A theory that suggests that job satisfaction is a two-dimensional construct; one dimension is motivation factors, the other hygiene factors

Two-tier wage system   Wage system where newly hired employees performing the same jobs as senior employees receive lower rates of pay

Unfair labor practices (ULPs)   Specific employer and union illegal practices that operate to deny employees their rights and benefits under federal labor law

Uniform Guidelines on Employee Selection Procedures   Procedural document published in the *Federal Register* to assist employers in complying with federal regulations against discriminatory actions

Union shop   Provision of the labor agreement that requires employees to join the union as a requirement for their employment

Union steward   Employee who as a nonpaid union official represents the interests of members in their relations with management

Upward communication   Communication flowing from employees to managers or supervisors

Validity   How well a test or selection procedure measures a person's attributes. See also content validity, construct validity, criterion-related validity, and predictive validity

Validity generalization   The extent to which validity coefficients can be generalized across situations

Verbal symbols   Words that stand for objects and abstractions

Vesting   A guarantee of accrued benefits to participants at retirement age, regardless of their employment status at that time

Voluntary protection programs (VPPs)   Programs that encourage employers to go beyond the minimum requirements of OSHA

Wage and salary survey   Survey of the wages paid to employees of other employers in the surveying organization's relevant labor market

Wage curve   Curve in a scattergram representing the relationship between relative worth of jobs and wage rates

Wage-rate compression   Compression of differentials between job classes, particularly the differential between hourly workers and their managers

Work permit/work certificate   Government document granting a foreign individual the right to seek employment

Work team   A job involvement technique whereby jobs are structured for groups rather than for individuals and team members are given discretion in matters traditionally considered management prerogatives, such as work scheduling, individual work assignments, and/or performance reviews

Workers' compensation insurance   Federal- or state-mandated insurance provided to workers to defray the loss of income and cost of treatment due to work-related injuries or illness

Yield ratio   The percentage of applicants from a recruitment source that made it to the next phase of the selection process

NAME INDEX

A

Aalberts, Robert J., 606
Aamondt, M. G., 222
Abel, Katrina L., 676
Abraham, Yohannan, 120, 382–383
Aburdene, Patricia, 299
Adair, John G., 36
Adams, Everett E., Jr., 532
Adams, J. Stacey, 508, 532
Adler, Nancy J., 721, 722
Adler, Ronald L., 753
Adler, Tina, 496, 568
Aldag, Ramon J., 292, 299
Alderman, Lesley, 456–457
Alexander, Elmore R. III, 567
Alexander, Kathleen, 53
Alexander, Keith L., 677
Alexander, Ralph A., 222
Allen, A. Dale, Jr., 678
Allen, Billie Morgan, 120
Allen, Gillian M., 186
Alley, William J., 404
Alsop, Ronald, 81
Amann, Robert J., 641
Amante, L., 186
Anderson, Janine, 187
Anfuso, Dawn, 495, 608
Anhalt, Rebecca L., 338
Antonini, Joseph E., 407
Arahood, Dale A., 420
Armshaw, Jim, 677
Arvey, Richard D., 221, 223, 224
Ash, Mary Kay, 72, 80
Ash, Ronald A., 152
Atchinson, Thomas J., 420
Atwood, Caleb S., 607
Austin, Nancy K., 338
Avolio, Bruce J., 223, 533

B

Babcock, Larry, 615, 641
Bacdayan, Paul, 532
Bacher, Jeffrey P., 420
Bachler, Christopher J., 496
Baer, R., 80
Bailey, Betty, 13
Baine, Susan Reynolds, 420
Baird, Lloyd S., 259
Baker, Margaret Ann, 568
Baker, N. C., 567
Baldwin, Timothy T., 532
Bales, John, 35
Balkin, David B., 381, 420
Ball, Donald A., 723
Balzer, William K., 338
Bannister, Brendan D., 339
Barani, L., 221
Barbanel, Cheryl, 457
Bardwick, Judith, 290, 299
Bar-Hillel, M., 222
Barling, Julian, 642

Barnett, Timothy R., 567, 606
Barnum, Darold T., 36, 78
Barreth, Charles A., 457
Barrett, Paul M., 120
Barrett, Richard S., 221
Barrick, M. R., 223
Bartholomew, Susan, 721
Bartlett, Christopher A., 683, 720, 723
Bartol, Kathryn M., 338
Bass, Bernard M., 533
Bassett, Glenn, 420
Baty, Wayne Marlin, 568
Baytos, Lawrence M., 35, 260, 420
Beadles, Nicholas, 642
Beamer, Linda, 569
Beatty, D. F., 185
Beatty, Richard W., 259, 339
Beck, David, 420
Becker, George, 627
Becker, T. E., 221
Behringer, Ken, 608
Beilinson, Jerry, 498
Belcher, David W., 420
Belcher, John G., Jr., 421
Ben-Abba, E., 222
Ben-Shakar, G., 222
Bennett, Rita, 298, 723
Bensimon, Henlen Frank, 569
Benson, Philip G., 339
Bentz, V. J., 223
Berger, Lance A., 381, 420
Bergmann, Marilyn A., 383
Bergmann, Thomas J., 383
Bergsman, Steve, 607
Berkeley, Arthur E., 676
Berkowitz, L., 532
Bernardin, H. John, 339
Bernstein, Aaron, 260, 458
Berun, Robert A., 641
Beutell, Nicholas, 293, 299
Bieber, Owen, 627
Bilu, Y., 222
Bingham, Walter Van Dyke, 9, 35
Bird, Allan, 721
Bixby, Michael B., 606
Bizones, William J., 642
Black, Stewart J., 721, 722, 723
Blackburn, Richard, 68, 80, 337, 338, 339
Blake, Robert R., 523, 524, 533
Blanchard, Kenneth H., 525, 533
Blau, F. D., 687
Bleakley, Fred R., 259
Block, Caryn J., 187
Block, Stanley B., 292, 299
Blocklyn, Paul L., 722
Bloom, Althea, 723
Bluestone, Irving, 631
Bluestone, Mimi, 79
Blunt, Peter, 722
Bohlander, George W., 80, 608, 642, 675, 678, 746
Bolick, Clint, 120
Bolles, Richard N., 271

Bongiorno, Lori, 298
Booth, I. MacAllister, 497
Borman, Stu, 187
Borman, W. C., 185
Boroski, John W., 185
Boudreau, John W., 36, 186
Bowen, David E., 338, 457
Bower, Catherine Downes, 53
Bower, John, 497
Boyd, Brian, 568
Boyle, Daniel C., 532
Boyles, Wiley R., 152
Bracken, David W., 754
Bradley, Ann K., 607
Bradt, Jeffrey A., 382, 420
Brady, Teresa, 120
Brammer, Lawrence M., 569
Brandt, Ellen, 721
Bratkovich, Jerrold R., 80
Bray, Douglas, 273
Breaugh, J. A., 186, 187
Breisch, Roger E., 339
Breisch, Walter E., 339
Brenner, Gary, 299
Bridges, William, 299
Briggs, Steven, 641
Brislin, Joseph A., 458
Britton, Paul, 419
Brockbank, Wayne, 36
Broderick, Renae, 36, 186
Brodzinski, James D., 496
Brookler, Rob, 607
Brooks, Brian, 721
Brooks, Mitchell, 224
Brooks, Susan Sonnsesyn, 290, 299
Brown, Donna, 79
Brown, Edwin L., 677
Brown, Helen Gurley, 298
Brown, Marlene, 221
Bruxelles, Mary, 35
Bryan, D. A., 222
Bryan, Leslie A., 261
Bryant, Alan W., 608
Buckham, Robert H., 338, 339
Buckley, M. Ronald, 186, 339
Budd, John W., 676
Buhler, Patricia, 187
Buller, Paul F., 338
Bunning, Richard L., 382, 419
Burgess, Leonard R., 382
Burris, L. R., 222
Burtt, Harold E., 36
Buzzotta, Victor R., 532
Byham, William C., 297, 532

C

Caldwell, David F., 186
Callahan, C., 222
Callahan, Madelyn R., 722
Caminiti, Susan, 186
Campbell, David, 289, 745
Campbell, Marshall H., 386, 677

ORGANIZATION INDEX

SUBJECT INDEX

Strikes, 651–653. *See also* Collective
    bargaining; Unions or
    unionization
  case on, 775–776
  declining number of, 653
  employer's warning on, 621
  in history, 7
  as management weapon, 637–638
  operations during, 654–655
  in public sector, 634
Strong Interest Inventory, 287
Strong Vocational Interest Blank
    (SVIB), 286–287
Structure, and leadership, 523
Structure, organizational, 71
Structured interview, 206–207, 210
Submission agreement, 669
Subordinate appraisal, 311
Substance abuse and drug testing, and
    job expectancy, 576, 578–580
Succession planning, 164
Suggestion programs, 511–515, 548–549
Sun Belt, 41
Supervisor appraisal, 309
Supervisors
  in alcoholism identification, 485
  and collective-bargaining
    preparations, 648
  HR role of, 5–6
  training of, 245–248
  and union avoidance, 638
  union impact on, 625
Supervisory Management, 18
Supplemental Security Income (SSI)
    Program, 433
Supplemental unemployment benefits
    (SUBs), 441
Supply analysis, on employees, 163–165
Survey data, 365–366
Surveys, of employee attitudes, 743–747
Symbols
  nonverbal, 538
  verbal, 537

T

Taft-Hartley Act, 596, 612, 614–615,
    620, 621
  and Civil Service Reform Act, 632
  emergency strike provisions of, 656
  on illegal subjects of bargaining, 647
  and secondary boycott, 654
  and union membership, 662–663
  and Wagner Act, 613
Tailored Clothing Technology
    Corporation (TC2), 659
Tardiness, and flextime, 146
Task analysis, 235
Task identity, and job characteristics
    model, 144
Task significance, and job characteristics
    model, 144

Tax Equity and Fiscal Responsibility Act
    (1982), 176
Taxes
  and ESOPs, 416
  on wage-earning Social Security
    recipients, 55
Tax Reform Act (1986), 447
Team appraisal, 312
Team bonuses, 393, 394
Team building
  and job involvement, 515–517
  by use of simulation exercises, 249
Teamsters, International Brotherhood of,
    618, 637
  Local 104, 666
Team training, 249
Teamwork, 69
  and internal equity, 346
  in self-managed teams (case), 768–771
Technical Assistance Training Institute
    (TATI), 92
Technological changes
  and HRP, 158
  and unions, 634–635
Technological elements in environment,
    43–45, 49
Technological illiteracy, 59
Technology, and work-team
    feasibility, 516
Technology secrets, and hiring of
    competitors' employees, 169
"Tech prep," 59
Telecommuting, 64
  and women in labor force, 56
Teleconferences, 546
Teletraining, 243
Temporary employees, 7, 63
  in future workforce, 156
Temporary help agencies, 176
Termination, and severance pay, 441
Terrorism
  international, 688
  in workplace, 558
Testers, anti-discrimination, 111–112
Tests
  for career counseling, 286–289
  employment, 202–205, 222n.27
Theft
  BIB and application forms as
    predicting, 196
  and reference checking, 197
Thematic Apperception Test (TAT), 521
Third-country nationals, 690
Thirteenth Amendment, 84
"30 percent rule," 370
Time standards, development of, 139
Title VII of Civil Rights Act (1964), 87,
    88–89, 96
  and affirmative action programs, 115
  and Americans with Disabilities
    Act, 91
  and bona fide occupational
    qualification, 103

and discharge decision, 596
and EEOC, 87, 106 (*see also* Equal
    Employment Opportunity
    Commission)
and 1991 Civil Rights Act, 92
and religious discrimination, 103–105
Toastmasters Clubs, 554
Tobacco smoke, 476
Top management, and appraisal
    program, 305
Total-quality management (TQM), 7,
    67–78
  factors in, 502
  and MBO, 327
  and performance appraisal, 68, 302, 312
*Toussaint v. Blue Cross and Blue Shield of
    Michigan*, 575–576
Towers Perrin, 28–29, 50
Toxic Substances Control Act (1976), 473
Trainers, success characteristics of,
    255–256
Training, 52, 126, 228, 231–233
  of appraisers, 313–315
  at AT&T Universal Card Services, 77
  auditing of, 732
  and career path, 270
  communication in, 536
  for employment interviewers, 209
  in Europe, 686
  for international assignment, 697–707
  leading corporate examples of, 59, 60
  and learning principles, 251–256
  of managers and supervisors, 245–248
  for minority managers, 282
  of nonmanagerial employees, 238–245
  off-the-job, 239, 241–245
  on-the-job, 239
  by OSHA, 466
  on recruitment (British Airways), 184
  for safety, 471
  and skill-based pay plans, 369
  special programs for, 248–251
  systems approach to, 233–234
    evaluation phase, 237
    meeting goals, 238
    needs assessment phase, 234–237
    training and development phase, 237
  and TQM, 68
  transfer of, 253–254
Training and Development Journal, 18, 238
Training validity, 238
Trait methods, in performance appraisal,
    316–320
Traits of leaders, 520–521
Transfer, 267
Transfer of training, 253–254
Transfer validity, 238
Transformational leadership, 527–528
Transnational corporation, 683
Transnational teams, 696
Transportation pooling, 451
Treasury Employees Union v. Von Raab, 578

PHOTO CREDITS